C   rca

THE ROUGH GUIDE

7.99
9/96.

D0539415

There are more than seventy Rough Guide titles covering
destinations from Amsterdam to Zimbabwe

Forthcoming titles include
Mallorca • Rhodes • Vietnam

Rough Guide Reference Series
Classical Music • Jazz • World Music

Rough Guide Phrasebooks
Czech • French • German • Greek • Italian • Spanish

Rough Guide Costa Rica Credits

Editor:	Samantha Cook
Series Editor:	Mark Ellingham
Production:	Susanne Hillen, Andy Hilliard, Alan Spicer, Judy Pang, Link Hall, Nicola Williamson, David Callier
Cartography:	Melissa Flack
Marketing & Publicity:	Richard Trillo (UK), Jean Marie Kelly, Jeff Kaye (US).

ACKNOWLEDGMENTS

Este libro es para Roxana, Enrique, Jonathan, Andrea y Montserrat Sánchez, de barrio la família, Sabanilla, Montes de Oca.

I am greatly indebted to Helena Chaverría and Mauricio Hernández of *Camino Travel* in San José, for their invaluable assistance, enthusiasm and support, and to their helpful staff, especially Lincy, Isabel and Adriana. Also to Ramón and Elizabeth Chaverría of *Casa de Finca* for their hospitality; Dieter Jungblut, for his friendship, whirlwind *boca* bar tour and Dominical; Peter Wohlleben of *Pitts Aviation* for his Piper Cherokee and CDs; Antonio Fonseca Herrera and family of the *Esquinas Rainforest Lodge* for their hospitality in Golfito; Emiliana Nuñez in Nosara; Flor Ugalde and the staffs of *Casa Ridgway* and the *Centro de los Amigos para la Paz* in San José; Ruud Bunting for bicycling advice; Gonzalo "the salsa demon" Alfaro for being an expert teacher; Mike Nicols for reporting back; John Liang and the *Tico Times* staff; Agustín Molina Marín for his hospitality in Limón (also to the fellows from the banana box factory for Carnaval); Silvia Brander for her account of Amubrí; Theresa Gaudet for her good company; Luis A Vivanco for advice on Drake Bay and background reading; Amos Bien and Rara Avis; Andrea Holbrook and *Selva Verde Lodge*; Paul Strassburger and the *Dundee Ranch*; Kristina Zdrilie and staff at *Sunset Tours* in Fortuna; Fernando Sandi Castro for hospitality in Los Chiles; *Albergue Buenavista* in Guanacaste; the *Belmar Hotel* in Monteverde; Patricia and Lenny of *Sano Banano* in Montezuma; Sr Mario Alfaro and the ICT staff at the Plaza de la Cultura; Dr Manuel Alonso of TUVA in Osa; Javier Herrera at the SPN HQ in San José; Rodolfo Tenorio, archeologist in Guayabo, all the *guardaparques*, especially William Vega in Corcovado and Délio Salazar in Manuel Antonio. In the UK and Canada, thanks to Jo Clarkson at *Trips*; Martin Mowforth of Plymouth University; Martin Diamond; Carolyn Emmett; Alex Wilks of *The Ecologist*; Elizabeth Agnew of *WWF Canada*; Steve Collins and Paul Raikes of *JLA*; and Mark Whatmore and Peter Eltringham, fellow *Rough Guide* authors. My thanks are especially due to Linda Taylor in London, and to Eric Young and Louise Dennys, who put me up in Toronto. I am also very grateful for the meticulous and supportive assistance I received from my editor, Sam Cook, to Sam Kirby for great maps, Nikky Twyman for eagle-eyed proofing, David and Narrell Leffman and Carol Pucci for help on *Basics*, and everyone in the production department, especially Susanne, Andy and Nicola.

   And *sobre todo*, to Nick Dennys for his continual support and friendship, without which I would not have been able to write this, or any other, book.

The quotations on p.134 and p.140 were originally published in *The Old Patagonian Express: By Train through the Americas* by Paul Theroux (UK, Hamish Hamilton, 1979/US, Pocket Books), © Cape Cod Scriveners Co, 1979. The quotation on p.162 was originally published in *What Happen: A Folk History of the Talamanca Coast*, edited by Paula Palmer (San José, Ecodesarrolos 1977).

This first edition published 1996 by Rough Guides Ltd, 1 Mercer Street, London WC2H 9QJ.

Distributed by the Penguin Group:
Penguin Books Ltd, 27 Wrights Lane, London W8 5TZ
Penguin Books USA Inc., 375 Hudson Street, New York, NY 10014, USA
Penguin Books Australia Ltd, 487 Maroondah Highway, PO Box 257, Ringwood, Victoria 3134, Australia
Penguin Books Canada Ltd, 10 Alcorn Avenue, Toronto, Ontario, Canada M4V 1E4
Penguin Books (NZ) Ltd, 182–190 Wairau Road, Auckland 10, New Zealand

Typeset in Linotron Univers and Century Old Style to an original design by Andrew Oliver.
Illustrations on p.1 and p.337 by Henry Iles. Illustrations in Part One and Part Three by Edward Briant.
Printed by Cox & Wyman Ltd, Reading.

416pp, includes index

A catalogue record for this book is available from the British Library.

ISBN 1-85828-136-9

Costa Rica

THE ROUGH GUIDE

Written and researched by
Jean McNeil

THE ROUGH GUIDES

LIST OF MAPS

Costa Rica	vi–vii
National Parks, Biological Reserves, Wildlife Refuges and principal private reserves	41
Chapter divisions	59
San José and surrounds	61
Central San José	72
The Valle Central and the Highlands	102
Alajuela	105
Heredia	117
Parque Nacional Braulio Carrillo	119
Cartago	125
Limón province and the Caribbean coast	135
Puerto Limón	141
Tortuguero village and Parque Nacional	151
Cahuita village	158
Parque Nacional Cahuita	165
Puerto Viejo de Talamanca	166
The Zona Norte	178
Fortuna	183
Puerto Viejo de Sarapiquí and around	195
Guanacaste	207
Liberia	216
Parque Nacional Rincón de la Vieja	222
Parque Nacional Santa Rosa	225
Parque Nacional Guanacaste	230
Tamarindo	238
Nicoya	244
The Central Pacific and Southern Nicoya	255
Monteverde	258
Santa Elena	261
Puntarenas	272
Montezuma	280
Playa Jacó	288
Quepos	292
Parque Nacional Manuel Antonio	299
The Zona Sur	303
Parque Nacional Chirripó	307
Golfito	318
Puerto Jiménez	324
Parque Nacional Corcovado	326

MAP SYMBOLS

32	Highway	⌒1500⌒	Contour
	Road	▲	Mountain peak
— —	Ferry route	ⓘ	Information Centre
▪▪▪▪▪	International boundary	⊠	Post Office
▪ ▪ ▪	Chapter division boundary	■	Building
✗	Airport	⊞	Church
☆	Bus stop	⊞	Cemetery
▲	Campground	▦	Park
∴	Ruins	▦	National Park
⏛	Gardens	▦	Reserves & Refuges
⚜	Waterfall	▧	Mangrove swamp
∿	Rocks	▨	Coral

CONTENTS

Introduction viii

PART ONE BASICS 1

Getting there from North America 3
Getting there from Britain 6
Getting there from Australasia 8
Red tape and visas 10
Insurance 11
Health 13
Information and maps 16
Costs, money and banks 18
Getting around 21
Accommodation 26
Eating and drinking 29
Mail, phones and telecommunications 34

The media 35
Crime and personal safety 37
Women travellers 38
Geography, climate and seasons 38
National Parks and Reserves 40
Outdoor activities 46
Public holidays and festivities 51
Shopping 52
Gay and lesbian Costa Rica 52
Travelling with children 53
Work, volunteering and study 54
Directory 56

PART TWO THE GUIDE 59

■ 1 SAN JOSÉ 61

■ 2 THE VALLE CENTRAL AND THE HIGHLANDS 100

■ 3 LIMÓN PROVINCE AND THE CARIBBEAN COAST 134

■ 4 THE ZONA NORTE 177

■ 5 GUANACASTE 206

■ 6 THE CENTRAL PACIFIC AND SOUTHERN NICOYA 254

■ 7 THE ZONA SUR 302

PART THREE CONTEXTS 337

A brief history of Costa Rica 339
Landscape and wildlife 351
Time running out: the tropical rainforest 361
Conservation and tourism 366
Books 372
Language 378
Glossary 382
Index 384

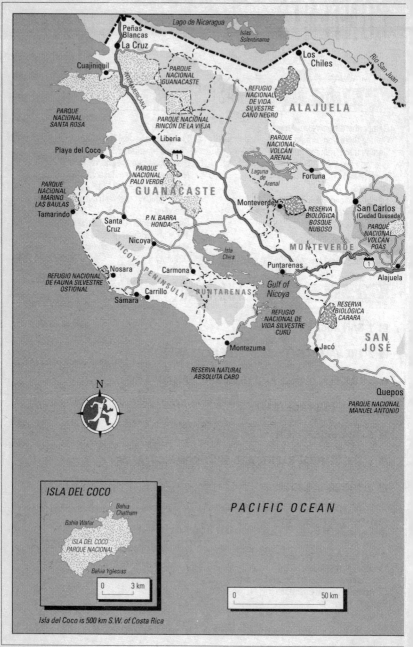

ISLA DEL COCO

Bahia Chatham

Bahia Wafer

ISLA DEL COCO
PARQUE NACIONAL

Bahia Yglesias

0   3 km

Isla del Coco is 500 km S.W. of Costa Rica

PACIFIC OCEAN

0   50 km

INTRODUCTION

As you fly over the Central American isthmus, Costa Rica spreads out beneath you like a whale basking in the sea, its narrow, mountain-ridged back clad with the barnacle-like forms of volcanos. To the north lies the broad bulk of Nicaragua, while to the south the crooked finger of Panamá reaches out to South America. On the Pacific coast, two peninsulas, the Nicoya and the Osa, clutch at the sea like crab's claws; by comparison the Caribbean coast – just 280km away at the country's widest point – is dead straight and raked by waves.

Despite its small size, Costa Rica possesses 5 percent of the world's total biodiversity, in part due to its position as a transition zone between North and South America, and also to a complex terracing of micro-climates created by differences in altitude. With one of the most enlightened and dedicated approaches to **conservation** in the world, the country has made an impressive effort to preserve its wildlands, and in the Americas is second only to Ecuador for the proportion (about 25 percent) of land it protects. Somewhat ironically, deforestation assails much of the remaining tropical forests to the extent that by the year 2000 there may be no significant patches of forest left outside the boundaries of protected areas.

In sharp contrast to the brutal internal conflicts in Guatemala or the grinding poverty of Nicaragua, Costa Rica has become synonymous with stability and prosperity, with a long democratic tradition, free and open elections, no standing army (it was abolished in 1948) and a Nobel Peace Prize to its name, won by former president, Oscar Arias. It has also become the prime **eco-tourism** destination in Central America, if not in all the Americas, due in no small part to its efficient self-promotion. The main draw is its complex system of national parks and wildlife refuges. In the last few years, hundreds of thousands of visitors – mainly from the United States and Canada – have come to walk trails through million-year-old rainforests, raft foaming whitewater rapids, surf on the Pacific beaches and climb the volcanos that punctuate the country's mountainous spine. More than anything it is the enduring **natural beauty** that impresses. Milk-thick twilight and dawn mists gather in the clefts and ridges divided by high mountain passes; on the Pacific coast, carmine and mauve sunsets go down into the sea like meteors; vaulting canopy trees and thick deciduous understories carpet large areas of undisturbed rainforest, and vestiges of high-altitude cloudforest offer glimpses into a misty, primeval universe, home to the jaguar, the lumbering Jurassic tapir and the truly resplendent quetzal.

So much is said about Costa Rica's rich plant and animal life that its **human population** often gets forgotten in all the hype. Costa Ricans enjoy the highest rate of literacy, health care, education and life expectancy in the isthmus. That said, it is certainly not the middle-class country that it's often portrayed to be, with a significant percentage of people living below the poverty line. While it is modernizing fast, and almost half the populace is concentrated in urban areas, the country still has the highest rural population density in Latin America and society still revolves around the twin axes of *campo* (countryside) and family. In part drawn by these "traditional" values, in recent years an estimated 35,000 North American citizens have come to settle here, most of them retirees, along with a sizable European population, prompting some foreign enclaves to be named "gringolandia".

One glib accusation you're almost certain to hear lobbed at the tiny nation is that it has no **culture** or **history**. It's certainly true that there are no ancient Mesoamerican monuments on the scale of Chichén Itzá or Tikal, and just 1 percent of the population is of indigenous extraction, so you will see little native Amerindian culture. Costa Rica's indigenous peoples experienced a rapid decline in the years immediately following the Spanish settlement of the country in 1560, largely due to Old World diseases such as smallpox and influenza. However, anyone who has time to spend, and whose Spanish is good enough, will find Costa Rica's character rooted in distinct local cultures, from the Afro-Caribbean province of Limón, with its Creole cuisine, games and patois, to the traditional *ladino* values embodied by the *sabanero* (cowboy) of Guanacaste. Above all, however long you spend in the country, and wherever you go, you're sure to be left with mental snapshots of *la vida campesina*, or rural life – whether it be aloof horsemen trotting by on dirt roads, coffee-plantation day-labourers setting off to work in the dawn mists of the Highlands, or avocado-pickers cycling home at sunset.

Where to go

Though everyone passes through it, hardly anyone falls in love with **San José**, Costa Rica's capital city and transportation hub. Often dismissed as an ugly sprawl, lacking in metropolitan ambience, it is much underrated, with a stirring setting amid jagged mountain peaks, some excellent cafés and restaurants, leafy parks, a lively university district and a good arts scene. The surrounding **Valle Central**, agricultural heartland of the country, is generally seen in terms of a series of easy day trips from the capital. Most popular are the volcanos: the huge crater of **Volcán Poás**, bubbling and simmering, and largely dormant **Volcán Irazú**, a strange lunar landscape high above the regional capital of **Cartago**.

Founded as a dairy farming community by American Quaker settlers in the early 1950s, **Monteverde** has become the country's number-one tourist attraction. It's the community-founded **Cloudforest Reserve** that pulls in the visitors, who flock here to walk trails through some of the only remaining pristine cloudforest in the Americas. Of the many **beaches**, **Manuel Antonio** wins the popularity contest, with its picture-postcard perfect Pacific setting. Others, particularly the **Nicoya Peninsula** beaches of Sámara and Nosara, are equally pretty, and far less touristed. The steamy **Caribbean coast** holds few good swimming beaches, many of them plagued by strong currents and sharks. However, this is the side of the country where you're most likely to see the seasonal mass-nestings of formerly endangered giant sea turtles, at the isolated community of **Tortuguero**, linked by a series of lazy lagoons to the earthquake-battered port of **Limón**.

Though nowhere in the country is further than nine hours' drive from San José – it's the condition of the roads, rather than distance, that determine the length of any journey – the far north and the far south are less visited than other regions. The broad alluvial plains of the **Zona Norte**, stretching up to the Nicaraguan border at the Río San Juan, are often overlooked, despite featuring active **Volcán Arenal**, which spouts and spews over the friendly tourist hangout of **Fortuna**, affording arresting nighttime scenes of blood-red lava illuminating the sky. It's in the north of the country, too, that you'll find some of Costa Rica's groundbreaking scientific **research stations**, including the tourist lodge and private rainforest reserve of **Rara Avis** and the **La Selva** biological station, both of which are superb destinations for birders and visitors with specialist interests in botany and the life of the rainforest. Off-the-beaten-path travellers and serious hikers will be happiest in the rugged **Zona Sur**, where you can climb to the highest point in the country, **Mount Chirripó**, in the national park of the same name. **Parque Nacional Corcovado**, probably the best destination in the country for walkers, is tucked away in the extreme southwest, on the outstretched feeler of the Osa Peninsula. Protecting the last significant area of tropical wet forest on the Pacific coast of the isthmus, Corcovado is also one of the only places in the country where you have a fighting chance of seeing some of the wildlife for which the country is so famed.

In the northwest, the cattle-ranching province of **Guanacaste** is often called "the home of Costa Rican folklore". It's difficult to find living and authentic examples of the folkloric tradition today, however, except perhaps in the traditional marimba music that you'll hear only at local fiestas and special occasions. *Sabanero* (cowboy) culture dominates here, with exuberant, rag-tag rodeos, and large cattle haciendas set amid a deforested, but nonetheless affecting, landscape. The province's **Parque Nacional Rincón de la Vieja** is one of the prime hiking destinations in the country, a superb, fantastical place dotted with ethereal volcanic mudpots and steam holes.

Limón province, which borders the Caribbean coast, is the polar opposite to traditional *ladino* Guanacaste, with about 30 percent of its population descended from Afro-Caribbeans. Brought to Costa Rica at the end of the nineteenth century to work on the construction of the San José–Limón railroad (the "Jungle Train", which no longer runs), the Jamaicans brought their language (Creole English), their Protestantism and the West Indian traditions that remain relatively intact today. In the Talamancan region to the south live the last significant populations of Bribrí and Cabecar indigenous peoples, although you cannot in general visit their communities.

When to go

Although Costa Rica lies between 8° and 11° north of the equator, **temperatures**, governed by the vastly varying altitudes, are by no means universally high, and can plummet to below freezing at the top of Mt Chirripó. Local **micro-climates** predominate and make weather unpredictable, though to an extent you can depend upon the **two-season** rule. From roughly May to mid-November you will have afternoon rains and sunny mornings. The rains are heaviest in September and October and while they can be fierce, will only impede you from travelling in the more remote areas of the country – the Nicoya Peninsula especially – where dirt roads become impassible to all but the sturdiest 4WDs. In the dry season most areas are just that: dry all day, with occasional blustery northern winds blowing in during January or February and cooling things off. Otherwise you can depend upon sunshine and warm temperatures.

In recent years Costa Rica has been booked solid during the **peak season**, the North American winter months, when bargains are few and far between. The crowds peter out after Easter, but return again to an extent in June and July. During peak times you have to plan well in advance, faxing the hotels of your choice, usually pre-paying or at least putting down a deposit by credit card, and arriving armed with faxed confirmations and a set itinerary. Travellers who prefer to play it by ear are much better off coming during the low or rainy season (euphemistically called the "green season" in an effort not to scare off the tourists), when many hotels offer discounts. The months of November, April (after Easter) and May are the **best times to visit**, when the rains have either just started or just died off, and the country is refreshed, green, and relatively untouristed.

TEMPERATURE AND RAINFALL

	Jan	Feb	Mar	Apr	May	Jun	Jul	Aug	Sep	Oct	Nov	Dec
Caribbean Coast												
Max temp °C	27	28	29	30	31	31	31	31	31	30	28	27
Min temp °C	19	21	22	23	24	24	24	24	23	22	20	20
Average rainfall in mm	137	61	38	56	109	196	163	170	244	305	226	185
San José												
Max temp °C	24	24	26	26	27	26	25	26	26	25	25	24
Min temp °C	14	14	15	17	17	17	17	16	16	16	16	14
Average rainfall in mm	15	5	20	46	229	241	211	241	305	300	145	41
Pacific Coast												
Max temp °C	31	32	32	31	30	31	31	30	29	29	29	31
Min temp °C	22	22	22	23	23	23	23	23	23	23	23	23
Average rainfall in mm	25	10	18	74	203	213	180	201	208	257	259	122

THE
BASICS

GETTING THERE FROM NORTH AMERICA

The easiest way to get to Costa Rica from the USA and Canada is to fly; there are daily non-stop flights to San José from LA and New York, as well as a number of other cities. Fares are very competitive, and airlines match each other almost to the dollar. There are also numerous air, hotel and car packages available, and a variety of escorted tours focusing on nature expeditions, wildlife, ecology or just relaxing on the beach.

You can also travel overland from the US through Central America, with connecting buses through Guatemala, Honduras and Nicaragua, but this is hugely time-consuming and generally uncomfortable.

SHOPPING FOR AIR TICKETS

Barring special offers, the cheapest of the airlines' published fares is usually an **Apex** ticket, although this will carry certain restrictions: you have to book – and pay – at least 21 days before departure, spend at least seven days abroad (maximum stay three months), and you tend to get penalized if you change your schedule. Some airlines also issue **Special Apex** tickets to people younger than 24, often extending the maximum stay to a year. Many offer youth or student fares to **under 25s**; a passport or driving licence are sufficient proof of age, though these tickets are subject to availability and can have eccentric booking conditions. It's worth remembering that most cheap return fares involve spending at least one Saturday night away and that many will only give a percentage refund if you need to cancel or alter your journey. Check the restrictions carefully before buying a ticket.

You can normally cut costs further by going through a **specialist flight agent** – either a **consolidator**, who buys up blocks of tickets from the airlines and sells them at a discount, or a **discount agent**, who in addition to dealing with discounted flights may also offer special student and youth fares and a range of other travel-related services such as insurance, car rentals, tours and the like. Bear in mind, though, that penalties for changing your plans can be stiff. Remember, too, that these companies make their money by dealing in bulk – don't expect them to answer lots of

AIRLINES IN NORTH AMERICA

Aero Costa Rica ☎1-800/237-6274
Direct flights from Atlanta, LA, Miami and Orlando.

Air Canada ☎1-800/555-1212 in Canada; ☎1-800/776-3000 in US
Connecting flights from Montréal.

American Airlines ☎1-800/433-7300
Direct flights from Cleveland, Dallas/Fort Worth, LA, Miami and Nashville.

Aviateca ☎1-800/284-2622
Direct flights from Houston and LA.

Continental Airlines ☎1-800/231-0856
Direct flights from Houston, Montréal and Toronto.

Iberia ☎1-800/772-4642
Direct flights from Miami.

Lacsa ☎1-800/225-2272
Direct flights from LA, Miami, New Orleans, New York, Orlando and San Francisco.

Mexicana ☎1-800/531-7921
Direct flights from LA via Mexico City.

Taca ☎1-800/535-8780
Direct flights from Houston and San Francisco.

United Airlines ☎1-800/241-6522
Direct flights from Houston, San Francisco and Washington, DC.

questions. Some agents specialize in **charter flights**, which may be cheaper than anything available on a scheduled flight, but again departure dates are fixed and withdrawal penalties are high (check the refund policy). If you travel a lot, **discount travel clubs** are another option – the annual membership fee may be worth it for benefits such as cut-price air tickets and car rental.

Don't, however, automatically assume that tickets bought through a travel specialist will be cheapest – once you get a quote, check with the **airlines** and you may turn up an even better deal. Be advised, also, that the pool of travel companies is swimming with sharks – exercise caution and *never* deal with a company that demands cash up front or refuses to accept payment by credit card.

Regardless of where you buy your ticket, the fare will depend on the **season**. The low season for flights from North America to Costa Rica is May through November; high season is December to May. **Fares** are steepest during the Christmas period, from mid-December through the first week in January. Flying at the weekend will bump up fares by about $50; all price ranges quoted below assume midweek, low-season travel. Student fares can be $30–100 cheaper.

FLIGHTS FROM THE US

Continental, American and *United Airlines,* along with *Taca*, an El Salvadorian carrier, and *Lacsa* (Costa Rican), fly **non-stop to San José** from

their gateway cities. Many discounters and consolidators use *Lacsa, Aero Costa Rica, Taca* or *Aviateca*, a Guatemalan airline.

The best low-season **fares** for direct flights from LA to San José (about 6hr) are around $680 round-trip; from New York (7hr 30min) $660; from Denver (7hr); and $460 from Miami (1hr 30min), Houston (3hr 30min) and New Orleans (5hr 30min). For a rundown of which airlines serve which cities, see the box opposite. Most require a three to five-day minimum stay and a maximum of 30 days. There are also some **charter flights** available: *LTU International Airlines*, a charter airline based in Miami, have offered round-trip fares for as low as $300 (tickets must be bought through a travel agent).

Some **tour companies** will sell you a discounted round-trip air fare even if you don't want to sign up for a tour. One California company, for example, recently offered a low-season fare of $580 round-trip from LA, including an air-conditioned jeep for seven days.

For those who wish to include Costa Rica in a flight itinerary that includes **Mexico or South America**, discounters offer fares that allow several stopovers. A ticket good for one year, for instance, starting in and returning to LA, and allowing stops in Costa Rica, Lima, Buenos Aires, Cape Town, Cairo, Athens and London, is about $2400. *Mexicana* makes connections from LA to San José via Mexico City, but this is not necessarily cheaper than taking a direct flight.

FLIGHTS FROM CANADA

There are **no direct flights from Canada** to San José. From Toronto *American* flies via Miami, and *Taca* via Houston. From Toronto and Montréal, *Continental* flies via Houston for a low-season fare of around C$840. Flights from Vancouver on *American* (via Dallas and Guatemala) and *United* (via LA and El Salvador) hover around C$870.

Air Canada has connecting flights from Montréal with *Continental*, and out of Toronto with *Taca* and *American*. There are also many **charter flights** out of the major cities, especially during the winter. These should be booked through travel agents.

PACKAGES AND ORGANIZED TOURS

There are a huge variety of **package tours** to Costa Rica from North America: check the travel sections of the Sunday papers for the latest offers. Typical of tours offered by **airlines** are *American Airlines'* three-day hotel packages, which, including transfers and a sightseeing tour

start at $180 for a hotel in downtown San José, rising to $350 for a hotel on Hermosa Beach.

The range of **fully escorted tours** is extremely wide. As an example, the Washington based *REI Adventures* offers combination 10-day biking, rafting and hiking tours for $1395, not including air fare. In Canada, *Adventures Abroad* is winning high marks among fans of low-key, small-group tours, offering two-week tours that include birdwatching, visits to tropical rainforests, volcanos and beaches for $1495 (land only) or $1995 including air fare from Miami. For specialist tours for gay and lesbian travellers see p.53.

OVERLAND TO COSTA RICA

There is good **overland bus service** between Guatemala, Honduras, Nicaragua and Costa Rica, and on south into Panamá, connecting with Costa Rica's international bus company, *Ticabus*.

Ticabus leaves **Guatemala City** daily for San José at 1pm. It's a two and a half-day trip, entailing nights (at your own expense) in San Salvador

NORTH AMERICAN SPECIALIST TOUR OPERATORS

Above the Clouds Trekking, PO Box 398, Worcester, MA 01602-0398 (☎1-800/233-4499).
Challenging treks, rafting through rainforests, guided ecological adventures.

Adventures Abroad, 1037 W Broadway, Suite 202, Vancouver, BC, Canada V6H 1E3 (☎1-800/665-2998).
Excellent, small-group tours with strong cultural focus.

American Airlines Fly Away Vacations (☎1-800/433-7300).
Hotel, sightseeing and car rental packages.

Backroads, 1516 5th St, Berkeley, CA 94710-1740 (☎1-800/462-2848).
Walking, biking and hiking vacations.

Eco-Adventures Special Interest Tours and Travel, 10020 N 27th St, Phoenix, AZ 85028 (☎1-800/525-6772).
Nature and wildlife tours, rafting, camping.

Elderhostel, 75 Federal St, Boston, MA 02110 (☎617/426-8056).
Extensive network of educational and activity programmes, cruises and homestays for people over 60 (companions may be younger).

Euro-Global Travel, 5670 Wilshire Blvd, LA, CA 90036 (☎1-800/235-5222).
Flight, hotel and car combination packages.

Green Tortoise Adventure Travel, 494 Broadway, San Francisco, CA 94133 (☎415/956-7500).
Inexpensive tours in Costa Rica and Central America, aboard converted buses.

Imagine Travel Alternatives, PO Box 13219, Burton, WA 98103 (☎1-800/777-3975).
Travel arrangements for independent travellers; some escorted small-group tours.

International Expeditions Inc, 1 Environs Park, Helena, AL 35080 (☎1-800/633-4734).
All-inclusive natural history tours.

Nature Expeditions International, 474 Willamette St, PO Box 11496, Eugene, OR 97440 (☎1-800/869-0639).
Small-group expeditions led by anthropology, biology and natural history specialists.

Questers Worldwide Nature Tours, 257 Park Ave South, New York, NY 10010 (☎1-800/468-8668).
Upmarket nature tours.

REI Adventures, PO Box 1938, Sumner, WA 98390-0800 (☎1-800/622-2236).
Biking, hiking, rafting tours; adventure travel; discounts to REI members.

and Managua. From Tegulcigalpa in **Honduras**, *Ticabus* leaves daily at 7.30am for San José, arriving 48 hours later (overnight in Managua, at your own expense). From **Managua** you can get a *SIRCA* (Nicaraguan) bus (Mon, Wed & Fri; 6.30am; ☎73833), or, more comfortably, a *Ticabus* (Tues, Thurs & Sat; 7am; ☎22094); in both cases the journey takes 11hr or more.

GETTING THERE FROM BRITAIN

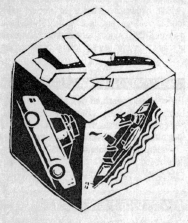

There are two main choices when it comes to flying from Britain to Costa Rica. One is to fly scheduled via the US, which gives you a variety of choices of airlines and cities in which you can potentially stop over. The other is on a scheduled flight via several European cities, whose carriers serve Costa Rica. Flights via Europe may be incrementally cheaper, but may also take longer, depending upon waiting time in usually more than one transfer point. The routings through the US, especially Miami, can get you to Costa Rica in as little as 13 hours – including changing planes – while via Europe you can expect to spend as much as 18 or 20 hours in transit.

Any reasonably direct routing to San José entails leaving from Heathrow; if you're flying from Ireland this is your only option. **Low season** to Costa Rica from the UK is generally April–November; at the **Christmas** period all airlines increase their fares shamelessly.

Getting to Costa Rica from the UK by air can be surprisingly **good value**, especially compared with fares from the US. Although there should be no problem fixing flexible return dates and six-month to a year ticket validity, few under-26 or student **discounts** apply – your best bet is to try a travel operator that specializes in student fares (see box opposite). One way to cut costs is to get on one of the very few **charter flights** from Europe, mainly from Germany; these operate only in the winter and should be booked through a travel agent.

The **cheapest low season air fare** from the UK is with *Viasa*, at £490 return. A popular route, this allows you one free stopover in either Caracas or Cartegena. *Avianca*, Colombia's national airline, has a fare of around £550 return with a stopover in Bogotá.

Via Europe, the best bets are with *KLM* and *Iberia*. While *Iberia* is usually slightly cheaper, at about £500, their London–Madrid–Miami/Santo Domingo–San José (plus sometimes a stop in Honduras, too) makes for a very long haul. However, their flights are frequent – London–San José and back daily except Tuesday – and they are accommodating about changing tickets. *KLM*, meanwhile, has better on-board service than *Iberia*, and will get you London–Amsterdam–Curaçao/Panamá City–San José relatively painlessly for about £550 (note that you can't get off the plane in Curaçao). They fly only twice a week, however, and it's sometimes difficult to find space on one of their flights if you want to change your dates.

Options on **US airlines** include *United*, who can route you practically anywhere, as they have the largest network of flights from the USA to Central and South America; they fly daily London–Washington DC/Miami–San José (if you go through DC you can travel to San José via Miami or Mexico City). *American Airlines* offer a £550 fare; you can stop over in Boston, New York, Philadelphia, Dallas, Chicago, LA or Miami for only £60 more. Theirs is the quickest, although not the most economical, routing, from

AIRLINES IN BRITAIN

American Airlines, 15 Berkeley St, London W1X 5AE (☎0181/572 5555).

Avianca, Linen Hall, Suite 246, 162–168 Regent St, London W1R 5TA (☎0171/437 3664).

British Airways, 156 Regent St, London W1R 5TA; 146 New St, Birmingham B2 4HN; 19–21 St Mary's Gate, Market St, Manchester M1 1PU; 66 Gordon St, Glasgow G1 3RS; 32 Frederick St, Edinburgh EH2 2JR (all enquiries ☎0345/222111).

British Midland Airways, Donington Hall, Castle Donington, Derby DE74 2SB (☎0345/554554).

Iberia, Venture House, 29 Glasshouse St, London W1R 5RG (☎0171-830 0011; Birmingham ☎0121/643 1953; Manchester ☎0161/436 6444).

KLM, Reservations (☎0181/750 9000); ticket office at Terminal 4, Heathrow.

United Airlines, 193 Piccadilly, London W1V 0AD (☎0181/990 9900).

Viasa, Venture House, 29 Glasshouse St., London W1R 5RG (☎0171/830 0011; Birmingham ☎0121/643 1953; Manchester ☎0161/436 6444).

Virgin Atlantic, Ashdown House, High St, Crawley, West Sussex RH10 1DQ (☎01293/747747).

FLIGHT AGENTS IN BRITAIN

APA Travel, 138 Eversholt St, London NW1 (☎0171/387 5337).

Campus Travel, 52 Grosvenor Gardens, London SW1W 0AG (☎0171/730 3402); 541 Bristol Rd, Selly Oak, Birmingham B29 6AU (☎0121/414 1848); 39 Queen's Rd, Clifton, Bristol BS8 1QE (☎0117/929 2494); 5 Emmanuel St, Cambridge CB1 1NE (☎01223/324283); 53 Forest Rd, Edinburgh EH1 2QP (☎0131/225 6111); 166 Deansgate, Manchester M3 3FE (☎0161/833 2046); 105–106 St Aldates, Oxford OX1 1DD (☎01865/242067).
Student/youth travel specialists, with branches also in YHA shops and on university campuses.

Council Travel, 28a Poland St, London W1V 3DB (☎0171/437 7767).
Flights and student discounts.

Journey Latin America, 14–16 Devonshire Rd, Chiswick, London W4 2HD (☎0181/747 8315; fax 0181/742 1312).
Very good fares; adept at multiple stops, stop-overs, open jaws, etc. Also tours (see p.8)

South Coast Student Travel, 61 Ditchling Rd, Brighton BN1 4SD (☎01273/570226).
Student experts, with plenty to offer non-students.

STA Travel, 86 Old Brompton Rd, London SW7; 38 Store St, London WC1E; personal callers at 117 Euston Rd, London NW1 (☎0171/361 6262 tele-sales for all three branches); 25 Queen's Rd, Bristol BS8 (☎0117/929 4399); 38 Sidney St, Cambridge CB2 (☎01223/366966); 75 Deansgate, Manchester M3; 14 Oxford Rd, Manchester M1 (☎0161/834 0668 for both); 88 Vicar Lane, Leeds LS1 (☎0113/244 9212); 36 George St, Oxford OX1 (☎01865/792800); and offices in Birmingham, Canterbury, Cardiff, Coventry, Durham, Glasgow, Loughborough, Nottingham, Sheffield and Warwick.
Discount flights, tours, accommodation and insurance with particularly good deals for students and people under 26.

Trailfinders, 42–48 Earls Court Rd, London W8 (☎0171/938 3366); 194 Kensington High St, London, W8 (☎0171/938 3939); 58 Deansgate, Manchester M3 2FF (☎0161/839 6969); 254–284 Sauchiehall St, Glasgow G2 3EH (☎0141/353 2224); 22–24 The Priory, Queensway, Birmingham B4 6BS (☎0121/236 1234); 48 Corn St, Bristol BS1 1HQ (☎0117/929 9000).
One of the best-informed and most efficient agents.

Travel Bug, 597 Cheetham Hill Rd, Manchester M8 5EJ (☎0161/721 4000).
Large range of discounted tickets.

London to San José via Miami. However, of all the US airlines, *American* has the most confusing range of **"shoulder seasons"**, when the price of the San José fare goes up above £600. Usually these are around Easter, and at long American weekends like Labor Day. *Continental* fly daily London–Houston–San José (an overnight stay in Houston is sometimes required).

Other options are to combine a flight, either scheduled or charter, from London to **Miami** on *Virgin Atlantic* or *British Airways* and buy your Miami–San José ticket separately. There may be some scope for finding rock-bottom fares to San José once you are in Miami from the airlines themselves, especially off-season (May–Nov). For ideas, see p.4.

PACKAGES AND ORGANIZED TOURS

A number of British operators offer **specialist tours** to Costa Rica; rainforest hiking, birdwatching and natural history tours are particularly popular. All those listed below offer one or all of these activities, as well as booking flights; *Reef and Rainforest* have the most detailed and specialized itineraries. Their 8-day tour costs around £1400 – but note that only the air fare from Miami is included; you have to pay for the London–Miami–London leg separately.

Walkers should contact their local ramblers' association, who may have information on group visits to Costa Rica. **Youth Hostel members** can contact the British IYHF (see p.29) for information on Costa Rica's hostels, some of which are included in small packages available from the *Albergue Toruma* in San José (see p.70).

SPECIALIST TOUR OPERATORS IN BRITAIN

Journey Latin America, 14–16 Devonshire Rd, Chiswick, London W4 2HD (☎0181/747 8315; fax 0181/742 1312).
Organized and tailor-made tours, from day trips to several days, including whitewater rafting, volcanos and birdwatching. Prices tend to be high but tours are of the highest standard.

Reef and Rainforest Tours, 3 Moorashes, Totnes, Devon, TQ9 5TN (☎01803/866965; fax 01803/865916).
Ecotours and "research programmes", on which you can work with scientists, collecting data, photographing animals and the like. Costa Rican programme includes a humpback whale research project off the coast of the Osa Peninsula. Also birding, natural history and "adventure" itineraries.

South American Experience, 47 Causton St, London SW1P 4AT (☎0171/976 5511; fax 0171/976 6908).
Tailor-made itineraries; the 19-day tour to Costa Rica ("the Turtle") takes in San José, Manuel Antonio, Tortuguero, Volcán Poás and Monteverde. Good value flights, too, plus fares with multiple stops.

Sunvil Holidays, 7–8 Upper Square, Isleworth, Middlesex (☎0181/568 4499).
Flexible fly-drive itineraries, with accommodation in a number of areas including Sámara and Nosara.

Trips Worldwide, 9 Byron Place, Clifton, Bristol BS8 1JT (☎0117/987 2626; fax 0171/987 2627).
Highly recommended for its great range of tours, some individually tailored, at varying prices. Friendly, knowledgeable staff.

GETTING THERE FROM AUSTRALIA AND NZ

From Australia only *United* offer a published fare through to Costa Rica. Otherwise you're looking at buying a ticket to LA or Mexico City combined with a separate fare to San José; this option usually involves a stopover in the carrier's home city. From New Zealand you have to fly via LA.

The **low season** for travel from Australia and New Zealand to Costa Rica is February and March, and mid-October to the end of November; confusingly, prices in Costa Rica itself are high at these times. **High-season** fares apply from December 1 to mid-January. All fares quoted below are low-season. Student and under-26 fares, where available, are about 10 percent cheaper.

From Australia *United* depart daily from Sydney and Brisbane to LA, with direct connection to San José ($2100). If you want to stop off in

AUSTRALASIAN AIRLINES

Air New Zealand, 5 Elizabeth St, Sydney (☎02/
9223 4666); cnr Customs and Queen streets,
Auckland (☎09/366 2424).

Cathay Pacific, Swire House, 8 Spring St,
Sydney (☎02/931 5500); 11th Floor, Arthur
Anderson Tower, National Bank Centre, 205–209
Queen St, Auckland (☎09/379 0861).

Garuda, 175 Clarence St, Sydney (☎02/334 9900);
120 Albert St, Auckland (☎09/366 1855).

Japanese Airlines, 17 Bligh St, Sydney (☎02/
9233 4500). No NZ office.

LAC No Australasian office.

MAS, 388 George St, Sydney (☎1800/269 998 or
02/9231 5066); Floor 12, Swanson Centre, 12–26
Swanson St, Auckland (☎09/373 2741).

Philippine, 49 York St, Sydney (☎1800/112 458).

Qantas, International Square, Jamison St, Sydney
(☎02/9236 3636); Qantas House, 154 Queen St,
Auckland (☎09/303 2506).

United Airlines 10 Barrack St, Sydney (☎02/9237
8888); 7 City Rd, Auckland (☎09/307 9500).

NOTE: ☎1800 toll free numbers apply only if
dialled outside the city in the address.

AUSTRALASIAN DISCOUNT AGENTS

Accent on Travel, 545 Queen St, Brisbane (☎07/
3832 1777).

Adventure World, 73 Walker St, N Sydney (☎02/
956 7766); 8 Victoria Ave, Perth (☎09/221 2300;
☎08/9221 2300 from Sept 1997).

Anywhere Travel, 345 Anzac Parade, Kingsford,
Sydney (☎02/663 0411).

Brisbane Discount Travel, 360 Queen St,
Brisbane (☎07/3229 9211).

Budget Travel, PO Box 505, Auckland (☎09/309
4313).

Discount Travel Specialists, Shop 53, Forrest
Chase, Perth (☎09/221 1400; ☎08/9221 1400 from
Sept 1997).

Flight Centres, Australia: Circular Quay, Sydney
(☎02/9241 2422); Bourke St, Melbourne (☎03/
9650 2899); plus other branches nationwide.
New Zealand: National Bank Towers, 205–225
Queen St, Auckland (☎09/309 6171); Shop 1M,

National Mutual Arcade, 152 Hereford St,
Christchurch (☎09/379 7145); 50–52 Willis St,
Wellington (☎04/472 8101); plus other branches
countrywide.

Passport Travel, 320b Glenferrie Rd, Malvern,
Melbourne (☎03/9824 7183).

STA Travel, Australia: 732 Harris St, Ultimo,
Sydney (☎02/9212 1255 or 9281 9866); 256
Flinders St, Melbourne (☎03/9347 4711); other
offices in Townsville, Cairns and state capitals.
New Zealand: Travellers' Centre, 10 High St,
Auckland (☎09/309 4058); 233 Cuba St,
Wellington (☎04/385 0561); 223 High St,
Christchurch (☎03/379 9098); other offices in
Dunedin, Palmerston North and Hamilton.

Topdeck Travel, 45 Grenfell St, Adelaide (☎08/
8410 1110).

Tymtro Travel, Suite G12, Wallaceway Shopping
Centre, Chatswood, Sydney (☎02/413 1219).

North America before heading on to Costa Rica,
with this fare they also offer coupons for up to
nine single flights (US$349 for the first three then
US$50–100 each). Other options that could
include Costa Rica are Cathay Pacific–United's
"Globetrotter" fare, which allows six stopovers
worldwide on their combined network (China
excepted) for between $2350–2900 and a five-
stopover deal to the US with Air New Zealand–
American from $2200.

Travelling to San José **via LA or Mexico
City**, the best-value deals from Brisbane, Sydney
and Melbourne – using example return fares of
$750 for San José–LA and $420 for San José–
Mexico City – are as follows: Garuda Indonesia
via Denpasar and LA ($2520; flat rate of $2350

from Cairns and Darwin); Philippine via Manila
and LA ($2350); MAS via Kuala Lumpur and either
LA ($2620) or Mexico City ($2290); Japanese
Airlines via Tokyo and LA ($2400), or Qantas via
LA and Miami ($2650). Add $750 to the above for
Perth departures (for transit to the east coast),
and $600 for flights from Darwin, except in the
case of the Garuda fare.

From **New Zealand** the best deals are out of
Auckland (add NZ$100 for Wellington depar-
tures), with Air New Zealand, MAS, Qantas or
United Airlines to LA, then on to San José with
United (NZ$2679). United also combine with a
variety of Asian carriers for **RTW** fares via LA,
Europe and Asia (NZ$2287), but not all allow
Costa Rica as a stopover.

An increasing number of Australasian operators offer **specialist tours** to Costa Rica; activity and natural history tours are particularly popular, and there are a number of good surfing packages.

AUSTRALASIAN SPECIALIST AGENTS

Adventure Associates, 197 Oxford St, Bondi Junction (☎02/389 7466).
Independent and escorted small-group tours, city stopovers and cruises in and around Costa Rica. Trekking, mountain biking, whitewater rafting, canal trips and sportsfishing.

Adventure Specialists, 69 Liverpool St, Sydney, 2000 (☎02/261 2927 or 1800/634 465).
Adventure trips (8–22 days) from San José, including whitewater rafting, rainforest hikes, National Parks and horseriding.

Adventure World, 73 Walker St, Sydney (☎02/956 7766 or 1800/221 931); branches in Melbourne, Brisbane, Adelaide and Perth; 101 Great South Rd, Remuera, Auckland (☎09/524 5118).
Five-day San José tour and accommodation package; 17-day rainforest tours from San José by bus, boat and foot through the National Parks, including Volcán Poás and Tortuguero.

Contours, 466 Victoria St, N Melbourne 3051 (☎03/329 5211).
Specialists in tour packages to the Caribbean, Central and South America: agents for the Costa Rican tour company Tikal Tours (see p.25).

Exodus, Suite 5, Level 5, 1 York St, Sydney 2000 (☎02/251 5430 or 1800/800 724); in New Zealand contact *Adventure World*.
Eight-week overland tours trucking between Mexico City and Panamá City; Costa Rican highlights include turtle-spotting and cloudforest tours.

Surf Travel Company, 12 Cronulla Plaza, Cronulla Beach, Sydney (☎02/527 4722); Kirra Surf Centre, cnr Gold Coast Highway and Coolangatta rd, Kirra, Queensland (☎075/99 2828); 6 Danbury Drive, Torbay, Auckland (☎09/473 8388).
Fly–4WD–accommodation surfing packages to Guanacaste, Golfito and Jacó; also overland surfing tours from LA.

Wiltrans/Maupintour, 189 Kent St, Sydney 2000 (☎02/255 0899).
All-inclusive 9-day guided tours from San José (Oct–July) through Parks and Refuges including Volcán Poás and Caño Negro. Also US–Central American cruises, some including stopovers in Costa Rica.

RED TAPE AND VISAS

Citizens of the US, Canada, the UK, Germany, Italy and Spain and most other western European countries can obtain a 90-day entry stamp for Costa Rica without needing a visa. Citizens of Australia, New Zealand, Ireland and France do not need a visa, either, but are only issued a 30-day entrance stamp. Whatever your nationality, you must in theory show your passport, valid onward ticket, visa for your next country (if applicable) and proof of "sufficient funds" (around $400 per month), but if you arrive by air the last is rarely asked for. Most other nationalities need a visa; always check first with the Costa Rican consulate concerning current regulations. It is likely that a 30-day visa will be issued at a cost of about $25.

Your **entrance stamp** is very important: no matter where you arrive, make sure you get it. You have to carry your passport (or a photocopy) with you at all times in Costa Rica. If you are asked for it and cannot produce it, you may well be detained and fined.

The easiest way to **extend** your entry permit is to leave Costa Rica for 72 hours – to Panamá or Nicaragua, say – and then re-enter, fulfilling the same requirements as on your original trip. You should, although it is at the discretion of the immigration officer, be given another 90- or 30-day stamp. If you prefer not to leave the country, you can apply for a permit or visa extension at the **Departamento de Migración**, in San José (see p.94): a time-consuming and often costly business. You'll need to bring all relevant documents – passport and 3 photographs, onward air or bus ticket – as well as proof of funds (credit cards and/or travellers' cheques). If you do not have a ticket out of Costa Rica you may have to buy one in order to get your extension. Bus tickets are more easily refunded than air tickets; some airlines refuse to cash in onward tickets unless you can produce or buy another one out of the country. Note that you will pay approximately 10 percent tax on all air tickets bought in Costa Rica.

If, for whatever reason, you **overstay** your 90- or 30-day limit, you must get an **exit visa** in order to be allowed to leave the country. This involves going to Migración in San José with your passport and onward ticket. The visa, normally granted after between 1 and 3 days, gives you 30 days in which to leave the country. This can be an expensive process; quite apart from the cost of the visa itself – about $15 – you will have to pay an overstayer's fine ($6 per month) and a departure tax of up to $50 when you leave, whether by land or air. These fees have been subject to abrupt change (always

> **COSTA RICAN EMBASSIES**
>
> **USA** 2114 S St NW, Washington, DC, 2008 (☎202/234-2945).
>
> **Canada** 135 York St, Suite 208, Ottawa, Ontario, K1N 5T4. (☎613/562-2855).
>
> **UK**, 14 Lancaster Gate, London W2 3LH (☎0171/562 2855).
>
> **Australia** 30 Clarence St, Sydney (☎02/261 1177).
>
> *No NZ contact*

upwards) recently, so make sure you ask exactly how much you will be required to pay and ensure that you have sufficient funds – either in colones or dollars – to fork out when you leave. To speed things up a bit, you can also go to a travel agency such as *Tikal Tours*, who have a good reputation for dealing with *trámites* (bureaucracy), handing them all the relevant documents. This is even more expensive, however, adding at least another $15 to the total cost.

Costa Rica has no such thing as a **Working Holiday Visa**. If you plan to stay for a long period, you need a Resident's Permit, which is extremely difficult to get hold of: you need to appoint a Costa Rican resident to act on your behalf (friend, family or a lawyer), fill in stacks of paperwork, and then wait as long as six months for your application to be processed. If you're **studying**, or on a **volunteer programme** (see p.54), the organization or school may sort out visas for you; check in advance.

INSURANCE

As for all Latin American countries, you should buy a comprehensive insurance policy when travelling to Costa Rica. Before buying, however, check that you're not already covered. Bank and credit cards (particularly *AmEx*) often have certain levels of insurance included, especially if you use them to pay for your trip. That said, however, normally the medical cover offered under these policies is not sufficient for Costa Rica, so read the small print carefully.

For Costa Rica you need **medical cover** to at least £1,000,000 or $2,000,000, covering all potential medical expenses plus repatriation. Make sure you take out insurance against **theft** of possessions and baggage, and buy a policy that offers to cover the cost of replacing your passport as well as theft of personal money.

If you plan to participate in **water sports**, or do some **hiking** or **skiing**, you'll probably have to pay a premium; check carefully that any policy you are considering will cover you in case of an accident. Note also that very few insurers will arrange on-the-spot payments in the event of a major expense or loss; you will usually be reimbursed only after going home. In all cases of loss or theft of goods, you will have to **contact the local police** within a certain time limit to have a report made out so that your insurer can process the claim.

NORTH AMERICAN COVER

Canadians are usually covered for medical mishaps overseas by their provincial health plans, while holders of official **student/teacher/youth cards** are entitled to accident coverage and hospital in-patient benefits. **Students** will often find that their student health coverage extends during the vacations and for one term beyond the date of last enrolment, while **homeowners' or renters'** insurance often covers theft or loss of documents, money and valuables while overseas, though conditions and maximum amounts vary.

After exhausting the possibilities above, you might want to contact a specialist **travel insurance** company; your travel agent can usually recommend one, or see the box below. Policies are comprehensive, but maximum payouts tend to be meagre. Most North American travel policies apply only to items lost, stolen or damaged while in the custody of an identifiable, responsible third party – hotel porter or airline, say, or luggage consignment. Premiums vary, so shop around.

The **best deals** are usually through student/ youth travel agencies – *ISIS* policies, for example, cost $48–69 for 15 days (depending on coverage); $80–105 for a month; $149–207 for 2 months, and on up to $510–700 for a year. If you're planning to do any "dangerous sports", figure on a surcharge of 20–50 percent.

BRITISH COVER

Most **travel agents** and **tour operators** will offer you insurance when you book your flight or holiday, and some will insist you take it. These are usually reasonable value, though, as ever, you should check the small print. If you feel the cover is inadequate, or want to compare prices, any travel agent, insurance broker or bank should be able to help. If you have a good "all risks" **home insurance policy** it may well cover your possessions against loss or theft when overseas, and many **private medical schemes** also cover you when abroad – make sure you know the procedure and the helpline number.

For Costa Rica, *Journey Latin America* (see p.8) has one of the most – if not *the* most – comprehensive deals around, covering you for up to £1,000,000 in medical expenses, the same in personal liability, and baggage up to £1250. Prices range from £40 for 8 days to £85 for 45 days (and more – their coverage goes up to 12 months). It can get pricey for 3 months or more; £165 for 3 months and then £50 for each subsequent month.

Other good policies are issued by *Campus Travel* or *STA*; *Endsleigh* (97–107 Southampton Row, London WC1B 4AG; ☎0171/436 4451); *Frizzell* (Frizzell House, County Gates, Bournemouth, Dorset BH1 2NF; ☎01202/292 333) and *Columbus* (17 Devonshire Square, London EC2M 4SQ; ☎0171/375 0011), who also offer an annual multi-trip policy for £125.

TRAVEL INSURANCE COMPANIES IN NORTH AMERICA

Access America, PO Box 90310, Richmond, VA 23230 (☎1-800/284-8300).

Carefree Travel Insurance, PO Box 310, 120 Mineola Blvd, Mineola, NY 11501 (☎1-800/645-2424).

International Student Insurance Service (**ISIS**) – sold by *STA Travel*, which has several branches in the US (see p.4).

Travel Assistance International, 1133 15th St NW, Suite 400, Washington, DC 20005 (☎1-800/ 821-2828).

Travel Guard, 1145 Clark St, Stevens Point, WI 54481 (☎1-800/826-1300).

Travel Insurance Services, 2930 Camino Diablo, Suite 300, Walnut Creek, CA 94596 (☎1-800/937-1387).

Travel agents in Australia and New Zealand offer their own insurance packages, often put together by *AFTA* or *Ready Plan*, typically at a cost of Aus\$125 for 16 days and Aus\$195 for 32

days. Be sure to check the policy if you intend to do participate in adventure sports; mountaineering with ropes, bungee jumping and scuba/assisted diving without an Open Water Licence are not covered.

HEALTH

Travelling in Costa Rica is generally very safe, health-wise. Food tends to be well and hygienically prepared, so bugs and upsets are normally limited to the usual "travellers' tummy". Water supplies in most places are clean and bacteria-free, and few of the infectious illnesses that cause periodic outbreaks in neighbouring countries, like cholera, exist as any real threat in Costa Rica.

In general, as in the rest of Latin America, it tends to be local people, often poor or without proper sanitation or quick access to health care, who contract infectious diseases. If you do fall ill or have an accident, medical treatment in Costa Rica is very good but *very* expensive: extensive health insurance is a must (see "Insurance").

Travellers who are concerned about keeping their immunizations up to date should ideally have a full course of **inoculations** before coming to Costa Rica – though none is a major risk, you might want to make sure that your polio, typhoid, and Hepatitis A and B jabs are up-to-date. An incurable illness and a potentially fatal one, **rabies** should also be taken seriously. There is a vaccine – a course of three injections that has to be started at least a month before departure – but it is expensive, serves only to shorten the course of treatment you need anyway, and is only effective for a maximum of three months. If you don't have a chance or time to get the shots, stay away from dogs, monkeys and any other potentially biting or scratching animals. If you get scratched or bitten, wash the wound at once, with alcohol if possible, and seek medical help *immediately*.

Sunstroke, dehydration and diarrhoea are the likeliest sources of illness in Costa Rica, one possibly

leading to the other, and capable of making you very sick indeed. Costa Rica is just 8° to 11° north of the Equator, which means blazing hot, directly overhead sun. To guard against **sunburn** take at least factor 15 sunscreen and a good hat, and wear both even on slightly overcast days, especially in coastal areas. Even in places where it does not feel excessively hot, like the relatively high altitude of San José and the surrounding Valle Central, protect yourself. **Dehydration** is another possible problem, so keep your fluid level up, and take rehydration salts (*Gastrolyte* is readily available). **Diarrhoea** can be brought on by too much sun and heat sickness. It's a good idea to bring an over-the-counter remedy like *Lomotil* from home – it should only be taken for short periods, however, as extensive use leads to constipation, which is equally uncomfortable and inconvenient while travelling.

COSTA RICA TRAVELLERS' FIRST-AID KIT

Among items you might want to carry with you, especially if you're planning to go hiking (see "Outdoor Activities", p.46), are:

- Antiseptic cream
- Plasters/band aids
- *Imodium* (*Lomotil*) for emergency diarrhoea treatment
- Paracetamol/aspirin
- Rehydration sachets
- Calamine lotion
- Hypodermic needles and sterilized skin wipes (more for the security of knowing you have them than any fear that a local hospital would fail to observe basic sanitary precautions)
- Iodine soap for washing cuts (guards against humidity-encouraged infections)
- Avon's *Skin-so-Soft* lotion for deterring a variety of biting insects
- Sulphur powder (fights sand fleas/chiggers that are ubiquitous in Costa Rica's beach areas)

WATER

The only areas of Costa Rica where it is best not to drink the tap water (or ice cubes, or drinks made with tap water) are the port cities of **Limón** and **Puntarenas**. Bottled water is available in these towns; drink from these and stick with known brands, even if they are more expensive. Though you'll be safe drinking tap water elsewhere in the country, it is possible to pick up the dreaded **giardia**, a bacterium that causes stomach upset and diarrhoea, by drinking out of streams and rivers: campers should pick up their water supplies from the National Park waterspouts, where it's been treated for drinking.

If you can't do this for some reason, the time-honoured method of **boiling** will effectively sterilize water, although it will not remove unpleasant tastes. A minimum boiling time of five minutes (longer at higher altitudes) is sufficient to kill micro-organisms. Boiling water is not always convenient, however, as it is time-consuming and requires supplies of fuel or a travel kettle and power source. **Chemical sterilization** can be carried out using either chlorine or iodine tablets or a tincture of iodine liquid. When using tablets it is essential to follow the manufacturer's dosage and contact time. Tincture of iodine is better; add a couple of drops to one litre of water and leave to stand for twenty minutes. **Pregnant women** or people with **thyroid problems** should consult their doctor before using iodine sterilizing tablets or iodine-based purifiers. Inexpensive iodine removal filters are recommended if treated water is being used continuously for more than a month or of it is being given to babies.

MALARIA AND DENGUE FEVER

Although some sources of information – including perhaps your GP – will tell you that you don't need to worry about **malaria** in Costa Rica, it is in fact a risk, although admittedly statistically small. Around 800 cases of malaria are reported annually, about half of these by tourists. If you want to make absolutely sure of not contracting the illness, and intend to travel extensively anywhere on the **Caribbean coast**, especially in Puerto Limón and south towards Cahuita and Puerto Viejo, you should take a course of prophylactics (usually *Chloroquine* rather than *Mefloquine*), available from your doctor or clinic.

Though a minimal health risk to travellers, some incidences of **Dengue Fever**, another mosquito-borne illness, have been reported in the past few years: local papers often carry scare stories about outbreaks in San José's suburbs and the area immediately south of Puerto Limón. A malady with symptoms very like malaria but characterized by extreme aches and pains in the bones and joints, along with fever and dizziness, Dengue is technically only fatal unless you get it twice, at which point it can become an haemorrhagic fever which is theoretically untreatable. There's no cure for first-time Dengue either, other than rest and painkillers, and the only way to avoid it is to make sure you don't get bitten by mosquitos.

SNAKES

Snakes abound in Costa Rica, but **snakebite** is statistically a small risk – there has been no instance of a fatal bite being received by a tourist in recent years. Most of the victims of Costa Rica's more venomous snakes are field labourers who do not have time or the resources to get to a hospital. Just in case, however, travellers hiking off the beaten track may want to take specific antivenins plus sterile hypodermic needles. If you're worried, you can buy **antivenin** at the University of Costa Rica's "snake farm" in Coronado, outside San José (see p.124), where herpetologists (people who study snakes) are glad to talk to visitors about precautions.

If you have no antivenin and are unlucky enough to **get bitten**, the usual advice is to catch or kill the specimen for identification, since administering the wrong antivenin can cause death, which rather defeats the purpose. For most travellers, though, it seems highly unlikely that they would be able to catch or kill the offending snake – nor should you even try, especially if faced with one of the larger vipers.

In general, **prevention** is better than cure. Before undertaking any activity where you're likely to come across a snake, stop off at the San José **Serpentario** (see p.79) and take a good look at some of Costa Rica's more poisonous specimens, so that you can theoretically identify – and avoid – them in the wild. As a rule of thumb, you should approach rainforest cover and grassy uplands – the kind of terrain you find in **Guanacaste** and the **Nicoya Peninsula** – with caution. Always watch where you put your feet. If you need to put out your hand for balance, look carefully at where you place it to make sure the vine you're grabbing isn't, in fact, a surprised snake. Be particularly careful in "sunspots" – places in dense rainforest cover where the sun

MEDICAL RESOURCES FOR TRAVELLERS

NORTH AMERICA

Center for Disease Control Hotline, Atlanta, GA (☎ 404/332-4555).
Latest information on health risks and precautions.

International SOS Assistance, PO Box 11568, Philadelphia, PA 19116 (☎1-800/523-8930; in Canada: ☎1-800/363-0263).
Members receive pre-trip medical referral info, as well as overseas emergency services designed to complement travel insurance coverage.

Travel Medicine, 351 Pleasant St, Suite 312, Northampton, MA 01060 (☎1-800/872-8633).
Sells first-aid kits, mosquito netting, water filters and other health-related travel products.

Medic Alert, 2323 Colorado Ave, Turlock, CA 95381 (☎1-800/432-5378; in Canada, ☎1-800/668-1507).
Sells bracelets engraved with travellers' medical requirements in case of emergency.

International Association for Medical Assistance to Travellers (IAMAT), 417 Center St, Lewiston, NY 14092 (☎716/754-4883); 40 Regal Rd, Guelph, ON N1K 1B5 (☎519/836-0102).
Non-profit organization supported by donations. Can provide a list of English-speaking doctors in Costa Rica, climate charts and leaflets on various diseases and inoculations.

UK

British Airways Travel Clinic, 156 Regent St, London W1 (Mon–Fri 9am–4.15pm, Sat 10am–4pm; ☎0171/439 9584). Appointment-only branches at 101 Cheapside, London EC2 (☎0171/606 2977) and at the BA terminal in London's Victoria Station (☎0171/233 6661); other clinics throughout the country (☎0171/831 5333 for the one nearest you).
Clinics and information helpline on ☎01891/224100.

Hospital for Tropical Diseases, 180–182 Tottenham Court Rd, London W1 (Mon–Fri 9am–5pm; ☎0171/636 6099).
Travel clinic for up-to-date information. Also a recorded message service on ☎01839/337722.

Masta Hotline, The London School of Hygiene and Tropical Medicine (☎01891/224100).
Information line run by the Medical Advisory Service for Travellers Abroad, giving up-to-date information on current health risks for travellers. Will send detailed health advice by return post.

AUSTRALASIA

Auckland Hospital, Park Rd, Grafton (☎3/797 440 in Auckland; ☎09/797 440 elsewhere).

Travel-Bug Medical and Vaccination Centre, 161 Ward St, N Adelaide (☎08/8267 3544).

Travel Health and Vaccination Clinic, 114 William St, Melbourne (☎03/9670 3871).

Travellers' Immunization Service, 303 Pacific Highway, Sydney (☎02/416 1348).

Travellers' Medical and Vaccination Centre, 428 George St, Sydney (☎02/9221 7133); 393 Little Bourke St, Melbourne (☎03/9602 5788); 29 Gilbert Place, Adelaide (☎08/8267 3544); 247 Adelaide St, Brisbane (☎07/3221 9066); 1 Mill St, Perth (☎09/321 1977; ☎08/9321 1977 from Sept 1997).

---

penetrates through to the ground or to a tree – snakes like to hang out there, absorbing the warmth. Above all, though, don't be too alarmed. Thousands of tourists troop through Costa Rica's rainforests and grasslands each year without encountering a single snake.

HIV AND AIDS

Though hospitals and clinics in Costa Rica use sterilized equipment, you may want to bring sealed hypodermic syringes anyway. **HIV** and AIDS (SIDA) is present in the country – travelling around you'll see corny government-sponsored educational directives (billboards aimed at heterosexual couples asserting "be faithful to your wife and save both your lives") – but it is not prevalent. That said, however, the same common-sense rules apply here as all over the world: condomless sex, especially in some of the popular beach towns, is a serious health risk. **Condoms** sold in Costa Rica are not of the quality you find at home; best bring them with you.

INFORMATION AND MAPS

The glossy promo bumf handed out by Costa Rican embassies and consulates is pretty to look at but largely useless, with remarkably little hard fact. With its emphasis on package operators, it is of minimal use to independent travellers.

Costa Rica no longer has a tourist office in North America, the UK or Australasia. US and Canadian residents can call a toll-free **tourist information hotline** (☎1-800/343-6332), which is answered by English-speaking ICT (see p.64) staff in San José. British and Australasian travellers should contact the nearest **embassy**.

INFORMATION

The best source of information about Costa Rica, and an obligatory stop before you head out into the *campo* (country) or to the *playa* (beach), is the **Instituto Costarricense de Turismo** (ICT) office in San José (see p.64).

Behind the counter, unannounced and unadvertised, are several key (and free) pieces of information. The staff will, on request, hand over a free map of San José, a complete bus and domestic airline timetable, as well as a full (although not necessarily up-to-date) list of practically all the hotels in the country with prices, addresses and telephone numbers, a list of museums and their opening hours, and details of many San José restaurants and nightclubs. The bus timetable is particularly useful, as staff will correct it on the spot with recent additions and changes. The **smaller ICT offices** at the Juan

Santamaría international airport and at the Peñas Blancas border crossing (into Nicaragua) don't offer the free timetables and hotel lists. Otherwise, there are very few tourist offices outside the capital. As a rule you have to rely on locally run initiatives, often set up by a small business association or the chamber of commerce, or hotels and tourist agencies.

A number of Costa Rican **tour operators**, based in San José, can offer information and guidance when planning a trip around the country; see p.25 for details.

MAPS

The maps dished out by the Embassy and the ICT are basic and somewhat out-of-date; it's best to arm yourself with general maps before you go. The best **road map**, a colourful spread giving a good rendition of all the major routes and National Parks, is the *Costa Rica Road Map* (1:650,000; Berndtson & Berndtson). It's available from good map stores or by mail from Hauptstr. 1a, D-82256 Fürstenfeldbruck, Germany (fax 08141/16280). Another excellent map, clearly marked with **contour** details, gas stations, National Parks, and roads, is *Costa Rica* (2nd edition; 1:500,000) available from *ITMB/World Wide Books and Maps* (see opposite). Road and park markings are less distinct on Nelles Verlag's large pull-out spread of *Central America* (1:1,750,000) focusing on *Costa Rica* (1:900,000), but it's handy if you are travelling **throughout the isthmus**. Buy it at specialist travel or map stores or write direct to Nelles Verlag, Schleissheimer Str. 371b, D-80935 München, Germany.

In Costa Rica it's a good idea to go to one of San José's two big downtown bookstores, *Librería Universal* or *Librería Lehmann* (see p.93), and pick through their stock of **cartographic** maps, which are contoured and show major topographical characteristics like river crossing points and high tide points. You buy them in sections; each costs about $2. You could also try going to the government maps bureau, the **Instituto Geográfico Nacional**, in San José at Av 20, C 5/7, which sells more lavishly detailed colour maps of specific areas of the country.

Considering it's such a popular hiking destination, there are unfortunately few good maps of Costa Rica's **topography** available outside the

MAP OUTLETS

NORTH AMERICA

Book Passage, 51 Tamal Vista Blvd, Corte Madera, CA 94925 (☎415/927-0960).

The Complete Traveler Bookstore, 199 Madison Ave, New York, NY 10016 (☎212/685-9007); 3207 Fillmore St, San Francisco, CA 92123 (☎415/923-1511).

Elliot Bay Book Company, 101 S Main St, Seattle, WA 98104 (☎206/624-6600).

Forsyth Travel Library, 9154 W 57th St, Shawnee Mission, KS 66201 (☎1-800/367-7984).

Map Link Inc, 25 E Mason St, Santa Barbara, CA 93101 (☎805/965-4402).

Open Air Books and Maps, 25 Toronto St, Toronto, ON M5R 2C1 (☎416/363-0719).

Phileas Fogg's Books & Maps, 87 Stanford Shopping Center, Palo Alto, CA 94304 (☎1-800/233-FOGG in California; ☎1-800/533-FOGG elsewhere in US).

Rand McNally*, 444 N Michigan Ave, Chicago, IL 60611 (☎312/321-1751); 150 E 52nd St, New York, NY 10022 (☎212/758-7488); 595 Market St, San Francisco, CA 94105 (☎415/777-3131); 1201 Connecticut Ave NW, Washington, DC 2003 (☎202/223-6751).

Sierra Club Bookstore, 730 Polk St, San Francisco, CA 94109 (☎415/923-5500).

Traveler's Bookstore, 22 W 52nd St, New York, NY 10019 (☎212/664-0995).

Ulysses Travel Bookshop, 4176 St-Denis, Montréal (☎514/289-0993).

World Wide Books and Maps, 736A Granville Street, Vancouver, BC V6Z 1G3 (☎604/687-3320; fax 604/687-5925).

*Rand McNally now has 24 stores across the US: call ☎1-800/333-0136 (ext 2111) for the location of your nearest store, or for **direct mail** maps.*

UK

Daunt Books, 83 Marylebone High St, London W1 (☎0171/224 2295).

John Smith and Sons, 57–61 St Vincent St, Glasgow (☎0141/221 7472).

National Map Centre, 22–24 Caxton St, London SW1 (☎0171/222 4945).

Stanfords*, 12–14 Long Acre, London WC2 (☎0171/836 1321); 52 Grosvenor Gardens, London SW1W 0AG; 156 Regent St, London W1R 5TA.

Thomas Nelson and Sons Ltd, 51 York Place, Edinburgh EH1 3JD (☎0131/557 3011).

The Travel Bookshop, 13–15 Blenheim Crescent, London W11 2EE (☎0171/229 5260).

The Travellers Bookshop, 25 Cecil Court, London WC2 (☎0171/836 9132).

*Maps by **mail or phone order** are available from Stanfords; ☎0171/836 1321.*

AUSTRALASIA

Bowyangs, 372 Little Bourke St, Melbourne, VIC 3000 (☎03/9670 4383).

Hema, 239 George St, Brisbane, QLD 4000 (☎07/3221 4330).

The Map Shop, 16a Peel St, Adelaide, SA 5000 (☎08/8231 2033).

Perth Map Centre, 891 Hay St, Perth, WA 6000 (☎09/322 5733; ☎08/9322 5733 from Sept 1997).

Speciality Maps, 58 Albert St, City, Auckland, New Zealand (☎09/307 2217).

Travel Bookshop, 20 Bridge St, Sydney, NSW 2000 (☎02/9241 3554).

country, and even within the country you'll find a lack of clear, detailed maps of the **National Parks**. Those given out at ranger stations are very general; your best bet is to get hold of the book *Parques Nacionales de Costa Rica/National Parks of Costa Rica* (separate editions in Spanish and English) printed by the National Parks Service (SPN) and available for about $2 from their main office in San José (see p.64). While rather cramped and none too detailed, and of little prac-

tical use for walking the trails, these maps (of all the Parks currently in existence) do, at least, show contours, and give a general idea of the terrain you will be covering, the animals you might see and the annual rainfall.

If you are going to be doing a lot of **driving**, pick up *The Essential Road Guide for Costa Rica* by Bill Baker ($9.95), widely available in San José bookstores, which features well-marked maps, tips and quite a bit of tourist information. Also available in San José is the *Guía Roja*, a locally produced compendium with maps impossible to find elsewhere, including detailed plans of the city and its suburbs, and regional maps.

INTERNET ACCESS

The easiest way to reach Costa Rica on the **internet** is through the Yahoo search program, although typing "Costa Rica" on any search mechanism on the World Wide Web will also get you to the right site. Yahoo have a countries search, by name, through which you will come to **RACSA**, Costa Rica's telecommunications company, which is fully wired, and features news summaries from the leading daily *La Nación*. RACSA's internet address is www.racsa.co.cr. Yahoo's country search also gets you through to pages set up by Costa Rica aficionados in the US – more chatty than informative, and spiked with personal opininons. In addition, the Universidad de Costa Rica and the Universidad Nacional in Heredia are both on the net; though these pages are probably of more use for prospective students, researchers and academics than for general or tourist information.

Beware **real-estate advertisements** on the internet. Costa Rica is property scam heaven, and there are lots of shady deals on the circuit; if you have any intention of buying property in the country, wait until you arrive. Of course, internet sites change rapidly; if in doubt try a country search to see what comes up.

If you want to bone up on ecological issues, some of them specific to Costa Rica, before you go, check out the **GreenNet**, which has a sometime conference called "green travel", promoting environmentally and culturally responsible tourism. Not all of this is fantastically useful, but it's worth checking into if you are serious about conservation, and "sustainable" and "responsible" tourism. For more info on GreenNet. call ☎0171/713 1941 in London, or join the Green Travel Conference by **e-mail** to green.travel @ igc.apc.org.

COSTS, MONEY AND BANKS

Costa Rica is the most expensive country in Central America. Just about everything – from ice-cream cones and groceries, to hotel rooms, meals and car rental – costs more than you might expect. Some prices, especially for upper-range accommodation, are analagous with those in the US, which never fails to astonish American travellers and those coming from the cheaper neighbouring countries.

The US **dollar** has long been the second currency of Costa Rica, and we quote dollar prices throughout the *Guide*. However, outside the tourist areas nobody really refers to dollars. The vast majority of Costa Ricans get paid in colones, and buy and sell in colones, and you would do well to get the hang of the currency soon after you arrive.

CURRENCY

Though the US dollar is often used in Costa Rica, the official currency is the **colón**, plural colones – named after Colón (Columbus) himself. It is divided into 1, 2, 5, 10 and 20 denomination coins. Notes start at 50, proceeding to 100, then 500, to 1000 and 5000. You'll often hear colones colloquially referred to as "**pesos**"; in addition, the 1000 is sometimes called the *rojo* (red). The colón floats freely against the American dollar, which means the **exchange rate** varies frequently; when this book went to press, it hovered at around 175 colones to $1, but inflationary pressures and devaluation inevitably mean that it will change over the lifetime of this edition.

Obtaining colones outside Costa Rica is virtually impossible: wait until you arrive and change some at the airport or border posts. If you miss banking hours then dollar bills in small denominations will do fine.

COSTS

Costa Rica has always been pricey, due to the relatively high (18–25 percent) **taxes** levied in restaurants and hotels; and more recently, the presence of the International Monetary Fund, whose policies, aimed at the restructuring of balance of payments deficit, has raised prices.

Even on a rock-bottom hotel and lunch-counter or takeout meal budget, you're looking at spending $20 a day for lodging, three meals and the odd bus ticket. Campers and hardy cyclists have been known to do it on $15 a day, but this entails sleeping either in your tent or in some pretty dire places. You will be far more comfortable if you count on spending at least $25 a day for accommodation and $10 for meals.

The good news is that some things are still inexpensive. **Bus** travel is geared toward Costa Ricans, not foreigners, so that stays cheap – about 25¢ to $1 for local buses, around $4 or $5 for long-distance (3hr or more), and never rising above $10. **Eating**, too, needn't be that pricey if you eat your main meal of the day at the good-value sodas (see "Eating and Drinking"; p.29), while fruit, beer, theatre seats and trips to the movies will all seem very reasonable to visitors from most other countries.

For notes on **tipping** in Costa Rica – who to tip, who not to tip, and roughly how much – see the *Directory* on p.57.

MONEY CHANGING AND BANKS

There are effectively no official **bureaux de change** in Costa Rica – the Juan Santamaría airport does have one, but it's very slow and rather surly. In general, official and legitimate money changing entails going to a bank or a (usually upper-range) hotel, or in outlying areas of the country, to whoever will do it – a tour agency, the friend of the owner of your hotel who has a Chinese restaurant . . .

Changing dollars into colones, try to avoid Costa Rica's **state banks**, *Banco Nacional* and *Banco de Costa Rica* (both with branches throughout the country). Slow and *trámites*-burdened, they will eat about an hour or two out of your

time. In addition, although they may be able to change dollars cash for colones, they will balk at travellers' cheques, especially the larger denominations. It's best to carry sufficient colones with you, especially in small denominations – you may have trouble changing a 5000 bill in the middle of the Nicoya Peninsula, for example. Going around with stacks of mouldy-smelling colones may not seem safe, but you should be all right if you keep them in a money belt, and it will save hours of time waiting in line. That said, however, if you are doing a lot of travelling, it's comforting to know that many of even the smallest end-of-the-world towns have a branch of at least one bank.

In sharp contrast to the state banks, efficient and air-conditioned **private banks**, the majority of which are in downtown San José, will relieve you of your dollars and give you colones in good time and good humour, requiring only your passport and about five minutes' processing time. Private banks in San José include *Bancoop, Banco Mercantil, Banco Lyon, Banco Metropolitano, Banco de San José, BANEX* and *Banco del Comercio* (for addresses, see San José's "Listings" on p.93). Outside San José you will want to try *Bancoop, Banco Popular* and, in some places, *Banco Lyon*. Private banks in Costa Rica can legally charge what they like for commission; the norm is about $3 per transaction.

Banking hours change slightly from branch to branch but tend to be Mon–Fri 9am–3pm for state banks and slightly longer – about 8am–3.30 or 4pm – for private ones. No banks in San José open on Saturdays, but a few provincial branches of private banks, such as *Banco Lyon* in Puntarenas and *Bancoop* in Liberia, open for a half-day in the morning. At present few, if any, **ATMs** in Costa Rica accept foreign credit cards.

If you're stuck in San José without cash in an emergency, you could approach the guys who hang out (currently) on the pedestrian mall at the western end of Avenida Central whispering "dólares" and "cambio". However, this should be used as only a last resort when you're absolutely stuck for colones; it is technically illegal and you could find yourself scammed.

CREDIT CARDS

Credit cards can come in very handy as a backup source of funds, and they can even save on exchange-rate commissions; just be sure someone back home is taking care of the bills if you're away for more than a month. You'll find

EMERGENCY CREDIT CARD PHONE NUMBERS	
American Express	☎233-0044
Diner's Club	☎257-2351
Mastercard	☎253-2155
Visa	☎257-1357

them especially useful in Costa Rica for making deposits for hotels via fax and for renting a car. In outlying areas, however, like the Talamanca coast, Quepos and Manuel Antonio and Golfito, some businesses levy a 6 percent charge for credit card transactions; you may be better off taking plenty of cash (see above).

In general, **Visa** and **Mastercard** are widely accepted, although retailers tend to accept only one or the other; it's handy to have both. **AmEx** is somewhat less useful, though you certainly won't have any problem using it in the higher-class hotels and paying for air tickets and rental cars. The **local Costa Rican credit card** is called *Su Tarjeta* (*ST*) and some retailers and hotels are only able to accept this.

Private banks in San José can give you **advances** (colones only) on your credit card with relative ease, though, again, most of them deal with one company only. *Banco de San José*, along with some others, deals with *Mastercard*, while *Banco Metropolitano*, *BANEX* and *Banco Lyon* will only give advances on *Visa*. Bring your passport (not a photocopy) as ID (*cédula*).

TRAVELLERS' CHEQUES

Undeniably the safest way to keep your money, **travellers' cheques** should be brought in US dollars only – Costa Rican banks will only stare blankly at other currencies. North American brands of travellers' cheques, including *AmEx*, *Citibank* and *Visa* are most familiar to Costa Rican banks; they'll change *Barclays* US$ for British travellers, too, although they might look askance for a minute before deciding they're legit. Do not expect to use travellers' cheques as cash in Costa Rica except in mid- or upmarket hotels and guest houses that regularly cater to foreigners.

The usual fee for travellers' cheque sales is 1 or 2 percent, and it pays to get a selection of denominations. Make sure to keep the purchase agreement and a record of cheque serial numbers safe and separate from the cheques themselves. In the event that cheques are lost or stolen, the issuing company will expect you to report the loss forthwith to their office in San José: most companies claim to replace lost or stolen cheques within 24 hours.

WIRING MONEY

Having **money wired** from home is never convenient or cheap, and should be considered a last resort. In Costa Rica you can organize to have money wired to *Western Union*, in San José at C 9, Av 2/4 (☎227-1103 or 257-1312), or the Costa Rican company, *Servicios Internacionales Unigiros SA* in San José at Av 1, C 1/3 (☎233-6640). Both companies' fees depend on the destination and the amount being transferred. The funds should be available for collection at the office within minutes of being sent. You can also have money wired directly from a **bank** in your home country to a bank in Costa Rica; a cumbersome process, because it involves two separate institutions. The person wiring the funds to you will need to know the telex number of the bank the funds are being wired to.

YOUTH AND STUDENT DISCOUNTS

Full-time students are eligible for the **International Student ID Card** (**ISIC**), which may entitle the bearer to some discounts at museums in Costa Rica. For Americans there's also a health benefit, providing up to $3000 in emergency medical coverage and $100 a day for 60 days in the hospital, plus a 24-hour hotline to call in the event of a medical, legal or financial emergency. The card, which costs $16 for Americans and $15 for Canadians, is available from *Council Travel*, *STA* and *Travel CUTS* (see p.4 for addresses). More useful is **local student ID**, available to visitors on language courses and other education programmes (see p.55); these may offer discounts at museums and theatres.

GETTING AROUND

Costa Rica's public bus system is excellent, cheap and quite frequent, even in remote areas. Getting anywhere by bus with a lot of baggage can be a problem, however, and between trips you should try to find somewhere secure to leave your luggage (your San José hotel, for example). Taxis regularly do long- as well as short-distance trips and are a fairly inexpensive alternative to the bus, at least if travelling in a group.

Car rental is more common here than in the rest of Central America, but as Costa Rica has one of the highest car accident rates in the world, driving can be hair-raising, to say the least. **Domestic airlines** are reasonably economical, especially since Costa Rica's difficult terrain makes driving distances longer than they look to be on the map. A number of **tour operators** in San José (see p.25) organize individual itineraries and packages with transport included; well worth checking out before making any decisions about heading out on your own.

Costa Rica's **Jungle Train** from San José to Limón used to be one of the prettiest rides in the Americas; that and the old service from San José to Puntarenas were suspended in 1990–1. It is unlikely that there will be a resurrection of passenger services in Costa Rica.

BY BUS

San José is the hub for virutally all bus services in the country; indeed, often it is impossible to travel from one place to another without back-tracking to San José. Different companies have semi-monopolies on various regions; for a rundown of destinations and routes, including international services, see p.95.

Some popular buses, like the service to Golfito, require **advance booking** of three days, though you may be lucky enough to get on without a reservation. Services to popular tourist areas – especially Monteverde – get booked up very fast, so for these you should buy your ticket at least five days in advance. Again, for more details, see p.95.

Even though there is no system of **bus passes** in Costa Rica, travelling by bus is by far the cheapest way to get around. The most expensive journey in the country (from Puerto Jiménez on the Osa Peninsula, to San José) costs $10, while fares in the mid- to long-distance range vary from $2.50 to $5. **Tickets** on most mid- to long-distance and popular routes are issued with

---

FINDING YOUR WAY AROUND COSTA RICAN TOWNS

In Costa Rica there is only one vision of urban planning: the **grid system**. However, there are a number of peculiarites that it is essential to come to grips with if you want to find your way around with ease. The following rules apply to all cities except Limón.

Typically, you'll see addresses written as follows: *Bar Esmeralda*, Av 2, C 5/7 (abbreviated from Avenida 2, Calles 5/7). This means that *Bar Esmeralda* is on Avenida 2, between Calles 5 and 7. *Bar Lotto*, C 5, Av 2, on the other hand, is on the corner of Calle 5 and Avenida 2. **Apartado** (Aptdo) means "postbox", and **bis** means, technically, "encore": if you see "Av 6 bis" in an address it refers to another Avenida 6, right next to the original one.

Many directions, in both written and verbal form, are given in terms of **metres** rather than blocks. In general, one block is equivalent to 100m. Thus "de la escuela President Vargas, 125 metros al sur, cincuenta metros al oeste", translates as "from the Presidente Vargas school, 125 metres south [one block and a quarter] and 50 west [half a block]". More confusingly, verbal directions are also commonly given in relation to **landmarks** which everyone – except the visitor – knows and recognizes, and, frustratingly, which may not even exist any longer. This is something to get the hang of fast: taxi drivers will often look completely bewildered if given street directions, but as soon you come up with a landmark, the proverbial light bulb goes on.

a date and a seat number; you are expected to sit in the seat indicated. Make sure the date is correct; even if the mistake is not yours, you cannot normally change your ticket or get a refund. Neither can you buy **return** bus tickets on Costa Rican buses, which can be quite inconvenient if heading to very popular destinations like Monteverde, Jacó and Manuel Antonio at busy times – you'll need to jump off the bus as soon as you arrive and buy your return ticket immediately to assure yourself a seat.

Costa Rica is a bus-riding nation, and buses have a pretty friendly atmosphere. Most do not have buzzers or bells to signal to the driver that you want to get off: do as Ticos do and perfect your whistle (they whistle loudly for a stop) or shout "¡parada!" If someone sees that the driver hasn't heard you they'll shout (or whistle) again for you. Similarly, if the driver starts to drive away and you're halfway out the back door trying to get off, your fellow passengers will erupt in spontaneous help. The majority of buses are in fairly good shape, although usually not air-conditioned. There is very little room for luggage, and anyone with long legs is at a disadvantage. Most comfortable are those that run the **border routes** from San José to Panamá or to Managua, with good seats, adequate baggage space and, sometimes, air-conditioning.

Though there are no **toilets** on the buses, drivers make (admittedly infrequent) stops on longer runs. Often a lunch or dinner stop will be made at a roadside restaurant or gas station; failing that, there is always a bevy of hardy food and drinks sellers who leap on to the bus proffering their wares.

DRIVING

Although outside the Valle Central there is very little traffic, if you're made nervous by the idea of dodging cows and potholes at 90km/hr, or big trucks looming up behind you and nudging your rear bumper in an effort to get you to go faster around that next blind hairpin bend, then you may choose not to drive in Costa Rica. The vast majority of cars are standard (manual) transmissions and, if you don't know how to operate one, this is not the place to learn. That is not to make driving in Costa Rica sound more dramatic or heroic than it is: it's perfectly possible to drive and survive.

Citizens of the US, Canada, UK, Spain, Germany, France and Italy need only a valid **driver's licence** or an International Driver's Licence to operate a vehicle in Costa Rica. Residents of other countries should check with their nearest Costa Rican consulate.

Car rental in Costa Rica is expensive. Expect to pay about $320 per week for renting a regular (non-4WD) vehicle, including insurance, and as much as double that for 4WD. Your "days" are calculated on a 24-hour basis: thus if you take a car on a Tuesday at 3pm for a week (7 days), you have to return it the following Tuesday at or before that time. The minimum age for rental is usually 25; you will need a credit card, either *Mastercard* or *Visa*, which has sufficient credit for the entire cost of the rental, both at the beginning and end of the rental period. The majority of

CAR RENTAL IN COSTA RICA

You have to exercise caution when **renting a car** in Costa Rica, where rental companies have been known to try to claim for "damage" they insist you inflicted on the vehicle. It is by far the best policy to rent a car through a Costa Rican **travel agent**. If you are travelling on a package, your agent will sort this out. Otherwise, go into an ICT-accredited travel agent in San José (see p.25) and ask them to arrange rental for you. This should be no more expensive than renting on your own and will help guard against false claims of damage and other accusations; rental companies will be less willing to make trouble with an agent who regularly sends them clients than with individual customers who they may not see again.

Make sure to **check the car** carefully before you sign off the damage sheet. Check the oil, brake fluid, gas (to make sure it's full) and that there is a spare tyre with good air pressure and a jack. Look up the Spanish for "scratches" and other damage terminology first, so you can at least scrutinize the rental company's assessment. Keep a copy of this document on you.

Take the maximum **insurance** (around $20/day) – which has no deductible – rather than the cheaper option. Because of the country's high accident rate, you need to be covered for damage to the vehicle, yourself, any third party and public property.

CAR RENTAL COMPANIES

NORTH AMERICA

Avis	☎1-800/331-1084
Budget	☎1-800/527-0700
Dollar	☎1-800/421-6868
Hertz	☎1-800/654-3001;
in Canada	☎1-800/263-0600
National	☎1-800/CAR RENT

UK

Avis	☎0181/848 8733
Budget	☎0800/181 181
Hertz	☎0181/679 1799

AUSTRALIA

Avis	☎1800/22 5533
Budget	☎13 2848
Hertz	☎13 1918

NEW ZEALAND

Avis	☎09/525 1982
Budget	☎09/309 6737
Hertz	☎09/309 0989

companies are based in San José, and you have to return the car there. The exception is *Elegante*, which has offices throughout the country. For a list of rental companies in San José, see p.93.

If you intend to drive in the rainy season (May–Nov), especially on the Nicoya Peninsula, or want to get to off-the-beaten-track places, or to Santa Elena and Monteverde, you'll need to rent a **4WD**. (Make sure someone explains the four-by-four function before you set out.) Indeed, if you intend to go to Monteverde from May through November, due to the condition of the roads, some car rental companies will refuse to rent you a regular car.

In recent years a system of high fines (*multas*) for infractions like **speeding** has been introduced in Costa Rica. The limit on the highways is either 75km/hr or 90km/hr; marked on the pavement or on signs. If you're caught speeding you could find yourself paying up to $150. Do not, under any circumstances, try to bribe a traffic cop; this could land you in far more serious trouble. If a motorist – especially a trucker – in the oncoming direction flashes his headlights at you, you can be almost certain that traffic cops with speed-trapping radar are up ahead.

Gas is reasonably priced, positively cheap, by European standards; about $10 a tank on a medium-sized compact or about $20 for a big 4WD.

BY AIR

Costa Rica's two **domestic air carriers** offer quite economical scheduled service between San José and many beach destinations and provincial towns. *Sansa* is the state-owned domestic airline; *Travelair* is its commercial competitor. Both fly small twin-propeller aircraft, servicing the same destinations.

Of the two, **Travelair**, which flies from Tobias Bolaños airport in Pavas, 7km west of San José, is more reliable and has more frequent service on some runs. **Sansa** is cheaper, but less reliable – make your reservations as far as possible in advance and even then be advised that a booking means almost nothing until the seat is actually paid for. Reconfirm your flight in advance of the day of departure and once more on the day of departure, if possible, as schedules are likely to change at short notice. *Sansa* also offers good-value packages, usually two or three nights in more popular areas like Manuel Antonio. They fly from Juan Santamaría airport, 17km northwest of San José.

For a rundown of *Sansa* and *Travelair* **schedules**, along with their addresses and phone numbers, see "Moving on from San José" on p.95.

While the fares will be at least double that of *Sansa* and *Travelair*, **air taxis** can work out as a

AIR CHARTER COMPANIES

Aero Costa Sol (☎441-1444; fax 441-2671; in the USA and Canada, ☎1-800/245-8420).
Planes with capacity for 7 maximum will fly you anywhere in the country; $235–820.

Aeronaves de America, from Tobias Bolaños airport in Pavas (☎232-1413 or 1176).
International and local charters.

Aerovias Isla del Coco (Coco Island Airways), from Tobias Bolaños airport, Pavas (☎296-3322; fax 296-3344).
Currently the only floatplane service in the country.

Helisa, Aptdo 1231-1007, San José (☎222-9219 or 255-4138; fax 222-3875).
Helicopter charter that can get you to places without airstrips – for example landing right on the beach.

SAETA (☎232-1474; fax 232-9514).
Pavas-based company for regular charter flights throughout the country, also volcano fly-overs for about $300 per planeload.

THE DJ PILOT

Pilot and air-taxi owner Peter Wohlleben offers one of the best experiences in Costa Rica in his Piper Cherokee single engine plane. Not only does he fly you anywhere you want to go (providing there's an airstrip), but he'll programme his vast collection of CDs so that you'll have a **musical accompaniment** to the amazing sights below.

Especially recommended are the early morning **volcano trips**. Banking at a 45° angle above Poás, Barva and Irazú – and sometimes Arenal, although planes can't get too close because of the activity – gives you the best volcano views in the country; the whole thing lifted from the amazing into the realm of the transformative by his well-chosen tunes (be they Irish folk or the theme from *Rocky*).

Most beach trips are in the range of $100 per person for four passengers; $115 for three, and $130 for two. Volcano fly-overs last between ninety minutes and two hours and cost $125 per person with a full load of 5; the price is higher if fewer people are travelling. Contact *Pits Aviation*, Aptdo 1442/1250, Escazú, San José (☎ and fax 228-9912).

reasonably cheap way to get to the beaches and more remote areas if several people split the expense (journeys can cost anywhere from $125 to $250 per planeload). Most charter planes operate from Tobias Bolaños airport in Pavas.

BY BICYCLE

Costa Rica's terrain provides easy **cycling** compared with neighbouring countries and, as there's a good range of places to stay and eat, you don't need to bring the extra weight of tent, sleeping bag and stove. Always carry warm **clothes** and a cycling jacket, however, wherever you are. As for **equipment**, rear panniers and a small handlebar bag (for maps and camera) should be enough. Bring a puncture repair kit, even if your tyres are supposedly unbustable. You'll need a bike with a **triple front gear** – this gives you 15 to 21 gears, and you will really need the low ones. Make sure, too, to carry and drink lots of **water** – 5 to 8 litres a day in the lowlands.

There is very little **traffic** outside the Valle Central, and despite their tactics with other cars – and pedestrians – Costa Rican drivers are probably the most courteous to cyclists in Central America. That said, however, bus and truck drivers do tend to forget about you as soon as they pass, sometimes cutting you off or forcing you off the road. **Roads** are generally good for cyclists, who can dodge the potholes and wandering cattle more easily than drivers, although bear in mind that if you cycle up to Monteverde, one of the most popular routes in the country, you're in for a slow trip: besides being steep there's not much traction on these loose gravel roads. Although road signs will tell you that cycling on the Interamericana (Pan-American Highway, or Hwy-

1) is not permitted, you will quickly see that people do, anyway.

San José's best **cycle shop** is *Mundo del Ciclismo*, at the corner of Paseo Colón and C 26. They have all the parts you might need, can fix your bike, and may even be able to give you a bicycle carton for the plane.

TOUR OPERATORS

The Costa Rican tourist boom of the last five years has led to a fast proliferation of **tour operators**. Market research shows that about 50 percent of travellers to Costa Rica arrive with only their return flight and the first few nights of accommodation booked; they then set about planning tours *in situ* in San José.

Wandering around the city, you face a barrage of tour agencies, and advertisements for tour agencies: if you want to shop around it could take some time to sort yourself out. The following is not a comprehensive list of tour operators in Costa Rica: such a thing would increase this book's size to that of a telephone directory. Those that we've listed are experienced, and commendable, offering a good range of services and tours. They are all licensed (and regulated) by the ICT.

There are scores of others – be especially wary of fly-by-night operators, of which there are plenty. You often see, for instance, posters advertising cheap "packages" to Tortuguero or to Monteverde, both for about $70 – less than half the price of regular packages. These cut-price tours are not packages at all, and never worth the price: in some cases you are responsible for your own transport, the accommodation is the most basic, and no tours, orientation or guidance is offered. This you can easily do on your own, for the same price or less.

TOUR OPERATORS IN COSTA RICA

Camino Travel, C1, Av 0/1 (☎257-0107 or 234-2530; fax 257-0243).
Young, extremely enthusiastic staff with high standards and a mainly European clientele. Experienced in both upmarket and independent travel; selling individual tours, and booking good-quality accommodation from their range of country-wide contacts. Can also help with bus and transport information and car rental. Convenient downtown office.

Caminos de la Selva, C 38, Av 5, 250m north of Centro Colón (☎255-3486).
Contact for serious walkers and birdwatchers, specializing in Volcán Barva, and the other Valle Central volcanos; they also plan itineraries anywhere in the country.

Central American Tours, 150m south of *Aurola Holiday Inn* (☎255-4111).
Whitewater rafting, hiking, Tortuguero and beach packages. Particularly good for booking, confirming and changing flights, representing many carriers. Very friendly, professional staff.

Costa Rica Expeditions, C Central, Av 3 (☎257-0766; fax 257-1665).
Longest established of the major tour operators, very often the "ground operators" for overseas tour companies; they have superior accommodation in Tortuguero, Monteverde and Corcovado. Also a superlative staff of guides, tremendous experience and resources. You can drop into their somewhat chaotic downtown office and talk to a consultant about individual tours.

Costa Rica Sun Tours, in Escazú, Av 7, C 3/5 (☎255-3418; fax 255-4410; Aptdo 1195).
All-round agency specializing in biking tours in the Valle Central. With good contacts in the Arenal area, including Arenal Observatory Lodge, they are also booking agents for Tiskita Lodge (near the Panamanian border and Golfito) and surfing contacts in the southwest, near Golfito.

Horizontes, C 28, Av 1/3 (☎222-2022).
Highly regarded agency known for intelligent programme concentrating on rainforest walking and hiking, volcanos and birdwatching, all with an emphasis on natural and cultural history. Specialists in mountain biking and horseback riding also.

OTEC, 275m north of the Teatro Nacional (☎222-0866 or 257-0166).
Large agency specializing in "adventure" tours including fishing, trekking, surfing and mountain biking, plus hotel reservations and car rentals. One of the few – if not the only – who claim to offer student discounts.

Sansa, C 24, Paseo Colón/Av 1 (☎222-6561).
Especially good for cheap air/hotel beach package accommodation at Nosara, Sámara, Manuel Antonio and Tamarindo beaches.

TAM Travel, Av 1, C 1/3 (☎222-3866; fax 222-3724).
Run the Banana Train (a tourist train from Turrialba to Siquerres to simulate part of the old Jungle Train experience). Expensive, catering to an upmarket, mainly North American clientele.

Tikal Tours, Av 2, C 7/9 (☎257-1494).
Long-standing company with experienced guides, selling packages and individual tours, including trips to Tortuguero, hiking packages and beach holidays. Also diving, surfing, horseback riding, hiking and rafting. Friendly and accommodating; can help with exit visas (see p.11).

CULTURE TOURS

The creation of tour agency owner Michel Brunel and Gail Nystrom of Santa Ana, near San José, **VNA Humanitarian Tours** is a new initiative dedicated to showing tourists the "other side" of Costa Rica and of tourism, appealing to tourists interested in the life of Costa Rican people as well as the lives of Costa Rican frogs, birds and forests. "Tours" run by VNA don't take you to the rainforest or whitewater rafting; instead you'll go to a women's prison, perhaps, or a girls' shelter, or visit a project aimed at helping street kids in Puerto Limón. What actually happens on the tours varies greatly according to the institution or community visited, but voyeurism is kept to a minimum and days are carefully planned to encourage an atmosphere of informal exchange and discussion. On the multi-day tours – to Limón, for example – accommodation is in the homes of local families. Prices vary depending upon the itinerary and size of the group, from about $50 to $70 for a day trip, including lunch, and from $150 for multi-day trips, breakfast, lodging and entrance fees. A portion of the proceeds is donated to the community and projects in question. For more information Contact Gail Nystrom (☎282-7368; Aptdo 458, Santa Ana Centro, Costa Rica).

ACCOMMODATION

Most towns in Costa Rica have a good range of places to stay, and even the smallest settlements have a basic *pensión* or *hospedaje*. The best budget accommodation tends to be found in less-touristed areas and caters more for nationals than foreigners. In the middle and upper price ranges, though facilities and services are generally of a very good standard, there has been a certain trend towards overpricing in recent years, and some hoteliers have decided they can pretty much charge what they please. If you don't mind spending $45–70 a night for accommodation (especially in San José, and especially in the high season) then you can stay quite comfortably. If you are on a tighter budget, it's going to be more of a struggle.

Officially, the Costa Rican tourist board classifies accommodation descending from "A", roughly analogous to 4 star, down the scale to "E" at rock bottom, but hoteliers themselves rarely use this distinction: the best indication of the quality of an establishment is price. The larger places to stay in Costa Rica are usually called **hotels**. *Posadas, hostals, hospejades* and *pensiones* are smaller, though *posadas* sometimes turn out to be quite swanky, especially in rural areas. *Casas* tend to be private guest houses, while *albergues* are the equivalent of lodges. **Cabinas** are common in Costa Rica, usually either a string of hotel rooms, motel-style, in an annexe away from a main building or hotel, or more often separate, self-contained units.

Usually – although not always – they tend toward the basic, and are most often frequented by budget travellers. More upmarket versions may be called "villas" or "chalets". Anything called a **motel** – as in most of Latin America – is likely not to be used for sleeping.

Few hotels except those at the upper end of the price range have **double beds**, and it's more common to find two or three single beds. **Single travellers** will generally be charged the single rate even if they are occupying a "double room", though this may not be the case in popular beach towns and at peak seasons.

Incidentally, wherever you are staying, don't expect to get much reading done in the evenings. Light bulbs are very wan, even in good hotels, and avid after-dark readers may actually want to bring their own **reading lamp** (plus adaptor for plug) with them. Also bear in mind that in Costa Rican hotels the term **"hot water"** can be misleading. Showers are often equipped with squat plastic nozzles: these are water heaters. Inside is an electric element, which heats the water coming through to a warm, rather than hot, temperature. Some of the nozzles have a button that actually turns on the element. Under no circumstances should you touch this button or get anywhere near the nozzle when wet – while the term commonly applied to these contraptions, "suicide shower", is tongue-in-cheek, there's a distinct possibility that you could get a shock. The trick to getting fairly hot water is not to turn on the pressure too high. Keep a little coming through to heat the water more efficiently.

RESERVATIONS

The accepted advice over the last few years, when the country has been chock-full at high season, has been to **reserve** well ahead for accommodation, especially for the good-value hotels in popular spots, and the youth hostels. Although we often give Apartado (post box) numbers in the *Guide*, it is far easier to reserve a room with a credit card by **fax**. Most hotels in Costa Rica, even some very low-priced budget ones, have fax numbers; these are listed with the phone numbers in the *Guide*.

In the **high season**, which lasts from around mid-November to Easter broadly corresponding

ACCOMMODATION PRICE CODES

All the establishments in this book have been given **price codes** according to the following scale. The prices quoted are for the least expensive double room in high season and do not include the 18.46 percent tax automatically added on to hotel bills. Wherever an establishment offers dorm beds the prices of these are given in the text.

① Less than $10	③ $20–30	⑤ $50–75	⑦ $100–150
② $10–20	④ $30–50	⑥ $75–100	⑧ $150 plus

with the dry months, you should fax the hotel or hostel well in advance, quoting – at least for the more upscale establishments – your credit card number. Once on the ground in Costa Rica, phone or fax to reconfirm your reservation. Some establishments require that you reserve and pay in advance – the more popular hotels and lodges require you to do this as far as 30 days ahead, although they will accommodate you any time if they have space.

While evidently good sense, for many travellers this level of pre-planning is impractical. If you prefer to be a little more spontaneous, you should travel in the **low season**, from roughly after Easter to mid-November, when you can safely leave making reservations until you arrive in the country. During these months it's even possible to show up at hotels on spec; there will probably be space and possibly even a low-season discount of as much as 50 percent. Another budget option is to arrange to **stay with a Tico family**; see p.68 for details.

PENSIONES AND HOTELS

When travelling, most Costa Ricans and nationals of other Central American countries stick to the bottom end of the market and patronize traditional *pensiones* (a fast-dying breed in Costa Rica, especially in San José) or established **Costa Rican-owned hotels**. If you do likewise you may well get a better price than at the tourist or foreign-owned hotels, although this is not a hard and fast rule. Though standards are generally high, at the lower end of the scale, by all means expect to get what you pay for – usually clean but dim, spartan rooms with cold-water showers. If you think you might have a choice or like to shop around, it's perfectly acceptable to ask to see the room first.

The majority of accommodation **catering to foreigners** is in the middle range, and as such is reasonably fairly priced – although still more expensive than similar accommodation in other Central American countries. Often hotels at the lower end of this price range will be very good value, however, giving you private bath with hot water, perhaps towels, and maybe even air conditioning – which, it has to be said, is not really necessary in most places; a ceiling fan generally does fine. At the upper end of this price range a few extras, like TV or breakfast, may be thrown in.

RESORTS AND LODGES

Costa Rica has several **resorts** scattered throughout the country. Some of them are swanky hotels in popular areas like Manuel Antonio, where you pay for creature comforts. Others are **rainforest-lodge** type accommodation which, while they may be rustic, offer superior service, personal attention, and excellent food and tours, all usually in an area of outstanding natural beauty – which is what you're paying for. The experience offered by these places is in general well worth the price, though due to the tourism "boom" they are becoming very expensive, obviously angling for the well-heeled North American market and putting themselves firmly out of reach of the budget traveller.

SOME ACCOMMODATION TERMS

Abanico	Ceiling fan
Ventilador	Desk fan
Aire-acondicionado	Air conditioned
Baño colectivo/ compartido	Shared bath
Agua caliente	Hot water
Agua fría	Cold water
Cama matrimonial	Double bed
Sencillo	Single bed
Impuestos	Taxes
Hora de salida	Check-out time (usually 2pm)

B&Bs

Until recently many hotels offered breakfast in their room rates as a matter of course, but this is becoming less common and, if breakfast is offered at all, it will probably cost extra. However, a new breed of **B&Bs** has sprung up in recent years, often owned by ex-pats and similar to their North American counterparts: rooms in homes or converted homes with a "family atmosphere". To find out more about B&Bs in Costa Rica, write to the Costa Rica Bed and Breakfast Group, c/o Debbi McMurray-Long, PO Box 025216-1638 Miami, FL 33102-5216, USA.

CAMPING

Though **camping** is fairly widespread in Costa Rica, gone are the days when people could pitch their tents on just about any **beach** or field. With more and more people coming to the country, local residents in small beachside communities, especially, are getting very upset with campers leaving their shit (literally and figuratively) on the beach. You'll have a far better relationship with locals if you ask politely whether it is OK to camp on the beach; if they direct you to a nearby campground, they are doing so not because they don't like the look of you, but in an attempt to keep their environment clean.

In the beach towns especially you will usually find at least one well-equipped **private campground**, with good facilities including lavatories, drinking water and cooking grilles. Staff may also offer to guard your clothes and tent while you're at the beach. Sometimes in these same towns you can find a hotelier, usually at the lower end of the price scale, willing to let you pitch your tent on the grounds and let you use their showers and washrooms for a charge – ask around or do a reconnaissance on foot. Though not all **National Parks** have campgrounds, the ones that do usually offer high standards and at least basic facilities, with lavatories, water, and often cooking grilles – all for around $2 per person per day. In some National Parks, you can sometimes bunk down at the **ranger station**, if you call well in advance; for more details, see p.42.

There are three general **rules** of camping in Costa Rica: firstly, never leave your tent unattended, or leave anything of value inside it unattended, or it may not be there when you get back. Never leave your tent open except to get in and out, unless you fancy sharing your sleeping quar-

WHAT TO BRING WHEN CAMPING IN COSTA RICA
Tent
Groundsheet
Backpack
Lightweight ("summer") sleeping bag, except for climbing Chirripó, where you may need a three-season bag
Rain gear
Mosquito net
Maps
Torch
Knife
Matches, in a waterproof box
Firelighter
Compass
Insect repellent
Water bottles
Toilet paper
Sunglasses
Sunblock
Plastic bags (for wet clothes/refuse)

ters with snakes, insects, coati or toads. Finally, take your refuse with you when you leave.

Costa Rica has just one **trailer park**, about 20km west of San José at San Antonio de Belén (☎239-0421); they provide electricity hook-ups in a clean and well-tended area just off the Interamericana.

YOUTH HOSTELS

Costa Rica currently has a small network of ten **youth hostels**, including San José's *Toruma*. While not rock-bottom cheap (many of them cost around $15–40 per night) they offer a good standard and all can be conveniently booked from *Toruma*. As with any accommodation in Costa Rica, if you're coming in the high season, hostel bookings should ideally be made three months in advance. Reserve by fax or phone with the hostel or through *Toruma*.

All hostels in Costa Rica follow conservation regulations based on the sustained development principle, working in harmony with nature. Most are in prime locations, near a National Park, beach or main town; more remote hostels, such as *Plastico* at Rara Avis in the Zona Norte, provide transport from the nearest town. Most have double, triple and family rooms, and bed linen, towels and soap are included in the price.

YOUTH HOSTEL ASSOCIATIONS

COSTA RICA

Red Costarricense de Albergues Juveniles ("RECAJ"), Aptdo 1355-1002, Paseo de los Estudiantes, Av Central, C 29/31, San José (☎ and fax 224-4085).

NORTH AMERICA

Hostelling International-American Youth Hostels (HI-AYH), 733 15th St NW, Suite 840, PO Box 37613, Washington, DC 20005 (☎202/783-6161).

Hostelling International/Canadian Hostelling Association, Room 400, 205 Catherine St, Ottawa, ON K2P 1C3 (☎613/237-7884 or 1-800/663-5777).

AUSTRALASIA

Australian Youth Hostels Association, Level 3, 10 Mallett St, Camperdown, NSW (☎02/565 1325).

Youth Hostels Association of New Zealand, PO Box 436, Christchurch 1 (☎03/799 970).

BRITAIN AND IRELAND

Youth Hostel Association (YHA), Trevelyan House, 8 St Stephen's Hill, St Albans, Herts AL1 (☎017278/45047). London shop and information office: 14 Southampton St, London WC2 (☎0171/836 1036).

An Óige, 39 Mountjoy Square, Dublin 1 (☎01/363111).

Youth Hostel Association of Northern Ireland, 56 Bradbury Place, Belfast, BT7 (☎01232/324733).

Scottish Youth Hostel Association, 7 Glebe Crescent, Stirling, FK8 2JA (☎01786/51181).

EATING AND DRINKING

The best way to describe the bulk of Costa Rican food is to apply that evasive adjective, "unpretentious". Ticos call their cuisine *comida típica* ("native" or "local" food). Simple it may be, but tasty nonetheless, especially when it comes to interesting regional variations on the Caribbean coast (Creole cooking) and in

Guanacaste (where there are vestiges of the ancient indigenous peoples' love of maize, or corn). For more on the cuisine of these areas, see the relevant chapters in the Guide.

Típico dishes you'll find all over Costa Rica usually include **rice** and some kind of meat or fish, often served as part of a special plate with coleslaw salad, in which case it is called a **casado** (literally, "married person"). Often called the "national dish of Costa Rica", the ubiquitous **gallo pinto** ("painted rooster") is a breakfast combination of traditionally red and white beans with rice, sometimes served with *huevos revueltos* (scrambled eggs). The heavy concentration on starch and protein belies the rural origins of Costa Rican food: *gallo pinto* is food for people who are going to go out and work it off.

Of the dishes found on menus all over the country, particularly recommended are **ceviche** (raw fish "cooked" in lime juice with coriander and peppers), **pargo** (red snapper), **corvina** (sea bass), and any of the ice creams and **desserts**, though these can be too sickly-sweet for many

GLOSSARY OF FOOD TERMS

Fruits

Anona	Custardfruit. Sweet, thick, ripe taste: one of the best fruits in the country	*Maracuyá*	Yellow fruit with bitter taste, often used in *refrescos*; delicious when sweetened
Carambola	Starfruit	*Moras*	Blackberries
Cas	Pale flesh fruit with sweet/sour taste, usally used for *refrescos*	*Naranja*	Orange
Fresas	Strawberries	*Papaya*	Papaya/pawpaw: large round or oblong fruit with sweet orange flesh.
Granadilla	Passion fruit: small yellow fruits, sharp and sweet		Best eaten with fresh lime juice; very good for stomach bugs
Guanábana	Soursop. Very large green mottled fruit, with sweet white flesh tasting like a cross between a mango and a pear; mostly found on the Caribbean coast	*Pejibaye*	A Costa Rican speciality, you'll find this small green/orange fruit almost nowhere else. Like its relative, the coconut, it grows in bunches on palm trees: the texture – thick and chewy – is unusual; the flavour, somewhere between nutty and bland, even more so
Guayaba	Guava, very sweet, usually used for making spreads and jams	*Piña*	Pineapple
Limónes	Lemons	*Sandía*	Watermelon
Mamones chinos	Red or yellow spiny-covered fruits that look diabolical but reveal gently flavoured lychee fruit inside; somewhat like peeled green grapes, but sweeter and more fragrant. Usually sold in small bags of a dozen on street corners or buses	*Tamarindo*	Typically a large pod of seeds, the tamarind fruit is the sticky, light-brown stuff outisde the seed itself; tart and sweet at the same time, it has a unique taste; best sampled first in *refrescos*
Mango	Mango	*Zapotes*	Large sweet orange fruit, with a dark-brown outer casing

Vegetables

Aguacates	Avocados (not to be confused with *abogados*: lawyers)	*Hongos*	Mushrooms
Chayote	Resembling a light-green avocado, this vegetable is tender and delicate when cooked, excellent in stews and with meat and rice dishes	*Palmito*	Heart-of-palm. The inner core of palm trees, usually eaten on salads; half-bitter taste and fibrous texture
Fruta de pan	Breadfruit; eaten more as a starch substitute than a fruit	*Plátanos*	Plantains; often fried and eaten as a sweet
		Zanahorias	Carrots

Dishes

Arreglados	Meat and mayonnaise sand-wiches on greasy bread buns	*Ceviche*	Raw fish, usually *corvina*, "cooked" in lime juice, onions, chillies and coriander
Arroz con pollo	Rice with chicken	*Chicarrones*	Pork rinds
...*con carne*	...with meat	*Chilasquilas*	Tortillas and beef with spices and battered eggs
...*con pescado*	...with fish	*Empanadas*	Patties, meat or vegetable.
...*con mariscos*	...with seafood	*Frijoles molidos*	Mashed black beans with onions, chilli peppers, corian-der and thyme
...*con camarones*	...with shrimp/prawns		
Bocas	Small snacks served with beer	*Gallo pinto*	"Painted rooster": rice-and-beans breakfast dish
Casado	Plate of meat or fish, rice and coleslaw salad, sometimes also served with fried plantains	*Gallos*	Small sandwiches

Dishes (continued)

Pan de maíz	Corn bread; white, rather than yellow	Tamal	One of the best local specialities, usually maize flour, chicken or pork, olives, chillies, and raisins, all wrapped in a plantain leaf: a kind of variation on the Greek dolmade
Picadillo	Potatos cooked with beef and beans		
Sopa negra	Black-bean soup with egg and vegetables		
Tacos	Tortilla filled with beef or chicken, cabbage, tomatoes and mild chillies	Tortilla	Thin, small and bland bread, served as an accompaniment to meals and, especially in Guanacaste, breakfast

Meat

Bistec	Steak	Lomito	Cut of beef (filet mignon)
Cerdo	Pork	Jamón	Ham

Fish and seafood

Atún	Tuna	Mariscos	Seafood
Corvina	Sea bass	Pargo	Red snapper
Langosta	Lobster	Trucha	Trout

Ingredients and condiments

Aceite	Oil	Frijoles	Beans
Aceitunas	Olives	Huevos	Eggs
Ajo ("al ajillo")	Garlic, in garlic sauce	Leche	Milk
Cebolla	Onion	Queso	Cheese
Cilantro	Coriander	Salsa	Sauce

Desserts

Cajeta	Dessert made of milk, sugar, vanilla and sometimes coconut	Queque seco	Pound cake
Helados	Ice cream	Tamal asado	Cake made of cornflour, cream, eggs, sugar and butter
Milanes	Delicate chocolate fingers	Tres leches	Boiled milk and syrup-drenched cake
Queque	Cake		

REGIONAL DISHES

Caribbean

Pan bon	Sweet glazed bread with fruit and cheese	Rice-and-beans	As the name indicates, and cooked in coconut milk
Patacones	Plantain chips, often served con frijoles molidos	Rundown	Meat and vegetables stewed in coconut milk

Guanacaste

Chorreados	Corn pancakes	Olla de carne	Meat stew: hearty and rich
Horchata	Hot drink made with corn or rice, flavoured with cinnamon	Pinolillo	Milky corn drink
		Rosquillas	Corn doughnut
Natilla	Sour cream	Tanelas	Scone-like corn snack

tastes. The fresh **fruit** is especially good, either eaten by itself or drunk in *refrescos* (see p.32.) Papayas, pineapple and bananas are all cheap and plentiful, along with some less familiar fruits like *mamones chinos* (a kind of lychee), *anona* (which tastes like custard) and *marañón*, whose seed is the cashew nut.

EATING OUT

Eating out in Costa Rica will cost more than you might think. Main dishes can easily run between $7–9. Then there's those sneaky **extra charges**: the service charge (10 percent) and the sales tax (15 percent), which bring the meal to a total of 25 percent more than the menu price. **Tipping**, however, is not necessary (for more, see p.57).

The cheapest places to dine in Costa Rica, and where most workers eat lunch, their main meal, are the ubiquitous **sodas**, halfway between the North American diner and the British greasy cafe. Sodas offer filling set *platos del día* (daily specials) and *casados*, combinations of rice, beans, salad and meat or fish, for about $3. Most do not add sales tax (although restaurants masquerading as sodas, like *La Perla* in San José, do). You usually have to go to the cash register to receive your bill. Sodas also often have takeout windows, where you can pick up snacks such as the delicious little fingers of bread and sugar called *churros*. Many sodas are **vegetarian**, and in general vegetarians do quite well in Costa Rica. Most menus will have a vegetable option, and asking for dishes to be served without meat is perfectly acceptable.

Because Costa Ricans start the day early, they are less likely to hang about late in restaurants in the evening, and establishments are usually empty or **closed** by 10 or 10.30pm. In general you need to be confident where the waiting staff are concerned: waiters and waitresses tend to leave you alone unless they are called for. **Non-smoking** sections are uncommon, to say the least, except in perhaps the most expensive establishments; if you're looking for a smoke-free environment, try the vegetarian sodas.

DRINKING

Mellow-tasting Costa Rican **coffee** is some of the best in the world, and it is usual to end a meal on a small cup. The best blends are export, which you can buy in stores and are served at some cafés. If you order it with milk (*café con leche*), it is traditionally served in a pitcher of coffee with a separate pitcher of heated milk, so you can mix it to your liking. Also good are **refrescos**, cool drinks made with milk (*leche*) or water (*agua*), fruit and ice, all whipped up in a blender. You can buy them at stalls, or in cartons – the latter tend to be sugary. You'll find **herb teas** throughout the country; those served in the Caribbean province of Limón are especially good. In Guanacaste you can get the distinctive **corn-based drinks** *horchata* and *pinolillo*, made with milk and sugar and with a grainy consistency.

In addition to the many imported American **beers**, Costa Rica has a few local brands, which are not bad at all. Most popular is *Imperial* (light draught, American-style), seconded by *Bavaria* (sweeter, more substantial and slightly nutty). Of the local low-alcohol beers, *Bavaria Light* is a good option; *Tropical* is a bit more watery.

Wine lovers will have to eschew their passion for the duration of their Costa Rican holiday; the country has no vineyards, and the imports available tend to be neither particularly good nor cheap, although you may get a decent bottle in a really swanky restaurant for an astronomical price. **Spirits** tend to be associated with serious drinking, usually drunk by men in bars, and rarely by local women in public. There is an indigenous hard-liquor drink, **guaro**, of which *Cacique* is the most popular brand. It's a bit rough, but good with lime sodas such as *Squirt* or *Lift*. For an after-dinner drink, try *Café Rica*, a creamy **liqueur** made with the local coffee.

BARS

Costa Rica has a variety of **places to drink**, from shady macho domains to pretty beachside bars, with some particularly cosmopolitan establishments in San José. The capital is also the place to find the country's last remaining **boca bars**, atmospheric places which serve *bocas* (tasty little snacks) with drinks; though historically these were free, nowadays, even in the most traditional places, it is becoming more common to be charged for them. (For more on San José's *boca* bars, see p.88.) In even the smallest town with any foreign population – either ex-pat or tourists – you'll notice a sharp split between the places frequented by locals and those that cater to foreigners. **Gringo grottos** abound, especially in the beach towns, with at least one bar aspiring to some kind of

COFFEE IN COSTA RICA

There are two types of **coffee** available in Costa Rica: **export quality** (*grano d'oro*), typically packaged by either *Café Britt* or *Café Rey*, and served in good hotels and restaurants, and the **lower-grade blend** usually sold for the home market. Costa Rica's export grade coffee is known the world over for being an excellently mellow and smooth Highland bean. The stuff produced for the domestic market, however, is another matter entirely. Some of it is even **pre-sweetened**, so if you ask for it with sugar (*con azúcar*), you'll get a saccharine shock. Among the best coffees you'll find in Costa Rica are **La Carpintera**, a smooth, rich, hard bean grown on Cerro de la Carpintera in the Valle Central, and **Zurquí**, the oldest cultivated bean in the country, grown for 150 years on the skirts of Volcán Barva. Strong, but with a silky, gentle taste, **Café el Gran Vito**, grown by Italian immigrants near San Vito in the extreme south of the country, is an unusual grade of export bean, harder to find than those grown in the Valle de el General and the Valle Central. Coffee **harvesting** in Costa Rica takes place from about November to January (summer) each year.

cosmopolitanism. These places tend to have a wide bar stock, at least compared to the limited *guaro* and beer menu of the local bars. In many places, especially port cities like Limón, Puntarenas and Golfito, there are the usual contingent of rough, rowdy bars where testosterone-fuelled machos go to drink gallons and fight; it's usually pretty obvious which ones they are – they advertise their seediness with a giant *Imperial* placard parked right in front of the door so you can't see what's going on in the dim depths inside.

Most bars typically **open** in the morning, any time between 8.30am and 11am, and **close** at around 11pm or midnight. In general **Sunday** night is dead, with many bars not open at all and others that close early, around 10pm or so. Though Friday and Saturday nights are, as usual, the busiest, the **best nights** to go are often those during the week, when you can enjoy live music, happy hours and other specials. The **drinking age** in Costa Rica is 18, and many bars will only admit those with a *cédula* (ID). A photocopy of your passport page is acceptable.

MAIL, PHONES AND TELECOMMUNICATIONS

Costa Rica's postal system, CORTEL is reasonably efficient, though you may have problems sending and receiving letters from remote areas. The Costa Rican state electronics company, ICE (Instituto Costarricense de Electricidad) provides international telephone, fax and internet services via RACSA, the telecommunications subsidiary.

MAIL

Even the smallest Costa Rican town has a **correo**, or post office, but the most reliable place to mail overseas is from San José's lime-green Baroque *Correo Central*, or main post office (see p.94). Airmail letters to Canada and the US cost 25¢ to 30¢; to Europe about 35¢. Letters generally take about 10 days to get to North America, or 2 weeks or more for Europe. Mail to Australasia can take 3 or 4 weeks and costs 40¢.

Most post offices have a **lista de correos** (Poste Restante, General Delivery); this is an efficient and safe way to receive letter mail, especially at the main office in San José. They will hold letters for up to 4 weeks at a charge of 10¢ a letter. Bring a photocopy of your passport when picking up mail, and make sure that correspondents address letters to you under your name as it appears on your passport.

One thing you can't fail to notice is the paucity of **mailboxes** in Costa Rica. In the capital, unless your hotel has regular mail pickup, the only resort is to hike down to the *Correo Central*. In outlying or isolated areas of the country you will have to rely on hotels' private mailboxes or on local businesses. In most cases, especially in Limón province, where mail is very slow, it is probably quicker to wait until you return to San José and mail correspondence from there. **Opening hours** for nearly all Costa Rica's *correos* are Mon–Fri 7.30am–5 or 5.30pm. Those in San José and Liberia also have limited Saturday hours.

Although CORTEL handles letters fairly efficiently, **packages** are another thing altogether – parcel service both coming and going is snarled in paperwork and labyrinthine customs regulations, besides being very expensive and very slow. If you must send parcels, take them unsealed to the *correo* for inspection.

TELECOMMUNICATIONS

Though calls **within Costa Rica** are relatively cheap, calling **long-distance** can work out very expensive: to the UK and Northern Europe you will pay about $15 for the first 3 minutes, and $4 for each minute thereafter. There are no reduced rates. Calls to the USA and Canada are considerably cheaper (though rates vary in relation to geographical distance); roughly about $2–3 per minute, with the cheapest period ($1.50 per min) between 10pm and 7am and at weekends.

You can **call collect** to virtually any foreign country from any phone or payphone in Costa Rica; simply dial ☎09 or ☎116 to get an English-speaking operator, followed by the country code, area code and number. *AT&T*, *MCI*, *Sprint*, *Canada Direct* or *UK Direct* calling-card holders can make **credit-card calls** from payphones in Costa Rica. Simply dial the relevant access code (see opposite); calls made will automatically be billed to your account.

PHONE NUMBERS IN COSTA RICA

The country code for the whole of Costa Rica is ☎506. There are no area codes. The 7-digit system of telephone numbers – used throughout this book – is relatively new, and you may still see numbers on business cards and advertisements given in the old 6-digit configuration. To check the new number, consult any telephone book; ICE offices also have free phone number conversion tables.

If you have to pay for the call on the spot, the best thing is to use a private line, perhaps from a hotel (expensive, due to the additional "line" charge the hotel may lay on, anywhere from 75¢ to $5) or from the San José *Radiográfica* office (see p.94), where you can make overseas calls, send and receive faxes, and use directories. It's not a good idea to use a payphone to make international calls with colones.

A number of annoying rules govern the use of **payphones** in Costa Rica: first, they are always occupied; second, the occupant will keep talking for ever, no matter how much you glare, pace and point to your watch. Third, a lot of payphones don't work – ask someone *"¿Está bueno/malo?"*

if you're in doubt. If you do manage to find one, they accept 5, 10 and 20 colones coins.

USEFUL NUMBERS	
International information	☎124
International operator (for call collect)	☎116 or ☎09
Calling-card access codes	
AT&T	☎114
Sprint	☎163
MCI	☎162
Canada Direct	☎161
UK Direct	☎167

THE MEDIA

Though as a rule, the Costa Rican media pumps out relatively anodyne and conservative coverage of local and regional issues – shadowing the antics of El Presidente and the political elite with burr-like tenacity – it is possible to find good investigative journalism, particularly in the daily *La Nación*. There are also a number of interesting local radio stations. TV output, on the other hand, leaves something to be desired.

NEWSPAPERS

In San José all **domestic newspapers** are sold on the street by vendors. Elsewhere you can find them in newsagents and in *pulperías* (general stores). All are tabloid format, with colourful, eye-catching layout and presentation.

Though the Costa Rican press is free, it does indulge in a certain follow-the-leader journalism. Leader of the pack is the daily **La Nación**, voice of the (right-of-centre) establishment and owned by the country's biggest media consortium; other highbrow dailies and television channels more or less parrot its line. Historically, *La Nación* has featured some good investigative reporting, for example with regard to the recent *Banco Anglo* corruption scandal and Costa Rica's continuing *narcotraficante* (drug-trafficking) problems. It also comes with a useful daily pull-out arts section, **Viva**, with listings of what's on in San José – the classifieds are handy for almost anything, including long-term accommodation.

No less serious, *La República* is slightly more downmarket; no matter what is happening in the world or Costa Rica, they have a tendency to slap a football photo on the front page. *Al Día* is the populist "body count" paper, good to read to get a feel of the kind of newspaper read by most Costa Ricans. **Alternative voices** include *La Prensa Libre*, the very good left-leaning evening paper, and the thoughtful weekly *Esta Semana*, which offers longer, in-depth articles and opinion pieces. *Mesoamerica*, based in San José, gives a solid weekly review and impartial analysis of politics, economics and society in Central America. You can consult it in libraries or receive a subscription from ICAS, Aptdo 1524-2050 San Pedro, Costa Rica. The *Semanario Universidad*, the voice of the University of Costa Rica, published weekly, certainly goes out on more of a limb than the big dailies, with particularly good coverage of the arts and the current political scene. You can find it on campus or in San Pedro; also in libraries.

Costa Rica's aspiration to *Newsweek*, *Rumbo*, is a rather dull weekly, featuring thinly researched articles on such sociological themes as jealousy and infidelity, alongside features on current politics in the region. Owned by the same group as *La Nación*, they also produce a dreadful women's magazine called *Perfil*.

Local **English-language** papers include the venerable and serious *Tico Times*, and the full-colour *Costa Rica Today*, intended specifically for tourists, with articles on activities and holidays. Both can be a good source of information for trav ellers: the ads regularly feature hotel and restaurant discounts. You can pick up recent copies of the *New York Times*, *International Herald Tribune*, *USA Today*, *Miami Herald*, *Newsweek*, *Time* and sometimes the *Financial Times* in the shop inside the *Gran Hotel Costa Rica* in downtown San José. Of the **San José bookstores** (see p.93) *Librerías Lehmann* and *Universal* keep good stocks of mainstream and non-mainstream foreign magazines (*Lehmann* has even been known to carry *The Advocate*); the Mark Twain library at the *Centro Cultural Costarricense-Norteamericano* also receives English-language publications. For publications in other languages, go to the relevant **cultural centre**.

Oddly enough, one of the best places in the entire country for domestic and foreign newspapers is in the provincial city of **Liberia**, where *Galería Fulvia* sells the major US newspapers and magazines along with *La Repubblica*, *Die Zeit* and *Le Monde*, and a number of other quality publications.

RADIO

There are many **commercial radio stations** in Costa Rica, all pumping out the Techno and House tunes-of-the-moment alongside a few salsa spots, annoying commercials, and the odd bout of government-led pseudo-propaganda promoting the general wonder that is Costa Rica.

Some of the more interesting **local radio stations** are non-mainstream and have only a limited airtime. One such is broadcast by Radio Matute, from the San José bar and nightspot *Casa Matute*, using the frequencies of Radio Emperador (104.7FM) and Radio Costa Rica (930 AM). Transmitted on weeknights from 8.30pm until midnight, Radio Matute is arts-oriented and often opens with a spot about culture in Costa Rica with a studio guest. After 10.30pm it features some of the most up-to-date playlist music in

Costa Rica, mixing salsa and merengue with some US and UK indie tunes. On Radio Alajuela (98.3FM/1280AM), also from 8.30pm to midnight, you'll hear Costa Rican singers and music along with some talk spots. Radio America Latina (780AM) has a fascinating advice show – how to live your life better, be happy, find God – broadcast from 10.30 to 11pm. Transmitting from the *Burger King Palace* in central San José, Radio Monumental (93.5FM/670AM) is a politically themed talk show. Another fascinating programme is *El Club del Taxista Costarricense* – "Costa Rican taxi driver's club" – broadcast by Radio Columbia (98.7FM/760AM) from 9.30 to 11pm. This social and political talk show, now in its 22nd year, was initially directed only at taxi drivers, but its populist, folksy appeal has led to it being adopted by the general population.

TELEVISION

Most Costa Rican households have a **television**, beaming out a diet of good Mexican/Venezuelan *telenovelas* (soap operas), and some not bad domestic news programmes. On the downside, Costa Rica is also the graveyard for 1970s American TV, the place where *The Dukes of Hazzard* and other such delights, dubbed into Spanish, come back to haunt you.

Channel 7 is the main home-grown station, particularly strong in local and regional news. Other than its news show, *Telenoticias*, Costa Rica has few home-grown products, and Channel 7's programming comprises a mix of bought-in shows from Spanish-speaking countries plus a few from the US. **Channel 6** is the main competitor, very similar in content; on **Channel 19** you'll see mostly dubbed programmes and movies from the US. The Mexican/Spanish cable channel **ECO** is good for news, and even has news spots from Europe. Many households, hotels and restaurants also receive **CNN**.

CRIME AND PERSONAL SAFETY

Costa Rica is generally considered to be a very safe country. Any crime that does exist tends to be opportunistic, rather than involving out-and-out assault. The main things travellers have to worry about are street mugging and pickpocketing.

In **downtown San José** you need to be wary at all times. Street crime, especially chain- and watch-snatching and pickpocketing, is on the rise, perpetrated by gangs of kids called *chapulines* (delinquents, literally "grasshoppers") too young to prosecute under Costa Rican law. This has been widely reported in the press; and gangs seem to come and go, doing a crime spree and then laying low for a while. Wear a money belt, and never carry anything of value – money, tickets or passport – in an outside pocket.

It has also been known for **luggage** to be stolen while you are distracted or while it is being kept supposedly secure in a left-luggage facility. Never hand your baggage to strangers, except the airport porters, who have official identification. If storing your luggage in a hotel or guest house while you are travelling around the country, make sure it is locked, has your name prominently written on it, and that you have left instructions for it not to be removed by anyone but yourself, under any circumstances.

Car theft – both of cars and things inside them – also occurs. You should not leave anything of value in a parked car – even locked in the trunk – anywhere in Costa Rica, day or night. In addition, never park your car on the street in San José, the Valle Central towns, Puntarenas or Limón; use the *parqueos* (guarded parking lots). Heavily touristed National Park parking places are also vulnerable.

The bottom line is that if you take the common-sense **precautions** outlined above, you should get by unscathed. In addition, keep copies of your passport, your air ticket and your travellers' cheques, plus your insurance policy at home; and, if possible, extra copies in your hotel. In Costa Rica you have to carry **ID** on you at all times, and for foreigners this means carrying your passport. A photocopy of your passport – of the first page and the one with your Costa Rican entry stamp – will do (the police understand tourists' reluctance to go about with their passports all the time), but if you are stopped and asked for ID, make sure you can produce the real thing – by going to your hotel, for example – just in case the police demand to see it.

Though in the winter of 1994–5 a couple of "ambushes" took place on the Guápiles Highway – one of them resulting in an American woman being shot dead – such situations are still *extremely* unlikely for tourists. Should the worst happen, the best thing to do seems to be to comply with demands.

REPORTING A CRIME

In the past year or so the **police** (*guardia*) presence in San José has increased dramatically. If you have anything stolen you will need to report the incident to the nearest police post: do this right away. In San José, the most convenient method is to head for the *Organismo de Investigación Judicial* (OIJ; ☎255-0122 or 222-1365) in the Tribunales de la Justicia, or La Corte (the Supreme Court) in San José between Av 6 and 8 and C 15 and 19. Theft is more unlikely in rural areas; if you do get robbed, go to the nearest *guardia rural* who will give you a report (you'll do better if you speak Spanish, or are with someone who does).

Any **tourist-related crime** (such as overcharging) can be addressed to the ICT, Aptdo 777-1000, San José. They have a good reputation for following up letters and reports of incidents. For a list of embassies in San José, see p.93.

EMERGENCY TELEPHONE NUMBERS	
All emergencies	☎911
Police	☎117
Fire	☎118
Traffic police	☎222-9330 or 9245

WOMEN TRAVELLERS

Travelling through Costa Rica, three things are immediately apparent with regard to the position of women. First, urban educated women play an active role in public life and in the workforce. Second, as the mothers and the heads of families, Costa Rican women are given respect by their peers, their children and to an extent by their husbands. Third, any woman under the age of thirty can invariably expect to be hissed at by men in the street.

Despite the fact that travelling solo as a female in some parts of the country is culturally foreign, in general people are friendly and helpful: women travelling on their own get the *pobrecita* (poor little thing) vote, because they're *solita* (all alone) without family or man. Nonetheless, Costa Rican men may throw out unsolicited comments (**piropos**, from *piropear*, to compliment) at women in the street. It's the usual stuff: *mí amor, guapa, machita* ("blondie") and so on, and if they don't feel like articulating a whole word, they may stare with an hilarious insistence, or they might hiss – there's a saying used by local women: "Costa Rica's full of snakes, and they're all men."

Blonde, fair-skinned women are in for a quite a bit of this, whereas if you look remotely Latin you'll get less attention. This is not to say you'll be exempt from these staggeringly unreconstructed compliments. Even in groups, women are targets. Walk with a man, however, and the whole street theatre disappears as if by magic. The accepted wisdom is to pass right by and pretend nothing's happening. If you're staying in Costa Rica for any time, though, you may want to learn a few responses in Spanish; this won't gain you any respect (men look at you and make *loca* [crazy] whirligig finger gestures at their temples), but it may make you feel better.

None of this is necessarily an expression of sexual interest: it has more to do with a man displaying his masculinity to his buddies than any desire to get to know you. Sexual assault figures in Costa Rica are low, you don't get felt up or groped, and you rarely hear *piropos* outside the towns. But for some women, unhappily, this machismo can be endlessly tiring, and may even mar their stay in the country.

GEOGRAPHY, CLIMATE AND SEASONS

For such a small country (51,000 square kilometres or 19,700 square miles), Costa Rica is home to an enormous diversity of terrain, climates and geographical zones. The startling, dramatic and quick changes in landscape that so fascinate visitors come from the stark contrast between mountains, tillable valleys, and the hot, tropical lowlands.

In much of Costa Rica the two-season rule of many tropical countries applies. The dry (Dec–April) and wet (May–Nov) **seasons** are most distinctly marked in the central Highlands. Although Costa Rica is in the northern hemisphere – it lies 8° to 11° above the equator – the dry season is referred to locally as *verano* (summer) and the wet *invierno* (winter) which can cause some confusion for North American and European visitors. March and April are usually the hottest months, while cool winds from the North American winter weather systems can make some days in December, January and February a bit cool.

VOLCANO REPUBLIC

Four **mountain ranges** traverse the country. Running roughly from northwest to southeast these are the low **Cordillera de Guanacaste**, the **Cordillera de Tilarán** – from which Volcán Arenal, one of the world's most active volcanos, sprouts – and the **Cordilleras Central** and **Talamanca**. Everywhere these ranges define the landscape, forming between their spines five distinct areas: the tropical lowlands of the Pacific and Caribbean coasts, the tropical plains of the Zona Norte, the Highlands of the Valle Central, and the low, broad lands of Guanacaste. More than sixty **volcanos** troop down Costa Rica's spine. Some are dormant or extinct, but there are eight active – or recently active – cones, testament to the active plate tectonics of the region, which lies near the meeting point with the Pacific Cocos plate and the Central Caribbean plate.

The fertile **Valle Central**, the geographical fulcrum of the country, is an intermountain plateau lying between the Cordilleras Central and Talamanca. Here you'll experience the classic Highland climate found in other Central American countries – the place where coffee grows, elites settle, and economic and industrial wealth gathers. The eastern slopes of the Cordillera Central – the **Atlantic Watershed**, as it's known, an area covered in our *Limón Province and the Caribbean Coast* chapter – is relatively flat, water-fed, hot and humid; ideal for fruit, especially banana, growing. The extreme southwest of Costa Rica – dealt with in our chapter on the *Zona Sur* – falls steeply away from the **Valle de el General**, drained by the wide Río Grande de Terraba, to fall quickly into heavily forested lowlands whose climate and geography is similar to the Atlantic areas: hot, humid and fairly swampy.

CLIMATES AND MICROCLIMATES

Although it is officially termed "subtropical", a virtual quilt of **microclimates**, with at least twelve bona fide climate zones in total, makes it impossible to describe Costa Rica's climate accurately in one shot. As a mountainous country with large tracts of low- and flatlands, **altitude** is the prime factor in determining temperature and vegetation. Temperatures can range from 35°C on either of the coasts, to below freezing atop Mount Chirripó; at 3500m, Costa Rica's highest point; these changes are extreme and localized.

In the **Valle Central**, including San José, the climate rosily called "perpetual summer", is a year-round 22–25°C. "Perpetual spring" is reserved for higher altitudes, which means it can actually be quite chilly in some of the higher mountain towns. The **Zona Norte**, and areas of the **Zona Sur**, like Golfito and the Osa Peninsula, can get oppressively hot and humid, with temperatures from 26–30°C. **Guanacaste**, in comparison, can also be very hot, but the effect here is mitigated by the area's relative dryness. The interior of the **Nicoya Peninsula** is quite warm, with a sea breeze cooling the beach towns. Along the Atlantic (Caribbean) coast, **Puerto Limón**, Tortuguero and Barra de Colorado are hot and humid year-round, receiving an enormous amount of rain. South of Puerto Limón, towards Cahuita and Puerto Viejo, there is a "little summer", or small and unpredictable dry season, in September and October, just when the Valle Central is getting drenched.

SEASONS

There is currently a move in Costa Rica to refer, somewhat euphemistically, to the wet season as the **"green season"**. No doubt this is because "wet" scares potentially paying visitors off with visions of monsoon-like deluges. In fact it is not all that wet, except in the Valle Central, where downpours, typically in the afternoon, can be fierce, especially in September and October. Even in the Valle Central, however, you'll experience plenty of sunshine early in the day. Ticos say that the hotter it is in the morning – and it can get quite fiercely hot in San José – the harder it will rain in the afternoon.

Access to some **National Parks**, especially Corcovado, is very limited in the rainy season – the Osa Peninsula on which Corcovado is located receives between 2500mm and 5000mm of rain a year, most of it between May and November. Driving is tougher in the wet season, and you'll need a sturdy 4WD to get you around the Nicoya Peninsula or up to Monteverde. Aside from these caveats, though, in general the wet season should not deter travelling in Costa Rica: it rains most of the year on the Atlantic side anyway, and Guanacaste and the Pacific coast do not have such a pronounced rainy season. Simply focus your activities in the period between about 7am and noon, bring an umbrella, be prepared to get drenched from time to time, and get used to your clothes smelling a little mouldy. If you are in Costa Rica during July and August and notice there's been no rain for days, you may have caught the **veranillo** (little summer), a fortnight or so of dry weather that usually occurs at this time.

Dry season days are characterized by more or less cloudless skies. The air is a pleasant temperature at higher altitudes and generally dry, with rare, unseasonal showers. The dry season is most pronounced in Guanacaste, the Nicoya Peninsula and the Valle Central.

NATIONAL PARKS AND RESERVES

Costa Rica protects 25 percent of its total territory under the aegis of a carefully structured system of National Parks, Wildlife Refuges and Biological Reserves; in all there are currently some 75 designated protected areas. Established gradually over the past thirty years, their role in protecting the country's rich fauna and flora against the expansion of resource-extracting activities and human settlement is generally lauded.

While these areas may be called different names (see below), they are all affiliated with the National Parks Service, or **SPN**, and its umbrella entity, MIRENEM, the Ministry of Natural Resources, Energy and Mines. The National Parks, which cover 12 percent of Costa Rica's protected land, provide more services and activities than the Refuges and Reserves, and tend to be more heavily touristed. Biologists, scientists and researchers from around the world make up a large portion of visitors.

Many people imagine Costa Rica's National Parks to be a kind of tropical version of those in North America. Some have the notion that they are huge outdoor zoos. However, it's important to get it straight from the start that you are in no way guaranteed to see any of the larger mammals that live within the Parks' confines – indeed it's very unlikely. As the SPN never tires of pointing out, the National Parks were not created specifically with **tourism** in mind, nor is it their – or the rangers' – exclusive function to cater to tourists, although the government and MIRENEM certainly recognize the invaluable cash flow brought by tourism.

In total the Parks and Reserves protect approximately 4 percent of the world's total **wildlife** species and **life zones**, among them rainforests, cloudforests, *páramo* – or high-altitude moorlands – swamps, lagoons, marshes and mangroves, and the last remaining patches of tropical **dry forest** in the isthmus. Also protected

PARK TERMINOLOGY	
Puesto	post (ranger post)
Sendero	trail
Area de acampar	camping area
Agua potable	drinking water
Peligro	danger
Area restringado	restricted area
Entrada/salida	entrance/exit

are areas of **historical significance**, including a very few pre-Columbian settlements, and places considered to be of immense scenic beauty – valleys, waterfalls, dry lowlands and beaches. Costa Rica has also taken measures to protect beaches where several species of **marine turtle** lay their eggs, as well as a number of active **volcanos**.

For a **history** of the Parks system in Costa Rica, see *Contexts*.

DEFINITIONS AND TERMS

A **National Park** (Parque Nacional) is typically a large – usually more than 1000 hectares – chunk of relatively untouched wilderness, dedicated to preserving features of outstanding ecological or scenic interest. These are the most-touristed of the protected areas, typically offering walking, hiking or snorkelling opportunities. A couple even have historical exhibits. Though habitation, construction of hotels and hunting of animals is prohibited in all National Parks, increasingly "buffer zones" are being designated around them, where people are permitted to engage in a controlled amount of agriculture and hunting. In most cases Park boundaries are surveyed but not demarcated – rangers and locals know what land is within the Park and what is not – so don't expect fences or signs to tell you where you are.

Although it also protetcts valuable ecosystems and conserves areas for scientific research,

National Parks, Biological Reserves, Wildlife Refuges & Principal Private Reserves

1. Parque Nacional Volcán Poás
2. Parque Nacional Braulio Carrillo
3. Parque Nacional Volcán Irazú
4. Monumento Nacional Guayabo
5. Parque Nacional Tapantí
6. Parque Nacional Volcán Arenal
7. Reserva Biológica Bosque Nuboso Monteverde
8. Parque Nacional Palo Verde
9. Reserva Biológica Lomas Barbudal
10. Parque Nacional Rincón de la Vieja
11. Parque Nacional Guanacaste
12. Parque Nacional Santa Rosa
13. Parque Nacional Marino las Baulas
14. Refugio Nacional de Fauna Silvestre Ostional
15. Parque Nacional Barra Honda
16. Reserva Natural Absoluta Cabo Blanco
17. Reserva Biológica de Guayabo y Negritos
18. Refugio Nacional de Fauna Silvestre Curú
19. Reserva Biológica Carara
20. Parque Nacional Manuel Antonio
21. Parque Nacional Marino las Ballenas
22. Reserva Biológica Isla del Caño
23. Parque Nacional Corcovado
24. Refugio Nacional de Fauna Silvestre Golfito
25. Parque Internacional la Amistad (Costa Rica & Panamá)
26. Parque Nacional Chirripó
27. Reserva Biológica Hitoy-Cerere
28. Refugio Nacional de Vida Silvestre Gandoca-Manzanillo
29. Parque Nacional Cahuita
30. Parque Nacional Tortuguero
31. Refugio Nacional de Fauna Silvestre Barra del Colorado
32. Refugio Nacional de Vida Silvestre Caño Negro
33. Parque Nacional Isla del Coco

a **Biological Reserve** (Reserva Biológica) generally has less of scenic or recreational interest than a National Park. Hunting and fishing are usually prohibited. A **National Wildlife Refuge** (Refugio Nacional de Vida Silvestre or Refugio Nacional de Fauna Silvestre) is designated to protect the habitat of wildlife species. It will not be at all obviously demarcated, with few, if any, services, rangers or trails, and is generally little visited by tourists.

There are also a number of **privately owned Reserves** and areas in Costa Rica, chief among them community-initiated projects such as the now-famous Reserva Biológica Bosque Nuboso Monteverde and nearby Santa Elena. While the money you pay to enter these Reserves does not go directly to the government (via the SPN), they are almost never money-grabbing places; the vast majority are conscientiously managed and have links with national and international conservation organizations. For more on how National Parks and protected areas link into Costa Rica's conservation strategy, see *Contexts*.

VISITING COSTA RICA'S PARKS

All National Parks have entrance **puestos**, or stations, often little more than a small hut where you pay your fee and pick up a general map. Typically the main ranger stations, from where the internal administration of the Park is carried out, and where the rangers sleep, eat and hang out, are some way from the entrance *puesto*. At some Parks you will only deal with the entrance hut, while at others it's a good idea to drop by the main station or administration centre, where you can talk to rangers (if your Spanish is good) about local terrain and conditions, enquire about drinking water, and use the bathroom. In some Parks, such as Corcovado, you can sleep in or camp near the main stations. Usually these provide very rustic but adequate accommodation, be it on a campsite or a bunk, and a good, collegial atmosphere. You'll need to call in advance via the SPN office in San José (see below).

Outside the most visited Parks – Volcán Poás, Volcán Irazú, Santa Rosa and Manuel Antonio – **opening hours** are somewhat theoretical. Many places are open daily, from around 8am to 4pm; where no official times are quoted, these are the times we have given throughout the *Guide*. There are **exceptions**, however: Manuel Antonio is closed on Monday and may be closed on Tuesday in the future, while other Parks may open a little

earlier in the morning. Unless you're planning on camping or staying overnight, there's almost no point in arriving at a National Park in the afternoon. In all cases, especially the volcanos, you should aim to arrive as early in the morning as possible to make the most of the day and, in particular, the weather (especially in the wet season). You'll usually find a ranger somewhere, even if he or she is not at the *puesto*. If you hang around for a while and call "¡*Upe!*" (what people say when entering houses and farms in the countryside), someone will appear.

It used to be crucial for anyone intending to do some independent hiking, or who wanted to visit several National Parks, to visit the **SPN headquarters** in San José to obtain detailed, up-to-date information, negotiate permits where required, and buy advance tickets (cheaper than those bought on the day). Now, however, under the new system of passes and fees (see below), the SPN has proposed allowing travel agents and local hotels to sell Park tickets. Though at present you can buy discounted advance tickets for Manuel Antonio at travel agents, it remains to be seen whether this system will be implemented, and whether it will work, on any large scale.

Whatever the situation when you arrive, it is still a very good idea to visit the SPN office. Things change fast and frequently in the Costa Rica Park system, and they will be the ones to keep you up-to-date. Plus, if you intend to visit any of the Parks that are governed by **restrictions** – chiefly Santa Rosa, Corcovado and Chirripó – this is where you should take care of the arrangements. See the individual accounts in the *Guide* for more details.

Information is given in this book both here and in the individual accounts in the *Guide* as to which **animals** inhabit the specific Parks. However, keep in mind that you are in **no way guaranteed** to see them – although you will, most likely, see some of the more common or less shy ones – and you would be very lucky indeed to spot the larger mammals such as the jaguar, ocelot or tapir.

PARK ORGANIZATION

In order to decentralize the National Park system and to shift some of the administrative and day-to-day responsibitilies to the areas in which the Parks are located, Costa Rica was formally divided in 1994–5 into eight conservation areas. It is useful to become familiar with these, as, in

GUARDAPARQUES

A **guardaparque** is a Park ranger, in some cases a semi-heroic figure, working long hours and long shifts – often 20 days on and 8 days off – for basic pay. You will sometimes see *guardaparques* in the more remote areas of the country setting out on foot, a rifle and a couple of sandwiches his or her only company – you may want to offer them a lift – off to patrol the Park against **poaching**. Poaching of animals, including the more famous and endangered ones such as the quetzal and the jaguar, for sale to zoos or individuals, is common, as is the hunting of animals for meat by locals within protected areas. *Guardaparques* also often go on patrol (*recorrido*) at night, solo, and armed only with a torch.

Many are locals, extremely knowledgeable about their patch of terrain, while others are university students of biology, botany or ecology who may have studied abroad and who are working for the SPN as part of their education. The Parks service also relies on a cadre of dedicated international **volunteers** to help out at both the San José office and the more remote ranger stations. If you fancy giving up some time, see p.54 for more details; you have to be pretty brave yourself to do this, as you are expected to do everything that a ranger does.

In general visitors to Costa Rica's National Parks will find *guardaparques* to be friendly and very informative. Though only part of their job is to provide tourist information – don't expect them to provide you with a *Jungle Book* repertoire of adventures – sometimes they will, if gently encouraged, tell you about their encounters with fearsome bushmasters or tapirs. Independent travellers and hikers might want to ask about the possibility of joining them "on patrol" during the day. In general you have to speak Spanish. This can be a great experience – and in some cases, especially if you are travelling alone, it's the only safe way to see the Park: some, like Corcovado, are not really safe to walk around solo.

the future, all Parks and Reserves will be discussed more and more in relation to the area to which they correspond.

In the middle of the country, the **CENTRAL VOLCANIC MOUNTAIN RANGE** contains the most accessible National Parks, near San José and easily visited on a day trip. Closest to the capital is **Braulio Carrillo** National Park, protecting tropical wet and cloudforest and with its own volcano, **Barva**. The little-known **Juan Castro Blanco** National Park sits above **Volcán Poás** National Park, one of the most-visited in the country; another volcano, **Irazú** National Park, lies to the southeast. Nearby is the archeological excavation of **Guayabo** National Monument, a pre-Columbian settlement on the slopes of the Cordillera Central.

The tiny **ARENAL** conservation area, in the west of the Zona Norte, comprises the relatively new Volcán Arenal National Park, established to protect the lava trails and the flora and fauna on the slopes of **Volcán Arenal**. You can still watch the nighttime eruptions, when lava streams down the sides of the mountain, for free – if the top isn't obscured by cloud, that is.

LA AMISTAD conservation area, located largely in the extreme south of the country and continuing east to encompass parts of the Caribbean province of Limón, includes giant **La Amistad International Park** – a joint venture betwen Costa Rica and Panamá that protects large areas of mammalian habitat and huge tracts of virtually impenetrable montane forests. Popular with hikers and backpackers, **Chirripó** National Park is named for Mt Chirripó, the highest point in Costa Rica, at 3820m. The wet and dense **Tapantí** National Park lies close to the Valle Central, while in the east, Limón province holds little-visited **Hitoy-Cerere** Biological Reserve, tiny **Cahuita** National Park, established to conserve some of the last remaining coral reef in Costa Rica, and in the southeast, **Gandoca-Manzanillo** Wildlife Refuge, an area of protected mangroves and low-lying swamps.

In the northeast corner of the country the **TORTUGUERO PLAINS** conservation area covers an enormous area of 133,000 hectares and comprises **Tortuguero** National Park, established to protect the nesting grounds of several species of marine turtle, and the wet lowland tropical forest of **Barra del Colorado** Wildlife Refuge. Largely impenetrable except by water, this area protects an enormous range of mammal and marine life, as well as some 400 different species of birds.

GUANACASTE conservation area, in the northwest of the country, includes **Guanacaste**, **Rincón de la Vieja** and **Santa Rosa** National

NATIONAL PARKS AT A GLANCE

National Park	Location	Wildlife	Topography	Activities
LA AMISTAD	border with Panamá	mammals, birds	rainforest	hiking
VOLCÁN ARENAL	136km NW of San José	birds, mammals	volcanic	volcano-watching, hiking
BALLENA	192km SW of San José	coral, mammals, fish	marine	diving, snorkelling
BARRA HONDA	330km E of San José (via Liberia)	bats, reptiles, birds	subterranean caves	caving
LAS BAULAS	301km NW of San José	turtles	beach, marine	turtle-watching
BRAULIO CARRILLO	20km N of San José	birds, reptiles, mammals	cloudforest, rainforest	hiking, birding
CAHUITA	195km SE of San José	coral, reptiles, mammals	marine, beaches	swimming, walking, snorkelling
CHIRRIPÓ	151km S of San José	mammals, birds (incl. quetzal)	mountain peaks, páramo	hiking, climbing
CORCOVADO	380km SW of San José	mammals, amphibians, reptiles	rainforest	hiking
GUANACASTE	250km NW of San José	butterflies, moths, birds, mammals	rainforest, tropical dry forest	hiking
GUAYABO NAT. MONUMENT	84km SE of San José	mammals, birds	rainforest	archeology, history, walking
VOLCÁN IRAZÚ	54km SE of San José	birds	volcanic	volcano-watching
ISLA DEL COCO	500km offshore from the Osa Peninsula	marine life	volcanic, rainforest	diving
MANUEL ANTONIO	132km SW of San José	mammals, marine life, reptiles	rainforest, mangroves, beaches	hiking, swimming
PALO VERDE	240km NW of San José	birds, mammals	limestone hills, savannah, mangroves	birdwatching, hiking
VOLCÁN POÁS	56km N of San José	mammals, birds	volcanic, dwarf cloudforest	volcano-watching
RINCÓN DE LA VIEJA	253km NW of San José	birds	rainforest, savannah	hiking, volcano-watching
SANTA ROSA	261km NW of San José	mammals, turtles	tropical dry forest	hiking, history, turtle-watching
TAPANTÍ	40km SW of San José	mammals, birds	primary montane forests	hiking
TORTUGUERO	254km NE of San José (via road/water)	turtles, mammals, birds	rainforest, beach	turtle-watching

Parks. It covers a wide variety of altitudes, from sea level to nearly 2000m at the top of Rincón de la Vieja volcano. Of most interest here are the surviving pockets of tropical dry forest and the good hiking trail up Rincon de la Vieja.

Straddling the Nicoya Peninsula and southern Guanacaste, **TEMPISQUE** covers **Palo Verde** National Park, **Las Baulas** National Marine Park, **Barra Honda** National Park, **Isla de Guayabo**, **Negrito** and **Pájaros Island** Biological Reserves and **Lomas Barbudal** Biological Reserve. This is a tremendously varied, if little visited, collection of protected areas, varying from subterranean caves in Barra Honda to turtles in Las Baulas to seasonal wetlands in Palo Verde, and well worth the effort of getting off the beaten track.

The **OSA** conservation area in the extreme southwest of Costa Rica protects some of the most diverse tropical forest in the Americas. Comprising **Corcovado** National Park on the Osa Peninsula, the **Golfito** Wildlife Refuge and the newly created Piedras Blancas National Park on the mainland, it also encompasses the Marine National Park **Ballena** and **Caño Island** Biological Reserve, both excellent snorkelling and scuba-diving destinations.

There's also a **satellite category** of parks that do not fit neatly into geographical or biological areas: **Manuel Antonio** National Park on the Pacific coast, protecting an area of astounding scenic beauty, including beaches and jungle trails; the Pacific lowland **Carara** Biological Reserve, a haven for crocodiles and other reptiles and amphibians; the unique and very localized habitat of **Cabo Blanco** Absolute Nature Reserve on the tip of the Nicoya Peninsula, and **Isla del Coco** National Park, offshore from the Osa Peninsula, which safeguards marine life and many endemic land-living species of reptiles and birds.

ENTRANCE FEES

In autumn 1994, MIRENEM and SPN increased the **entrance fees** to the vast majority of Costa Rica's Parks by more than 1000 percent. Overnight, entrance into Manuel Antonio or Poás – just to mention two of the most popular – jumped from $1.50 to $15 for foreigners (Costa Ricans and foreign residents continue to pay the lower rate). Offered little publicity to explain this meteoric rise, many people, among them tourists, tour agencies and operators, were furious. Debates raged in the national press, with many long-time visitors to Costa Rica asserting they were never going to come back, owing to the money-grabbing policies of the government, eager to milk rich foreigners of their hard-earned holiday money. The government and SPN, for

PARK AND REFUGE CATEGORIES

Category "A"

The following "high impact" Parks and Refuges typically receive the most visitors and have the least capacity for accommodating large numbers. They cost $15 to enter on the same day, or $10 if ticket bought a day or more in advance.

- Carara
- Chirripó
- Volcán Irazú
- Isla del Caño
- Manuel Antonio
- Volcán Poás
- Guanacaste/Santa Rosa

Category "B"

These Parks and Refuges are less visited but still popular. They cost $15 to enter on the same day, or $7 if ticket bought a day or more in advance.

- Volcán Arenal
- Braulio Carrillo

- Cabo Blanco
- Cahuita
- Corcovado
- Guayabo National Monument
- Palo Verde
- Rincón de la Vieja
- Tapantí
- Tortuguero

Category "C"

Little-visited Parks and Refuges. They cost $15 to enter on the same day, or $5 if ticket bought a day or more in advance.

- La Amistad
- Barra Honda
- Hitoy-Cerere

Isla del Coco doesn't belong to any of the above categories; everyone (Costa Rican and foreign) pays $15 per day to enter.

their part, were quick to point out that the whole system of protected areas is under-resourced, beleaguered and in need of as much financial help as it can get.

Now that the dust has settled, it seems that it was the way the whole thing was handled, rather than the actual rise in fees, that created the resentment. Many tourists are happy to support Costa Rica's impoverished Parks; they just feel the rise was a bit much and a bit fast. Learning from this, MIRENEM and the ICT joined forces to publicize the 1995 restructuring of Parks into "categories" (see p.45), and the concurrent new fees.

Until December 1997 the following system will apply. The **"Green Pass"** enables tourists to buy a carnet of 4 entrance tickets to National Parks and some designated Wildlife and Biological Refuges, for $29, whatever category they fall into. The pass will be valid for 30 days after you enter the first Park, and each ticket will be transferable – in other words, you can sell them on to someone else if you don't use them. You can, of course, buy separate entrance tickets to the Parks, which are cheaper if bought in advance from the SPN office in San José; they cost $15 if bought at the gate on the day, whatever the category.

OUTDOOR ACTIVITIES

Costa Rica is famous for year-round outdoor "adventure" tourism and outdoor activities, and in recent years has seen a proliferation of well-organized day trips, packages and guided outings. In many ways the country is becoming much better set up for groups of this kind than for the individual traveller who wants to rough it on his or her own.

HIKING AND WALKING

Almost everyone who comes to Costa Rica does some sort of **hiking** or **walking**, whether it be through the rainforest, on grassy uplands or drylands, or ambling along beaches or trails in Parks with less demanding terrain.

From lowland tropical forest to the heights of Mount Chirripó, there are opportunities for walking in all kinds of terrain; often for considerable distances. Make sure to **bring** sturdy shoes or hiking boots, and a hat, sunblock, umbrella and lightweight rain gear. It helps if you bring binoculars, too, even if you don't consider yourself an avid birder or animal-spotter; it's amazing what they pick up that the naked eye misses. In certain areas, like Corcovado – where you'll be doing more walking than you've ever done before, unless you're in the Marines – most people also bring a **tent**. In the high *páramo* of Chirripó, you'll need to bring at least a **sleeping bag**.

There are a number of things you have to be careful of when hiking in Costa Rica. Chief danger is **dehydration**: always carry lots of water with you, preferably bottled, or a canteen.

In 1992 two hikers were killed in Barra Honda National Park when they ventured along unfamiliar trails in the midday heat without sufficient water and became lost. To protect yourself against sunstroke, bring a hat and sunscreen. Use both, even if it is cloudy.

Many hikers **get lost** every year, although they are nearly almost always found before it's too late. If you're venturing into a remote area with which you are unfamiliar, bring a map and a compass and make sure you know how to use both. To lessen anxiety if you do get lost, make sure you have matches, a torch and, if you are at a fairly high altitude, warm clothing. It gets cold at night above 1500m, and it would be ironic to end up with hypothermia in the tropics.

You have to watch out for **snakes** in all parts of Costa Rica, and need to be particularly wary at dawn or dusk – before 5.30am or after 6pm. Theoretically you should not be out walking at these times, anyway, especially on trails where snakes hang out at the end of the day because they have absorbed the day's warmth. Many snakes start moving as early as 4.30pm, particularly in dense cloudforest cover. When walking, look where you step. When reaching for balance or a handhold, look where you put your hand. In grassy uplands like Rincón de la Vieja or around Volcán Arenal – among others – be careful of long grass and stick to the trails. In Cahuita and Manuel Antonio National Parks, watch out for "hanging vines" which may really be snakes in clever disguise.

All that said, however, most hikers and walkers, while they may encounter snakes, are very rarely bitten, especially if they stay alert. For more information on specific snakes in Costa Rica, see *Contexts*. For general health precautions and information on obtaining antivenin, see "Health", on p.14.

WHITEWATER RAFTING

After hiking and walking, **whitewater rafting** is probably the single most popular activity in Costa Rica. Some of the best rapids and rivers to be found south of Colorado are here, and a mini-industry of rafting outfitters, most of them in San José, has grown up. Elsewhere in the country your hotel or lodge might provide a guided rafting trip as an inclusive or extra tour.

Whitewater rafting entails getting in a rubber dinghy with about eight other people – including a guide – and paddling, at first very leisurely, downstream one of the rivers listed below, working together with the guide to negotiate exhilarating rapids of varying difficulty. Overall it's very **safe**: the ample life-jackets and helmets help. **Wildlife** you are likely to see from the boat, as well as from the river banks, are crocodiles, caimans, lizards, parrots, toucans, herons, kingfishers, iguanas and butterflies. Most trips last a day, though some companies run overnight or weekend trips. They **cost** between $70 and $80 for a day, including transport, equipment and

lunch. **Dress** to get wet, with sunscreen, a bathing suit, shorts and surfer sandals or gym shoes.

Rafters classify their rivers from Class I (easiest) to Class IV (pretty hard; to venture on to one of these you need to know what you're doing). The **most difficult** rivers in Costa Rica are the Class III–IV Río Reventazón and Pacuaré (both reached from the Valle Central via Turrialba), and some sections of the Río Naranjo around Manuel Antonio National Park. **Moderately easy**, Río Sarapiquí (Zona Norte) is a Class II river with some Class III rapids. The **gentlest** of all is Corobicí (in Guanacaste), a Class I flat water.

SWIMMING

Costa Rica has many lovely **beaches**, most of them on the Pacific coast. You do have to be careful swimming at many of them, however, as more than 200 **drownings** occur each year – about 4 or 5 a week. Most are unnecessary, resulting from **rip tides**, strong currents that go from the beach out to sea in a kind of funnel. Rip tides are created by an excess of water coming into the beach and seeking a release for its extra energy. When the water finds an existing depression on the ocean floor, or creates one from its own force, it forms a kind of swift-moving current, much like a river, over this depression. Rip tides are always found on beaches with relatively **heavy surf**, and can also form near river estuaries. Some are permanent, while some "migrate" up and down a beach.

People who die in rip tides do so because they **panic** – it *is* undeniably unnerving when you find yourself being carried at what seems an alarming rate, 6 or 10km an hour, out to the wide blue ocean. They also try to swim against the current, which is a useless enterprise. The combination of panic and an intense burst of energy exhausts people fast, causing them to take in water. Tragically, many people who die as a result of rip currents do so in water that is no more than waist-high. The important thing to know about rip tides is that, while they may drag you out to sea a bit, they won't take you far beyond the breakers, where they lose their energy and dissipate. They also won't drag you under – that's an **undertow** – and there are far fewer of those on Costa Rica's beaches. The best **advice** if you get caught in rip currents is to relax as much as possible, float, call for help from the beach, and wait until the current dies down. Then swim back towards the beach at a 45° angle; not straight in. By swimming back more or less parallel to the beach you'll avoid getting caught in the current again.

The other thing you have to be careful of is fairly heavy **swells**. Waves that might not look that big from the beach can have a mighty pull when you get near their break point. Many people are hurt coming out of the sea, backs to the waves, which then clobber them from behind. Best come out of the sea sideways, so that there is minimum body resistance to the water.

In addition to the above **precautions**, never swim alone, don't swim at beaches where turtles nest (this means, more often than not, sharks), never swim near river estuaries (pollution and rip tides), and always ask locals about the general character of the beach before you swim.

RIP TIDES IN COSTA RICA

Some of the most popular and frequented beaches in Costa Rica are ironically also the worst for **rip tides**:

Playa Doña Ana (Central Pacific)

Playa Jacó (Central Pacific)

Manuel Antonio's Playa Espadilla (Central Pacific)

Playa Bonita (Limón)

Punta Uva (Limón)

Cahuita, the first 400m of beach (Limón)

For more **information** on beaches and safety measures, call the Costa Rican **Lifesaving Association** in Quepos (☎777-0345).

DIVING AND SNORKELLING

Though **diving** is less of a big deal in Costa Rica than in Belize or Honduras' Bay Islands, there are a few scuba outfitters concentrated in specific areas. The best places for diving in Costa Rica are on the **Pacific coast** in the extreme northwest. Santa Elena Bay's Murciélago and Catalina Islands provide great diving, as does Isla del Coco – although the last is much more difficult and very expensive to get to.

You can also theoretically **snorkel** all along the Pacific coast. Playa Flamingo in northern Guanacaste has clear waters but not a lot to see; Bahía Ballena in the Dominical area in the southwest is also starting to be discovered as a snorkelling destination. For people who want to see **reefs** and an abundance of underwater life, the small reef near Manzanillo on the Caribbean coast is the best; Cahuita's has suffered in recent years from erosion and is dying.

DIVING OUTFITTERS IN COSTA RICA

Deep Sea Scuba ☎289-8191
Week-long courses, starting off in a swimming pool and then heading to the northern Guanacaste beaches for a minimum of 4 sea dives.

Diving Safaris ☎670-0012
Costa Rica's oldest diving outfitter, offering training courses and certification as well as excursions. They concentrate on the Gulf of Papagayo (Bahía Culebra) in northwestern Costa Rica, and can take you to the Murciélago islands in the extreme northwest. Cheapest one-day tours are about $50.

Ecotreks ☎228-2029
Diving in the Playa Flamingo area of Guanacaste; also a variety of tours from day trips to full PADI courses for about $275.

SURFING

Surfing is very good on both of Costa Rica's coasts, although there are certain beaches that are suitable during only parts of the year. You can surf all year round on the **Pacific**: running north to south the most popular beaches are Boca de Barranca, Naranjo, Tamarindo, Jacó, Hermosa, Quepos, Dominical and, in the extreme south near the Panamá border, Pavones. On the **Caribbean** coast the best beaches are at Puerto Viejo and Punta Uva further down the coast. Call the 24-hour **Costa Rican Surf Report hotline** for the latest on conditions (☎233-7386).

The **north Pacific Coast and Nicoya Peninsula** is probably the prime surfing area in the country, with a wide variety of breaks and lefts and rights of varying power and velocity. **Playa Naranjo** gives one of the best breaks in the country (Dec–March). Within Santa Rosa National Park, it has the added attraction of good camping facilities, though you need your own 4WD to reach them. **Playa Potrero Grande**, only accessible by boat from Playas del Coco, offers a very fast right point break.

Moving down to the long western back of the Nicoya Peninsula, **Playa Tamarindo** has three sites for surfing, the downside being the rocks that plague parts of the beach. While they don't offer a really demanding or wild ride, Tamarindo's waves are very popular due to the large number of hotels and restaurants in the town nearby. **Playa Langosta**, just south of Tamarindo, offers right and left point breaks, a little more demanding than Tamarindo. **Playa Avellanas** has a good beach break, locally called the *Guanacasteco*, with very hollow rights and lefts, while **Playa Nosara** offers a fairly gentle beach break, with rights and lefts. Remote and difficult to reach, Playas Coyote, Manzanillo and Mal País have consistent lefts and rights and several points.

Near Puntarenas on the **Central Pacific Coast**, **Boca Barranca** is an estuary with a very long left, while **Puerto Caldera** has a good left. **Playa Jacó** is not always dependable for good beach breaks, and the surf is not too big. Further south, **Playa Hermosa** is better, with a very strong beach break. Next door **Playas Esterillos Este**, **Oese** and **Bejuco** offer similarly good beach breaks.

On the **south Pacific** coast, **Playita Manuel Antonio** is good when the wind is up, with beach breaks, and left and right waves. Southwards, **Dominical** offers great surfing, with strong lefts and rights, and beautiful surroundings. Down at the very south of the country, past Golfito, **Playa Pavones** boasts one of the longest left points in the world, very fast and with a good formation.

The best surfing beaches on the **Caribbean** coast lie towards the south, from **Cahuita** to **Manzanillo** villages. **Black-Sand Beach** at Cahuita has an excellent beach break, with the added bonus of year-round waves. **Puerto Viejo** is home to *La Salsa Brava*, one of the few legitimate "big waves" in Costa Rica, a very thick, tubular wave formed by deep water rocketing towards a shallow reef. Further south **Manzanillo** has a very fast beach break, in lovely surroundings and with good camping.

Further north towards **Puerto Limón** are a couple of beaches that, while not in the class of Puerto Viejo, can offer experienced surfers a few good waves. **Playa Bonita**, a few kilometres north of Limón, is known for its powerful and dangerous left; only people who really know what they are doing should try this. Similarly, the left breaking waves at **Isla Uvita**, just off the coast from Puerto Limón, are considered tricky.

FISHING AND SPORTSFISHING

Costa Rica has hit the big time in the lucrative **sportsfishing** game. Both coasts are blessed with the kind of big fish serious anglers love – marlin, swordfish, tarpon and snook among them. The most obvious characteristic of sportsfishing is its tremendous **expense**: some 3- or 4-day packages run upwards of $3000. **Quepos** and **Golfito** have long been good places to do a little fishing, while some areas, like **Barra del Colorado** in the northeast and **Playa Flamingo** in Guanacaste, have turned into monothematic destinations, where a rather expensive brand of sportsfishing is really all that's on offer. Although good fishing is possible all year round, **January** and **February** are the most popular months.

Sportsfishing is just that: sport. The vast majority of fish are returned to the sea alive. Marty Bernard's *No Frills Sportsfishing Tours* (☎228-4812) are nearly famous in Costa Rica for teaching total amateurs how to snag huge tarpon and *guapote* (rainbow bass) in a day; they offer a "no fish, no pay" deal and all-inclusive day tours for $500, which, odd though it may seem, is a good price. See the accounts of Barra del Colorado in Limón province (p.148), Los Chiles in the Zona Norte (p.189), Quepos in the Central Pacific (p.291) and Golfito in the Zona Sur (p.317) for local sportsfishing opportunities.

Casual anglers can find cheaper and more low-key fishing opportunities in the many fresh **rivers** abounding in **trout**, or in **Laguna de Arenal**, where **rainbow bass** fishing is especially good.

BIRDWATCHING

One oft-repeated statistic you'll hear about Costa Rica is that the country boasts more than 850 species of birds (including migratory ones), a higher number than in all of North America. Consequently, **birding** is impressive, and it's likely that at the very least you'll spot hummingbirds, scarlet macaws, toucans, kingfishers and a variety of trogons. The resplendent quetzal, found in the higher elevations of Monteverde, Braulio Carrillo National Park, and the Talamanca mountain range, is elusive, but can still be spotted.

Serious birders have a few **tour operators** to choose from, all of them in San José. Of those listed on p.25, *Horizontes* and *Costa Rica Expeditions* are good bets, and *Caminos de la Selva* have a 15-day tour devoted exclusively to birdwatching. In addition, *San José Travel* (☎221-0593) and *Geotur* (☎234-1867) run popular 1-day **quetzal-spotting** trips.

BICYCLING AND MOUNTAIN BIKING

Only certain places in Costa Rica lend themselves well to **mountain biking**: where trails have good surfaces (not seas of mud) and there's something to see along the way or to aim for at the end. In general the **best areas** for extensive biking are Corcovado National Park, Montezuma village to Cabo Blanco Absolute Nature Reserve on the Nicoya Peninsula, and Santa Rosa National Park in Guanacaste. The Fortuna and Volcán Arenal area is also increasingly popular: you can bike to see the volcano (although not up it) and around the pretty Laguna de Arenal.

There are plenty of **bike rental shops** throughout the country; you may also be able to rent one from local tour agencies. Prices are most often around $7 an hour; or up to $60 or so for the day. See "Getting Around" for more on independent cycling around Costa Rica.

BIKING TOURS IN COSTA RICA
Costaricabike   ☎225-3939
Day trips to the Valle Central's Guayabo National Monument and surroundings, and overnight trips to Volcán Arenal.

Ecotreks   ☎ and fax 289-8191
Good one-day mountain-biking tour up one of the Valle Central volcanoes. Fairly priced at $65.

Ríos Tropicales   ☎233-6455; fax 255-4354
Day bike-rides up and around Poás and Irazú volcanoes with this whitewater rafting specialist (see p.47); also a 10-day coast-to-coast tour on demand.

SEA AND RIVER KAYAKING

More than twenty rivers in Costa Rica provide good **kayaking**, especially the Sarapiquí, Reventazón, Pacuare, General and Corobicí. The small towns of Turrialba, in the Valle Central, and Puerto Viejo de Sarapiquí, in the Zona Norte, are good bases for customized kayaking tours, with a number of specialist operators or lodges that rent boats, equipment and guides.

Sea kayaking has become increasingly popular in recent years. This is an activity for the experienced only, and should never be attempted without a guide. The number of rivers, rapids and streams pouring from the mountains into the oceans on both coasts can make currents treacherous, and any kind of boating, especially kayaking, is potentially dangerous without proper supervision.

HORSERIDING

Almost everywhere you go in Costa Rica, with the exception of waterlogged northern Limón province, you should be able to hook up with a **horseback tour**. Guanacaste is probably the best area in the country for riding, where a cluster of excellent haciendas (working cattle ranches) also

HORSERIDING TOURS
ATEC, Puerto Viejo de Talamanca (see p.169).
Specializing in tours to the Kéköldi Bribrí indigenous reserve near Puerto Viejo, with some horseback rides on the beach.

Dundee Ranch (see p.286) and **Hacienda Doña Marta** (see p.286), near Orotina in the Central Pacific.
Horseback tours through pockets of rainforest, Pacific tropical dry forest, grasslands, mango plantations and rivers.

Paradise Mountain Trails   ☎282-7720
Rides in the Valle Central, near Barva, Turrialba and Irazú volcanos.

Robles Tours   ☎237-2116
Tours on the hilly flanks of Volcán Barva.

Rancho Savegre near Quepos in the Central Pacific (☎777-0528).
Great rides through rainforest, mangroves and grasslands; also on the beach, through raging rivers.

Tropical Adventure Tours ☎222-8974
Half-day tours to the Kéköldi Reserve and the nearby Gandoca-Manzanillo Wildlife Refuge.

cater to tourists, offering bed, breakfast and horse rental. They're covered in detail in our chapter on *Guanacaste*.

Riding on the **beach** on the Nicoya Peninsula, especially at Montezuma in the south and Sámara on the west coast, is also very popular. Horses are rented by the hour. However, there has been a history of mistreatment of horses in these places – overworking them and not allowing them sufficient water in the midday heat. Don't expect the animals here to be in as good shape as sleek thoroughbreds back home, but if you see any extreme cases of mistreatment complain to the local tourist information centre or local residents.

PUBLIC HOLIDAYS AND FESTIVITIES

Though you shouldn't expect the kind of colour and verve that you'll find in *fiestas* in Mexico or Guatemala, Costa Rica has its fair share of holidays and festivals, or *feriados*, when all banks, post offices, museums and government offices close. In particular, don't try to travel anywhere during *Semana Santa*, Holy (Easter) Week: the whole country shuts down from Holy Thursday until after Easter Monday, and buses don't run. Likewise, the week from Christmas to New Year invariably causes traffic nightmares, overcrowded beach towns and a suspension of services.

Provincial holidays, like Independence Day in Guanacaste (July 25) and the Limón Carnaval (the week preceding October 12) affect local services only, but nonetheless the shutdown is drastic: don't bet on cashing travellers' cheques or mailing letters if you're in these areas at party time.

January 1 New Year's Day. Celebrated with a big dance in San José's Parque Central.

March 19 *El día de San José* (St Joseph's Day). Patron saint of San José and San José province.

Ash Wednesday Country-wide processions; in Guanacaste, marked by horse, cow and bull parades, with Guanacastecan bullfights (in which the bull is not harmed) in Liberia.

Holy Week *Semana Santa*. Dates vary annually but businesses will often close for the entire week preceding Easter weekend.

April 11 Juan Santamaría Day. Public holiday to commemorate the national hero who fought at the Battle of Rivas against the American adventurer William Walker in 1856.

May 1 *Día de los trabajadores* (Labor Day).

June 20 St Peter's and St Paul's day.

July 25 Independence of Guanacaste Day (Guanacaste province only). To mark the annexation of Guanacaste from Nicaragua in 1824.

August 2 Virgin of Los Angeles Day. Patron saint of Costa Rica.

August 15 Assumption Day and Mother's Day.

September 15 Independence Day, with big patriotic parades celebrating Costa Rica's independence from Spain in 1821.

October 12 *El día de la Raza* (Columbus Day). Limón province only, marked by Carnaval, which takes place in the week prior to October 12.

November 2 All Soul's Day.

Christmas Week The week before Christmas is celebrated in San José with fireworks, bullfights and funfairs.

December 25 Christmas Day. Family-oriented celebrations with trips to the beach. Much consumption of apples and grapes.

SHOPPING

Compared with many Latin American countries, Costa Rica does not have an impressive crafts or artisan tradition. However, there are some reasonable souvenirs to buy, such as carved wooden salad bowls, plates and trays. Wherever you go you'll see hand-painted wooden replica ox-carts, originating from Sarchí, a small town in the Valle Central; these are perennial favourites, though their aesthetic appeal is something of a mystery.

Reproductions of the pre-Columbian pendants and earrings displayed in San José's Museo Nacional, the Museo de Oro and the Museo de Jade are sold both on the street and in shops. Much of the stuff is not real gold, however, but gold-plated, which chips and peels: make sure before you buy.

Costa Rican **coffee** is one of the best gifts to take home. Make sure you buy export brands *Cafe Britt* or *Cafe Rey* and not the hideous lower-grade sweetened coffee sold locally. It is often incrementally cheaper to buy bags in the supermarket rather than in souvenir shops;

cheaper still to buy beans at San José's **Mercado Central.** If you want your coffee beans roasted to your own taste, go to the *Café Gourmet* in San José (p.86) for excellent beans and grinds. For more on coffee, see p.33.

In the absence of a real home-grown crafts or textile tradition, generic **Indonesian** dresses and clothing – batiked and colourful printed cloth – are widely sold in the beach communities of Montezuma, Cahuita, Tamarindo and Quepos (near Manuel Antonio). In some cases this craze for all things Indonesian extends to slippers, silver and bamboo jewellery and so on; prices aren't bad.

If you have qualms about buying goods made from **tropical hardwoods**, ask the salesperson what kind of wood the object is made from. Avoid mahogany, laurel and purple heart. Other **goods to avoid** are coral, anything made from tortoise shells, and furs such as ocelot or jaguar.

Consumer goods manufactured anywhere other than Costa Rica have a 100 percent tax levied on their importation, so you should bring many of the items listed below from home.

THINGS TO BRING FROM HOME

Batteries	Tampons	Contraceptive pills
Film	Spare spectacles prescription	Electrical adaptor (the 2-prong American-style one)
Binoculars	Contact lens supplies	Umbrella (make sure it's sturdy and compact, especially if coming in the rainy season; those sold in Costa Rica tend to be flimsy)
Watches (plastic, digital is best)	Condoms	
Alarm clock	Non-soap facial cleansers and shower gels	
Cassette tapes	Combination lock	
Insect repellent	Towel	

GAY AND LESBIAN COSTA RICA

Costa Rica has a good reputation among gay and lesbian travellers. The Manuel Antonio area, in particular, has become very popular in recent years, although as yet there is no gay/lesbian guest house or hotel there.

By Central American standards Costa Rica has a large gay community, and to a smaller extent a

sizable lesbian one, though confined pretty much to San José. In San José there is also a large community of **transvestite/transexual** prostitutes (*travestís*). Although there have been some incidents of police harassing gays in bars, in general you will be met with respect, and there is no need to assume that everyone will be a raving hetero-Catholic poised to bash gays. Part of this tolerance is due to the subtle tradition in Costa Rican life and politics, summed up in the Spanish expression *quedar bien*, which translates roughly to mean "to not rock the boat", or "to leave well alone". People don't ask you about your sexual orientation or make assumptions, but they don't necessarily expect you to talk about it unprompted, either.

There are few formal **contacts** in Costa Rica for gay and lesbian travellers, and it is difficult to find an entrée into gay life (especially for women) without knowing local gays and lesbians. The two easiest **points of contact** for foreigners are *La Torre* (also known as *Tonite*), a mainly gay disco in San José (see p.89). The other is the University of Costa Rica. You can check with the

GAY/LESBIAN TRAVEL CONTACTS

Different Drummer Tours, PO Box 528, Glen Ellyn, IL 60137 (☎1-800/645 1275).
Scheduled and customized international tours; occasionally include Costa Rica.
Different Strokes Tours, 1841 Broadway, New York, NY 10023 (☎1-800/688 3301).
Customized international tours. Seven nights in Costa Rica (San José and a beach resort) for around $700 including lodging, ground transport and some meals, but not the flight.

Vida Estudantíl office on the fourth floor of Building A for gay-oriented events. See "Drinking and Nightlife" in our *San José* chapter for details of other bars.

TRAVELLING WITH CHILDREN

Costa Ricans love kids, and travellers with children will be very well received. However, a certain amount of red tape and bureaucracy governs the bringing of children, of any nationality, to the country if you wish to stay for more than 30 days.

Officially, if one parent, rather than both, is travelling with their child, that child is not permitted to remain in Costa Rica for **more than 30 days** unless the travelling parent asks permission, in person, supported by the other parent's request in writing, from the Costa Rican Child Protection Agency, the *Patronato Nacional de la Infancia*, C 19, Av 6, San José (in the Tribunales de la Justicía complex).

That said, the Costa Rican authorities take a very dim view of this method, preferring that both parents are "on the ground" with the child when permission to stay longer is requested. It becomes even more tricky if a child is coming to Costa Rica without his or her parents: in this case you have to contact the Costa Rican embassy or

consulate in your home country to get a notarized permit.

Far more convenient is the option of **crossing the border** to Panamá or Nicaragua for a few days when your 30 days and those of your child run out; you can then re-enter with the same rights and under the same conditions (see p.10).

CONTACTS FOR TRAVELLERS WITH CHILDREN

Rascals in Paradise, 650 Fifth St, #505, San Francisco, CA 94107 (☎1-800/U RASCAL).
Scheduled and customized itineraries in the US, Mexico, Caribbean, Belize and Costa Rica, built around activities for kids.
Travel with Your Children, 45 W 18th St, New York, NY 10011 (☎212/206 0688).
Publisher of Family Travel Times, a newsletter that comes out ten times a year. The $55 annual subscription includes the use of a call-in advice line.

WORK, VOLUNTEERING AND STUDY

Language study tours to Costa Rica and volunteer work projects (many of which are tax-deductible for travellers from the USA) are extremely popular. Costa Rica is one of the best places to learn Spanish in the Americas, partly because of the appeal of so many outdoor activities and the country's celebrated political and economic stability.

VOLUNTEER WORK AND RESEARCH PROJECTS

There's a considerable choice of **volunteer work** and **research projects** in Costa Rica, some of which include food and lodging. Many of these can be organized from the US (see box). As an example, *University Research Expeditions* sends teams each year on 2-week expeditions to replant lost trees and measure soil and plant characteristics. The team shares a rented house in a rural

VOLUNTEER CONTACTS IN THE US

Caribbean Conservation Corp, PO Box 2866, Gainesville, FL 32602, USA (☎1-800/678-7853; in Costa Rica: ☎225-7516).
Volunteer research work on marine turtles at Tortuguero.

Global Service Corps, 1472 Filbert St, #1405, San Francisco, CA 94109, USA (☎415/922-5538).
Service programmes in Costa Rica.

University Research Expeditions, University of California, Berkeley, CA 94720-7050, USA (☎510/642-6586).
Environmental studies, animal behaviour.

Volunteers for Peace, 43 Tiffany Rd, Belmont, VT 05730, USA (☎802/259-2759).
Membership organization which serves as clearing house and organizer of volunteer work projects.

VOLUNTEER PROGRAMMES IN COSTA RICA

Amigos de las Aves, 32-4001 Rio Segundo de Alajuela (☎441-2658).
Works to establish breeding pairs of scarlet and great green macaws. Volunteers are welcome to help care for the birds; no food or lodging offered.

ANAI (☎224-6090 or 3570; fax 253-7524).
Based in southern Talamanca, training people to farm organically and manage forests sustainably. Volunteer programme (May–July) to help protect the Gandoca-Manzanillo Refuge and the turtles that come to the Caribbean coast each year. Also work on ANAI's experimental farm; officially a minimum of 6 months, but 3-month stays can be arranged. Lodging and food included.

ANAO, The National Association of Organic Farming (☎223-3030).
Volunteer places on organic farms; lodging and meals provided.

APREFLOFAS (Association for the Preservation of Flora and Fauna), Aptdo 917, 2150 San José (☎240-6087).
Accepts volunteers to help protect National Parks and Reserves. The work can be risky, and there's no food or lodging.

ARBOFILIA (Association of Tree Protection), Aptdo 512, Tibas 1100 (☎240-7145).
Helps communities to plant native trees; accepts a few volunteers each year.

ASVO (Association of Volunteers for Service in Protected Areas), contact the director of International Voluntary Programmes (☎222-5085).
Government-run scheme, enabling volunteers to work in the National Parks. Between 800 and 900 volunteers help guard protected areas, write reports and give environmental classes. Minimum 2 months; no lodging or food.

CEDARENA (Legal Centre for the Environment and Natural Resources; ☎224-8239).
Accepts lawyers or people with experience in the legal area of conservation to help with paperwork. Usually a minimum of 3 months, but some exceptions.

Monteverde Conservation League, Proyecto de San Geraldo, Aptdo 10581-1000, San José (☎645-5053).
Volunteer places on various projects in the cloudforests of Monteverde. Lodging not included.

SEJETKO (Cultural Association of Costa Rica), Aptdo 1293-2150 Moravia (☎234-7115).
Volunteers needed to help defend indigenous reserves, work in rural development conservation and other projects. Lodging, meals and insurance included. Programmes usually last about a year.

YISKI Conservationist Association, Aptdo 1038-2150, Moravia (☎297-0970).
Sponsors various conservation volunteer groups.

area of southern Costa Rica. Cost is around $1595, including meals and ground transport.

A good **resource** in the USA for language study and volunteer work programmes is *Transitions Abroad*, a bi-monthly magazine focusing on living and working overseas (write to Dept TRA, Box 3000, Denville, NJ 07834, USA). In Australasia, for current details of student exchanges and study programmes, contact the consul or *AFS*, PO Box 5, Strawberry Hills, Sydney 2012 (☎02/281 0066), or PO Box 6342, Wellington, New Zealand (☎04/384 8066). British travellers should contact the Costa Rican Embassy.

STUDY PROGRAMMES AND LEARNING SPANISH

As with most things, you will pay more in Costa Rica for a course in Spanish, than in Guatemala or Mexico. There are so many schools in **San José** that choosing one can be a problem. Though you can arrange a place through organizations based in the US (see below), the best way to choose is to visit a few, perhaps sit in on a class or two, and judge the school according to your own personal-

ity and needs. This is not always possible, though, especially in high season (Dec–April) when many classes will have been booked in advance. At other times the drop-in method should be no problem at the majority of the schools we've listed.

Some of the **language schools** mentioned in the box below are Tico-run, some are arms of international (usually North American) education networks. Whatever the ownership, instructors are almost invariably Costa Ricans who speak some English. School noticeboards are an excellent source of information and contact for travel opportunities, apartment shares and social activities. Most schools have a number of Costa Rican families on their books with whom they regularly place students for homestays.

If you don't fancy going back to school, one of the most engaging language study programmes available to Costa Rica is the **"Language School on Wheels"** offered by Green Tortoise, the California-based company known for its low-cost and adventurous bus tours. If you want **private tuition**, any of the schools we've listed can recommend a tutor. Private rates run from $10 to 30 (£7–20) an hour.

US CONTACTS FOR STUDY PROGRAMMES IN COSTA RICA

Council on International Educational Exchange (CIEE), 205 E 42nd St, New York, NY 10017 (☎212/661-1414).
Non-profit parent organization of Council Travel and Council Charter, CIEE runs work- and study-abroad programmes and a voluntary service programme. It also publishes two excellent resource books, Work, Study, Travel Abroad *and* Volunteer!

Global Exchange, 2017 Mission St, #303, San Francisco, CA 94103 (☎415/255-7296).
Educational/research trips including Mexico, Central and South America.

Green Tortoise Adventure Travel, 494 Broadway, San Francisco, CA 94956 (☎415/956-7500).
"Language School on Wheels" with native speaker while touring the country on a converted bus. Two weeks cost $600, including meals.

The Institute for Central American Development Studies (ICADS), Dept 826, PO Box 025216, Miami, FL 33102 (fax 506/234-1337).
Monthly intensive Spanish programmes and semester and academic year programmes that include internships in Costa Rica in women's studies, environment/ecology, public health, journalism and agriculture.

Institute of International Education, 809 UN Plaza, New York, NY 10017 (☎212/984-5413).
Publishes an annual study-abroad directory.

International Schools Services, PO Box 5910, Princeton, NJ 08543 (☎609/452-0990).
Places teachers in schools in Central American countries.

Total Immersion Spanish, ISLS, Dana G Garrison, 1011 E Washington Blvd, LA, CA 90021 (☎1-800/765-0025; fax 213/765-0026).
Five year-round institutes to choose from. Live with a Costa Rican family while taking 3–6hr of intense language classes a day. Programmes from 1 week to 6 months.

Unipub, 4611-F Assembly Drive, Lanham, MD 20706 (☎1-800/274 4888; in Canada, ☎1-800/233-0504).
Distributes UNESCO's encyclopedic Study Abroad.

World Learning Summer Abroad Program, Kipling Road, PO Box 676, Brattleboro, VT 05302 (☎1-800/345 2929).
Summer programme for high-school students.

Worldteach, 1 Elliot St, Cambridge, MA 02138-5705 (☎1-800/483-2240).
Places teachers in schools in Costa Rica.

LANGUAGE SCHOOLS IN COSTA RICA

Central American Institute for International Affairs (ICAI), Aptdo 10302, Otoya 1000, San José (☎233-8571; fax 221-5238).

Spanish tuition, cultural events and field trips, with an emphasis on conversation. Good resources include a reference library, international directories and a travel office that can arrange weekend excursions. Minimum six students per class. Two or four-week programme, 4hr study a day, Mon–Fri.

Centro Cultural Costarricense-Norteamericano, Spanish Programme c/o Aptdo 1489-1000, San José (☎225-9433).

Not really a Spanish school, but a centre for cross-cultural exchange. Unrivalled facilities, including the Mark Twain Library, which has an excellent stock of English-language publications and a similar range in Spanish, a theatre, and gallery.

Centro Linguistico Conversa, Aptdo N17, Centro Colón 1007, San José (☎221-7649).

Well-established institute that also teaches English to Ticos. Thorough approach, with some concentration on grammar. Students have access to the centre's 5-acre farm 10km outside San José. Classes have a minimum of six; 5hr 30min daily tuition is the norm. Four-week programme, including a homestay. Accommodation either with a Tico family, in a separate lodge with private bath and bedrooms, or at their farm. At the latter two, daily transport is included in the cost.

Costa Rican Institute of Language and Latin Dance. Av 0, C 25/27 (☎233-8938 or 8914; fax 233-8670).

Small, friendly and Costa Rican-owned, with multi-national clientele (many Germans and Swiss). Dance classes every afternoon, and trips to discos to practise those hard-learned steps. Conversational, current-affairs approach.

Institute for Central American Development Studies (ICADS), Aptdo 3, 2070 Sabanilla, San José (☎225-0508; fax 234-4337).

Conversational emphasis, concentrating on culture, environment and political issues. Field trips and volunteer internships, where you can visit schools and orphanages. Month-long courses; five days a week; 4hr 30min tuition a day. Also full semester and summer sessions to coincide with US university semesters.

Instituto Latinoamericano de Idiomas (ILISA), Dept 1420, Aptdo 1001, 2050 San Pedro, San José (☎225-2495; fax 225-4665).

Small, locally owned and operated, classes usually with about four students. Mon–Fri, 4hr a day. Two and four-week programmes, some with homestay.

Mesoamerica Language Institute, Aptdo 1524, C 5, Av 2, San Pedro, San José, 2050 (☎234-7682; fax 224-8910).

Classes of just three or four people go out into the city for mini-field trips. Also 6hr Spanish survival course with emphasis on the absolute essentials of communication. Classes Mon–Fri; flexible tuition length; homestay available.

DIRECTORY

BUSINESS HOURS Hours fluctuate from establishment to establishment, but generally banks will be open Mon–Fri 9am (some earlier)–3pm; government offices 8am–5pm and stores 9am–6pm or 7pm. A two-hour lunch break between noon and 2pm is common, though more and more stores are staying open through this period. Stores but not services are open Saturdays, and most things are closed on Sundays.

DANCING Costa Ricans *love* to dance, and it's common to see children who have barely learned to stand up grooving and bopping, much encouraged by their equally animated parents. Consequently, there are many good discos, which tend to be concentrated in San José. It has to be said that your popularity at discos or house parties will have something to do with how well you can dance; if you're really keen you might want to take salsa and merengue lessons before you come. Fitting in at a disco is somewhat easier for women, who simply wait to be asked to dance; not only are men expected to go out and hunt down female dance partners but also to lead, which means you have to know what you're doing. For a list of dance schools in San José, see p.87.

DEPARTURE TAX   Currently $17 if leaving by air – for Costa Ricans and foreigners – but check with your travel agent or airline in Costa Rica before you leave. The tax is not included in the price of your air ticket. You must leave sufficient funds in dollars or colones to pay it, and will be expected to show the stamp that confirms payment to the migración officer when you leave. If you're leaving overland, the tax is less – about $10 – but this varies according to whether you need a visa and what kind of visa you have. See the relevant accounts in the *Guide* of crossing into Nicaragua and Panamá for details, and/or check in advance with the consulates.

ELECTRICITY   The electrical current in Costa Rica is 110 volts – the same as Canada and the US – although plugs are two-pronged, without the round grounding prong.

:LANGUAGE   The language of Costa Rica is Spanish. Although tourists who stay in top-end-of-the-market hotels will find that "everyone speaks English" (a common myth perpetrated about Costa Rica) your time here will be vastly more meaningful if you arm yourself with at least a 500-word Spanish vocabulary. Communicating with *guarda-parques* and people at bus stops, asking directions and ordering *bocas* – not to mention finding salsa partners – is facilitated by speaking the language. For more on Costa Rican Spanish, see *Contexts*.

LAUNDRY   Very few laundrettes exist in Costa Rica, and the ones that do are practically all in San José. Furthermore, laundrettes are rarely self-service – someone does it for you – and charge you by the kilo. Most hotels will have some kind of laundry service, although charges are often outrageously high. For a list of laundrettes in San José, see p.94.

PHOTOGRAPHY   Film is extremely expensive in Costa Rica, so bring lots from home. Although the incredibly bright equatorial light means that 100ASA will do for most situations, remember that rainforest cover can be very dark, and if you want to take photographs at dusk you'll need 200 or even 400ASA. San José is the only place in the country where you can process film; for a list of processors, see p.94.

PROSTITUTION   Prostitution is legal in Costa Rica. While there is streetwalking (largely confined to the streets of San José, especially those in the red-light district immediately west and south of the Parque Central), many prostitutes work out of bars. Bars in San José's "Gringo Gultch", more or less on C 7, Av Central/5, tend to cater to and attract more foreign customers than the bars in the red-light district, which are frequented by Ticos. Steetwalkers around C 12 look like women but are not. *Travestís* are transexual or transvestite prostitutes who do not take kindly to being approached by jokers.

TIME   Costa Rica is in North America's Central Standard time zone (same time as Winnipeg, New Orleans and Mexico) and 6hr behind GMT.

TIPPING   Unless service has been exceptional, you do not need to leave a tip in restaurants, where a 10 percent service charge is automatically levied. Taxi drivers are not usually tipped, either. When it comes to naturalist guides, however, the rules become blurred. Many people – especially North Americans, who are more used to tipping as a matter of course – routinely tip guides about $3 or $4 per day. If you are utterly delighted with a guide it seems fair to offer a tip, although be warned that some guides may be made uncomfortable by your offer – as far as many of them are concerned, it's their job.

TOILETS   You'll notice a lack of public toilets in Costa Rica. The only place you will find so-called "public" conveniences – they're really reserved for customers – is in fast-food outlets in San José, gas stations and roadside restaurants. When travelling in the outlying areas of the country you may want to take a roll of toilet paper with you; but note that except in the poshest hotels – which have their own sewage system/septic tank – you should not put toilet paper down the toilet. Sewage systems are not built to deal with paper, and you'll only cause a blockage. There's always a receptacle provided for toilet paper.

PART TWO

THE

GUIDE

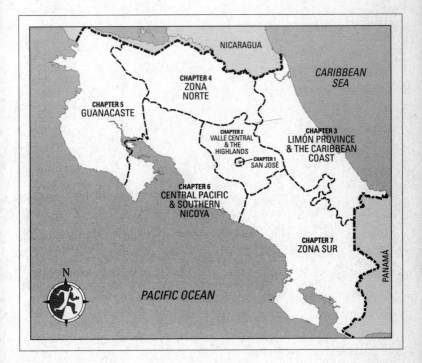

NICARAGUA

CARIBBEAN SEA

CHAPTER 4
ZONA NORTE

CHAPTER 5
GUANACASTE

CHAPTER 2
VALLE CENTRAL
& THE
HIGHLANDS

CHAPTER 1
SAN JOSÉ

CHAPTER 3
LIMÓN PROVINCE
& THE CARIBBEAN
COAST

CHAPTER 6
CENTRAL PACIFIC
& SOUTHERN
NICOYA

CHAPTER 7
ZONA SUR

PANAMÁ

N

PACIFIC OCEAN

CHAPTER ONE

SAN JOSÉ

S prawling smack in the middle of the fertile Valle Central, **SAN JOSÉ**, the only city of any size and administrative importance in Costa Rica, has a spectacular setting, ringed by the jagged silhouettes of soaring mountains – some of them volcanos – on all sides. At night, from high up on one of those mountains, the valley floor twinkles like a million Chinese lanterns, while on a sunny morning the sight of the blue-black peaks pink-shearing the sky is undeniably beautiful.

That's where the compliments end, however. Costa Ricans who live outside the capital are notoriously hard on the place, calling it, with a mixture of familiarity and contempt **"Chepe"** – the diminutive of the name José – and writing it off as a maelstrom of stress junkies, rampant crime and other urban horrors. Poor Chepe is much maligned by just about everyone – you're hard pressed to find one among the 800,000 odd *Joséfinos* willing to say much good about their city's pothole-scarred streets and car dealership architecture, not to mention the choking black diesel fumes, kamikaze drivers and chaotically unplanned expansion. Travellers, meanwhile, talk about the city as they do about bank line-ups or immigration offices: it's a pain, but it's unavoidable. That said, however, while most visitors simply see the city in passing before heading out to Costa Rica's "real" attractions, for anyone with a little more time it is worth getting to know Chepe a bit better – many people even end up perversely fond of the place, modern malls, fast-food outlets, neon billboards and all.

San José has a sprinkling of excellent **museums** – some doubly memorable for their bizarre locations – a couple of elegant buildings and landscaped parks. Cafés and a few art galleries dot the streets and, occasionally, wandering around the leafy, flowered *barrios* **Amón** and **Otoya** you could be under the impression you were walking through the streets of an old European town. In the gridlock

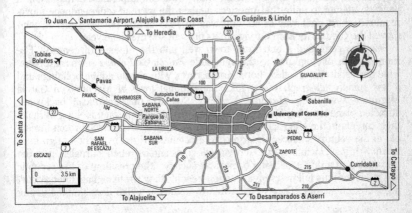

centre things are more hectic, with vendors of fruit, lottery tickets and cigarettes jostling one another on street corners and seemingly thousands of shoestores tumbling out onto sidewalks. You can just about see order straining to prevail above the chaos, but walking around town means, more often than not, keeping your eyes glued to the ground to avoid stepping in deep open drains or in one of the boxes of multi-coloured clucking chicks sold by street-corner hopefuls. **Street crime** is on the rise, and pedestrians adopt the defensive posture (bags clutched securely, knapsacks worn on the front, determined facial expression) that you see in so many other big cities. All in all, walking in San José is a stressful experience, which is lamentable, because exploring on foot is really the best way to get around.

San José is beginning to suffer from pressure on land due to the population density in the Valle Central and to rural migration, and today one in four Costa Ricans lives within the San José metropolitan area. Most of them – lower, middle and upper-middle class – live in the **suburbs**, some of which, like comfortable **Escazú** and hip **San Pedro**, home to the campus of the University of Costa Rica, merit visits in themselves.

Some history

If the early story of San José were fictional, you feel sure that its author would have been Gabriel García Marquez. San José began life in 1737 as a thatched-roofed cottage, constructed at the insistence of the Catholic church in order to give a focal point to the scattered populace surrounding the community. For as much as forty years thereafter **Villa Nueva de la Boca del Monte**, as it was cumbersomely called, remained a muddy village of a few squalid adobe houses. There was little if any reason to develop the site into a larger settlement, until coffee was first planted in the Valle Central in 1821 (see p.104), beginning the process of so-called development.

The single most crucial event in determining the city's future importance was **Guatemala's declaration of independence** from the Spanish crown in 1821, at which time Mexico's self-proclaimed emperor, General Agustín de Iturbide, ordered Costa Rica's immediate annexation to his seat. This demand caused a rift between citizens of Heredia and Cartago, who suported the move, and those of Alajuela and San José, who saw it for what it was: an imperialist demand and a panicky attempt to unite the Americas against the wave of Independence movements. A short **civil war** broke out, won in 1823 by the *independentistas*, who moved the capital city from Cartago to its present site the same year.

San José remained a one-horse town well into the nineteenth century. The framed sepia photographs in the venerable *Balcón de Europa* restaurant show wide dirt roads traversed by horse-drawn carts, with simple adobe buildings and a few spindly telegraph wires. Like the fictional town of Macondo in García Marquez' novel, *One Hundred Years of Solitude*, this provincial backwater attracted piano-teaching European flotsam – usually young men looking to make their careers in the hinterland – who would wash up on the drawing-room threshold of the country's nascent bourgeoisie. Accounts written by early foreign tourists to San José, including two German scientists and a French journalist, give the impression of a tiny, stultifying backwater society: "the president of the republic has to sit with his followers on a wooden bench", they wrote, aghast after attending a church service. They were invited to homes in which dark-skinned young women bound tight in white crinoline dresses would sit patiently conjugating French verbs. Costa Rica's earliest cultural affiliations and aspirations lay with France. Even the mansions of former *finqueros* (coffee barons) in San José's *barrio* Amón – especially the Alianza Francesa – resemble mansions in New Orleans or Port-au-Prince with their delicate French ironwork, Moorish-influenced latticework, long, cool corridors of deep-blooded wood and brightly painted exteriors.

By the mid-1800s, fuelled largely by the tobacco boom, the city had acquired the trappings of bourgeois prosperity, with leafy parks, a few paved avenues and some fine examples of European imitative architecture. Grand urban houses, many of which have survived successive earthquakes, were built to accommodate the new class of burgeoning burghers, coffee middlemen and industrialists; this Europhile aspiration culminated in 1894 with the construction of the splendid **Teatro Nacional** – for which every molecule of material, as well as the finest craftsmen, were transported from Europe.

In this century San José has come to dominate nearly all aspects of the country. Not only the seat of government, since the 1970s it has become the Central American headquarters for many foreign non-governmental organizations, raising its international profile considerably. Multinationals, industry and agribusiness base their national and regional offices here, and at times it seems to be a largely middle-class city, populated by an army of office and embassy workers, neatly suited and sporting briefcases.

Arrival

Arriving in San José is neither disconcerting nor challenging, even if you speak no Spanish. All the machinery to get you into town is well oiled and there is less opportunistic theft than at other Central and South American arrival points.

By air

International **flights** arrive at Juan Santamaría International airport, 17km northwest of San José and 3km southeast of Alajuela (☎441-0744). The **ICT office** (daily 8am–4pm; ☎442-1820 or 8542) can supply maps and give advice on accommodation. There's a **correo** (Mon–Fri 8am–5pm) next to the departure tax window and a **bank** upstairs (Mon–Fri 6.30am–6pm, Sat, Sun & holidays 7am–1pm); colones are not necessary for taxis but you will need them for the bus.

Many flights from North America and Europe arrive late at night or early in the morning. At these times, and if you are arriving with more than one piece of luggage, the best way to get into San José is by **taxi** ($10–12). The rank is right outside the arrivals gate, and drivers will approach you when you're barely out of the door. The airport is connected to the city via the Autopista General Cañas, one of the better roads in the country, and the ride into town takes about twenty minutes in light traffic.

Though the Alajuela–San José **bus** stops right outside the airport, this is an inter-city service, not really geared up for travellers. You can just about get away with it if you are carrying a backpack, but the seats are small and there are no real luggage racks inside. Look for the beige/orange *Station Wagons Alajuela* bus; check before you ride, however, that it is on its way to San José and not Alajuela. Similarly with the black/red *Tuasa* bus doing the San José–Alajuela–Heredia run, even though it may say "San José" on the front. Fare is about 70 colones (equivalent of 25¢ – but you can only pay in local currency) and should be paid to the driver (all buses every 3min 5am–10pm, every 15min 10pm–5am). The journey takes around thirty minutes. The bus drops passengers in town at Av 2, C 12/14, which can mean a hike to your hotel. However, taxis hang around out front of this small terminus, or can be flagged down on Av 2.

By bus

International buses from Nicaragua, Honduras, Guatemala and Panamá pull into the *Ticabus* station, Av 4, C 9/11 (☎221-8954), next to the yellow Soledad church. Many buses arrive at odd hours: if you want to take refuge before setting off to look for a room, head for one of several 24-hour eating spots nearby on Av 2. One of the cheapest is the *Casa del Sandwich* on the corner of C 9. There's a taxi rank around the corner on the stretch of Av 2 between C 5 and 9. Coming from Managua on *Sirca*, you will arrive at the terminal at C 7, Av 6/8 (Mon–Fri 8am–5pm, Sat 8am–1pm; ☎223-1464). Taxis can be flagged down on C 7.

The closest thing San José has to a **domestic bus station** is **La Coca-Cola**, so named for an old bottling plant that used to stand on the site. Just west of the Mercado Central at Av 1/3 and between C 16 and 18, the main entrance is off C 16. Buses arrive here from the north and west, including Monteverde, most of the beaches of the Nicoya Peninsula, Liberia and Puntarenas. The name La Coca-Cola not only applies to the station proper – which is quite small and the arrival point for only a few buses – but also the surrounding area, where many more buses pull in. Like many bus stations, La Coca-Cola is well on its way to being an unredeemed hell-hole: noisy, hemmed in by small, confusing streets crammed with busy market traders, and invariably prowled by pickpockets. Anywhere in the La Coca-Cola area it is very hard not to look like a confused gringo, thus increasing the chances of opportunistic theft: best to arrive and leave in a taxi. Be especially careful of your belongings around the **Tilarán terminal**, also used by buses from Monteverde. For details on getting out of the city from La Coca-Cola, see "Moving on from San José" on p.95.

Information

San José's **ICT office** is beneath the Plaza de la Cultura, Av Central, C 3/5 (Mon–Fri 9am–5pm, Sat 9am–1pm; ☎222-1090); enter down the steps leading off C 5. They have free city maps, leaflets and binders in which you can check out photos of hotels before you book, but the crucial information is behind the counter in the form of the super-organized staff and, more importantly, the computerized print-

SAN JOSÉ'S STREET SYSTEM AND ADDRESSES

San José, along with all Costa Rican towns of any size, is intersected by **Avenida Central**, which runs east–west, and **Calle Central**, which runs north–south. From Av Central parallel avenidas run odd numbers to the north and even numbers to the south. From Calle Central, even-numbered calles run to the west and odd numbers to the east. Avenidas 8 and 9, therefore, are actually quite far apart from one another. Similarly, Calles 23 and 24 are at opposite ends of the city. When you see **bis** (literally "encore" – again) in an address it refers to a separate street, usually a dead end, next to the avenida or calle to which it refers. Av 8 bis, for example, is between Avs 8 and 10. **"0"** in addresses is shorthand for "Central": thus Av 0, C 11 is the same as Av Central, C 11.

While foreigners may use street numbers in San José, locals, and especially taxi drivers, rarely do: instead directions are given in relation to local **landmarks**, buildings, businesses, parks or institutions, or according to the nearest intersection. People use **metres** to signify distance: in local parlance 100 metres equals one city block. For more on finding your way around Costa Rican towns, see p.21.

out of the national bus schedule (reliable and accurate), details of all the hotels in Costa Rica (less so), and lists of restaurants, nightclubs and museums in San José.

The National Parks Office

Things change fast in Costa Rica's Parks system, making San José's **National Parks Office** (SPN), C 25, Av 8/10 (Mon–Fri 8am–4pm; ☎257-0922; fax 223-6963) an essential stop. They offer up-to-date information, passes – cheaper here than at the park entrances; see *Basics* – maps and information booklets (100–200 colones), as well as a telephone and radio accommodation-booking service for any of the National Parks for which special arrangements are needed. Staff are extremely helpful, and although at present information is in Spanish only, they are taking lessons in English; try to talk to the knowledgeable Sr Javier Herrera Retana.

City transport

Once you've got used to the potholes, San José is easily negotiated on foot. There is really little need to take the **city buses**, unless you are going out to Parque la Sabana, which is about a thirty-minute walk west along Paseo Colón; to Escazú, about twenty minutes' ride to the west, or to the University of Costa Rica and San Pedro, about ten minutes' ride to the east.

After 10pm the buses stop running and **taxis** become the best way to get around. These days most *Joséfinos* and travellers alike advise against walking alone after dark, especially if you are a woman. Be especially **wary** of the streets around La Coca-Cola, roughly from C 12 to 16 and between Av 1 and 3; *barrio* México in the northwest of the city, and the red light districts of C 12 around Av 8 and 10, and Av 4 to 6 and C 4 to 12, just southwest of the centre.

The dangers are mainly mugging, purse-snatching or jewellery-snatching, rather than rape or serious assault. Despite the warnings, however, many people, even single women, walk around without encountering problems. But taxis are so cheap that it is not worth taking the risk.

Buses

Most *Joséfinos* travel by **bus**. Fast, cheap and frequent, buses reach every one of San José's neighbourhoods and suburbs, generally running from 5am until 10 or 11pm. The bulk of the city routes and a few suburban ones originate and end in front of the twin 1960s monolith-style towers on Av 2 between C 5 and 7 (across from the *Esmeralda* restaurant) – probably San José's ugliest landmarks. **Bus stops** are marked on metal signs underneath shelters painted with advertisements, and sometimes have green metal benches. *"Haga fila"*, which you will see on each sign, means "line up", and Ticos will appreciate it if you do. The buses are generally marked with their routes. They're supposed to stop automatically at every stop, but if you see yours coming it is safest to flag it down, just to make sure. **Fares** are usually between 20–35 colones (12–20¢), except for the faster and more comfortable *busetas de lujo* (luxury buses) to the suburbs, which cost about 50 colones (30¢), payable either to the driver or his helper when you board.

USEFUL BUS ROUTES

The following is a rundown of the main inner-city routes, all of which stop in town on Av 2, between C 3 and 9 (near the big Coca Cola sign).

SABANA–CEMENTERIO travels west along Paseo Colón to Parque Sabana, and is ideal for going to any of the shops, theatres and restaurants clustered around Paseo Colón, the Museo de Arte Costarricense or Parque Sabana.

SABANA–ESTADIO runs basically the same route, with a tour around Parque Sabana. Good for the neighbourhoods of Sabana norte and Sabana sur.

SABANILLA–BETHANIA, LA U runs east through Los Yoses and beyond to the suburb of Sabanilla.

SAN PEDRO or TRES RIOS buses will also take you east through Los Yoses and on to the University of Costa Rica and the hip neighbourhood of San Pedro. Other buses to San Pedro are: Vargas Araya, Santa Marta, Granadilla, Curridabat and Cedros.

Taxis

Taxis are cheap and copious, except during a rainstorm or late at night. Licensed vehicles are red with a yellow triangle on the side, and licence plates which say "SJP" for "San José Publico". A ride anywhere in the city costs between 125 and 250 colones (80¢–$1.50): about double that to get out to the suburbs. The starter fare – about 100 colones – is shown on the red digital read-out. Always make sure the meter is on and running (ask the driver to "toca la maría, por favor"); drivers may claim their meters are not working and, though technically they have to have an official letter stating that this is the case posted in their cab, this is very unlikely due to the *trámites* (bureaucracy) involved. So if the meter is not working, or if you suspect the cab driver of wanting to charge you "gringo fare", agree a sum before you start out. Most drivers are honest and scrupulous; don't immediately assume they will try to cheat you. But a few might try tricks like faking flat tyres and stopping off to get gas while leaving the meter running. In these situations the best thing is to get out, pay the fare on the meter and flag down another taxi, unless you are in the middle of nowhere.

Taxi companies in San José can be phoned from anywhere in the city and will come to your door. Calling a taxi from a hotel will slap on a twenty percent surcharge – universally applied, as the taxi company usually has some arrange-

---

PEDESTRIAN SAFETY IN SAN JOSÉ

You have to be careful when crossing the street in San José; the national newspapers often feature letters written by the relatives of dead or injured pedestrians, wondering why drivers here are so aggressive. That said, plenty of people do cross the street and live to tell the tale. Some ground rules:

• You can't see the traffic lights easily (they are hung about 5m above your head) so watch the traffic and other pedestrians.
• Look over your shoulder before you cross.
• Run if it looks like the light is changing.
• Run anyway.
• If you jaywalk, never take your eyes off the direction in which traffic could theoretically come.
• Don't expect anyone to stop for you under any circumstances. You have to get out of their way, not vice versa.

---

ment with the hotel in question. Similarly, after midnight, taxis from the El Pueblo shopping and entertainment centre charge forty percent extra. These are institutionalized gringo fares; if you feel you have been done seriously wrong, however, note the license plate number and the driver's personal number – if you can get it from him – and make an official complaint in person to the Dirección General de Transport Automotor, Departamento de Taxis, at C 7, Av 18. The larger companies are *Coopealfaro* (☎221-8466); *Coopeguaria* (☎226-1366); *Coopeirazú* (☎254-3211); *Coopetaxi* (☎235-9966); *Coopetico* (☎221-2552); and *Coopeuno* (☎254-6667).

By car and bike

There is no need to **rent a car** specifically for getting around San José – indeed, most Ticos advise foreigners against driving in the city, at least until they are familiar with the local style of driving. If you *are* driving, take very seriously the warnings that cars should never be left on the street anywhere near the city centre. They are guaranteed to be broken into or stolen. Secure **parqueos** (guarded parking lots) dot the city; if you rent a car, use them. Check their opening times, however, as although many are 24-hour, most close at 8 or 8.30pm. For a list of car **rental companies** see *Listings* on p.93.

It is generally not a good idea to **cycle** in San José, either. Diesel fumes, potholes and un-cycle-conscious drivers do not make for a pleasant ride. In the suburbs or in the Parque la Sabana it is easier and less hazardous to your health.

Accommodation

San José has few good rooms in the budget to moderate range, especially in the high season, and the rock-bottom hotels tend, with a few exceptions, to be depressing cells that make the city seem infinitely more ugly than it is. If you are flush, however, San José is yours for the choosing.

Though staying in the **centre of town**, where there are a number of budget hotels, is convenient, the payoff is noise and pollution. Avenidas 2 and 9 are especially bad for bus noise. The very cheapest rooms are in the insalubrious area immediately around La Coca-Cola, but are best avoided unless you've got an early bus to catch.

STAYING WITH A COSTA RICAN FAMILY

There is no better way to learn about life off the tourist trail and to practise your Costa Rican Spanish than staying with a Tico family. Usually enjoyable, sometimes transformative, this can be a fantastic experience, and at the very least is sure to provide some genuine contact with Costa Ricans.

One of the better established "B&B with a family" organizations in San José is **Turcasa** (contact Eva Guzmán; ☎221-6161 or 257-5169), who offer three categories of accommodation, from A to C, ranging from $12 to $18 a night. A is the "*Lujosa*" (luxury) option, which usually gets you private bath, TV and phone; B means that you will share a bathroom with other guests, while C gets you a bathroom shared with your host family. Most of the homes are in San Pedro, Montes de Oca and Guadaloupe (east of the city). Tell *Turcasa* if you have any special needs, and they will do their best to find a family that suits you (and whom you suit). Restrictions are few, and vary according to the household. Stays can last anything from week to a month, and many travellers use the family home as a base while touring the country. You'll have your own key, but in most cases it would be frowned upon if you brought someone home for the night. The one rule that always applies is that guests and hosts communicate in Spanish.

Other points of contact include ads in the **Tico Times**, although homestays listed here tend to be expensive, and the (Spanish) classifieds in *La Nación*. **Language schools** may be able to put you in contact with a family even if you are not a student at the school in question, while the bulletin boards at the **University of Costa Rica** work well for students who want to live with a family or share with other students. In the last case, however, you are more likely to be sharing with fellow foreigners – it is very hard to find an apartment or house-share with Tico students as most of them live at home while going to university.

Not too far from downtown, in quieter areas such as **Sabana Sur**, **Paseo Colón**, **Los Yoses** and *barrios* **Amón** and **Otoya**, are a group of more expensive hotels, many of them in old colonial homes. Within a ten- or fifteen-minute bus ride from the city centre, the suburbs of **Escazú** and **San Pedro** are also worth checking. Escazú, technically a separate town and not part of San José, is known, quite fairly, as Gringolandia, the stamping ground of American ex-pats and businesses catering to their interests. The vast majority of the B&Bs here are owned by foreign nationals, and prices are higher than elsewhere in town. Street names and addresses are particularly confusing in this area; best call ahead to get clear directions or to arrange pick-up. Studenty San Pedro is closer to the centre, with better connections to downtown and a more cosmopolitan atmosphere, with bars and restaurants within walking distance. It's a great place to stay, but unfortunately there are only a few hotels, most of them expensive.

Despite the proliferation of hotels, San José does get booked up in **high season**, between December and April, and especially over Christmas and Easter. In general it is best to call or fax ahead for reservations. Almost all hotels listed below do a weekly discount and in the wet season (May–Nov) rates drop considerably.

Central San José

L'Ambiance, C 13, Av 9/11 (☎222-6702; fax 223-0481; Aptdo 1040-2050, San José; international postal address: c/o Interlink 179, PO Box 526770, Miami, FL 33152, USA). Venerable mansion hotel in quiet area. From the Presidential Suite to ordinary doubles the rooms are exquisitely furnished, with a Southern Plantation-house atmosphere. No kids under 10. ⑦.

Bellavista, Av 0, C 19/21 (☎223-0095). Rare good value close to the centre but far enough away to be less hectic. Retro rooms are a bit dark and musty, but it's a friendly place, with lively murals depicting scenes from *Caribeña* life (it's close to the Limón bus stop). ③.

Bienvenido, C 10, Av 1/3 (☎221-1872 or 233-2161). Once a cinema, the enormity of this place is belied by its modest exterior. One of the best downtown budget options, with small clean rooms with private bath. Near La Coca-Cola; great if you want to catch an early bus. Avoid arriving on foot at night, however, as the area is dodgy. ②.

Cacts, Av 3 bis, C 28/30 (☎221-2928 or 6546; fax 221-8618; Aptdo 379-1005, San José). Small, quiet, spotless hotel. Some new rooms, but the older rooms, upstairs particularly, are nicer; those with shared bath are best value. All have ceiling fans, hot or heated water. Small café, bar and TV lounge. Friendly owners can help with travel reservation and confirmation. ④.

Casa Leo, Av 4 bis, C 15/17 (☎222-9725). Small, friendly guesthouse with dorms and basic private rooms with shared bath. The train passing right outside the door every morning before 6am can be a disadvantage, however. ①–②.

Casa Ridgway, C 15, Av 6/8 (☎ 233-6168 or 221-8299; fax 224-8910). Affiliated to the adjacent *Friends' Peace Center*, this friendly Quaker guesthouse is San José's best budget option, a great place to meet other travellers. College atmosphere, with discussion groups, alcohol ban and "quiet time" after 10pm. Single-sex dorms, singles and triples, with kitchen, communal showers, laundry and luggage storage. Dorms $8. Reserve in high season. ②.

Cinco Hormigas Rojas, C 15, Av 9/11 (☎257-8581). *Dueña* Mayra Güell is an artist who has decorated the bright rooms in this small, very good-value B&B with her wonderful paintings. She also offers breakfast, advice and tour information. It's a private house in the quiet *barrio* Otoya, 200m east of the back of the INS building and 25m north. ③.

Costa Rica Inn, C 9, Av 1/3, casa 154 (☎222-5203; fax 223-8385; from the USA ☎1-800/637-0899; from Canada and Europe ☎318/263-2059; USA address: PO Box 59, Arcadia, LA 7100). Weird 1950s decor and not entirely noise-free, but this friendly, atmospheric and labyrinthine old house in the centre of town gives rare good value in this price range. ③.

Don Carlos, C 9, Av 9 (☎221-6707; fax 255-0828). Elegant landmark hotel, filled with replicas of pre-Columbian art. Small rooms, and it's often full with a devoted clientele; you have to reserve and pay in advance, but they don't accept credit cards. ⑤.

D'Raya Vida, on an extension of Av 11 and C 15 (☎223-4168; fax 223-4157). Quiet, friendly B&B-style place in an impressive columned house with stylish rooms, library and huge winding staircase. The owners can recommend hotels in the rest of the country. ⑥.

Edelweiss, Av 9, C 13/15 (☎221-9702; fax 222-1241). Elegant, heavy dark wood furniture and pretty decor (check the lovely tiles in the shower). Rooms away from the front are the best. They serve an excellent healthy breakfast, with some of the best brown bread in San José. Most amenities associated with this price range, but no TV. English and German spoken. ⑤.

Galilea, Av 0, C 11 next to Plaza de la Democracía (☎223-6925; fax 223-1689). Clean rooms, friendly management, and lots of maritime imagery on the walls (the *dueño* used to be a boat captain). Affordable low season and weekly rates. Popular, so book ahead in high season. ④.

La Gema, Av 12, C 9/11 (☎257-2524; fax 222-1074). South of the centre in a relatively quiet area, this small hotel is surprisingly light, with an open courtyard planted with leafy trees. Rooms are good, but walls a bit thin: the lighter upstairs rooms are the best. ④.

ACCOMMODATION PRICE CODES

All the establishments in this book have been given price codes according to the following scale. The prices quoted are for the least expensive double room in high season, and do not include the national 18.46 percent tax automatically added on to hotel bills. Wherever an establishment offers dorm beds the prices of these are given in the text. For more details see p.26.

① less than $10	③ $20–30	⑤ $50–75	⑦ $100–150
② $10–20	④ $30–50	⑥ $75–100	⑧ $150 plus

Grano d'Oro, C 30, Av 2/4 (☎255-3322; fax 221-2782; Aptdo 1157-1007, Centro Colón, San José; USA address: PO Box 025216-36, Miami, FL 33102-5216). Beautiful, individually decorated rooms, all non-smoking with TV and phone, in a quiet area west of the centre, attracting a mainly American clientele. Excellent breakfast served in the restaurant, which is highly respected in its own right. ⑥.

Kékoldi, Av 9, C 3 bis (☎223-3244; fax 257-5476). New hotel – "we're new, young, hip, friendly" – with large rooms and whimsical, bright decor. An alternative to ye olde mansion houses, but overpriced. ④.

Mansion Blanca Inn, C 9, Av 10 (☎222-0423; fax 222-7947). Roomy, opulent interior; yellow and green with mirrors. The street-facing upstairs rooms inevitably get noise, but management are very friendly and this is good value in this price range. Breakfast included. ④.

Oak Harbour Inn, Av 3, C 18 bis (☎256-0041 or 221-1829; fax 233-0442). Small new hotel owned by a very friendly Chilean family. Large comfortable rooms with bath and hot water and a dizzying array of services: fax, free maps, tour service, kitchen, TV/video lounge, laundry, luggage storage. Near La Coca-Cola, but on a side street so there is minimal bus noise. ②.

Pensión de la Cuesta, Av 1, C 11/15 (☎ and fax 255-2896; in Italy: ☎ and fax 045/8010085 or 8348340). Italian-owned, pink, colonial-style wooden house, tranquil and tasteful. The previous owner was an artist – hence the gold masks on walls and decorated bedsteads. Decor is bright but some rooms can be gloomy; those at the front are noisy. Laundry, luggage storage, tours and car rental; and bring your sax – you can play instruments here. ②.

Principe, Av 6, C 0/2 (☎222-7983; fax 223-1589). Basic old hotel, nothing special but affordable, friendly and very clean. Street-facing rooms are light but noisy; interior ones quiet but musty. TV lounge, laundry service and heated water. ③.

Ritz, C 0, Av 8/10. Very friendly, clean central hotel with its own tour service, frequented by Swiss travellers. Pension rooms (shared bath) are half the price of those with private bath and heated water. Breakfast in the pretty dining area costs extra. ②–③.

Santo Tomás, Av 7, C 3/5 (☎255-0448; fax 222-3950). Another "colonial-style" mansion house, decorated with burnished wood, Persian rugs and soft lighting. Rooms vary widely in size, character and price. Quiet and elegant, in *barrio* Amón, near downtown. ④.

Taylor's Inn, Av 13, C 3 bis (☎257-4333; fax 221-1475). One of the better "old colonial" options: a lovely old house in historic *barrio* Amón, with beautiful rooms, some decorated with modern art. Very helpful staff and management. ⑥.

Tica Linda, Av 2, C 5/7; brown metal door with small sign (☎233-0528). Central hotel that is unusual in being characterful, cheap, clean and respectable, with tiny rooms and dorms. *Bar Esmeralda* next door churns out mariachi all night which, added to the noise of buses and fellow occupants, makes for little sleep. Dorms $4. Cold water only. Luggage storage. ①.

Torremolinos, C 40, Av 5 bis (☎222-5266; fax 255-3167). A rarity: downtown, two blocks from Parque la Sabana, with a good pool, jacuzzi, gym and sauna. Very good value, especially in low season. ⑤.

Toruma, Av 0, C 29/31 (☎ and fax 224-4085). Beautiful hostel with Neoclassical exterior and high ceilings. Good place to meet people, to reserve for hostels and tours, and arrange onward travel. Book at least three months in advance in high season. Luggage storage, safe, laundry, 11pm curfew; non-smoking. Single-sex dorms with shared bath; from $9 for IYHF members, $12 for non-members (membership available at desk). ①–②.

Vesuvio, Av 11, C 13/15 (☎221-7586 or 8325; fax 221-8325). What this place lacks in decor (long, institutional corridors) it makes up for by being quiet and affordable. Rooms are cosy if a bit claustrophobic, with TV, bath, phone and fan. Bar/restaurant and safe parking. ④.

San Pedro

Casa de Finca, 2km east of San Pedro on the road to Tres Ríos (☎225-6169; Aptdo 1049, San Pedro 2050). Beautiful former house of a *finquero* (coffee baron), in spacious landscaped gardens. Quiet and rural, yet easy to get into town by bus (20min). Lovely rooms, large bathrooms and an elegant dining area – *dueño* Sr Chaverría is a wonderful cook. ⑤.

Casa Yemaná, Aptdo 372-2050 San Pedro, Montes de Oca (☎225-3652; fax 225-3636). Where "women come together and live, work, despite differences in class, education, and sexual orientation", this women-only feminist centre also operates as a guesthouse and holds Spanish classes. Communal kitchen. Near the university, 10min by bus from downtown. ②.

La Granja, 50m south of the *Antiguo Higuerón* landmark tree, off Av 0 in *barrio* la Granja, San Pedro (☎225-1073; fax 234-1676). Great IYHF-affiliated hostel in a pink house with pretty garden, near the university, bars and restaurants. Some singles; most rooms have shared shower. TV lounge, and free breakfast for members. Members pay $13. ②.

Milvia, 100m north and 200m east of *Muñoz y Nanne* supermarket (☎225-4543; fax 225-7801). Lovely old house in residential area. Beautifully decorated, with fountain, sun terrace and mountain views. TV and fridge in all rooms; restaurant and bar. Free breakfast. ⑦.

Escazú

Casa de las Tias, 100m east of *Restaurant El Che* (☎289-5517; fax 289-7353). Owned by a well-travelled Costa Rican couple, this friendly, atmsopheric place has individually decorated rooms with private bath and hot water. Quiet, although in town; no children under 12. ④.

Park Place B&B, on the left-hand side of road up the hill (☎228-9200). Small, nicely decorated B&B with lounge, fireplace, use of kitchen, and a good view from upstairs verandah. Large private bath. ④.

Posada del Bosque, Aptdo 669-1250 (☎228-1164; fax 228-2006). Very quiet, homey place, in large landscaped grounds. Comfortable no-smoking rooms with shared bath. Breakfast served in conservatory. ⑤.

Posada El Quijote, Bello Horizonte (☎289-8401; fax 289-8729). Spacious rooms with bath, hot water and cable TV in private house with lovely garden and views. ⑤.

The City

Few travellers come to San José for the sights, and on first impressions it's easy to see why most people bed down for a night and then get straight out. A city of nondescript buildings, energized by a fairly aggressive street life – umbrella-wielding pedestrians pushing through narrow streets, noisy food stalls, homicidal drivers – San José is certainly not a place that exudes immediate appeal.

Scratch the surface, though, and you'll find a civilized city, with plenty of places to walk, sit, eat, meet people, go dancing and enjoy museums and galleries. It's also reasonably manageable, without the level of chaos and crowds that plagues most other Latin American cities; all the attractions are close together, and everything of interest can be covered in a couple of days. Of the museums, the exemplary **Museo de Oro Precolumbiano**, and the **Museo de Jade**, which houses the Americas' largest collection of the precious stone, are the major draws. Less visited, the **Museo Nacional** offers a brutally honest representation of the country's colonization and some interesting archeological finds, while the **Museo de Arte y Diseño Contemporáneo** displays some of the most striking work in the Americas. San José is also a surprisingly **green** city, or, at least one with quite a bit of public space, with paved-over plazas and small, carefully landscaped parks punctuating the centre of town.

The centre is subdivided into little neighbourhoods (*barrios*) that flow seamlessly in and out of one another: *barrios* **Amón** and **Otoya**, in the north, are the prettiest, lined with the genteel mansions of former coffee barons, while further out, **La California** and **Los Yoses** are home to the *Toruma* youth hostel and the National Parks Office.

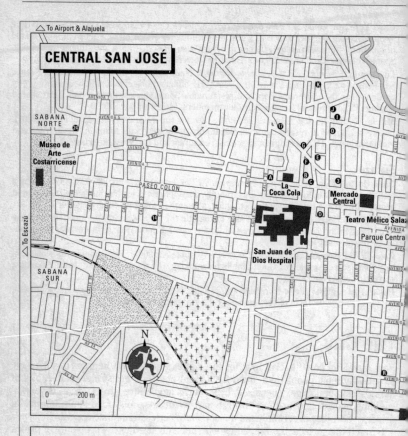

CENTRAL SAN JOSÉ

Hotels

1.	L'Ambiance	14.	Grano de Oro
2.	Bellavista	15.	Kéköldi
3.	Bienvenido	16.	Mansión Blanca Inn
4.	Cacts	17.	Oak Harbour Inn
5.	Casa Leo	18.	Pensión de la Cuesta
6.	Casa Ridgway	19.	Principe
7.	Cinco Hormigas Rojas	20.	Ritz
8.	Costa Rica Inn	21.	Santo Tomás
9.	D'Raya Vida	22.	Taylor's Inn
10.	Don Carlos	23.	Tica Linda
11.	Edelweiss	24.	Torremolinos
12.	Galilea	25.	Toruma
13.	La Gema	26.	Vesuvio

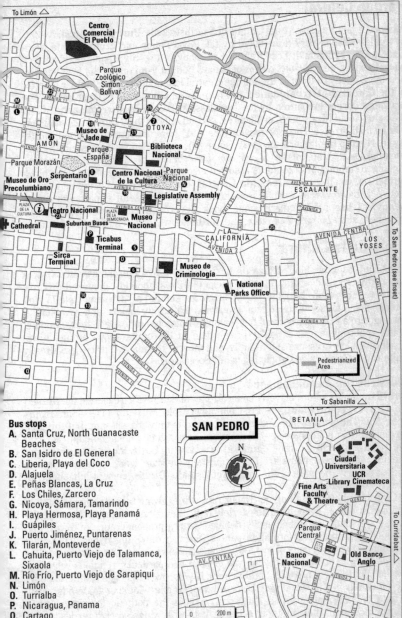

To Limón △

Centro
Comercial
El Pueblo

Parque
Zoológico
Simón
Bolívar

Río Torres

AVENIDA 15

AVENIDA 13

AVENIDA 11 BIS

AV 11 BIS

AVENIDA 9

OTOYA

Museo de Jade

Biblioteca Nacional

AMÓN

Parque
España

Parque Morazán

Serpentario

Centro Nacional de la Cultura

Parque
Nacional

ESCALANTE

AVENIDA 3

AVENIDA 1

Museo de Oro
Precolumbiano

AVENIDA 5

Legislative Assembly

AVENIDA CENTRAL

Teatro Nacional

PLAZA
DE LA
CULTURA

PLAZA
DE LA
DEMOCRACIA

Museo
Nacional

LA
CALIFORNIA

LOS
YOSES

Cathedral

Suburban Buses

AVENIDA 2

AVENIDA CENTRAL

△ To San Pedro (see inset)

Ticabus
Terminal

Sirca
Terminal

Museo de
Criminología

AVENIDA 2

National
Parks Office

AVENIDA 12

Pedestrianized
Area

To Sabanilla △

Bus stops
A. Santa Cruz, North Guanacaste
   Beaches
B. San Isidro de El General
C. Liberia, Playa del Coco
D. Alajuela
E. Peñas Blancas, La Cruz
F. Los Chiles, Zarcero
G. Nicoya, Sámara, Tamarindo
H. Playa Hermosa, Playa Panamá
I. Guápiles
J. Puerto Jiménez, Puntarenas
K. Tilarán, Monteverde
L. Cahuita, Puerto Viejo de Talamanca,
   Sixaola
M. Río Frío, Puerto Viejo de Sarapiquí
N. Limón
O. Turrialba
P. Nicaragua, Panama
Q. Cartago
R. Golfito

SAN PEDRO

N

BETANIA

CALLE MANO

Ciudad
Universitaria

UCR

Fine Arts
Faculty
& Theatre

Library Cinemateca

MUNÓZ

△ To Curridabat

Parque
Central

AV

AVENIDA CENTRAL

Banco
Nacional

Old Banco
Anglo

AV CENTRAL

0   200 m

Parque Central

As good a point as any to start a tour of San José is the **Parque Central**, Av 2, C 2/4, a landscaped park punctuated by tall Royal Palms and centring on a weird Gaudíesque bandstand. Less frantic than many of the city's squares, it's a nice place to snack on *mamones chinos* or papaya bought from one of the fruit vendors nearby. Directly in front of the Parque Central looms the huge columnar exterior of the **Catedral Metropolitaneo**, newly restored but of little interest inside. The northeast corner is marked by the Neoclassical **Teatro Melico Salazar**, C 0, Av 2, one of Costa Rica's premier theatres, second only to the *Teatro Nacional* a few blocks further east. The *espectaculos* (see p.91) here are touristy but well worth-while. Next to the theatre, *La Perla* (see p.86), one of San José's best **sodas**, is a great place to stop off for a *café con leche* before heading into the narrow, contained hubbub of C 2 and its assorted electronics and shoe shops. One block further on, you'll come to **Avenida Central** – in the process of being pedestrian-ized – a narrow east–west thoroughfare lined with useful department stores (*Universal* has a particularly good book department), the cavernous book/stationery shop *Librería Lehmann*, and, further down, a clutch of fast-food outlets.

Plaza de la Cultura

The bland, concrete-block **Plaza de la Cultura**, on Av Central between C 3/5, is constantly crowded with rampaging packs of Tico schoolkids, confused gringos, crafts vendors and hopeful pickpockets. A huddle of **artisans' stalls** sell hammocks, chunky Ecuadorean sweaters, leather bracelets and jewellery – earrings are a particularly good buy – along with more mundane T-shirts, wooden crafts and trinkets, all at lower prices than in the crafts shops around town. Traders are low-pressure and friendly, and most of the marked prices are already quite fair, so aggressive bargaining is not necessary.

Museo de Oro Precolumbiano

The Plaza de la Cultura cleverly conceals one of San José's treasures, the **Museo de Oro Precolumbiano**, or Pre-Columbian Gold Museum (Tues–Sun 10am–5pm; $6). The bunker-like underground space is unprepossessing, but the gold on display is truly impressive – all the more extraordinary if you take into account the relative paucity of pre-Columbian artefacts in Costa Rica (compared with Mexico, say, or Guatemala). The exquisitely delicate work on show here is almost entirely the work of the master goldsmiths **Diquis**, ancient inhabitants of southwestern Costa Rica.

Objects are cleverly hung on transparent wires, giving them the impression of floating in space, suspended mysteriously in their perspex cases. Most of the pieces are small and unbelievably detailed, with a preponderance of disturbing, evil-looking **animals**. Information panels (Spanish only) suggest that the chief function of these portents of evil – frogs, snakes and insects – was shamanic. The *Ave de Rapiña*, or bird of prey, seems to have had particular religious relevance for the Diquis: there are tons of them here; hawks, owls and eagles, differing only incrementally in shape and size. Look out, too, for angry-looking arachnids, ready to bite or sting; jaguars and alligators carrying the pathetic dangling legs of human victims in their mouths; grinning bats with wings spread; turtles, crabs, frogs, iguanas and armadillos, and a few spiny, unmistakable lobsters. The only fish in evidence is the shark. In addition to the animal representations, bell

COSTA RICAN GOLD

Little, if anything, is known of the early prehistory of the **Diquis,** responsible for most of the work you see at the Museo de Oro Precolumbiano. The history of gold metallurgy in the New World is fairly well documented, however, recorded earliest (around 2000 BC) in Peru, from where it spread northwards. By 700–900 AD metallurgy was fully developed in Mexico and south into the isthmus; all the ancient peoples favouring more or less the same methods and styles. Most of the gold work was in fact done with gold-copper alloy (called *tumbaga*), and featured extremely intricate shapings, with carefully rendered facial expressions and a definite preference for ingenious but rather diabolical-looking zoomorphic representations – growling peccaries, threatening birds of prey, and a two-headed figure, each mouth playing its own flute. Many of these objects show no sign of having been worn – no grooves in the pendant links, from which they would have been suspended, modern style, on chains – and were, archeologists believe, intended for ceremonial burial. Some were even "killed" or ritually mutilated before being entombed.

The Diquis would have obtained the gold by panning in rivers, and it is speculated that in Osa at least, the rivers routinely washed up gold at their feet. Although the Diquis were the undisputed masters of design, according to archeological digs in the Reventazón valley, gold extraction and fashioning – usually into breastplates – also featured among the peoples of the Atlantic watershed zone. Diquis *caciques* (chiefs) and other social elites used their gold in the same way it is used today – to advertise wealth and social prestige. Ornaments and insignias were often reserved for the use of a particular *cacique* and his family, and these special pieces were traded as truce offerings and political gifts between various rules, maintaining contacts between the *caciques* of distant regions.

When Columbus first came ashore in 1502, he saw the local (Talamancan) peoples wearing gold mirror pendants and headbands and immediately assumed he had struck it rich – hence the country's name. An early document of a subsequent expedition to the Caribbean coastal region of Costa Rica, now housed in archives in Cartago, contains the impressions of native gold recorded by one Spaniard on Diego de Sojo's 1587 expedition, crazed with gold fever: "The rivers abound with gold . . . and the Indians extract gold with calabashes in very large grains . . . from these same hills Captain Muñoz . . . took from the tombs of the dead . . . such a great quantity of gold as to swell two large chests of the kind in which shoes and nails for the cavalry are brought over from Castile."

pendants are also common, with two round spheres ("bells") dangling from little squares of gold.

Sharing the building, the marginally absorbing **Museo de Moneda** (entrance included in Gold Museum fee) displays a collection of Costa Rican coins with minute variations in their design. Look out for the 5-colón note, decorated with a delicate, brightly coloured panorama of Costa Rican society.

Teatro Nacional

Half-Parthenon, half Paris Opéra, San José's heavily columned, grey-brown **Teatro Nacional** sits on the corner of C 5 and Av 2, tucked in behind the Plaza de la Cultura. The theatre's marbled stairways, gilt cherubs and red velvet carpets would look more at home in old Europe than in Central America: you won't find such impressive elegance anywhere else between here and the Manaus Opera House in deepest Amazonia.

The story of the Teatro Nacional – which celebrates its centenary in 1997 – is an intriguing one, illuminating the industrious no-nonsense attitude of the city's coffee bourgeoisie, who demonstrated the nascent national pride and yearning for cultural achievement that came to characterize Costa Rican society in the twentieth century. In 1890 the world-famous prima donna Adelina Patti was making a tour through the Americas, but could not stop in Costa Rica as there was no appropriate theatre. Mortified, and determined to raise funds for the construction of a national theatre, the wealthy coffee farmers responded by levying a tax on every bag of coffee exported. Within a couple of years the coffers were full to bursting; European craftsmen and architects were employed, and by 1897 the building was ready for its inauguration, a stylish affair with singers from the Paris Opéra performing Faust.

All red plush and gold (though if you look closely you'll see the gilt beginning to wear away), the theatre remains in remarkably good condition, despite the dual onslaught of the climate and a succession of earthquakes. The latest, in 1991, closed the place for two years – the huge marble staircases on either side of the entrance still have wooden supports strapped on them like slings. Above all it is the details that leave a lasting impression: plump cherubim, elegantly numbered boxes fanning out in a wheel-spoke circle, heavy hardwood doors and intricate glasswork on the bathrooms.

Even if you're not coming to see a performance, you can wander around in the post-Baroque splendour, or just satisfy yourself with a coffee and a sandwich in the elegant café.

Around the Parque España

Three blocks east and two blocks north of the Plaza de la Cultura, tall-treed **Parque España** is surrounded by a number of the city's most intriguing sights. On the eastern corner, facing Av 5, is the **Edificio Metálica** (Metal Building, also known as the *Escuela Metálica*), so-called because its exterior is made entirely out of metal plates shipped from France at the turn of the century. Though the prospect sounds dour, the effect – especially the bright multi-coloured courtyard as seen from the **Museo de Jade**, high above – is, while slightly military, also very pretty. Fronting the *Edificio Metálica*, **Parque Morazón** – more a concrete-paved square than a park proper – is a useful orientation point, centring on the landmark grey-domed bandstand floridly known as the Templo de Música.

Museo de Jade

On the north side of the Parque España rises one of the few office towers in San José: the INS, or Institute of Social Security, building. This uninspired edifice is home to one of the city's finest museums, the **Marco Fidel Tristan Museo de Jade** (Jade Museum) on the eleventh floor (Mon–Fri 9am–3pm; free). The scale of the jade on show – the sheer amount of it – is staggering; this is the largest collection of American jade in the world.

As in China and the East, jade was much prized in ancient Costa Rica as a stone with religious or mystical significance. It was and is still considered valuable because of its (mineralogically speaking) rarity. Only slightly less hard than quartz, it is well known for its durability, and lends itself well to weaponry and to cutting tools like axes and blades – Neolithic civilizations assigned it great significance as an object of power. As no quarries of the stone have been found in Costa

Rica, the big mystery for archeologists is to discover how the pre-Columbian societies here got hold of so much of it. The reigning theory suggests that it came from Guatemala – where one of the only six known jade quarries in the world exists at the Motagua valley – or was perhaps traded or sold down the isthmus by the Olmecs of Mexico. This also goes some way to explaining the presence of Maya insignia on some of the pieces – symbols that had no meaning for Costa Rica's pre-Columbian inhabitants.

The museum displays are ingenious, subtly back-lit to show off the multi-coloured and multi-textured pieces to full effect. Jade exhibits an extraordinary range of nuanced colour, from a milky-white green through soft grey and blue to deep green, most prized of all by the inhabitants of the Americas c. 600 BC. No two pieces in the collection are alike in hue and opacity, though as in the Gold Museum, you'll see a lot of **axe-gods**: anthropomorphic bird/human forms shaped like an axe and worn as a pendant. One entire room devotes itself to male fertility symbols, and you'll also see X-shaped objects used to support the breasts of women of standing – a kind of proto-bra.

Incidentally, the **view** from the museum windows is one of the best in the city, taking in the sweep of San José from the centre to the south and then west to the mountains.

Museo de Arte y Diseño Contemporáneo

Sprawling across the entire eastern border of the Parque España, the former National Liquor Factory, dating from 1887, today houses the *Centro Nacional de la Cultura, Juventud y Deportes* (Ministry of Culture, Youth and Sports, known as CENAC), entered from the corner of C 15 and Av 3. The attraction here is the cutting edge **Museo de Arte y Diseño Contemporáneo**, or Museum of Contemporary Art and Design (Tues 1pm–5pm, Wed & Fri–Sun 10am–5pm, Thurs 10am–9pm; 75¢). Opened in 1994 under the direction of dynamic prize-winning artist Virginia Pérez-Ratton, it's a highly modern space, with a cosmopolitan, multi-media approach – recent exhibits include a wall of skateboards mounted installation-style and painted in aggressive electric colours. Other exhibits include Costa Rica's entries for the various international Biennales and, upstairs, the gallery of industrial and furniture design – very Bauhaus, very impressive. There's also a theatre in the CENAC complex; a wander around during the day offers interesting glimpses of dancers and musicians rehearsing.

Barrios Amón and Otoya

Weaving its way up the hill from the Parque España and the INS, the historic **barrio Amón** leads seamlessly into another old *barrio*, **Otoya**. Chock full of historic buildings, lined with the former homes of the Costa Rican coffee gentry, these two neighbourhoods are among the most attractive in San José, and after decades of neglect they are currently undergoing something of a rediscovery by hoteliers, café and restaurant owners and residents.

More than 100 years old, Amón especially is home to some fine examples of the tropical architectural style best described as "neo-Victorian": low-slung wooden houses girthed with wide verandahs and iron railings. Striking examples include the **Alianza Francesa building** at C 5 and Av 7, the turreted **Bishop's Castle**, Av 11 bis and C 3, and the grand old **Casa Verde de Amón** hotel, (C 7 and Av 9). Two blocks north of Parque España, at Av 11 and C 7/9, is the entrance to the **Parque Zoológico Simón Bolívar** (Tues–Fri 8am–4pm, Sat &

Sun 9am–5pm; free). There are plans to move this zoo to a location outside San José sometime in the next two years, but until then the zoo should be avoided by animal lovers. A peculiar counterpoint to Costa Rica's supposed commitment to preserving its flora and fauna, it keeps the beasts in pitifully cramped conditions. All the same, it continues to draw Tico families on Sundays and great gaggles of schoolchildren on weekdays, making it in no way a relaxing place to spend time.

Centro Comercial El Pueblo

The cluster of shops, restaurants, bars and discos that make up the **Centro Comercial El Pueblo** – known simply as "El Pueblo" – lies about 200m north of the Simon Bolivar Zoo across the Río Torres. El Pueblo is a tourist trap in the best sense of the word: a sensible initiative to give both tourists and Ticos – who love it – an attractive, atmospheric place to shop, eat, drink and dance, all within virtually the same building. A winding maze of adobe-type edifices, El Pueblo's whitewashed exteriors and wide dark wooden staircases evoke the kind of colonial architecture that finds it hard to survive in Costa Rica, thanks to the knock-down blows of successive earthquakes. The souvenir and crafts shops tend to be a little expensive in comparison to those downtown; still, it's a nice place to wander about and perhaps have lunch. Walking to El Pueblo can be awkward. Most people take a taxi, which, depending upon where it is hailed, should cost no more than $1.50. Butterflies flutter in the adjacent **Spirogyra Jardín de Mariposas** (daily except Tues 9am–4pm; $5); daily guided tours at 3.30pm point out particularly unusual and pretty examples.

Around the Parque Nacional

Bordered by Av 1 and 3 and C 15 and 19, San José's **Parque Nacional** is, in park terms – the density and arrangement of green things, rather than concrete – the best open space in downtown San José. Almost jungle-like in places, with a tall canopy of mop-headed palms and thick deciduous trees, and punctuated by stone benches, it is a popular hang-out for courting couples, construction workers on break, and older men discussing the state of the nation. At night pickpockets and potential muggers take over: walking through it after dark is not a good idea.

You can hear government debates Costa Rican-style at the **Palacio Nacional**, at the corner of C 15 and Av Central. The fun starts at 4pm, but check first whether the Legislature is in session. At the top end of Av 3 between C 21/23, the **Museo Ferrocarríl**, or Railway Museum (Mon–Thurs 9am–4pm, Fri 9am–3.30pm; 75¢), was the terminus for the old "Jungle Train" (see p.137). Today it holds a largely photographic collection dedicated to the famed train that once ran from San José to Limón before being dealt two blows in quick succession: one by the April 1991 earthquake and another by the government, who took the decision not to finance its repair. It's worth a look, especially for railway enthusiasts, but doesn't merit a trip in its own right.

Biblioteca Nacional and Galería Nacional de Arte Contemporáneo
Down the hill one block and opposite the Parque Nacional, the modernist **Biblioteca Nacional** is Costa Rica's largest and most useful library (Mon–Fri 8.30am–4.30pm). Anyone can go in, to rifle through the newspaper collection to the right of the entrance on the ground floor, or even to use the bathrooms. On its

southwest corner the **Galería Nacional de Arte Contemporáneo** (Mon–Sat 10am–1pm & 2–5pm; free) features small and often quirky displays of work by local artists.

Serpentario

Lurking on the second floor of a nondescript building on the corner of Av 1 and C 9, the **Serpentario** (Mon–Fri 9am–6pm; $3) is one of Costa Rica's most useful attractions, where aghast tourists and fascinated schoolboys wander amid glass cases of snakes, poison dart frogs and the odd lizard. The *serpentario* can be an unnerving experience, giving rise to any number of paranoid "escaped snakes" fantasies, but seeing the reptiles in the flesh can help identify them if you see them in the *selva*; especially handy when it comes to some of the more poisonous species that call Costa Rica home, including the fer-de-lance, bushmaster and jumping and eyelash vipers. Other snakes – thankfully – live elsewhere: look out for the Burmese python, who lies curled up in the biggest case doing a deft impression of an eighteen-wheeler transport truck tire.

Museo Nacional

Heading one block south to Av Central, then one block east, you'll come to the concrete **Plaza de la Democracía**, yet another of the city's soulless squares just one aesthetic marker up from a paved parking lot. Constructed in 1989 to mark President Oscar Arias' key involvement in the Central American Peace Plan, this expanse of terraced concrete slopes gently up toward a fountain and the impressive fortress edifice of the **Museo Nacional** (Tues–Sat 8.30am–5pm, Sun 9am–5pm; $1) which crowns the top of the square.

The museum, more than a century old (and that *is* old for Costa Rica) only came to its current location – the renovated former Bellavista Barracks – after some upheaval. Bullet holes blasted during the **1948 insurrection** (see contexts) can still be seen on the south side of the building's thick walls. The collection, though rather haphazard, gives a fascinating introduction to the story of Costa Rica's **colonization**, with national pride sacrificed in the truthful depiction – some information panels are in English – of just how slowly culture and education have advanced here. The most lasting impression is of a country struggling well into the twentieth century to extricate itself from terrible cultural and social backwardness. A grisly series of drawings, deeply affecting in their simplicity, tells the story of the fate of Costa Rica's **indigenous** people at the hands of the Spanish settlers. Violence, it appears, was meted out in both directions, and beheadings, hangings, clubbings, shooting of priests, the pouring of liquid gold down throats, infanticide and suicide as a means of resistance in the indigenous community are all mercilessly depicted. In the same room are examples of **colonial art**; without exception religious (and dreadful, for that matter), degrading and replacing indigenous art forms with scores of lamentable gilt-and-pink Virgin Marys.

Highlights elsewhere include petroglyphs, pre-Columbian stonework, and wonderful anthropomorphic gold figures in the **Sala Arqueológica**. This is the single most important archeological exhibition in the country; the grinding tables and funerary offerings, in particular, show precise geometric patterns and incredible attention to detail, but the really astounding pieces are the "flying panel" **metates**, corn-grinding tables used by the Chorotega peoples of present-day Guanacaste, each with three legs and meticulously sculpted from a single piece of volcanic stone.

Museo Criminalógico

Between Av 6 and 8 and C 17 and 19, about three blocks south and two east of the Plaza de la Democracía, the Courts of Justice (*La Corte*) house the **Museo Criminalógico** (Mon, Wed & Fri 1–4pm; free), a bizarre gathering of horrible deeds, photo-accounts of severed limbs and other grisly bits. In addition to the more sensationalist displays of body parts pickled in formaldehyde, there are informative explanations of the history and execution of law enforcement in the country. You'll never feel the same again about saying "peace-loving" and "Costa Rica" in the same sentence when you walk out of this place.

Los Yoses and La California

The neighbourhoods of **Los Yoses** and **La California** run parallel to each other, the former on the south side of Av Central and the latter on the north, all the way east from the Museo Nacional to San Pedro. Mainly residential, Los Yoses is home to foreign embassies and the National Parks Office (see p.65), while commercial La California runs into *barrio* Escalante and *barrio* Dent, two of the nicest of San José's residential districts. Walking through *barrio* Escalante is the way to go east: a much better alternative to bus-choked Avenida Central.

Lurking in *barrio* Escalante, 100m east and 150m north of the pretty Iglesia Santa Teresita, the unusual **Museo Dr Rafael Angel Calderón Guardia** (Tues–Sun 10am–5pm; 75¢) is dedicated to Costa Rica's president of the immediate pre-Civil War years. Creator of the national university, the much-heralded Costa Rican social security system, the promulgation of the constitution and the workers' code, Calderón was essentially a socialist-minded president who met his downfall in 1944 when it seemed to other members of the ruling elite that his reforms were simply too expensive. Oddly modernist, with Bauhaus chairs and spare colour scheme, most of this elegiac – occasionally cheesy – museum is devoted to his early years as a helper of the poor.

Homesick tourists should head for the pleasant courtyard reading room in the Neoclassical **Goethe Institut**, Av Central and C 29, a former coffee plantation house that stocks German-language newspapers and has a good café, or to the **Centro Cultural Costarricense-Norteamericano**, just 100m north of the *Am-Pm* supermarket on the corner of Av Central and C 37 in *barrio* Dent (Mon–Fri 7am–7pm, Sat 9am–noon; ☎255-9433 for library). At the latter you'll find a huge back stock of English-language publications – the *Miami Herald*, *New York Times* and *USA Today* – as well as all the main Costa Rican dailies. There's also an art gallery, the Eugene O'Neill theatre, café and CNN beamed out on the communal TV.

San Pedro

First impressions of **San Pedro** can be offputting: Avenida Central appears to be little more than a strip of gas stations, broken-up sidewalks, and dull malls. Walk just a block off Av Central, however, and you'll find a lively combination of university student ghettos and elegant old residential houses, home to some of the city's best bars, restaurants and nightlife, catering to students, professors, residents and professionals.

Buses to San Pedro from the centre of town stop opposite the small **Parque Central**, with its bubblegum-orange bandstand and monument to John F Kennedy. Walking north from the *parque*, through three blocks of solid sodas, bars, restaurants and abandoned railway tracks, you come to the cool, leafy and beautifully landscaped campus of the **University of Costa Rica** (UCR), one of the finest in Central America and certainly the most prestigious educational institution in Costa Rica. Founded in 1940, the university has in the past been accused of being too rigidly academic, "elitist" and too opposed to change (shades of Ivy League here), but the overall campus atmosphere is busy, egalitarian and stimulating.

The best places to hang out on **campus** are the frenzied and cheap cafeteria in the building immediately to the right of the library (there's an excellent **bookstore** across from the back entrance of the cafeteria), the *comedor universitario*, or **dining hall**, and the *Faculdad de Bellas Artes*, which has a wonderful open-air **theatre** used for frequent concerts. The theatrical productions are usually stimulating, among them an innovative production of *Othello* that drew obvious parallels with the OJ Simpson story. Noticeboards around campus, particularly in front of the *Vida Estudantíl* office (Building A, fourth floor), keep you up to date with what's going on; try also to get hold of a copy of *Semana Universitaria*, the campus newspaper. The three or four square blocks surrounding the university are lined with some of the liveliest bars and restaurants in San José: in most of them you'll feel more comfortable if you're under thirty. For Spanish-speakers this is a great place to meet people, watch movies and browse around the several well-stocked bookstores (one of the best is *Librería Macondo*, 100m before you come to the university proper; look for the lime-green storefront).

Theoretically it's possible to walk to the campus from Los Yoses, but this entails dealing with a huge and threatening roundabout – the one with three fountains. This is not recommended, as there are no provisions at all for pedestrians.

Around the Mercado Central

Northwest of the Parque Central and the commercial centre between Av Central and 1, and C 6 and 8, San José's **Mercado Central** is open from about 5am until 5pm daily except Sunday. Much more orderly than the usual chickens-and-*campesino* Latin American city markets, it is still something of an experience: entering its labyrinthine interior, you're assaulted by colourful arrangements of strange fruits and vegetables, dangling sides of beef and elaborate, silvery ranks of fish. Occasionally the Mercado Central can resemble the Eighth Circle of Hell – choking with unfamiliar smells and an almighty crush of people – while at other times you'll face a relaxed wander through wide uncrowded alleys of rural commerce. It's certainly the best place in town to get a cheap bite to eat, and the view from a counter stool is fascinating, as traders and their customers jostle for *chayotes*, *mamones*, *piñas* and *cas*. With a little Spanish, and a pinch of confidence, shopping for fruit and vegetables here can be miles cheaper than in the supermarket.

The surrounding streets, which even in the daytime can look quite seedy (in sharp contrast to the roads just one or two blocks east), are also full of noisy traders and determined shoppers. All this activity encourages **pickpockets**, and in this environment *turistas* stick out like sore thumbs. Take only what you need and be on your guard.

Two blocks east and one block north of the Mercado Central, in the *Correo Central*, C 2, Av 1/3, the **Museo Postal, Telegráfico y Filatelico** (Mon–Fri 8am–4pm; free), exhibits old pieces of telegraphic equipment – relics of interest to buffs only. Far more appealing is the pretty **flower market** in the square opposite, where carnations, orchids, begonias and scores of lush blooms create a blaze of colour and fragrance.

Paseo Colón and Parque la Sabana

Clustered around the main entrance to La Coca-Cola, off C 16, shops selling women's underwear, cosmetics and luggage compete for space with a variety of cheap snack bars and drinks stalls. Two blocks south, however, the atmosphere changes, as Av Central turns into **Paseo Colón**, a wide boulevard of upmarket shops, restaurants and car dealerships. At the very end of the *paseo*, a solid expanse of green today known as **Parque la Sabana** was until the 1940s San José's airport, and now is home to the country's key art museum. To get to the parque, take the Sabana Cementerio bus from Av 2, or walk (20–30min from downtown).

Parque la Sabana

The bright orange neocolonial edifice of the old air terminal in **Parque la Sabana** has been converted into the attractive **Museo de Arte Costarricense** (Tues–Sun 10am–5pm; $2), with a good collection of mainly twentieth-century Costa Rican paintings. Of the permanent exhibits highlights include the outstanding landscapes of Teodorico **Quirós**, with their Cézanne-inspired panoplies and palettes of russets and burnt siennas, along with Enrique Echandi, Margarita Berthau, abstract painter Lola Fernández, and a scattershot selection of foreign artists including **Diego Rivera** and Alexander Calder. The **Salon Dorado** upstairs is remarkable; four full walls of bas-relief wooden carvings overlaid with sumptuous gold, portraying somewhat idealized scenes of Costa Rica's history since pre-Columbian times. On the western wall are imagined scenes from the lives of the indigenous peoples, followed on the north wall by Columbus' arrival, when almost immediately we see them fallen to their knees, solemnly praying. Other golden representations include the Costa Rican agrarian gods of horses, oxen and chickens, and an image of this very building as San José's airport, little biplanes buzzing around it like mosquitos.

On the southwest corner of Sabana Park, across the road, the quirky natural science museum **Museo de Ciencias Naturales La Salle** (Mon–Fri 8am–3pm; $1), is in the Ministry of Agriculture and Livestock complex. Walk right in, and after about 400m you'll see the painted wall proclaiming the museum; the entrance is at the back. It's an offbeat collection, with displays ranging from pickled fish and snakes coiled in formaldehyde to some rather forlorn taxidermy exhibits – age and humidity have taken their toll. Highlights include the model of the huge **baula**, or leatherback turtle, the biggest reptile on earth, and the **dusky grouper**, a fish well in the running for first prize in the Ugliest Animal in the World contest. Tons of crumbly fossils and an enormous selection of pinned butterflies (twelve cases alone of titanium-bright Blue Morphos) finishes off the collection. Real turtles, virtually motionless, doze off in the courtyard garden. The Sabana Estadio **bus** (see p.66) stops right outside the museum. Note, on your right as you go by, the futuristic air traffic control tower shape of the **Controlaría de la República**: this is the government's administrative headquarters.

Incidentally, Sabana is one of the better places in San José to **jog**. The cement track is usually full of serious runners in training, but you can run fairly safely all around the park. There's a small, dank changing hut, shower and lavatory beside the track; you can leave your bag securely with the *señora* who takes the money (10am–4pm only).

Eating

It used to be said that nobody goes to Costa Rica for the food. However, while it's still true that in most of the country you'll eat nothing more exotic than rice-and-chicken, the standard of cuisine in the capital has improved dramatically in the last couple of years. For a Central American city of its size, San José has a surprising variety of **restaurants** (Italian, macrobiotic, even Thai), along with simple places that offer dishes that begin and end with rice (rice-and-shrimp, rice-and-chicken, rice-and-meat). For really good down-home *típico* cooking, you'll get the best deals at the more upmarket restaurants that do grills or barbecues (*churrascos*).

Many of the city's best restaurants are in the relatively high income and cosmopolitan neighbourhoods of **San Pedro**, along **Paseo Colón**, and in **Escazú**, but wherever you choose, eating out in San José can set your budget back on its haunches. Prices are generally steep, and the 23 percent tax on restaurant food can deliver a real death-blow. The cheapest places are in the centre, especially the sodas and snack bars, where the restaurant tax doesn't apply. A sit-down lunch of the *plato del día* at a **soda** will rarely set you back more than $5, or for a quick sugar fix you could feast on *churros* dispensed over the counter. Healthier choices include *empañadas* and sandwiches to take out – combine this with a stop at one of the fruit stalls on any street corner and you've got a quick, cheap lunch. Remember to wash fruit bought at stalls thoroughly. The pieces of papaya and pineapple sold in neatly packaged plastic baags have been washed and peeled by the vendors and should be all right, but if in doubt wash again. Snacks sold at the **Mercado Central** are as tasty as anywhere, and there's a good cluster of sodas popular with office workers hidden away in the *Galería* shopping arcade, Av 2, C 5/7. The sodas along the entrance to the **University of Costa Rica** are all much of a muchness, serving bland lunches eaten with plastic cutlery to the blasting accompaniment of bad 1970s TV shows, but the food is filling and cheap and the eavesdropping is free.

Cafés also abound: some, like *Giacomín*, have old-world European aspirations; others, *Spoon* for example, are resolutely Costa Rican, with *Joséfinos* piling into order birthday cakes or grab a **coffee**. Most cafés serve exclusively export Costa Rican coffee, with its mild, soft flavour – for something different, try *Café Gourmet*, which offers numerous blends and roasts. Wherever you go you're likely to get *café con leche* served in the traditional way – a pitcher of coffee and a pitcher of heated milk, so that you can mix to your liking. For more on coffee, see p.33 in *Basics*. **Bakeries** (*pastelería*, *repostería*) on every corner sell generally high-quality cakes, breads and pastries – most of them thick with white refined flour. Chains to head for include *Trigo Miel*, *Schmidt* and *Giacomín*. The city's fantastic **ice cream** is another source of woe to dieters. Of the major chains – *Pops*, *Mönpik*, *Baloons* – *Pops* is the best, with particularly good fruit flavours.

Working *Joséfinos* eat their main meal between noon and 2pm, and at this time sodas especially can get very busy. Many restaurants close at 3pm and open again for the evening. For the **best tips** on the restaurants and cafés of the moment, check the weekly (Spanish) newspaper *Esta Semana,* whose witty, smart and very discerning restaurant critic, "Juarena", writes the *Buen Comer* column. In the listings below we have given a phone number only for places where you might need to **reserve** a table.

Restaurants

Antojitos, Los Yoses, 50m before the fountain roundabout on Av 0. Cheap, filling, Mexican food, not wholly authentic, but good for late-night snacks and cheap all-you-can-eat buffets. Draught beer and an outside terrace where you can sit and watch the 4WDs whizz round the fountain. Mariachi Fri and Sat from 10pm. Daily 11am–midnight.

Ave Fenix, San Pedro, 150m before Parque Central as you come in on Av 0. No-nonsense Chinese place, frequented by the Chinese community. Dinner costs $15 or so.

Balcón de Europa, C 9, Av 0/1. City landmark: the food, largely pasta and Italian staples, is nothing special, but the atmosphere is great. Sepia photos of the early days line the wood-panelled wall, along with annoying snippets of "wisdom". Monster cheeses dominate the dining room, as does the game strummer who serenades each table. Closed Sat.

Biajua, 50m west and 300m south of the *Mas x Menos* supermarket, San Pedro (☎225-0613). San José's most ambitious restaurant, offering *Nueva Cocina Costarricense*, a hybrid of nouvelle, Californian and local cuisine. Results sound delicious – *lomito* (tenderloin) on eggplant, *pejiballe* crème fraiche, red snapper stuffed with plantain in avocado sauce – but don't always live up to expectations. Innovation doesn't come cheap, either: expect to pay $70 for two with wine. Mon–Sat 7–11pm.

Café Mundo, Av 9, C 13/15, in the *Villa Borghese* building. Beautiful decor, relaxed, European atmosphere, and the best food (and prices) in San José. Try the delicate wok-cooked chicken, peppers and black beans, or inventive soups such as orange and tomato. Great cakes, too; take out a huge chocolate chip cookie and you won't need to eat for the rest of the day. It gets frantic at about 1pm so arrive early. Mon–Fri 11am–6pm.

Café 1900, 100m north of La Iglesia de Fatima, Los Yoses. Peruvian restaurant – originally a tea/coffee house – oddly done up in flowery chintz wallpaper. At lunch choose from pisco sours, big salads and crepes; for dinner try a shrimp entrée (about $7). The fish in spicy sauce is particularly good. Mon–Fri 11.30am–3pm & 6–10pm, Sat 7–11pm, Sun noon–4pm.

Caruso, 200m north of the *Centro Cultural Costarricense-Norteamericano* in *barrio* Dent (☎224-4801). One of the very best Italian restaurants in the city. Cool elegant interior, superb service and a varied menu including carpaccio and exquisitely cooked pasta. A good place for a special dinner; about $40 with wine for two.

Casa Blanca, San Pedro, 50m south of *Caccio*. Small restaurant in a private house; a good bet for lunch. Superior and cheap *casados*, very well cooked.

La Cascada, behind *Centro Comercial Trejos Montalegre*, Escazú (☎228-0906). This difficult to find place (no sign) with unpromising decor is the best steak house in San José. Hugely popular, it's often full of Tico families, especially on Sunday afternoon. The hunks of beef are fantastic, and the terrifically filling plates all come with rice and veg.

Cocina de Leña, El Pueblo. *Típico* food, superbly cooked, in rustic, down-homey surroundings (big wooden tables, gingham tablecloths, menus on paper bags). Good for a quiet, upscale night out; dinner costs around $35 for two.

Fellini, Av 4a, C 36, 200m south of the Toyota dealership, Paseo Colón (☎222-3520). Italian food with Latin American touches. Very upmarket, with marbled floors and grave waiters, and posters of *Amarcord* adorning the walls. Cheapest choice is risotto, about $5; the lobster salad or *scallopina* is worth the extra.

La Galería, 125m west of the ICE building in Sabana Norte (☎234-0850). Intriguing combination of German and local cuisine, including well-cooked *lomito* (tenderloin), *corvina* (bass) and some more traditionally German dishes like Wiener schnitzel and great desserts. Dinner for two will set you back about $45. Mon–Fri noon–2.30pm & 7–11pm; evenings only Sat.

Grano d'Oro, C 3, casa 251, 150m south of Paseo Colón (☎253-3322). Upscale restaurant with changing menu. Beautifully spare decor; the kitchen door is usually open so you can see artistry in action. Amazing desserts; try the tiramisu and strawberry cream cheese. Call ahead and bring plenty of funds. Breakfast from 7am; lunch after 11am; dinner hours are "flexible".

Lubnán, in front of the Mercedes Benz dealership on Paseo Colón, C 22/24. Lebanese restaurant; the sixteen-dish meze selection, with tasty *babagonoush*-like pastes, shish kebabs and the like, is a meal in itself. Tues–Sat 11am–3pm & 6–11pm, Sun 11am–6pm.

Machu Picchu, C 38, 125m north of Paseo Colón (☎222-7384). Appetizers, including *ceviche* and Peruvian *bocas* are more interesting than the main dishes. Great atmosphere; the only truly South American feel in town (kitsch velvet llama pictures on the walls help). Around $30 for two with beer or wine. Mon–Fri 11.30am–3pm & 6–10pm.

Marisqueria La Princesa, north side of Parque la Sabana. Doesn't look much from the outside but this is one of San José's best restaurants, with seafood at very low prices; the shrimps with garlic (*camarones con ajillo*) are about half the price you find them elsewhere. It also has a breezy, open-air feel as the sides are open to the street.

La Masía de Triquel, Av 2, C 40. Consistently dependable Catalan cuisine – the place to go if the desire for paella hits you. Bet on spending at least $35 for dinner for two. Tues–Sat noon–2pm & 7–11pm, Sun noon–4pm.

Mazorca, 200m east and 100m north of San Pedro church. Macrobiotic restaurant just east of the entrance to UCR. Tasty bread, soups, peanut butter sandwiches and macrobiotic cakes make a welcome change from greasy *arroz con pollo*. Homey, simple decor and a plain menu; also takeout. Mon–Fri 9am–8pm, Sat 9am–2pm.

Nimbé, just before you get to San Miguel de Escazú, on the left. Excellent authentic Costa Rican food, favourite of the local gentry. Crepes of *corvina* and eggplant are pricey but miraculously tasty, or try fish in *pejibaye* sauce. In an old colonial building where you can sit outside as well as in. Marimba on Sunday.

Poás Taberna and Restaurant, Av 7, C 3/5. The sign says "Eat in the Jungle" – not quite, but it's solid *típico* food served in a room of plants, tame birds and trees. A good downtown lunch, quite cheap; dinner costs around $20 for two.

Il Pomodoro, San Pedro, 150m east of the entrance to UCR. Sooner or later, everybody ends up at The Tomato, one of the best pizza places in the city. Proper large pizzas, including a great vegetarian special, served in cheerful large restaurant popular with university crowd. Cheap draught beer served in mugs and pitchers. Around $18 for two.

Restaurante Campesino, C 7, Av 2. The name means "peasant restaurant", reflecting the prices, which are extra good value, rather than the quality of the food, which is high. The menu is almost exclusively chicken, succulently roasted over a wood fire. Not more than $7 for a good filling dinner.

Tin-Jo, C 11, Av 6/8 (☎221-7605). Quiet, popular and fairly formal Chinese/Thai place; lemongrass soup, bean thread salad in lime juice, and coconut milk curries are particularly recommended. Dinner with wine is around $40 for two; skip the alcohol, or go for lunch, and you'll get away with half that.

La Trancha, on the road to Aserrí, 12km from downtown. This miraculous restaurant, little known by tourists, serves up the best *churrasco* this side of Brazil, eaten at great tree-trunk tables. Also known as the *mirador*, or "lookout", it sits high on the mountainside south of San José and has the most stupendous views. Take a taxi (and a sweater – it can get chilly) or a suburban bus to Aserrí and ask the driver where to get off.

Sodas

Castro, Av 10, casa 279. Simple fluorescent decor, 1970s vinyl, and slightly rough-around-the-edges neighbourhood belie the treats inside. This is where local families take their kids for an Sunday ice-cream treat; good fruit salads, too.

La Cocina de Bardolino, C 21, Av 6, 100m east from *La Corte*. Watch the Argentine owners prepare exquisitely fresh chicken and beef *empañadas* while keeping their eyes glued on the TV soccer game. Images of *La Patria*, including Maradona posters, abound.

Comedor Universitario, *Centro de Recreación*, UCR. Three extra-cheap lunch options – chicken and rice, salad and *refresco* – every weekday; none of them gourmet but the prices are good and the somewhat frantic atmosphere is interesting.

Delicias, C 23, Av 0, near the *Toruma* hostel. Plain soda where squashed office workers are barked at by waitresses in a 1950s time warp. Very cheap *plato del día* – so filling you'll never eat again. A takeout window sells alarming-looking cakes and pastries.

Don Sol, Av 7, 50m northeast of the Parque España. Excellent vegetarian bargains, popular with office workers, in a quiet part of *barrio* Amón. The special for $1.75 isn't huge; the larger vegetarian *casado* gets you lentils, brown rice, beans and fried plantain plus *refresco* for $2. Cafeteria-style self-service, Mon–Fri lunch only.

La Fogata, Av 0, next to *Mas x Menos*. Chicken-and-chips joint with open-air soda atmosphere and cheap lunch specials ($2.50 for two pieces of chicken, fries and a drink). One of the best deals in town; takeout service, too.

La Perla, C 2, Av 2, across from the Parque Central. Pricey, and grudging – to say the least – service, but huge portions; try the steak sandwich with fries, scrambled eggs on toast, or the extra good *refrescos*. Streetlife streams by outside; open 24 hours.

Shakti, C 13, Av 8. Fantastically filling *platos del día* include *sopa negra* or salad, a big hearty vegetarian *casado*, *refresco* and tea or coffee, all for only $2.50. Popular for lunch, so go early or late for a seat. Mon–Fri 11.30am–3pm.

Tapia, southeast corner of Parque la Sabana. Huge place, open on to the street with views of Parque la Sabana. Especially good for late-night snacks, with sandwiches and burgers for those weary of *casados*.

Vishnu, Av 1, C 1/3. Obligatory pit stop for vegetarians. Friendly pink-and-green-shirted waiters are bizarrely reluctant to show you the menu (*Joséfinos* must know it by heart) but eventually relent and bring out delicious *platos del día*, soups, fruit salads and yoghurt – even a dieters' selection. A *plato del día*, *refresco* and *café con leche* costs about $4.

Cafés and bakeries

Café Gourmet, C 7, Av 9. Small, quiet, aromatic café with excellent export-quality coffee, freshly roasted beans, and friendly staff who will answer any questions about the entire coffee process, from bean to cup. Tasty desserts and snacks.

Café la Maga, 100m east of the church, Av 0, San Pedro. Currently one of the most popular places in town day or night, this café/bar doubles as an art gallery, and stocks an enormous array of magazines dealing with Latin American and Spanish art, culture and literature. Film club ($21 per annum), with more than 100 videos. Daily 11am–midnight.

Café Mundo, Av 9, C 13/15. Sit in the cool green upstairs café and enjoy great coffee – with free refills – and the most delicious gateaux in the city. Mon–Fri noon–6pm.

Café Parisienne, *Gran Hotel Costa Rica*, Av 2, C 3/5. Wonderful place to sit and have coffee and cake on a sunny day, complete with wrought-iron chairs and trussed-up waiters. San José's closest thing to European street-café elegance, and one of the few establishments in the city that do continental breakfast.

Le Petit Café, 500m south of the Antiguo Higuerón/Mobil gas station, San Pedro. Family-run café run serving quiches, cakes, crepes and very good cappuccino. Daily 11am–7pm.

Ruiseñor, *Centro Comercial Casa Alameda*, Los Yoses. Old-world European style and service. If you sit upstairs on the the outdoor terrace you can watch the diplomats come and go. Upmarket, with prices to match.

Spoon, Av 0, C 5/7. Full of *Joséfinos* ordering birthday cakes. Coffee is somewhat bitter but served with mix-it-yourself hot milk; the choice of cookies and cakes is endless.

Teatro Nacional, Av 2, C 3/5. Sandwiches and pastries served in a tranquil mint-green setting – also good for watching the goings-on in the square in front of the *Gran Hotel Costa Rica*.

Drinking and nightlife

San José's nightlife is gratifyingly varied, with scores of **bars** and **live music** venues. Many bars don't offer music during the week but change character drastically come Friday or Saturday, when you can hear jazz (live or taped), blues, upcoming local bands, rock and roll, or South American folk music. That said,

LEARNING TO SALSA IN SAN JOSÉ

One of the best ways to prepare yourself for San José nightlife, and to meet people, is to take a few **salsa lessons** at one of the city's many *academias de baile*. You don't necessarily need a partner, and you can go with a friend or in a group. The tuition is serious-minded, but the atmosphere is usually relaxed. The best in San José are: *Bailes Latinos*, in the Costa Rican Institute of Language and Latin Dance, Av 0, C 25/27 (☎233-8938; fax 233-8670); *Malecón*, C 17, Av 2 (☎222-3214), and *Merecumbé*, which has various branches, the most central of which is at San Pedro (☎ and fax 224-3531). For more on salsa and merengue see *Contexts*.

activity is not relentlessly weekend-oriented: it's possible, with a little searching, to hear good live music on Wednesday, and encounter a packed disco floor on a Monday or Tuesday. People do stay out later on the weekends, but even so, Ticos aren't known for burning the candle at both ends, and most places close by 2 or 3am, earlier on Sunday.

Downtown features a number of places with American names that attract gringos in packs; in **Los Yoses**, Av Central features a well-known "yuppie trail" of bars, packed with middle- and upper-middle-class Ticos conspicuously consuming, enjoying a few beers and generally revelling. It starts roughly at *El Cuartel de la Boca del Monte*, where the crowd is relatively mixed, and reaches its peak at *Rio*, a hugely popular American-style bar with an outdoor terrace. On Friday and Saturday nights the road outside is lined with young Ticos posing on their car hoods, chatting or having a beer – all longing to be as close as they possibly can to *Rio*, even if they can't get in. **San Pedro** nightlife is obviously geared toward the university population, with a couple of very studenty bars. Those looking for local atmosphere should head for a **boca bar**, or seek out places to hear **peñas**: slow, acoustically accompanied folk songs that come from the Andean region, and grew up out of the leftist revolutionary movements of the 1970s and 1980s.

It's well worth experiencing one of the city's **discos**: even if you don't dance, you can watch the Ticos burn up the floor. For traditional **salsa**, merengue, cumbia and soca try *La Plaza, Cocloco, Las Risas, Infinito, Salsa 54*, and the traditional *El Gran Parqueo* in working-class Desamparados. DJs at these places intersperse the Latino playlist with reggae and a bit of jungle from Jamaica, the US, the Dominican Republic and sometimes even from Limón, and then do a House set, usually playing internationally popular, if somewhat out of date, tunes. For **reggae** – hugely popular with young *Joséfinos* – head for *Dynasty*. Because locals are usually in couples or groups, the atmosphere at most places is non-"scene"; if you are asked to dance you needn't worry that anyone expects more than that. The only exception might be if you go as a single woman, which is quite uncommon here and usually taken as a sign of availability. In general, the **dress code** is relaxed: most people wear smart jeans and men need not wear a jacket. **Cover charges** run to about 700¢ or $4, though the big mainstream discos at El Pueblo charge slightly more than places downtown.

San José is one of the best places in Central (possibly Latin) America for **gay** nightlife. Establishments come and go without much notice other than on the grapevine; if you have a contact in the local lesbian and gay scene you can hunt down small local clubs, often without addresses and certainly without telephone

BOCA BARS

In Costa Rica **bocas** – "mouths" in Spanish – are the tasty little snacks traditionally served free in bars. *Boca* bars are a largely urban tradition, and although you find them in other parts of the country, the really famous ones are all in San José. Because of mounting costs, however, and erosion of local traditions, few places serve these gratis any more. Several bars have a *boca* menu, among them *Chelles Taberna* in downtown San José or *La Villa* in San Pedro, but the authentic **boca bars** are concentrated in suburban working- or lower-middle-class residential neighbourhoods. They have a distinctive convivial atmosphere – friends and family getting together for a good night out – and are very busy most nights. Saturday is the hardest night to get a table; get there before 7.30pm or so. You'll be handed a menu of *bocas* that have no prices; they're free, but the catch is that the beer costs about twice as much as elsewhere ($2 as opposed to $1). Nevertheless, the little plates of food are generous enough to make this a bargain way to eat out. One beer gets you one *boca*; keep drinking and you can keep eating. You'll do better if you speak Spanish, but you can get by with point-and-nod. **Typical bocas** include deep-fried plantain with black bean paste, small plates of rice and meat, shish kebabs, *tacos* or *empañadas*; nothing fancy, but the perfect accompaniment to a cold beer.

Bar México, opposite the church in *barrio* México, northwest of the city. Old working-class *boca* bar, one of the most authentic and well-known in the city. These days *barrio* México is a pretty rough neighbourhood, at least in San José's terms, so get there by taxi; the driver will know where to let you off. Mon–Fri 3pm– midnight, Sat 11am–midnight, closed Sun.

Los Perales and El Sesteo, in the eastern suburb of Curridabat. Both places are hard to find on your own, but taxi drivers will know them by name. About 100m apart from each other on the same street, with a varied clientele – although conspicuously few foreigners. Mon–Sat 7pm–midnight.

numbers. The venues in our listings are established places that are unlikely to disappear or ressurrect themselves as something else.

A note on Costa Rican **rock music**: there are a few groups who have made it big at home and to an extent elsewhere in the region. Local favourites include *Marfil*, the granddaddy of Costa Rican rock bands, hard-working, hard-touring *K-lor*, or *Café con Leche*, the local answer to grunge.

For full details of **what's on**, check the *Viva* section of *La Nación* or in *Espectaculos*, the fortnightly listing of culture and entertainment.

Bars and live music

Akelare, C 21, Av 4/6. Huge college-bar-style place with a varying live music scene; usually rock. Loud (big sound system), and a great outdoor patio. Busy on Friday and Saturday nights, otherwise a bit forlorn. No cover during the week; weekends $2.

Los Andes, across the street from the UCR library and cafeteria, San Pedro. University hang-out with low-key atmosphere, cold beer, good snacks and regular acoustic music, including *peñas*. Mon–Sat 11am– midnight.

Los Balcones, in El Pueblo. Regular *peñas* and other acoustic music and an outdoor terrace make this the nicest bar in El Pueblo. Open daily until 2am; no cover.

Bar Shakespeare, C 28, Av 2/4. Quiet, friendly place that attracts a large English-speaking clientele and people on their way to art-house films at the *Sala Garbo*, adjacent, or the *Teatro Laurence Olivier*. Occasional jazz. Daily 3pm–midnight.

Caccio, 200m east and 25m north of the San Pedro church. Insanely popular student hang-out with guys wearing baseball caps and singing along to the *St. Elmo's Fire* theme song. Packed tables are great for meeting people: another bonus are the baskets of pizza and cheap cold beer. Mon–Sat 11am–midnight.

Charleston, C 11, Av 4/6 across from the yellow Iglesia Soledad. Nice ambience near the centre in an old house, one wall lined with flowers, plants and old photos. Well-stocked bar; taped music is a mixture of Latin, fusion, straight jazz. Live jazz some nights. Closed Sun.

Chelles Taberna, C 9, Av 0/2 (☎221-1369). More like an English pub than a Latin American tavern, with smooching couples, serious guys in leather jackets and surly bar staff. Good range of drinks and cheap, tasty *bocas*. Open 24 hours.

Contravía, 100m south of the *Nueva China* restaurant on Av 0, San Pedro (☎253-6589). San José's best venue for live blues and rock, with consistently good acts. Clientele is mostly university or otherwise hip. Open 6pm–midnight.

El Cuartel de la Boca del Monte, Av 1, C 21/23. Indescribably popular with the beautiful young things. Well-stocked bar, great food, and some of the best live music in town from up-and-coming bands (Wed only). Go early, before 8.30pm. There's a door policy of sorts, but the bouncers never seem to turn anyone away. Small cover ($2.50) most nights.

La Esmeralda, Av 2, C 5/7. Landmark institution, offering a bit of "local colour". It's the headquarters of the Mariachi bands union, who congregate ready to dash off in a taxi at a moment's notice to serenade or celebrate. In the meantime, they whoosh by your table in colourful swirls of sombreros and sequins. Mon–Sat 11am–dawn.

Las Risas, C 1, Av 0/1. One of the best downtown bars, on three floors. The disco at the top is good, with a small floor and lively young crowd. Bring ID or the bouncers won't let you in.

Rock Olas, in the *Centro Comercial Cocorí*, just before the fountain in Los Yoses. Owned by the manager of *Marfil*, Costa Rica's best-known rock band. Choose from a request sheet of rock, blues, merengue and salsa, currently spanning 1950–79 (he adds a year each year). A couply place: single women are not really welcome, as they're trying to deter prostitutes . . .

Sand, in the *Centro Comercial Cocorí*. Spartan, friendly venue with great, up-to-the-moment playlist of metal, grunge, even a bit of garage. Pretty loud; the young crowd don't go to converse. Live music on Sunday, and darts for homesick English. Daily 7pm–midnight.

Soda Blues, C 11, Av 8/10. CD music most nights, and Thursday there's live *musica latina* and blues – interesting combination. Beer-and-*boca*s special for 75¢.

El Tablado, next to the *Toruma* hostel, Los Yoses. Currently closed but so often resurrected that it's worth a mention. Every few months, because of the noise level of the live rock bands the *Toruma* people complain and it shuts down. When it's open, its packed out with high school and university students.

La Villa, 125m north of the old *Banco Anglo*, San Pedro. San José's best bar for beer and conversation. Atmospheric old house, frequented by students and "intellectuals", and plas-tered with interesting political and theatrical posters. Mercedes Sosa on the CD player, occa-sional live *peñas* and tasty *bocas*.

Gay and lesbian nightlife

La Avispa, C 1, Av 8/10. Landmark San José lesbian disco-bar where men are welcome. Friendly atmosphere, simple dance floor and mainly Latin music. Tues–Sat 8pm–2am, Sun 5pm–2am. Thurs–Sun cover $5.

Déjà Vu, C 2, Av 14/16. Men only really, though no policy as such is posted anywhere. Hot and hopping atmosphere, with serious salsa, merengue and House. The neighbourhood isn't great at night; watch yourself.

La Torre, C 7, Av 0/1. Predominantly male crowd, but unpredictable; heterosexuals are welcome and it often fills with straight couples. Hip tunes and energetic dancing. Wed–Sat 7.30pm–4am, Sun 2.30pm–midnight; cover $4 on Wed, Sat & Sun.

Discos

Cocoloco, El Pueblo. Smart, well-dressed clientele, small dance floors, and the usual Latin techno-pop/reggae/merengue mix. Daily 8pm–midnight; 2am weekends.

Dynasty, in *Centro Comercial del Sur*, Desamparados, south of central San José (next to the old Pacific Railway station). Excellent *caribeña* tunes with reggae, odd sample of garage, soca, merengue and calypso. Young, hard-dancing crowd.

El Gran Parqueo, Desamparados. Very traditional venue, with almost wholly working-class Costa Rican clientele. Live bands play merengue and salsa on the spot to a packed crowd of smart-looking expert older dancers who make the cement floor smoke. Minimal cover.

Infinito, El Pueblo. Similar to *Cocoloco*, but with an older, smarter crowd; the DJs here are pretty good. Mon–Fri 8pm–midnight; till 2am at weekends.

La Plaza, across from El Pueblo. Archetypical Latin American disco. Designed like a giant bull ring, the huge round dance floor is packed with merengue dancing couples and superb waiters who twirl in their truncated tuxedos when business is slack. There's also a bar with a big TV screen flashing out a steady diet of music and sport. Daily from 8pm.

Salsa 54, C 3, Av 1/3. Downtown alternative to the El Pueblo discos, this joint plays the favoured mix of Latin and American tunes, but as the name implies, goes heavy on the salsa and merengue. The best place to dance in San José proper, attracting the most talented *salseros*.

The arts and entertainment

Considering decreasing financial support from the national government, the quality of the arts in San José is very high. *Joséfinos* especially like **theatre**, and there is a healthy cadre of venues for a city this size, showing a variety of inventive productions at affordable prices. If you speak even a little Spanish it's worth checking to see what's on.

Costa Rica's **National Dance Company** has an impressive repertoire of classical and modern productions, some by Central American choreographers, arranged specifically for the company; again, ticket costs are low. The city's premier venues are the *Teatro Nacional* and the *Teatro Melico Salazar*; here you'll see performances by the **National Symphony Orchestra** and **National Lyric Opera Company** (June–Aug), as well as from visiting orchestras and singers – usually from Spain or other Spanish-speaking countries. A number of

---

CASA MATUTE

The huge former home of a Colombian millionaire, **Casa Matute**, C 21, Av 10, 100m south of the court buildings (daily 8pm–3am; ☎222-7806), is Costa Rica's most exciting entertainment complex. A very plush arts and cultural centre with its own radio station, it includes an acoustic music venue, theatre space, a good (expensive) outdoor restaurant and a maze of bars – one of which specializes only in whiskey, and one with 57 wines. Although the high cover charge at the weekend (up to $7) limits the clientele somewhat, *Casa Matute* has really changed the face of San José nightlife – not only do local artists, photographers and poets have a space specifically geared to their needs, but the city now has a place for young well-to-do Ticos who want to dress up and hit the town. Get a schedule from *Casa Matute* or watch the listings in the *Viva* section of *La Nación*.

cinemas show the latest American movies, almost always subtitled and never dubbed; for Spanish-language art movies, head for the *Sala Garbo, Cinemateca* and the Law faculty cinemas at the university.

Though obviously geared up for tourists, the **Fantasía Folklórica** held every Tuesday night in the *Melico Salazar* is the only forum in which traditional dances and songs of the Costa Rican countryside are performed. Shows vary between representations of, for instance, Guanacastecan dance and music, and historic spectaculars such as the current long-running production *Limón, Limón*. Not nearly as cheesy as they sound, they're generally well staged and good fun if you like musicals.

For **details of performances**, check the *Viva* section of *La Nación* and the listings in the *Tico Times*, which also distinguish between English- and Spanish-language films and productions. There is also a fortnightly brochure distributed to hotels and other tourist haunts called *Info-Spectacles*, which lists much of what is going on in the city.

Cinemas

Bellavista, Av 0, C 17/19 (☎221-0909). American blockbusters.

California, C 23, Av 1 (☎221-4738). Huge, barn-like space; never full and has good popcorn.

Capri 1 and 2, C 9, Av 0 (☎223-0264). Downtown cinema for blockbusters.

Cinemateca, University of Costa Rica, San Pedro. Arty movies.

Colón, Paseo Colón, C 38/40 (☎221-4517). Plush, American-mall-cinema-style, with the more ambitious American films.

Faculdad de Derecha Cinema, Faculty of Law, University of Costa Rica, San Pedro (☎225-9175). Occasional European and art films.

Sala Garbo, C 42, Av 2/4 (☎222-1034). Popular art-house cinema.

Universal, Paseo Colón, C 26/18 (☎221-5241). Highly rated American movies.

Variedades, C 5, Av 0/1 (☎222-6104). Old theatre with a rococo-Gaudí exterior; shows good foreign and occasionally Spanish-language films.

Theatres

Teatro de la Aduana, C 25, Av 3/5 (☎221-5205). Elegant mid-sized space, which often hosts the National Theatre Company.

Teatro del Angel, Av 0, C 11/13 (☎222-8258). Musicals and light comedies, from a former Chilean company who fled (actors, directors and all) Pinochet's Chile in the 1970s to re-establish themselves in San José.

Teatro Bellas Artes, University of Costa Rica, San Pedro, Faculdad de Bellas Artes (☎253-4327). Generally excellent and innovative student productions with new spins on classical and contemporary works.

Teatro de la Carpa, Av 0, C 29/33 (☎234-2866). Sometime home of the English-language Little Theatre Company and run by the wife of the president of the National Theatre Company, this orange clapboard house is a kind of museum to Costa Rica's recent theatrical history, with fascinating posters and reviews on the walls. Large proscenium-arch performance space with a lovely café/restaurant, and a children's theatre that hosts workshops.

Teatro Chaplin, Av 12, C 11/13 (☎223-2919). Small space for alternative drama, new plays and mime.

Teatro la Comedía, Av 0, C 11/13 (☎233-0307). As the name suggests, comedy (plays, not stand-up) only.

Teatro Eugene O'Neill, *Centro Cultural Costarricense-Norteamericano*, Los Yoses (☎225-9433). Modern theatre mounting up-to-date independent productions.

Teatro Laurence Olivier, in the *Sala Garbo* building, C 28, Av 2 (☎223-1960). Modern, theatre mounting contemporary productions, plus sometime jazz concerts and film seasons.

Teatro la Mascara, C 13, Av 2/4 (☎255-4250). Sex comedies and burlesques.

Teatro Melico Salazar, C Central, Av 2 (☎221-4952). San José's "workhorse" theatre, featuring a wide variety of performances, including *Fantasía Folklórica*.

Teatro Nacional, C 5, Av 2 (☎221-1329). San José's premier theatre, where you'll see all the prestige productions – opera, ballet and concerts, as well as drama.

Shopping and markets

San José's **souvenir and crafts shops** are well-stocked and in general fairly pricey; it's best to buy from larger ones, run by government-regulated crafts cooperatives, from which more of the money filters down to the artisans. You'll see an abundance of **pre-Columbian gold jewellery copies**, Costa Rican liqueurs (*Café Rica* is best known), T-shirts with jungle and animal scenes, weirdly realistic wooden snakes, leather rockers from the village of Sarchí (see p.111), walking sticks, simple leather bracelets, hammocks, and a vast array of woodcarvings, from tiny miniatures depicting everyday rural scenes through salad bowls to giant, colourfully hand-painted **Sarchí ox-carts**. Look out too for *molas*, hand-made and appliquéd clothes, mostly shirts, occasionally from the Drake's Bay region of southwestern Costa Rica but more usually made by the Kuna peoples of Panamá.

ANDA, Av 0, C 5/7. Indigenous crafts including wooden masks, colourful *molas*, and bags and reproductions of Chorotega pottery.

Atmósfera, C 5, Av 1 (☎222-4322). Elegant gallery-like space selling jewellery, large pieces of furniture and woodwork.

CANAPI, C 11, Av 1 (☎221-3342). Large shop with a good stock of wooden bowls, serving spoons, walking sticks and boxes.

La Casa del Indio, Av 2, C 5/7 (☎223-0306). Jewellery and indigenous art; some replicas of Diquis goldwork.

La Casona, C 0, Av 0/1 (no phone). Great for browsing, a large marketplace of stalls selling the usual local stuff along with Guatemalan knapsacks and bedspreads; the quality at some stalls is pretty poor, however, and there's not one good T-shirt in evidence.

Hotel Don Carlos, C 9, Av 9 (☎221-6707). One of the best places in the city for pre-Columbian artefacts and jewellery reproductions.

Mercado Central, Av 0/1, C 6/8 (no phone). *The* place to buy coffee beans. Make sure they are export quality (ask for *Grano d'Oro* or golden bean, which is the prime export crop).

Mercado Nacional de Artesanía, C 22, Av 2 bis (☎223-0122). One of the largest stocks of souvenirs and crafts in the country, featuring all the usuals: hats, T-shirts, Sarchí ox-carts, jewellery, woodwork including snakes and walking sticks.

Tienda de la Naturaleza, Curridabat, 1km past San Pedro on Av 0 (☎253-2130). The shop of the *Fundación Neotropica*, this is a good place to buy the posters, T-shirts and other paraphernalia painted by English artist Deirdre Hyde that you see all over the country. She specializes in the landscapes of tropical America and the animals who live there; her jaguars are particularly good.

Sol Maya, Paseo Colón, C 18/20 (☎221-0864). Guatemalan arts and crafts and a selection of indigenous art that tends toward the expensive.

Listings

Airline offices In all the following, the first numbers are downtown offices; the last number is the airport office, if it applies. *Aero Costa Rica*, 200m north of *La Hispanidad*

(☎253-4753; ☎441-6094); *Aeronica*, C 11/13 (☎233-2483; ☎441-1744); *Air France*, Av 1, C 4/6 (☎222-8811); *Alitalia*, C 38, Av 3 (☎222-6138); *American*, Paseo Colón, C 26/28 (☎257-1266; ☎441-1168); *Aviateca*, Paseo Colón, 100m north of the *Banco de Costa Rica* (☎255-4949; ☎441-7651); *Continental*, C 19, Av 2 (☎233-0266; ☎442-1904); *Copa*, C 1, Av 5 (☎223-7033; ☎441-4742); *Iberia*, C 40, Paseo Colón (☎221-3311; ☎442-1932); *KLM*, C 1, Av 0/1 (☎220-4111; ☎442-1922); *Lacsa*, C 1, Av 5 (☎231-0033; ☎441-6244); *Ladeco* (☎641-1444); *LTU*, Av 9, C 1/3 (☎257-2990); *Lufthansa*, C 5, Av 7/9 (☎221-7444); *Mexicana*, C 1, Av 2/4 (☎222-7147 or 1711; ☎441-9377); *SAM*, Av 5, C 1/3 (☎233-3066); *Sansa*, Av 5, C 1/3 (☎221-5774; ☎441-1064); *TACA*, C 1, Av 1/3 (☎222-1790; ☎441-5090); *United Airlines*, Sabana Sur (☎220-2027 or 4844; ☎441-8025); *Varig*, Av 5, C 1/3 (☎221-3087; ☎441-6244); *Viasa*, Av 5, C 1/3 (☎231-0033; ☎441-6244).

Banks *Banco de Costa Rica*, Av 2, C 4/6 (Mon–Fri 9am–3pm; ☎255-1100); *Banco Nacional*, Av 0/1, C 2/4 (Mon–Fri 9am–3pm; ☎255-5044); *Banco Mercantil*, Av 3, C Central/2 (Mon–Fri 9am–3pm; ☎255-3636); *Banco Lyon*, C 2, Av 0/1 (Mon–Fri 8am–4pm; ☎221-2611; *American Express* travellers' cheques only); *Banco Metropolitano*, C Central, Av 2 (Mon–Fri 8.15am-4pm; ☎257-3030; *Visa* only); *BANEX*, C Central, Av 1 (Mon–Fri 8am–5pm; ☎257-0522; *Visa* only); *Banco de San José*, C Central, Av 3/5 (☎221-9911; *Visa* and *Mastercard*); *Banco del Comercio*, 150m north of the Cathedral (☎233-6011; *Visa* only).

Bookstores *The Bookshop*, Av 1, C 1/3 (☎221-6847) sells mainly new English-language books, some hardcovers imported from the US (expensive due to import duties), literary fiction, children's books, calendars, postcards and wrapping paper; *Book Traders*, Av 1, C 3/5, on the second floor in the back of the Omni building (☎255-0528) has occasional good secondhand finds but is mainly flooded with blockbusters and old *National Geographics*; *Chispas*, C 7, Av 0/1 (☎223-2240; fax 224-9278) sells new and secondhand, with the best selection of fiction in English in town, also a good guide book and Costa Rica section (English/Spanish), plus *New York Times*, *El País* and English-language magazines and a small tour agency in the back; *Lehmann*, Av 0, C 1/3 (☎223-1212) has a good selection of fiction and non-fiction, more downmarket than *Universal*, with lots of children's books, and a good stock of foreign magazines and Costa Rica guides; *Macondo*, opposite the entrance to the university in San Pedro, is probably the best bookshop in town for literature in Spanish, especially from Central America, as well as academic disciplines such as sociology and women's studies; *Universal*, Av 0, C Central/1 (☎222-2222) is strong in Spanish books, fiction, titles on Costa Rica (in Spanish), and cartographic maps of the country.

Car rental In all the following, the first telephone numbers belong to downtown offices; the last number is the airport office, if it applies. *ADA*, Av 18, C 11/13 (☎233-7733 or 222-7929; ☎441-1260; fax 233-5555); *Adobe*, C 7, Av 8/10 (☎221-5425; fax 221-9268); *Avis*, C 42, Av Las Americas (☎222-6066; in the US: ☎1-800/331-1212); *Budget*, Paseo Colón, C 30 (☎223-3284; fax 255-4966; ☎ and fax 441-4444; in the US: ☎1-800/472-3325); *Economy*, in the Datsun dealership, Sabana Norte (☎231-5410 or 220-1838); *Elegante*, C 10, Av 13/15, *barrio* México (☎221-0066 or 233-8605; in the US: ☎1-800/582-7432); *Hertz*, C 38, Paseo Colón (☎223-5959; fax 221-1949; ☎441-9366); *National*, C 36, Av 7 (☎233-4044; fax 233-2186; ☎441-6533); *Thrifty*, C 3, Av 13 (☎255-4141; fax 223-0660); *Tico*, Paseo Colón, C 24/26 (☎222-8920; fax 222-1765; ☎443-2078).

Embassies and consulates *Argentina*, Av 6, C 21/25 (☎221-6869); *Austria*, Edificio Nagel, Av 4, C 36/38 (☎255-3007); *Belize*, in Rohrmoser, 25m west and 75m south of the Plaza Mayor (☎231-7766 or 232-6637); *Bolivia*, Av 2, C 19/21 (☎233-6244); *Brazil*, Av 2, C 20/22 (☎233-1544 or 1092); *Canada*, 6th floor, Edificio Cronos, C 3, Av 0/1 (☎255-3522 or 228-5154; fax 223-2395); *Chile*, in Los Yoses, 50m east and 225m west of the Automercado (☎224-4243); *Colombia*, C 29, Av 1 (☎221-0725 or 255-0937); *Denmark*, 11th floor, Edificio Centro Colón, Paseo Colón, C 38/40 (☎257-2695 or 2696); *Ecuador*, in Sabana Sur, 100m east and 125m south of the Colégio de Médicos (☎232-1503 or 231-1899); *El Salvador*, in Los Yoses, Av 10, C 33/35 (☎224-9034); *Finland*, 9th floor, Edificio Centro Colón, Paseo Colón, C 38/40 (☎257-0210); *France*, in Curridabat, 200m south and 25m west of the San

José Indoor Club (☎225-0733); *Germany*, in Rohrmoser 200m north and 50m west of the Residencial España (☎232-5533); *Guatemala*, on the road to Pavas from Sabana Oeste (☎231-6645 or 6654); *Honduras*, in Los Yoses, 300m east and 200m north of ITAN (☎234-9502); *Mexico*, Av 7, C 13/15 (☎222-5528 or 5485); *Netherlands*, in Los Yoses, Av 8, C 35/37 (☎234-0949); *Nicaragua*, Av 0, C 25/27 (☎222-2373 or 233-8747; Mon–Fri 8am–noon; visas issued but 24hr turnaround minimum – more like 48hr); *Norway*, 10th floor, Edificio Centro Colón, Paseo Colón, C 38/40 (☎257-1414); *Panamá*, 100m east and 50m north of the *Hotel Torremolinos*, off Paseo Colón at C 40, Av 5 bis (☎221-4784; fax 257-4940); *Peru*, in Los Yoses, 200m south and 50m west of the Automercado (☎225-9145); *Spain*, C 32, Paseo Colón/Av 2 (☎222-1933; fax 221-2908); *Switzerland*, 4th floor, Edificio Centro Colón, Paseo Colón, C 38/40 (☎221-4829; fax 255-2831); *UK*, 11th floor, Edificio Centro Colón, Paseo Colón, C 38/40 (☎221-5566 or 5816; fax 233-9938); *USA*, in Pavas, opposite the Centro Comercial – take bus to Pavas from Av 1, C 18 (☎220-3939; 8am–4pm Mon–Fri; after hours ☎220-3127);*Venezuela*, in Los Yoses, Av 2, C 37/39 (☎225-5813 or 8810).

Film processing San José is the only place in the country you should try to get film processed. That said, it's expensive and quality is low: wait until you get home if you can. Bearing in mind these caveats, try *Universal*, Av 0, C 0/1 (process Fuji only, can do 1hr); *IFSA*, Av 2, C 3/5 (☎223-1444; process Kodak only; 1hr); *Dima*, Av 0, C 3/5 (☎222-3969).

Hospitals The city's public (social security) hospital is *San Juan de Díos*, Paseo Colón, C 14/16 (☎222-0166). Of the **private hospitals** foreigners are most often referred to *Clínica Biblica*, Av 14, C Central/1 (☎223-6422 or 221-3922); basic consultation and treatment (ie a prescription of a course of antibiotics) costs about $100 in the first instance. *Clínica Americana*, Av 14, C Central/1 (daily and holidays; ☎222-1010) is also good.

Immigration Costa Rican *Migración* is on the airport highway, opposite the Hospital México (take an Alajuela bus and get off at the stop underneath the overhead catwalk). Go here, early, for visa extensions and exit visas. Larger travel agencies can take care of the paperwork for you for a fee (anywhere from $10 to $25).

Laundry *Burbujas*, 50m west and 25m south of the *Mas x Menos* in San Pedro (☎224-9822); *Lava Más*, C 45, Av 8/10, next to *Spoon* in Los Yoses (☎225-1645); *Lava y Seca*, 100m north of *Mas x Menos* next to Autos San Pedro (☎224-5908); *Lavamatic Doña Anna*, C 13, Av 16; *Sixaola* (one of a chain), Av 2, C 7/9 (☎221-2111).

Libraries and cultural centres *Biblioteca Nacional* (see p.78); *Centro Cultural Costarricense-Norteamericano* (see p.80); *Goethe Institut* (see p.80); *Alianza Francesa*, (see p.77) stocks *Le Monde* and some magazines in French.

Post office *Correo Central*, C 2, Av 1/3, two blocks east and one block north of the Mercado Central (Mon–Fri 7am–5pm, Sat 7am–noon). The *lista de correos* is a safe way to receive mail; they'll hold letters for up to 4 weeks (10¢/letter; bring passport).

Sports The Sports Complex behind the *Museo de Arte Costarricense* on Parque la Sabana, has a gym, running track and Olympic-size pool ($3). The park, which also has tennis courts, is as good a place as any for jogging, with changing facilities and shower; in the morning there are lots of other runners about (there have been reports of assaults on lone joggers in the evening and it is wise to stay away from the heavily forested northeastern corner of the park – otherwise it is perfectly safe). Parque de la Paz in the south of the city is also recommended for running; in San Pedro you can jog at UCR campus. Swim at Ojo de Agua, 17km northwest of town (bus from Av 2, C 20/22; 15 min). The *Club Deportivo Cipresses*, set in nice suburban landscaped grounds 700m north of La Galera in Curridabat (☎253-0530) has day membership ($7) giving access to weights, machines, pools and aerobics classes. *Gymnasio Perfect Line*, downtown, on the 6th floor above the *Soltano* store (☎221-0537) has a weights room and regular step classes.

Telephone offices *Radiográfica*, C 1, Av 5 (☎223-2720 or 221-3303) is a state-run telecommunications shop where you can use directories, make overseas calls, send and receive faxes (☎223-1609 or 233-7932; 75¢). The *ICE* (*Instituto Costarricense de*

Electricidad) office next door on Av 5 has the same services at slightly higher prices. For more details on Costa Rica's telephone system, see p.34 in *Basics*.

Moving on from San José

San José is the **transportation hub** of Costa Rica. Most bus services, all express bus services, flights and car rental agencies are located here. Wherever you are in the country, technically you are never more than nine hours by highway from the capital, with the majority of destinations being only four or five hours by road. Eventually, like it or not, all roads lead to San José.

The tables on pp.96–98 deal with **express bus services** from San José. Regional bus information is covered in the relevant accounts in the *Guide*. As schedules are given to change, and because this is a quick reference rather than a bible, exact departure times are not given here. Details are given where necessary in the separate accounts of the individual destinations; for a full timetable when you arrive, ask at the ITC office (see p.64).

BUS COMPANIES IN SAN JOSÉ

A bewildering number of **bus companies** use San José as their hub: the following is a rundown of their head office addresses, and/or phone numbers and the abbreviations that we use in the tables overleaf.

ALF	*Transportes Alfaro*, C 14, Av 3/5 (☎222-2750).
BA	*Barquero* (☎232-5660).
BL	*Autotransportes Blanco*, C 12, Av 9.
BM	*Buses Metropoli* (☎272-0651).
CA	*CARSOL Transportes*, C 14, Av 3/5 (☎221-1968).
CL	*Coopelimón*, Av 3, C 19/21 (☎223-7811).
CO	*Coopecaribeños*, Av 3, C 19/21 (☎223-7811).
CPT	*Coopetragua* (☎223-1276).
CQ	*Autotransportes Ciudad Quesada*, C 16, Av 1/3 (☎255-4318).
EM	*Empresa Esquivel* (☎666-1249).
ME	*Transportes MEPE*, Av 11, C Central/1 (☎257-8129).
MO	*Transportes Morales*, C 16, Av 1/3 (☎223-5567 or 1109).
MRA	*Microbuses Rapidos Heredianos*, C1, Av 7/9 (☎238-8392 or 3277).
MU	*Transportes Musoc*, C 16, Av 1/3 (☎222-2422).
PU	*Pulmitan*, C 14, Av 1/3 (☎222-1650; in Liberia ☎666-0458).
S	*SIRCA*, C 7, Av 6/8 (☎222-5541 or 223-1464).
SA	*SACSA*, C 5, Av 18 (☎233-5350).
Tica	*Ticabus*, C 9, Av 4/6 (☎221-8954 or 9229).
TIL	*Autotransportes Tilarán*, C 14, Av 9/11 (☎222-3854).
TRA	*TRALAPA*, C 20, Av 1/3 (☎221-7202).
TRC	*TRACOPA*, Av 18, C 2/4 (☎221-4214 or 223-7685).
TRS	*Transtusa* (☎556-0073).
TU	*Tuasa* (☎222-5325 or 233-7477).
Tuan	*Tuan* (☎441-3781).

DOMESTIC BUS SERVICES FROM SAN JOSÉ

The initials in the ☎ column correspond to the bus company that serves this route; see p.95 for telephone numbers. Where advance purchase is mentioned, it is advised, and strongly recommended in the high season (HS), or at weekends; ie from Friday to Sunday (WE). You need buy your ticket no more than one day in advance unless otherwise indicated. NP = National Park; WR = Wildlife Refuge, NM = National Monument.

TO	FREQUENCY	BUS STOP	DISTANCE	DURATION	☎	ADV/PURCHASE
Alajuela (and airport)	every 5min	Av 2, C 10/12	17km	30min	TU	no
Volcán Arenal see Fortuna						
Braulio Carrillo NP see Guápiles						
Playa Brasilito	2 daily	C 20, Av 3	320km	6hr	TRA	yes (WE)
Cahuita	3 daily	Av 11, C 0/1	195km	4hr	ME	yes (HS)
Caño Negro WR see Los Chiles						
Cartago	every 10min	C 5, Av 18	22km	45min	SA	no
Los Chiles	2 daily	C 16, Av 1/3	217km	5hr	CQ	no
Chirripó NP see San Isidro						
Playa Coco	1 daily	C 14, Av 1/3	251km	5hr	PU	yes (WE)
Corcovado NP see Puerto Jiménez de Osa						
Playa Flamingo	2 daily	C 20, Av 3	320km	6hr	TRA	yes (WE)
Fortuna	3 daily	C16, Av 1/3	130km	4hr 30min	BA	yes (HS)
Golfito	3 daily	Av 18, C 2/4	339km	8hr	TRC	yes (3 days)
Guápiles	26 daily	C 12, Av 7/9	30km	35min	CPT	no
Guayabo NM see Turrialba						
Heredia	every 10min	C 1, Av 7/9	11km	25min	MRA	no
Playa Hermosa	1 daily	C 12, Av 5/7	265km	5hr	EM	no
Volcán Irazú	1 on Sat, 1 on Sun	Av 2, C 1/3	54km	1hr 30min	BM	no (but go early)
Playa Jacó	2 daily	C 16, Av 1/3	102km	2hr 30min	MO	yes (WE)
Playa Junquillal	1 daily	C 20, Av 3	298km	5hr	TRA	no
Liberia	8 daily	C 14, Av 1/3	217km	4hr	PU	no

TO	FREQUENCY	BUS STOP	DISTANCE	DURATION	CL/CO	ADV/PURCHASE
Limón	14 daily	Av 3, C 19/21	162km	2hr 30min	TIL	no
Manuel Antonio NP *see* Quepos						
Monteverde	2 daily	C 14, Av 9/11	167km	3hr 30min	TIL	yes (3/5 days)
Nicoya	8 daily	C 14, Av 3/5	296km	6hr	ALF	no
Nosara	1 daily	C 14, Av 3/5	361km	6hr	ALF	no
Palmar Norte/Sur	6 daily	Av 18, C 2/4	258km	5hr	TRA	no
Playa Panamá	1 daily	C 12, Av 5/7	265km	5hr	EM	no
Volcán Poás	1 on Sun	C 12, Av 2/4	55km	1hr 30min	TU	no (but go early)
Playa Potrero	2 daily	C 20, Av 3	320km	6hr	TRA	yes (WE)
Puerto Jiménez de Osa	2 daily	C 12, Av 7/9	378km	9hr	BL	yes
Puerto Viejo de Sarapiquí	6 daily	Av 11, C 0/1	97km	4hr	check with ITC	no
Puerto Viejo de Talamanca	3 daily	Av 11, C 0/1	210km	4hr 30min	ME	yes
Puntarenas	26 daily	C 16, Av 10/12	110km	2hr	PU	no
Quepos	3 daily	C 16, Av 1/3	145km	3hr 30min	MO	yes (3 days)
Sámara	1 daily	C 14, Av 3/5	331km	6hr	ALF	yes (WE)
San Carlos/Ciudad Quesada	14 daily	C 16, Av 1/3	110km	3hr	CQ	no
San Isidro	13 daily	C 16, Av 1/3	136km	3hr	TRC/MUS	no
Santa Cruz	5 daily	C 20, Av 1/3	274km	5hr	TRA	no
Sarchí	34 daily	C 8, Av 0/1	152km	1hr 30min	Tuan	no
La Selva, Selva Verde etc *see* Puerto Viejo de Sarapiquí						
Tamarindo	1 daily	C 20, Av 3	320km	6hr	TRA	yes (WE)
Turrialba	17 daily	C 13, Av 6/8	65km	1hr 30min	TRS	no
Zarcero	14 daily	C 16, Av 1/3	177km	2hr	CQ	no

INTERNATIONAL BUS SERVICES FROM SAN JOSÉ

Codes given under the ☎ column correspond to the relevant bus company (see p.95).
Advance purchase – at least a week in advance, particularly for Managua and Panamá
City – is necessary for all routes.

TO	FREQUENCY	BUS STOP	DISTANCE	DURATION	☎
David, Panamá	2 daily	Av 18, C 2/4	400km	9hr	Tica
Guatemala City (overnight in Managua & El Salvador)	1 daily	Av 4, C 9/11	1200km	60hr	Tica
Managua, Nicaragua	Mon, Wed, Fri, Sat	Av 4, C 9/11	450km	11hr	Tica
Managua, Nicaragua	Wed, Fri, Sun	C 7, Av 6/8	450km	13hr	S
Panamá City	1 daily	Av 4, C 9/11	903km	20hr	Tica
Paso Canoas (for Panamá)	5 daily	Av 18, C 2/4	349km	8hr	TRC
Peñas Blancas (for Nicaragua & Santa Rosa NP)	4 daily	C 14, Av 3/5	293km	6hr	CA
Sixaola (for Panamá)	3 daily	Av 11, C 0/1	250km	6hr	ME
Tegulcigalpa, Honduras (overnight in Managua)	1 daily	Av 4, C 9/11	909km	48hr	Tica

DOMESTIC FLIGHTS FROM SAN JOSÉ

Sansa, C 24, Paseo Colón/Av 1
(☎223-4179; reservations ☎233-3258 or 0397; fax 255-2176).

TO	FREQUENCY	DURATION
Barra del Colorado	1 Mon, Thurs, Sat	30min
Golfito	1 Sat, Mon, Tues; 2 Wed, Thur, Fri	45min
Nosara	1 Mon, Wed, Fri	1hr 25min
Palmar Sur	1 Tues, 2 daily Wed–Sat & Mon	1hr 30min
Puerto Jiménez	daily except Sun	1hr 15min
Quepos	2 daily Mon–Sat, 1 Sun	20min
Sámara	1 Tues, Thurs, Sat, Sun, 2 Mon, Wed, Fri	1hr 45min
Tamarindo	1 Tues, Thurs, Sat, Sun, 2 Mon, Wed, Fri	40min
Tambor	1 daily	20min

Travelair, Tobías Bolaños airport, Pavas (☎220-3054 or 232-7883; fax 220-0413).

Barra del Colorado	1 daily	30min
Golfito	1 daily	1hr 15min
Nosara	1 daily	1hr 25min
Palmar Sur	1 daily	1hr 30min
Quepos	1 daily (low season)	20min
	3 daily (high season)	20min
Sámara	1 daily	1hr 45min
Tamarindo	1 daily	40min
Tambor	1 daily	20min

Domestic flights from San José are run by *Sansa*, the state airline, and *Travelair*, a commercial company. *Sansa*, who fly from Juan Santamaría International airport, 17km northwest of the city, change their schedules frequently: best phone ahead or double-confirm when booking. *Travelair*, more reliable in terms of schedules, fly from Pavas airport, 7km west of the city. Although the table below gives as accurate a rundown of the routes as possible, flight durations are subject to change at the last minute. Some of the routings, particularly those to Nicoya Peninsula, tend to be roundabout, with one or two stops quite usual. Note that advance purchase (14 days) is necessary to ensure yourself a seat during the high season, especially for Quepos, Sámara and Tamarindo. Both companies have offices and agents throughout the country in most of the destinations they serve, or you can book and pay for tickets at a travel agent.

Sansa check-in is at the San José office (see p.93) one hour before departure; they lay on a free bus to get to you the airport and in some cases have free transfers to your hotel at your destination. Fares range from $35 and up one-way, to $70–80 return for most destinations. *Travelair* is typically $10–15 more expensive.

CHAPTER TWO

THE VALLE CENTRAL AND THE HIGHLANDS

osta Rica's **Valle Central** (literally "Central Valley") and surrounding Highlands form the cultural and geographical fulcrum of the country. A huge, wide-hipped inter-mountain plateau at elevations between 3000 and 4000m, the area – often also referred to as the *Meseta Central*, or "Central Tableland" – has a patchwork-quilt beauty, especially when lit by the early morning sun, with staggered green coffee terraces set in sharp contrast to the blue-black summits of the surrounding mountains. Many of these are **volcanos**: the Valle Central is contained within a nearly complete "ring of fire", formed by smoking Poás in the northwest, precipitous Irazú to the southeast and largely dormant Barva and Turrialba in the east. Though there have been no *bona fide* eruptions since Irazú blew its top in 1963, Poás and Irazú periodically spew and snort, raining a light covering of fertile volcanic ash on the surrounding farmland.

Although it occupies just six percent of the country's total landmass, the Valle Central supports roughly two-thirds of Costa Rica's population. The most fertile land in the country, it is also home to the four most important cities – San José, covered in Chapter One, and the provincial capitals of **Alajuela**, **Heredia** and **Cartago**. Tremendous pressure on land is noticeable even on short forays from San José. Urban areas, suburbs and highwayside communities blend into each other, and in places you'll see every spare patch of soil planted with coffee bushes, fruit trees or vegetables.

Chief attractions, of course, are the volcanos, especially **Parque Nacional Irazú** and **Parque Nacional Poás**, and **Volcán Barva**, sheltered within the huge **Parque Nacional Braulio Carrillo**, but there's also **whitewater rafting** on the Reventazón river near Turrialba, and rainforest hiking at **Parque Nacional Tapantí**. Most people use San José as a base for forays into the Valle Central; while the **provincial capitals** each have their own strong identity, with the exception of Alajuela – nearer than the capital to the airport – they have little to entice you to linger. If you do want to get out of the city and stay in the Valle Central, the nicest places are the lodges and inns scattered throughout the countryside.

Mountainous terrain and narrow, winding, unlit roads can make **driving** difficult, if not dangerous. Many Ticos commute from the Valle Central and Highlands to work in San José, so there is a fast, efficient and frequent **bus** network plying the town routes; but some interesting areas – notably Poás, Irazú and Tapantí – remain frustratingly out of reach by public transport, either through distance or inconvenient schedules. In many cases the only (expensive) recourse is to rent a car or take a taxi from the nearest town, or join an organized tour from San José.

Some history

Little is known about the **indigenous** inhabitants of the Valle Central, except that they had lived in the valley for at least 12,000 years, cultivating corn and grouping themselves in small settlements like the one excavated at **Guayabo**, near Turrialba. In 1559 King Philip of Spain and his New World administrators in the Spanish Crown seat of Guatemala decided that it was high time to **colonize** the area between modern-day Nicaragua and Panamá. The Valle Central was chosen mainly for its fertility and because it was far enough from both coasts to be safe from pirate raids; in 1561 the first *conquistadors* of Costa Rica founded a permanent settlement, **Garcimuñoz**, in the west of the region. Three years later Juan Vazquez de Coronado founded another settlement at modern-day Cartago, but the history of the Valle Central, like the rest of the country, has less to do with the development of towns and urban culture than with agriculture and farming.

The first **settlers**, just like those who went to the other countries of the Central American isthmus, dreamed of easy riches and new-found status, and expected to be met with a ready-made population of slave labour. Though they did find land rich in agricultural potential, little else conformed to their expectations: no settlements, no Bishop (he was in Nicaragua), no churches, no roads (until 1824 there was only the Camino Real, a mule path to Nicaragua, and a thin ox-cart track to Puntarenas), no Spanish currency, no way of earning cash and, crucially, far less free labour than they had hoped.

The indigenous inhabitants of the Valle Central proved largely unwilling to submit, either to the system of slave labour, called *encomienda,* or to the taxation forced upon them. Some tribes and leaders collaborated with the settlers, but in general they did what they could to resist the servitude the Spanish tried to impose, often fleeing to the jungles of Talamanca. The settlers, then, had little alternative but to leave for elsewhere, vent their frustrations in fights among themselves – unruliness and resentments prevailed for the first hundred years or so of colonization – or settle down and till their own fields, which, eventually, they did. Ironically, many of the first families ended up living as much in a "primitive" state as those peoples they had hoped to exploit. No materials for fabric were available or could be bought, so the immigrants had little choice but to don rough clothes of goatshair and bark. Currency was scarce, and cash-earning activities almost non-existent, so in 1709 the cacao bean – also the currency of the indigenous peoples the immigrants supplanted – was adopted as a kind of barter currency and used as such until 1850.

Throughout the 1700s the *criollo* (meaning a Spaniard born in the New World, rather than in Spain) *campesinos* spread ever westward in the Valle Central. A population of yeoman farmers developed; almost wholly independent, they lived on isolated farms, rarely venturing into "towns", which barely existed until well into the eighteenth century. To an extent Costa Rica's avoidance of the dual society that characterizes other isthmus countries, in which the poor are miserably poor and the rich exceedingly rich, rests upon this initial period of across-the-board poverty and backwardness. Because the Spanish newcomers did not succeed in constructing a properly colonial society, there was an absence of large-scale servitude on big farms in the Valle Central.

Though some twentieth-century historians point to this period as the crucible in which modern-day Costa Rica's largely middle-class society and devotion to the principles of independence and social equality were born, more recent theories (including those expressed in writing by political scientist, former

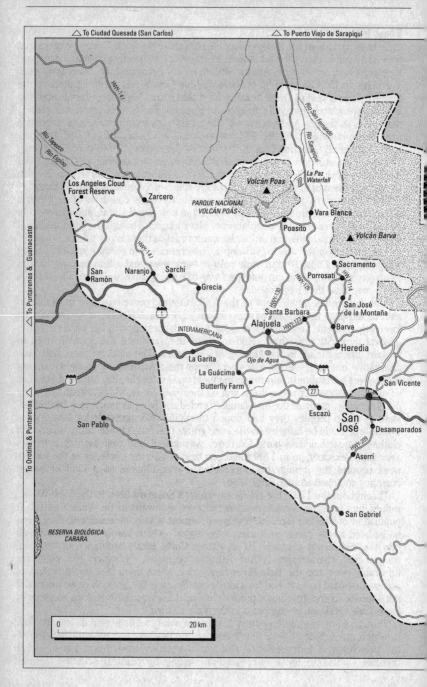

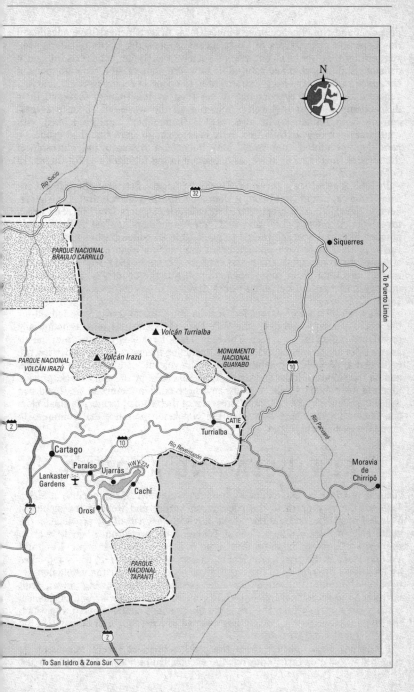

president and Nobel peace prize winner Oscar Arias Sánchez) have questioned this depiction of the roots of Costa Ricans' supposedly innate egalitarianism, suggesting that the nascent *criollo* society was quite conscious of social divisions and, in fact, manufactured them where none existed. Though many of the *conquistadors* were from Extramadura, the poorest region in Spain, and had acquired their titles by conquest rather than by inheritance, they and their descendants thought themselves superior to the waves of "poor peasants" coming from Andalucía. In turn, settled "commoner" families looked with contempt upon new arrivals, and there is evidence to show that, had economic conditions permitted, they would have imposed a system of indentureship of the *mestizo* (mixed-race) stock, as happened in the highlands of Nicaragua, El Salvador and Guatemala.

In 1808, Costa Rica's governor, Tomás de Acosta, first brought **coffee** here from Jamaica; a highland plant, it flourished in the Valle Central. Legislators, keen to develop a cash crop, offered incentives to farmers – in 1821, San José's town council offered free land and coffee seedlings to the settlers, while families in Cartago were ordered to plant 20 to 25 coffee bushes in their back yards. In 1832 there were enough beans available for export, and real wealth – at least for the exporters and coffee brokers – came in 1844, when the London market for Costa Rican coffee opened up. It was the country's main source of income until war and declining prices devastated the domestic market in the 1930s.

Coffee is still a major earner for Heredia and Cartago provinces – indeed for the whole country – and today the Valle Central remains the most economically productive region in Costa Rica. The huge black tarpaulins you see from the air as you fly in are flower nurseries. Fruits, including mangoes and strawberries, are cultivated in Alajuela; vegetables thrive in the volcanic soil near Poás and Irazú, and on the slopes of Irazú and Barva, Holstein cattle, prized dairy stock, provide much of the country's milk. Venture anywhere outside the urban areas and you will see evidence of the continued presence of the yeoman farmer, as small plots and family holdings survive despite the population pressure that continues to erode the available farmland.

ALAJUELA AND AROUND

Alajuela province is vast, extending from **Alajuela** town, 20km northwest of San José, all the way north to the Nicaraguan border and west to the slopes of Volcán Arenal. The account here deals only with that part of the province on the south side of the Cordillera Central, spanning the area from Alajuela itself to the town of Zarcero, 59km northwest, up in the Highlands. **Parque Nacional Volcán Poás** is the area's principal attraction, with some great trails and lakes on its slopes; the ride up to the crater gives good views over the whole densely populated, heavily cultivated province, passing flower-growing *fincas*, fruit farms and the occasional coffee field. In general the **climate** is good; Alajuela is considerably warmer than San José, and the province contains two towns which the National Geographic Society has deemed to have the "best climates in the world" – Atenas and **La Garita**.

People also head out here to see the crafts factories at **Sarchí**, famous for its coloured wooden ox-carts; **Zoo-Ave**, the exceptional bird sanctuary and zoo just outside town on the way to La Garita; and the **Butterfly Farm** at La Guácima. There's also the little-visited **Los Angeles cloudforest**, a miniature version of the better-known cloudforest at Monteverde, and **Ojo de Agua**, a thermal water-fed swimming and recreation complex near the Juan Santamaría airport, popular with *Joséfinos* as a place to escape the city.

Alajuela

With a population of just 35,000, **ALAJUELA** is nonetheless Costa Rica's "second city". Indeed, on first sight there's little to distinguish it from San José, until the pleasant realization dawns that walking down the street you can smell bougainvillea rather than diesel. This is still a largely agricultural centre, with a **Saturday market** that brings hundreds of farmers from the surrounding area, selling their fruit, vegetables, dairy products and flowers.

Founded in 1657, Alajuela's most cherished historical figure is the drummer-boy-cum-martyr **Juan Santamaría**, hero of the battle of 1856, who sacrificed his life to save the country from the avaricious desires of the American adventurer William Walker (see p.228). Today Santamaría is celebrated in his own **museum**, about the only formal attraction in town. All in all, Alajuela can be "done" in a morning or afternoon, but it makes a convenient base for the arts-and-crafts-oriented village of **Sarchí** or to the butterfly farm at **La Guácima**. Above all it is

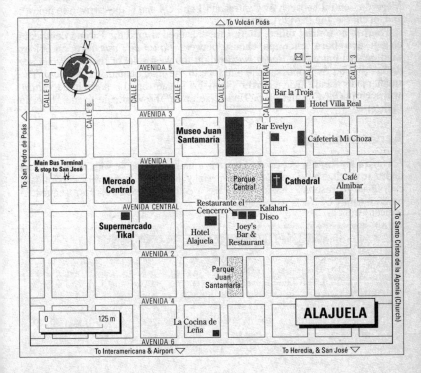

a useful place to stay for travellers who have to catch early morning flights; the **airport** is less than 3km away, about five minutes by bus in comparison to thirty to forty minutes from San José.

If you're here in mid-October, it's worth stopping to see the **Festival of San Geronado**, the patron saint of Alajuela, which takes place on the 16th. It's a very dignified affair, with well-ordered, flower-strewn parades and performances by school kids' orchestras in the Parque Central.

Arrival, orientation and information

Red/black *Tuasa* **buses from San José** arrive at the bus terminus area west of the centre; an inhospitable confusion of stalls, supermarkets and shoe stores. The beige/orange *Station Wagon Alajuela* drops you off about half a minute's walk from the Parque Central. If **driving**, take the *pista* to the airport (General Cañas Highway), which is also the road to Puntarenas. The turnoff to Alajuela is 17km from San José – don't use the underpass or you'll end up at the airport.

Alajuela's peaceful **Parque Central** (officially called Plaza del General Tomás Guardia) forms the focal point of the grid of streets, skirted by Avenida Central and Calle Central, the town's main thoroughfares. Like in San José, calles and avenidas go up by twos, and even more so than in San José, no one pays attention to street numbers, instead giving directions in relation to known **landmarks**. Most popular are *Supermercado Tikal* on Av Central between C 8 and 10; the Mercado Central between Av Central and 1 and C 4 and 6; the *correo* (see below); and, of course, the Parque Central.

There is no **tourist office. Banks** are clustered around the Parque Central: to change **travellers' cheques**, choose between *Banco de Costa Rica*, one block west on Av Central; the *Banco Nacional* on the west side; or the *Creditel/Banco de San José* on Av 3 opposite the entrance to the Juan Santamaría museum. The small, modern and efficient **correo** (Mon–Fri 7.30am–5pm) is north of the centre, at the corner of C 1 and Av 5. **Taxis** line up on the west side of the Mercado Central.

Accommodation

Alajuela's few **hotels** get booked up very quickly by people with early morning flights to catch. The *Hotel Alajuela*, especially, is often full: it is very important to call ahead to reserve. Outside town are a couple of good **resorts**, frequented predominantly by North Americans.

ACCOMMODATION PRICE CODES

All the establishments in this book have been given price codes according to the following scale. The prices quoted are for the least expensive double room in high season, and do not include the national 18.46 percent tax automatically added on to hotel bills. Wherever an establishment offers dorm beds the prices of these are given in the text. For more details see p.26.

① less than $10	③ $20–30	⑤ $50–75	⑦ $100–150
② $10–20	④ $30–50	⑥ $75–100	⑧ $150 plus

In town

Charly's Albergue, 200m north and 25m east of Parque Central (☎441-0115). Eleven large clean rooms with private bath and hot running water. Also a lounge with TV and kitchen area. Mainly gringo crowd. ③.

Hotel Alajuela, southwest corner of Parque Central and C 2 (☎441-1241 or 6595; fax 441-7912; Aptdo 110-4050). Comfortable, quiet hotel for an older, well-heeled clientele. Clean, pleasant rooms, some with kitchenettes. ④.

Hotel Villa Real, 100m south of the *correo* (☎441-4856). Operated by Fabio and friends, this budget travellers' hang-out is a great place to meet people, from Panamanian jazz musicians to surfers. Rooms are clean and bright with Guatemalan print blankets and colourful wall hangings, and there's a lounge, small kitchen, and library. The only drawbacks are the shared bathroom and noise in the evenings. ②.

Around Alajuela

Chatelle Country Resort, from the *Fiesta del Maíz* restaurant on the road through La Garita, turn left and drive 1.5km (☎448-7781; fax 448-7095; Aptdo 755, Centro Colón, San José). Hexagonal chalets, with conical wooden roofs inspired by Bolivian village architecture. Very quiet, with kitchen, terrace, pool, a restaurant serving international food, and great views. Airport pick-up and tours available. ⑧.

Orquideas Inn, 5km outside Alajuela on the road to Poás (☎443-9363; fax 443-9740; Aptdo 394, Alajuela). Spanish hacienda-style country inn with enormous rooms, landscaped gardens, attentive service, and pool. Adults only; mostly older clientele. ⑦.

The Town

Alajuela's few attractions are all less than a minute's walk from the Parque Central, though you'll have to go further to get to the large Baroque church east of the centre. Colonial buildings surround the park, their aesthetic effect ruined somewhat by the *Pepsi-cola*-banner-festooned storefronts. Most impressive is the sturdy-looking whitewashed former jail that now houses the **Juan Santamaría Cultural-Historical Museum** Av 3, C Central/2 (Tues–Sun 8am–6pm; free). Inside this fortress-like edifice, through the pretty tiled courtyard lined with long wooden benches, the dark, silent exhibition rooms are devoted to a nook-and-cranny, rather than corner, of regional history. The curiously monastic atmosphere is almost more interesting than the small collection, which runs the gamut from mid-nineteenth-century maps of Costa Rica to crumbly portraits of figures involved in the battle of 1856. A modern and comfortable auditorium hosts talks and conferences on topics of regional interest.

That's about it for sightseeing in the centre; the white domed no-name **Cathedral** which flanks the eastern end of the Parque Central was badly damaged in a 1990 earthquake and is still closed for repairs, while one block south of the Parque Central the small **Parque Juan Santamaría**, a paved-over empty plaza, centring on a jutting statue of the national hero, is something of a disappointment. Outside the centre, the town is leafy, quiet and residential, once in a while giving pretty views of the blue mountain ridges and bright green carpet of the Valle Central. Five blocks east of town is the church **Santo Cristo de la Agonía**; constructed in 1935, it looks older, Baroque in style, in two-tone cream. Inside there's a lovely wooden altar, bright and gilt-edged, with naif Latin American motifs, and gilt-painted columns edging the bright tiled floors. Realist murals, apparently painted from life, show various stages in the development of Christianity in Costa Rica, depicting Monsignors and indigenous peoples as well as good middle-class citizens gathering to receive The Word.

Eating, drinking and nightlife

Lunches and **pastries** are particularly plentiful and cheap in Alajuela, which has a number of good places to eat. Generally derided by *Joséfinos* for its (lack of) **nightlife** – many people still live in and around the centre, so pressure from residents means that bars close earlier than in the capital, at around 11pm – Alajuela does have two cinemas, one great bar, and a disco. On Sunday morning or Thursday evening the local **forty-piece band** plays orchestral and local favourites in the open-air gazebo in the Parque Central.

Bar Evelyn, C Central, Av Central/1. Small cosy place with no particular "scene", where you can sit at booths or at small bar.

Bar la Troja, Av 3, C 1/3 (☎441-4856). In a 100-year-old adobe house, this youthful bar is the most popular in town. Nice atmosphere, with a courtyard, small garden, gallery exhibiting local art, and even a serpentarium. Live rock or jazz Tues–Sat; they also organize surf and rafting outings.

Café Almibar, Av Central, C 1/3. Clean and quiet café, a favourite with locals for pastries and biscuits served with *café con leche*.

Cafeteria Mi Choza, C 1, 150m south of the *correo*. Superior, cheap breakfasts and lunches. Closes at 2pm and gets very busy – arrive early.

El Cencenerro, south side of Parque Central. Around for eighteen years or so, this steakhouse is an Alajuela institution and the only restaurant in town with any pretensions, serving succulent beef dishes for $7.

Las Cocinas de Leña, C 2, Av 6. Upscale establishment, particularly recommended for filet mignon and chicken cordon bleu, both cooked in a wood stove which give them a grilled, aromatic taste.

Joey's Bar and Restaurant, south side of the Parque Central. Open to the park, serving burgers and *típico* dishes. Extensive bar stock, too. Cable news and US sports on TV over the bar. Open 7am–midnight.

Kalahari, next to *Joey's* on south side of Parque Central. The only disco in Alajuela proper, highly popular with locals. Merengue and salsa only. Tues–Sun 8.30pm–2am.

Repostería las Espigas, C 1, Av 3. Expertly baked *pain au chocolat*, *pan dulce*, cakes and healthy breads. Small; takeout only.

MOVING ON FROM ALAJUELA

The fast and frequent red/black *Tuasa* bus to **San José** and **Heredia** stops at Alajuela's **main bus terminal**, in the covered enclosure north of Av Central. Even if your bus says "Alajuela–San José", check with the driver if it goes direct to San José or to Heredia first. **Naranjo** and **Sarchí** buses also leave from here.

Other **local buses**, to Grecia and **La Guácima Abajo** for the **Butterfly Farm**, leave from the unpaved lot south of the main terminal. It's a confusing area, with stops not well marked; ask around to make sure you are waiting at the right place. There is also a stopping service (*Station Wagons Alajuela*) to San José and the airport every few minutes from the centre of town, 100m south of Parque Central.

Around Alajuela

The most popular excursions in the Valle Central lie within 30km of Alajuela, including **Volcán Poás**, one of the most visited National Parks in the country. Closer to town, **La Guacimá Butterfly Farm** and the aviary at **Zoo-Ave** are

THE STRAWBERRY TRAIL

You can't fail to notice that the area around Volcán Poás is practically the only place in the country where **strawberries** are grown. Two fruit-related **restaurants** make possible stops on the way from Alajuela to the volcano; *Chubascos*, about 15km from Alajuela on the road to Poás, is famous among Ticos for superlative local cuisine, including the usual *casados* and large lunch plates, but succulently cooked with extra-fresh ingredients. If you try nothing else, sample the strawberry *refresco*, which is absolutely the best anywhere. *Las Fresas*, on the road to San Pedro de Poás, has fantastic wood-oven-cooked pizzas and several strawberry dishes. It's closed on Wednesday.

unabashed tourist attractions, while slightly further afield, in the northwest of the province, you can visit the crafts-making enclave of **Sarchí** and the atmospheric mountain town of **Zarcero**.

Parque Nacional Volcán Poás

PARQUE NACIONAL VOLCÁN POÁS (daily 8am–3pm; $15 on the day, $10 in advance) just 55km from San José and 37km north of Alajuela, is one of the most easily accessible active volcanos in the world, with a history of eruptions that goes back 11 million years. Poás' last gigantic blowout was on January 25, 1910, when it dumped 640,000 tons of ash on the surrounding area. In 1989 the Park was closed much of the year, due to the intensity of the volcano's spewings, and from time to time you may find that Poás has been closed due to sulphurous gas emissions, so it is worth checking conditions before you set off with the **National Parks Service** or the ICT in San José.

Outside the park, on the flanks of the volcano, **La Paz**, the most photographed waterfall in Costa Rica, is near Varablanca, about 4500m northeast of the hamlet of Poásito. From Poás, take the road east from Poásito for 3km, turn left at the crossroads, and about 10km further north you will see, quite unmissably, the waterfall tumbling down the cleft between Volcáns Poás and Barva. You can park and take pictures from the lookout point.

You need to get to the volcano before the clouds roll in, which they inevitably do, as early as 10am, even in the dry season (Dec–April). Poás has blasted out three craters in its lifetime: due to more or less constant activity, the appearance of the **main crater** (2704m) is subject to change. At present it's a large area, ripped 1500m wide, filled with murky moss-green water from where sulphurous gases waft and broil. Although it's an impressive sight, you only need about fifteen minutes' viewing and picture-snapping.

The Park features a few very well-maintained, short and unchallenging **trails**, which take you through a strange, otherworldly landscape, dotted with smoking, sizzling fumaroles (steam vents) and tough ferns and trees valiantly holding up against regular scaldings with sulphurous gases (the battle-scarred *sombrilla de pobre*, or poor man's umbrella, looks the most woebegone). Poás is also home to a rare version of cloudforest called **dwarf** or **stunted cloudforest**, a combination of pine-needle-like ferns, miniature bonsai-type trees, and bromeliad-encrusted ancient arboreal cover, all of which has been stunted through an onslaught of cold (it can get down to below freezing up here), continual cloud cover, and acid rain from the mouth of the volcano.

The **Crater Overlook trail**, which, as it name suggests, winds its way around the main crater, is only 750m long, along a paved road. A side trail (1km; 20–30min) heads off through the forest to the pretty, emerald **Botos Lake**, which fills an extinct crater and makes a good spot for a picnic. Named for the pagoda-like tree commonly seen along its way, the **Escalonia trail** (about 1km; 30min) starts at the picnic area (follow the signs), taking you through ground cover less stunted than that at the crater. **Birds** ply this temperate forest: among them, the ostentatiously colourful quetzal, the robin, and several species of hummingbird. Although a number of large **mammals** live in the confines of the Park, including coyotes, and wildcats such as the margay, you're unlikely to spot them around the crater. One animal you probably will come across, however, is the small, green-yellow **Poás squirrel**, which is found nowhere else in the world.

Getting to Volcán Poás

It is possible to get to Poás by public transport, but not ideal; to arrive early enough to be absolutely sure of a **cloud-free view** many people rent a car or a taxi, which, added to the admission charge, can hike the price of a visit up to as much as $60. A weekly private **"tourist bus"** leaves San José at 8am every Sunday from in front of La Merced park (also known as Parque Braulio Carrillo, not to be confused with the National Park of the same name; see p.118) on C 12 between Av 2 and 4. This is a small modern minibus, and though theoretically the company – *TURASA* – puts on another if there is excess demand, in order to secure a seat you should arrive at least an hour (more in the high season) before departure. The **return fare**, which doesn't include the Park fee, is $4. The bus makes a stop at the small hamlet of **Poásito**, perched high on the flank of Volcán Poás, where *Restaurante El Poás* has washrooms and refreshments; as there are currently no food and drink facilities at the volcano, make sure to stock up here. It arrives at the Park at around 10am, returning to San José at 1.30pm, which theoretically leaves ample time for hiking and crater-viewing – however, as it is common for the crater to be obscured by cloud by 10am, many visitors are left disappointed.

Sunday is by far the most popular day to visit the volcano; to get there mid-week, and avoid the crowds, you'll need to fork out for a taxi, as **public transport** is practically impossible. There's a bus from Alajuela as far as San Pedro de Poás, from where it is a 18km walk to the hamlet of Poásito, and another 10km to the volcano entrance. It's not even feasible to hitch these distances; traffic is sparse and tour buses and groups are unlikely to pick you up. A **taxi** from San Pedro de Poás (ask anywhere in the village) to the Park will cost between $25 and 30, waiting time included; the same price, roughly, as a taxi from Alajuela right to the entrance at Poás (again, waiting time included). Taxis from **San José** cost as much as $45 or 50; not so bad if split between four or five people.

The **visitor centre**, which used to house an "interpretive exhibit" and snack shop, is currently closed, due to damage inflicted by a recent spewing. Consequently there is nowhere to **eat or drink** at the volcano; if you're not on the weekly minibus from San José, which makes a refreshment stop (see above), do as Ticos do and pack a picnic lunch. Make sure to bring water and ideally a thermos of coffee, along with a sweater, **rain gear** and an umbrella. No **camping** is allowed in the Park.

Accommodation near the Park

If you want to get a really early start, to guarantee a view of Poás' crater, there are plenty of places to stay in the vicinity. There is no budget accommodation, however; with the exception of one, the establishments below are comfortable **"mountain lodges"** on working dairy farms, and you'll need a car to get to them.

Juanbo Mountain Resort, Restaurant and Cabins, 15km from Poás on the road between Varablanca and the La Paz waterfall (☎482-2099). On a dairy farm, set on a ridge of the continental divide between volcanos Barva and Poás. Cabinas with great views and a very good restaurant serving nouvelle cuisine (fried camembert with chutney sauce is good), open for breakfast, lunch and dinner to non-guests. ④.

Poás Volcano Lodge, 16km from Poás on the road from Poásito, just short of Varablanca (☎ and fax 441-9102; Aptdo 5723-1000, San José). Working dairy farm, with patches of private protected forest on the grounds and beautifully furnished rooms evoking a combination of English cottage, Welsh farmhouse and American Shaker. ⑤.

La Providencia Ecological Reserve, 1km from the Park entrance on the slopes of Poás (☎232-2498). Rustic cabinas on another working dairy farm, near the top of Poás, with spectacular views across to Volcán Arenal and the Talamanca mountains. The owners prepare excellent local food and rent out horses for trots up the volcano. ⑤.

Lo Que tu Quieras ("Whatever you want"), 5km before the Park entrance (☎482-2092). The cheapest option around here. Three small cabinas, with heated water and a restaurant. ②.

Sarchí and around

Touted as the centre of Costa Rican arts and crafts, especially **furniture making**, the village of **SARCHÍ**, 30km northwest of Alajuela, is a commercialized place – firmly on the tourist trail but without much charm. Its setting is pretty enough, between precipitous verdant hills, but don't come expecting to see picturesque scenes of craftsmen sitting in small historic shops, blowing glass, sculpting marble or carving wood. The **fábricas de carretas** (ox-cart factories) and the **mueblerías** (furniture factories) are large factory showrooms strung out along the main road and, granted that in the larger *fábricas* you can watch the painting and assembly of local crafts, there's not much to actually see. Nevertheless, the ox-carts and leather rocking chairs are cheaper here than anywhere else in the country; most people come on half-day shopping trips from the capital or stop on their way to Zarcero and the Zona Norte.

The **Sarchí ox-cart** is a kaleidoscopically coloured, painted square cart meant to be hauled by a single ox or team of two oxen. Moorish in origin, the designs can be traced back to immigrants from the Spanish provinces of Andalucía and Granada. Full-scale carts ($250–300) are rarely sold, but a number of smaller-scale versions are made for tourists (about $60). Faced with the question "But what, exactly, am I going to do with this at home?" the salespeople in Sarchí deftly whip off the top of the miniature cart to reveal a bar area with room for several bottles, a serving tray and an ice section. They sell like hotcakes.

Besides the carts, Sarchí tables, bedsteads and **leather rocking chairs** (about $70) are the most popular items. Other crafts are much the same as you'll see all over Costa Rica: wiggly wooden snakes, hand-polished wooden boxes and bowls, T-shirts and walking sticks, and the ubiquitous hokey wooden "home sweet home" wall hangings. Many of the *mueblerías* will freight-mail your ox-cart if you arrange this in advance.

FÁBRICAS DE CARRETAS AND CRAFT SHOPS IN SARCHÍ

Fábrica Chaverrí, Sarchí Sur, on the left-hand side of the road as you enter the village (☎454-4412; fax 454-4421). Sarchí's largest ox-cart factory, with a huge showroom. In the back you can wander around the painting workshop and see hundreds of ox-carts-in-progress. There's also a small soda where you can eat lunch outside at picnic tables and a free *Café Britt* kiosk. They will also arrange shipping and transport for souvenirs. Credit cards accepted.

Mercado de la Artesania, Sarchí Sur. Roadside mall-like group of shops and restaurants, arranged in a courtyard. Snazzy and pricey, with boutiques sell-

ing everything from Guatemalan vests to gold jewellery. Ox-carts are available from *Originales Sarchí* (☎454-4980; fax 454-4327) who can arrange freight transport (about $25 for a small cart, $90 for a big one to the US or Europe). There's also a *heladería* and a moderately priced fish restaurant, *La Troja*. The *Banco Nacional* can change dollars (Mon–Fri 8.30am–noon & 1–3.30pm).

Lalo Alfaro, at the north end of Sarchí Norte, on main road. The only *fábrica* where you can see actual working ox-carts being made for actual working oxen to pull. Not too many tourists here.

The village itself is spread out and divided into two halves. Large *fábricas* line the main road from **Sarchí Sur**, in effect a conglomeration of *mueblerías*, to the residential area of **Sarchí Norte**, which climbs the hill. Besides the shops and factories, the only thing of interest is Sarchí Norte's bubblegum coloured pink-and-turquoise **church**, looking out from atop the hill. Inside, the tiles are delicate pastel shades of pink and green; in the little park fronting the church, stone benches are painted with the same colourful designs you see on the ox-carts.

If you have time on the way to Sarchí, stop off to see the remarkable fin-de-siècle church in the small town of **GRECIA**, some 18km northwest of Alajuela. After their first church burned down, the prudent residents of Grecia decided to take no chances and built the second out of metal, for which pounded sheets had to be specially made and imported from Belgium. The rust-coloured and white-trimmed result is surprisingly beautiful, with an altar that is a singular testament to Latin American Baroque froth, made entirely from intricate marble and tottering up into the eaves of the church like a wedding cake.

Grecia is also the place to stop if you want to make the only **bungee jump** in the country: *Tropical Bungee* (☎233-6455) organize leaps from the bridge over the Río Colorado, just 8km west of the village. From San José there's a bus to Grecia every hour on the hour (or when full) from La Coca-Cola (5am–7pm; 1hr).

Sarchí practicalities

It goes without saying that if you intend to buy a large item, it's best not to come to Sarchí by public transport, as buses are always crowded and seats are tiny. However, if you have no choice, local **buses** from Alajuela run approximately every thirty minutes from 5am to 10pm. Buses back (via Grecia) can be hailed on the main road from Sarchí Norte to Sarchí Sur. From **San José** an express service (1hr–1hr 30min) runs from La Coca-Cola daily every thirty minutes from 5am to 10pm; the return schedule is the same. You could also take the bus to Naranjo from La Coca-Cola, every hour on the hour, and switch there for a local service to Sarchí. Call the *Tuan* bus company for information.

There is hardly anywhere to **stay** in Sarchí; though you could try the cabinas rented by the hardware store on the main street just above the church in Sarchí Norte. Enquire at the "rooms for rent" sign (☎454-4425; ②). For **lunch** or a snack, try the *Restaurant Nuevo Abuelo* on the corner of the central plaza; *Soda Donald* beside the soccer field is the only other place for a *refresco* or ice cream.

The *Banco Nacional* on the main road beyond the church **changes dollars and cheques** (Mon–Fri 8.30am–3pm), as does a smaller branch in the *Mercado de Artesanía*. If you need a **taxi** to ferry you back and forth between Sarchí Sur and Sarchí Norte, or to Alajeula or Zarcero, they can be called (☎454-4028) or hailed on the street.

Los Angeles Cloudforest Reserve

A private 800-hectare reserve, 60km or so from Alajuela, **LOS ANGELES CLOUDFOREST RESERVE** ($15) is often described as a cheaper and less crowded alternative to the Monteverde cloudforest (see p.264); that said, however, it is nowhere on the same scale. Climbing from 700m to nearly 2000m, Los Angeles is home to a number of habitats and microclimates, including, of course dark, impenetrable cloudforest, often shrouded in light misty cloud and resounding with the calls of monkeys.

Two rather short trails provide a good introduction to rainforest walking and the cloudforest habitat. Both are easy, along wooden boardwalks covered with non-slip corduroy. The third, much longer, trail (about 18–20km; 8hr hike in total), takes you to the junction of the Ríos Balsa and Espino, through a change in elevation and concurrently differing vegetations, and along paths that are cut but not fitted with corduroy. The administration offers **guided walks** for about $10 and **horseback rides** in the reserve for about $15 per hour. Ask at the *Hotel Villablanca* (see below).

Practicalities

Los Angeles can be reached from Hwy-141, the Naranjo–Zarcero road. The *Hotel Villablanca* in the reserve is signed from Naranjo, about 24km northwest of Alajuela. Take a left at the small village of Palmito north of Naranjo; then just follow the signs, turning right at an unpaved road leading to Villablanca. You can **stay** in the reserve at *Hotel Villablanca*, 20km north of San Ramón (☎228-4603; fax 228-4004; ⑦). Twenty chalets each have a fireplace and large well-fitted bathroom; there's a restaurant on site and a lounge with TV.

Zarcero

ZARCERO, 52km northwest of Alajuela on Hwy-141, sits virtually at the high point of this stretch of the Cordillera Central, in an astounding landscape where precipitous inclines, falling into deep gorges and valleys, are scaled by contented Holstein cattle. First impressions of Zarcero itself are of a pleasant mountain town, with crisp fresh air and ruddy-faced inhabitants. Head for the central plaza, however, where a pretty white church gleams in the sun, and you'll see the work of local Evangelisto Blanco, who has let vent his Doctor Seuss-like imagination, fashioning fabulous topiary sculptures – an elephant, a light bulb, a strange bird – and vaulting, Gaudí-esque archways from vines and hedges. There's little else to see in town, but Zarcero is also famous for its fresh, white, relatively bland

cheese called *palmito* (heart-of-palm, which is what it looks like). You can buy it from any of the shops near the bus stop on the south side of the central plaza.

Practicalities

Buses from San José to Zarcero leave hourly between 5am and 7.30pm from La Coca-Cola (1hr 30min). There are no **hotels** and only a few places to **eat**, all of which are around or near the central plaza, including *Restaurante Germanios* and *Pizzería Casa del Campo*, both serving cheap, good, local food. Next door to the latter, a bakery and sweet shop sells fresh and delicious cookies and cakes.

The bus stop for San Carlos/Ciudad Quesada and the **Zona Norte** is on the northwest corner of the central plaza (hourly; 1hr).

South of Alajuela

Twelve kilometres southwest of Alajuela, **La Guácima Butterfly Farm** (daily 9.30am–4.30pm, last tour at 3.30pm; $15, $10 with student ID) breeds valuable pupae for export to zoos and botanical gardens all over the world. Tours begin with an audiovisual exhibit introducing the processes involved in commercial butterfly breeding. Guides explain all aspects of butterfly life, including their cruelly short lifespan, while flashes of jewel colours flutter prettily around the mesh-enclosed breeding area. The farm also has beautiful views over the Valle Central; in the wet season make sure to go early, as the rain drives butterflies to ensconce themselves, and clouds obscure the views.

Buses from San José to La Guácima leave from Av 1, C 20/22, daily except Sunday at 11am and 2pm – the trip takes two hours, so get the earlier service. Return buses to the capital leave at 12.15pm and 3.15pm. From **Alajuela** buses marked "La Guácima Abajo" leave from the area southwest of the main bus terminal; the Butterfly Farm is practically the last stop, and they will let you off at the gates. Return buses pass the gates of the farm at about 11.45am, 1.45pm, 3.45pm and 5.45pm; get to the stop a little early just to make sure.

The largest aviary in Central America, **Zoo-Ave** (daily 9am–4.30pm; $4.50, $2 with student ID), at Dulce Nombre, 5km northeast of La Garita, is just about the best place in the country – besides the wild – to see the fabulous and many-coloured birds of Costa Rica's dense lowland forests and alpine heights. This is an exceptionally well-run exhibition, with large clean cages and carefully tended grounds. Many of the birds fly free, fluttering around in a flurry of raucous colours: look out for the kaleidoscopic *lapas* – **scarlet macaw** – and wonderful blue **parrots**. Other birds include chestnut mandibled **toucans** and the very fluffy **tropical screech owls**. There are also some **primates**, from monkeys to marmosets, again in large and well-tended areas. A sign in one of the enclosures says "There are 50 iguanas in this area. Can you find any?" – but there's not an iguana in sight, not *one* – camouflage experts should study these shy, skilled creatures. Ideally, you need a minimum of an hour to see everything. The La Garita bus from Alajuela passes right by Zoo-Ave, leaving from the area southwest of the main terminal. The trip takes about fifteen minutes.

Several kilometres beyond Zoo-Ave, the small hamlet of **LA GARITA** is known for its climate, chosen by the National Geographic Society as one of the best in the world. Fruits, ornamental plants and flowers flourish here, but the only reason to stop, really, is if you happen to be going through to **Jacó Playa** (see p.286) on the weekends when *Restaurante Fiesta del Maíz* ("Corn party") is open.

This is a very popular stop for Ticos heading from San José to Jacó, serving cheap (under $5) entrées and snacks, all made from corn. Many have no English translation and are endemic to Costa Rica, but all are pretty tasty, good with a cold drink. Open only Friday to Sunday and on holidays, the restaurant is on the left-hand side as you head toward the Pacific coast, opposite *Restaurante El Jardín*.

HEREDIA AND AROUND

Heredia province stretches northeast from San José all the way to the Nicaraguan border, skirted on the west by Hwy-9, the old road from San José to Puerto Viejo de Sarapiquí. To the east, the Guápiles Highway, Hwy-32, provides access to Braulio Carrillo and to Limón on the Caribbean coast. The moment you leave San José for **Heredia**, the provincial capital, the rubbery leaves of coffee plants spring up on all sides; in the section of the province covered in this chapter, the land is almost wholly given over to coffee production, and there are a number of popular **"coffee tours"**, especially to the *Café Britt finca* near Heredia town.

In the Valle Central, the province's chief attractions are **Parque Nacional Braulio Carrillo**, easily accessible from San José, where rainforest walks are laid out on well-maintained trails, and – officially within the Park, but approached by an entirely different route – dormant **Volcán Barva**, which offers a good day's climb. Just outside the Park, the **Rainforest Aerial Tram** allows you to see the canopy of primary rainforest from above, causing minimal disturbance to the animals and birds.

Heredia

Just 11km northeast of San José, **HEREDIA** is a lively city, boosted by the student population of the UNA, the Universidad Nacional, at the eastern end of town, and famed among Ticos for its **soccer team**, one of the best and most popular in the country. The town centre is prettier than most, with a Parque Central flanked by tall palms and a few historical buildings. Small and easy to navigate, Heredia is a natural jumping-off point for excursions to the nearby historical hamlet of **Barva** and to the town of **San José de la Montaña**, a gateway to **Volcán Barva**. Many tourists also come to sample the **Café Britt tour**, hosted by the nation's largest coffee exporter, about 3km north of the town centre.

Arrival and information

From **San José** *Microbuses Rapidos Heredianos* leave every ten minutes from 5am to 10pm. Another bus runs from C 12, Av 2 (every 20min), and after 10pm a night bus leaves from the marked stop at Av 2, C 4/6. Buses pull in to Heredia at the corner of C Central and Av 4, a stone's throw south of the Parque Central. There's also an unpredictable **train service** between the University of Costa Rica in San Pedro, San José and Heredia, but this is an on-again, off-again phenomenon; call *Intertren* (☎226-0011) to check.

There is no **tourist office** in town. *Banco Nacional* at C 2, Av 2/4 (Mon–Fri 8.30am–3.30pm) and *Banco de Costa Rica*, C1, Av 6, **exchange currency** and travellers' cheques, but it can be a time-consuming process. The **correo** is on the northwest corner of the Parque Central (Mon–Fri 7.30am–5.30pm). **Taxis** line up on the east side of the Mercado Central, between Av 6 and 8.

Accommodation

Decent accommodation in **downtown** Heredia is pretty sparse. It's unlikely, in any case, that you will need to stay in town; San José is within easy reach, and nearby there are some nice **B&Bs** as well as a couple of **"country resort"** type hotels, including one of the finest in the country. Although they are all accessible by bus, it's easier to drive.

Downtown

Hotel Heredia, C 6, Av 3/5 (☎237-1324). Homey whitewashed house in quiet residential area north of the centre. Decor is a bit dowdy, but rooms with bath are perfectly serviceable and clean. A reassuring sign says emphatically that it does *not* rent rooms by the hour. ②.

Verano, at the western entrance of the Mercado Central (☎237-1616). Cheap and very friendly, but otherwise devoid of charm. ①.

Around town

Cuesta de Sanchez, 4km north of Heredia (☎237-9851). Small *posada*: clean, rustic, friendly and comfortable. ③.

Finca Rosa Blanca, on the road between San Pedro de Barva and Santa Barbara de Heredia (☎269-9392; fax 269-9555). One of the best hotels in the country, like some beautiful giant white bird roosting above the coffee fields. Eight themed suites; the famous Tower Suite, with wraparound windows and a romantic four-poster, is continuously booked. Pool in the offing, but no TV (the idea is to relax). Excellent cuisine – Cuban, Californian and French – by hotel's own chef. Meals and tax included in package rates. ⑧.

Los Jardines B&B, 2km north of the Parque Central, before Barva village (☎260-1904). A good bet just outside town; comfortable rooms in a modern house with hot water and shared bath. Very friendly family owners will arrange airport pick-up. ③.

La Posada de la Montaña, San Isidro de Heredia, 8km northeast of Heredia (☎ and fax 268-8096; in USA: c/o PO Box 308, Greenfield, MO 65661). Rustic, comfortable rooms at varying prices. Some are suites with cable TV, kitchen, living room and fireplace (it gets chilly up here). Airport pick-up on request. ⑤.

The Town

Heredia's lay-out conforms to the general Costa Rican pattern; centring on a **Parque Central** and church, from which a grid of streets fan out before quickly becoming residential. The Parque Central is quiet, draped with huge mango trees and palms; its plain **Basílica de la Inmaculada Concepción**'s unexciting squat design – "seismic Baroque" – has kept it standing through several earthquakes since 1797. North of the Parque, the old colonial tower of **El Fortín**, "The Fortress", features odd gun slats, which fan out and widen from the inside to the exterior, giving it a medieval look. You cannot enter or climb the tower.

East on Avenida Central, the **Casa de la Cultura**, an old colonial house with a large breezy verandah, displays local art, including sculpture and painting by the schoolchildren of Heredia. The **Mercado Central** is a clean, orderly place, its wide aisles lined with rows of fruit and veg, dangling sausages and plump prawns.

The uncharacteristically light interior makes it a nicer place to shop than the markets in either San José or Alajuela.

Eating and drinking

Perhaps because of the student population, Heredia is crawling with excellent cafés, patisseries, ice-cream joints and the best vegetarian/health food **restaurants** outside San José. **Nightlife** is low-key, restricted to a few local salsa spots.

Azzura Italiana, southwest corner of Parque Central. Upmarket café with superior Italian ice cream, cappuccino, espresso, and fresh sandwiches.

Bar/Restaurante Mariscos, C6, Av 4. Uninspiring decor but good seafood and regular *típico* menu. Their business card says nothing of the food or service but does mention that "Jesucristo es la Solución".

Centro de Amigos, C Central, Av Central/2. Costa Rican cuisine served in big, comfortable booths until unusually late. Daily 11am–4am.

Deli Pollo, west side of the Parque Central. Fast-food type place, popular with students for lunch. Quick and filling chicken-and-potatoes or rice dishes for around $2.

Fresas, C 7, Av 1. Large and popular American-style restaurant with some outdoor seating. Typical soda food, with emphasis on just what the name implies – strawberries – with strawberry fruit cups, fruit salads and the like. About $6 for lunch.

Italian Patisserie, C Central, Av 6/8. Great coffee, from a gleaming silver espresso machine, ideally accompanied by the elaborate, tasty cakes on display. The modern, minimalist decor is welcome after the usual plastic-and-formica café/soda interiors.

Natura, C7, Av Central/1. Plant-adorned back area and wooden, rustic decor. Good vegetarian food; sandwiches made to order, yoghurt, sweets and coffee. Lunch only Mon–Fri.

Soda La Rustica, in the Mercado Central. Good cheap *casados* and *refrescos* and ungrudging counter service.

Yerbabuena, C7, Av Central/1. Macrobiotic vegetarian food served in small light dining area upstairs. Also sells brown and grain breads, cookies and cakes and macrobiotic delights such as bags of dried kelp. Lunch only Mon–Fri.

MOVING ON FROM HEREDIA

Heredia has no central bus terminal. A variety of **bus stops**, marked and signed, are scattered around town, with a heavy concentration around the Mercado Central. Buses **to San José** depart from C Central, Av 4 (about every 10min).

From the Mercado Central, local buses leave for **San Joaquín de Heredia**, **San Isidro de Heredia** and the swimming complex at **Ojo de Agua**. Buses to **San Rafael de Heredia** and on to **San José de la Montaña** depart from near the train tracks at Av 10 and C Central/2. For **Barva** and **Santa Barbara de Heredia** the stop is at C Central, Av 1/3. All leave fairly regularly, about every thirty minutes.

Around Heredia

North and east of Heredia the terrain climbs to higher altitudes, reaching its highest point at **Volcán Barva**, at the western entrance of the wild, rugged **Parque Nacional Braulio Carrillo**. Temperatures are notably cooler around here, the landscape dotted with dairy farms and conifers. Though the area in general gives a good picture of coffee-oriented agriculture and provincial Costa Rican life, none of the villages surrounding Heredia town offer much to persuade you to linger. The exception is for church aficionados, who could make jaunts out to a number of pretty **churches**, from the old colonial structure in **Barva** to **San Rafael**'s white and silver edifice, set high above the Valle Central, and the jolly twin-towered churches of **Santa Barbara de Heredia** and **San Joaquín de Heredia**.

Parque Nacional Braulio Carrillo

Many people only experience **PARQUE NACIONAL BRAULIO CARRILLO**, 20km northeast of San José (daily 8am–4pm; $15 on the day, $7 in advance), from the window of a bus on the way to the Caribbean coast. And, in fact, this isn't a bad way to see the place, giving majestic views of cloud and foliage rising up precipitously on both sides, and small white fingers of water cascading down sheer rock in the distance. Cool and often shrouded in cloud, with dense forest cover, much of the park is inaccessible to walkers, though there are a couple of well-maintained trails.

Named after Costa Rica's third, and rather dictatorial, chief of state, who held office in the mid-1800s, the Park was established in 1978, mainly to protect the land from the possible effects of the Guápiles Highway that was then in construction between San José and Limón. If not for the intelligent foresight on the part of the National Parks system, the whole stretch of the Park on both sides of the highway might have been a solid strip of gas stations and motels. As it is, after walking a kilometre or so from the highway, the sounds of the traffic disappear, and the Park becomes pristine and silent.

Braulio Carrillo's dense forested cover gives you a good idea of what much of Costa Rica used to look like about fifty years ago, when approximately three-

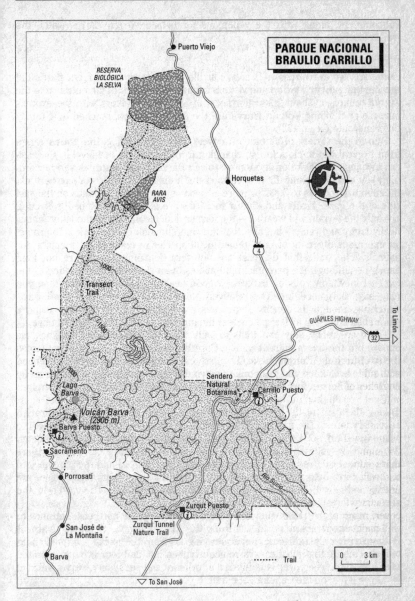

quarters of the country's total terrain was virgin rainforest. **Quetzals** have been sighted in the higher altitudes, as well as toucans, trogons and eagles, but while the Park is home to large mammals like the jaguar and ocelot, it is rare to see them. Braulio Carrillo is, however, one of the few places you are likely to spot a **bushmaster** (*matabuey*), the largest venomous snake on the subcontinent, along with the venemous fer-de-lance (*terciopelo*) – watch the trails closely.

Visiting the Park

There are two **entrances** to Braulio Carrillo. The majority of walkers start off at the **Zurquí ranger station** and visitors centre, 500m south of the entrance to the Zurquí tunnel, or about 20km northeast of San José. Walkers with the express purpose of climbing **Volcán Barva** use the *puesto* at Barva, reached by a totally different route (see p.122).

Due to the variety of altitudes it covers, Braulio Carrillo's **life zones** range from tropical wet to cloudforest, changing from 50m above sea level in the eastern lowlands to 2906m on the top of Volcán Barva. **Temperatures** vary accordingly – it can be a chilly 15°C or less on the trails from the Zurquí *puesto*, while the mercury rockets to 30°C or more as soon as you hit the lowlands on the east side of the Park. **Trails** and **visitor facilities** are not very developed, reflecting not only the terrain and weather – the former difficult and steep, the latter fantastically foggy and rainy – but also that the chief function of this Park is to protect an enormous diversity of flora (about 6000 species of plants) and a habitat for animals. The trails that do exist are not very demanding – they're not long enough – although the perennial mud makes them slippery, which, added to the fog that inevitably rolls in, makes it a good deal more dark and eerie than you may have bargained for. The relatively undisturbed cover yields good **birdwatching**, though its density sometimes renders everything invisible: using a pair of binoculars on a clear patch near the highway might be more productive.

There are really only two trails to walk from this entrance of the Park (as opposed to the Barva entrance). The **Capulin Loop trail** leads off from across the road from the Zurquí *puesto*. The first few hundred metres are steep, fenced with railings to keep you from falling down the highwayside rocks, but it rapidly levels out. After another few hundred metres you come to a fork: keeping straight will get you higher up into primary forest, where it becomes dense and dark. Taking the path to the right, you follow the lower side of the loop, through secondary forest. The primary forest section of the loop is about 1500m long, the secondary 1km, so you can walk the whole thing in about an hour if you steam through. Give yourself an hour more if you want to stop and look at the tanagers that frequent the tree limbs, or, if you're lucky, the quetzal and the bare-necked umbrella bird, both much more difficult to spot. In the primary forest, trees are heavily laden with mosses, strangler vines and epiphytes. The cover in the secondary forest is more open.

The other short trail begins at the Carrillo *puesto,* at the northeast entrance to the park, about 15km northeast from the Zurquí *puesto*. **Sendero Natural Botarama** is only 1km long, never straying far from the *puesto* – a good thing too, as it's here that most cars have been broken into and tour groups assaulted (see opposite). The cover is a mixture of primary and secondary, very similar to what you'll find on the Capulin Loop trail.

Practicalities

Getting to Braulio Carrillo **independently** couldn't be easier. From **San José**, buses to Guápiles, Siquerres and Puerto Viejo de Sarapiquí drop you at the Zurquí *puesto*, where you can pay your entrance fee and then walk to the start of the trails. On the way back buses will stop when flagged down – unless they are

SECURITY AT BRAULIO CARRILLO

Braulio Carrillo has suffered a number of **security problems** in recent years. Its proximity to San José and situation just off the Guápiles Highway has made it attractive to **thieves** as well as to hikers; cars left anywhere along the highwayside are often broken into. Worse, there were reports in 1992/3 of **armed robbers** assaulting groups of tourists on the paths. Several tour operators have subsequently **dropped hiking trips** to Braulio Carrillo, and while the ranger on duty may be able to keep an eye on your car, it is unfortunately the case that walking the trails is no longer as safe as it once was. Tell the ranger which trail you are on and how long you expect to be, and check with the staff at the National Parks office in San José for updated information. Remember, too, that while these are alarming stories, they are also isolated incidents.

full. You could also arrange in advance for a **taxi** from San José to come and pick you up (about $35) since the Zurquí *puesto* is only 20km from the city.

One of the few operators still organizing excursions to Braulio Carrillo, *Los Caminos de la Selva* run a specialist **birdwatching tour** for a full day with guide and transport included. Call or fax ☎255-3486 for prices and details.

Rainforest Aerial Tram

The invention of American naturalist Donald Perry, the **Rainforest Aerial Tram** lies just beyond the eastern boundary of Braulio Carrillo (daily 6am–4pm; $45; San José office: C 7, Av 7; ☎257-5961; fax 257-6053). Funded by private investors, and the product of many years' research, most of it carried out at nearby Rara Avis in the Zona Norte (see p.196), the tram is an innovation in rainforest tourism, the first of its kind in the world. Its premise is beautifully simple: twenty **overhead cable cars**, each holding five passengers and one guide, run slowly along the 1.7km aerial track, skirting the tops of the forest and passing between trees, providing eye-level encounters along the way. The ride affords a rare glimpse of birds, animals and plants, including the epiphytes, orchids, insects and mosses that live inside the upper reaches of the forest and, largely silent, it cuts down on the propensity for animals to be frightened by the oncoming thudding of feet. However, Perry is quite insistent that people should not come expecting to see particular animals – "that's a zoo," he says. Perry's book, *Life Above the Jungle Floor* (for more on which, see *Contexts*), tells how he risked life and limb to get this project operational. Committed to protecting the rainforest canopy and also the jungle floor, he would not allow the construction firm erecting the high-wire towers for the tram to use tractors; they were unable to secure a powerful enough helicopter in Costa Rica, but Nicaragua's Sandinistas came to the rescue, loaning one of their MI-17 combat helicopters (minus the guns) to help erect the poles.

Surrounding the tram track is a 354-hectare **private reserve** used by researchers to study life in the rainforest canopy. A few short loop trails and a basic lodge are planned, along with a restaurant, visitor centre and parking area.

Practicalities

Less than an hour from San José, and easily accessible, the aerial tram turnoff is on the northeast border of Braulio Carrillo, about 7km beyond the (signed) bridge over the Río Sucio, on the right hand side. From the turnoff it's another

1500m walk or drive. To get there **by bus**, catch the Guápiles service and ask the driver to drop you at the entrance. The return Guápiles–San José bus will stop when flagged down, unless full. It is advisable to wear a hat, insect repellent, and bring binoculars, camera and rain gear.

Most San José travel agencies offer **one-day trips** to the tram; about $50, including pick-up at all the major hotels. Currently this fee allows you as many tram rides as you like (45 min each way) and access to the ground trails. Special early morning birdwatching trips and torchlit night rides (until 9pm) will soon be added – many canopy inhabitants become active and visible only in the dark.

North of Heredia to Volcán Barva

The colonial village of **BARVA**, about 2km north of Heredia, is really only worth a brief stop on the way to Volcán Barva to have a look at the huge cream **Baroque church**, flanked by tall brooding palms, and the surrounding adobe-and-tiled-roof houses. Though Barva was founded in 1561, most of what you see today dates from the 1700s. *Soda Chaporro* sells ice cream and *refrescos* and has a small patio out front facing the soccer field – **buses** to San José de la Montaña (for the volcano) and San Rafael de Heredia (for the *Hotel Chalet Tirol*; see p.123) stop right outside.

Another kilometre north, the **Café Britt finca** (daily tours at 11am & 3pm; $15) grows one of the country's best-known coffee brands and is the most important exporter of Costa Rican coffee to the world. Costumed guides take you through the history of coffee growing in Costa Rica, demonstrating how crucial this export crop was to the development of the country, with a rather slick multimedia presentation and thorough descriptions of the process involved in harvesting and selecting the beans. It all ends on a free tasting and, of course, the inevitable stop in the gift shop; they can pack and mail coffee to the US. The *finca* offers a pick-up from most San José hotels for $7.

Volcán Barva

The small village of **San José de la Montaña**, 20km northeast of Heredia, is the chief gateway to dormant **VOLCÁN BARVA** (hours and admission as for Braulio Carrillo), a popular destination for walkers and climbers. Though the volcano is located within Braulio Carrillo National Park, covered on pp.118–121, you can't reach it via the Zurquí entrance on the Guápiles Highway. Rather you have to enter and pay your Park fee at the Barva *puesto*, a ranger station and entrance point 13km northeast of San José de la Montaña.

The **main trail** (3km; about 1hr) up Barva's slopes begins at the village of Porrosatí (also shown on some maps and buses as "Paso Llano"), at the western edge of Braulio Carrillo, ascending through dense deciduous cover, climbing 3000m before reaching the **cloudforest** at the top. Along the way you'll get panoramic views over the Valle Central and southeast to Volcán Irazú; if you're lucky – bring binoculars – you might see the elusive, jewel-coloured quetzal (though these nest-bound birds are usually only seen at their preferred altitude of 3600m or more). At the **summit**, you'll find the green/blue **lake** that fills the old crater, surrounded by dense forests that are often obscured in cloud. Before embarking on the walk, pick up a **map** from the National Parks headquarters in San José – although the trail is short, it's easy to get lost. Take a compass, water and food, a sweater and raingear – and leave early in the morning to enjoy the clearest views of the top. Be prepared for serious mud in the rainy season.

The **Transect Trail**, heading from Barva to the Zona Norte, is not recommended. The National Parks Service are pretty emphatic about advising hikers not to do it: foolhardy adventurers get lost every year in the attempt.

Practicalities

Numerous **tour operators** organize hiking expeditions to Barva, usually day trips, inclusive of transport, picnic lunch, and experienced guide. Prices run between $80 and 100. Contact *Los Caminos de la Selva* (☎255-3486); *Horizontes* (☎222-2022) or *Costa Rica Expeditions* (☎257-0766). *Robles Tours* (☎237-2116; fax 237-1976) also offer a very pretty horse ride in the area around Sacramento, just outside the Park boundary, including a lunch at their own country *posada*. They lay on coffee, naturalist guides and, if the weather is good, will take you up to the Lago Barva. All these tours run on request – in other words, when there is enough demand to put a group together – and it may be difficult to go during the wet season when fewer people are travelling.

Daily **buses** (at around 6.30am, 11am & 4pm) run from Heredia to San José de la Montaña, and on to Porrosatí (usually labelled "Paso Llano"). At Porrosatí signs point to the Barva *puesto*. Bus drivers will help with directions – ask before getting off. The only convenient bus from Porrosatí to Heredia leaves at 5pm, though there is also one at 1pm. Otherwise it's a case of getting a taxi – ask in either of the restaurants mentioned below, or in the village.

If you want to stock up on energy before climbing, two small local **restaurants** serve *típico* food; the *Campesino*, about three and a half kilometres beyond Porrosatí and the *Sacramento* about 500m or so further on. Beyond here the road is in poor shape; any vehicle other than a tough jeep should probably be left at one of the restaurants.

There are a number of good, if pricey, **places to stay** around Volcán Barva; *Cabanas de la Montaña Cypresal*, in San José de la Montaña (☎221-6455; fax 221-6244; ⑥), has rustic, very comfortable rooms, with fireplace and private bath, plus a small pool and restaurant. *Hotel Chalet Tirol*, high in the pine-covered mountains near San Rafael de Heredia (☎267-7371 or 7070; fax 267-7050; Aptdo 7812, San José 1000; ⑦) is a well-run resort with little Swiss chalets and a gourmet French restaurant. It's ideal for hikers, as they have their own small cloudforest with trails over high, green terrain. The hotel also arranges airport pick-up and tours, plus birdwatching and trout fishing in nearby rivers.

East of Heredia

The small village of **SAN VICENTE DE MORAVIA**, about 7km northeast of San José, is a well-known centre for handicrafts; ceramics and leather mostly, but also some wooden bowls and jewellery. There are a dozen or so shops in town, most of them ranged around the Parque Central, with little variety in the price or quality of goods. Most sell the same kind of stuff you find all over the country – wooden walking sticks, snakes, serving bowls, mini ox-carts – but a few specialize in different crafts. Worth a look are *Artesanía Bribrí,* which sells masks and leather goods made by the **Bribrí** indigenous peoples of the Talamanca coast (see p.172); the local landmark *Caballo Blanco*, one of the oldest such stores in Costa Rica, specializing in leather bags, belts and knapsacks; and a small complex of arts and crafts stores called the *Mercado de Artesanías Las Garzas*.

About 6km east of Moravia, in a cluster of small villages known commonly as Coronado, lies the hamlet of **DULCE NOMBRE DE CORONADO**. Budding herpetologists will want to stop by the **Instituto Clodomiro Picado**, or "snake farm" (Mon–Fri 9am–4pm; free), where a variety of poisonous species are bred for research, their venom used in the commercial production of antivenin. Most of the action occurs at feeding time, when you can watch live mice and toads being guzzled by the hungry reptiles; Friday afternoon visitors have a special treat, as this is when the snakes' venom is extracted. The institute also sells pre-prepared antivenin which you can take on the road with you, but in general the serum needs to be refrigerated; ask the staff for instructions. To get to the snake farm **by bus**, a local service leaves San José from Av 3, C 3/5, which will let you off at San Isidro de Coronado, the neighbouring hamlet. From there it is a 1km walk (follow signs). Staff at the institute will know the return bus times.

CARTAGO AND AROUND

With land made fertile by the deposits from Volcán Irazú, **Cartago province** extends east of San José and south into the Cordillera de Talamanca. The section covered in this chapter is a heavily populated, farmed and industrialized region, centring on **Cartago** town, a major shopping and transporation hub for the southern Valle Central. Dominated by the soaring wide-girthed form of **Volcán Irazú**, the landscape is varied and pretty, patched with squares of rich tilled soil and pockets of pine forest. Though at Cartago you can see Costa Rica's most famous church, the fat Byzantine **Basílica de Nuestra Señora de Los Angeles**, the town itself is seldom used as a place to stay, and many of the Valle Central attractions are visited on day trips from San José. Most popular is the volcano, but there's also the mystically lovely **Orosí valley**, the orchid collection at **Lankaster Gardens**, and the wild, little-visited **Parque Nacional Tapantí**.

Connected to San José by a good divided-toll highway, it takes about forty minutes by car to reach Cartago, from where there are road connections to Turrialba on the eastern slopes of Irazú, Parque Nacional Tapantí and the Orosí valley, and south via the Interamericana over the hump of the Cordillera Central to San Isidro and the Valle de el General.

Cartago

CARTAGO, meaning "Carthage", was Costa Rica's capital for three hundred years before the centre of power was moved to San José in 1823. Founded in 1563 by Juan Vazquez de Coronado, like its ancient namesake the city has been razed a number of times, although in this case by **earthquakes** instead of Romans – two, in 1823 and 1910, conspired to practically demolish the place. Most of the fine nineteenth-century and fin-de-siècle buildings were destroyed, and what has grown up in their place – the usual assortment of shops and haphazard modern

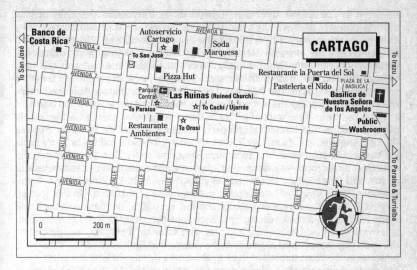

buildings – is not particularly aesthetically appealing, although the town does have a pretty **Parque Central** centring on a ruined **church** (*Las Ruinas*).

Nowadays Cartago's chief function is as a busy market and shopping centre, with some industry around its periphery. Its prize possession is its soaring **cathedral**, or basilica, dedicated to La Negrita, Costa Rica's patron saint.

Arrival, information and accommodation

SACSA runs frequent local **buses** to Cartago from San José (40–45 min). You can also pick up a stopping service from any of the stops on Av 2 past C 19 or so – they run along Av Central and out through San Pedro. In Cartago buses sometimes do a bit of a tour of town, stopping at virtually every block; wait to get off at the Parque Central, where you'll be dropped right in front of **Las Ruinas**.

Like the other provincial capitals in the Valle Central, Cartago has no **tourist office**. *Banco de Costa Rica*, Av 4, C 5/7 (Mon–Fri 8.30am–3.30pm, with a stop for lunch) and *Banco Nacional*, C 3, Av 2 (same hours), will change **travellers' cheques** but it's bound to take a while. The **correo** is at C 1, Av 2/4 on the right-hand side (Mon–Fri 7.30am–5pm). **Taxis** leave from the rank at *Las Ruinas*.

As for **staying** in Cartago: to put it bluntly, don't do it. While the widespread claim that Cartago hotels do little but turn over beds by the hour may be overstated, it's not too far from the truth, and there is, at the time of writing, nowhere "suitable" for tourists to stay in town. Getting stuck in Cartago overnight is an unlikely scenario, however, as there is 24-hour bus service to San José.

The Town

There's little to see in central Cartago; as usual, it focuses on its **Parque Central**, a leafy, tranquil square enclosed by Avenidas 1 and 2, and Calles 1 and 2, and bordered by *Las Ruinas*, the ruined **Iglesia de la Parroquía**. Originally built in 1575, the church, destroyed by a number of earthquakes, was stubbornly rebuilt by Cartagoans every time, until eventually the giant earthquake of 1910 vanquished it for good. Only the elegantly tumbling walls remain, enclosing pretty subtropical gardens; unfortunately they are locked more often than not, but you can peer through the iron gate at the fluffy blossoms flowering inside. If you inspect the sides and corners of the ruins carefully you'll see where the earthquake dislodged entire rows of mortar, sending them several centimetres beyond those above and below.

From the ruins it's a walk of no more than five minutes east to Cartago's only other attraction: the **cathedral**, properly named **Basílica de Nuestra Señora de Los Angeles**, at C 16 and Av 2. Casualty of a 1926 earthquake, Cartago's basilica was rebuilt soon after, in a decorative Byzantine style. This huge cement-grey structure, its elaborate wood-panelled interior soaring into complex parabolas and arches and lightened by lovely stained-glass, is home to **La Negrita**, the representation of the Virgin of Los Angeles, patron saint of Costa Rica. On this spot on August 2, 1635, the Virgin reportedly showed herself, in the form of a dark doll made of stone, to a poor peasant girl. Each time the girl took the doll away from where she had found it, keeping it to play with at home, it mulishly reappeared on the spot; this was seen as a sign, and the church was built soon after. August 2 is now one of the most important days in the Costa Rican religious calendar, when hundreds of pilgrims make the journey to Cartago to visit the tiny black statue of the Virgin, tucked away in a shallow subterranean antechamber beneath the crypt. It is a tradition in this grand, vaulting church for pilgrims to shuffle all the way down the aisle toward the altar on their knees, rosaries fretting in their hands as they whisper a steady chorus of Hail Marys. On August 2, many of them will have shuffled from as far as San José to pay their respects. In the antechambers of the cathedral, you'll see silver *ex-votos* or, in Spanish, *promesas,* of every imaginable shape and size, including horses, planes, grasshoppers (representing plagues of locusts), hearts with swords driven through them, arms, fingers and hands. This is a Latin American tradition stretching from Mexico to Brazil, whereby the faithful deposit representations of whatever they need cured, or whatever they fear, to the power of the Almighty.

There are good clean **public washrooms** across the street from the cathedral's southwest side, next to the holy water vendors.

Eating and drinking

There are few **restaurants** in Cartago, and certainly nowhere remarkable. The town does, however, boast several good **pastry shops**, where you can grab something to take out and eat on one of the benches in front of the basilica. As for **nightlife**, any bars or clubs must be local, very well-kept, secrets.

Ambientes, Av 1, C2/4. Restaurant with outdoor bar and garden. Good *típico* food and, like the name says, a nice ambience.

Autoservicio Cartago, C 4, Av 4. Ice cream of all description and flavours.

Pastelería el Nido, C 12, Av 4, 200m west of the basilica. Superior pastries and pies, plus delicious moist carrot cake.

Pizza Hut, C 2, Av 2/4. Popular with Ticos for cheap salad-and-pizza lunches.

La Puerta del Sol, C 16, Av 4. Simple *casados* and rice, with a small garden at the back.

Soda Marquesa, Av 4, C 4/6. A particularly good deal on burgers – about $1 – and ice cream. They also have a takeout window. Look out for the pink and green building.

MOVING ON FROM CARTAGO

To get back to **San José**, hop on whichever bus happens to be loading up in the covered area on Av 4, C 2/4. Buses leave every ten minutes between 5am and midnight, and about every hour otherwise. Local buses are frequent and reliable; for **Paraíso** use the stop on the south side of Las Ruinas; for **Orosí** catch a bus at C 4, Av 1, and for **Cachí** and **Ujarras**, the bus leaves from C 6, Av 1/2 (roughly hourly 5am–4pm).

Around Cartago

Dominating the landscape, **Volcán Irazú**, part of the mighty Cordillera Central, is the most popular excursion in Cartago province. Less visited and fairly off the beaten track, **Parque Nacional Tapantí**, recently upgraded from its former Wildlife Refuge status, is one of the closest places to San José for rainforest hiking; if you have your own transport, it makes a good day excursion or weekend trip. The Park lies in the pretty **Orosí valley**, which boasts a couple of churches at Ujarras and Orosí.

On the eastern slopes of the Cordillera Central, not officially in the Valle Central, the small town of **Turrialba** is something of a local hub for watersports, with Ríos Reventazón and Pacuaré, two of the best **whitewater rafting** rivers in the country, nearby. Turrialba has also become a small centre for river kayaking – whitewater kayaking, in effect – with one or two specialist tour operators in town. In addition, the town is the gateway to **Monumento Nacional Guayabo**, the most important ancient site in Costa Rica. A good two hours from San José, both are best reached via Cartago.

Parque Nacional Volcán Irazú

The blasted-out lunar landscape of **PARQUE NACIONAL VOLCÁN IRAZÚ** (daily 8am–4pm; $15 on the day, $10 in advance) is affectingly dramatic, reaching its highest point at 3432m and giving fantastic views on clear days to the Caribbean coast. Famous for having had the gall to erupt on the day President John F Kennedy visited Costa Rica on March 19, 1963, Irazú has been more or less calm since; but while its **Diego de la Haya crater** is far less active, in terms of bubblings and rumblings, than Poás' (see p.109), its deep depression, and the strange algae-green lake that fills it, is an undeniably impressive sight.

Situated 32km north of Cartago, a journey that is almost entirely uphill, the volcano makes for a long but scenic trip, especially early in the morning, before the inevitable **clouds** roll in. Up at the top there is very little vegetation, and what does grow has an unsettling, otherworldly quality, struggling to survive in this strange environment. There is little to actually *do* in the Park after viewing the crater from the mirador; there are no official trails, though it is possible to clamber along the scraggly slopes of a few outcroppings and dip into grey-ash sand dunes. Whatever you do, watch your step, as volcanic ash crumbles easily and there are a few places where it looks perfectly possible to be pitched into the ominous-looking lake.

Practicalities

A visit to Irazú is strictly for **day-trippers** only: there is nowhere to stay within the Park, and camping is not allowed on the slopes. As with Volcán Poás, only one

public excursion bus runs to the Park, at weekends and on all public holidays, leaving from in front of San José's *Gran Hotel Costa Rica* (information on ☎272-0651 or 551-9795; fax 272-2948). The cheerful "Volcano Express", a yellow school-bus emblazoned with a psychedelic "Irazú", leaves at 8am sharp; it's a good idea to be there an hour early to make sure you get a seat. The bus stops to pick up passengers at **Cartago** (from *Las Ruinas*) at 8.30am. Return fare is about $4 from San José and $2.25 from Cartago, which does not include the Park entrance fee.

The bus pulls in at the crater parking area, where there are toilets and an infor-mation board, along with a **snack wagon** serving sandwiches and welcome steaming cups of coffee (it can get **cold** at the summit – bring a sweater). Tico families bring picnics and set up lunch at the tables provided, determined in the face of the chilly temperatures, but they tend to look pretty shivery. At about 1pm the bus sets off from the volcano back to San José, making a refreshment stop at the **Bar/Restaurante Linda Vista**, poised above Cartago, with wonderful views from its large picture window. Business cards from all over the world line the walls, along with fluttering, fragile paper currencies – a good place to bone up on your (endangered) Argentinian australs and Guatemalan quetzals. The food is quite tasty, too. You can also get to Irazú on any number of half-day **tours** run by travel agencies in San José; whisking you back and forth in a private modern minibus, they cost around $45, not including the entrance fee.

The only **place to stay** – for groups of between six and twelve people – near Irazú is at *Hacienda Retes*, a 150-year old oak-log farmhouse set at 2700m facing the volcano. With fantastic wraparound views from the enormous upstairs veran-dah, the hacienda is surrounded by old oak forests, home to quetzals, woodpeck-ers and hummingbirds. You need to book in advance; accommodation is in bunks only (☎253-8146; fax 253-9937). They also specialize in **horseback riding tours** for non-residents, including a three-hour ride to the volcano. Lunch is at the farm-house; call to reserve.

Lankaster Gardens

Quite how much you get from a trip to **Lankaster Gardens** (daily 8.30am–3.30pm; $5), 6km southeast of Cartago, depends upon the time of year and how strongly you feel about orchids. **Orchids** are the main attraction at this tropical garden and research station, and while there are always some in bloom at any given time, the wet season (May–Nov) is less rewarding than the dry. March and April are the best months, when the gardens are alive with virulent reds, purples and yellows. A huge area, carefully and attractively landscaped, Lankaster Gardens houses a bewildering array of plant and flower species; it's difficult to resist photo opportunities, as ostenta-tious, elaborate blooms thrust themselves at you out of the undergrowth.

To get to the gardens by **bus from San José**, take the Cartago service, get off at *Las Ruinas*, and change to a Paraíso bus (see p.127). Get off when you see the very pink *Casa Vieja* restaurant, litte more than ten minutes out of town. A gravel road stretches off to your right, with an orange sign for the gardens: it's a one-kilometre walk along this road, turning right at the fork.

The Orosí valley

West of the small town of **Paraíso**, 8km south of Cartago, the road drops down a ski-slope hill to descend into the deep bowl of the **Orosí valley**. Church fans will want to make a trip to **Orosí** and **Ujarras**, pretty villages both, and each accessible by bus via Paraíso; annoyingly, although they lie less than 8km apart, you can't get direct from one to the other, and have to backtrack to Paraíso. A good place to **overnight** nearby is the *Albergue Linda Vista*, a friendly family house with lovely views over the valley. From the main road into Paraíso, turn right at the Parque Central, drive straight as if to go out of town, and then turn right at the sign (☎574-7632; ③).

Ujarras

Set in a beautiful corner of the Orosí river valley, in a flat basin at the foot of precipitous hills, the tiny agricultural hamlet of **UJARRAS**, about 10km southeast of Cartago, is home to the ruins of the church of **Nuestra Señora de la Limpia Concepción**. The church was built in 1693 on the site of a shrine erected by a local fisherman who claimed to have seen the Virgin in a tree trunk, but was abandoned in 1833 after irreparable damage from flooding – earthquakes are not the only foes of Costa Rican churches. Today the orangish limestone ruins are lovingly cared for, with a full-time gardener's genius in evidence in the landscaped grounds. The ruined interior, reached through what used to be the door, is now a grassy, roofless enclosure fluttering with birds; despite its dilapidation, you can identify the fine lines of a former altar.

Right across the road is a small outdoor **swimming pool** popular with local families, open in the dry season (Dec–April) only. The prospect of a cool swim after a walk around the ruins is welcoming: Ujarras has its own little microclimate and it can get very hot. Avocados grow nearby and you'll see plantation workers bicycling home at the end of the day, bulging sacks of the fruit slung over their backs.

To get to Ujarras by **bus from Cartago**, take one of the hourly services from *Las Ruinas* that goes via Paraíso to Cachí. Cachí is some 6km beyond Ujarras; ask to be dropped at the fork for Ujarras, or get off when you see *Restaurante Típico Ujarras*. From here it's 1km to the ruins. To get back to Paraíso and Cartago just flag the bus down at the same spot – currently the bus passes by the fork for Ujarras at about fifteen minutes past the hour. **Driving**, take Hwy-224 south from Cartago, signed to Paraíso and Cachí, which makes a circular trip around Lake Cachí. Extremely winding and steep, this route affords fantastic views over the valley as you descend the last few kilometres. If you want to **stay** nearby, the one option is *Paraíso de Cataratas*, in a stupendous, if perilous-looking, position just above the village (☎574-7893; ④). There are few facilities at the ruins; toilets, but nowhere to eat. The closest **restaurant**, *Restaurante Típico Piccolo*, on the road to the church, is not always open.

Orosí

One of the most picturesque small villages in Costa Rica, nestling in a little topograpical bowl between gloomy, thick-forested hills, **OROSÍ** also boasts the **church of San José de Orosí** (1735). Sitting squat against the rounded pates of the hills behind, this simple, low-slung adobe structure, single-towered and roofed with red tiles, has an interior devoid of the hubris and frothy excess of much of Latin American church decor. Adjacent, the **Religious Art Museum**, also called the **Museo Franciscano** (officially daily 9am–noon & 1–5pm; 75¢) is a fascinating little place, filled with *objectos de culto* such as icons, religious paintings and ecclesiastical furniture, along with a faithful recreation of a monk's tiny room. If the sun's out, you might want to check out the two **swimming pools** in the village: *Los Patios* (Mon–Fri 8am–4.30pm; $1.50) or *Balneario Termal Orosí* (daily 7.30am–4.30pm; $1.25).

Regular **buses** leave Cartago for Orosí from the stop on C 4, Av 1 (6am–10pm; Mon–Fri every 30 min; Sat & Sun hourly). The trip takes about forty minutes. The last service back to Cartago via Paraíso leaves at 5pm from the stop on the main street in front of the church. By **car**, take the road from Cartago to Paraíso, turn right and drive straight ahead until you begin to descend the precipitous hill to the village. You can grab a bite to **eat** at S*oda Nido* and *Restaurante Coto* on the main road; the latter serves beer on its outdoor terrace facing the church.

For **taxi** service, ask at the *Restaurante Coto* or go to the rank on the north side of the main square. A 4WD taxi up the hill to Paraíso should cost about $10, or you could hire one to take you to Parque Nacional Tapantí (see below) for about $15. There is nowhere to **stay** in Orosí.

Parque Nacional Tapantí

Rugged, pristine **PARQUE NACIONAL TAPANTÍ** (daily 8am–4pm; $15 on the day, $7 in advance) receives one of the highest average rainfalls (a whopping 5600mm) in the country – if you *really* want to get wet, go in October. Altitude in this watershed area ranges from 1220 to 2560m above sea level and contains two life zones; low mountain and premontane rainforest. It is chock full of **mammals** – about 45 species live here, including the tapir (*danta*), the brocket deer (*cabro de monte*), the mountain hare (*conejo de monte*) and wildcats, along with **birds** such as the golden oriole, falcons, doves, hawks and the famous quetzal. Because of the wet, frogs, salamanders and snakes abound.

Tapantí's **trails** are relatively short and densely wooded. The Camino Principal, or main road, about 4km long, leads off from the *puesto* at Quebrada Segunda (Second Creek), 12km from Orosí. From this wide trail lead three walks under much denser cover: the **Sendero Natural Arboles Caidos** to the east, and the **Senderos Oropendola** and **Pantanoso** to the west. All provide anywhere from ninety minutes to three hours' walking. Towards the end of the main trail, **Sendero La Pava** leads to the Río Grande de Orosí and a mirador from where you can see a high waterfall. Whenever you go, bring **rain gear** and dress in layers. If the sun is out it can be blindingly hot, whereas at higher elevations, when overcast and rainy, it can feel quite cool. Despite its low numbers of visitors, Tapantí has good services, with washrooms and drinking water at regular intervals along the trails.

Getting to Tapantí by public transport is difficult. From Cartago, take the bus to Orosí, where you can stay on the bus until its final stop, the tiny hamlet of Río Macho, and walk the final 9km to the refuge. It's easier, however, to get off in Orosí and take a jeep taxi from there ($10–15). **Driving** from Orosí, turn right at the coffee factory *Beneficiadora Renex* and continue for 10km along a bad road (4WD in rainy season). You can **stay** with the park rangers at the *puesto* (②); call ahead to reserve at the SPN office in San José (see p.65). On the road to the Park the *Kiri Lodge* (④) organizes trout fishing trips in the many nearby rivers, and also serves great trout **lunches**.

Turrialba and around

Though the pleasant agricultural town of **TURRIALBA**, 45km east of Cartago on the eastern slopes of the Cordillera Central, has sweeping views over the rugged eastern Talamancas, there's little to keep you here long. Tourists are most likely to see it as part of a trip to the archeological monument of **Guayabo**, or even more likely, on the way to a **whitewater rafting** or **kayaking** trip on the Ríos Reventazón or Pacuaré. Many of the mountain-lodge-type hotels nearby have guided walks or horseback rides up dormant **Volcán Turrialba**, which, with its lack of trails, is otherwise inaccessible to casual or independent visitors.

Accommodation in and around Turrialba

While Turrialba isn't yet really a tourist town, it has some perfectly decent places to stay, from simple hotel rooms in town to the – considerably more expensive – "mountain lodges" nearby, which offer luxurious rooms, good home-cooked food (which usually costs extra), guided treks and horseriding. Some of the accommodation listed below is at a **higher altitude** than Turrialba's pleasantly refreshing hillside position; bring a sweater or light jacket.

Albergue la Calzada, 500m before the entrance to Monumento Nacional Guayabo (☎556-0465). Large country house, with rustic, very comfortable rooms and excellent local food. The friendly owners know the area well and can advise on excursions. ③.

Albergue de Montaña Pochotel, 2km from Turrialba. Simple accommodation and *típico* food in an astounding situation with volcano views in all directions. Camping also allowed. ③.

Casa Turire, 20km southeast of Turrialba (☎531-1111; fax 531-1075). Country-resort-type place with pool, six-hole golf course, horseback riding and tours. Lovely views of the Río Reventazón. ⑦–⑧.

Guayabo Lodge, Santa Cruz de Turrialba, 20km from Monumento Nacional Guayabo (☎ and fax 556-0133). This dairy farm, in a small hamlet near Turrialba, has been owned for years by the family of the current President of Costa Rica. They have recently turned it into a comfortable country lodge, offering farm tours, rides up to Volcán Turrialba, and visits to Guayabo, and will collect you from San José. Packages available. ⑤.

Interamericano, southeast corner of Turrialba, near the old train station (☎556-0142). Basic, clean and very friendly, with a kitchen where you can cook snacks. The proprietor can hook you up with sea kayaking tours. The best budget deal in town. ②.

Turrialba Volcano Lodge, Aptdo 1632-2050, San José (☎ and fax 273-4335). Quiet, modern, simply furnished farmhouse on the flanks of Volcán Turrialba; accessible over a badly rutted road, 4WD only (call for directions). Six rooms with private bath. ox-cart rides, horseback tours to Turrialba crater with Spanish-speaking guides, and hotel pick-ups from San José. ⑥.

Wagelia, Av 4, Turrialba, just beyond the gas station on the way in from Cartago (☎556-1566). Small, clean, basic rooms with TV and phone. ④.

Monumento Nacional Guayabo

The most accessible ancient archeological site in Costa Rica, **MONUMENTO NACIONAL GUAYABO** lies 19km northeast of Turrialba and 84km from San José (daily 8am–3.30pm; $15 on the day, $7 in advance). Discovered by explorer Anastasio Alfaro at the end of the nineteenth century, Guayabo was only excavated in the late 1960s. Administered by MIRENEM, the Ministry of Mines and Resources – which also controls Costa Rica's National Parks system – today Guayabo suffers from an acute shortage of funds, and although the current site covers about 50 acres, only a small part has been excavated. With the recent withdrawal of the annual US aid grant, the future looks even grimmer.

Guayabo belongs to the archeological/cultural area known as **Intermedio**, which begins roughly in the province of Alajuela and extends to Venezuela, Colombia and parts of Ecuador. Archeologists believe that Guayabo was inhabited from about 1000 BC to 1400 AD; most of the heaps of stones and basic structures now exposed were erected between 300 and 700 AD. The central mound is the tallest circular base unearthed so far, with two staircases and pottery remains on the very top. Like the prehistoric peoples of Stonehenge, the people of Guayabo brought stones to the site from a great distance – probably from the banks of the Río Reventazón – and petroglyphs have been found on 53 of these stones. Other than this, little is known of the people who lived here, though excavations have shown that they were particularly skilled in water conducting. At the northern end of the site you can see the stone **tanque de captación**, where they stored water conducted by subterranean aqueducts from nearby springs. Other conclusions drawn are that this community was led by a chief, a *cacique*, who had both social and religious power. There are no clues as to why Guayabo was abandoned; hypotheses include an epidemic, or maybe war with neighbouring peoples.

At the **entrance hut** you can pick up a leaflet, written in the "voice" of Brúl, a Bribrí word for armadillo, that points out orchids, a petroglyph and *guarumo* trees; but it has to be said that there is still not a great deal to see, as you can't get very close to the excavated mounds of stone. If, however, you find your imagination fired by this Lost Eden – and your Spanish is up to it – try and speak to resident archeologist and *guardaparque* Sr Rodolfo Tenorio. In the face of disappointment from visitors familiar with the magnificent Maya and Aztec cities of Mexico or Guatemala – cultures contemporaneous with that at Guayabo – Tenorio is adamant that the development of a civilization cannot necessarily be gauged by its ability to erect vast monuments or group itself into fabulously complex communities. Facing the considerable difficulties posed by the density of the rainforest terrain, the Guayabo peoples managed not only to live in harmony with an environment that remains hostile to human habitation, but also constructed a complex system of water management, social organization, and expressed themselves through the "written language" of petroglyphs. The extent to which they mastered their environment and integrated their lives with the surroundings, Tenorio argues, shows an adaptability that can be measured against the Aztecs and the Maya, societies which had far longer to develop.

Getting to Guayabo by bus can be done, but is a bit inconvenient, entailing a stay of two nights. Every weekday a bus leaves Turrialba for Guayabo at 5.15pm; you can bed down at *Albergue la Calzada* (see p.131) and visit in the morning. The return bus leaves at 5.30am. On Monday and Friday only, an extra Guayabo service leaves Turrialba at 11.10am. It is also possible to **walk** back to Turrialba down the gravel road (4km, downhill) and intercept the bus that goes from the hamlet of Santa Teresita to Turrialba. It passes by at *about* 1.30pm – double-check times with the *guardaparques*, or at *la Calzada*, otherwise you might be left standing at the crossroads for another 24 hours. **Driving** from Turrialba takes about thirty minutes. The last 4km is on a bad gravel road – passable with a regular car, but watch your clearance. *Green Tropical Tours*; Aptdo 675-2200, San José (☎ and fax 255-2859) offer a **day trip** to the monument, including pick-up at a San José hotel, breakfast, guided tour, lunch in Turrialba and a visit to Cartago's basilica.

CATIE

Specializing in tropical agriculture research, **CATIE**, or *Centro Agrónomo Tropical de Investigación y Enseñanza*, set in the valley 4km east of Turrialba and 70km from San José (☎556-1149), has the oldest Agricultural Sciences degree in Costa Rica. In the surrounding 1000 hectares they grow more than 2400 types of coffee bean and 450 kinds of cacao plants. At least a quarter of Costa Rica's internal produce and about half the actual labour force are at some time engaged in agricultural activity; part of CATIE's mandate is to develop technological innovations to modernize tropical agriculture, and to evolve and preserve sustainable agricultural practices for the smallholders who make up a significant part of Costa Rica's farmer population. The centre hosts occcasional open days with activities and workshops about local agriculture; visitors with a special interest should give three days' advance warning before coming.

travel details

Buses

San José to: Alajuela (constant; 20min); Braulio Carrillo (every 30min; 35min); Cartago (constant; 40min); La Guacima Abajo for the Butterfly Farm (2 express daily except Sun; 40min); Heredia (constant; 15min); San Pedro de Poás (1 weekly; 1hr 30min); Sarchí (17 daily; 1hr 30min); Turrialba (17 daily; 1hr 30min); Volcán Irazú (1 Sat & Sun; 1hr 30min); Volcán Poás (1 weekly; 2hr); Zarcero (12 daily; 2hr).

Alajuela to: La Guacima Abajo, for the Butterfly Farm (4 daily; 20min); San José (constant; 20min); Sarchí (constant; 1hr); Zoo-Ave (constant; 15min).

Braulio Carrillo to: San José (every 30min; 35min).

Cartago to: Lankaster Gardens (every 30min; 10min); Orosí (every 1hr 30min Mon–Fri, hourly Sat & Sun; 30min); Paraíso (every 1hr 30min Mon–Fri, hourly Sat & Sun; 30min); San José (constant; 40min); Río Macho, via Orosí, for Tapantí (1hr 30min); Ujarras (every 1hr 30min Mon–Fri, hourly Sat & Sun; 30min).

Heredia to: San José (constant; 15min); Volcán Barva, via San José de la Montaña (3 daily Mon–Sat, 2 daily Sun; 1hr).

Orosí to: Cartago (every 1hr 30min Mon–Fri, hourly Sat & Sun; 30min).

Sarchí to: Alajuela (constant; 1hr); San José (17 daily; 1hr 30min).

Turrialba to: Guayabo (1 daily Mon–Fri; 1hr+).

Ujarras to: Cartago, via Paraíso (every 1hr 30min Mon–Fri, hourly Sat & Sun; 30min).

Volcán Barva to: Heredia, via San José de la Montaña (3 daily Mon–Sat, 2 daily Sun; 1hr).

Volcán Poás to: San José (1 weekly; 2hr).

CHAPTER THREE

LIMÓN PROVINCE AND THE CARIBBEAN COAST

We were at the shore and travelling alongside a palmy beach. This was the Mosquito Coast ... Massive waves were rolling towards us, the white foam vivid in the twilight; they broke just below the coconut palms near the track. At this time of day, nightfall, the sea is the last thing to darken: it seems to hold the light that is slipping from the sky; and the trees are black. So in the light of this luminous sea, and the pale still-blue eastern sky, and to the splashings of the breakers, the train racketed on towards Limón.

Paul Theroux *The Old Patagonian Express*

The Miskito coast (in Spanish, *Mosquito*) is just part of huge, sparsely populated **Limón province**, which sweeps south in an arc from Nicaragua right down to Panamá. Hemmed in to the north by dense jungles and swampy waterways, to the west by the mighty Cordillera Central – an effective wall that it cost at least 4000 lives to break through during the building of the track for the Jungle Train (see p.137) – and to the south by the even wider girth of the Cordillera Talamanca, Limón can feel like a lost, end-of-the-world place. While the coast is undeniably the main attraction, anyone hoping to find the palm-fringed sands and tranquil crystalline waters that the word "Caribbean" conjures up will be disappointed; excepting a couple near Puerto Viejo de Talamanca, Limón has no really good **beaches** to speak of. Most are battered, shark-patrolled shores, littered with driftwood that has travelled thousands of kilometres, and with huge, bucking skies stretching out to sea. Here, however, you can watch gentle giant sea **turtles** lay their eggs on the wave-raked beaches of **Tortuguero**; snorkel coral reefs at **Cahuita** or Punta Uva; go surfing at **Puerto Viejo**; drift along the **jungle canal** from Tortuguero to Barra del Colorado, or try animal- and bird-spotting in the many mangrove **swamps**. The interior of Limón province is criss-crossed by the powerful Río Reventazón and Río Pacuaré, two of the best rivers in the Americas for **whitewater rafting**.

Although Limón remains an unknown for the majority of visitors – especially those on package tours – it holds much appeal for eco-tourists and off-the-track travellers. The province has a highest proportion of **protected land** in the country, from **Refugio Nacional de Fauna Silvestre Barra del Colorado** on the Nicaraguan border, to **Refugio Nacional de Vida Silvestre Gandoca-Manzanillo** near Panamá in the extreme south. That said, however, the Wildlife Reserves and National Parks offer only mitigated resistance to the considerable threats to ecological integrity presented by full-scale fruit farming, logging, mining and tourism.

Traditionally neglected and underfunded by Highland-oriented government, Limón suffered a further blow from the 1991 **earthquake**, which heaved the Caribbean coast up in the air about 1.5 metres. Already ill-maintained roads, bridges and banana railroads were destroyed, including the track for the famous **Jungle Train** from San José to Puerto Limón, one of the most scenic train rides anywhere in the world. Today, an air of neglect still hangs over much of the province, from housing and tourist infrastructure to basic sanitation. Despite this, however, more than anywhere else in Costa Rica the Caribbean coast exudes a **cultural diversity**, a feeling of community and a unique and complex local history. The only town of any size, **Puerto Limón**, is part of a very old community of "black" Central American coastal cities – like Bluefields in Nicaragua and Livingston in Guatemala. A typical Caribbean port, it has a large (mostly Jamaican-descended) **Afro-Caribbean** population. In the south, near the Panamanian border, live several communities of indigenous peoples from the **Bribrí** and **Cabécar** groups. None of these people have been well-served by the national government: until 1949 blacks were effectively forbidden to settle in the Valle Central or the Highlands, according to a law supposedly promulgated but

CREOLE CUISINE IN LIMÓN PROVINCE

Creole cuisine is known throughout the Americas from Louisiana to Bahía for its imaginative use of **African-originated spices** and vegetables, succulent fish and chicken dishes, and fantastic sweet **desserts**. You should make an effort to sample Limón's version by eating at any one of the locally run restaurants dotted along the coast. These are often family affairs, usually run by respected older generation Afro-Caribbean women. Sitting down to dinner at a red gingham tablecloth, with a cold bottle of *Imperial* beer, reggae on the squeaky old boombox and a plate full of coconut-scented rice-and-beans is one of the real pleasures of visiting this part of Costa Rica. However, note that many restaurants, in keeping with age-old local tradition, serve Creole dishes like rice-and-beans and rundown on weekends only, serving simpler dishes or the usual Highlands rice concoctions during the week.

Everyone outside Limón will tell you that the local speciality, **rice-and-beans** (in the lilting local accent it sounds like "rizanbin") is "comida muy pesada" (very heavy food). However, this truly wonderful mixture of red or black beans and rice cooked in coconut milk is no more *pesada* – and miles tastier – than traditional Highland dishes like *arroz con camarones*, wherein everything is fried. It's the coconut milk that gives it a surprising lift. **Pan Bon** (not, as it is commonly thought, "good bread": "bon" actually derives from "bun", brought by English-speaking settlers), another local speciality, is sweet bread glazed and laced with cheese and fruit; it is often eaten for **dessert**, as are ginger biscuits and plantain tarts. **Rundown** (said "rondon" – to rundown is to cook) is harder to find, mainly because it takes a long time – at least an afternoon – to prepare. This is a vegetable and meat or fish stew in which the plantains and breadfruit cook for many hours, very slowly, in spiced coconut milk. Some restaurants – *Springfields* in Limón, *Miss Junie's* in Tortuguero, *Soda Marley* in Puerto Viejo and *Miss Edith's* in Cahuita – have it on their menus as a matter of course, but it is usually best to stop by on the morning of the day you wish to dine and request it for that evening.

Favoured **spices** in Limonese Creole cooking include cumin, coriander, peppers, chillies, paprika, cloves and groundspice. The vegetables are those you might find in a street market in West Africa, the northeast of Brazil, or Kingston, Jamaica. Native to Africa, **Ackee** (in Spanish *seso vegetal*), was brought to the New World by British colonists. It has to be used in knowledgeable hands because its sponge-cake-like yellow fruit, encapsulated in three-inch pods, is poisonous until the pods open. The fruit is served boiled and looks like scrambled eggs; it goes well with fish. **Yucca**, also known as manioc, is a long pinkish tuber, similar to the yam, and is usually boiled or fried. Local yams can grow as big as 25kg, and are used very much like potato in soups and stews. Another native African crop, the huge melon-like **breadfruit** (*fruta de pan*), is more a starch substitute than a fruit, with white flesh that has to be boiled, baked or grated. **Pejiballes** (*pejibaye* in Spanish – English-speaking people in Limón pronounce it "picky-BAY-ah") are small green or orange fruits, looking a little like limes. Though you'll see them sold on the street in San José, boiled in hot water and skinned, they are most popular in Limón. They're definitely an acquired taste; at once salty and bitter. Better known as heart-of-palm, **palmito** is served in good restaurants around the world as part of a tropical exotic salad. It originates here, on giant plantations near Siquerres and Las Horquetas. **Plantains** (*plátanos* in Spanish), the staple of many Highland dishes, figure particularly heavily in local Creole cuisine. They are deliciously sweet when baked or fried in fritters. Right at the other end of the health scale, **herbal teas** are a speciality of the province, available in many restaurants: try wild peppermint, wild basil, soursop, lime, lemon grass or ginger.

for which documentary evidence does not exist. While the indigenous communities have a degree of autonomy, their traditional territories have long since been eaten up by government-sanctioned mineral exploration and banana plantations.

There are few options when it comes to **getting around** Limón province. From San José to Puerto Limón you have a choice of just two roads, while from Puerto Limón south to the Panamá border at Sixaola there is but one narrow and badly repaired route (not counting the few small local roads leading to the banana *fincas*). North of Puerto Limón there is no public land transport at all: instead, private *lanchas* ply the coastal **canales** (canals) – dug in the late 1960s in order to bypass the treacherous breakers of the Caribbean – connecting the port of Moín, 8km north of Puerto Limón, to Río Colorado near the Nicaraguan border. There are also several scheduled **flights** a week from San José to Barra. A good, frequent and quite reliable **bus** network operates in the rest of the province, with the most efficient and modern routes from San José to Puerto Limón and to Sixaola. Gas provision is generally poor, except for on the highway from San José: take a spare can with you if you plan to do much driving south of Puerto Limón and/or down into Panamá. **Language** can also be a problem: while English is spoken widely along the coast (not just in Limón but also in Tortuguero and Barra, due to the many Miskito-descended people from Nicaragua who were taught English in school), do not expect it from everyone. Your best bet is to make your first approaches in Spanish; people can then choose in which language to answer you.

The area's diverse **micro-climates** mean there is no "best" time to visit the Caribbean coast. In Tortuguero and Barra del Colorado, it is very wet all year round, with a small dry spell in January and February. South of Limón, September and October offer the best chance of rainlessness.

Some history

Although the Limón coast has been populated for at least 10,000 years, little is known of the ancient indigenous **Bribrí** and **Cabécar** groups who inhabited the area when Columbus arrived here, just off the coast of present-day Puerto Limón, on his fourth and last voyage to the Americas in 1502. Well until the mid-eighteenth century the only white people the Limón littoral saw were British **pirates**, rum-runners and seamen from the merchant vessels of the famous Spanish Main, plying the rich waters of the post-Conquest Caribbean, bringing commerce and often mayhem. Nefarious buccaneers often found refuge on Costa Rica's eastern seaboard, situated as it was between the two more lucrative provinces of Panamá and Nicaragua, from which there was a steady traffic of ships to raid. Their presence, along with the difficult terrain, helped deter full-scale settlement of Limón.

The province's development was inextricably linked to two things, themselves related: the **railway** and **bananas**. In 1871 it was decided that Costa Rica needed a more efficient export line for its coffee crop than the long, meandering river journey from Puerto Viejo de Sarapiquí to Matina, midway between Tortuguero and Puerto Limón, from where beans were shipped to Europe. The other main coffee port was Puntarenas on the Pacific coast (see p.271), which required boats to go the long way round. An American, **Minor Keith**, was contracted to build a railroad across the Cordillera Central from San José to Puerto Limón; to help pay for the laying of the track, he planted bananas along its lowland stretches. Successive waves of Highlanders, Chinese, East Indian (still locally called

ETHNICITY IN LIMÓN PROVINCE

"An anthropological Galapagos" is the ingenious term used by journalist and travel writer Peter Ford in his book *Tekkin a Waalk*, to describe the ethnic and cultural oddities encountered in Limón, where the Caribbean meets Central America. There's no doubt that the province provides a touch of multi-culturalism lacking in the rest of Costa Rica's relatively homogeneous Latin, Catholic society. Limón is characterized by intermarriage and racial mixing: it is not unusual to find people on the coast who are of combined Miskito, Afro-Caribbean and Nicaraguan ancestry. Though the first black inhabitants of the province were the slaves of the British pirates and mahogany-cutters who since the mid-1700s had lived in scattered communities along the coast, the region's ethnic diversity is in a major part due to the labour-contracting schemes of Minor Keith (see above). After the construction of the Jungle Train, many of the Afro-Caribbean railway workers stayed on in Costa Rica, where land ownership rights were in some cases more liberal than those of their native countries. They were soon joined by turtle fishermen who had settled in Bocas del Toro, Panamá, and who migrated north to escape the the Panamanian war of independence from Colombia in 1903. With them the settlers brought their religions – unlike the rest of Costa Rica, most Afro-Caribbeans in Limón province are Protestant.

Regardless of race or religion, the coast settlers were resourceful and independent. Like the pioneers of North America, they not only planted their own crops, bringing seeds to grow breadfruit, oranges, mangoes and ackee, all of which flourished and grew alongside native coconuts and cocoa, but also made their own salt, charcoal, musical instruments, shoes and brewed their own spirits – red rum, *guarapo*, cane liquor and ginger beer.

Limón's diversity has never been appreciated by the ruling and economic elite of the country. Official – legislated, even – racial discrimination against the province's Afro-Caribbean inhabitants was in force until 1949, when the new Constitution granted them full citizenship. Black *Limonenses* now make up between 25 and 30 percent of the province's population and are a sharply contrasting and separate entity from the rest of the country.

Hindus) and Italian immigrant labourers were brought in for the gruelling construction work, only to succumb to yellow fever. In the final stages, some 10,000 Jamaicans and Barbadians, who were thought to be immune to the disease, were contracted, many of them staying on to work on the railroad or in banana plantations. In 1890 the **Jungle Train** first huffed its way from San José via Turrialba and Siquerres to Limón, bringing an abrupt end to the Caribbean coast's period of near-total isolation. This was also the beginning of Costa Rica's **banana boom**: initially planted along the tracks, the fruit soon prospered in the ideal climate and conditions here. Keith eventually founded the United Fruit company, which made him far more wealthy than the railroad ever could.

San José to Puerto Limón

There are two land routes from the capital to Puerto Limón, one of which, the Guápiles Highway (Hwy-32), is one of the best-maintained roads in the country. The narrower, older route, Hwy-10, often called the **"Turrialba road"**, runs through Turrialba on the eastern slopes of the Cordillera Central before following the old switchbacking San José–Limón train tracks through a pristine, dense and mountainous landscape, gutted by the deep cuts of the Ríos Pacuaré and Reventazón. It joins the Guápiles Highway near **Siquerres**, about three-quarters of the way to Limón. Considered dangerous and difficult to drive, the Turrialba road now carries very little traffic, as it takes about four hours as opposed to the two-and-a-half or three hours on the Guápiles Highway.

That said, however, the **Guápiles Highway**, despite its good condition, is so often fog-shrouded that it is only half-jokingly referred to as the "Highway to Heaven" such is its accident and fatality record. Nevertheless, the vast majority of buses and cars take this road, which begins in San José at the northern end of C 3, and proceeds to climb out of the Highlands to the northeast. This part is visually impressive, with Volcán Barva on your left and Volcán Irazú on your right. It then winds its way through Braulio Carrillo National Park (see p.118), over the hump of the continental divide, and down from the mountains into a very brief spell of foothills before opening out into a long stretch of flat lowlands for the final 80km or so to Puerto Limón. The road is not as scenic as you might suspect, hewn as it is from straight-dropping walls of mountain carpeted with thick intertwining vegetation. While one side is solid rock, the other is, in places, a sheer phantasmagoric drop that you cannot quite see, only imagine – all the worse – with only the enormous huge-leaf common plant known as the "poor man's umbrella" (*sombrilla de pobre*) growing by the roadside to break the monotony.

There are no **restaurants or gas stations** for the first 57km beyond the toll booth (about 25¢) at the entrance to Braulio Carrillo National Park. The first gas station appears on the left after climbing down from the mountains proper – look for the green/white Castrol sign – before the Las Horquetas turnoff.

Guápiles

GUÁPILES, about 50km east of San José, is the first town of any size, a supply point for the banana plantations of the Río Frío and a waystation for the *bananero* workers. The few **hotels** in town cater mainly to plantation workers and have cold water and thin walls. The one exception – the only place on the entire San José–Limón route that offers much comfort – is the comparatively swish *Hotel Suerre* (☎710-7551; fax 710-6376; ⑤), a country club with pool, gym and exercise room, poolside bar, and a good restaurant (all of which non-guests are welcome to use on a pay-as-you-use or day basis).

Siquerres

Many of the package tours to Tortuguero (see p.150) make a brief stop at **SIQUERRES**, 1km northeast of the Guápiles Highway at Km-99 from San José, en route to picking up the boat at the small village of Hamburgo de Siquerres on the Río Reventazón. As the rusted hulks of freight cars and track-scarred streets show, Siquerres – which means "reddish colour" in a Miskito dialect – used to be a major railway hub for the Jungle Train, which carted people, bananas and cacao to the Highlands. Along with Turrialba it was a place where black train drivers, engineers and maintenance men would swap positions with their "white" (Spanish, *mestizo*, European or Highland) counterpart, who would then take the train into the Valle Central, where blacks were discouraged from travelling until 1949. Though the Jungle Train no longer runs, trains still haul bananas and machinery to and from Siquerres – mainly servicing the innumerable banana towns or *fincas* nearby (easily recognizable on detailed maps from their factory-farmed names of Finca 1, 2, a, b, and so forth). There's little to see in town today, though it's worth taking a look at the completely **round church** on the western side of the soccer field. Built to mirror the shape of a Miskito hut, its indigenously authentic shape shelters a plain, wood-panelled interior.

From Siquerres it is a relatively easy flat-road drive east about 57km to Limón; though the road is well-maintained, note that truck and bus drivers love to make up time by speeding and/or overtaking on these stretches, and that buses may stop with little warning to pick up passengers. Outside the window you'll see macadamia nut farms set alongside small banana plots, flower nurseries and clear-cut areas, dotted with humble roadside dwellings.

Puerto Limón and around

To the rest of the country, **PUERTO LIMÓN**, more often simply called Limón, is Costa Rica's *bête noire*, a steamy port raddled with slum neighbourhoods, bad sanitation and drug-related crime. The traveller is apt to be kinder to the city than the Highland Tico, although Paul Theroux's first impressions in *The Old Patagonian Express* are no encouragement: "The stucco fronts had turned the colour and consistency of stale cake, and crumbs of concrete littered the pavements. In the market and on the parapets of the crumbling buildings there were mangy vultures. Other vultures circled the plaza. Was there a dingier backwater in all the world?"

Not much has changed in the fifteen years or so since Theroux went through town, though the vultures have crept off to wherever vultures go. Many buildings, damaged during the 1991 earthquake, whose epicentre was just south of Limón, lie skeletal and wrecked, still in the process of falling down. Curiously, however, with its washed-out peeling oyster-and-lime hues Limón can be almost pretty, in a sad kind of way, with the pseudo-beauty of all Caribbean "slums of empire" as St Lucian poet Derek Walcott put it.

There's very little to do; Limón has never been in the same Caribbean port league as Veracruz in Mexico or Cartagena in Colombia, lacking those cities' architecture and dilapidated elegance. It's a working port but a neglected one, since the big-time banana boats started loading at the deeper and excellent natural harbour of **Moín**, 8km up the headland toward Tortuguero. Generally speaking, tourists come to Limón for one of three reasons: to get a **boat to Tortuguero** from Moín, to get a bus south to the **beach towns** of Cahuita and Puerto Viejo, or to join in the annual Carib-fest and Carnaval-like celebration of **El Día de la Raza** (Columbus Day) during the week preceding October 12.

Arrival, information and orientation

Arriving in Limón can be unnerving at night; best get here in daylight if only to orientate yourself. *Coopelimón* and *Coopecaribeños* **buses** do the **San José–Limón** run, starting at 5am and continuing hourly until 7pm (2hr 30min–3hr). You should buy your ticket a day in advance if travelling on a Friday or Sunday; more during Carnaval, even though extra buses are laid on. Buses come into town from San José along Av 1, parallel to the docks and the old railroad tracks, pulling in at Limón's main bus station 100m east and 50m south of the mercado.

To Hospital, Springfields & Moin △

Bars
Apartments Cocori & Restaurante Tia María
Maribú Caribe

PORTETE

Main Docks
Tortuguero Canal

Boathouse
for Lanchas
to Tortuguero

Hotel Jardín Tropical
Hotel Matama
Cabinas Maeva

MOIN

N

Isla Uvita

Puerto Limón

CALLE 6

CALLE 5

CALLE 4

CALLE 3

CALLE 2

AVENIDA 6

AVENIDA 5

CARIBBEAN SEA

Helennik Souvenirs
Radio Casino

Hotel Nuevo Internacional

Sea Wall (Malecón)

To Moín ☆

AVENIDA 4

To Cahuita, Puerto Viejo & Sixaola ☆

Soda La Estrella

Hotel Teté

Mercado

Hotel/Restaurante Park

AVENIDA 3

Soda Yans

Hotel Acón

Banco Costa Rica

Restaurante Brisas del Caribe

Municipalidad (Town Hall)

AVENIDA 2

Banco Nacional

Supermarket

ICE Telephone

Hotel Miami

Restaurante Mares

Coopelimón Stop (To/From San José) ☆

CALLE 1

Parque Vargas

Mural

Pizzería Il Macarrone

AVENIDA 1

To Cahuita, Puerto Viejo & San José

PUERTO LIMÓN

Docks

0   100 m

Arrivals **from the south** – Cahuita, Puerto Viejo and Panamá (via Sixaola) –
disembark at the *Transportes MEPE* stop at C 3, Av 4, 100m north of the mercado.
Buses from Moín pull in at C 4, Av 4, near the landmark *Radio Casino*.

For **information** on the Caribbean coast, you'll need to contact the San José
ICT (☎233-1733, ext. 277): there is no official tourist office in the entire province.
Tour agencies can provide basic information, however, and you could try the
Hellenik souvenir shop, 200m north of the mercado. *Banco Nacional*, C 3, Av 2,
across from the mercado, and *Banco de Costa Rica*, on Av 2, 150m east of the
mercado, offer **exchange facilities** (Mon–Fri 8.30am–3pm); at weekends try a
large hotel like the *Maribú Caribe*. **Mail service** from Limón is dreadful – you're
better off posting things from San José. However, if you're desperate, the *correo*
lies 200m west and 100m south of the mercado at the *CORTEL* office, C 5, Av 1
(Mon–Fri 8am–5pm). **Telephone calls** (international, too) can be made from the
ICE office, Av 2, C 5/6 (Mon–Fri 8am–4pm). Note that during **Carnaval** everything shuts for a week, making banking and posting impossible. Should you need
medical care, head for Hospital Dr Tony Facio Castro, at the north end of the
malecón (☎758-2222).

LIMÓN PATOIS

Limón patois combines **English phrases**, brought by Jamaican and Barbadian immigrants to the province in the last century, with a Spanish slightly different to that spoken in the Highlands. The traditional greeting of the area; "What Happen?" ("Whoppin?") is used less and less these days, but is still a stock phrase, equivalent to the Spanish ¿Qué Pasa? ("What's going on?"). You'll also hear the Spanish-speaking Costa Ricans' "adiós" ("hello" rather than goodbye in Costa Rica; see p.380), "Que le vaya bien", or "Que Díos le accompañe" switched for the more laconic "Okay" or "all right" (both hello and goodbye) in Limón.

Do not, however, assume that everyone speaks English. While English might be spoken in the home, and among older Limón inhabitants, Spanish is the language taught at school and, among the younger generation, used on the street. Young people often have only a smattering of colloquial English expressions. Older *Limonenses* sometimes refer to Spanish speakers as "Spaniamen", which comes out sounding like "Sponyaman".

While Limón is not quite the mugger's paradise it is sometimes portrayed to be in the Highland media, standing on the sidewalk and looking lost is not recommended, nor is carrying valuables (most of the hotels listed opposite have safes). When trying to **find your way around**, bear in mind that even more than in other Costa Rican towns, nobody refers to calles and avenidas in Limón. The city does have street numbers, but there are virtually no signs. However, if only for the purposes of map-reading, it's useful to know that avenidas run more or less east–west in numerical order, starting at the docks. Calles run north–south, beginning with C 1 on the western boundary of Parque Vargas by the malecón. To confuse things further, unlike other towns in Costa Rica, calles and avenidas in Limón run sequentially: Avs 1, 2 and 3 are just one block away from each other, instead of being separated into twos by a grid system. Though the city as a whole, including its suburbs, is very spread out, **central Limón** covers no more than about ten blocks.

Accommodation

It's worth shelling out a bit for a **room** in Limón, especially if travelling alone; this is most certainly a place where the comfort and safety of your hotel makes a difference to your peace of mind. The better places fill quickly at weekends, when *Limonenses* who live and work in the Highlands come back to visit friends and family. If you're arriving on a Friday, call or fax ahead.

Staying **downtown** keeps you in the thick of things, and many hotels have communal balconies, perfect for relaxing with a cold beer above the lively street activity below. The downside of this is noise, especially at night; if you want to hear gentle waves lapping in the breeze, your best bet is the *Park Hotel*, which stands on a little promontory all its own, quite close to the sea. The nicest hotels, however, are outside town, about 4km up the spur road to Moín, at **Portete** and the small, somewhat misnamed **Playa Bonita**. A taxi up here costs less than $1.50, and the bus to and from Moín runs along the road every twenty minutes or so. Allow an hour to walk into town. In all but the most upscale places, avoid drinking the **tap water**, or use a filter or chlorine tablets.

Hotel prices rise by as much as fifty percent for **Carnaval** week, and to a lesser extent during *Semana Santa*, or Easter week, and between July and October. December, January and February which (confusingly) are elsewhere in the country considered high season, are the cheapest times to come.

Limón has its share of dives, which tend to fill when there's a big ship in town. None of the places listed below is rock-bottom cheap. If this is what you're after, you'll find it easily enough; but always ask to see the room first and make sure to inspect the bathroom.

ACCOMMODATION PRICE CODES

All the establishments in this book have been given price codes according to the following scale. The prices quoted are for the least expensive double room in high season, and do not include the national 18.46 percent tax automatically added on to hotel bills. Wherever an establishment offers dorm beds the prices of these are given in the text. For more details see p.26.

① less than $10	③ $20–30	⑤ $50–75	⑦ $100–150
② $10–20	④ $30–50	⑥ $75–100	⑧ $150 plus

In town

Acón, Av 3, C 2/3 (☎758-1010; fax 758-2924; Aptdo 528, Limón). Doubles only in this basic, clean hotel. Can be noisy; there's a popular weekend disco upstairs. Private parking. ④.

Miami, Av 2, C 4/5 (☎758-0490; fax 758-1978; Aptdo 266, Limón). Friendly place with clean rooms with ceiling fans; check the bathrooms, however, as they can be grubby. ③.

Nuevo Internacional, Av 5, C 2/3 (☎758-0662 or 0532; Aptdo 288, Limón). Light, bright and scrupulously clean, but with paper-thin partition walls. Private bath with electric showers. Rooms with fans are about half the price of a/c. ②.

Park, Av 3, C 1 and the malecón (☎758-3476; fax 758-4364). Recently renovated, the best choice in town, popular with Ticos and travellers alike. Three choices: sea view (most expensive), street view, and *plana turista* (no view, cheapest). Good restaurant, too. Reserve. ④.

Teté, Av 3, C4/5 (☎758-1122; fax 758-0707; Aptdo 401, Limón). Nothing special but clean, well-cared for and central; the best value downtown in this price range. Rooms on the street can be noisy but have balconies; rooms inside are a little darker. Friendly reception staff. ③.

Portete and Playa Bonita

Apartments Cocorí, Playa Bonita (☎758-2930; in San José ☎257-4674). Beautiful setting and the best value in Playa Bonita, although not greatly comfortable or creatively furnished. Friendly family reception and a lively outdoor bar/restaurant with nice view, right by the sea. Downstairs rooms have a/c, upstairs have fans. Slim but adequate self-catering facilities. ④.

Cabinas Maeva, Portete; look for the blue-and-white sign (☎758-2024). Cute yellow hexagonal cabinas nestled in palms, with a beautiful pool and Neoclassical statuary. Restaurant. ④.

Jardín Tropical, Playa Bonita (☎758-1244). New, upmarket hotel with jacuzzi/pool and waterfall. Open-air restaurant and a thatched bar in landscaped gardens with tall palms. Cramped rooms – the family suite is most spacious – with phone, a/c, hot water and TV. ④.

Maribú Caribe, Portete (☎758-4543; fax 758-3541; Aptdo 623, Portete). Sea-facing complex of round, thatched-roof huts with decor suspended around 1965; a favourite with the banana company execs. Very luxurious: quiet, with a good pool and bar/restaurant. The somewhat pricey restaurant overlooking the sea is not part of the hotel. ⑥.

Matama, Playa Bonita. Nice enough hotel with comfortable bungalow rooms, pool, bar and restaurant – all marred by the owners' insistence on having a tiny private zoo, the most unhappy of whose sorry inhabitants is the caged jaguar. ⑤.

The Town

Fifteen minutes' walk around Puerto Limón and you've seen the lot. **Avenida 2**, known locally as the "market street", is for all purposes the main drag, touching the north edge of Parque Vargas and the south side of the **Mercado Central**. The market is as good a place as any to start your explorations, and at times seems to be full of the entire town population, with dowager women minding their patch while thin men flutter their hands, clutching cigarettes and gesticulating jerkily to animated chatter. The produce looks very healthy: *chayotes*, plantains, cassava, yucca, beans and the odd banana (most of the crop is exported) vie for space with bulb-like cacao fruit, baseball-sized tomatoes and forearm-thick carrots. The sodas and snack bars are good places to grab a bite.

Shops in Limón close over lunch, between noon and 2pm, when everyone drifts toward **Parque Vargas** and the malecón to sit under the shady palms. A little shabby today, the park, at the easternmost end of C 1 and Av 1 and 2, features a sea-facing **mural** by artist Guadalupe Alvarea, depicting colourful and evocative images of the province's tough history. On the left of the semicircular wall, indigenous people are shown making crafts – later suppressed and destroyed by the Catholic missionaries. Next comes Columbus; ships being loaded with coffee and bananas by women wearing vibrant African cloth, and the arrival of the Jungle Train, with a wonderful Chinese dragon to symbolize the Chinese labourers who came to work on its construction. The park is also home to nine **sloths**, who live in the tall Royal Palms; no one seems to be able to confirm whether they're two-toed or three-toed – take binoculars and a field guide to be the first to set this to rest. There's a shrine to sailors and fishermen at the end of the central promenade, and a bandstand, now much dilapidated, which hosts occasional concerts. From here the **malecón** (a thin ledge where it is hardly possible to walk, let alone take a seaside promenade) winds its way north. Avoid it at night, as muggings have been reported.

Around the park, you'll see the large blue-and-white justice court, and the evocative *Municipalidad*, or **Town Hall**, with its sour yellow facade and peeling Belle Epoque grillework. The landmark *Radio Casino* building, on the corner of C 4 and Av 4, almost across the street from the Cahuita bus stop, is home to an excellent community-service station, broadcasting by and for *Limonenses* with call-in chat shows, international news and good music, including local and imported reggae. As for other activities in town, forget **swimming**. One look at the water at the tiny spit of sand next to the *Park Hotel* is enough discouragement; JAPDEVA, the harbour authority, used to run a public pool, but this is now closed. Pollution, sharks, huge banana-carrying ships and sharp, crumbly exposed coral make it practically impossible to swim anywhere nearby; the nearest possibility is at **Playa Bonita**, though even that is plagued by dangerous rip tides.

There are few **excursions** worth making from Limón. Day trips up the *canales* to Tortuguero (see p.150) take three to five hours (with animal-spotting) one-way; you then have to turn round immediately and motor back down without seeing the turtles or the village. A better possibility for a short boat trip is up the **Río Matina** from Moín, but without a guide you are unlikely to spot many animals.

Carnaval in Limón

Though in the rest of Latin America **Carnaval** is usually associated with the days before Lent, somewhat ironically, Limón takes Columbus' arrival in the New

World – October 12 – as its point of celebration. The idea was first brought to Limón by a local man named Arthur King, who had been away working in Panamá's Canal Zone and was so impressed with that country's Columbus Day celebrations that he decided to bring the merriment home with him. Today **El Día de la Raza** (Day of the People) is basically an excuse to party. Ticos from the Highlands descend upon Limón as if they'd never heard the words "crack" and "mugger" in association with the place. Buses are packed, hotels brim, and revellers hit the streets in search of this year's sounds and style. Rap, rave, ragga – in Spanish and English – is hot, and Bob Marley lives, or at least is convincingly resurrected, for Carnaval week.

Carnaval can mean whatever you want it to, from noontime displays of Afro-Caribbean dance to Calypso music festivals, bull-running, afternoon children's theatre, colourful *desfiles* (parades) and massive firework displays. Most spectacular is the **Grand Desfile**, usually held on the Saturday before October 12, when Afro-Caribbean costumes – sequins, spangles, fluorescent colours – parade the streets to a cacophony of tambourines, whistles and blasting sound systems.

Instead of taking place in Limón's streets as it has in years past – there were some problems with "sanitation" according to the national press, and the whole event was threatened with closure – most of Carnaval's nighttime activity now occurs within the fences of JAPDEVA's huge docks and parking lot. This might sound like a soulless location, but it is a well-managed affair, and while you may not be dancing in the streets you are at least getting a chance to dance. The over-all atmosphere – even late at night – is unthreatening, with young bloods and grandparents alike enjoying the music. Kiosks dispense steaming Chinese, Caribbean and Tico food, and on-the-spot discos, complete with dance floor, light show and live band or DJ, compete on the bass volume. **Cultural Street**, which runs from the historic Black Star Line (the shipping company that brought many of the black immigrants here) is an alcohol-free zone, popular with family groups, where kids can play games at small fairgrounds to win candyfloss and stuffed toys. Elsewhere bars overflow into the street, and the impromptu partying builds up as the night goes on.

Eating, drinking and entertainment

Though Limón has a surprising variety of places to eat, there is only one completely authentic restaurant in town – *Springfields* – to sample the wonderful local Caribbean or **Creole** cuisine (see p.136). It's best to heed warnings not to sit outside to eat at the restaurants in town, especially around the Mercado Central, where tourists are prime targets for – often aggressive – beggars. Gringos in general and women especially should avoid most **bars** – especially those that have a large advertising placard blocking views of the interior. If you want to drink, stick to places like *Mares* or *Brisas del Caribe*. **Playa Bonita** is a great place for lunch or an afternoon beer if you are tired of town.

In town

Brisas del Caribe, C 1, Av 2. Clean restaurant/bar with a good view of Parque Vargas. Except on the nights when the sound system is blasting, this is a quiet place to have a coffee or beer and not be bothered except by having to collar a bored waiter. No exciting food, just the usual rice, *casados* and sandwiches, and a worthy *medio casado* (half *casado*) for $2.

Mares, Av 2, C 3/4. *The* gringo hang-out, exuding café elegance with comfortable cushioned chairs, small glass tables, huge plant-dotted interior and a nice view of the mercado. Varied, reasonably priced menu, featuring sandwiches and burgers.

Hotel/Restaurante Park, Av 3, C1 and the malecón, 50m north of Parque Vargas. The only restaurant in town where you feel you might actually be in the Caribbean – sea breezes float in through large slatted windows and all you can see is an expanse of blue sea and cloud. If you stick to *arroz con pollo* and the like, the food is not too bad.

Pizzería Il Macarrone, C 4, Av 1/2. Excellent Italian pizzeria, somewhat incongruous in this very Caribbean city. Large pizzas, with thin crust and fresh toppings cost about $6 and are enough for three; not a bad price for the best pizza in Costa Rica (and passable red Italian wine!). Credit cards even accepted.

Soda la Estrella, C 5, Av 3/4. The best lunch in town. Top marks for soda staples: excellent *refrescos*, coffee, snacks, basic plates and daily specials, all with very cordial service.

Soda Yans, Av 2, C 5/6. Very popular with locals, this vaguely upmarket-looking place has a certain urban cachet. Small menu; some local dishes.

Springfields, north of the end of the malecón, across from the hospital. People in the know say *Springfields* used to be better; but it is still *the* place to eat in Limón. Authentic Creole cuisine on gingham tablecloths, cooked and served by people who know what they're doing. Go before 8pm and do not walk along the malecón alone at night.

Portete and Playa Bonita

Johnny Dixon's, on the beach. Nice place for local food and cold beer; music some nights.

Kimbambu, on the beach. Bar serving Caribbean food; staples include ceviche, fish, soup, chicken and cold beer.

Maribú Caribe, Portete. Cheerful poolside bar/restaurant for excellent food and *refrescos* (not to mention very friendly waiters).

Tía María, at the *Apartments Cocorí*. Very pleasant bar/restaurant with good sea views.

MOVING ON FROM LIMÓN

Heading north to **Tortuguero**, shallow-bottomed private *lanchas* make the trip up the canals from the docks at Moín. If you have arranged in advance to take one, it is crucial to get to the docks early (preferably 7am). The bus stop for Moín is at C 4, Av 4/5, 100m north of the mercado, around the corner from *Radio Casino*, but the bus leaves more or less when it wants to, so a taxi ($2) is a better option, especially if you've just arrived on the 5am bus from San José.

    Buses to San José start running at 5am from the main bus station and continue hourly until 7pm. Buy your ticket a day in advance if travelling on a Friday or Sunday. The ticket windows for *Coopelimón* and *Coopecaribeños* are side by side; *Coopetraga* (☎758-0618) also has services to **Siquerres** and **Guápiles** from where you can connect with buses to the capital. Destinations **south of Limón** are served from the *Transportes MEPE* (☎221-0524) office and stop at C 3, Av 4, 100m north of the mercado. There are four buses a day to Cahuita and Puerto Viejo (currently 5am, 10am, 1pm & 4pm). The **Sixaola** bus stops in Cahuita, but does not go into Puerto Viejo (it stops at El Cruce – "the cross" – from where it is about 5km walk to the village on a gravel road). Two buses (6am & 2.30pm) go direct to **Manzanillo** village in the heart of the Gandoca-Manzanillo Wildlife Refuge, via Puerto Viejo.

    Taxis line up on the north side of the mercado, and also on Av 2 around the corner from the San José bus stop. They regularly do long-haul trips to Cahuita and Puerto Viejo ($40–50), and to the banana plantations of the Valle de Estrella ($25). Prices are per carload, so if you are in a group this can be far more convenient than taking the bus.

South of Puerto Limón

Thirty kilometres south of Limón and 1km before the coastal road crosses the wide Río Estrella, the small wildlife sanctuary **Aviarios del Caribe** offers **B&B** accommodation on an 88-hectare island in the river's delta (fax 798-0374; Aptdo 569 7300, Limón; ⑥). The sanctuary features a 45-minute walking trail, which has an observation platform for **birdwatching** (255 species have been sighted; bring binoculars); you may also see white-faced, howler and spider monkeys. Canoes and bicycles are for rent at about $10 an hour. Owners Judy and Luis Arroyo offer several excursions, including a three-hour **kayak tour** ($35) through the delta, spotting caimans, river otters, and birds. This is a great place to stay, with four rooms with fans and bath with hot water, a small library and a games room. Because of its size, it's best to fax ahead. To reach *Aviarios del Caribe* by bus from Limón take the Cahuita service and ask to be dropped off at the entrance, which is before the Río Estrella bridge.

The Río Estrella region is one of the prime areas in the country for growing bananas and cacao. **Fincas** lace the countryside, some of which you can visit; look for the company signs and pull up by the processing plant, which will be a zinc-roofed, hangar-sized building in the middle of town. Several buses a day leave from the Cahuita stop in Limón to **Penshurst**, a banana/cacao *finca* town on the Río Estrella. The turnoff to Penshurst is just after the Río Estrella bridge, on the right (going south).

Reserva Biológica Hitoy-Cerere

Sixty kilometres south of Limón by road, a three-hour trip best done with your own car, the **RESERVA BIOLÓGICA HITOY-CERERE** (daily 8am–4pm; $5 in advance, $15 on the day) is one of the least visited National Reserves in Costa Rica. Sandwiched between the Tanyí, Telier and Talamanca indigenous reservations, this very rugged, isolated terrain – 9154 hectares of it – offers no information, campsites or washrooms, though there is a ranger station at the entrance. Especially if you're planning on hiking the one trail (see below), stop by the Parks Headquarters in San José beforehand – they or you may be able to call ahead and speak to the Hitoy-Cerere ranger about current conditions.

The name comes from the Bribrí language: *hitoy,* meaning "woolly" (the rocks in its rivers are covered with algae, and everything else is covered with a soft fuzz of moss); and *cerere,* meaning "clear waters", of which there are many. It is one of the wettest Reserves in all Costa Rica, receiving a staggering 4m of **rain** per year in some areas, with no dry season at all. Its complicated biological profile is due to its changing altitude. The top canopy trees are very tall indeed – some as high as 50m – and epiphytes, bromeliads, orchids and lianas grow everywhere under the very dense cover. **Wildlife** is predictably abundant, but most of the species are nocturnal and rarely seen, although you might spot three-toed sloths, and perhaps even a brocket deer. You'll probably hear howler monkeys – whitefaced monkeys live here, too. Pacas and frogs abound, many of them little-studied and considered rare. More visible are the 115 species of **birds**, from large black vultures to hummingbirds, trogons and dazzling blue kingfishers.

Hitoy-Cerere's **Espavel trail** is a tough 9km long, leading south from the ranger station through lowland and primary rainforest past clear streams, small waterfalls and beautiful vistas of the carpeted green Talamanca hills. Only **experienced tropical hikers** should attempt it, bringing compass, rubber boots, rain gear and water. The trail begins at a very muddy hill; after about 1km, in the secondary forest and open area, you'll notice the white-and-grey wild cashew trees (*espavel*) for which it is named. Follow the sign here; it leads off to the right and cuts through swathes of thick forest before leaving the Reserve and entering the Talamanca reservation, which is officially off limits.

From here the trail continues up a steep hill and ends at the Río Moín, 4.5km from the start. All there is to do now is turn back, taking care to negotiate the numerous fallen trees, tumbled rocks and boulders. Many of them were felled by the 1991 earthquake; older casualties are carpeted in primeval plants and mosses. The only possible respite from very dense jungle terrain is along the small dried river beds, following streams and tributaries of the Ríos Cerere and Hitoy.

Getting to Hitoy-Cerere under your own steam is complicated. Take the bus from Limón to Valle de Estrella, and get off at the end of the line at a banana town called (confusingly) both **Fortuna** and **Finca Seis** (Finca Six). There's 15km yet to go to the Reserve, most of it through banana plantation. A local 4WD taxi – ask at the plantation office – can take you there for about $25, and will return to pick you up at a mutually agreed time. The nearest **accommodation** is at *Aviarios del Caribe* or in Cahuita or Limón.

Refugio Nacional de Fauna Silvestre Barra del Colorado

Poised at the tip of Costa Rica near the border with Nicaragua, 99km straightshot northeast from San José, **REFUGIO NACIONAL DE FAUNA SILVESTRE BARRA DEL COLORADO** was created specifically for the preservation of the area's abundant fauna. A large, isolated tract, very sparsely populated (by humans, at least), it is crossed by Río Colorado, which branches out before Barra to meet the Caribbean, and Río San Juan, which peters out north of the border in Nicaragua. Almost all traffic in this area is by water.

BARRA DEL COLORADO is the only settlement of any size, a small, quiet village inhabited by a mixed population of Afro-Caribbeans, Miskitos, Costa Ricans and significant numbers of Nicaraguans, many of whom spilled over the border during the Civil War. The village is divided into two halves: Barra Sur and the larger Barra Norte, opposite each other near the mouth of the Río Colorado. Tropical hardwoods are still under siege from illegal logging around here – you may witness giant tree trunks being towed along the river and into the Caribbean, from where they are taken down to Limón.

Very few people come to Barra on a whim. As far as tourism goes, **sports-fishing** is the place's *raison d'être*, and numerous lodges offer packages and transportation from San José. Tarpon and snook, two big-game fish prized for their fighting spirit, ply these waters in droves, as does the garfish, a primeval throwback, looking something like a cross between a fish and a crocodile. The **season** runs from January to May and September to October.

Because of the impenetrability of the cover, there is little for non-fishing tourists to do in Barra other than birdwatch or crocodile-watch from a boat in one of the many waterways and lagoons. The usual sloths and monkeys are in residence, and you'll certainly hear the wild hoot of howler monkeys shrieking through the absolutely still air. If you are really lucky, and keep your eyes peeled

THE RÍO SAN JUAN AND THE NICARAGUAN BORDER

Heading to or from Barra from the Sarapiquí area in the Zona Norte (see p.195) entails a trip along the Río Sarapiquí to the mighty **Río San Juan**. Flowing from Lago de Nicaragua to the Caribbean, the San Juan marks most of Costa Rica's border with Nicaragua, and the entire northern edge of the Barra del Colorado Wildlife Refuge. Costa Ricans have the right of travel on the river, although it is theoretically in Nicaraguan territory (the actual border is the bank on the Costa Rican side, not the midpoint of the river), but there is no official entry point between the two countries along this stretch; it is technically illegal to attempt to cross here. For details on crossing into Nicaragua see p.192.

One bizarre phenomenon local to this area, and unique in the world, is the migration of **bull sharks** from the saltwater Caribbean up the Río San Juan to the freshwater Lago de Nicaragua, making the transition, apparently without trauma or difficulty, from being saltwater to freshwater sharks.

You'll notice the chainsaw's work much in evidence, especially at the point where the Sarapiquí flows into the Río San Juan; the **lumber industry** has long had carte blanche in this area, due to the non-enforcement of existing anti-logging laws. The **Nicaraguan side** of the Río San Juan, part of the country's huge Indio Maíz reserve, looks altogether wilder than its southern neighbour, with thick primary rainforest creeping right to the edge of the bank. Partly because of logging, and the residual destruction of banks, the Río San Juan is silting up, and even shallow-bottomed *lanchas* get stuck in this once consistently deep river. It is a far cry from the days in the 1600s and 1700s when pirate ships would sail all the way up and through to Lago de Nicaragua, from where they could wreak havoc on the Spanish Crown's ports and shipping.

on the water, you might catch a *manatí* (manatee, or sea cow) going by underneath. These large, benevolent seal-like creatures are on the brink of becoming an endangered species. You can't swim here – though you may see locals risking life and limb to do so – as this is **shark** territory.

It is very, very **hot**, and painfully **humid** around Barra. Wear a hat and sunscreen and, if possible, stay under shade during the hottest part of the day. February, March and April are the driest months, but there is no season when it does not rain.

Practicalities

In sheer terms of the time it takes you to get there, Barra is one of the most **inaccessible** places in the country. Most people arrive either by **lancha** from Tortuguero (45min) or Puerto Viejo de Sarapiquí (3hr downriver, twice that upriver), both lovely trips – from Puerto Viejo especially, as you come in partly on the Río San Juan. If you do this, be sure to have your passport to show at Nicaraguan border checkpoints. *Lanchas* arrive in Barra Sur, or, if you ask, will take you directly to your accommodation.

The **flight** from San José to Barra (landing at Barra Sur) affords stupendous views of volcanos, unfettered lowland tropical forest, and the coast stretching practically all the way up to Nicaragua. Currently *Sansa* flies from San José (6am on Mon, Thurs & Sat), returning on the same days, while *Travelair* flies daily, currently leaving San José at 6am and returning at 6.55am.

Accommodation

Because of Barra's inaccessibilty and its emphasis on fishing, literally no one comes here for just one night. Most lodges are devoted exclusively to **fishing packages**, although you could, theoretically call in advance and arrange to stay as an independent, non-fishing guest. The lodges can provide details of their individual packages; generally they comprise meals, accommodation, boat, guide and tackle, and some may offer boat lunches, drinks and other extras. The only lodge in the area that doesn't cater to sportsfishers, *Samay Laguna*, also brings most of its guests to the area on packages from San José. The only place at all geared up for **independent travellers** is *Tarponland*, which has a few cabinas. While all of the accommodation in this area is comfortable, some tends toward the positively rustic, and you should certainly not expect frills such as air conditioning.

Río Colorado Fishing Lodge, Barra Sur (☎232-4063; fax 231-5987; in the US: ☎1-800/243-9777). Elegant old lodge, with comfortable rooms, bar with US cable TV, dining room with a pretty view of Barra Norte and good food. ⑥.

Samay Laguna Lodge, 15min by *lancha* south from Barra Sur (☎228-9912; ☎ and fax 236-7154; Aptdo 12767-1000, San José). The best away-from-it-all experience in this part of the country, on the deserted stretch of beach between Barra and Tortuguero. Two German brothers have done a good job of integrating the lodge in the community, offering boat tours, jungle hikes, horse rides on the beach, turtle tours to Tortuguero and trips along the Ríos Colorado and San Juan to Puerto Viejo de Sarapiquí. You can fly in or out, take your own canoe, and go sportsfishing, although this is not their speciality. Good value 2- and 3-day packages from San José. ④.

Tarponland Bar and Restaurant, next to the airstrip in Barra Sur. Older, large lodge, one of the only places in town where you can get a cold drink and meal. Moderately priced, with simple, screened rooms with fans, and private or shared baths. Attached are the cheaper and more basic *Salsa Olandia* cabinas. ②.

PACKAGES IN BARRA DEL COLORADO

Casamar (☎441-2820; fax 433-9287; Aptdo 825, San José; in the US: PO Box 787, Islamorada, FL 33036; ☎1-800/327-2880). Comforable two-storey cabins, open during the fishing season only. Fishing packages only, at around $2000 per week.

Isla de Pesca, (☎223-4560; fax 221-5148; Aptdo 8-4390, San José 1000; in the US: c/o *Costa Sol Intl*; ☎1-800/245-8240; fax 305/539-1123). Pretty chalet-style cabins, some of the most comfortable in Barra, with overhead fans, hot water, and small verandah. Fishing packages from 3 to 7 nights cost in the region of $1000.

Silver King Lodge (☎288-0849; fax 288-1403; in the US: c/o *Rainforest Excursions*). Comfortable specialist fishing lodge, with big rooms, bar and restaurants, and US TV. $1195 for 3-day package.

Parque Nacional Tortuguero

Though isolated – 254km from San José by road and water, or 83km northwest of Limón – **PARQUE NACIONAL TORTUGUERO** ($15 on the day, $7 in advance) is one of the most visited National Parks in Costa Rica. As the name implies – *tortuguero* means turtle-catcher in Spanish, and turtle-catchers have long flourished in this area – this is one of the most important nesting sights in the world for the **green sea turtle**. One of only eight species of marine turtles in the world, it lays its eggs here between July and October, joined by the hawksbill.

First established as a protective zone in the 1960s, Tortuguero became a National Park in 1975. It's big – 18,946 hectares to be exact, and 35km long – protecting not only the turtle nesting beach, but also surrounding forests, canals and waterways. (There are no distinct boundaries, but everyone in the area knows which areas are protected and which are not.) It's also very **wet**, except for a short dry season during February and March: otherwise it receives over 6000mm of rain a year. A combination of impenetrable tropical rainforest, with coastline vegetation, mangrove swamps and lagoons, it's the **water** that defines Tortuguero. This soggy environment hosts a wide abundance of species – fifty kinds of **fish**, numerous **birds**, including the endangered green parrot and the vulture, and some 160 **mammals**, some under the threat of extinction. Due to the waterborne nature of most transport and the impenetrability of the ground cover, it's difficult to spot them, but howler, white-faced and spider monkeys lurk behind the undergrowth, along with the fishing bulldog bat, which fishes by sonar,

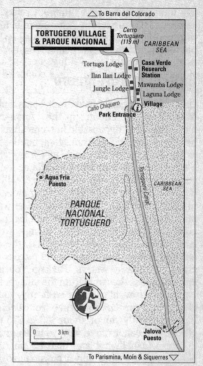

and a variety of large rodents, including the window rat, whose internal organs you can see through its transparent skin. You may spot the little-understood West Indian manatee, or sea cow, swimming beneath the water. Jaguars used to thrive, but are slowly being driven out by the encroaching banana plantations at the western end of the Park. It's the **turtles** that draw people here, however, and the sight of the gentle beasts tumbling ashore and shimmying their way up the beach to deposit their heavy load before limping back, spent, into the dark phosphorescent waves can't fail but move even the most hard-hearted viewer.

The most popular way to see Tortuguero is on one of literally hundreds of **packages** that use the expensive "Jungle Lodges" across the canal from the village. These are usually two-night, three-day affairs, although you can certainly go for longer. Accommodation, meals and transport (which otherwise can be a bit tricky) are taken care of, while guides point out wildlife along the river and canals on the way. The main difference between tours comes in the standard of accommodation; check the reviews of the lodges on p.154 to help you choose. With a little planning, you can also get to Tortuguero **independently** and stay in cabinas in the **village**, which is a more interesting little place than initial impressions might suggest. Basing yourself here allows you to explore the beach at leisure – though you can't swim – and leaves you in easy reach of restaurants and bars.

As elsewhere in Costa Rica, logging, economic opportunism and fruit plantations have had their effects on Tortuguero. Sometimes advertised by package tour brochures as a "Jungle Cruise" along "Central America's Amazon" the journey to Tortuguero is Amazonian indeed, taking you past tracts of **deforestation** and lands cleared for cattle – all outside the official boundaries of the Park, but together with banana plantations, encroaching on to its western fringes.

Getting to Tortuguero

Until the 1991 earthquake, tour boats and a weekly cargo boat would travel from Moín, north of Limón, up the Limón–Nicaragua canal. Sadly the earthquake made the canal unpassable in some areas to all but the most shallow-bottomed of boats; *lanchas* still go from Moín, but the bulk of the traffic has shifted elsewhere.

The journey up the canals to Tortuguero is at least half the experience. Expect a three- or four-hour trip (sometimes longer) by *lancha*, depending upon where you embark – if on a package tour, it will probably be **Hamburgo de Siquerres** on the Río Reventazón; if travelling independently, you'll find it logistically easier to leave from **Moín** (see p.146). Either way you'll pass palm and deciduous trees, mirror-calm waters, and small stilt-legged wooden houses, brightly painted and poised on the water's edge – along, of course, with acres and acres of cleared land. Quite apart from the wildlife, the canal is a hive of human activity, with *lanchas*, *botes* (large canoes) and *pangas* (flat-bottomed outboard-motored boats) plying the glassy waters. Package tourists are disgorged at whichever of the lodges, across the canal from the village, they are booked into.

If you're travelling **independently**, you'll need to get to the Moín docks early, ideally by 7am. *Lanchas* leave from behind the large blue-and-white boathouse. Fares currently run at about $65 to $75 per person, less if you're travelling in a group. You can arrange with your boatman when you would like to be picked up to return (usually not later than 1.30pm, to avoid getting stuck in the dark). Get a phone number from him if possible, so you can call from Tortuguero village if you change plans. The *lanchas* drop you at Tortuguero dock, from where you can walk to the village accommodation, or take another *lancha* across the canal to find space at the more expensive tourist lodges. If you haven't booked a hotel, beware that in the high (turtle-nesting) seasons, accommodation in the village can fill up quickly, so finding a place to sleep should be your first concern.

The Village

The static, heat-stunned village of **TORTUGUERO** lies at the northeastern orner of the Park, on a thin spit of land between the sea and the Tortuguero canal. With its exuberant foliage of wisteria, oleander and bougainvillea, the whole place has the look of a carefully tended tropical garden. Tall palm groves and clean, mowngrass expanses are punctuated by zinc-roofed wooden houses, often elevated on stilts. This is classic Caribbean style: washed-out, slightly ramshackle and pastelpretty, with very little to disturb the torpor until after dark.

A dirt path runs through the village north–south – the "main street" from which narrow paths go off to the sea and the canal. Smack in the middle of the village stands one of the prettiest churches you'll see anywhere, pale yellow and quiet, with a small spire and an oval doorway – it's the one in the photo on the back cover of this book. At the octagonal ranch-roofed building just north of the Park information kiosk (see below), look out for the semi-naif **jungle murals**, a bright display of sloths lazing on lianas, jaguars pacing and palms swaying.

Enrique's **souvenir shop** (Mon–Fri 8am–7pm), at the northern end of the village across from the small *muelle*, is very well-stocked with T-shirts, wooden carved souvenirs and cards, with prices more or less in line with those of San José. If the sun here is getting to you, this is the place to pick up a hat or sunscreen.

Information

A display on the turtles' habits, habitat and history surrounds the **information kiosk** in the centre of the village. Officially you should buy tickets for turtle tours here (see p.156), but it operates under eccentric hours, so if no one's there, go to the **ranger station**, south of the village, where you officially enter the Park.

The **pulpería**, 50m south of the information kiosk, houses a **public phone** (☎710-6716). This is the number to call to reserve village accommodation, but bear in mind it is not foolproof: you need to speak Spanish, and should leave a Costa Rican number where the hotelier can call you back. There are more phones at *Enrique's*, and *Miss Junie's* restaurant (see p.154). The *Centro Social la Culebra*, next to the *pulpería*, has details of **boat rental** and **tours**, as well as anything that's happening in the way of nightlife.

Though there is a **correo** in the middle of the village, mail may take three or four weeks just to make its way to Limón. If villagers are heading to Limón they might offer to carry letters for you and post them from there; gratifying if you are staying here for any length of time. Tortuguero has only a fortnightly doctor service; emergencies and health problems should be referred to the Park's administration headquarters, north of the village, near the airstrip.

Village accommodation

Staying at Tortuguero on the cheap entails bedding down in one of the independent **cabinas** in the village. **Camping** on the beach is not allowed, though you can set up tent at the Park's central administration headquarters at the very northern tip of the village, as well as at the mown enclosure at the **ranger station** (about $2 per day) at the southern end of the village, where you enter the Park. It's in a sheltered situation, away from the sea breezes, and there is water and toilets. Bring a ground sheet and mosquito net, and make sure your tent is waterproof.

Brisas del Mar (or *El Bochinche*) east side of village. Very basic, with shared outside bathrooms, cold water and stuffy rooms (no fans), though it does, as the name suggests, get the odd sea breeze. Can get noisy Wed and Sat nights, when its bar hosts a good disco. ①.

Cabinas Merry Scar, east of the *pulpería*, before the beach. Well-run place with clean small rooms that can get stuffy, and separate, spick-and-span bath. Family atmosphere; the friendly *dueña* or her daughters will cook simple meals on request (about $4 extra). ①.

Cabinas Sabina, east of the information kiosk, on the beach. Very simple (and very green) cabinas whose attraction is their setting on a nice strip of sand. Rooms are basic and dark; the toilet and shower are outhouse-type, but clean. Upstairs has better ventilation. Rules to vacate by 10am are strictly enforced. Good restaurant and popular bar. ①.

The lodges

Staying at Tortuguero's **lodges**, most of which are across the canal from the village, has its drawbacks. You're pretty much duty-bound to eat the set meals included in your (not cheap) package, and – unless you're at the *Laguna* or *Mawamba* – if you want to explore the village and the beach on your own you have to get a *lancha* across the canal (free, but inconvenient, nonetheless). The lodges only rent rooms to independent travellers if they have space, which they rarely do, owing to Tortuguero's perennial popularity. Though prices vary, and none is officially posted for non-package tours, they hover between ④ and ⑤. To locate the lodges listed here, see the map on p.151.

Ilan-Ilan Most basic and cheapest of the lodges. Very prefab looking, cabin-type accommodation in small grounds. Nothing fancy, but private rooms with bath and set meals. ④–⑤.

Jungle Lodge, owned and operated by *COTUR* (☎233-0155; fax 233-0778; Aptdo 1818, San José 1002). Friendly, comfortable place in its own gardens, with a not-bad restaurant. Large private baths – this is the only lodge that has running hot water – and your own verandah. Free canoes and footpath to a lagoon. The second-cheapest tour/accommodation (after *Ilan-Ilan*) and a good deal. ④–⑤.

Laguna Lodge (☎ and fax 225-3740). Small, very attractive hotel with rustic wooden cabins. Peaceful atmosphere and personal service, ideal for those who don't like large *turista* lodges. Convenient village location, with easy access to the beach and full tour services. ④–⑥.

Mawamba Lodge (☎223-2421; fax 222-4932; Aptdo 6618, 1000 San José). Upmarket lodge, the best place to go if money is no object, as the village and ocean are just a walk away. ④–⑤.

Tortuga Lodge, owned by *Costa Rica Expeditions* (☎257-0766; fax 257-1665). The plushest lodge in the area, but rather far-flung. Large rooms, with private baths, and elegantly landscaped grounds with lots of walking opportunities. Meals are usually extra and, while of the "all you can eat" variety, are not cheap ($10 for breakfast). ④–⑤.

Eating, drinking and nightlife

Tortuguero village offers good downhome food, typically Caribbean, with wonderful fresh **fish**. The disadvantages are the prices, which tend to be high, and the lack of places for **breakfast** (though the *dueña* of *Cabinas Merry Scar* has been known to whip up something for a few dollars if you ask nicely).

Centro Social la Culebra has a **disco**, generally agreed to be rather rough; *Bar Brisas del Mar* is better, with a large, semi open-air dance floor and a good sound and light system (when it is not visiting Limón). You can hear the sea from your table and atmosphere is low-key and inviting.

Miss Junie's, north end of village path, 50m before the central Park administration. Sizeable dining room, with gingham tablecloths and cool white walls. Miss Junie is a local who does solid Caribbean food – red beans, jerk chicken, rice, chayote and breadfruit, all on the same plate – with ice-cold beers to boot. She cooks for the Park rangers, so you need to ask a day in advance or in the morning whether she can fit you in.

Pancana Restaurante, on the path to *Cabinas Merry Scar*, east side of the village. A pretty house, otherwise known as *Jacob and Edna's*, this restaurant is famous in the area for succulent baked goods and Caribbean food. Open 6am–8pm.

Restaurant Sabina, east of the information kiosk, on the beach. Great outdoor site next to the sea, with a backdrop of crashing waves and clean breezes. The fresh fish is especially good, but prices are high (twice as expensive as similar dishes in San José, for example), and it can cost more to eat here than to stay the night at the cabinas next door. Open 6am–11pm.

Soda el Tucan, next to the *pulpería*. Soda staples rather than Caribbean food, including rice and chicken and *casados* as well as cool *refrescos* and lunch deals.

Visiting the Park

Most people come to Tortuguero to see the **deshove**, or egg-laying of the turtles. Few are disappointed, as the majority of tours during laying **seasons** (March–May & July–Oct) result in sightings of the moving, surreal procession of the reptiles from the sea to make their egg-nests in the sand. While turtles have been known to lay in the daylight (the hatchlings wait under the cover of sand until nightfall to emerge), it is far more common for them to come ashore in the relative safety of night. Nesting can take place turtle-by-turtle: you can watch a single mother as she comes ashore and scrambles up the beach or, more strikingly, in groups (*arribadas*) when dozens emerge from the sea at the same time to form a colony, marching up the sands to their chosen spot, safely above the high tide mark. Each turtle digs a hole in which she lays eighty or more eggs; the collective whirring noise of sand being dug away is extraordinary. Having filled the hole with sand to cover the eggs, the turtles begin their course back to the sea, leaving the eggs to hatch and return to the waves under the cover of darkness. Incubation takes some weeks; when the hatchlings emerge they instinctively follow the light of the moon on the water, scuttling to safety in the ocean.

Although Tortuguero is by no means the only place in Costa Rica to see marine turtles nesting (they use the Pacific beaches too), three of the largest kinds of

TURTLING

For hundreds of years the fishermen of the Caribbean coast made their living **culling** the seemingly plentiful supplies of turtles, selling shell and meat for large sums to middlemen in Puerto Limón. Initially they were hunted for local consumption only, but around the turn of the century and into the first two decades of the 1900s, the fashion for turtle soup in Europe, especially England, led to large-scale exportation.

Turtle-hunting was a particularly brutal practice. Spears were formed from long pieces of wood, taken from the *apoo* palm or the *rawa*, fastened with a simple piece of cord to a sharp, barbed metal object. Standing in their canoes, fishermen hurled the spear, like a miniature harpoon, into the water, lodging the spear into the turtle's flesh. Pulling their canoes closer, the fishermen would then reel in the cord attached to the spear, lift the beasts into the canoes and take them ashore dead or alive. On land, the turtles might be beheaded with machetes, or put in the holds of ships, where they could survive a journey of several weeks to Europe if they were given a little water.

Today, turtles are protected, their eggs and meat a delicacy. Locals around Tortuguero are officially permitted to take two turtles a week during nesting season for their own consumption – the unlucky green turtles are considered most delicious. As the recent sharp decline in the populations of hawksbill, green and leatherback turtles has been linked, at least in part, to **poaching**, the National Parks administration have adopted a firm policy to discourage the theft of turtle eggs within the Park boundaries, and rangers are armed. Meanwhile, should you find a turtle on its back between July 10 and September 15, do not flip it over, as in most cases it is being tagged by researchers, who work on the northern 8km of the 35-km long nesting beach.

It is not just the acquisitive hand of humans that endangers the turtles. On land, a cadre of **animals**, among them coati and racoons, regularly ransack the nests in order to eat the unborn reptiles. Once the hatching has started – the darkness giving them a modicum of protection – the turtles really have their work cut out for them, running a gauntlet of vultures, barracudas, sharks and even other turtles (the giant leatherback has been known to eat other species' offspring) on their way from the beach to the sea. Only about 60 percent – an optimistic estimate – of hatchlings reach adulthood, and the survival of marine turtles worldwide is under question.

endangered sea turtles regularly nest here in large numbers. Along with the **green** (*verde*) turtle, named for the colour of soup made from its flesh, you might see the **hawksbill** (*carey*), with its distinctive hooked beak; and the ridged **leatherback** (*baula*), the largest turtle in the world, which can easily weigh 300kg – some are as heavy as 500kg and reach 5m in length. They come ashore here because of the high concentrations of their prime food source, sargasso, nearby, around the Miskito Cays off the coast of Nicaragua. The green turtles and hawksbills nest most concentratedly from July to October (August is peak month), while the mighty leatherbacks may come ashore from March to May.

Turtle tours, led by certified guides, leave at 8pm every night from the village. Tickets ($25 including the Park entrance fee) are sold from the information kiosk in the village between 4 and 6pm on the day. Guides are instructed to make as little noise as possible so as not to alarm the turtles, allowing them to get on with their business; everyone must be off the beach by 10pm. Some packages include the price of taking a turtle tour; on others you pay for it separately on the spot at your lodge. Check with your tour operator.

A single, generally well-maintained, self-guided **trail** (1km), the **Sendero Natural**, starts at the ranger station at the entrance, passing two ranger huts and skirting west around the *llomas de sierpe* (swamp). As for that long, wild, wind-raked **beach**, you can amble for up to 30km south and enjoy crab-spotting, birds, and looking out for truck-wheel-like turtle-tracks. Swimming – even paddling – is emphatically not recommended, due to heavy waves, turbulent currents and sharks that are so audacious as to zoom around in waist-deep water. Remember that you'll need to **pay Park fees** to walk on the beach or along the trail.

Other activities around Tortuguero

Almost as popular as the turtle tours are Tortuguero's **boat tours** through the *caños*, or lagoons, to spot animals and birds – dignified looking herons, cranes and kingfishers, for example. For a *Jungle Book* adventure, take a tour with Mr Damma, a Miskito, originally from Nicaragua, who with his son Castor has an assured knowledge of the jungle and its creatures. Their photo album is full of picture after picture of surprised gringos holding caimans, spotting yellow eyelash vipers, swinging ecstatically from lianas and drinking from *skowa-skowa*, a water-full vine. They do an occasional overnight camping trip in the deep jungle (you have to build your own tent) and a 6.30am wildlife-spotting tour paddling along pristine *caños* (4hr; price negotiable). Damma lives next to the *Cabinas Merry Scar*, on the ocean side of the village. He needs at least a day's notice for an overnight tour, which are not always possible.

Most lodges have **canoes** you can take out on the canal – a great way to get around if you are good with a paddle, but do stick to the main canal as it is easy to get lost in the complex lagoon system northwest of the village. In the south of the village, Ruben, 50m north of the ranger station, right by the water, rents traditional Miskito-style boats for about $8 an hour, or $15 with a guide/paddler.

It is also possible to climb **Cerro Tortuguero**, an ancient volcanic deposit looming 119m above the flat coastal plain 6km north of the village. A climb up the gently sloping side leads you to the "peak", from which there are good views of flat jungle and inland waterways. Accessible only by *lancha*, this is a half-day hike, and you must go with a guide – ask at the village information kiosk or at the ranger station. Some of the lodges offer the guided climb as part of their packages.

Cahuita village and Parque Nacional Cahuita

The tiny village of **CAHUITA**, 43km southeast of Limón, is reached on the paved Hwy-36 from Limón to Sixaola on the Panamanian border. Like other villages on the Talamanca coast, especially Puerto Viejo (see p.165) and Manzanillo (see p.173), it has recently become a byword for relaxed, cheap "Caribbean" holidays, with a laid-back atmosphere, opportunities for a little forest walking, and the added appeal of great Afro-Caribbean food and cultural diversity. Though it is mainly wet all year round, the local "dry" season is between March and April, and from September to October.

You can swim on either of the village's two beaches, although neither is fantastic: the first 400m or so of the narrow white sand beach is particularly dangerous on account of rip tides. **Black-Sand Beach**, at the northern end of the village, is littered with fallen trees from the 1991 earthquake and driftwood, although you can swim in some places. Near the village, the **Parque Nacional Cahuita** was formed mainly to protect one of the only living coral reefs in Costa Rica, near Punta Cahuita; many people come here to **snorkel** and take glass-bottomed boat rides. The beach south of Punta Cahuita – sometimes called **Playa Vargas** – is better for swimming than those in the village, as it is protected from raking breakers by the coral reef, but is slightly awkward to get to. Backing the shores, a trail leads through the vast area of thick vegetation and mangrove swamps.

Cahuita started its days as a fairly sheltered bay populated by *cawi* trees, known in Spanish as *sangrilla* ("bloody" – the tree has a sap as thick and red as human blood). The name – Cawayta – comes from the Miskito words, *cawi* and *ta*, which means "point". Most of the inhabitants are descended from the Afro-Caribbean settlers from the Bocas del Toro area of Panamá and from workers brought to help build the Jungle Train. Older residents remember the days when a little fishing, small-scale farming and some quadrille dancing were the centre of local life. Now Cahuita, along with the rest of the Talamanca coast, has become very popular with backpackers and surfers, who idealize this semi-Rasta culture as a cool, relaxed paradise. Admittedly it is a relief to escape the homogeneity of Highland and Pacific Costa Rican culture and, as a beach town, Cahuita is culturally more arresting than anything you find on the Pacific coast. But in many ways, like Puerto Viejo, it is a case-study example of the unhappy clash between tourism and local communities; communities that have lost the happy, easy-going veneer that travellers like to assign to them. While tourism has undeniably brought prosperity, it has also brought cultural confusion and dislocation.

There's a drugs scene in Cahuita, with crack as well as the traditional ganja around, and some problems with opportunistic theft. In past years this area of the coast has attracted its share of "drug tourists", a problem that the government is attempting to combat with a hysterical propaganda campaign. Locals also tell stories of women travellers who come to town looking for a Rasta man to call their own for a few days. The arrangement seems to be that the woman pays the bills for a few days, and in return gets a short-term friend. This point begs a mention here only to warn non-interested single females to watch out for potentially difficult situations. Some local men can be pretty aggressive in their approaches, and no woman put in such a situation would agree that, for them, Cahuita is a friendly, easy-going place. The bottom line, then, is to be on your guard in Cahuita. Lock your door and

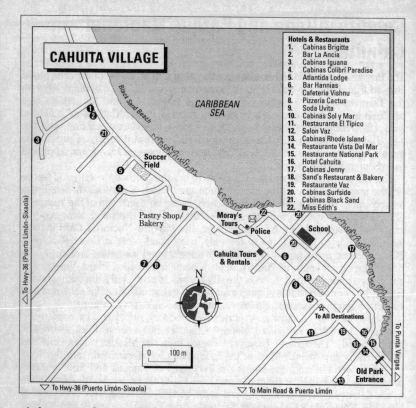

CAHUITA VILLAGE

Hotels & Restaurants
1. Cabinas Brigitte
2. Bar La Ancia
3. Cabinas Iguana
4. Cabinas Colibrí Paradise
5. Atlantida Lodge
6. Bar Hannias
7. Cafeteria Vishnu
8. Pizzería Cactus
9. Soda Uvita
10. Cabinas Sol y Mar
11. Restaurante El Típico
12. Salon Vaz
13. Cabinas Rhode Island
14. Restaurante Vista Del Mar
15. Restaurante National Park
16. Hotel Cahuita
17. Cabinas Jenny
18. Sand's Restaurant & Bakery
19. Restaurante Vaz
20. Cabinas Surfside
21. Cabinas Black Sand
22. Miss Edith's

windows, never leave anything on the beach, and avoid walking alone in unlit places at night. Nude or topless bathing is definitely unacceptable, as is wandering though the village wearing no more than a bathing suit. With just a bit of common sense, most travellers really enjoy the community and atmosphere here.

Arrival and information

Cahuita, like Puerto Viejo and Manzanillo to the south, was long cut off from the rest of the country – even from Limón – by the absence of a road. Before the Río Estrella bridge was built in the mid-1970s, a journey from Limón to Cahuita would involve a train ride, a canoe ferry across the Río Estrella, and a bus over a dirt road. Since the opening of the Guápiles Highway in 1987 things have changed dramatically.

Nowadays the easiest way to get to Cahuita from San José by **bus** is on the modern, comfortable Sixaola service (3–4hr). Taking a bus from San José to Puerto Limón (3hr) and then changing for Cahuita (4 daily) is only marginally cheaper than the *directo* bus and will increase travelling time by an hour, at least. In Cahuita, buses stop at the shelter on the small scruffy park across from the bar-disco *Salon Vaz*, whose walls are painted with the current **bus schedules** to Limón, San José and Sixaola.

Information

If you're coming to Cahuita **from Puerto Viejo**, be sure to pick up a copy of ATEC's *Welcome to Coastal Talamanca* (see p.167), which has good local maps and a directory of local-owned accommodation and businesses in Cahuita. The only sources of **visitor information** in the village itself are the tour companies: *Moray's Tours*, in the north, on the sea side (supposedly daily 8am–6pm; ext 216) has a small map of the village, while at *Cahuita Tours*, 200m north of *Salon Vaz* (daily 7am–noon & 1.30–7pm; ext 232 or ☎ and fax 758-0652), you can get up-to-date national newspapers and occasionally the *Tico Times*. They also sell **stamps**, offer **currency exchange** and have a phone for **international calls**. They dial for you and keep track of time used, charging about 75¢ on top of the cost of the call. There's a public **phone** at *Soda Uvita*, next door to *Salon Vaz*.

TELEPHONE NUMBERS IN CAHUITA

At present Cahuita has just **one phone number** for the entire village: ☎758-1515. Everyone who has a phone is assigned an extension number, which you have to request from the operator. This system is obviously more suited to the days when Cahuita was a small, little-visited village, and there is talk among residents of the phone company installing individual lines. People are sceptical, however, about how soon this will actually happen, but bear in mind the situation may have changed before you get there.

There are no **banks** in town – the nearest are in Bribrí, 20km away by road, or Limón. Your best bet for changing money is *Cahuita Tours* (see above). Established restaurants like the *National Park* and upscale hotels like the *Atlantida Lodge* have been known to change money, but you should not necessarily expect them to. *Atlantida* gives guests cash advances on credit cards for a 6 percent charge. The small **police station** (*guardia rural*) is on the last beach-bound road at the north end of the village; the *correo* next door has erratic hours to say the least (supposedly Mon–Fri 7am–4pm). The **doctor** comes to town every few days: bill posters announce his or her arrival a couple of days in advance.

Accommodation

Though Cahuita is popular with budget travellers, it is not especially cheap, although if you are travelling in a group it is possible to cut costs. Most **cabinas** charge per room and have space for at least three or four people. Though most tend to be of the concrete-block cell variety, standards are high, with fans, mosquito nets, clean sheets and bathrooms. Upstairs rooms are slightly more expensive, with sea breezes and occasional ocean views.

The **centre** of the village has scores of options, the best of which are listed below; staying here is convenient for restaurants, bars and the Park. There is also accommodation in all price ranges along the long (3km or so) road that runs by the sea north along **Black-Sand Beach**. It's quieter here, and the beach is not bad. However, women (even travelling in groups) and those without their own car are better off staying in town. A number of rapes and muggings have been committed along the Black-Sand Beach road, thus far always at night. You can, of course, take a taxi from the *National Park* restaurant in town, but this is not always convenient. Wherever you stay in Cahuita, make sure there are bars on the windows and a sturdy lock on the door. The combination of cash-carrying travellers (the nearest banks are in Bribrí and Limón) and a crack problem have made tourists' rooms easy prey. You should **book ahead** on weekends during the Highland dry season (Dec–April).

In the village, the site at *Cafeteria Vishnu* ($2.50), is a good place to **pitch a tent**, with breakfast on your doorstep. You can also camp in the Park (see p.165).

In the village

Cabinas Jenny, on the beach (ext 256). Beautiful rooms, especially upstairs (more expensive) with high wooden ceilings, sturdy bunks, mosquito nets, fans and wonderful sea views, but no hot water. Deck chairs and hammocks provided, and good stout locks on all doors. The owner sometimes offers breakfast. ②–③.

Cabinas Rhode Island, on the road to the right, opposite *National Park* restaurant (ext 264). Good budget option set slightly back from the village, close to the Park and beach. Near two restaurants, so can be noisy at night. Locally managed, with cell-like rooms, but clean sheets and good locks and window bars. ②.

Cabinas Surfside, opposite the school (ext 246; Aptdo 360, Puerto Limón). One of the best budget options in town: the concrete cell rooms are dark and none too special, but very popular with the budget crowd. Good restaurant frequented by locals. ②.

Hotel Cahuita, next to the *National Park*, 50m north of the old Park entrance (ext 201). Locally managed hotel with friendly motel-style accommodation around a slightly chaotic courtyard. Ground floor rooms are dark, with poor bathrooms, but sheets are clean, and they offer economical single rates. Small pool, bar and restaurant, and laundry service. ②.

Sol y Mar, across the street from *Hotel Cahuita* (ext 237). Decor at this hospitable place is nothing special, but upstairs rooms are particularly good: airy, bright and clean, with table fans and pretty sea views from verandahs. ④.

Black-Sand Beach

Atlantida Lodge, next to soccer field on the road to Black-Sand Beach, about 1km from the village (ext 213). Best of the pricier options: friendly, with the nicest pool in town, patio, pretty grounds, and good security. Cool rooms, decorated in tropical yellows and pinks, with heated water. Filling breakfasts included. ⑤.

Cabinas Algebra, 2km or so up Black-Sand Beach road (in Puerto Limón: ☎758-2623). Comfortable, basic, clean and quiet cabina rooms, some from town but with good, plant-entangled, *Banana Restaurant* on site. ③.

Cabinas Black Sand, 500m past the soccer field (ext 251). Pleasant, clean cabina rooms, a step up from the usual. Some have balcony (sea views) and private bath. ③.

Cabinas Brigitte, next to *Bar la Ancla* (no phone). Very basic, and rather dark, with cold water and mosquito nets. Outdoor shared bath and showers, painted in Rasta Nation colours. Popular restaurant too, serving cheap health food. ①–②.

Cabinas Colibrí Paradise, opposite soccer field (ext 263). Charming octagonal-shaped little houses, roomier than most cabinas, with hammocks outside. Also a house for rent ($75 per night) with TV and video. Reached on a narrow, muddy path; bring a torch at night. If driving from Limón, take the first road (unsignposted) into Cahuita before the main road. Accepts credit cards; rare in this price range. ③.

Cabinas Iguana, 200m south of *Bar la Ancla* on small sideroad (no phone; Aptdo 1049, Puerto Limón). Good, very friendly, budget accommodation in lovely wood-panelled cabinas set back from the beach. Big screened verandah, laundry service, and a small tourist kiosk (paperback books, some in German). Also two apartments and a three-bedroom house ($25–40 per night) with kitchen. ③.

Chalet Hibiscus, 2500m north of village on right (in Puerto Limón: ☎758-1543; fax 758-0652). Two luxury houses on small point by the sea, with beautiful views, sleeping 6 or 7. The largest is open and breezy, with verandah and hammock, rustic wooden decor and an unusual wood-and-rope spiral staircase. Good security, and friendly owners. ⑥.

Hotel Magellan, 3km up Black-Sand Beach, on small signposted road leading to left (fax 758-1453; Aptdo 1132, Puerto Limón). Relatively new, very comfortable hotel, in beautiful gardens dotted with Pre-Columbian sculpture and a small pool. Hacienda-style rooms have rattan furniture and running hot water. Continental breakfast, bar and restaurant. ⑤.

The Village

Cahuita proper comprises just two puddle-dotted, gravel-and-sand streets running parallel to the sea, intersected by a few cross-streets. Jewellery and crafts-sellers have set up on the road by the beach; though it seems like anything nailed down has been turned into some kind of small business, you'll still see a couple of private homes among the haphazard conglomeration of signs advertising cabinas and restaurants. Few locals drive (bicycles are popular) but tourists do, kicking up dust with their 4WDs.

Cahuita's main street runs from the Park's former entrance at Kelly Creek to the northern end of the village, marked more or less by *Moray's Tours*. Beyond here it curves round and continues two or three kilometres north along **Black-Sand Beach**. The sea-battered green *Salon Vaz* is the focal point of the village. You don't need to go inside to catch the tunes; by 10.30am, even on Sunday, high-volume reggae and soca blasts from its near-gutted interior, while the snap of pool cues and dominoes can be heard from within. Opposite *Salon Vaz*, the forlorn and ill-maintained **park** is of little interest except as a bus terminal; you could, if you wished, fight your way through the rubbish to take a look at the three small busts to Cahuita's founding fathers.

A number of people take visitors out on to the coral reef in **glass-bottomed boats**; try Chapan at *Marisquera de Langosta*, near *Cabinas Jenny* ($20). One-day **scuba diving** tours are run by both *Moray's* and *Cahuita Tours* for around $100 (equipment included). **Snorkelling** expeditions run by the tour companies cost around $6 per day plus rental (about $10); if you go snorkelling on your own, you have to enter the Park from the Puerto Vargas *puesto*, and swim out to the reef from the beach on this side of the point. Note the signs indicating treacherous currents. Wear shoes, as you will have to walk over exposed coral, and watch out for prickly black sea urchins. Though you can **surf** at Cahuita, Puerto Viejo (see p.166) has better waves. Bring your own board; as yet there is nowhere in either village to rent equipment.

Though the tour agencies in Cahuita offer combination "Indian"/beach excursions by jeep, if you are genuinely interested in visiting the **Bribrí indigenous reserves**, including the KéköLdi reserve near Puerto Viejo, the best – most environmentally and politically aware – expeditions are run from Puerto Viejo by ATEC (*Associación Talamanqueña de Ecoturismo y Conservación*; see p.169).

Eating

Cahuita has plenty of places to eat fresh local **food**, and there's a reasonably cosmopolitan selection. At the small café on the sideroad leading to *Cabinas Iguana*, ingredients are exported from Italy, and they serve some of the finest sandwiches, espresso and cappuccino in the country.

As with accommodation, **prices** are not low (dinner starts at $7) – breakfast is by far the cheapest meal of the day ($3–4). **Service** (with the possible exception of the *National Park*) tends to be laid-back: leave yourself lots of time to eat.

PIRATES AND GHOSTS

According to local history, in the 1800s the coastal waters of the Caribbean crawled with pirates. Two **shipwrecks** in the bay on the north side of Punta Cahuita are locally believed to be pirate wrecks, one Spanish and one French. You can sometimes see the Spanish wreck on glass-bottomed boat tours to the reef, although it has been (illegally) picked over and the only thing of interest that remains are carbuncled manacles – an indication of the dastardly intentions of the ship's crew.

In her excellent collection of local folk history and oral testimony, *What Happen*, sociologist Paula Palmer quotes Selles Johnson, descendant of the original turtle-hunters, on the pirate activity on these shores:

> *. . . them pirate boats was on the sea and the English gunboats was somewhere out in the ocean, square rigger, I know that. I see them come to Bocas, square rigger. They depend on breeze. So the pirate boats goes in at Puerto Vargas or at Old Harbour where calm sea, and the Englishmen can't attack them because they in Costa Rican water . . . so those two ships that wreck at Punta Cahuita, I tell you what I believes did happen. Them was hiding in Puerto Vargas and leave from there and come around the reef, and they must have stopped because in those days the British ship did have coal. You could see the smoke steaming in the air. So the pirate see it out in the sea and they comes in here to hide.*

Where you find pirates you also find pirate **ghosts**, it seems, doomed to guard their ill-gotten treasure into infinity. Treasure from the wrecks near Old Harbour, just south of Cahuita, is said to be buried in secret caches on land. One particular spot, guarded by a fearsome headless spirit dressed in a white suit, has attracted a fair share of treasure hunters; no one has yet succeeded in exhuming the booty, however, all of them fainting, falling sick or becoming mysteriously paralysed in the attempt.

Bananas, at *Cabinas Algebra*. Rustic, plant-entwined verandah with great atmosphere. Simple, tasty food from a varied menu; sometimes candlelit at night.

Cafétería Vishnu, in the village. Breakfast place with not a *gallo pinto* in sight. Instead try yoghurt and granola, Indian bread and herb tea, or Swiss, Canadian or Hawaiian breakfasts – all variations on eggs. Ten percent service, not included on menu prices. Daily 7–9am.

Margaritaville, at the end of Black-Sand Beach, 3500m from the village. Canadian-owned, serving good wholesome home-baked bread and local fish and greens. Dinner only, open erratically, more often in the high season (Dec–April). There is talk of moving into the village.

Miss Edith's, northern end of village. The *doyenne* of Creole food, *Miss Edith's* is justifiably popular with tourists; go early to get a table, especially on weekend nights. Great rice-and-beans, rundown and *pan bon*, and occasionally home-made ice cream and herbal teas. Traditional decor, with clean tables covered with gingham cloths. Daily from 6.30am.

Pastry Shop, north of the village. A small roadside kiosk selling the best of local baked goods, including *empañadas*, *pan bon*, brownies and home-baked bread.

Restaurante National Park, at the old Park entrance at southern end of village. Highly recommended, unusual strawberry *refrescos* and tasty *bocas* (try the *patacones* – fried plantains and mashed black beans), along with *casados*, good grilled fish and rice-based dishes. Pleasant situation, and live music most nights.

Restaurante Vaz, 50m north of old Park entrance. A locals' restaurant with an extensive menu concentrating on seafood. Bright and breezy blue and white decor, all scrupulously clean.

Sand's Restaurant and Bakery, opposite *Salon Vaz* in the centre of the village. Even better than the sand-floor restaurant is the bakery, which sells fantastic banana bread, corn bread, banana spice cake, lemon pie and other goodies – handy to stock up for bus rides.

El Típico, off the main road south of the village. Open-air place good for lunchtime *casados* and Tico food; extensive menu of fish, rice and chicken. Tables and stools hewn from tree trunks, with plants and baskets hanging from every conceivable nook. Open 7.15am–10pm.

Nightlife and entertainment

Nightlife in Cahuita revolves around having a beer and listening to music. Cahuitans also their own small **theatre company**, *Teatro Maraca*, which performs regularly in the local school.

Bar la Ancla (aka *"Reggae Bar"*), 2km up Black-Sand Beach. Lively bar with vivid Africa tricolour decor: even the signposts are yellow, red and green. Very popular with locals and tourists alike, with reggae on the sound system, cold beer, and sea breezes from across the road. They also do pasta and Tico dishes as well as breakfast ($3–4).

Bar Hannia, centre of the village, 25m north of *Sand's* (look for interlocking black and white hands painted on outside). Friendly bar with good cold beer, relatively loud music at night, and a reportedly drug-free atmosphere maintained by Lloyd, the local owner.

Restaurante National Park, at the old Park entrance at southern end of village. Extensive drinks menu, often live music at weekends, and nice atmosphere. Some tables outside.

Salon Vaz, centre of the village. Everybody goes to this down-at-heels dance hall. Sweaty backroom atmosphere and good music, mostly reggae. It looks forbidding, but is safe enough; though women will face a bit of cruising.

Parque Nacional Cahuita

At 1067 hectares, **PARQUE NACIONAL CAHUITA** (daily 8am–4pm; officially $15 on day, $7 in advance, but see box on p.164) is one of the smallest in the system, covering the wedge-shaped piece of land from Punta Cahuita back to the

CAHUITA CORAL

Arcing around Punta Cahuita, the **arrecife de Cahuita**, or Cahuita reef, comprises 600 hectares of coral. It is one of just two snorkelling reefs to speak of on this side of Costa Rica; the other is further south at **Refugio Nacional de Vida Silvestre Gandoca-Manzanillo** (see p.171). Corals are actually tiny animals, single-celled polyps, that secrete limestone, building their houses around themselves. Over centuries the limestone binds together to form a multi-layered coral reef. The coral thrives on algae, which, like land plants, transform light into energy to survive; reefs always grow close to the surface in transparent waters where they can get plenty of sun.

Unfortunately, Cahuita's once-splendid reef is **dying**, soured by agricultural chemicals from the rivers that run into the sea here (the fault of the banana plantations, again), and from the silting up of these same rivers caused by topsoil run off from logging and the upheaval of the 1991 earthquake. The species that survive are common **brain coral**, grey and mushy like its namesake, **moose horn coral**, which is slightly red, and sallow grey **deer horn coral**. In water deeper than 2m, you might also spot **fan coral** wafting elegantly back and forth.

This delicate ecosystem shelters more than 120 species of **fish** and the odd green **turtle**. **Lobsters**, particularly the fearsome-looking spiny lobster, used to be common but are also falling victim to the reef's environmental problems. Less frail is the blue **parrotfish**, so called because of its "beak"; actually teeth soldered together. Environmentally incorrect, the parrotfish won't leave the coral as it finds it, and instead gnaws away at its filigree-like structures and spines. Hence the white sand beaches along this part of the coast; formed by shards of excreted coral.

COMMUNITY ACTION IN CAHUITA

In the autumn of 1994, the National Parks service, in consultation with the ICT, raised entrance fees for foreign nationals to all its parks. Fees leapt 1000 percent overnight, going from $1.50 for everybody to $15 for foreigners and $1.50 for Costa Ricans and foreigners with residency (for more on this, see *Basics*). In Cahuita, where an estimated two-thirds of the 3000 residents are in some way dependent upon tourism, villagers were particularly enraged at this sudden, unilateral action. The new fee is particularly damaging to Cahuita's status as a "budget" destination – given that most cabina accommodation in the village costs around $15 a night, raising the Park fees doubles the cost of visiting the village in one fell swoop. Cahuita Park is also in the position of being essentially – not counting the one, rather dull trail, and the coral reef – a beach. Who, residents reasoned, would pay such a price simply to go to the beach, when there were just as good (and free) beaches further south around Punta Uva and Manzanillo?

Fuelled by the prospect of losing their livelihoods, Cahuitans divested the ranger at the Kelly Creek *puesto* of his station, erecting a sign saying "Please do not pay to go into the Park. Community Protest". The National Parks service responded by advising tourists to avoid Cahuita, accusing it of unruliness, lawlessness and a general "bad" reputation – part of what the community saw as an ongoing propaganda campaign against them. Cahuitans then launched a suit against the government, asserting that charging foreigners more than Ticos was discriminatory, contravening Costa Rica's constitution, which stipulates that everyone (including foreigners) is equal under law. In the middle of the furore, the minister of natural resources, René Castro, was quoted as saying that the area attracted budget, drug-taking travellers who "experiment with attitudes we do not want in our country", adding that they should "find themselves another country to visit". Castro's brother Mauricio, president of the National Parks Foundation, plunged the government's collective foot in its mouth even further, saying that Costa Rica did not want the type of tourists who "hang out on the beach and take drugs, as is the problem in Cahuita and Montezuma".

Meanwhile, the Constitutional Court has not yet ruled on this sensitive issue, which has extensive legal and financial implications, for the National Parks service in particular; in the meantime there are no entrance fees to the beach if entered from the south end of Cahuita village, no rangers, and no park infrastructure or services. At Puerto Vargas, where there are rangers, you must pay the fees.

main highway from Puerto Limón to Sixaola and, crucially, the *arrecife de Cahuita*, or the coral reef about 500m offshore. On land, Cahuita protects the littoral, or coastal, rainforest, a lowland habitat of semi-mangroves and tall canopy cover which backs the gently curving white sand beaches of Playa Vargas to the south of Punta Cahuita and Playa Cahuita to the north. **Birds**, including ibis and kingfishers, are in residence, along with white-faced (*carablanca*) monkeys, sloths and snakes, but the only animals you're very likely to see are howler monkeys, and perhaps coati, who do well scavenging near the north section of the Park, where bins overflow with rubbish left by day-trippers.

The Park's one **trail** (7km), skirting the beach, is a very easy, level walk, with a path so wide it feels like a road, covered with leaves and other brush, and a few fallen trees and logs. Stick to the trail, as snakes abound here. The Río Perzoso, about 2km from the northern entrance, or 5km from the Puerto Vargas trailhead, is not always fordable, unless you like wading through chest-high water when you can't actually see how deep it is. Similiarly, at high tide the beach is impassable in places: ask the ranger at the Puerto Vargas *puesto* about the *marea*, or tide schedules. Walking this trail can be unpleasantly humid and buggy: best to go in the morning. It's also very likely to rain, and despite the dense cover of tall trees, you'll still get wet.

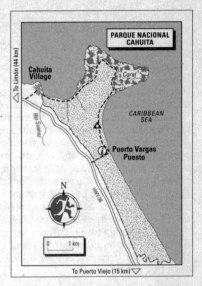

Many **snorkellers** swim the 200 to 500m from Puerto Vargas out to the reef. Again, you should ask about currents, although the beach here is calmer than the one next to Cahuita village.

Practicalities

There used to be an entrance at the north of the Park, immediately south of the village, called Kelly Creek. Now you can only officially enter from **Puerto Vargas**, 4km south of the village, reached along the Limón–Sixaola road. The Puerto Vargas ranger station has good **camping facilities** ($2 per day) complete with barbecue grill, pit toilets and showers, but no drinking water. Take water and insect repellent, and a torch. Theft is a problem around here, so do not leave your things unattended: ask the ranger for advice, as he or she may be able to look after your things. Be careful, too, not to pitch your tent too close to the high tide line; ask the rangers where it's safest to camp.

MOVING ON FROM CAHUITA

The **bus schedule** from Cahuita is painted on the side of *Salon Vaz*. There are four buses daily to **Limón**, where you can connect for **San José**, but if you're in a hurry to reach the capital, it is faster and easier to take the the *directo* service, which doesn't stop (3 daily; 4hr). Call *Transportes MEPE* in San José for information.

For **Puerto Viejo**, take the local bus (9am, 11am & 1pm), which takes thirty minutes to one hour and stops right in the village. The express service from San José to **Sixaola**, which stops in Cahuita at around 10am, 5.30pm and 7.30pm, does not go right into Puerto Viejo but drops you at the crossroads (El Cruce; a 5-km walk). Whichever bus you take, be at the bus stop about 20 minutes early, as services have been known to leave before the scheduled time.

Puerto Viejo de Talamanca and around

The 12km stretch between the langorous hamlet of **PUERTO VIEJO DE TALAMANCA**, 18km southeast of Cahuita, and Manzanillo village is prime territory for holiday-makers. Though not spectacular for swimming, the **beaches** – Playa Chiquita, Punta Uva and Manzanillo – are the most picturesque on the entire coast; there's plenty of accommodation, and for now, at least, it's a good deal more relaxed than Cahuita.

It's **surfing** that really pulls the crowds; the stretch south of _Stanford's_ restaurant at the southern end of the village offers some of the most challenging waves in the country and certainly the best on the Caribbean coast. Puerto Viejo's famous twenty-metre **"La Salsa Brava"** crashes ashore between December and March and from June to July; September and October, when La Salsa Brava goes away to wherever big waves go, are the quietest months of the year.

The **village** itself lies between the thick forested hills of the Talamanca mountains and the sea, where locals bathe and kids frolic with surfboards in the waves. It's a quiet and dusty place, but well-cared for, with pretty hand-painted signs pointing to restaurants and cabinas, and rasta red, green and gold splashed all over the place. The main drag through the centre, potholed and rough, is criss-crossed by a few dirt streets and an offshoot road that follows the shore. Like Cahuita, Puerto Viejo has drawn many Europeans to take up residence here, looking for an easier life and setting up their own cabinas, restaurants and sodas. And, also like Cahuita, most locals are of Afro-Caribbean descent.

Signs of **indigenous culture** are more evident here than in Cahuita; the **KéköLdi** reserve, inhabited by about two hundred Bribrí and Cabécar peoples, skirts the southern end of Puerto Viejo, and ATEC has a strong presence in the town (see p.169).

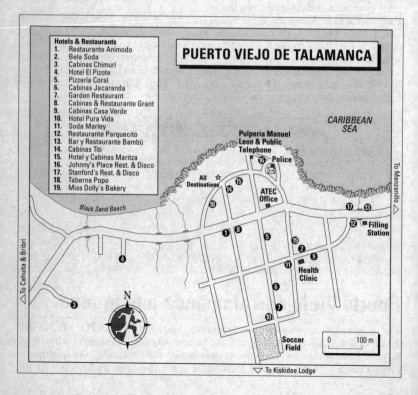

Hotels & Restaurants
1. Restaurante Animodo
2. Bela Soda
3. Cabinas Chimurí
4. Hotel El Pizote
5. Pizzería Coral
6. Cabinas Jacaranda
7. Garden Restaurant
8. Cabinas & Restaurante Grant
9. Cabinas Casa Verde
10. Hotel Pura Vida
11. Soda Marley
12. Restaurante Parquecito
13. Bar y Restaurante Bambú
14. Cabinas Titi
15. Hotel y Cabinas Maritza
16. Johnny's Place Rest. & Disco
17. Stanford's Rest. & Disco
18. Taberna Popo
19. Miss Dolly's Bakery

PUERTO VIEJO DE TALAMANCA

CARIBBEAN SEA

To Manzanillo ▷

Pulpería Manuel Leon & Public Telephone

Police

All Destinations

ATEC Office

Black Sand Beach

Filling Station

◁ To Cahuita & Bribrí

Health Clinic

N

Soccer Field

0   100 m

▽ To Kiskidee Lodge

Arrival

Theoretically you could walk along the beach from Cahuita to Puerto Viejo (a good 15km, and one whole day's walk) but this is not wise. Tides cut you off from time to time, leaving you the grim option of crashing through the jungle that backs the beach; there's a creek to be forded, and robberies have been reported.

Local bus services **from Cahuita** to Puerto Viejo leave at 9am, 11am and 1pm (about 1hr 30min), stopping at *Taberna Popo*, right beside the seafront. **From San José** the 3.30pm bus to Puerto Viejo arrives approximately five hours later. Taking the bus to Limón and changing there for Puerto Viejo (4 daily) is only marginally cheaper, and will increase travelling time by an hour, at least. You can also get to Puerto Viejo on the express service to **Sixaola**. Note that some services – including the Sixaola bus – don't go right into the village, but stop at **El Cruce**, about 5km outside – ask to be sure. You could hitch from El Cruce, but there's little traffic, and it's a hot, dusty walk; instead, call one of Puerto Viejo's two public phones (see below) to book a **taxi** to pick you up (at least $5).

Information

Puerto Viejo has no **tourist information** per se, but the **ATEC** office on the main road (Mon–Sat 9am–noon & 1–5pm) sells a cheap booklet, *Welcome to Coastal Talamanca*, which includes an invaluable list of locals who have particular expertise – from traditional medicine to surfing. Though emphatically not a travel agency, they can arrange exemplary tours or recommend locals to talk to about diving and snorkelling on the Manzanillo reef, or getting to Refugio Nacional de Vida Silvestre Gandoca-Manzanillo (see p.171). They also have a small library of books on the area, plus nature guides, field guides and guidebooks, which, in a gesture of astounding good faith, they may lend you. For **horse rental**, speak to Antonio at *Caballos Antonio*, 500m southeast from the *pulpería* next to *Earl Brown's* restaurant, or Mauricio Salazar at *Cabinas Chimurí*.

Resident medic Doctor Rosa León runs a **health clinic** across from *Bela Soda*, about 100m back from the main road. You can get **gas** at the south end of the village, across the road from *Stanford's* in the house right next to the billboard sign for the *Las Palmas* hotel. For film and essentials, head for *Pulpería Manuel León*, which also has one of the two public **phones** in town (☎758-0854). The other is at the *Hotel Maritza* (☎758-3844). There is no **bank**.

Accommodation

Due to its increasing popularity, there's been a mushrooming of places to stay in and around Puerto Viejo in recent years. The vast majority of accommodation in the **village** is in simple cabinas, usually without hot water, and sometimes without water altogether. More upscale establishments line the **coast** south of the village. You can **camp** on the beaches, but rock-bottom budget travellers usually forsake their tent for a night and stay at the lovely and very cheap *Kiskidee*.

Though you should **reserve** during the surfing seasons (Dec–March & June–July), this can be tricky from outside the country: mail (addressed simply to the establishment, Puerto Viejo, Limón, Costa Rica) may take up to two months; few businesses have a fax number, and several have no phone. One option if you are already in Costa Rica is to call *Hotel Maritza* or the *Pulpería Manuel León* (☎758-0854), tell them which place you would like to make a reservation for, and ask them to call you back at an appointed time. Admittedly awkward, this is currently the only way to do it.

Cabinas Casa Verde, south of the main road. Lovely, good-value cabinas with very clean showers and outside toilets. Also ceiling fans, mosquito nets and space to sling hammocks. Bamboo and plant decor, with shell mobiles and pieces of washed-up coral in the rooms. ③.

Cabinas Chimurí, 20min walk from the village towards the Sixaola–Cahuita road (signed). Owned by Mauricio Salazar, an indigenous Bribrí, and president of ATEC, these A-frame hatched huts, set back from the road, have balconies with nice views. Small kitchen and very tasty breakfasts included in highly reasonable price. ③.

Cabinas Grant, on the main road. Small, spotless, locally run cabinas with hammock space. Cold water, soap and towels and ceiling fans. Some singles. Restaurant on site. ②.

Cabinas Jacaranda, north of the soccer field. Basic but very clean budget option, with lively Guatemalan fabrics. Unscreened windows but mosquito nets, table fans, and clean shared bath with cold water only. ①–②.

Cabinas Maritza, attached to *Hotel Maritza*. Cheerful cabinas with colourful mural. Bike rental, a collection of poison dart frogs and small turtle pond on the premises. Parking. ①.

Cabinas Titi, right in the centre of the village, around the corner from the bus stop. Clean and orderly cabinas owned by *Taberna Popo*. Can be noisy at night. ①.

Kiskidee, along the path from the soccer field (signed). Well worth the 15-min trek up the hill – bring a torch at night – this is one of the most beautiful, tranquil lodges in all Costa Rica, and at budget rates. Large verandah, good for bird- and animal-spotting, and spacious bunk accommodation. No fans, but mosquito nets and outdoor toilet. Kitchen privileges cost $1.50 extra (stock up on food at the *pulpería*). ①.

Hotel Maritza, 100m southeast of bus stop (☎758-3844). Rooms with private bath and balconies upstairs. Also a bar, lounge and tours. Unusually, accepts credit cards. ②.

El Pizote, on main road. Most expensive place around this side of Playa Chiquita, catering for wealthy surfers and Americans. Luxury laurel-wood cabins with huge verandahs in large landscaped gardens planted with tropical fruits. Tours include diving off Punta Uva, hiking and snorkelling. Meals included. ⑥.

Hotel Pura Vida, near the soccer field. Popular budget option with seven rooms; it tends to fill quickly. Rooms have ceiling fans and mosquito nets, and there's a verandah. Sink inside but toilets are shared. Friendly owners (with friendly Rottweiler). ①.

Eating, drinking and nightlife

Puerto Viejo has a surprisingly cosmopolitan range of **places to eat**. Good, traditional **Creole food** is served at *Soda Marley*, and ATEC can put you in touch with village women who cook typical regional meals on request; one such, Miss Dolly, sometimes sells her baked goods at a little shop at the west end of the village.

Puerto Viejo, quiet during the day, begins thumping at **night**; the bass-heavy music usually emanates from *Taberna Popo* and *Stanford's*, probably the most popular place in town, dominated by well-honed surfers. There are also a couple of **discos**, though women alone and in groups should be prepared to fend off advances and might find the atmosphere a bit heavy. *Johnny's Place* is good; a restaurant-disco with sea view. A quieter option is to have a beer at *Parquecito* or *Taberna Popo*, and you'll find a lot of travellers sipping stiff drinks at *Bambú*, next door to *Stanford's*, which has a narrow verandah facing the sea.

Animodo, on the main road in the village. New Italian restaurant with great food – gnocchi, cannelloni ($7–10) and proper Italian wine. Jazz on the stereo makes a change from reggae. Simple, rustic decor, with lovely mobiles twirling above your head. Outdoor terrace area.

Garden Restaurant, near the soccer field. Vegetarian, Asian and Caribbean cuisine cooked by Vera, a Trinidadian/Canadian woman who has an excellent gourmet pedigree from Toronto restaurants *Bamboo* and *Squeeze Club*. Prices are not low (the fantastic breakfasts are cheapest) but the food is exquisite and atmosphere relaxing. Nov–June only, 5–10pm.

Grant, on the main road. Rustic wooden upstairs restaurant, with views of the village and out to sea. Plain Tico food, with good lobster and rice (Nov–Jan only). Breakfast 7–10am; closes 8pm.

ATEC AND TOURS TO THE KÉKÖLDI RESERVE

The *Associación Talamanqueña de Ecoturismo y Conservación*, or **ATEC**, is a grass-roots organization set up by members of the local community – Afro-Caribbeans, Bribrí indigenous peoples and Spanish-descended inhabitants. As well as being able to tell you where to find **locally made products** such as banana vinegar, guava jam and coconut oil, and jewellery made from coconut shells, seashells and bamboo, they arrange some of the most authentic and interesting **tours** in Costa Rica. If you're spending even just a couple of days in the Talamanca region, an ATEC-sponsored trip is a must; to reserve a tour, go to their Puerto Viejo office at least one day in advance.

Chief among the organization's aims is to give local people a chance to demonstrate their pride in and knowledge of their home territory, to show them that this expertise can be profitable, and that they themselves can make a living off tourism without selling their land or entering into more exploitative business arrangements. In this spirit ATEC has trained about fifteen local people as guides, who get about two-thirds of the individual tour price. Whereas many of the hotel-organized excursions to the indigenous reserves take you in cars, ATEC promote horseback and hiking tours. There's a strict maximum of six people, and they visit places on a rotating roster, so that local hamlets do not have to deal with foreigners traipsing through every day.

One of the most popular tours is to the **KéköLdi reserve**, which touches the water just a few kilometres southeast of Puerto Viejo at Playa Cocles ($15; ATEC take care of the permission fee). This tour does not lead, as you might expect, to villages where indigenous peoples live in "primitive" conditions. The Bribrí speak Spanish (as well as Bribrí) and wear Western clothes. But underneath this layer of integration lie vital preservations of their culture and their traditional way of life, and this is what the local guides illustrate and explain. Although the area has seen some strife between the reserve dwellers, their neighbours, and foreign hotel developments, these altercations remain largely on the level of policy. For the tourist, there is no overtly apparent ill-feeling or violence between the groups.

Treks usually last about three hours, traversing dense rainforest and the Talamanca hills. They start near the road to Puerto Viejo – where **Bribrí crafts**, including woven baskets and coconut shell carvings, are on sale – passing cleared areas, coca plantings and very small homesteads, then into secondary, and then finally primary, cover. In this old forest the guide may take you along the same trails that have been used for centuries by Bribrís on their trips from their mountain homes down to the sea, and point out the traditional medicinal plants (curing everything from malaria to skin irritations). A tour may involve discussions about the permanent reforestation programme in which the Bribrí have been involved, and might perhaps visit the iguana breeding farm the local community have established.

ATEC's **Afro-Caribbean tours** have an historical and educational bent. Locals whose families have been in the area since the eighteenth century take you on walks through the villages and in the jungle, telling you about old farming techniques, and traditional plant remedies. Some tours include time in the Refugio Nacional de Vida Silvestre Gandoca-Manzanillo Wildlife Refuge (see p.171).

Parquecito, across the bridge from the gas station. Locally run restaurant with sea view, cross-breezes, cold beer and a fish-oriented menu. Good atmosphere, quieter than *Stanford's*, opposite.

Pizzeria Coral, on the road to the soccer field. Tasty, if pricey, Italian food. Low-key atmosphere on the outdoor patio and quick service along with a small, well-balanced menu heavy on pizza. Breakfasts – traditional Costa Rican as well as healthy yoghurt and granola – are cheaper. Popular place to have a beer, too.

Soda Marley, south of the main road. Small, locally run place that comes a very close second to the *Garden Restaurant* for the best food in town. Certainly the nicest place to have lunch, served on a little terrace. The red snapper is a treat, perfectly cooked with onions and sauce, and the delicate coconut rice-and-beans must be the best in the province.

Stanford's, opposite *Parquecito*. Local institution right on the sea, with laid-back good-time atmosphere. Popular with surfers, who keep an eye on the waves and their buddies from the upstairs verandah. Noisy or lively, depending on how you look at it, with a beautiful view. The music is reggae but the food is Highland, with rice-and-everything predominating.

MOVING ON FROM PUERTO VIEJO

The bus from Puerto Viejo **to San José** (5hr) leaves at 7am, travelling via Cahuita. There are also four buses direct **to Cahuita** (9am, 1pm, 4pm & 5pm; 30min–1hr), and you can get there on the "express" (a misnomer) service to Limón (usually the last bus of the day, around 5pm). Note that as this is "express" you will be asked to pay the full fare to Limón, even if you are getting off along the route.

To get to **Sixaola** and Panamá by bus, you have to flag down the San José–Sixaola service at El Cruce. The bus should get here any time between four and five hours after it has left the capital, but arrival time varies; check with locals. Otherwise get the bus to Cahuita and pick up the San José–Sixaola service there (see p.165).

South from Puerto Viejo to Manzanillo

The stretch south of Puerto Viejo, dotted by tiny hamlets of **Playa Cocles**, **Playa Chiquita**, **Punta Uva** and **Manzanillo**, the main village, is one of the most appealing on the entire Caribbean coast. All the visual trappings of a pristine tropical paradise are here, with palm trees leaning vertiginously over calm beaches, purples, mauves, oranges and reds all fading into the sea at sunset, and a milk-like twilight mist wafting in from the Talamancas. There's a low-hassle atmosphere, and excellent accommodation strung along the Puerto Viejo–Manzanillo road, but transport is infrequent, and you'll do best with a car, especially to explore the **Refugio Nacional de Vida Silvestre Gandoca-Manzanillo**, which borders the area. Take care, though, on the single-track, no guard-rails bridges (the one just before Manzanillo as you approach the *Almonds and Corals Tent Camp*, which comes on a slight turn and then has a steep uphill section, is the trickiest). The road from Puerto Viejo to Manzanillo was only built in 1984 – electricity came five years later – and despite the mini-invasion of hotels and cabinas, local life remains much the same as ever, with subsistence householders fishing for still-abundant lobster and supplementing their income with tourism-oriented activities.

Manzanillo Playa, in a small bay a couple of kilometres before the village, is the least driftwood-strewn of all the beaches on this shore, backed with jungle and mangrove swamps that are home to howler monkeys, toucans and many other birds. Just walking along the sand with a pair of binoculars is rewarding for birders. Bear in mind, though, that it is very swampy, and mosquitos and sand-flies thrive: bring your repellent and *Avon Skin-so-Soft* lotion.

Accommodation

The dirt road from Puerto Viejo to Manzanillo is lined with a number of places to stay, ranging from basic **cabinas**, popular with surfers, through entire vacation houses to a unique **tent camp** near the village.

Aguas Claras, Playa Chiquita (☎233-9265; fax 221-2589). The best choice for families or groups, these lovely wooden houses, painted in bright Caribbean style, have mosquito nets, sitting area, balcony, clean bathroom, cold water, fully equipped kitchen, and electricity. Set in jungle-like gardens, with a natural path leading to the beach, 200m away. Weekly rates $300; can sleep 7 or 8. ⑤.

Almonds and Corals Tent Camp, 2km north of Manzanillo village; operated by *GEO Expeditions* (see p.173). Unique place 100m from Manzanillo beach, with 24 super-luxurious tents, elevated from the ground, with electricity, beds, tea- and coffee-making facilities – all the comforts, basically, of a hotel. Judging from the number of mosquitos around here, not a bad idea. Good for families, offering a range of tours, snorkelling equipment ($10), mountain bikes ($8), restaurant and parking. ④.

Kashá Hotel and Spa, Playa Chiquita (☎288-2563; fax 232-2056). Six bungalow-style rooms, with two double beds each; screens, fans, cold water in Italian-tiled bathrooms, and verandah with hammock. There's even a gym (small, with rusty equipment). Spacious covered restaurant (rates include breakfast) and small bar. ⑤.

Miraflores, Playa Chiquita (☎233-5127; fax 233-5390; Aptdo 7271, San José 1000). Rustic, comfortable lodge opposite the beach, on an old cacao plantation with tropical flowers in the grounds. Lovely decor: Bribrí paintings, carvings and objets d'art. Upstairs is better and brighter with mosquito nets, mirrors and high bamboo ceilings. Outside breakfast area. ④.

Hotel Punta Cocles, 5km south of Puerto Viejo. Large (60 rooms) upscale hotel with big restaurant and parking. Only place along this stretch of coast with a/c, but the atmosphere is sterile and bathrooms are not that clean. All in all overpriced. ⑥.

Villas del Caribe, Punta Cocles/Playa Chiquita (☎233-2200; fax 221-2801; Aptdo 8080-1000, San José). Actually within the KéköLdi indigenous reserve, this hotel – part-owned by Canadian government minister Maurice Strong – is at the forefront of a local dispute over its alleged illegal building. Very comfortable accommodation, with loft-like rooms, hot water, fan and organic garbage disposal. Lovely grounds with great sunset views, but no pool. No restaurant either, but takeout nearby at *Lapalapa* (call in advance and walk 50m to collect). Credit cards accepted. A good deal for groups of 4 (5 at a pinch) and in low season. ⑤–⑦.

Walaba, 8500m south of Puerto Viejo (☎234-2467). Friendly, three-storey rustic lodge, across the road from the beach. Wooden decor and big verandah; fully equipped, bright rooms with fans and cold water, but no cooking facilities. Very good value. ③.

Eating and drinking

Lapalapa, 50m north of *Villas del Caribe*. The best place along this coast for a meal or drink. Great fish menu and French cuisine, Caribbean music and bar snacks. Tree-trunk tables with kerosene lamps and huge dripping candles. Very basic rooms for rent. Open 9am–1am.

Naturales, Old Harbour, south of Puerto Viejo. Excellent, great value, health food. Breakfast with wholewheat bread, 100 percent natural juices, salad, milkshakes and sandwiches, all for less than $2.

Soda Aquarius, Playa Chiquita. Breakfast, dinner, coffee and *refrescos* kept going all day. Healthy, fresh local food.

Refugio Nacional de Vida Silvestre Gandoca-Manzanillo

In the very southeast corner of the country, bordering Río Sixaola and the international frontier with Panamá, the little-visited but fascinating **REFUGIO NACIONAL DE VIDA SILVESTRE GANDOCA-MANZANILLO**, which incorporates the small hamlets of Gandoca and Manzanillo and covers 5000 hectares of land and a similar area of sea. The refuge was established to protect some of Costa Rica's last few **coral reefs**, of which **Punta Uva** is the most accessible. You can **snorkel** happily here. There's also a protected **turtle-nesting beach** south of the village of Manzanillo, and tracts of mangrove forests and **swamp**, including the last *orey* swamp in the country. More than 358 **bird** species have been identified, many of them rare; ten years ago there were sightings of the endangered harpy eagle, believed to be extinct in the rest of the country due to deforestation. Other species include the *manatí*, tapir and American crocodile, who hang out on the river estuary, but, as usual, you're unlikely to see them.

VISITING A BRIBRI RESERVE

A personal account by Silvia Brander

Amubri is a town in the Talamancan mountains, about 20km southwest of Bribrí. As it is within the Reserva Indígena Talamanca, you officially need a permit (and a good reason) to visit. Silvia Brander visited Amubri as the guest of someone who knew the village and the villagers well. Individual travellers are discouraged by CONAI, the National Commission on Indigenous Affairs, from visiting places like Amubri, in order to control the cultural impact of potentially large numbers of travellers who may go looking, somewhat voyeuristically, for colourful "indian" life. If you want to visit Amubri (or indeed any settlement within an indigenous people's reservation) apply to CONAI, Av 8, C 23/25 in San José (☎221-5496) or to the Barrio los Corales regional CONAI office in Limón (☎758-3996), or ask at ATEC in Puerto Viejo (see p.167).

I am a keen traveller and always enthusiastic about making new discoveries. Chance often plays a very important part – as it did during my recent visit to Costa Rica. In the *Ritz Hotel* in San José, a meeting place for travellers, I met a globetrotter, who had been living on an indigenous reservation in Amubri, in the Talamanca region, for a few months. He invited me to come and visit him there, and I took up his offer without delay. I took the bus to Bribrí via Limón and Cahuita. Most people do not get off the bus in Bribrí, but stay on to the Panamanian border so that they can leave the country and come back to get a new entry stamp in their passports. Bribrí itself is a sleepy, provincial village where life centres around the village square. People go shopping, meet for a drink in the restaurant, and watch other people. The few tourists that do stop here are a special attraction.

I travelled from Bribrí to my destination in a converted old school bus. The dirt track is very bumpy. There are also fords through streams, and a couple of very precarious-looking bridges on the way to Suretka, where, already in the dark, I had to walk to the river. There boatmen were waiting on the bank to ferry the passengers over the river. These little boats are the reservations' only connection with the outside world – with the exception, I am told, of one or two smugglers' tracks leading to Panamá.

A banana truck and a beaten-up old minibus were waiting on the opposite bank of the river to take passengers the remaining 7km to the village. Some knowledge of Spanish is an absolute must if you want to make any kind of contact with the locals, and although mine is very limited, it was enough to find that there was only one place visitors could say, a *posada* belonging to the village's missionary station. Four hundred colones a night got me a simple room with running water, a shower and cooking facilities in the mission house. I had hardly got settled in when my first

If you want to take an **organized trip**, *GEO Expeditions* (☎272-2024 or 4175; fax 272-2220), based in San José, have years of experience running innovative tours in the Gandoca–Manzanillo area, including trips to local Bribrí communities, a dugout canoe trip to Punta Mona, biking and snorkelling at the Punta Uva coral reef, along with jaunts to Hitoy-Cerere Biological Reserve (see p.147), Tortuguero (see p.150) and Bocas del Toro in Panamá (see p.175).

Camping is permitted within the refuge, but is really only feasible on the beach, due to proliferation of mosquitos, snakes and other biting creatures inland. In **MANZANILLO** the only **place to stay** is at the basic *Cabinas Maxi* (①), which also serves great **lobster** in season – just ask around for George or Maxi. Four kilometres from Manzanillo down a rough track, **GANDOCA**

visitors arrived; a couple of kids from the village who wanted to play cards, a pastime to which my friend from the *Ritz* had introduced them. They drew me into the game for what turned out to be a really enjoyable evening.

Waking up in the morning, I saw the place properly for the first time. The Catholic Mission is the centre of the village, together with a church, clinic, school, inn and a few scattered buildings – that's about it. One of these buildings is the village kitchen, where you can get warm meals if you order them in advance. The general store sells basic necessities. The Bribri's simple houses are scattered around the reservation; most live next to their work, which means cultivating bananas, cocoa, citrus fruits, maize and beans, but a few make a living outside the reservations. I mostly got to know men and boys, as these were the ones who moved more freely in public spaces. The women and girls work in the houses and tend to be shy of strangers, as they are brought up to be.

It really is quiet. The banana truck and the old bus are the only motorized vehicles in Amubri – except, of course, for the small aeroplane owned by the village priest, Father Bernadito, which is kept for emergencies. (I never actually saw it; and the overgrown landing strip in the middle of the village was the only evidence that it really did exist.) Mass, by the way, is celebrated on Sunday mornings, and the priest delivers his message so audibly that we had no difficulty in following the proceedings from our breakfast table at the *posada*. When there is something to celebrate, there is home-brewed "chica" (beer made of maize or yucca) and good home cooking. The normal diet is a little more monotonous: a lot of beans, maize and rice, enriched with fruit, vegetables and sometimes a little meat or fish. Costa Rica's national dish, *gallo pinto*, is well-known here, too. Wild pig, hunted and caught by the villagers, is a special delicacy. I found the fruit juices particularly wonderful.

With my friend I went on several expeditions, crossing wobbly suspension bridges with wonderful views over the mountains, or wading though rivers to nearby settlements. On the way we sucked coca leaves – a refreshing delicacy. Once I was even able to take a dip in the river. There were hundreds of butterflies fluttering on the bank. We also went by boat on an expedition to the Río Yorkin, which forms the border with Panamá: the river is mostly calm, with a couple of dangerous parts which our boatsman negotiated skilfully.

When night falls, the village is even quieter. You can hear mysterious noises out in the wilderness. Animals who do not show themselves in the daylight hours appear – toads and beetles visited us. And a spider wove her cobweb in front of the window every evening. By daybreak each morning she had eaten up her work again.

provides access to the estuary of the Río Gandoca. Bird-spotting is great here, and boat trips are organized from the village. Get there by walking from Manzanillo, or drive (access from the Sixaola road) about 6km via the banana *fincas* of Daytonia, Virginia and Finca 96. You'll need 4WD.

Gandoca-Manzanillo has one fairly demanding but rewarding **trail** (5.5km), passing primary and secondary forest, and some secluded, pretty beaches on its way from **Manzanillo** to **Monkey Point** (Punta Mona). It can get extremely hot, and mosquitos are usually out in force, so carry plenty of water, sunscreen and repellent. Beginning at the northeast end of Manzanillo village, it proceeds along the beach for 1km. After crossing a small creek and entering a grove of coconut trees, it becomes poorly marked and easy to lose, but should be just about visible as it climbs up a small bluff. The trail then drops to lower ground and a few small shark-infested beaches before heading inland. Some of these up-and-down sections are quite steep, and if it has been raining (as it invariably has) then mud and mosquitos may combine to make the trip unpleasant.

However, the trail offers great opportunities for spotting birds and wildlife; you're effectively guaranteed a sight of chestnut-mandibled and keel-billed **toucans**. The tiny flashes of colour darting about on the ground in front of you are **poison dart frogs**; watch where you're stepping, and avoid touching them. Punta Mona, the end of the trail, is flanked by a shady beach, from where you can see across to Panamá, only about 8km to the south. From here you return to Manzanillo the same way.

The KéköLdi indigenous reserve

About two hundred Bribrí and Cabécar peoples live in the 250-hectare **KéköLdi indigenous reserve**, which begins just a few hundred metres south of Puerto Viejo and extends inland into the Talamancas. The reserve was established in 1976 to protect indigenous culture and the ecological resources of the area, but nevertheless the communities and land remain under constant threat from logging, squatters, tourism and banana plantations. The worst problems arise from poor surveying of the boundaries of the reserve and less than stringent government checks on construction in this area, which, the inhabitants claim, has led to several hotels being built illegally on their land. The story of all the bungling, red tape and wranglings surrounding the formation of these reserves is wittily told in Anachristina Rossi's novel, *La Loca de Gandoca*, which is available in Spanish only, in San José.

The main obstacle to understanding between the indigenous peoples and their neighbours has been, historically, their irreconcilable views of land, and especially the forest. In sum, the Bribrí and Cabécar see the forest as an interrelated system of cohabitants all created by and belonging to Sibö, their god of creation, while the typical *campesino* view is that of a pioneer – the forest is an obstacle to cultivation and therefore civilization, to be conquered, tamed and effectively destroyed. Travelling around the Talamanca coast, you'll see large **ceibas**, or silk cotton trees, with their distinctive seeds, which look like large black pill capsules, and are usually scattered all over the ground beneath. These seeds were traditionally used as mattress and pillow stuffing. Believed sacred by the Maya, the *ceiba* was also significant for the Bribrí as the mother of Tbekol, the Big Snake.

Bribrí and the Panamanian Border

From Puerto Viejo the paved road (Hwy-36) continues to **BRIBRÍ**, about 10km inland southwest, arching over the Talamancan foothills, and revealing the green bowls of valleys from here all the way to Panamá. This is banana country; with little to see, even in Bribrí itself, largely devoted to administering the affairs of indigenous reserves in the Talamanca mountains. Bribrí does, however, have a **bank** (*Banco Nacional* – it changes money, but allow half a day), one basic **place to stay**, *Cabinas Picuno* (☎258-2981; ①), and a couple of simple **restaurants**.

From here a dusty gravel road winds the 34km through solid banana *fincas* (Fields, Olivia, Margarita, Paraíso, Daytonia) on to **Sixaola**. Locals cross the border here to do their shopping in Panamá, where most things are cheaper. The majority of foreigners who cross into Panamá do so simply because their tourist visa for Costa Rica has expired and they must leave the country for 72 hours; however, with the pristine island of **Bocas del Toro** just over the border, it's an inviting prospect even for those who don't need an extension.

The border and on into Panamá

Sixaola–Guabito is a small crossing that does not see much foreign traffic, and for the most part formalities are simple, but you should get here as early in the morning as possible. There's nowhere decent to stay before you get to Bocas del Toro – and you should leave time to look for a hotel once there – and bus connections in Panamá can be tricky.

The Sixaola–Guabito border is open daily from 8am to 4pm Panamá time (one hour ahead of Costa Rica). There is a toll of about $1.50. At the moment most nationalities need a visa or tourist card to cross into Panamá for thirty days; the Panamanian consulate in San José issues them both, or you can get a tourist card from the office of *Copa*, the Panamanian airline, in San José (see p.93).

There is nowhere to **stay** in Guabito, the tiny hamlet on the Panamanian side of Río Sixaola. Best catch the bus to the banana town of Changuinola (every 30min; 7am–5pm) or arrange a taxi (ask at the border post), which will make the thirty-minute trip for about $15. The bus continues on to Almirante – though you may need to change at Changuinola – from where you can get a water taxi to **Bocas del Toro**, a small, little-inhabited island, with beautifully clear water, great for snorkelling and swimming. **Hotels** include *Botel Thomas*, right on the sea (②); *Bahia*, the grand-looking but basic former local headquarters of the United Fruit company (②), and the friendly *Pension Miss Peck* (①).

Connections with the **rest of Panamá** from this northeast corner are tenuous. Fifty kilometres southeast of Almirante is a banana town called Chiriquí Grande, which is connected to the rest of the country by road, but, frustratingly, is not accessible by road from Almirante. You can, however, get there by taking a ferry from Almirante, then hopping on the public bus across the Cordillera Central to Chiriquí (not to be confused with Chiriquí Grande) on the Interamericana, east of the city of David (from where there are bus connections to Panamá City and back to San José). This road has spectacular views of the continental divide.

travel details

Buses

San José to: Cahuita (3 daily; 4hr); Puerto Limón (12 daily; 2hr 30min–3hr); Puerto Viejo de Talamanca (3 daily; 4hr); Sixaola, for Panamá (3 daily; 6hr).

Puerto Limón to: Cahuita (4 daily; 1hr); Puerto Viejo de Talamanca (4 daily; 1hr); San José (12 daily; 2hr 30min–3hr); Sixaola, for Panamá (1 daily; 3hr).

Sixaola to: Cahuita (4 daily; 2hr); Puerto Limón (1 daily; 3hr); Puerto Viejo de Talamanca (4 daily; 2hr); San José (4 daily; 6hr).

Boats

Barra del Colorado to: Puerto Viejo de Sarapiquí (private *lanchas* only; 3–4hr). Note that the trip from Puerto Viejo de Sarapiquí (in the Zona Norte, see p.201) takes 6hr.

Moín docks to: Tortuguero (private *lanchas* only; 4hr).

Flights

At present the service between San José and Tortuguero has been dropped; it may, however, be resumed in the future. Call *Sansa* or *Travelair* to check (see p.98).

San José to: Barra del Colorado (1 daily Mon, Thurs, Sat; 30min).

Barra del Colorado to: San José (1 daily Mon, Thurs, Sat; 30min).

other in Costa Rica. There are, however, several places to buy Guatuso **crafts**: rather folksy, with a preponderance of decorated drums covered in snakeskin and small wooden carvings. Excavations of several old Guatuso **tombs** in the area every now and again turn up jade and pottery artefacts, which you can see in San José's Museo Nacional (see p.79).

Irregular **buses** (about 2 daily) from Fortuna to Guatuso leave from the stop next to the *Hotel La Fortuna* and around the corner from *El Jardín* restaurant.

The far north

The **far north** of the Zona Norte is an isolated region, in many ways culturally – as well as geographically – closer to Nicaragua than to the rest of the country. Years of conflict in the Civil War made the region more familiar with CIA men and arms runners than with tourists, but most of the area, and certainly any tourist destinations, are quiet now. Los Chiles, near the Nicaraguan border, is the only village of any size: the drive up there, along the stretch of good tarmac road from San Carlos, takes you through a dead, flat landscape broken only by roadside shacks – many inhabited by former Nicaraguan refugees – illuminated by the cool mint blue of television screens within. Tourist facilities are practically non-existent, and between the small village of Muelle, 8km from San Carlos, and Los Chiles, you encounter 74km of highway virtually uninterrupted by settlements of any size, with the llanura de Guatusos stretching hot and interminably to the west.

Most tourists are here to see **Refugio Nacional de Vida Silvestre Caño Negro**, a vast wetlands area and – at 192km from San José – one of the most remote Wildlife Refuges in Costa Rica. No longer a well-kept secret, it is possible to visit Caño Negro on a day trip from the capital or on an excursion from Fortuna or one of the larger hotels in the Zona Norte. You can also go independently, although this, as everywhere in Costa Rica, is becoming more complicated.

During the Nicaraguan Civil War, **Los Chiles**, nearly 200km from San José but right next to the border, was a Contra supply line. Nowadays, though, there is a climate of international cooperation, helped by the fact that many of the residents are of Nicaraguan extraction or immigrants to Costa Rica, and the area is gently opening up to tourism. A committed group of local hoteliers, restaurateurs and boatmen have formed a local tourism association with help from the ICT, and crossing the border is straightforward (though make sure your documents are in order). Despite these initiatives, bear in mind that you will have a hard time finding people who speak English; the further north you head, the more Spanish you'll need.

Incidentally, the Río San Juan is technically Nicaraguan territory – the border is on the Costa Rican side of the bank – but through a treaty the two nations have established that Costa Rica has the free use of the river.

Los Chiles

Few tourists make it all the way to **LOS CHILES**, a border-post town just 3km from the Nicaraguan frontier. Indeed, other than soaking up local colour, there is little to actually do in town, which has a static, end-of-the-world feel; it is possible, however, with a little forward planning, to rent a boat or horse to go to **Caño Negro**, 25km downstream on the Río Frío (see p.192).

Another reason to stay in Los Chiles these days, if conditions permit, is to cross the Nicaraguan border. Non-Nicas and non-Ticos have only been able to cross here for the past two years, however, and the majority of travellers still cross at Peñas Blancas on the Interamericana.

Arrival
For a long time cut off from the rest of Costa Rica by the lack of a good road, the current highway – built only in 1982 – is in generally excellent condition. Two buses per day run from La Coca-Cola in **San José** "direct" to Los Chiles (in reality, they stop frequently, and always in San Carlos). The journey takes more than five hours. From **San Carlos** there are ten daily services between 5am and 7pm (2hr 30min). The San José bus stops right outside the Mercado Central, while buses arriving from San Carlos often stop close to the docks, about 25m beyond *Los Petates* restaurant towards the river.

Returning from **Los Chiles to San Carlos**, buses currently leave at 4.45am, 5.15am, 6.15am, 7.45am, 9am, 11am, 12.30pm, 2pm, 3pm and 4pm.

You can also charter an **air taxi from San José** to Los Chiles (see p.23). Planes land next to the *guardia civil* post on the edge of town.

Driving from San Carlos, Hwy-141 heads north along a poor, potholed road through the tiny settlements of Florencia and Muelle. However, beyond Boca de Arenal, it is 84km straight through to Los Chiles on a good tarmac road which is passable all year round. *Bombas* line the way at regular intervals.

Information
Although Los Chiles has no **tourist information** as such, everyone in town knows the current bus schedules and the river-boat departure for the Nicaraguan border. You'll need Spanish to ask around. **Migración** (Mon–Fri 8am–5pm; ☎471-1061) can answer more detailed enquiries, but note that it often closes before 5pm – get there about 3pm to be safe. Linked to the local tourism initiative, Fernando and Mohammed Sandi Castro at *Los Petates* restaurant, 50m east of the *muelle* (dock), are great sources of local information, as is Nelson Leiton, who runs a small **travel agency**, *Servitur*, at *Cabinas Jabirú* (see below).

Los Chiles might seem like the end of the world, but it has most of the facilities you'll need: you can supposedly **change dollars** and travellers' cheques at the *Banco Nacional* on the north side of the soccer field (Mon–Fri 8am–3.30pm); that said, however, its safest to bring an adequate supply of colones. Full postal services, including fax, are offered at the **correo** in the Mercado Central (Mon–Fri 8am–4pm). The **police station**, or *guardia civil* (☎471-1103), is on Hwy-141 from San Carlos at the entrance into town. For **supplies** – milk, ice cream, chocolate and other basics – head for the *Dos Piños* general store across from *Los Petates*, 50m east of the *muelle*.

Accommodation
If you're intending to cross the border, you may well need to **stay the night** in Los Chiles. The most comfortable accommodation in town, the cool and spotless *Cabinas Jabirú*, 200m north of the centre (☎471-1055; ①–②) offers private

bath, hot water and fans and a laundry service. Other good options include the long-established *Las Carolinas*, one block from the *guardia civil* on the road into town (☎471-1151; ①). A pension-style hotel with room for forty, it lacks something in the decor department – rooms are *very* pink – but is comfortable enough, and has some singles with shared bath, for the lowest prices in town. The basic rooms with private bath and cold showers at *La Central* (no phone; ①), at the northeast corner of the soccer field, are nothing special, but clean. Two kilometres outside town on the road to San Carlos, the *Guaípil Lodge* (no phone; ②) has ten cabinas perched near a small tributary of the Río Frío. Rooms are suburban-motel-style, but comfortable, with fans and hot water, and there's a bar and restaurant.

The Town

Los Chiles is laid out on a small grid of wide, dusty, uneventful streets. The highway peters out somewhere beyond the town in the direction of the Río San Juan, leaving literally nowhere to go but the river. There's no traffic to speak of – just a few *campesinos* ambling along on their horses, huge workhorse trucks rumbling by with the red dust of the tropical forest soil caked around their axles, and children nipping past on creaky bikes – probably the most excitement you'll encounter will be the clumps of youths sitting in the middle of the road idly chatting.

There is little to see around the usually deserted **main "square"** (actually an ill-kempt soccer field), although the tumbledown houses lining the right-hand side on the way to the river have a certain atmospheric melancholy. Faded grey two-storey structures, they show wooden latticework of surprising delicacy, and French doors opening off the tall, narrow porch. They have such a haunted look it is difficult to believe they are only forty or fifty years old: some of the first buildings to be built in the area, they evoke a forlorn, France-in-the-tropics feel.

The only sign of any activity is at *migración* and the adjacent docks, where young kids frolic in the river, and at the new bunker-like **Mercado Central**, 200m northeast of the soccer field. Besides the *Dos Piños* store, this is the only place in town to buy fresh food. If it's souvenirs you're after, *Los Petates* restaurant sells a small selection of **handicrafts**. Best buys include small wooden carvings, Guatuso-made drums, fearsome iguanas carved in wood, and *naif*-style, very colourful and delicate landscape/jungle paintings from the Solentiname islands of Lago de Nicaragua.

Though less well known for it than Barra del Colorado (see p.148), Los Chiles is a great spot for **tarpon-fishing**. Outside January to April – when fishing is not permitted – a number of locals take tourists out in their own *lanchas*. Enquire at the dock, *Los Petates*, or with *Servitur*. Martin Bernal takes three or four people, while Victor Rojas has a larger boat that can accommodate 23. Provision of rods and tackle varies, and you need a licence. For details of fishing tour specialists and operators, see p.49 in *Basics*.

Eating and drinking

In town, *Los Petates* is currently the only **restaurant** proper, serving good Tico home cooking and sandwiches. However, owners Mohammed and Fernando are opening up a larger *Rancho*-style place, 2km outside town near the *guardia civil* post, which may well supersede the restaurant in town. Ask around when you arrive.

CROSSING INTO NICARAGUA

Although in the past only Costa Ricans and Nicaraguans were allowed **transit across the border** at Los Chiles, it is now possible for anyone to enter, by boat, into Nicaragua from here. The service usually departs the *muelle* from Monday to Friday at 8am, but this is always worth checking with officials in either Los Chiles or at the Nicaraguan consulate in San José. The Los Chiles *migración* are, for immigration officials, approachable, and groups of Nicas or Ticos hanging around the office may be able to attest to current boat times.

Some nationalities need **tourist visas** before they are allowed transit into Nicaragua. Requirements are constantly in flux, so always check with the consulate in San José, the only point in the country that can issue the necessary documentation (allow at least 24hr for processing). The **Nicaraguan border patrol** is at the 3km point upriver from Los Chiles. Make sure they stamp your passport, as you will need proof of entry when leaving Nicaragua. There is also a **police check south of Los Chiles** on the highway to San Carlos and Fortuna. Don't worry if they signal you over – this is mainly to guard against Nicaraguans entering or staying in Costa Rica illegally.

From the border control point it is a 14km trip up the Río Frío to the small town of **San Carlos de Nicaragua**, on the southeast lip of huge Lago de Nicaragua. You'll need at least a bit of cash upon arrival; change a few colones for cordobas at the Los Chiles bank. From San Carlos de Nicaragua it is also possible to cross the lake to **Granada** and on to **Managua**, but again check with the consulate in San José; this is an infrequent boat service and without forward planning you could end up stuck in San Carlos for longer than you'd hoped.

In the relatively new atmosphere of political stability in Nicaragua, there are tentative plans for one-day **river tours** from Los Chiles to Nicaraguan San Carlos, Lago de Nicaragua, and even the Solentiname islands in the lake. Visitors may even be able to see the fortress San Juan – also called the Castillo de la Concepción or Fortaleza – which is one of the oldest Spanish structures (1675) in the Americas, built as a defence against the English and pirates (often one and the same) plying the Río San Juan. All that said, however, bear in mind that there remains some controversy about Costa Rican tour operators taking tourists into Nicaraguan territory without informing Nicaraguan officials, and it is currently in dispute whether tourism constitutes the "trade" purposes for which Costa Rica is allowed to use the river.

There's just one official **bar**, next to *Los Petates*. Dingy and uninviting it may be, but it does at least serve ice-cold beers – very welcome in this steamy climate. Avoid the dark booths off to the side, however, which are reserved for a different type of trade.

Refugio Nacional de Vida Silvestre Caño Negro

The largely pristine **REFUGIO NACIONAL DE VIDA SILVESTRE CAÑO NEGRO** ($2), 25km west of Los Chiles, is one of the best places in the Americas to view huge concentrations of both migratory and indigenous **birds**, along with mammalian and reptilian **river wildlife**. Until recently well off the beaten tourist track – partly because of its isolated location, so far from San José – nowadays more and more tours are being offered to an area that has been on the itineraries of specialist birdwatching excursions for years.

SÍ-A-PAZ TRANSNATIONAL PARK

The tropical wetlands and river-fed rainforest between Caño Negro in Costa Rica and the southern shores of Lago de Nicaragua is land designated by the two governments for a transnational conservation initiative dubbed **"Sí-a-Paz"** ("Yes to peace").

The timing couldn't be more perfect. Pressures threatening the projected Sí-a-Paz region have increased dramatically in the past few years. Serious threats to the ecological survival and integrity of the area are manifold: multinationals wanting to buy land for plantation crops; illegal logging; refugees from the Nicaraguan Civil War returning to squat and clear land, and the increasingly serious toxic runoff of chemicals down the tributaries of rivers on the Costa Rica side that flow into the wide Río San Juan. At the time of writing the transnational park was yet to be delineated or set up, but both governments claim to be committed to the project.

Caño Negro is created by the seasonal flooding of the Río Frío, so, depending upon what time of year you go, you may find yourself whizzing around a huge broad lake in a motorboat or walking along mud-caked riverbeds. There's a three-metre difference in the water level between the rainy season (May–Nov), when Caño Negro is at is fullest, and the dry season (Dec–April); note that the rainy season is not necessarily the best time to see the most wildlife, because while the mammalian population of the area stays more or less constant, the birds vary widely (see p.194). In the dry season you'll see enormous flocks of birds mucking about in the mud together or washing their feathers; the **best time** of all to visit for birders is between January and March, when the most migratory species are in residence.

Unless you're an expert in identifying wildlife, the most rewarding way to enjoy the diverse flora and fauna of Caño Negro is to use the services of a **guide** who knows the area and can point out animals and other features of river life as you motor down to the refuge. However, it is not always possible to find trained guides, and the prices of organized tours can be prohibitive for many travellers. Usually, though, as in many places in Costa Rica, locals know quite a bit about wildlife in the area and, if you're travelling in on one of the *lanchas* from Los Chiles, you may be lucky enough to hook up with a boatman who can identify many animals. They may not be as stimulating as a professionally trained guide (and they usually will not speak English), but they'll improve your trip nonetheless. Asking at the docks or in either *Los Petates* or *Servitur* in town might turn up someone.

Getting to Caño Negro

An increasing number of **tour outfitters** run trips to Caño Negro from San José, the more upscale Zona Norte hotels, and Fortuna. Prices vary widely, but in general the trip to Caño Negro is a little more expensive than many expeditions because of the distances involved and – in the wet season – the amount of time spent in the boat simply getting there. Wherever you're coming from, in the wet season all tours stop in Los Chiles, while during the dry months it's possible to drive straight to the Refuge, bypassing the town altogether.

From San José *Horizontes* (☎222-2022) runs three-day/two-night tours to Caño Negro, including a stop at Volcán Arenal, with accommodation at the *Tilajari Resort Hotel* (see p.181). All meals, accommodation, transport and guides are included. Tours **from Fortuna**, including transport by air-conditioned minibus, launch, bilingual guide, and lunch by the river, cost around $40 with *Aventuras Arenal*; a little more with *Sunset Tours*.

The **journey to Caño Negro** from Los Chiles varies according to season. In wet months, you'll be transported by boat all the way into the lake, formed by the swelling of the river, that forms the main part of the Refuge. The rest of the year, boats, vehicles or horses (itineraries vary – check with your tour operator) travel down the Río Frío or along the dirt road to the entrance of the Refuge, from which point it is possible to walk (if the water is very low) or take a horseback tour.

You can also get to Caño Negro **independently**. Driving is easy enough in the dry season, while in the wet season a boat leaves from the Los Chiles docks (Tues & Thurs only; 7.30am; for information call ☎460-1301); on other days you can take your pick from several *lanchas*. Get there early in the morning and ask around for prices: expect to pay at least $65 per boat for the five-hour return trip. The people at Los Chiles' *Servitur* can recommend someone reliable, as can Fernando and Mohammed at *Los Petates*; they also have a Caño Negro video to give you a taste of what you'll see. Note that the first 25km of the trip down the Río Frío (taking an hour or more by *lancha*) does not take you through the Wildlife Refuge, which begins at the mouth of the large flooded area and is marked by a sign poking out of a small islet. Make sure your boatman takes you right into Caño Negro.

If you take a tour, the **entrance fee** is included. If not, you should pay at the ranger station on the north side of the lake.

WHAT TO SEE IN CAÑO NEGRO

Migratory birds such as storks, ducks, herons and cormorants join an abundant variety of permanent residents: caimans, iguanas, snakes, osprey eagles, kingfishers, "Jesus Christ" lizards, yellow turtles, "yellow-footed" birds (*patas amarillas*) and egrets (*garças*). The largest colony of the Nicaraguan **grackle** also makes regular appearances here, the only place in Costa Rica where they nest. Land animals, including **jaguars**, have been spotted, but it is very rare to see them.

Among the more unusual inhabitants of Caño Negro in the wet season is the **garfish**, a kind of in-between creature straddling fish and mammal. This so-called "living fossil" is a fish with lungs, gills and a nose, probably looking its oddest while it sleeps, drifting along in the water; again, it's rare to see one. The **tarpon** can get truly huge – up to 2m in length – and you'll often see its startling white form splashing out of the water, arcing its huge fin and long body.

Other creatures to watch out for include the ubiquitous pot-bellied **iguanas**; **swimming snakes**, heads held aloft like periscopes, bodies whipping out behind (don't get too close and do not touch; in most cases they will be fleeing from you); the elegant, long-limbed **white ibis** that rests on river-level branches and banks, and the sinuous-necked **anhingas** (snakebirds), who impale their prey on the knife-point of their beaks before swallowing.

Howler monkeys (*monos congos*) will often sound the alarm as you approach. To see them, look up into the taller branches of riverside trees. It is best to have **binoculars** to distinguish their black hairy shapes from the densely leaved trees. Speaking of which, it is very difficult to spot a **sloth** because this is exactly what they look like – a dense clump of leaves. Not only do they move very little during the day, they are also very well camouflaged by the green algae that often covers their brown hair. For the best chances of catching sight of one, use binoculars to scan the middle and upper branches of the trees, and especially the V-intersections of branches, keeping an eye out for what will initially look like a dark mass. The rows of small grey triangles are **bats**, literally hanging out on the underside of branches.

Accommodation

Though not in the Refuge itself, *Caño Negro Lagoon Lodge* occupies a prime spot on the banks of the Río Frío, across the river (☎ and fax 446-0124; ④); its simple palm-thatched **cabins** have fans and cold water. To get there by car, take the turnoff to the left, 10km south of Los Chiles, and then drive 6km further along the bad dirt road. You can also reach the lodge by boat; ask around in Los Chiles.

Camping is permitted in Caño Negro, but no formal facilities are provided and there's a charge of around $4, payable to the ranger. A better option is to stay at the **ranger station** (☎460-1301; ①). This is more common in the dry season: call from the public telephone at Caño Negro, or from the SPN office in San José, to reserve. Facilities at the station are variable: you may be able to pay for a meal, but bring your own supplies just in case.

The Sarapiquí region

Steamy and tropical, carpeted with fruit plantations, the eastern part of the Zona Norte around Puerto Viejo de Sarapiquí bears more resemblance to the hot and dense Caribbean lowlands than the plains of the north and, despite the toll of deforestation, it shelters some of the best preserved **premontane rainforest** in the country. North by northwest from the Las Horquetas turnoff on the Guápiles Highway, the Sarapiquí area makes a parabolic arc around the top of Braulio Carrillo National Park (see p.118) and stretches west to the village of San Miguel, from where Arenal and the western lowlands are easily accessible by road.

South of Puerto Viejo de Sarapiquí, the area around the small town of **Las Horquetas** is home to the biggest *palmito* (heart-of-palm) plantations in the world. This and banana cultivation make up the bulk of the local economy, alongside more recent ecotourism initiatives such as the research station **La Selva**, and the rainforest lodges of **Rara Avis** and **Selva Verde**. The region's chief tourist attractions, these lodges offer access to some of the last primary rainforest in the country. The largest settlement, **Puerto Viejo de Sarapiquí**, is primarily a river transport hub and a place for the fruit plantation workers to stock up on supplies and have a beer or two. A sleepy town, it attracts few visitors in itself.

There are two options when it comes to getting **from San José or the Valle Central** to Puerto Viejo. The western route, which takes a little more than three hours, goes via Varablanca and the La Paz waterfall, passing the hump of Volcán Barva. Characterized

by winding mountain roads and plenty of potholes, this route offers great views of velvety smooth green hills clad with coffee plantations, which turn, eventually, into rainforest. Faster (1–1hr 30min) and less hair-raising – although somewhat less scenic – is the route via the **Guápiles Highway** through Braulio Carrillo National Park, switching off to the left at the Las Horquetas/Puerto Viejo turnoff at the base of the mountain pass. If you are on an all-in package to one of the lodges and you have transport included, it is likely that your driver will take the latter route.

Unsurprisingly the region receives a lot of **rain** – as much as 4500mm annually, and there is no real dry season (although less rain is recorded Jan–May), so rain gear is essential.

Rara Avis

RARA AVIS, a private rainforest reserve 17km south of Puerto Viejo, and about 80km northeast of San José, offers one of the most thrilling and authentic "ecotourism" experiences – if not *the* best – in Costa Rica, featuring both primary rainforest and some secondary cover dating from about thirty years ago. This general area, bordering the northeast tip of pristine Braulio Carrillo National Park, is home to a number of **palm species** known nowhere else (those found in Chiriquí, Panamá, are now extinct because of deforestation). Huge ancient hardwood trees, smothered by lianas, "walking" palms (that shift a metre or so in their lifetime), ancient primitive ferns and mosses, orchids and other flowering plants are also common.

Established in 1983 by American Amos Bien, a former administrator of Estación Biológica La Selva, with Trino, a a local squatter *campesino*, Rara Avis was intended to be both a tourist lodge and a private rainforest preserve, dedicated to the conservation, study and farming of the area's biodiversity.

The ultimate objective of Rara Avis is to show that the rainforest can be profitable for an indefinite period, giving local smallholders a viable alternative to clearcutting for their cattle. Rara Avis supports a number of endemic plants that have considerable economic potential, including *geonoma epetiolata*, or the stainedglass palm, which was until recently believed to be extinct. Another significant part of the Rara Avis mandate is to province alternative sources of employment in Las Horquetas, 15km away, where most people work for the big fruit companies or as day-labourers on local farms.

Rara Avis also functions as a **research station**, accommodating student groups and volunteers whose aim is to develop rainforest products – orchids, palms and so forth – as crops. Aims to create sustainable management for forest hardwoods have recently been dropped, however, as there is no longer sufficient forest in the Las Horquetas area. For more on rainforest management and sustainability, see *Contexts*.

Getting to Rara Avis

Some **packages** to Rara Avis include private transportation from San José (check with your travel agent or ground operator when you buy your package). If time is short, then this can be worth it, but with some planning it is perfectly possible – and more economical – to get there **independently**, by taking the bus from San José to the turnoff for the small village of Las Horquetas de Sarapiquí, where a tractor-pulled cart makes the final 15km of the journey.

As the tractor for Rara Avis leaves daily at 9am, you have to take the 7am bus to Río Frío/Puerto Viejo de Sarapiquí from San José. Make sure to get the express (*directo*) service via the Guápiles Highway (the bus via Heredia leaves thirty minutes earlier and takes the long western route to Puerto Viejo). If in doubt, ask people at the bus stop or the driver.

It takes between an hour and ninety minutes from San José to get to the turnoff for Horquetas. The *directo* bus does not go through Horquetas, but continues along the highway, so ask the driver to let you off at the Cruce (cross, or turnoff) for Las Horquetas. From here **taxis** will take you to the Rara Avis office in Horquetas (all accommodation at the lodge is pre-booked, so they will know you are coming, but you should call and double-check that a taxi is waiting for you).

Getting to Rara Avis **from Horquetas** is at least half the fun, though not exactly comfortable. The uphill flatbed-tractor journey to the lodges takes two to four hours depending upon the condition of the "road" (actually a horrendously muddy rutted track). The pluses of this mode of transport include the sheer excitement – there's much multi-lingual cheering when the heroic tractor driver revs the tractor for the fifth time and finally, squelching and sputtering, gets you up that slippery hill – and an exhilarating open-air view of the surrounding landscape with plenty of time for toucan-spotting. Minuses include pain (every part of anatomy not tied down bounces to high heaven), choking diesel fumes and a few worrying moments as the tractor slithers and slides up pitted hills.

If you have booked ahead to take the tractor and do by any chance miss it, **horses** are available for hire from villagers ($15) until noon – any time after that is too late as the trip takes several hours. Ask at the Rara Avis office when you arrive. The horses can get as far as the *El Plástico Lodge* (see below); if you are staying at the *Waterfall Lodge*, you'll have to walk the last 3km on a rainforest trail as the road is impassable for horses by that point.

Leaving Rara Avis, the tractor departs at about 2pm. This means that it often arrives in Horquetas too late to rendezvous with the last bus for San José, which passes through at 5.15pm daily. If you miss this bus, the Rara Avis office in Horquetas can arrange for a taxi (about $25 per carload) to the Guápiles Highway, from where you can flag down a Guápiles–San José bus (passing by hourly until 7pm).

Accommodation

There are two **places to stay** at Rara Avis. The cheaper is the IYHF-affiliated *El Plástico Lodge* ($45 per person), in a cleared area 12km from Horquetas. *Plástico*, as everyone calls it, is named after a convicts' colony that used to stand on the site, in which the prisoners slept underneath plastic tarpaulins. It has dirt floors downstairs, bunk-style beds and cold water, a covered but open-view communal dining table and a sitting area. Despite its rusticity, it's all very comfortable, and probably the only way to see Rara Avis on the – relatively – cheap. *Plástico* maintains radio contact with the outside world, but there's no phone.

The road from *Plástico* to the more comfortable *Waterfall Lodge* (⑧) is only 3km, but it's uphill, through dense rainforest, and takes at least an hour by tractor on a broken corduroy road which looks as if it's been hit by an earthquake. If you are in good shape, however, the best way to get there is to hike the (fairly obvious) trail through the rainforest – you'll have been given a map at the Rara Avis office in Horquetas. This should take about an hour: do not, under any circumstances, leave the trails, which are in good condition despite year-round mud.

WHAT TO SEE AT RARA AVIS

Rara Avis' **flora** is as diverse as you might expect from a premontane rainforest. The best way to learn to spot different flowers, plants, trees and their respective habitats is to go on a walk with one of the knowledgeable guides, who typically have lived at Rara Avis or nearby for some time. Especially interesting plants include the **stained-glass palm tree**, a rare specimen much in demand for its ornamental prettiness, the **walking palm**, whose fingertip or tentacle-like roots can propel it over more than 1m of ground in its lifetime, as it "walks" in search of water. **Orchids** are numerous, as are non-flowering bromeliads, heliconias, lianas, primitive ferns and other plants typically associated with this dense rainforest cover.

A mind-boggling number of **bird species** have been identified at Rara Avis, and it is likely that there are yet to be discovered. As well as the fearsome black, turkey and king vultures and the majestic osprey eagle, you might see four types of kites, ten types of hawk owls, hummingbirds, pretty Amazon and green kingfishers, woodpeckers, both chestnut-mandibled and keel-billed toucans, robins, warblers, great-tailed grackle, and the unlikely named black-crested coquette, great potoo and tiny hawk.

Among the more common **mammals** are monkeys, tapirs, ocelots and jaguars, though the last three are rarely seen. Along with other vipers, the **fer-de-lance** and **bushmaster snakes**, two of the most venomous in the world, may lie in wait, so take extra care on the trails, and look everywhere you step and put your hand.   Rara Avis' **butterfly farm** (for which a nominal visiting fee of $2 is asked – you don't have to pay, but it goes towards the farm's upkeep) is at the *Plástico Lodge*. **Boa constrictors** hang out around here; ask if any have been spotted lately. If you do see one, be careful; boas, generally quite torpid, can get aggressive if bothered.

Set above a picture-perfect cascade, the *Waterfall* has running hot water, private baths, and spacious balconies complete with hammocks and fantastic views of utterly pristine rainforest and hot, flat lowland plains stretching towards the Caribbean. It's an idyllic place to stay; the only sounds heard at five or six in the morning are the echoing shrieks of birds and *monos congos* (howler monkeys), and the light, even first thing, is sheer and unfiltered, giving everything a wonderfully shimmering effect. Meals, cooked by local women and served at three set times a day, are delicious. Odd as it may sound, some of the best "cuisine" in Costa Rica is to be had right here in the middle of the jungle, especially if you've been eating the bucketfuls of *arroz* concoctions served elsewhere. Breakfasts are heaped platters of eggs and cheese, *gallo pinto*, corn muffins, fresh fruit and wonderful coffee, while lunches and dinners are filling, delicately flavoured dishes with a variety of meat and vegetables. Vegetarians should have no problem at all. Beer and snacks are kept in a small "tuck shop": you take your own and keep track of your bill. There's also a phone from which you can make international calls (so much for rustic isolation).

Due to its popularity, you should **book** accommodation in Rara Avis well in advance from Aptdo 8105, San José 1000 (☎253-0844; fax 221-2314), or through a travel agent. Rates include guided walks and meals, as well as transportation by tractor from and to Las Horquetas. Although it is quite possible to stay for one night, because of the relative difficulty of access it is best to stay for two or more to get the most out of a trip.

Visiting Rara Avis

Just below the *Waterfall Lodge*, a 50m-high waterfall on the Río Atelopus plummets into a deep pool before continuing the river's slide down towards lower ground. **Swimming** in the pool, icy cold and shrouded in a fine mist, is a wonderful experience, but don't even consider it without a guide. Occasional *cabezas* up in the highlands swell the river and cause sudden rushing torrents; three people were swept to their deaths in 1992.

Rara Avis also has a network of very good **trails**: there are at least four around *Plástico*, not including the two ("Atajo" and "Catarata") that lead up to the *Waterfall Lodge*. From the *Waterfall* nine or so trails weave through fairly dense jungle cover. All are well-marked, and give walks of thirty minutes to several hours depending upon the pace. While guided walks are fun and informative, guests are welcome to go it alone: you'll be given a map at the lodge receptions. Staff do ask that you let them know which trail you are following and how long approximately you intend to be. Rain gear is essential at all times. At *Plástico* birdwatchers can buy a table of **birds** in the area (about 10¢), and tick them off.

Estación Biológica La Selva

A fully equipped research station, **ESTACIÓN BIOLÓGICA LA SELVA**, 93km northeast of San José and 4km southwest of Puerto Viejo, is owned and operated by the Organization of Tropical Studies (OTS), an international group of institutions dedicated to the study of rainforest and tropical areas. La Selva is probably the best place to visit in the Sarapiquí region if you are a botany student or have a special interest in the scientific life of a rainforest and, like Rara Avis, it is a superb birder's spot, with more than 400 species of indigenous and migratory birds. An equally staggering number of tree species – some 450 – have been identified, as well as 113 species of mammals. Many leading biologists from various countries have at one time studied here, and its facilities are extensive – a large swatch of pre-montane rainforest shouldering the northern part of Braulio Carrillo National Park forms the natural laboratory, while the research facilities comprise lecture halls and extensive labs along with **accommodation** for the scientists and students who make up the majority of its residents.

Though tourists are secondary to research at La Selva, visitors are welcome, providing there is space – it's impossible to overstate La Selva's popularity, and in the high season it is sometimes booked months in advance, even for day trips. Be sure to reserve way in advance by fax if you are coming between November and April. Visiting in the low season (roughly May–Oct) is a safer bet, but even then call first; if you come on spec, staff will simply turn you away.

Visiting La Selva

La Selva is impressively geared up to cope with its many visitors, with a reception, dining room, shop (selling posters, T-shirts, maps and a small selection of books) and visitors' centre. The ground cover extends from primary **forest** through abandoned plantations to pastureland and brush, crossed by an extensive network of about 25 **trails**. Varying in length from short to more than 5km long, most are in very good condition, clearly and frequently marked. Some, however, are "real" trails, with no corduroy, cement blocks or wire netting to help you get a grip, and many become very muddy indeed. Tourists tend to stick to

NEW VIEWS ON THE RAINFOREST

Many people unaccustomed to the **rainforest** approach it with the kind of awe reserved for great architectural or engineering feats. The idea that a rainforest is like a cathedral, a monolith, to be admired in hushed and humbled voices, is strangely intermingled with its metaphorical role as the epitome of the pristine, a latter-day Eden. Regeneration and decay is quick in tropical climes, but it has always been assumed that the highly complex and intertwined mechanisms that make a rainforest take centuries, even millennia, to regenerate themselves.

The tropical rainforest in the Sarapiquí region, and especially that within La Selva's natural laboratory, has long been thought to be representative of premontane, or ancient and relatively untouched, rainforest cover. But recent research into the history of La Selva's forests has raised new theories about the **regenerative capacities** of rainforests – ideas that are bound to be considered controversial by conservationists.

Unlike temperate-zone deciduous trees, those that make up the tropical rainforest do not form rings, so traditionally scientists have had to resort to other tactics, like examining the soil layer for clues, to determine the age of a given piece of forest. Recent findings – pottery pieces, two thousand year-old charcoals, burial sites, an ancient hearth, and tools used to cultivate crops like maize and yucca – unearthed in La Selva suggest, in the broadest sense, that early rainforests around here may have been slashed, burned and inhabited by generations of indigenous peoples. Meanwhile, contemporaneous evidence provided by scientists working in the Darién Gap and in the Amazon basin presents the possibility that rainforests throughout the Americas may be more resilient to disturbances than previously thought.

At the 1993 Ecological Society of America conference, La Selva researchers announced new data illustrating that between about 2000 and 800 years ago the Reserve's forest was put under the scythe by indigenous people to make space for, typically, corn plantations, small villages and *pejibaye* patches. For rainforest scientists the chief benefit of this information is that certain puzzles surrounding seemingly natural patterns of plant distribution may be solved. But in a wider sense it suggests that, far from being static, immovable monoliths of untouched biodiversity, rainforests may be the products of constant change and adaptation – or at least more so than has previously been thought.

Scientists at La Selva and elsewhere are quick to say that these findings do not sanction clear-cutting or any other modern form of rainforest destruction. Researchers admit that, while it may be possible to cultivate the land in a sustainable or regenerative fashion, the kind of agriculture they believe pre-Columbian people to have practised in the rainforest in no way resembles the massive plantation-style cultivation, logging, large squatter settlements, and other threats to the rainforest that we witness today.

the main trails within the part of La Selva designated as the Ecological Reserve, next to the Río Puerto Viejo. These trails, the **Camino Circular Cercano**, the **Camino Cantarrana** and the **Sendero Oriental**, radiate from the river research station and take you through dense primary growth, the close, tightly knotted kind of tropical forest for which the Sarapiquí area is famous.

The simple **map** they hand you at reception leads you adequately around the main trails, but for more detail the OTS-published booklet, *Walking La Selva*, sold at the station shop, gives a comprehensive, annotated trail-by-trail account.

Practicalities

To get to La Selva **from San José**, the least expensive option is to take the Río Frío–Puerto Viejo bus (see below), which, if you ask, drops passengers off at the entrance to the road leading to the station. Note, however, that it is a two-kilometre walk down the road from the junction. The OTS (☎240-5033 or 6696; fax 240-6783) also lays on a weekly bus from its office ($10); though mainly reserved for researchers and students, it is worth asking if they can fit you in. Taxis make the four-kilometre trip **from Puerto Viejo** for about $5.

If you want to **stay** at La Selva, you *must* book in advance (☎240-5033 or 6696; fax 240-6783; Aptdo 676, San Pedro 2050). The tourist rate (⑥) is not cheap, but proceeds go towards the maintenance of the station. Researchers and students with scientific bona fides stay for less (④). Rates include three meals a day, served in the communal dining hall. Most accommodation is in cabins with dorm beds and shared bathrooms, unless any of the singles or doubles normally reserved for researchers are free.

Though most people prefer to stay at La Selva, visiting on a day trip allows you to walk the trails and have a hearty lunch of *típico* food at the station's dining room. A **day visit** costs about $20 (including lunch); again, you have to reserve in advance, whatever time of the year you come.

Puerto Viejo de Sarapiquí

Just short of 100km northeast of San José, **PUERTO VIEJO DE SARAPIQUÍ** (known locally as Puerto Viejo, not to be confused with Puerto Viejo de Talamanca on the Caribbean coast) is the epitome of the steamy jungle town. The Río Sarapiquí is the focal point for the 6000 local inhabitants, and most cargo, both human and inanimate, is still carried by river to the Río San Juan and the Nicaraguan border in the north, and to the canals of Tortuguero and Barra del Colorado in the east.

An important hub for banana plantation workers and those who live in the isolated settlements between here and the Caribbean coast, Puerto Viejo is of little of interest to independent travellers except as a jumping-off point to visit the nearby jungle lodges.

Arrival

Numerous **buses** leave San José for Puerto Viejo and the small settlement of Río Frío (they'll be marked "Río Frío"). The service that goes **via Las Horquetas** (the fast route, via the Guápiles Highway through Braulio Carrillo) currently departs at 7am, 9am, 10am, 1pm, 3pm and 4pm. Although the schedule handed out by the ICT indicates that this 97km trip takes four hours, in reality it can be as quick as ninety minutes. Buses from San José to Puerto Viejo **via Heredia** (ask the driver if you are unsure which bus you're on – there's nothing on the front indicating which route it takes) are more likely to take around three hours. They leave at 6.30am, noon and 3pm, returning from Puerto Viejo at 8am and 4pm – although the last has been known to end up in La Virgen, some 12km west of Puerto Viejo.

Accommodation

The **accommodation** situation in Puerto Viejo de Sarapiquí is pretty good considering the town's size, though Friday and Sunday nights can get booked up with plantation workers. To really get to know the dense rainforest in the region, however, you may prefer to stay at one of the bona fide **jungle lodges** nearby, or at one of the good, privately owned hotels near the town (see opposite).

Mi Lindo Sarapiquí, on the main street (☎760-6281; ③) is the best-known spot in town, with a good restaurant that doubles as a bar at night. Ask behind the counter in the restaurant for rooms, as there is no reception. A good fall-back, *Cabinas Monteverde*, next to the *Monteverde* restaurant (☎760-6236; ②) has small, very basic rooms: pleasant enough, with cold-water shower and fans. Also on the main street, *El Bambú* (☎ and fax 766-6005; Aptdo 1518-2100, Guadalupe; ④), does not quite live up to its aspirations to be a small-scale resort, but is still the plushest accommodation in town, with fans, colour TV and hot water as well as a restaurant, bar and full tour service.

The Town
Puerto Viejo's one main street runs from the Cruz Roja at the entrance to the town and curves around towards the river and the small dock adjacent to it. The town "centre" lies across from the large well-manicured soccer field, where well-dressed schoolchildren gather to watch the local team practise.

A strange mixture of tropical langour and industriousness, Puerto Viejo does get a bit more lively on Friday evenings when the banana and the palmito plantation workers get paid. But in general it is a well-ordered place, relatively clean and cared for. There's an efficient, full-service **Banco de Costa Rica** (Mon–Fri 8am–3.30pm) on the main street and a **correo** (Mon–Fri 7am–5pm) on the corner where the main street joins the street to the *muelle*. Locals hang out around the **taxi rank** next to the soccer field (there is a taxi line-up sign). If none is parked you'll see plenty roving around the area – look out for tough-looking red 4WDs. They'll theoretically take you anywhere and prices are more or less fixed. The charge to La Selva and Selva Verde is about $5; about $25 to Rara Avis.

Eating and drinking
There are only two places to get a decent **meal** in Puerto Viejo: *Mi Lindo Sarapiquí* and *Monteverde*, both on the main street. There's little to choose between them – both places dish up good *típico* food – but the staff at *Mi Lindo* are somewhat more used to seeing tourists and have a smattering of English. At night they both double as gratifyingly laid-back **bars** and are good places to sit and have a beer. A few **fruit stalls** on the main street sell seasonal treats such as *mamones chinos*, the spiky lychees that look like vivid sea anemones, while the soda near the *muelle* by the river serves drinks, the usual *empañadas* and other super-starchy **snacks**. It's pleasant to while away time here by the slow-moving Sarapiquí with a cold beer, watching the activity at the docks.

Accommodation around Puerto Viejo de Sarapiquí

Although La Selva, Selva Verde and Rara Avis are the prime tourist destinations in this area, there are also a number of very attractive **hotels** and **lodges** dotted around Puerto Viejo that allow you to experience something of the **rainforest**. In general they are reasonably priced and accessible, and some offer packages from San José. If you are travelling by bus and the accommodation is west of Puerto Viejo, you should take the San José–Río Frío bus via Heredia (see above). Anything in Puerto Viejo itself or east is faster reached by the service to Río Frío–Puerto Viejo via the Guápiles Highway.

El Gavilán, 4km north of Puerto Viejo (☎234-9507; fax 253-6556; Aptdo 445-2010, San José). A former cattle *finca*, this lovely secluded lodge offers many excursions: hiking, swimming, river trips to Tortuguero (see p.150) and horseback rides. Guides are available. Simply furnished, comfortable rooms have hot water and fan. Packages cost about $400 for 2 nights/ 3 days, including transport from San José. Overnight rates include breakfast. No alcohol served. Hard to find, so call for directions or take a taxi. ④.

Islas del Río, 6km west of Puerto Viejo, 2km west of Chlilamate (☎761-6898 or 233-0366; fax 233-9671). IYHF-affiliated, with good rustic rooms with heated water. A small network of trails on site allows for walking, horseback riding. Discounts (30 percent) available for members; make reservations with *Toruma* in San José. ④–⑥.

Oro Verde, 3km from the Nicaraguan border on the banks of the Sarapiquí (☎233-6613; fax 233-7479; Aptdo 7043-1000, San José). Reached from Puerto Viejo by *lancha* (2hr), this private biological preserve protects 2500 hectares of land in an area under threat from logging and squatters. Rooms are rustic and comfortable, with shared or private bath (cold water only). Good dorms, too, accommodating groups up to 15. Guided nature tours, walking on site, and full meals ($17 extra). Very good value 2-night/3-day packages from San José include transport, meals and guide. ②–⑤.

La Quinta, about 7km west from Puerto Viejo, and 5km east of La Virgen (☎ and fax 761-1052). On the banks of the Río Sardinal, near Selva Verde, this comfortable lodge offers swimming, biking, horseback riding and birdwatching. All rooms have ceiling fans and hot water. Meals are extra. ④.

Rancho Leona, La Virgen, 12km west of Puerto Viejo (☎761-1019). Specialists in kayaking, offering good river trips both nearby (the Sarapiquí) and further afield (Reventazón, Caño Negro). You don't have to kayak to enjoy it here, though: they have comfortable rustic bunk rooms, some with verandahs, in lovely landscaped gardens. Good value short kayaking packages (2 nights/1 day) available. ③.

Sarapiquí Ecolodge, 4km south of Puerto Viejo, across the river from the La Selva Biological Station (☎253-2533 or 766-6122; fax 253-8645) is a family home and working farm, offering many of the same facilities and activities as La Selva, including horseriding, good birdwatching excursions, boat trips and hiking (all cost extra). No luxury accommodation here, but the bunks are comfortable enough. ⑤.

MOVING ON FROM PUERTO VIEJO DE SARAPIQUÍ

Puerto Viejo is a hub for the entire Zona Norte and eastern side of the country. From here it's possible to travel back to the **Valle Central**, either by the Guápiles Highway (1hr 30min or more) or via Varablanca and Heredia (3hr or more). You can also cut across country west to **San Carlos** (3 daily; 2–3 hr) and on to **Fortuna** (3–4hr) to reach Volcán Arenal, from where you can easily travel, via Tilarán (see p.271), on to **Monteverde** and **Guanacaste**.

By river it is possible to continue from Puerto Viejo north to the **Río San Juan** and **Nicaragua**. A public boat ($2.50) leaves the Puerto Viejo dock daily at 11am and returns from the small riverside village of La Trinidad – which has a few basic places to stay – the following day at 5am. It will drop you off at the private Oro Verde Preserve (see above) if you ask.

The public boat doesn't get you to Barra or Tortuguero on Costa Rica's Caribbean coast. To get to either of these places, a pleasant journey along the Ríos Sarapiquí and San Juan can take anywhere between four and seven hours (you're going upstream) by *lancha* and is fairly pricey if you're travelling independently – unless you happen to be with a group of eight or so other people. Ask at the Puerto Viejo dock, or in the soda above it, where local boatmen will be able to advise on availability and will quote about $300 for the trip (8–10 maximum capacity). For a full rundown of routes within the Zona Norte, see p.205.

Selva Verde Lodge

One of the premier rainforest lodges in Costa Rica, if not the Americas, **SELVA VERDE LODGE** sits amid 500 acres of preserved forest alongside the Río Sarapiquí, near the village of Chilamate de Sarapiquí 5km west from Puerto Viejo and 103km from San José. Softening the collision between tourist and rainforest, this private rainforest reserve is owned and operated by the US-based *Holbrook Travel*, specialists in ecological and adventure holidays.

Selva Verde is an impressive complex of accommodation, dining hall, lecture rooms and a lovely riverside bar/patio where monkeys chatter above and the Sarapiquí bubbles below. Connected by a series of elevated walkways or ground-level paths, it is set in landscaped tropical gardens rather than dense overgrowth, and appears to have mastered its environment to the extent that it's as if the staff have had a word with the animals – among them the dreaded fer-de-lance snake – and told them to behave themselves and not bother the tourists. And while it is full of very friendly, dedicated people and some of the most knowledgeable naturalist guides in Costa Rica, unless you can cope with the *Sheraton*-in-the-Jungle aspect of the place it may be best to rough it elsewhere. Comfort-lovers are well rewarded, though, by the very tasty food and super-comfortable rooms. And the hiking opportunities, wildlife-spotting and birding is unquestionably excellent, as are refreshing swims in the Sarapiquí. Whitewater rafting, horseback riding, riverboat rides and visits to a banana plantation are among the many activities offered.

Getting to Selva Verde

Taxis from Puerto Viejo to Selva Verde cost about $5. If you're driving, watch for a green gate and a large orange building (the lodge's library and community centre) on the left-hand side of the road from Puerto Viejo. Coming from the west on Hwy-9 via Heredia, look out for a large pasture field beyond which the Río Sarapiquí can be seen. Then the shallow driveway with its "Selva Verde" sign comes into view. If you come to the village of Chilamate (signed) then you've gone too far.

Accommodation

Selva Verde Lodge (☎766-6077 or 6266; fax 766-6011; ⑤–⑥) is owned and operated by the US company *Holbrook Travel* (you can reserve through their office in Gainesville, FL; ☎1-800/451-7111). Reservations should be made at least thirty days in advance, and the first night must be pre-paid. Children under twelve stay for free. Bear in mind that much of the time the lodge, which has a long-established link with the *Elderhostel* organization in the USA (see p.5), is full of tour groups or study groups. Rates include all meals, good showers with hot water, and full mosquito netting. Accommodation is in two complexes of elevated bungalows, the *River Lodge* – from which the Sarapiquí's gentle chatter can be heard – or the *Creek Lodge*, so named for a dried-up creek nearby. The former is slightly more expensive because of its tranquil location: the rooms with river views are best. Each has a hammock for daytime swings. After dark, rooms are lit by electricity, so night owls at least have the option of reading (everybody at Selva Verde seems to go to bed early – the bar and barbecue area empties out by 9pm).

Visiting Selva Verde

The whole of Selva Verde's 200-hectare area offers an excellent variety of walks along well-marked trails through primary and secondary forest, riverside, swamps and pastureland. Unless you've come as part of a pre-paid, all-inclusive package, you'll need to pay for the activities below: they cost between $15 (for guided walks) and $45 (for a half-day whitewater rafting). If you are energetic, tour costs can add up.

Across the road from the lodge, a network of easy **self-guided rainforest trails** weaves through a section of premontane forest, offering rewarding bird-watching. It's difficult to get lost (you'll be given a map at reception), and they all eventually loop round to the main trail. They start out from a small botanical and butterfly garden, where the vision of dozens of butterflies fluttering through the fluorescent display of colour gives you a taste of the raucous flora that can grow in this climate. For expereienced rainforest walkers or botany enthusiasts, however, the **guided walks** through the denser section of premontane forest across the Río Sarapiquí are more rewarding. Guides are absolutely top-notch (highly qualified people originally from the Sarapiquí area, some with self-taught English) and will point out poison dart frogs, primitive ferns, complex lianas, make uncannily authentic bird calls to get the attention of trogons and toucans, and generally give you a very good and informative time.

The most popular activity at Selva Verde, however, is **whitewater rafting** on the Class III (easy–moderate) Río Sarapiquí (May–Nov only). The trip is thrilling enough, though experienced rafters might regret the lack of any really scary rapids. **Riverboat rides** leave from Puerto Viejo, too, giving a good introduction to wildlife in the area – though admittedly, animal-watching is better from more pristine spots like Caño Negro or Tortuguero (see p.150). The banks of the Sarapiquí are, at least in Costa Rican terms, heavily populated, and on one side are packed for long stretches with banana plantations. What this trip does offer, however, is the rather dubious opportunity to observe at first hand the problems caused by the plastic pesticide bags used in banana plantations, caught up in the water or tangled around the lower branches of trees, poisoning the river and its wildlife.

Selva Verde's **reference library and community centre**, built largely for the people of the small community of Chilamate, 1km down the road, is open to guests, with excellent books in Spanish and English and a paperback section where you can swap your own.

travel details

Buses

San José to: Fortuna (3 daily; 4hr 30min); Los Chiles (2 daily; 5hr); Puerto Viejo de Sarapiquí and Río Frío (via Guápiles Highway, 6 daily; 1hr 30min–3hr; via Heredia, 3 daily; 3–4hr); San Carlos (14 daily; 3hr); Tilarán (4 daily; 4–5hr).

Fortuna to: San Carlos (7 daily; 1hr); San José (express, 1 daily; 4hr 30 min); San Rafael de Guatuso (2 daily; 1hr); Tilarán (1 daily; 1hr).

Los Chiles to: San Carlos (10 daily; 2hr 30min).

Puerto Viejo de Sarapiquí to: San Carlos (3 daily; 3hr); San José (via Guápiles Highway, 7 daily; 1hr 30min–3hr; via Heredia, 2 daily; 3–4hr).

San Carlos to: Fortuna (7 daily; 1hr); Los Chiles (10 daily; 2hr 30min); Puerto Viejo de Sarapiquí (3 daily; 3hr); San Rafael de Guatuso (5 daily); Tilarán (2 daily; 2hr).

Tilarán to: Fortuna (1 daily; 1hr); San Carlos (1 daily; 2hr); San José (4 daily; 4–5hr); Santa Elena, for Monteverde (1 daily; 3–4hr).

Boats

Puerto Viejo de Sarapiquí to: Barra del Colorado and Tortuguero (variable; 4–7hr); Río San Juan and Nicaragua (1 public boat daily).

CHAPTER FIVE

GUANACASTE

Those features in which the inhabitants of Guanacaste resemble Nicaraguans and differ from the rest of Costa Rica, so far as I could learn, are: their racial character, the Indian element being furnished by the Chorotegan tribe not found east of the Cordillera de Tilarán; many peculiar idioms not in use elsewhere in Costa Rica; a farm life of different character; the use of the marimba as a musical instrument; and certain peculiar dances ...

Amelia Smith Calvert and Philip Powell Calvert,
A Year of Costa Rican Natural History

Considering it was written in 1910, biologist Smith's observation of the cultural profile of Guanacaste is still remarkably apt. For the inhabitants of the Valle Central – whom *Guanacastecos* still sometimes call *Cartagos*, an archaic term dating back to the eighteenth century when Cartago was Costa Rica's capital – **Guanacaste province**, hemmed in by mountains to the east and the Pacific to the west, and bordered on the north by Nicaragua, is distinctly Other. Though little tangible remains of the dance, music and folklore for which the region is famous, there is undeniably something special, affecting even, about the place. Granted that much of the **landscape** has come about essentially through the slaughter of tropical dry forest, it is still some of the prettiest you'll see in the country, especially in the wet season, when wide open spaces, stretching from the ocean across savannah grasses to the brooding humps of volcanos, are washed in a beautifully muted range of earth tones, blues, yellows and mauves. Its **history**, too, is distinct. If not for a very close vote in 1824, it might have been part of Nicaragua, which would have made Costa Rica very small indeed.

The dry heat, relatively accessible terrain and panoramic views make Guanacaste the best place in the country for **walking** and **horseback riding**, especially around the mud pots and stewing sulphur waters of **Parque Nacional Rincón de la Vieja**, and through the tropical dry forest cover of **Parque Nacional Santa Rosa**. For many travellers, however, Guanacaste means only **beaches**: specifically those where the **Nicoya Peninsula** joins the mainland (roughly two-thirds of the mountainous peninsula is in Guanacaste, with the lower third belonging to Puntarenas province, covered in our chapter on *The Central Pacific and Southern Nicoya*), which range from simple hideaways to the controversial **Papagayo Project**, a mega-resort aimed at the North American winter market. That said, however, many of the province's beaches are not particularly beautiful, nor are all of them great for swimming, though some are used as nesting grounds for several species of **marine turtles**. The only **towns** of any significance for travellers are the provincial capital of **Liberia**, and **Nicoya**, the main town of the peninsula. If you are overnighting on the way to **Nicaragua**, La Cruz makes a useful base.

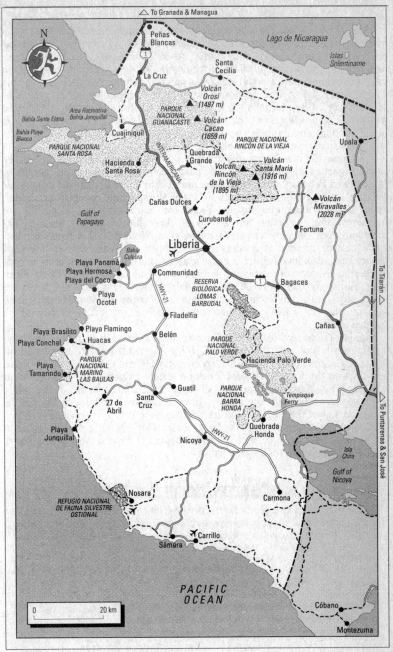

Much of Guanacaste has long been put under pasture for cattle ranching, and a huge part of the region's appeal is the **sabanero** (cowboy) culture, based around the hacienda (ranch) and *ganado* (cattle). As in the USA, in Costa Rica the *sabanero* has come to be a mythical figure – industrious, free spirited, monosyllabic to the point of mysticism, a skilful handler of animals and the environment – and his rough, tough body, clad in jeans with leather accoutrements, to symbolize "authenticity". (Women get assigned a somewhat less exciting role in this rural mythology: the *cocinera*, or cook.) In reality, however, the life of the *sabaneros* is hard, working often in their own smallholdings or as *peones* (farm workers) on large haciendas owned by relatively well-off ranchers.

To witness the often extraordinary skills of the *sabaneros*, head for the smaller towns – particularly on the Nicoya Peninsula – where during the months of January and February weekend **fiestas** are held in the local *redondel de toros*, or bullring. Unlike Spain, no gory kills are made: the spectacle comes from amazing feats of bull riding and roping. You'll see cowboys riding alongside the Interamericana, too, often towing two or three horses behind them as big transport trucks steamroller past on their way to Nicaragua. This dependence on cattle culture has its downside, however; much of Guanacaste is degraded pastureland, abandoned either because of its exhaustion by grazing or as a result of continually poor domestic and foreign prices and markets for Costa Rican meat. Although impressive efforts to regenerate former tropical dry forest are under way – at Parque Nacional Santa Rosa and **Parque Nacional Guanacaste**, for example – it is likely that this rare life zone/forest will never recover its original profile.

Highland Ticos tend to describe Guanacaste as a virtual **desert**, liberally applying the words "*caliente*" (hot) and "*seco*" (dry). Certainly it is dry, in comparison to the rest of the country: parts of it receive only 500mm of rain a year, ten times less than on the Caribbean coast. To some extent irrigation has helped, but in summer (Dec–March) Guanacaste still experiences some drought. This is when you'll see an eerie landscape of bare, silver-limbed trees glinting in the sun, as many trees shed their leaves in order to conserve water. The province is significantly greener, and prettier, in the "wet" season (May–Nov), generally agreed to be the **best time** to come, with the added benefit of fewer travellers and lighter rainfall than in the rest of the country.

THE TREES OF GUANACASTE

Trees blossom in a strange way in the dry lands of Guanacaste, flowering literally overnight and then, just as suddenly, shedding their petals to the ground, covering it in a carpet of confetti colours. Many people insist upon referring to Guanacaste as the "Texas of Costa Rica", and it even has its own yellow symbol to compete with the yellow rose of that state: the **corteza amarilla**, which bursts into a wild Van Gogh blaze of colour in March, April and May, all the more dramatic for being set against an otherwise Cézanne landscape of burnt siennas, muted mauves and sallow yellows.

In November the deciduous **guachepelín** tree blooms, with its delicate fern-like leaves; in January it's time for the pastel-pink floss of the **poui**, followed in March by the equally pretty **tabebuia rosea**. By the end of the dry season the red flowers of the **malinche** explode into colour.

Today Guanacaste is a province on the verge of great change. It remains to be seen what long-term effects the Papagayo Project might have, and if the spanking new, inexplicably stalled international **airport** near Liberia ever gets up and running (it was first scheduled to open in 1992) the province may become many tourists' first, and perhaps only, glimpse of the country. For now, **access** to most of Guanacaste is easy, facilitated by the straight-shot Interamericana, which runs right through to the Nicaraguan border at Peñas Blancas – watch out, though, for falling mangos, dead monkeys and iguanas; not to mention cyclists, school children and traffic cops. Modern, comfortable **buses** ply this road, with good services to Cañas, Liberia and the border. The National Parks of Rincón de la Vieja and Santa Rosa are trickier to reach, however, and bus travellers should bet on some walking, taxiing and hitching. All the beaches are accessible by bus and car, although the roads are not in fantastic shape, and journeys from San José can take at least five hours – those on the top half of the Nicoya Peninsula are the easiest to get to.

Some history

Due to significant excavations in the area, along with contemporaneous Spanish accounts, Guanacaste's **pre-Columbian** history is better documented than in the rest of Costa Rica. Archeologists have long been interested in the **Chorotegas** – considered to have been the most highly developed of all Costa Rica's scattered and mutually isolated pre-Columbian peoples, but whose culture predictably went into swift decline after the Conquest – and in the entire area of Guanacaste. In archeological terms it belongs to the **Greater Nicoya Subarea**, a pre-Columbian designation that includes some of western Nicaragua, and which continues to throw up buried clues to the extent of communication between the Maya and Aztec cultures to the north and smaller groups inhabiting Mesoamerica from the fifth to fifteenth centuries.

Historically part of the administrative entity known as the **Captaincy General of Guatemala**, Guanacaste was annexed to Nicaragua in 1787. In 1812, the Spanish rulers about-faced and donated the province to Costa Rica, so that it could increase its territory to a point where it had sufficient land to be officially represented in the Captaincy. When the modern-day Central American nations declared independence from Spain, and the Captaincy was dissolved in 1821, Guanacaste found itself in the sensitive position of being claimed by both Costa Rica and Nicaragua. In an 1824 vote the province's inhabitants made their allegiances clear: the *Guanacastecos* in the north, traditionally cattle ranchers with familial ties to Nicaragua, voted to join that country, while the inhabitants of the Nicoya Peninsula wished to maintain links with Costa Rica. The peninsular vote won out, by a slim margin.

As the nineteenth century progressed, **cattle ranching** consolidated and began to dominate the landscape, providing the mainstay of the economy until well into the 1900s. Despite the continuing presence of the cattle culture and the *sabanero* in Guanacaste, however, beef prices have been dropping in Costa Rica for some years now: in 1993–94 meat exports declined 17 percent. In contrast, as in the rest of the country, **tourism** is becoming increasingly important to the local economy. Large-scale tourism, however, is new here, and the development represented by the Papagayo Project has engendered raging debate about the direction tourism should take.

PRE-COLUMBIAN GUANACASTE

Greater Nicoya (today Guanacaste) was an archeological and cultural buffer zone between the complex cultures of the Aztecs and the Maya to the north, and the simpler tropical forest agrarian cultures to the south, who had more in common with prehistoric peoples of the Amazon basin. Although Greater Nicoya was occupied from an indeterminate date by the **Nicoyans** (about whom little is known) much of what is taken as historical and archeological fact about the region is about the peoples known as the **Chorotegas**, who may have arrived in Nicoya in 800 AD – some sources date their arrival as late as the fourteenth century – fleeing social and political upheavals far to the north.

The central Mexican empire of Teotihuacán, near the Mexico City of today, had fallen into disorganization in about 650 AD, and was abandoned about one hundred years later, at the same time that the Classic Maya civilizations of modern-day Yucatán and northern Guatemala also collapsed. New **fragmented groups** were created; some forged migratory, largely militaristic, bands. In the eighth century, harassed by their territorial enemies, the Olmecs, groups of Maya and Aztecs migrated south. Among them were the people who would become known as Chorotegas. The word *Chorotega* derives from either their place of origin, Cholula, or from two words in the Chorotegan language: *cholol* (to run or escape), and *teca*, (people – "the people who escaped").

Evidence of immediate and long-term cultural upheaval in the area after 800 AD includes a significant increase in the number of Nicoyan **burial sites** found dating from around this time. The use of elite-associated objects like ceremonial skulls, jades and elaborate metates suddenly declined, almost to the point of disappearance, and populations seem to have migrated from the interior toward the coasts. While this evidence could suggest a natural disaster (a volcanic eruption, perhaps) it also bears the hallmarks of what could be termed an invasion.

The Chorotegas' first contact with the **Spanish** was not fortuitous. The 1522 Spanish expedition from Panamá up the Pacific coast to Nicaragua spawned many adventure stories for the leader, Captain Gil González, to tell Carlos I of Spain, but brought considerable dismay to the indigenous people of Greater Nicoya, not to mention smallpox, the plague and influenza. Imprisonment and slavery followed, with coastal peoples raided, branded and sold into slavery in Panamá and Peru. The demise of the Chorotegas from the sixteenth century was rapid and unreversed.

The Río Tempisque area: north to Liberia

From San José the Autopista General Cañas leads 95km to the Puntarenas turnoff and the Interamericana (Hwy-1). For Guanacaste and Nicaragua, you turn off to the right, heading north. Eventually, neat white fences of cattle *fincas* begin to appear, with stretches of cleared land on both sides of the highway. Heading north to Liberia you pass the turnoff for Las Juntas de Abangares on your right, one possible route to Monteverde and Santa Elena (see p.256), while on the left is the road to the Río Tempisque, Guanacaste's principal drainage river, and the ferry across its estuary. Beyond Cañas, protected areas administered by the **Area de Conservación Tempisque** (ACT) encompass **Parque Nacional Palo Verde**, an important site for migratory birds, **Reserva Biológica Lomas Barbudal**, and the deep underground caves of **Parque Nacional Barra Honda** on the Nicoya Peninsula, just across the Río Tempisque (see p.250).

Excavations in Guanacaste and the Nicoya Peninsula reveal something of **Chorotega belief systems** and social arrangements. Excavations near **Bahía Culebra** unearthed pottery shards, utensils and the remains of hearths, along with a burial ground holding than twenty females, children and infants. Chorotega villages were made up of longhouse-type structures – common to many indigenous cultures of the Americas – inhabited by entire extended families, and centred on a large square, site of religious ceremonies and meetings.

Like the Maya and Aztecs, the Chorotegas had a belief system built around **blood-letting** and **sacrifice** of animals and humans. Although it is not known whether beating hearts were ripped from chests, virgins were definitely thrown into volcano craters; all in the appeasement of their Gods, of whom little is known, but who no doubt spent their spare hours lolling in the luscious aphrodisiac realm of those who have had their appetites fulfilled. Chorotegas also believed in **yulios**, the spirit alter ego that escaped from their mouths at the moment of death to roam the world for ever. Although pagan, Chorotega priests shared a number of duties and functions with the Catholic priests who worked to destroy their culture. Celibate, they may also have heard confessions and meted out punishments for sins.

The Chorotega **economy** was based on maize (corn). They also cultivated tobacco, fruit, beans and cotton, using cacao beans as currency. Women ran the marketplace. All land was held communally, as was everything that was cultivated and harvested, which was then distributed throughout the settlement. This plurality did not extend to social prestige, however. Three strata characterized Chorotega society: at the upper echelon were chieftains (*caciques*), warriors and priests; in the middle were the commoners, and at the bottom were the slaves and prisoners of war. The Chorotegas were the only indigenous peoples in Costa Rica to have a written **language**, comprising hieroglyphs similar to those used by the Maya, and were also skilled artisans, producing ornamental jewellery and jade, and colouring cotton fabrics with animal and vegetable dye. They also made the bulk of the distinctive **ceramics** so celebrated in the country today, many of which can be seen in San José's Museo Nacional (for more on Chorotega pottery, see p.243).

Few Chorotega **rituals** are documented. One known practice was the formation of a kind of human maypole, consisting of *voladores*, or men suspended "flying" (actually roped) from a post, twirling themselves round and round while descending to the ground. Originating with the Aztecs, and still performed in the Mexican state of Veracruz, the display is no longer seen in Costa Rica.

The **ACT head office**, on the Interamericana across from the turnoff to Parque Nacional Palo Verde, is not set up for tourists, though they can advise on current road conditions. For general information, it's best to head for the office of the Amigos de Lomas Barbudal in Bagaces.

Bagaces

BAGACES is a very hot town, only worth a stopoff for the **Amigos de Lomas Barbudal office**, about 300m east of the Parque Central (Tues & Thurs–Sun 8–11am & 1–4pm, Weds 8–10am & 2–6pm; ☎671-1062; fax 671-1029), which has photographs of all the Reserves and Parks in the area, printed information and brochures (Spanish only), and generally good advice. Staffed by a limited force of local volunteers, however, it is sometimes closed, even during office hours. Run on a shoestring, this serious and committed local organization very much appreciates contributions, no matter how small, and will tell you exactly how they intend to use your colones. Other than the office, there's nothing to see in

---

ACCOMMODATION PRICE CODES

All the establishments in this book have been given price codes according to the
following scale. The prices quoted are for the least expensive double room in high
season, and do not include the national 18.46 percent tax automatically added on to
hotel bills. Wherever an establishment offers dorm beds the prices of these are
given in the text. For more details see p.26.

| ① less than $10 | ③ $20–30 | ⑤ $50–75 | ⑦ $100–150 |
| ② $10–20 | ④ $30–50 | ⑥ $75–100 | ⑧ $150 plus |

Bagaces besides the unusual **bullring** (*redondel de toros*) a few hundred metres
beyond, in the direction of the mountains. Unlike most Guanacastecan bullrings,
which are made of wood and palm thatch, this one is a kind of cement mini-
Roman Coliseum, with a definite Fellini-esque air.

Parque Nacional Palo Verde

About 30km west of Cañas on the east bank of the Río Tempisque, **PARQUE
NACIONAL PALO VERDE** (daily 8am–4pm; $15 on the day, $7 in advance)
was created in 1982 specifically to preserve the habitat of **migratory birds** who
nest in the estuary of the Tempisque, and a large patch of relatively undisturbed
lowland dry forest. With a distinctive topography featuring ridged **limestone
hills** – unique to this part of the country, and attesting to the fact that areas of
Guanacaste were once under water – the Park shelters about fifteen separate
habitats, and huge ecological diversity. In the dry season, which around here
lasts from December to May, Palo Verde can dry out into baked mud flats, while
in the wet, extensive flooding gives rise to saltwater and freshwater lakes and
swamps, creating marshes, mangroves and other habitats favoured by migratory
birds. Little-visited by tourists, it is mainly of interest for serious **birders**, but
what you see depends on the time of year – the **best months** by far are at the
height of the dry season, when most of the 250 or so migratory species are in
residence. In the wet season, flooding makes parts of the Park inaccessible.

With one of the largest concentrations of **waterfowl**, both indigenous and
migratory, in Central America, there are more than 300 species of birds here,
among them the Costa Rican endangered jabiriú stork and black-crowned night
herons. Further from the river bank, in the tree cover along the bottom and
ridges of the limestone hills, you may be able to spot toucans and perhaps an
increasingly rare scarlet macaw.

From the administration building (see below), two **trails** lead up to the top of
hills, from where you can see the expansive mouth of the Tempisque to the west
and the broad plains of Guanacaste to the east. A number of other **loop trails**,
none more than 4km long, run through the Park; walking these you've got a good
chance of seeing a collared peccary, which are abundant in this area. Another
common mammal you may see or hear foraging in the undergrowth is the coatimundi; white-tailed deer are also around, but they are very shy and likely to dart
off at the sound of your approach. For longer treks, try the **Bosque Primario**
trail (about 7km), through, as the name suggests, primary forest cover, or walk
the 6km (dry season only) to the edge of the Río Tempisque from where you can
see the aptly named **Isla de los pájaros** (Bird Island). Square in the mouth of
the river, the island is chock-full of birds all year round, with black-crowned night

herons swirling above in thick dark clouds. Many hotels and tour agencies in the province offer boat trips around the island, but landings are not permitted, so you have to content yourself with bird-spotting and taking photographs from the boat.

Check with rangers regarding conditions before walking on any of the trails: access due to flooding (and perhaps bee colonies) are constantly subject to change, and the Río Tempisque walk in particular can be muddy and unpleasantly insect-ridden in all but the driest months. You should bring plenty of water, as the heat is considerable and humidity higher than further north in Guanacaste. A note on **safety** in Palo Verde: in recent years swarms of **Africanized bees** – sometimes sensationally termed "killer bees" – have taken to colonizing the area. Africanized bees *are* aggressive, and may pursue – in packs – anyone who unwittingly disturbs one of their large, quite obvious, nests. The usual advice is to cover your head and run in a zigzag pattern so that you can dodge the cloud of pursuing bees; a nightmarish scenario, but one, luckily, that occurs very rarely. However, take special care if you are sensitive to stings, and ask the rangers regarding the presence of nests on or around trails.

Practicalities

Getting to Palo Verde takes a while, though it is possible with a regular non-4WD in the dry season. From Bagaces, the 30km route southwest is well-signed, with an obvious turnoff from the Interamericana to the left (opposite ACT head office, where you should check out current road conditions). There are signs all along the road to the Park, but at large intervals, and the road forks unnervingly from time to time without (currently) indicating which way to go. If in doubt, follow the tyre tracks, made by the rangers. Once you turn off, it is nearly 30km (a 45-min drive) to the entrance hut, and another 9km to the administration building and the limestone outcroppings.

The Organization for Tropical Studies (**OTS**) has a field station at Palo Verde, originally set up for comparative ecosystem study and research into the dry forest habitat. If you contact their San José office (☎240-5033 or 6696 or 9938; fax 240-6783) in advance you may be able to stay in the rustic **field station** (②), providing it is not full up with scientific researchers. Otherwise, the most comfortable **place to stay** nearby is the *La Ensenada Lodge* (☎223-6653; fax 289-5281; ⑥). A working cattle ranch recently opened to tourists, they offer birdwatching tours on their land. Rooms are rustic, in cabins with private bath and fans, and small verandahs with pretty views over the Gulf of Nicoya. It's 20km west of the Punta Morales junction on the Interamericana (follow signs). You can **camp** ($2 per day) at the small site next to the administration building, where there are lavatories, but it is best to radio ahead from the SPN office in San José. You might also be able to **eat** with the ranger for about $10 a day on top of the camping fees – a good bet, as there's nowhere else to go for food in the area.

Reserva Biológica Lomas Barbudal

Created by locals for locals, **RESERVA BIOLÓGICA LOMAS BARBUDAL** ($2) is an impressive, though small-scale, initiative about 20km west of Bagaces. Home to some of the last vestiges of **tropical dry forest** in the region, the Reserve was temporarily closed by a scrub/forest fire in early 1994 that scorched much of the surrounding land. Vegetation still looks a bit ravaged, but for the hardy and opportunistic *jaragua,* a type of grass imported from Africa that you see throughout Guanacaste.

Lomas Barbudal means "bearded hills" and that's just what they look like – although less so since the fire – with relatively bare pates surrounded by side-burns of bushy deciduous trees. Stretches of open grassland, savannah-like, are punctuated only by the thorny-looking twisting **shoemaker's tree**, and criss-crossed by rivers and strips of deciduous woods that hug their banks. The Reserve also features isolated examples of the majestic **mahogany** and **rose-wood**, whose deep blood-red woods are so coveted as material for furniture.

With two swimmable rivers, a small network of trails designed and cleared by local volunteers, and a visitor centre, Lomas Barbudal is also rich in **wildlife**: you'll hear howler monkeys, at least, even if you don't spot one, and this is practically the only place along the entire Guanacaste coast where you have a reasonable chance of seeing the **scarlet macaw**. Like Parque Nacional Santa Rosa to the north, Lomas Barbudal hosts an abundance of **insects** – some 200 to 300 **bee species** alone, around 25 percent of the species of bees in the entire world. Those allergic to stings or otherwise intolerant of the insects might want to give Lomas Barbudal a miss; they're everywhere, including aggressive Africanized bees (see Palo Verde, above).

Practicalities

Although theoretically you could take a **taxi** (about $30) to Lomas Barbudal from Bagaces (ask at *Amigos de Lomas Barbudal*; drivers will wait), it is best reached with your own transport. Take the road north from Bagaces, and after about 7km follow the road off to the left. The administration office lies 6km further, prettily set on the banks of the Río Cabuyo. You can **camp** ($2.50 per night), but bring your own water and food; there are no lavatories.

TROPICAL DRY FOREST

With its mainly deciduous cover, Guanacaste's **tropical dry forest**, created by the combination of a Pacific lowland topography and relative aridity (in summer, from November to March approximately, almost no rain falls on lowland Guanacaste), looks startlingly different depending upon the time of year. In the height of summer, trees have stripped themselves bare, having shed their leaves – not in response to cold, like their northern autumnal cousins, but in an effort to conserve water – and the landscape takes on a melancholy, burnt-sienna hue. In April or May, when the rains come, the whole of Guanacaste perks up and begins to look comparatively green, although the dry forest never takes on the lush look of the rainforest.

The story of the **demise** of the tropical dry forests in Mesoamerica is one of nearly wholesale destruction. In all, only about 2 percent of pre-Columbian dry forest survives, and what was once a carpet stretching the length of the Pacific side of the isthmus from southern Mexico to Panamá now exists only in bedraggled and sieged pockets. Today dry forests cover just 518 square kilometres of Costa Rica, almost all in Guanacaste, concentrated around the Río Tempisque and, more signifi-cantly, north in Parque Nacional Santa Rosa. Due to deforestation and climatic change, tropical dry forests are considered a **rare life zone**. Their relative dryness means they are easily overrun by **field fires**, which ranchers light in order to burn off old pasture. In their wake spring up hardy grasses such as the imported African *jaragua*, which gives much of Guanacaste its African savannah-like appearance.

Along with the leafy trees, tropical dry forest features **palms** and even a few **evergreens**. At the very top of a good thick patch of dry forest you see the umbrella

Liberia and around

True to its name (it means "liberty"), the spirited provincial capital of **LIBERIA** has a distinctively free-thinking and open feel, its wide clean streets and blinding white houses the legacy of the pioneering farmers and cattle ranchers who founded it. At present most travellers use Liberia simply as a jumping-off point for **Parques Nacionals Rincón de la Vieja** and **Santa Rosa**, an overnight to or from the beaches of Guanacaste, or a stopoff on the way to Nicaragua. It's worth getting to know it better, however, for Liberia is actually one of the most appealing towns in Costa Rica.

Known colloquially as the **"Ciudad Blanca"** (white city), with its whitewashed houses, it is the only town in the country that seems truly "colonial". Many of the white houses still have their **Puerta del Sol**, an architectural feature left over from the colonial era and particular to this region – corner doors that were used, ingeniously, to let the sun in in the morning and out in the late afternoon, thus heating and cooling the interior throughout the day.

Liberia has everything you might need for a relaxing stay of a day or two – well-priced accommodation, a very helpful tourist office, a good bookstore, a couple of nice places to eat and drink, and a cinema showing startlingly original films. This may all change, of course, when the **international airport** starts pumping in the passengers in the next few years, but for now it's the epitome of dignified (if somewhat static) provincialism, with a strong identity and atmosphere all its own.

Several lively local **festivals** take place in Liberia, the most elaborate of which is **July 25**, *El día de la independencia*, celebrating Guanacaste's independence

form of **canopy trees**, although these are much shorter than in the tropical rainforest. Dry forest is a far less complex ecosystem than the humid rainforest, which has about three or four layers of vegetation (see p.361). Like temperate zone deciduous forests, the tropical dry forest has only two strata. The ground shrub layer is fleshed out by thorn bushes and tree ferns, primitive plants that have been with us since the time of the dinosaurs. Unlike rainforest, dry forest has very few epiphytes (plants growing on the trees), except perhaps for bromeliads (the ones that look something like upside-down pineapple leaves). The most biologically diverse examples of tropical dry forest are in the lower elevations of **Parque Nacional Santa Rosa**, where the canopy trees are a good height, with many different species of deciduous trees. There are also some pockets of mangroves and even a few evergreens in the wetter parts of the Park.

Tropical dry forests can support a large variety of **mammal life**, as in the Parque Nacional Santa Rosa–Parque Nacional Guanacaste corridor. Deer and smaller mammals such as the coatimundi and paca are most common, along with large cats, such as the jaguar and ocelot, provided they have enough room in which to hunt. You may see the endangered **scarlet macaw**, who likes to feed on the seeds of the sandbox tree, in a very few remaining pockets of Pacific dry forest, including Lomas Barbudal and, further south, around Río Tarcoles and Carara (see p.285), itself a transition zone between the dry forests of the north and the wetter tropical cover of the southern Pacific coast. However, it's the staggering number and diversity of **insects** that they support which makes the tropical dry forests of northern Guanacaste of most interest to biologists and entomologists: there are more than 200 types of bee in Lomas Barbudal, for example, and a large number of butterflies and moths in Parque Nacional Santa Rosa.

from Nicaragua with parades, horseshows, cattle auctions, rodeos, fiestas and roving marimba bands. If you want to attend, make your bus and hotel reservations as far in advance as possible and buy that straw hat. The last week in September is known as the **Semana Cultural Liberia Ciudad Blanca**, offering similar goings-on but without the wild patriotic revelry of July's celebration; there's no need to book buses and hotels in advance.

Arrival and information

Buses from San José pull in to Liberia's clean and efficient bus station on the western edge of town near the exit for the Interamericana. It's at most a ten-minute walk to the centre of town seven blocks east (or northeast, to be absolutely exact; because Liberia is set on a **northeast slant** it is difficult to get the usual bearings). **Drivers** enter from the obvious intersection (with traffic lights and three gas stations) off the Interamericana and turn right into a divided **Avenida Central**, lined with mango trees and centring on the *sabanero* monument. No one refers to calles and avenidas in Liberia: almost everything is described in terms of distance from the **church** or the **Gobernación**, the white house on the south side of the **Parque Central**.

Information

Liberia's supremely helpful **tourist office** is five minutes' walk south from the Parque Central (Mon–Sat 7.30–11.45am & 1.30–4.45pm, Sun 7.30am–1.30pm; ☎666-1606), in the same building as the Museo de Sabanero (see p.218). Erica Rivas and her colleagues have computers showing images of the beaches and hotels, will make phone calls to book hotels or ask directions, and will even place international calls and faxes at cost. In the high season especially, they also func-

tion partially as a **tour service**: with local operators they arrange group outings such as "Culture of Guanacaste" (a rather staged visit to "ye olde Wild West" including a trip to a working cattle ranch), or crocodile- and bird-watching in Parque Nacional Palo Verde. The office is a non-profit-making service, and any contributions, however small, are appreciated.

Another invaluable source of **information**, *Galería Fulvia*, inside *Centro Comercial Bambú*, 100m north of the church, has one of the best stocks of **foreign magazines and newspapers** in the country, from *Miami Herald* and *Newsweek* to *El País*, *La Prensa de Nicaragua*, *La Republica* and *Der Stern*. They also sell second-hand English-language paperbacks and guidebooks; if you bring in two used books plus 100 colones you get one free. A kind of one-woman promotional board for Guanacastecan art and literature, Fulvia publishes *Ruzafa Chorotega*, her own bi-monthly review, containing poetry, anecdotes and a local events calendar, as well as a calendar of local services (from *abogados* to *zapaterías*), activities and bus schedules. She also draws, paints and displays the work of local artists.

The efficient **correo**, 500m west and 100m north of the church (Mon–Fri 7.30am–5.30pm), is a bit hard to find: it's the low-slung white house across from an open field bordered by mango trees. Perhaps anticipating the influx of foreign money the airport might bring, **banks** in Liberia have mushroomed in the last few years. Of these *Bancoop* (Mon–Fri 8am–4pm, Sat 8am–2pm), is recommended for fast, *trámites*-free dollar exchange. Their tiny office is hidden in back of the small shopping centre across from the comisaría de policía, 50m west of the Parque Central. Just 50m from the entrance to the Interamericana on Av Central, *Banco Popular* has a pretty fast change facility.

Though Liberia is small enough to walk around, many locals cycle; you can **rent bikes** from *Mountain Bike Guanacaste*, near 3 gas stations corner and signed from the Interamericana.

Accommodation

Liberia is the most convenient place to spend the night along this northern stretch of the Interamericana. Standards are generally very high and, though dirt-cheap places are scarce, the ones that do exist are good. Because of tourist traffic to and from the beaches, Liberia is chock-full in the dry season, especially weekends, and it is imperative to have a **reservation** before you arrive. At other times, midweek especially, there's no problem with space.

Bramadero, 3 gas stations corner (☎666-0371). The setting, beside the *bombas* on the Interamericana, isn't the loveliest, but convenient for the beaches and popular with Ticos. Nondescript, basic rooms, good restaurant, plus pool. ④.

Hostal Ciudad Blanca, 200m south and 150m east of the Gobernación (☎666-2715). New hotel with modern, comfortable rooms, a/c, TV, private bath and ceiling fans. Spotless, with a lovely breakfast terrace and bar. Liberia's best mid-price option. ④.

Las Espuelas, 2km south of town, on the right (☎666-0144). The best upscale hotel in the region, with friendly staff, low-slung hacienda architecture, a/c, cable TV, nice pool, restaurant (good steaks), and poolside bar. ⑥.

Hotel Guanacaste, 300m south of the bus station (☎666-0085). Popular, friendly budget IYHF-affiliated hotel, with a traveller-friendly restaurant where you can start a conversation as well as have a cold beer. Rooms are simple, clean and dark. Reservations recommended. $20 without IYHF card, $12 with. ②.

Hotel Liberia, 50m south of the Gobernación (☎ and fax 666-0161). Established, friendly hotel, with secure parking and basic, box-like rooms. Probably the cheapest in town. ①.

Hospedaje Paso Real, 400m south of the church (☎666-1112). The very friendly *dueña* of this huge historic family home runs a very genial house with TV lounge. Not particularly cheap for basic, clean rooms, but a good atmosphere. Breakfast costs 400 colones extra. ④.

El Sitio, from 3 gas stations corner turn left on to road to Nicoya and drive 100m (☎666-1211; fax 666-2059). Comfortable motel-style accommodation with TV, private bath with hot water, pool and restaurant. Convenient if you are heading out to Nicoya. ⑤.

The Town

Liberia's wide streets are used more by cyclists than motorists and shaded by mango trees that plop their ripe fruit at your feet full-force in March and April. The town is arranged around its large **Parque Central**, properly called Parque Mario Cañas Ruiz and dedicated to *el mes del annexion*; the month of the annexation (July), celebrating the fact that Guanacaste is not in Nicaragua. The **church** in the *parque* is modern, and generally considered unattractive – the kindest view is that its startlingly modernist form looks a little out of place in this very traditional town. About 600m away at the very eastern end of town, the colonial **Iglesia de la Agonía** is more arresting, with a mottled yellow facade like a peeling, washed-out banana. On the verge of perpetual collapse – it has had a hard time from those earthquakes – it's almost never open, but you could try shoving the heavy wooden door and hope the place doesn't collapse around you if it does give way.

If you're interested in **souvenir shopping**, *Artesano Maya* about 100m east of the church, sells Guatemalan duffel bags, knapsacks and a truly splendid collection of small rugs and bedspreads, all at better prices than in San José (Mon–Sat 8am–1pm & 2–6.30pm).

Museo de Sabanero

To learn something of daily life on the old hacienda *ganadera*, or cattle ranch, head for the tourist office, which also houses the **Museo de Sabanero**, or Cowboy Museum (Mon–Sat 7.30–11.45am & 1.30–4.45pm, Sun 7.30am–1.30pm; free). The exhibit is fascinating in a small-scale way, displaying objects that you might have found in the big ranch houses, or *casonas*, that formed the nucleii of ranch communities. The *casona* consisted of a *zaguán*, where the *sabaneros* kept their *aperos* (tack); the *cocina de leña,* or wood stove, where meals were cooked;

the *corrales de piedra,* or distinctive stone corrals, and the *corrales de ordeño y remonta,* where livestock were branded.

Entering the museum from the tourist office, you pass an enormous wooden hacienda table – if a table can be said to ooze integrity this one does – and come into the musty, low-lit world of the old adobe house. Here you'll see the taut skins of former cattle: bridles, chaps, boots, and the *sabanero*'s distinctive high-backed saddle, kept in place by a lariat wound around the horse's tail. Also on show are twirling, ferris-wheel spurs, old hacienda chairs, lariats smoothed with age, elaborate whips, branding irons and several unidentifiable tools and instruments of bovine torture. It's a small, immensely dignified collection, perfectly in tune with its cool, dark surroundings.

Eating, drinking and entertainment

Liberia has several **restaurants** that are particularly good for breakfast and lunch. Local treats include the ubiquitous **natilla** (soured cream) eaten with eggs or *gallo pinto* and tortillas. For a real feast, try the various **desayunos guanacastecos** (Guanacastecan breakfasts): *sabanero* or, more properly, **criollo** food, made to be worked off with hard labour. For rock-bottom cheap **lunches**, head for the stalls in the bus terminal, *Las Tinajas* or *Rancho Dulce* in town, or at a number of fried chicken places. You can pick up Guanacastecan **corn snacks** from stalls all over town and at 3 gas stations corner.

There's little **drinking** to be done in Liberia, though the bar at the *Hostal Ciudad Blanca* is a nice place for a beer, as are *Las Tinajas* or *Pizzería Pronto*. The one **disco,** *Kurú,* next to the *Pokopí* restaurant, is lively with salsa and merengue, especially on weekends and *feriados*. The main Saturday evening activity, however, involves parading around the Parque Central in local fashion finery, hanging out, having an ice cream, and maybe going to the movies. The **Cine Olimpia,** 100m north of the church, is the most astonishingly up-to-date provincial cinema in Costa Rica, showing new art-house movies alongside action-adventure blockbusters.

LA COCINA GUANACASTECA: CORN COOKING

Corn is still integral to the regional cuisine of Guanacaste, thanks to the Chorotegas, who cultivated maize (corn), to use in many inventive ways. One pre-Columbian corn concoction involved roasting, then grinding, the maize, and combining the meal-like paste with water and chocolate to make the drink *chicha*. Although you can't find this version of *chicha* any more you can still get **grain-based drinks** in Guanacaste, such as **horchata** (made with rice or corn and spiced with cinnamon), or *pinolillo* (made with roasted corn), both milky and sweet, with an unmistakably grainy texture.

Corn also shows up in traditional Guanacastecan snacks such as **tanelas** (like a cheese scone, but made with cornflour) and **rosquillas**, small rings of cornflour that taste like a combination between tortillas and doughnuts. You can buy these at roadside stalls and small shops in Liberia, and from hawkers at both ends of the Tempisque ferry. Served throughout the country, **chorreados** crop up most often on menus in Guanacaste: they're a kind of pancake made (again) with cornflour and served with *natilla*, the local version of sour cream.

Restaurants and sodas

Donde Marcos Cafeteria, 200m east of the church. Friendly, outdoor terrace, good for breakfast if you can't handle the noise at the *Jardín de Azúcar* (see below). Nice service and even nicer *repostería* (desserts): chocolate cake plus *refrescos* and *café con leche*. Open 7.30am–6pm.

Hostal Ciudad Blanca, 200m south and 150m east of the Gobernación. A really nice place, with a good choice of drinks, in a semi-open-air tiled hotel terrace.

Jardín de Azúcar, 100m from *Banco de Costa Rica* on other side of street. But for the ear-splitting Latinopop, this place *would* be wonderful. Great breakfasts include *Americano* (ham, egg, toast, plus coffee or tea) and *Guanacasteco* (*gallo pinto, natilla, tortillas* and eggs). Go later for Liberia's cheapest grilled fish in garlic. Also a *jardín de niños* (kid's section).

Pizzería Pronto, 200m south of the church. The most cosmopolitan place in town for good, cheap pizzas and drinks. In an old tile-decorated adobe house, cool, dark and pleasant inside.

Pokopí, 100m from 3 gas stations corner on the Interamericana, on the road to Nicoya, across from *Hotel el Sitio*. Fastidiously clean (they mop the floor every two seconds) and with Tropico-naif toucans and the like decorating the walls. Good gringo food includes huge, dripping burgers ($3), and very tasty *pargo en ajillo* (snapper in garlic butter; about $7).

Rancho Dulce, 50m south of the Gobernación. Tiny soda serving *casados*, sandwiches, *empañadas* and *refrescos*: great for a cheap lunch. You can sit at the tiny outdoor stools (if you have a small bottom) or tables.

Las Tinajas, west side of Parque Central. Nice outdoor tables on verandah of old house with park view. Good for a *refresco* or beer, and very basic *casados* and rice combinations. Sells the *Tico Times*.

MOVING ON FROM LIBERIA

As well as having good connections with **San José** (8 direct *Pulmitan de Liberia* buses daily) Liberia is also the main regional hub, giving easy access to Guanacaste's Parks and beaches, and the Nicaraguan border.

For **Parque Nacional Santa Rosa**, take a La Cruz or Peñas Blancas (Nicaraguan border) bus (5.30am, 8.30am, 11am, 2pm & 6pm; 2hr) from the Liberia station. Take the earliest bus you can to give yourself more time for walking – though bear in mind that the Park won't be officially open until after 7.30am – and ask the driver to let you off at Santa Rosa. If you want to get to the Park's Murciélago sector, however, take the Cuajiniquil service (daily; 3pm; 1hr 30min). The return bus is at 7.30am, so, allowing for a day in the Murciélago sector, it's a three-day trip. For **Parque Nacional Guanacaste**, take the 3pm bus to Quebrada Grande village, from where it's a walk of at least two hours. If you're heading for the border, regular buses run to **La Cruz** (hourly; 1hr). Services to **Bagaces** and **Cañas** leave the station at 5.45am, 1.30 and 4.30pm, taking about forty minutes to an hour.

There are direct services to the more northerly of Guanacaste's **beaches**: for Playas Hermosa and Panamá, two buses leave daily (11.30am & 7pm; 1hr). Playa del Coco is served by three or four services per day (5.30am, 12.30pm, 4.30pm and, high season only, 2pm; 1hr). You can also get to **Santa Cruz** (hourly; 5.30am–7.30pm; 1hr), from where you can hook up with buses to Tamarindo, Junquillal and beaches further south. Buses for **Nicoya** leave on the hour from 5am to 7pm (2hr). Buses to **Puntarenas** leave at 5am, 8.30am, 10am, 11am and 3pm (3hr).

Colectivo taxis, shared between four or five people, can be good value if you're heading for **Parque Nacional Rincón de la Vieja** or the haciendas near **Las Espuelas ranger station**. They line up at the northwest corner of the Parque Central, and charge about $60. If you don't have much luggage, you could also **rent a bike** from *Mountain Bike Guanacaste* (see p.217).

Parque Nacional Rincón de la Vieja

The beautifully dry landscape of **PARQUE NACIONAL RINCÓN DE LA VIEJA** (daily 8am–4pm; $15 on the day, $7 in advance), about 30km northeast of Liberia, varies from rock-strewn savannah to patches of tropical dry forest and deciduous trees, culminating in the blasted-out vistas of the volcano crater. The land here is actually alive and breathing: Rincón de la Vieja last erupted in 1991, and rivers of lava/magna still broil beneath the thin epidermis of ground, while brewing **mud pots** (*pilas de barro*) bubble, and puffs of steam rise beatifically out of lush foliage, signalling sulphurous subterranean springs. This is great terrain for **camping, riding** and **hiking**, with a comfortable, fairly dry heat – although it can get damp and cloudy at the higher elevations around the crater. **Birders**, too, get excited about Rincón de la Vieja, as there are more than 200 species in residence.

Getting to the Park

The local dry season (Dec–March especially) is the **best time** to visit Rincón de la Vieja, when hiking and visibility as you ascend the volcano are more pleasant. There are two **entrances**, each with a ranger station. From Liberia most people travel through the hamlet of Curubandé, about 16km northeast, to the **Las Espuelas ranger station**. The other ranger station, **Santa María**, lies about 25km northeast direct from Liberia. The **casona** that houses the ranger station is a former retreat of US president Lyndon Baines Johnson, who sold it to the SPN, and, at more than 110 years old, is ancient in Costa Rican terms.

Both routes are along stony roads, not at all suitable for walking. People do, but it's tough, uninteresting terrain, and it is really more advisable to save your energy for the trails within the Park itself. Options for getting here **from Liberia** include renting a *colectivo* taxi or hitching. Some people hike out to the Interamericana gas stations; if your Spanish is up to it you could hitch a lift from a truck driver there and ask what he'd charge. Split between a group this can work out significantly cheaper than a taxi. At the other end of the scale, you could rent a car (4WD is crucial), and stay in one of the upscale, good-value tourist lodges; these also offer **packages** from San José, with transport included.

Accommodation

The Rincón de la Vieja area boasts some very good **lodges**, which provide pick-ups ($10–25 return) from Liberia hotels; in some packages this transport is included. Most of the lodges offer their own tours, either on horseback or by foot; some go into the National Park lands and some don't. Staying at *Buenavista* you

---

BORDER CHECKS IN GUANACASTE

Driving along the Interamericana north of Liberia, do not be surprised to see a blue-suited *policia de transito* (traffic cop) or a light-brown-suited *guardia rural* (border policeman) leaping out, kamikaze-like, into the highway directly in front of you, expecting you to stop. Do so, and show him your driver's licence and passport (which you must have on you at all times – see *Basics* p.37). Other times they will pull you over. These are routine checks, mainly to deter the entry of undocumented Nicaraguans into Costa Rica. The nearer the border you get, the more frequent the checks become; either by traffic police or the border authorities. Make sure to drive carefully: knocking over a policeman is not a good move.

can go on tours to the crater without paying the fees, as they own the land from which the crater is accessed.

You can **camp** at the Santa María station ($2 per person per day) where there are lavatories and water, or near the Río Colorado at the Las Espuelas station; take cooking utensils, food, water plus canteen, sweater, rain gear, compass and mosquito repellent. If you have a sleeping bag, and ask in advance, you can also stay inside the rustic **bunk rooms** in the ranger station, a bit musty and dark, but at least you have a roof over your head. Call the Santa Rosa administration centre; see p.226.

Albergue de la Montana Rincón de la Vieja, 5km northwest from the *Guachepelín*; follow signs (☎666-2369; fax 666-0473). The nearest lodging to the Las Espuelas ranger station. IYHF affiliated but not cheap; rustic, with cold showers. Choice of bunks, doubles with bath or full board (the food is good, if pricey). All tours, including guides and horses plus transport from Liberia, cost extra. Members should book in advance from *Toruma*. ③–④.

Buenavista Lodge, 31km northeast of Liberia, near the hamlet of Cañas Dulces (☎ and fax 695-5147). Quiet, comfortable, working cattle ranch, with stupendous views over Guanacaste, and trails through ranch land, pockets of rainforest on the flanks of the volcano, and up to the crater. A very friendly ranching family make you feel at home, though Pancho the monkey is a bit of a pain – the pet peccary is more fun. Private or shared bath, with welcome hot water (it's cool up here). Filling, tasty meals cost extra, as do horseback and hiking tours, but they are very reasonably priced (8hr jaunt to the crater $40). To get here, best call ahead and ask for transfer from Cañas Dulces (accessible from Liberia by bus); they will send a 4WD and, if driving, you may be able to leave your car at the house of their driver. ④.

Hacienda Guachepelín (☎442-2818 or 2695; fax 442-1910). Lovely unpretentious house on a working ranch, converted into a friendly tourist lodge, the historic *Guachepelín* is one of the nicest places to stay in the entire country. Choice of doubles decorated with cowboy ephemera, simple rooms with bunks ($6–14 per person), and a cheaper bunk house annexe, good for groups. Verandah with Sarchí leather rockers, and TV lounge (electricity until 10pm). Meals cost extra. There's a waterfall 5min away, and well-marked trails; they even have their own mud pots. Guides are available for a variety of tours, including riding/hiking to the volcano. Pick-up from Liberia is free if you stay at the *Hotel Guanacaste*; otherwise it costs about 4000 colones. Packages available. ③.

Miravieja Lodge, 25km north of Liberia in the hamlet of San Jorge (☎666-2004 or 1045). Very basic, clean lodge surrounded by fruit trees: you can pick yourself a mango in season. It's reached via a garbage dump (4WD-only road), but persevere. ②.

Rinconcito, San Jorge (☎666-0626). Basic accommodation in an annexe on a family farm; friendly, with advice on transport, guides and directions. Cold water only. ②.

Visiting the Park

Rincón de la Vieja's **main trail*** leads from both ranger stations to the summit of the volcano to view the active crater. Whether on foot or horseback or a combination of the two, this is quite simply one of the best hikes in the country, if not *the* best. A variety of elevations and habitats reveals hot springs, sulphur pools, bubbling mud pots, fields of purple orchids – the *guaria morada*, the national flower – plus a great smoking volcano at the top to reward you for your efforts. **Animals** in the area include all the big cats (but don't expect to see them), the shy tapir, red deer, collared peccary, two-toed sloth, and howler, white-faced and spider monkeys. There's a good chance you will see a brilliant flash of fluttering blue – this is the **blue morpho** butterfly, famous for its electric colours. **Birders** will have a chance to spot the weird-looking three-wattled bellbird, the Montezuma oropendola, the trogon and the spectacled owl, among others.

It's 18km from the Santa María ranger station to the top of the volcano, a fairly leisurely hike of around two days. From the Las Espuelas station the summit is much closer, some 7km, and can be reached in in few hours, but, unless you walk very fast indeed, you'll still probably want to **camp** along the way – most likely at the crater. You see far more by starting out at Santa María, which enables you to follow a number of minor trails leading off from the main one. From Las Espuelas, you miss out on the mud pots, though you can, of course, head back towards them before doubling back and continuing up to the crater.

From the Santa María ranger station you come to a trail, **Bosque Encantado** (Enchanted Forest), which leads to a small forest with a couple of hot springs and a waterfall. Back on the main trail, 1km beyond the Bosque Encantado, is a sign for the **aguas thermales**, or hot springs. This is roughly a three-kilometre walk; the springs are next to a creek, which hikers love to leap into after a wallow in the thermal pool, imitating a sauna effect. At the moment the temperature is about right for soaking, but you should *never* jump into any thermal water without **checking** first at the ranger station regarding the current temperature.

Back on the main trail, after a further 5km or so, you'll come upon a *Pilas de Barro* sign, leading to the **mud pots**; listen out for strange bubbling sounds, like a large pot of water boiling over. Mud pots, which should be treated with respect, are formed when mud, thermally heated by subterranean rivers of magma, seeks vents in the ground, sometimes actually forcing itself out through the surface in

---

*Rincón de la Vieja is getting more and more popular, and it is likely that the trails will soon become over-walked. If you stay at one of the lodges (see opposite) and take their summit tours, either by horseback or foot, note that you may pass through different territory than is covered here. Also, bear in mind that Rincón de la Vieja is an active volcano, and the trail described above may have been altered due to periodic lava flows. Always check current conditions at one of the ranger stations before setting out.

great thick gloops. It's a surreal sight; grey-brown muck blurping and blopping out of the ground like slowly thickening gravy. Back on the main trail, a side trail is signed to the geothermal **hornillas** (literally, "stoves"); mystical-looking holes in the ground exhaling elegant puffs of steam. You almost expect to stumble upon the witches of *Macbeth*, brewing spite over them. Make sure not to go nearer than a metre or so, or you'll be steamed in no time. The combined effect of all these boiling holes is to make the landsape a bit like brittle Swiss cheese – tread gingerly, and look carefully where you're going, to avoid the ground crumbling underneath you. Many hikers have been scalded by blithely strolling too close to the holes.

About 1km past the *hornillas* is a **camping area**; the river beyond is the only place on the entire trek to fuel up on water. On the other side of the river you come to the **Las Espuelas** ranger station, from where it is an uphill walk to the summit, passing the tree line and a second campsite. The forest here becomes similiar to lower montane rainforest, densely packed, and lushly covered with epiphytes and mosses. Cool mist and rain often plague this section of the trail: if you are anywhere near the crater and lose visibility, which can happen very suddenly, it really is best to sit down and wait out the weather rather than stumbling around in the fog with a volcanic crater somewhere in front of you.

At the **summi**t (1916m), Rincón de la Vieja presents a barren lunar landscape, a smoking hole surrounded by black ash, with a pretty freshwater **lake**, Lago los Jilgueros, to the south. Quetzals are said to live in the forest that rims the lake; as usual, however, you're unlikely to see them. When clear, the **views** up here are the reward for the uphill sweating: Lago de Nicaragua shimmering silver-blue to the north; to the southeast the hump of the Cordillera Central, and to the west the Pacific Ocean and spiny profile of the Nicoya Peninsula. You can get hammered by wind at the top; bring a sweater and windbreaker.

Parque Nacional Santa Rosa

Established in 1971, **PARQUE NACIONAL SANTA ROSA** (daily 8am–4pm; $15 on the day, $10 in advance), 35km north of Liberia, and 260km from San José, was the first National Park in Costa Rica's system, established to protect the increasingly rare dry tropical forest. Today it's one of the most popular, due to its good trails, great surfing (though poor swimming), prolific turtle *arribadas,* and historical and cultural interest in the form of the **casona**, a fortress-cum-farmhouse whose proximity to Nicaragua, made it a prime target for would-be interlopers. It's also, given a few official restrictions, a great destination for **campers**, with a couple of sites on the beach.

All in all Santa Rosa has an amazingly diverse topography for its size, ranging from mangrove swamp to deciduous forest and savannah. Home to 115 species of mammals – half of them bats – 250 species of **birds** and 100 of **amphibians** and **reptiles** (not to mention 3800 species of **moths**), Santa Rosa is prime biological investigation territory, attracting researchers from all over the world. Jaguars and pumas prowl the park, but you're unlikely to see them; what you may spot – at least in the dry season – are coati, coyotes and peccaries, often snuffling around watering holes.

The appearance of the Park changes drastically between the **dry season**, when the many streams and small lakes dry up, trees lose their leaves, and thirsty animals can be seen at known waterholes, and the **wet months**, greener but afford-

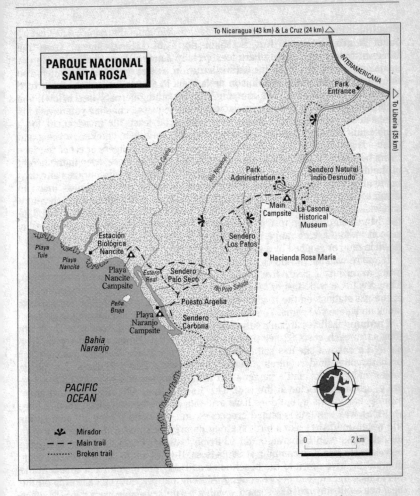

ing fewer animal-viewing opportunities. From August to November, however, you may be able to enjoy the sight of hundreds of **Olive Ridley turtles** (*llora*) dragging themselves out of the surf and up Playa Nancite by moonlight; September and October are the months of heaviest arrival. You need a permit to watch the *arribadas*: in an attempt to avoid the disturbance caused by big tour groups *à la* Tortuguero (see p.150), these are only given to individuals or small groups. Provided there is space (25 is the maximum), there should be no problem; though you can, theoretically, be able to pick them up from the administration centre, its best to ask in advance at the SPN office in San José, as the rules may well change.

Though too rough for swimming, the picturesque **beaches** of Naranjo and Nancite, about 12km down a bad road from the administration centre, are popular with serious **surfers**. They're also great places to rest out a while (outside turtle season) camping and walking a little on the nearby trails.

Practicalities

Santa Rosa's **entrance hut** is 35km north of Liberia, signed from the Interamericana. After paying Park fees, pick up a map and proceed some 6km or so, taking the right fork to the **administration centre** (☎695-5598), which also administers Guanacaste and Rincón de la Vieja Parks. As well as checking road conditions and showing your camping/turtle-watching permits (see below), you could ask the rangers here if you can join them on patrol, enabling you to visit off-the-beaten-track trails, and make reservations (at least 3hr in advance) for a simple lunch in the *comedor*. The food – *casados* with fish, chicken or meat and salad – is good, and this is a great place to get talking to rangers or other tourists. From here two rough roads lead to the beaches; to drive these, even in the height of the dry season, you need a sturdy 4WD. Administration discourages any driving at all beyond the main road; nevertheless, people – surfers, mainly – insist on doing so, and survive. Most people park their vehicle at the administration centre and walk. One thing is for sure: don't try to drive anywhere in the Park (including the Murciélago sector to the north, and the road to Cuajiniquil) in the rainy season without asking rangers about the state of the roads. You could get bogged down in mud or stopped by a swollen creek.

If you're walking, a ranger or fellow tourist will probably give you a ride, but bring **water** just in case – five litres, at least, for two people, even on a short jaunt. The easy-to-carry bottles of *Montaña* water (the ones with a plastic handle) sold at the gas stations on the road outside Liberia, are particularly good for walkers: stock up before you come. You can also buy **drinks** at the administration centre.

Camping facilities at Santa Rosa are some of the best in the country. There are four sites: each costs $2 per person, payable at the administration centre. The shady **La casona** site has bathrooms and grill pits; **Playa Nancite** has no water or bathrooms (and requires a permit; see below); **Playa Naranjo** has picnic tables and grill pits, and a ranger's hut with outhouses and showers plus, apparently, a boa constrictor in the roof. The **Estero Real** site, next to a mangrove swamp, has no water, but does have grill pits and outhouse toilets. Staying here you may well see cruel-grinned crocodiles and the blind fishing bat that skims the water and fishes like a bird, spotting its prey by sonar and ensnaring it with its claws. As with Corcovado and Chirripó National Parks, however, there are some **restrictions** on camping at Santa Rosa. If you want to stay for several days, or want to drive down to the beach sites and stay there, you need to ask at the SPN office in San José before coming. Although at present you can camp on the beaches – outside *arribada* season – with a permit, available from the SPN office or the administration centre, regulations are liable to change. You should also check the state of the facilities; the roads in the Park are occasionally closed, and you have to bring your own food, water and supplies. Wherever you camp, watch your fires (the area is a tinderbox in the dry season), take plastic bags for your food, do not leave anything edible in your tent (it will be stolen by scavenging coati) and, of course, carry plenty of water.

Visiting the Park

Many of Santa Rosa's **trails** are used for scientific research, not really intended for tourists and thus not well-signed. If you do set off to walk, it's a good idea to pay for a ranger as a guide – ask at the administration centre. Prices range from $10 to $15. If you walk only one trail in the entire Park, make it the very short (1km) and undemanding **Sendero Natural**, which provides an introduction to the unique features of the tropical dry forest. Curving round from the road just before the *casona*, it is signed as the **Sendero "Indio Desnudo"**, after the peeling-bark trees of the same name (also tongue-in-cheekily called "sunburnt tourists trees"). Along the trail you'll see acacia and **guapinol** trees, whose colloquial name is "stinking toe", on account of its smelly seed pods. Look out for monster iguanas hiding innocuously in tree branches, and for the ubiquitous bats.

From the administration centre a rough track (signposted) leads past *La casona* camping area, with several trails branching off on the way. Some of these may be restricted at any one time for research purposes; check first at the administration centre, however, as you can usually walk where you wish as long as you let someone know. After about 5km you come to a fork, bearing left to Playa Naranjo, and right to Playa Nancite, both of them about 3km further on.

A lovely grey sand beach, **Playa Nancite** is as lustrous as a wet seal's skin when the tide has just gone out. It is also the nesting home of the **Olive Ridley turtles**, a species that nest only here and at Ostional near Nosara in the Nicoya Peninsula. With none of the large tour groups you find at other Costa Rican turtle beaches, it's a great place to watch the **arribadas**, during which around 8000 turtles – which on average weigh around 40kg – come ashore on any given evening, virtually covering the beach. According to SPN estimates, more than eleven million eggs can be deposited by the turtles during a single *arribada*.

Due to rip currents Playa Nancite is no good for swimming but, as is usually the case, it's good for **surfers**, with huge rolling, tubular waves. For the best surf, though, you should head for Naranjo. Theoretically you can hike between the two (2hr) on a narrow trail across the rocky headland, which opens out on top in a hot, dry scrub cover, but you have to watch the tide; the trail crosses the deep tidal Estero Real, the drainage point for two rivers. Ask for the *marea* (tidal times) from the administration centre before setting out.

Santa Rosa's **casona** (Big House), one of Costa Rica's most famous historical sites, was for many years the centre of a working hacienda until the land was expropriated for the National Park in 1972. It's an impressive sight, this formidable wooden and red-tiled country fortress, and you can just about envision the dramatic events that have taken place in its corrals and on its doorsteps. **Plaques** (in Spanish) outside the house recount the derring-do at the *casona*, with resumes of the battles of *20 de Marzo 1856* (the confrontation of William Walker's *filibusteros* against the Costa Rican forces; see p.228), of 1919 against upstart Nicaraguans (again), and of 1955, against yet another Nicaraguan – the dictator Anastasio Somoza, whose hulk of a tank can still be seen, rusting and abandoned, along a signed road just beyond the entrance hut.

Like all old houses, the *casona* has the fragrant, slightly musty odour of wood comfortable in itself. It is now entirely given over to **exhibitions**, and you are free to clamber up and down the worn steps and wander around the dark ample rooms. One wing concentrates on archeology, with plaques explaining the unique history of Guanacaste, some lovely **petroglyphs**, and the dusty skulls of long-dead animals. In the main house are formal oil portraits of hacienda owners and presidents, and old family **photographs** of *peones* who worked on the hacienda over the years: fine-looking sepia-toned *sabaneros* and *cocineras* lined up together, staring rigidly at the camera. Most interesting is the **kitchen**, showing a table set for the *sabaneros'* morning coffee, a stone kiln-like hole used for cooking, and the *choreador de café* (like a cafetière) among other domestic relics. The **barn** is also worth a look, filled with harnesses and saddles quietly gathering dust.

THE GREAT PRETENDER: WILLIAM WALKER

Born in Tennessee in 1824, **William Walker** was something of a child prodigy. By the age of 14 he had a degree from the University of Nashville, notching up degrees in law and medicine just five years later before setting off to study at various illustrious European universities. However, upon his return to the US, Walker proceeded to fail in his chosen professions of doctor and lawyer and, somewhat at a loose end, landed up in California in 1849 at the height of the gold rush. Here he became involved with the **pro-slavery** organization Knights of the Golden Circle, who financed an expedition, in which Walker took part, to invade Baja California and Mexico in a kind of Lebensraum manoeuvre to secure more land for the United States. Though this expedition failed, Walker, undeterred, soon put his mind to another plan. Intending to make himself overlord of a Central American nation of five slave-owning states, and then to sell the territory to the US, in June 1855 Walker invaded Nicaragua. The next logical step was to secure territory for the planned eleven-kilometre long canal between Lago de Nicaragua and the Pacific. Gaining much of his financial backing from Nicaraguan get-rich-quick militarists and North American capitalists who were quick to see the benefits of a waterway along the Río San Juan from the Pacific to the Atlantic, in 1856 William Walker, and several hundred mercenary troops, invaded Costa Rica from the north.

Meanwhile, Costa Rican president **Juan Rafael Mora** had been watching Walker's progress with increasing alarm and, in February 1856, declared war on the usurper. Lacking military hardware, Costa Rica was ill-prepared for battle, and Mora's rapidly gathered army of 9000 men was a largely peasant-and-bourgeois

Murciélago sector

Few tourists go to Santa Rosa's **Murciélago sector**, which juts out to the north of the Park. It's a kind of reforestation laboratory; pasture land and cattle ranch slowly being regenerated, with a beach that's safe for swimming. To get there, drive along the Interamericana from the main Santa Rosa entrance about 10km north to the hamlet of **Cuajiniquil**. The road is poor, with two creeks to cross in the wet season; it's practically impossible to get there without your own vehicle, and even then you'll need high clearance. From Cuajiniquil, be sure to take the dirt road and not the paved one, which heads in the wrong direction to Punta Morros. After another 15km, the road ends in the **Area Recreativa Junquillal** (not to be confused with Playa Junquillal on the west of the Nicoya Peninsula; see p.241) and the pretty **Playa Blanca**. A small, white sand beach where you can actually swim without risking your life, Playa Blanca is one of the most isolated and least visited in the country, with a ranger station and camping area with water and toilet facilities. **Border checks** (see p.221) are particularly vigilant in this area. As usual, have your passports and all documents in order.

Just 30km from the border, Murciélago is home to the remains of the training grounds used by the CIA-backed **Contras** during the Nicaraguan civil war. They're overgrown and scrubby today, with no sign that anything was ever there. It was also the location of the famous "secret" airstrip built, on Oliver North's orders, in direct violation of Costa Rica's declared neutrality in the conflict. Originally given the go-ahead by President Alberto Monge, the airstrip was eventually destroyed under Arias' subsequent administration – a unilateral action that eventually led to the US diminishing its financial and political support for Costa Rica.

band, armed with machetes, farm tools and the occasional rusty rifle. Marching them out of San José through the Valle Central, over the Cordillera de Tilarán and on to the hot plains of Guanacaste, Mora got wind that Walker and his band of 300 *filibusteros* were entrenched at the **Santa Rosa casona**, the largest and best-fortified edifice in the area. Although by now Mora's force was reduced to only 2500 (we can only guess that, in the two weeks that it took them to march from San José, heat exhaustion had left many scattered by the wayside), on 20 March 1856 they routed the *filibusteros*, fighting with their *campesino* tools. Mora then followed Walker and his men on their retreat, engaging them in battle again in Nicaraguan territory, at **Rivas**, some 15km north of the border, where Walker's troops eventually barricaded themselves in another wooden *casona*. It was here – and not, as is commonly thought, at Santa Rosa – that **Juan Santamaría**, a lowly nineteen-year-old drummer boy, volunteered to set fire to the building in which Walker and his men were barricaded, flushing them out, and dying in the process. Walker, however, survived the fire, and carried on filibustering, until in 1857 a US warship was dispatched to put an end to his increasingly embarrassing (for the US government, who had covertly backed him) antics. Undeterred after a three-year spell in a Nicaraguan jail, he continued his adventuring until being shot dead by the Honduran authorities the same year.

Meanwhile, Mora, no devotee of democracy himself, rigged the 1859 Costa Rican presidential election so that he could serve a second term – despite his military victories against Walker, there was strong popular opposition to his domestic policies – and was deposed later that year. He attempted a coup d'état, but was subsequently shot in 1860, the same year that his former nemesis met his Waterloo in Honduras.

Parque Nacional Guanacaste

Located 36km north of Liberia on the Interamericana, much of **PARQUE NACIONAL GUANACASTE** (hours and admission as for Santa Rosa) was not long ago under pasture for cattle. Influential biologist DH Janzen, editor of the seminal volume *Costa Rican Natural History*, who had been involved in field study for many years in nearby Santa Rosa, was instrumental in creating the Park virtually from scratch in 1991. Raising over $11 million, mainly from foreign sources, he envisioned creating a kind of biological corridor in which animals, mainly mammals, would have a large enough tract of undisturbed habitat in which to hunt and reproduce. The **Santa Rosa–Guanacaste** (and, to an extent, Rincón de la Vieja) **corridor** is the result of his work, representing one of the most important efforts to conserve and regenerate tropical **dry forest** in the Americas.

With tropical wet and dry forests and a smattering of cloudforest, and covering the slopes of the dormant volcanos Orosí and Cacao, Parque Nacional Guanacaste also protects the **springwell of the Río Tempisque**, as well the Ríos Ahogados and Colorado. More than 300 species of **birds** have been recorded, while mammals lurking behind the undergrowth include jaguar, puma, tapir, coati, armadillo, two-toed sloth and deer. It's also thought that there are about 5000 species of **butterflies** and moths alone.

Few people come to Parque Nacional Guanacaste, and you may hear from both the SPN in San José and the administration at Santa Rosa (see p.226) that there's nothing to see. It's true in a way, as the only primary rainforest exists at the upper elevations and, of the three biological stations, you are currently allowed to visit only the one on Volcán Cacao. **Trails** are being cut, however, and there are pre-

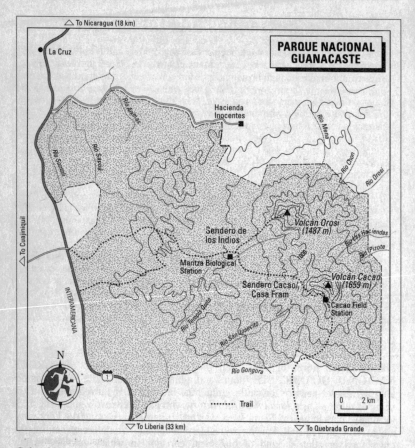

PARQUE NACIONAL GUANACASTE

Columbian **petroglyphs** lying around at a place called El Pedregal, near the Maritza field station at the bottom of Volcán Orosí. Ask the rangers at the entrance about the best way to see them; they are not on any currently existing trail, nor are they marked.

Practicalities

Facilities at Guanacaste are still at a minimum. **Access** is very difficult, unless (as usual) you've got a Range Rover or some other tank of a vehicle. While the dirt and gravel road from the highway is passable most of the way, the boulders from hell appear 3km from the entrance; at this point you have to ditch non-4WD vehicles and walk. To get there, take the exit for Potrerillos on the right-hand side of the Interamericana, 10km south of the Santa Rosa turnoff. At Potrerillos turn right for the hamlet of Quebrada Grande (on some maps called Garcia Flamenco) and continue for about 8km. You can **camp** at the main ranger station and there is a rustic, simple **lodge** at Cacao field station. Call the SPN or Santa Rosa administration to check if it is open and how much they charge for people to stay.

La Cruz, the haciendas and the border

Set on a plateau overlooking Bahía Salinas and the Pacific Ocean to the west, the tiny town of **LA CRUZ** is the last settlement of any size before the border, just 20km away, and makes a useful refuelling stop if you are heading up to Nicaragua. Though if you're staying any length of time in the area you'd do far better at one of the nearby working **cattle ranches** that have a sideline as tourist lodges (see below), La Cruz itself has a few nice, fairly affordable **places to stay**. The best budget bet is the friendly *Cabinas Santa Rita*, across from *la corte*, the courthouse (☎679-9062; ②), where the clean, simple rooms have private bath (cold water). Across the street from the bus station, *Cabinas Maryfel* (☎679-9096; ①) is even more basic, with dark, clean rooms. For a **meal** go where the locals go for a proper dinner out: *Ehecatl*, well known throughout the entire province for its seafood, and its lovely views over Bahía Salinas. *Bar y Restaurante Thelma*, 200m north of the *bomba* is another good choice; friendly *dueña* Thelma serves good Guanacastecan specialities, *casados* and rice dishes.

Hacienda accommodation around La Cruz

Colinas del Norte, 5km beyond La Cruz on the Interamericana (☎679-9132; fax 679-9064). Once a simple, friendly family cattle ranch, now being transformed by new Italian *dueños* into a resort with a pool and disco in the offing. At present they offer horseback trips on the ranch, and the restaurant does good pizza with home-made mozzarella. ④.

Los Inocentes, about 17km along the right turn (for Santa Cecilia), 3km before La Cruz (☎679-9190). Longest-established hacienda in the area, friendly and well set up for tourists, but still functioning as a working ranch. Horseback tours, excellent food (around $25 a day for 3 meals) and you can even hang out and ride with the *peones*. Volcán Orosí hovers prettily in the background. ⑦.

Las Salinas, Bahía Salinas (☎233-6912 in San José). Essentially a trailer park with a few cabinas next to the beach, this nice little place has a great setting. You can swim quite safely, and the owners will arrange horseback rides, and help with directions. Camping possible; $5. ④.

The border: Peñas Blancas

Peñas Blancas (8am–noon & 1–5pm, closes at 4pm on the Nicaragua side) is emphatically a border post and not a town, with just one or two basic sodas and no hotels. Prepare yourself for *trámites* hell whichever way you cross; the procedure here is as ponderous as any in Central America. By bus or by car you'll be lucky to get through in less than ninety minutes; if you cross on a *Tica* or *SIRCA* bus (between San José and Managua), the bus waits for all passengers to be processed, so you could find yourself hanging around for as long as four or five hours. Both Costa Rican and Nicaraguan border officials are quite strict, and demand that all paperwork be in order. Make sure you have your passport and any necessary visa before you come.

You can pay the border exit fee (about $1 either way) in dollars, but will get change in córdobas or colones. Be warned that, if you are one of those unlucky nationalities (Canadians, Australians and New Zealanders, for example) who need **visas**, you should have already obtained them in San José (around $25, or $15 for a 72-hr transit visa). You get your exit stamp at the Costa Rica office and up to *three* Nicaraguan entrance stamps at the Nicaraguan migración. Make sure you've got them all or you'll have trouble leaving again. The border offices are 4km apart; regular minibuses ($2) whisk you, airport-style, between the two. The Costa Rican border **tourist office** is helpful and organized; its Nicaraguan counterpart unfortunately is not. You can buy **bus tickets** to San José and Liberia next door to the tourist office. **Moneychangers** hang out on both sides of the border: reliable, on the whole, and certainly the fastest way to change cash.

An **alternative** way to cross into Nicaragua from Liberia is to take a Peñas Blancas service, then pick up a local bus to **Rivas**, the first Nicaraguan town of any size, 37km beyond the border. This might not be convenient if you are going all the way to Managua, but the formalities are far less cumbersome than on the *Tica* and *SIRCA* services. As there's so much regular local traffic and fewer (potentially visa-holding) foreigners on these buses, they are generally processed as an entire entity, which can save hours.

Whichever route you take, you should aim to get to the border as **early** as possible. Buses on the border routes leave early in the morning, and fizzle out completely by 2 or 3pm. If you arrive any later than this you are left with no alternative but to take a costly taxi into Nicaragua or back to Liberia.

The Guanacaste beaches

The **beaches of Guanacaste** are scattered along a rocky coastline from Bahía Culebra to Sámara on the west of the Nicoya Peninsula. Few of those in the north could truthfully be called beautiful – especially in the wake of tourist developments such as the controversial **Papagayo Project**, a giant package-holiday complex in Bahía Culebra. Things improve as you head south – though there's another development north of the pretty beach of **Conchal** – towards **Parque Nacional Marino las Baulas**, where droves of leatherback **turtles** come ashore to lay their eggs between October and February. If it's a good swim you want, however, best head down to **Tamarindo**, or better still to **Sámara** or **Nosara**, on the Nicoya Peninsula. The beaches here have drawn pockets of foreign nationals in pursuit of Paradise, and the cosmopolitan enclaves – and inflated prices – are in sharp contrast to the rest of the region. Inland, the small towns of **Nicoya** and **Santa Cruz** are of little interest in themselves, but do have reasonably priced accommodation and places to eat and, as the main transportation hubs for the area, are pretty much unavoidable. Beaches of the southern peninsula are covered in our chapter on *The Central Pacific and Southern Nicoya*.

It can take a long time to get to the Guanacaste coast from San José (5hr minimum, unless you fly) and in some places you feel very remote indeed. There are few settlements of any size, and only a desultory scattering of hotels. **Getting around** can take time, too, as the beaches tend to be separated by rocky headlands or otherwise impassable formations, with barren hilly outcroppings coming right down to the sea, carving out little coves and bays, but necessitating considerable backtracking inland to get from one to the other. Travelling by **bus** is particularly tricky, and you'll need determination and some fancy footwork to intercept the infrequent local services. By far the most popular option is to explore with a **rental car**, which allows you to beach-hop with relative ease. Roads are not bad, if somewhat pothole-scarred, and you'll do best with **4WD**, though this can work out a bit expensive. Another possibility, for couples or small groups, is to **hitch**, as there is a fair amount of tourist traffic around here.

Bahía Culebra

Once a quiet area washed by the sheltered, clear blue waters of **Bahía Culebra** (Snake Bay), the little-populated **Gulf of Papagayo** was the perfect candidate for Costa Rica's first big **mega-development**. Though the Spanish-based Barceló group have already built a large, resort-type hotel in Playa Tambor in the south of the Nicoya Peninsula (see p.278), the **Papagayo Project** is the first to swallow up a whole area and cover it with villas, hotels, sports facilities and the like. Most of

THE PAPAGAYO PROJECT

The **Papagayo Project** covers nearly the entire Bahía Culebra, encompassing the once tranquil Playas Panamá and Hermosa. Over the next fifteen years about 14,000 rooms – that's 28,000 people, the population of a small Costa Rican town – are planned, making it the largest tourism development in Central America (there are currently a total of 13,000 hotel rooms in the whole of Costa Rica).

Designed to include large hotels, time-share villas and condos, a shopping mall and a golf course, the project has caused considerable **controversy** in Costa Rica; the government, doubly hit by the pull-out of US economic aid and the iron fist of the International Monetary Fund, needs to find ways to encourage foreign investment (and therefore hard currency); conservationist groups, on the other hand, are concerned about the **environmental impact** of such projects. Large-scale tourism developments run directly in the face of "ecotourism", a concept that Costa Rica has worked hard to make virtually synonymous with the country. Ecotourism is traditionally defined as being made up of small-scale, locally owned operations that allow for some kind of commune with nature. Resorts on the scale of Papagayo, on the other hand, are seen to isolate tourists within an artificial context. The main developer, the Mexican firm Situr, has come under a lot of flak for its handling of the project, and has been called upon by Costa Rican Ombudsman Rodrigo Carazo to defend itself. Situr's line is that the type of tourism represented by the Papagayo Project benefits from being carefully planned, and **contained**, so that its destructive capacity can be mitigated. Situr also claim that they will spend up to $150 million on developing area **infrastructure**, including waste treatment plants and roads – two things sorely lacking in other areas of Costa Rica that have experienced an unexpected "boom", such as the area from Quepos to Parque Nacional Manuel Antonio.

Environmentalists and locals are still concerned, however, about alleged legal violations and titular favouritisms granted to Situr by the government, including a 49-year lease on the land, as opposed to the customary twenty-year leases permitted by national law. They have also been accused of building roads without permits from the proper authorities, cutting trees illegally – including existing endangered mangroves – illegally, and dredging the Río Tempisque beyond the limits specified in the permits. None of these alleged infractions have been proven or proscecuted, but the allegations are remarkably similar to those levelled against the Barceló group, who developed Bahía Ballena on the southern Nicoya Peninsula (see p.278). What is highlighted by the accusations is less the morality of large developers or the viability of large-scale tourism, but the problem of how to ensure that large foreign nationals, often powerful investors in the local economy (and in the national balance of payments) can be brought to account for infringements of national law and for environmental degradation or destruction. As for the effect of the arrival of thousands of short-stay foreigners each year on the **cultural integrity** of a region made up of small, scattered localities, you only have to look at Cancún, that jewel of the Yucatán, to be worried.

the tourists who'll come here will be on package holidays, mostly from North America, and will land at Liberia's new international airport.

Playa Panamá used to be a lovely, semi-deserted spot – a nice, calm beach where you were unlikely to encounter another soul. These days it's an eyesore, with half-built constructions scattered over hills and noisy trucks lumbering back and forth loaded with building materials. It is impossible to tell, right now, what it will look like when finished (the first stage will be completed in 1996, but the project intends to grow over a fifteen-year period), but the general opinion is that it's to be Costa Rica's Cancún – with all that implies. Two **buses** daily arrive from Liberia, arriving noonish and around 8pm. The turnoff for Playa Panamá is 3km north of the more travelled turnoff for Coco, all on a good paved road.

Playa Hermosa ("Pretty Beach"), on the southern edge of the Bahía Culebra, 10km north of the nearest beach to the south, Playa del Coco, is something of a misnomer. The water may be relatively calm, clean and good for swimming, but the tiny grey-sand beach itself is scruffy and strewn with garbage. In the wet season, however, Hermosa is wonderfully quiet, and you may well have it to yourself but for the odd cow that has ambled down from pasture.

If you want to **stay** on the beach, there are two places to choose from; rather rundown cabinas that mar the overall look of the place even further. *Cabinas Playa Hermosa*, with private bath and ceiling fans (☎ and fax 670-0136; ②) is the most comfortable. Next door, the much more basic *Cabinas Vallejo* (☎670-0417; ①), has shared bath and cold water. Continuing down the road you come to the **self-catering** *Villa Boni Mar* (☎670-0397; ④), where apartments for up to eight people cost around $45 a night, with weekly discounts. *Hotel el Velero* (☎ and fax 670-0330; ⑥) has a good restaurant, two-storey rooms with balconies, and a pool, but the plushest place in Hermosa is without a doubt the *Condovac la Costa* (☎221-8949; fax 222-5637; ⑦) with cable TV, pool, restaurant and disco, plus a nice view of the ocean, and full tours service, including sportsfishing and snorkelling.

Playa Hermosa is easily accessible by **car** from Liberia. Take the turnoff to the right just after the hamlet of Comunidad – signposted to Playas Hermosa, Panamá and Coco – and continue for several kilometres over the good paved road. There's another turnoff to Hermosa and Panamá on the right.

Playa del Coco

Thirty-five kilometres west of Liberia, with good road connections, **Playa del Coco** was the first Pacific beach to hit the big time with weekending Costa Ricans from the Valle Central. Unfortunately you can't really swim here any more, due to the slicks of oil and fuel bleeding out from the many boats anchored in the bay. The water at **Playita Blanca**, a kilometre walk away (low tide only) at the other side of the point, is cleaner, though still hardly compares to the beaches further south. Nevertheless, its accessibility and budget accommodation make Coco a useful place for a couple of days' jaunt or, if you have a car, as a base to explore the better beaches nearby. Restaurants are good, too, and there are various snorkelling and diving tours.

Arrival and information

Direct **buses** (5hr) leave San José for Coco daily at 10am, returning at 9.15am. You can also get to Coco on local services from Liberia (see p.220), returning to Liberia at 7am, 9.15am (high season only), 2pm and 6pm (1hr). The town itself spreads out right in front of the beach, with a tiny **parquecito** as the focal point. Minimal services include a tiny **correo** (Mon–Fri 7.30am–5pm), and public **telephones** on either side of the *parquecito*. You can **change money** at *Flor de Itabo* (see below); at *Pizzería Pronto* the *dueño* offers Interlink, private mail, PO boxes and money transfer.

Of the various souvenir-shops-cum-tour-outfits, *Paseos de Golfo Papagayo*, 50m from the beach, on the main road (☎670-0354), specializes in **sportsfishing** and boat tours. The English-speaking staff at *Rich Coast Diving*, about 300m from the beach on the main road (☎670-0176) organize **snorkelling**, scuba trips and rent out mountain bikes. **Taxis** gather in front of the *Restaurant e Cocos* by the beach.

Accommodation

Coco has lots of fairly basic **cabinas**, catering to weekending nationals and tourists. In the high season, you should make sure to **reserve** for weekends, but can probably get away with turning up on spec midweek, when rooms may be a little cheaper. In the low season, too, bargains abound. There's **camping** ($4) at the Ojo Parqueo, 75m from the beach on the main road; they will keep an eye on your belongings, and also sell water.

Cabinas Catarina, 100m before the *parquecito* on main road (☎670-0156). Basic, clean cabinas set up for budget weekenders, with ring cookers, laundry, private bath, cold water and ceiling fans. ②.

Cabinas Chale, 50m from the beach, 500m beyond the *parquecito* (☎670-0036). Slightly pricier than the others, with big rooms plus fridges (useful if you don't want to walk into town for a beer), and a pool, unusual in this category. ③.

Hostal el Coco, 100m beyond *Cabinas Chale* (☎685-5422). New cabinas near the beach; comfortable, clean and friendly. Shared or private bath, fans and free breakfast. ④.

Flor de Itabo, on the main road coming into town, about 1km from the beach (☎670-0011 or 0292; fax 670-0003). The best, most expensive, hotel in Coco, with lower off-season rates. Tasteful and friendly, decorated with lovely dangling shell moblies. Rooms have private bath, a/c, hot water and TV. They will change money for non-guests and, even better, you can use the pool for 400 colones. ⑤.

Hotel Anexo Luna Tica and **Cabinas Luna Tica**, 100m left of where the road ends at the beach (☎670-0279). Rooms in both are about the same price, and good value, but the hotel is a bit breezier than the cabinas, with some fans and a/c. Breakfast included in both. ③.

Eating, drinking and nightlife

Coco has two very distinct types of **restaurants**, **sodas** and **bars**: those catering to nationals and those that make some sort of stab at cosmopolitanism to hook the gringos. Nightlife is generally quiet during the week, but things get livelier at the weekend, when the **disco** starts up.

California Café, 50m from beach. The San Francisco crowd who run this cheery meloncoloured restaurant offer treats such as home-made lasagne and roast beef sandwiches.

Coconuts, opposite the *parquecito*. Coco's disco, especially lively at the weekend, playing the usual mix of salsa, reggae and the occasional Techno tune. Open until midnight or later.

Restaurante Cocos, right by the beach. Popular place in prime position. Good for seafood lunches, but the music is *very* loud; it doubles as a bar in the evening.

Flor de Itabo, in the *Flor de Itabo* hotel. The most ambitious food in town, with prices to match; the fillet of beef and fresh shrimp are recommended if you feel like splashing out. Open 6.15am–9.30pm. The popular *Havana Bar* is open until 11pm.

Restaurante Hemingway, about 50m before the beach. Travellers' hangout recommended for the all-you-can-eat breakfast buffet (from 7am), with pancakes, juices and *gallo pinto*. BBQ some nights 6–9pm.

Pizzería Pronto, 500m before the beach on the right-hand side as you enter Coco. Green salad and large pizzas for about $7 – the *jalapeña* is good; the *pequeña* better value at $4 – served beneath a pleasant rancho canopy. Daily except Tues 11.30am–10pm.

Playa Ocotal to Conchal

Past the rocky headland south of Coco, the upscale enclave of **Playa Ocotal** is reached by taking the turnoff to the left (signed) at the *Don Humo* restaurant. Ocotal and its surrounds have lovely views over the ocean and off to the Papagayo gulf from the top of the headland, and the small beach is better for swimming than Coco, but the real attraction are the marlin and other "big game" fish that buzz through these waters. Ocotal **hotels** are usually tied in with very good **sportsfishing** packages – one of the most highly rated is the *Bahía Pez Vela* (☎221-1586; fax 221-3594; ⑥) with simply furnished, comfortable cabinas and a nice restaurant overlooking the sea.

The best **mid-range** place to stay is *Villa Casa Blanca* (☎ and fax 670-0448; Aptdo 176, Playa del Coco 5019; ⑤) a small, quiet B&B that offers boat tours, deep-sea fishing, scuba diving to the Islas Murciélago up near Santa Rosa, and horseriding trips. There's even a tennis court on the grounds.

Playas Flamingo and Brasilito

Despite its name, there are no flamingos at the upmarket, very expensive gringo ghetto of **Playa Flamingo**. It does, however, have a pretty white-sand beach and great sportsfishing: almost all the resort-style hotels in the area cater to **fishing** enthusiasts or sun worshippers on packages. It is approached along the road to small, unappealing **Playa Brasilito**, a scruffy beach with darkish sand; about 5km beyond it you see Playa Flamingo's marina. This is more or less the centre of the community, with the larger **hotels** spread out along the beach. The *Aurola Playa Flamingo* (☎233-9233; fax 654-4060; ⑧) is one of the largest places to stay, with a good pool, several restaurants and a casino. The *Flamingo Marina Resort* (☎257-1431; fax 221-8093; ⑥–⑦) has fully equipped suites with jacuzzis, a restaurant and tour service. Both can arrange air charter service or will pick you up from the airstrip.

By **car**, Playas Flamingo and Brasilito are reached via the road that veers off from the Liberia–Nicoya road to Belen; they're signposted from the hamlet of Huacas, 25km beyond Belen. Getting to Flamingo **from San José**, *Tralapa* runs direct buses (2 daily; 6hr), while the *Hotel Herradura* puts on private air-conditioned buses along the same route (Mon, Wed & Fri 9am; return Tues, Thurs & Sat; $45 return). There are two buses from **Santa Cruz** (see p.243), arriving at Brasilito, Flamingo and Potrero beach, several kilometres north, early in the morning or mid-afternoon.

Playa Conchal

Though the construction of the Spanish-owned resort-style *Melia* hotel, between Playa Brasilito and **Playa Conchal** ("Shell Beach"), threatens to disrupt the peace and quiet of the area, for now Conchal, set in a steep broad bay and protected by a rocky headland, is an appealing place. Swimming is good here, and there's a pretty, light-coloured beach formed, as its name implies, from crushed shells. The end near the shabby *Marisquería el Encanto* restaurant – the only one – is a bit garbage-strewn; head to the right for cleaner sands.

About 1km before you reach Playa Conchal, in a secluded spot up on the hill, the *Hotelito la Paz* (☎654-4259; fax 680-0280; ④–⑤) is a great **place to stay**, run by friendly Tico/Swiss management, with a pool, a restaurant serving seafood, pizza and good breakfasts. They also have a house for rent: good value at $60, with terrace and kitchen with fridge (sleeps six maximum). The owners offer a complete tour service and even occasional *yoga del sonido* – "sound yoga" – in which you make sounds in the water and feel your cells vibrate. To **get to Conchal** from Flamingo, you have to backtrack inland, turning right at the village of Matapalo.

Parque Nacional Marino las Baulas

On the Río Matapalo estuary between Conchal and Tamarindo, **PARQUE NACIONAL MARINO LAS BAULAS** ($2) is less a National Park than a Reserve, created to protect from developer speculation the nesting grounds of the **leatherback turtles** (*baulas*), who come ashore in droves from October to February. The largest reptile in the world, the leatherback can reach a truly astounding size (over 5m long) and bulk, which, combined with the armour-like aspect of its shell, makes you wonder how it manages to swim. They lay their eggs at **Playa Grande**, a beautiful beach with a great wide sweep of bay and light-grey sand. Outside laying season you can surf and dash into the waves, but swimming is a bit rough, plagued by rip tides.

As yet Las Baulas has none of the infrastructure – or the usual entrance fees – of Costa Rica's other National Parks. There are **restrictions**, however, on turtle-viewing. Playa Grande is one of the most important spots for leatherback nesting in the country, and in the past has been a magnet for tour groups from upmarket Guanacaste hotels as well as day-trippers from Tamarindo and Coco. Nowadays, however, numbers of visitors are regulated. You are not allowed any more to walk on the beach during *arribadas* (get the rangers to tell you stories of what people used to do to harass the turtles and you'll see the logic of this). Unless you arrive by boat from Tamarindo (see below) you have to be led by official Park guides to the **viewing platforms**, leaving the turtles in peace to go about their business. Unauthorized tours still arrive, however, principally boat trips from Tamarindo, whereby local boatmen land on the beach, often while there are turtles present. If you buy a tour to Las Baulas from Tamarindo, ask first whether they have permission from the Park personnel.

To **drive to Las Baulas**, take the road from Huacas to Matapalo, and turn left at the soccer field. During the wet season, **4WD** is recommended for this stretch. Most people, however, visit the park by **boat** from Tamarindo, entering at the southern end rather than from the Matapalo road.

Playa Tamarindo

Perennially popular, **Playa Tamarindo** may not be the most beautiful beach in the world, but it is one of the nicest in Guanacaste, stretching for a couple of kilometres over a series of rocky headlands. **TAMARINDO** village, which has a sizable foreign community, boasts a great selection of restaurants – you'll even find cappuccino and *pain au chocolat* – a varied, lively beach culture (for which, read beautiful young things parading up and down the sand), and a healthy nightlife. There's a price to pay for the cosmopolitan atmosphere, however, as everything costs that bit more in Tamarindo.

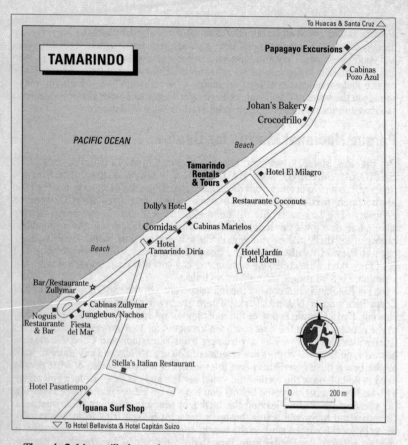

To Huacas & Santa Cruz

TAMARINDO

Papagayo Excursions

Cabinas
Pozo Azul

Johan's Bakery

Crocodrillo

PACIFIC OCEAN

Beach

**Tamarindo
Rentals
& Tours**

Hotel El Milagro

Dolly's Hotel

Restaurante Coconuts

Comidas

Cabinas Marielos

Beach

Hotel
Tamarindo Diría

Hotel Jardín
del Edén

Bar/Restaurante
Zullymar

Cabinas Zullymar

Noguis
Restaurante
& Bar

Junglebus/Nachos

Fiesta
del Mar

N

Stella's Italian Restaurant

Hotel Pasatiempo

0   200 m

Iguana Surf Shop

To Hotel Bellavista & Hotel Capitán Suizo

Though **fishing** still plays a large part in the local economy, Tamarindo's transformation from village to beach resort has been rapid, with the usual associated problems. Locals worry about drugs, for example, and the loss of community – that said, community spirit was in full force recently in the initiative led by newcomers and long-time residents to pick up detritus left by weekenders and campers.

The beach attracts a combination of enthusiastic surfers and weekending *Cartagos* who arrive with enormous cooking pots and set up their children and radios on the beaches. **Swimming** is not great, as the waves are fairly heavy, rip tides are common, and there are a number of submerged rocks: ask around regarding conditions. Most people are content to paddle in the rocky coves and tide-pools south of the town, while **surfers** swoop and zoom in the waves at adjacent Playa Langosta.

North of the Tamarindo river estuary begins the long sweep of Playa Grande, where the **leatherbacks** lay their eggs. Turtles also come ashore at Tamarindo, in much smaller quantities. Officially, Tamarindo is within the boundaries of Las Baulas Park, in so far as the ocean covered by the protected area extends out in an arc, encompassing Tamarindo beach. The SPN has bought up the beach south

SURFBOARDS AND TURTLE TOURS

A number of outfitters in Tamarindo rent **surfboards** and windsurfing equipment; among them, **Iguana Surf Shop**, south of the village loop (they break for lunch between 2 and 2.30pm). In addition, numerous operators offer **turtle tours** to Las Baulas in nesting season (about $12 per person); these are not permitted by the Park administration to land on the beach. Contact **Papagayo Excursions** at the northern entrance to the village (☎680-0859; fax 225-3648), who also rent windsurfing boards, or **Tamarindo Rentals and Tours**, further south on the main road.

of Tamarindo to Playa Langosta, too, preventing further hotel development and allowing turtles to continue coming ashore – though in far fewer numbers that at Playa Grande – along this entire stretch.

There's little to do in the village itself, though the international community makes for some interesting **shopping**: *Bambola Tienda* in *Noguis Restaurante and Bar* sells hats, sarongs and hand-painted dresses; *Galería Doña Luna* next door has a good selection of pricey but unique mobiles.

You can **fly** into Tamarindo on *Travelair* and *Sansa* (see p.98), and both have offices in town; **buses** arrive by the village loop at the end of the road. The loop effectively constitutes Tamarindo's small centre, with a circular *parquecito* populated by pecking chickens and surrounded by restaurants. The small *Banco Nacional*, about 500m north of the loop, may be able to **change dollars** (Mon–Fri 8am–3pm); there are **public telephones** on the *parquecito*.

Accommodation

Many of Tamarindo's **hotels**, especially at the top end of the scale, are overpriced. Mid-range the selection is better, but budget travellers are not well served in this chic enclave and Tamarindo offers fewer low-season discounts than other Pacific beach towns. You can **camp** at *Tito's* ($5) at the south end of the beach; he also rents horses for reasonable prices.

Bellavista, coming into town from the south, take a left before the village loop, turn right up the hill and follow signs (☎ and fax 654-4036; Aptdo 143-5150, Santa Cruz). Hilltop cabinas with pool and spectacular sea views. Spotless and well-designed, with fans, coffee-maker, kitchen, bathroom, hot water and loft beds. Can sleep 5; great low season deals. ⑤–⑥.

Cabinas Marielos, about 800m from village loop (☎ and fax 654-4041). Basic rooms, light and clean, with fan, cold water and use of small kitchen, in pleasant colourful grounds. Professional, helpful *dueña*; but a very tough reservation and advance deposit policy. ③.

Capitán Suizo, south end of beach (☎ and fax 680-0853). New, upmarket place with cabin-type rooms with fridge, a/c and ceiling fans, sunken bathtub, hot water and outside shower. Buffet breakfast, cocktail bar, pool and beach views. Good discounts in low season. ⑥–⑦.

Dolly's, on main road opposite *Cabinas Marielos* (no phone). Friendly place and, as the only cheap option in town, fills up fast. Very basic rooms with flimsy beds and fan, or better, quieter upstairs rooms with sea view. All have private bath. Bar and restaurant. ②–③.

Jardín del Eden, take the road in front of *El Milagro* and continue up the hill (☎654-4111). Nicely decorated, comfortable villas, all very pink, set in attractively landscaped grounds. Each has hot water, a/c and good sea views. Pool, jacuzzi, bar and restaurant add to the resort atmosphere. A place to splurge; some villas have room for 3. ⑥–⑦.

El Milagro, 1km before the village loop (☎441-5102; fax 441-8494). Nicely decorated cabinas with fans, private bath and hot water. Poolside restaurant serves great food, and the European owners speak a million languages. Good mid-range choice. ④.

Pasatiempo, south of the village loop (fax 654-4223). Popular, smallish rooms with ceiling fans and hot water; larger rooms (sleeping 5) are a better deal. Nice pool, friendly management, plus lively restaurant and bar. ④.

Pozo Azul, on road into town (☎680-0147). Geared towards weekending nationals, this older complex of cabinas offers a small kitchen and pool, and run-down but clean rooms. Rooms with fan are cheap; price rises steeply for a/c. ②–④.

Tamarindo Diría, north of the village loop (☎289-8616; fax 289-8727). Right on the beach, with views of ocean or street (some street rooms have jacuzzis to make up for the lack of water outside the window). Tasteful rooms with fridge and TV, plus tennis court, restaurant and direct beach access. Low season deals and weekend rates. ⑥–⑦.

Zullymar, at the village loop (☎226-4732). Clean, spacious cabinas with carved wooden doors, one with trilobite motif, set in pleasant grounds scattered with reproduction pre-Columbian art. Rooms with fan and cold water cheaper than a/c and heated showers. ②–④.

Eating, drinking and nightlife

Tamarindo's cosmopolitan profile has led to a proliferation of **restaurants**, some of them very good, ranging from Indonesian to Italian. If you have a craving for hamburgers and nachos, make a beeline for *Junglebus* and *Nachos*, in the village loop. **Nightlife** focuses on the restaurants and bars in the centre of the village, many of them geared towards surfers.

Coconuts, on the main road into town. Sandwiches, herb teas, stunning cakes, espresso and cappuccino for breakfast and lunch; at night dine by candlelight on Indonesian crossed with Japanese and European cuisine, to a classical music accompaniment. They show videos some evenings. Main courses $10–12. Dinner 6–10pm.

Comidas, next to *Cabinas Marielos*. Some of the best cheap lunches in town, featuring *típico* food, generous *casados*, rice dishes, *refrescos* and coffee.

Crocodillo, on the main road into town. Well-cooked local food at reasonable – for Tamarindo – prices. Try the *arroz con camarones* or taberna bass fillet. The back opens on to the beach; the front is a bar reached by crossing a small stone bridge.

Fiesta del Mar, east side of the village loop. Suffering from competition from beach bars and gringo joints, but still serves great grouper, skate and snapper.

Johan's Bakery, next to *Crocodillo*. Small bakery serving delicious fresh croissants, *pan dulce*, swiss rolls, banana cake, pizza, waffles and apple flan for breakfast. Daily 6am–8pm.

Milagro, in the *Hotel el Milagro*. Respected restaurant with a changing menu of European dishes and a pleasant poolside setting.

Noguis Restaurante and Bar, in the village loop. Best sea view in town. Creative lunches such as eggplant and tomato or zucchini and cheese sandwiches, or tricolore salad for about $2. Full range of tropical cocktails.

MOVING ON FROM TAMARINDO

A direct bus to **San José** leaves at 5.45am, and one to **Liberia** at 6am (1–2hr), or you could take a bus to **Santa Cruz** at 6.45am, and from there (see p.242) hook up with **local services** to Liberia or San José (call ☎221-7202 for schedule information).

Continuing down along the west coast of the peninsula is only really possible if you have your own transport, especially **4WD**. It's trickier by bus, although you can pick up occasional services to Sámara or Nosara from Santa Cruz and Nicoya. A more convenient, if expensive, option is to take a **long-distance taxi** from *Dolly's*: destinations include Nicoya, Santa Cruz, Liberia, Nosara and Sámara. Fares run between $30 and $80. You can also **fly** back to San José with either *Travelair* or *Sansa*.

Stella's, 500m back from the town; take left road from *Tamarindo Resort Club* and follow signs. One of Tamarindo's best restaurants, with good Italian pasta and fresh fish cooked in excellent, inventive sauces. Main courses $8–12. Closed Sun.

Bar/Restaurante Zullymar, right in front of the *parquecito*. Popular place for a cold beer to the accompaniment of crashing waves; restaurant serves seafood and *típico* dishes.

South from Tamarindo to Playa Junquillal

It's not possible to continue straight on down the coast from Tamarindo: to pick up the road south you have to return a couple of kilometres inland to the hamlet of Villareal. Don't head south in the rainy season without a 4WD, and not at all unless you like crossing creeks; there are plenty on this stretch, and they can swell worryingly fast in the rain. In the dry months you should be all right with any vehicle as far as the surfing beach of **Avellana**, 11km south of Tamarindo, and then to Junquillal, 10km beyond, but it may not do the car any good, and further south the roads become discouragingly rough. If you want to stay along the west coast of Nicoya, especially in more isolated spots like Junquillal, it's best to reserve ahead to avoid getting stranded.

Playa Junquillal is a lovely, if expensive, spot, with a long, relatively straight beach. It's ideal for **surfing**, pounded by breakers crashing in from their thousand kilometre journeys, but far too rough for swimming. If you're looking for seclusion, however, it's a great place to hang out for a few days, with little activity and nothing at all in the way of nightlife. There are several very good **hotels**, many perched up above the beach on a small cliff, with stupendous views. None is cheap, but they may offer packages or weekly discounts. The friendly *Hotel Iguanazul*, 3km north (☎668-0783; ⑥) has a great setting overlooking the sea, with bright rooms decorated with indigenous art, plus its own pool, bar and restaurant. They offer fishing, diving and horseback tours, as well as excursions to Las Baulas. Call ahead and ask about their bus service to and from San José. *Guacamaya Lodge*, 2km south (☎221-1000 or 223-2300; ④) is good value, with very comfortable, semicircular rooms, lovely views over Junquillal, friendly management and a pool. In Junquillal itself, *Cabinas/Hotel Junquillal* (no phone; ②), is the only place that offers anything like cheap accommodation, with basic cabinas with cold water. You can also **camp** on their grounds ($5).

One **bus** daily arrives in Junquillal from San José (via Santa Cruz). This service currently gets you to Junquillal after dark: as with all the places along the west coast of Nicoya, make sure to have booked a room in advance. The bus returns to San José at 5am.

Santa Cruz

Generally seen by travellers as little more than somewhere to pass through on the way from Liberia or San José to the beach, the sprawling town of **SANTA CRUZ**, inland some 30km from Tamarindo and 57km south from Liberia, is actually "National Folklore City". Much of the music and dance that are considered quintessentially Guanacastecan originate from here, like marimba and various complex, stylized local dances, including the *Punto Guanacasteco*. *El punto* rivals Scottish country dancing for its complexity, and has been adopted as the national dance. That said, however, they're not exactly dancing in the streets in Santa Cruz; life is actually rather slow, much of it lived out in contemplative fashion on the wide verandahs of the town's old houses.

Santa Cruz has little of interest to keep you in town any longer than it takes to catch the bus out, especially since a fire in 1993 destroyed much of the town centre and the older buildings. There isn't much in the way of services, either, apart from the **Banco Nacional** on the way into town (Mon–Fri 8.30am–3.30pm). In the unlikely event that you need a **hotel**, choose from the *Diría* (☎680-0080; fax 680-0442; ④) which has a pool and rooms with TV, or *Hotel la Estancia* (☎680-0476; ③) where rooms have TV, private bath and fans, but can be stuffy. For **food**, join the locals at the popular *Coopetortilla*, a tortilla factory just off the central plaza that has its own restaurant selling chicken, Guanacastecan *empanadas*, and sweet cheese bread, as well as, of course, tortillas.

Santa Cruz is something of a regional **transportation** hub, with good connections inland and to the coast. *Tralapa* run five buses daily to **San José** (4.30am, 6.30am, 8.30am, 11.30am & 1pm; 5hr), and there are numerous **local services** to Liberia (hourly; 5.30am–7.30pm). A number of buses leave for **Tamarindo**, including a direct service at 8.30pm (about 1hr), returning at 6.45am. For **Junquillal**, a bus leaves at 6.30pm and returns to Santa Cruz at 5am. You can also

DANCE AND MUSIC IN GUANACASTE

In their book *A Year of Costa Rican Natural History*, Amelia Smith Calvert and Philip Powell Calvert describe their month on Guanacaste's **fiesta** circuit in 1910, starting in January in Filadelfia, a small town between Liberia and Santa Cruz, and ending in Santa Cruz. They were fascinated by the formal nature of the functions they attended, observing: "The dances were all round dances, mostly of familiar figures, waltzes and polkas, but one, called 'el punto' was peculiar in that the partners do not hold one another but walk side by side, turn around each other and so on."

At Santa Cruz, they witnessed: "All the ladies sat in a row on one side of the room when not dancing, the men elsewhere. When a lady arrived somewhat late then the rest of the guests of the company, if seated, arose in recognition of her presence. The music was furnished by three fiddles and an accordion. The uninvited part of the community stood outside the house looking into the room through the open doors, which as usual were not separated from the street by any vestibule or passage." The Calverts were also delighted to come across *La giganta*, the figure of a woman about 4m high; actually a man on stilts "with a face rather crudely moulded and painted". What exactly *La giganta* represented is little known, but she promenaded around the streets of Santa Cruz like an Edwardian goddess, long white lace trailing, while her scurrying minders frantically worked to keep her from keeling over.

Outside of the occasional local fiesta, today the only places you'll come across many of the dances of Guanacaste, as well as its music, are in specialist, Spanish-only **publications**. For enthusiasts, *La danza popular costarricense* by Bonilla and Guayacán (San José, 1989), comes complete with diagrams. *La musica en Guanacaste* is a musicologist's collection of tunes and lyrics, by Jorge Luis Acevedo, who has also written a more accessible publication, *Antología de la música guanacasteca*. For a good overall description of musical and dance styles, as well as the folklore of the Santa Cruz region, search out *Santa Cruz Guanacaste: una approximación a la historia y la cultura popular* by Roberto Cabrera, which includes accounts of hacienda life in the eighteenth and nineteenth centuries, plus vivid descriptions of bull-riding and other Guanacastecan cultural events. All these titles are available in San José's *Librería Universal* (see p.93) or in libraries. For further details, see "Books" in *Contexts*.

get to **Playas Flamingo** and **Brasilito**, via Tamarindo, with two services daily leaving at 6.30am and 3pm (1hr 30min). They return to Santa Cruz at 9am and 5pm (call ☎221-7202 or 680-0392 for schedule information).

Guaitíl

The one place in Guanacaste where you can see crafts being made in the traditional way, **GUAITÍL**, 12km east of Santa Cruz, is well known throughout the country for its ceramics, and the best place in the country to buy them. On the site of a major Chorotega potters' community, the present-day artisans' co-operative was founded more than twenty years ago by three local women whose goal was to use local traditions and their own abilities as potters and decorators for commercial gain. Today the artisans are still mainly women, keeping traditions alive at the distinctive, large, dome-shaped kilns, while the men work in agricultural smallholdings.

Potters in Guaitíl use local resources and traditional methods little changed since the days of the Chorotegas. To make the clay, local rock is ground on ancient metates, which the Chorotegas used for grinding corn. The pigment used on many of the pieces, *curiol*, comes from a porous stone that has to be collected from a nearby natural source, a four-hour walk away, and the ceramic piece is shaped using a special stone, also local, called *zukia*. *Zukias* were used by Chorotega potters to mould the lips and bases of plates and pots; treasured examples have been found in Chorotega graves. Every house in Guaitíl seems to be in on the trade. Pottery is either sold in front of people's homes on little roadside stalls, or in the *Artesanía Co-op* on the edge of the soccer field. Some of the houses are open for you to wander inside and watch the women at work. Wherever you buy, don't haggle and don't expect it to be dirt cheap, either. A large vase can easily cost $20 or $25. Bear in mind, too, that this is decorative, rather than functional, pottery, and may not be that durable.

Guaitíl is on the old road to Nicoya; **to get there** from Santa Cruz, head east on the smaller road instead of south on the new road.

CHOROTEGA POTTERY

The chief characteristics of **Chorotega pottery** are the striking black and red on white **colouring**, called *pataky*, and a preponderance of panels, decorated with intricate anthropomorphic snake, jaguar and alligator motifs. Archeologists believe that pieces coloured and designed in this way had elite-associated functions; possibly as mortuary furniture for *caciques* (chiefs) or other high-ranking individuals. In the Period VI (an archeological denotation for the years between 1000 BC and 500 AD) the *murillo appliqué* style emerged, an entirely new, glossy, black or red pottery with no correlation anywhere else in the region, but mysteriously similar to pottery found on Marajó Island at the mouth of the Amazon in modern-day Brazil, thousands of kilometres away.

After the Conquest, predictably, pottery-making declined sharply. The traditional anthropomorphic images were judged to be pagan by the Catholic Church and subsequently suppressed. Today you can see some of the best specimens in San José's Museo Nacional, or watch them being faithfully reproduced in Guaitíl.

Nicoya

Bus travellers journeying between San José and the beach towns of Sámara and Nosara need to make connections at the country town of **NICOYA**, the main settlement of the peninsula. Set in a dip surrounded by low mountains, it's a hot place, permeated by an air of infinite stasis; but undeniably pretty, nonetheless, with a lovely **Parque Central**, centring on a preserved white adobe church (earthquake-battered, structurally unstable and currently closed), draping bougainvillea and aggressive-looking plants. There's a considerable Chinese presence; many restaurants, hotels and stores are owned by descendants of Chinese immigrants.

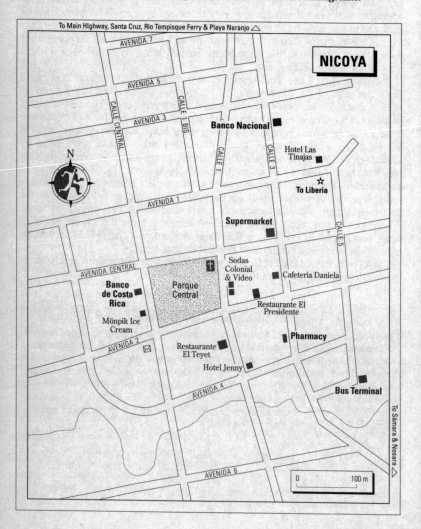

To Main Highway, Santa Cruz, Río Tempisque Ferry & Playa Naranjo

NICOYA

AVENIDA 7
AVENIDA 5
AVENIDA 3
AVENIDA 1
AVENIDA CENTRAL
AVENIDA 2
AVENIDA 4
AVENIDA 6

CALLE CENTRAL
CALLE 1 BIS
CALLE 1
CALLE 3
CALLE 5

N

Banco Nacional

Hotel Las Tinajas

To Liberia

Supermarket

Sodas Colonial & Video

Cafeteria Daniela

Banco de Costa Rica

Parque Central

Restaurante El Presidente

Mönpik Ice Cream

Pharmacy

Restaurante El Teyet

Hotel Jenny

Bus Terminal

To Sámara & Nosara

0   100 m

Practicalities

Eight **buses** a day arrive in Nicoya from San José, a journey of around six hours. Some take the long way round via the road to Liberia, but most take the Tempisque ferry (only slightly shorter; you spend less time on the road but more time in line waiting for the ferry. Call ☎222-2750 for more information). In addition, buses arrive from a number of regional destinations, including Liberia (14 daily), Santa Cruz (17 daily) and Sámara (3 daily). Most buses arrive at Nicoya's spotless new bus station, on the southern edge of town, a short walk from the centre. The Liberia service, however, pulls in across from *Hotel las Tinajas*. As usual, you'll find most **services** around the Parque Central, including the *correo* (Mon–Fri 7.30am–5.30pm), the *Banco de Costa Rica* (Mon–Fri 7am–3pm), and **taxis**. For the latter you can also call *Coopetico* (☎658-6226).

The friendly *Hotel Jenny*, 200m south of the Parque Central (look for sign; ②) is the cheapest **place to stay**, with old, basic rooms with a/c, TV and phone. *Las Tinajas*, 100m north and east of the Parque Central, has dark rooms inside the main building, an old house, and lighter cabinas in the back. Good **restaurants** include the *Cafetería Daniela*, 100m east of the park, for breakfast and pastries; the sodas *Colonial* and *Video* by the park for large *casados* and, for Chinese food, the restaurants *Tey-et*, across from the *Hotel Jenny*, and *El Presidente*.

Moving on from Nicoya, **buses** to Sámara leave at 8am, 3pm and 4pm (2hr), and there is one daily service to Nosara, at 1pm (2hr). You can also get to San José (6 daily; 6hr), Liberia (14 daily; 2hr) and Santa Cruz (15 daily; 40min).

Playa Sámara

Although on the map a road runs the 35km between Nicoya and the coast at Nosara, it's only negotiable with 4WD. Most drivers, and all buses, take the longer, paved route through **Playa Sámara**, from where you can loop north back up the coast. The scenery from Nicoya to Sámara, 30km south, is rolling, rather than precipitous, although there are a couple of particularly nasty corners punctuated by crosses marking the drivers who didn't make it. As you approach Sámara at the *Bar Rancho* and gas station, the right-hand road branches off into a creek, sometimes deep. On the left hand a new road is being built that will make land access much easier to Sámara, and will no doubt change the character of the village in one fell swoop.

At present, however, for sheer size and safety for **swimming**, Sámara is probably the best beach in Costa Rica, especially now that local residents and visitors have tackled the litter problem that once plagued its wide, flat sands. The waves break on a reef about a kilometre out, so the water near the shore is actually quite calm – a rarity for the Pacific coast. It's a great place to relax – midweek, especially – as even at the busiest times there's little action other than weekenders tottering by on stout *criollo* **horses** (available for rent at $5 per hour) and the occasional dune buggy racing up the sand.

On Sunday the town turns out in force to watch the local **soccer** teams who play on the village field as if they're Brazil and Uruguay battling it out for the World Cup – even weekending Ticos shun the beach for the sidelines. Ninety minutes' walk south along good flat sands (avoid the trees by the beach, or you'll be attacked by biting insects) is **Playa Carrillo**, less popular than Sámara but also safe for swimming.

Arrival and information

Sansa and *Travelair* **planes** from San José come in at the airstrip 6km south of town at Carrillo, where 4WD taxis can take you to Sámara for about $6. The express **bus** from San José leaves at noon and gets in about six hours later, stopping about 50m in front of the beach right at the centre of the village. The express bus **back to San José** currently leaves at 4am, and there are buses **to Nicoya** at 5.30am and 6.30am (2hr).

Sámara's **correo** (Mon–Fri 7.30am–5pm), a small shack really, 50m before the entrance to the beach, offers minimal services. **Pulpería Mileth**, near where the buses come in, is stocked with all the things you need: potato chips, suntan lotion, bottles of cold water, and they also have the village public **telephone**.

Accommodation

Staying in Sámara is getting pricier, with few cheap cabinas. Though during the low season most hotels can offer better rates than the ones listed here, at high season weekends you should have a **reservation** no matter what price range you aim for. The best budget option is to **camp**: especially popular on weekends, *Camping Coco*, on the beach, is clean and well-run with cooking grills ($2.50). At the north end of the beach *Camping Playas Sámara* is also clean, with toilets and showers ($3).

Cabinas Belvedere, across street from *Hotel Marbella*, first left as you come into town from Nicoya (no phone). Clean, basic cabinas with heated water. Not quite rock-bottom but one of the cheaper options in town, with breakfast included. ③.

Cabinas Magaly, north of the soccer field, entrance off road to Nosara (no phone). Noisy, none too clean, close to the disco; but a reliable fallback. Shared bath, and cold water. ②.

Casa del Mar, set back from beach, 50m north of entrance to beach on the left (☎232-2241). Downstairs rooms are clean and white, but lack light. Better rooms upstairs with shared bath and palm-fringed sea view. Currently undergoing a change in management, so may change its name. ③–④.

Giada, about 100m before you come to the beach, on the left (☎ and fax 685-5004). Fairly upscale, with spotless rooms, good beds, overhead fans, private baths and tiled showers. Upstairs rooms are better for views and breeze. Dollar exchange for guests only. ④.

Hospedaje Katia, northern end of the beach (no phone). You have to walk along the beach to get to this very basic place, where rooms have walls, a bed and little else. Shared bath. ①.

Hotel Marbella, first left as you come into town from Nosara, 50m along road (☎ and fax 233-9980). One of the better places to stay in town with clean rooms and swimming pool. The helpful management also rents bikes. Takes *AmEx*. ④.

Hotel Playa Sámara, by the soccer field (☎680-0750; fax 233-5503). Old, run-down and rambling, above the town disco. Rooms have private baths and fans but are pretty grim. ②.

Hotel Sámara Beach, in the centre of town on the left as you enter (☎233-9398; fax 233-9342). The swishest option, with a/c rooms, bar and restaurant. Accepts *AmEx*. ⑤.

Eating, drinking and nightlife

There are a couple of very nice places to **eat** in Sámara, where you can enjoy a cold beer or two by the lapping waves. **Nightlife** is quiet, though things hot up on Saturday nights when the village's one disco comes into its own.

Bahía, on the beach. Bar/restaurant with beautiful views from outdoor tables beneath the palms. Lovely place for *típico* food and a beer with the waves at your feet. Daily 8am–9.30pm.

Colochos, next to *Hotel Sámara Beach*. Moderately priced ($4) seafood, starring the usuals: *pargo* (snapper) and *corvina* (bass).

Soda Mi Abuelo, on the beach. *Típico* food, popular for lunch.

Soda Sindhy, in the middle of the village, about 75m before the beach. Open-air soda; service is slow, but it's clean, and serves generous heapings of *típico* food.

Sámara Beach, by the soccer field. Disco-bar; very popular on holiday weekends, when people go wild to salsa and merengue.

South from Sámara

The stretch south of Sámara is for off-road driving nuts only, and should be not be attempted without **4WD** (make sure the clearance is good; the Suzuki Sidekicks rented out by many agencies may be too low). You need a good **map**, because roads go haywire in this part of the peninsula, veering off in all directions, unsigned and heading to nowhere, some ending in deep creeks (unpassable even by Range Rovers and Land Rovers at high tide). South from **Carrillo**, it gets even tougher, as dirt roads switch inland and then along the beach through the hamlets of Camaronal, Quebrada Seca and Bejuco, all just a few kilometres apart but separated by frequent creeks and rivers. You should preferably not drive down here alone, as it's highly likely you'll get stuck (in the rainy season it's almost a certainty, whatever vehicle you have) and settlements are few and far between. There are **gas stations** in Sámara and Cobano: bring a spare can with you, just in case. Be sure also to carry lots of drinking water and food, and, if possible, camping gear. You can **camp** on the deserted beaches or, if you speak good Spanish, you might be able to rent a room in someone's house.

Nosara and around

The drive from Sámara 25km north to the village of **NOSARA** is pretty; a shady, secluded stretch along dirt and gravel roads punctuated by a few creeks – it's passable with a regular car (low clearance) in the dry season but you'll need a 4WD or high clearance in the wet. The road follows a slightly inland route; you can't see the coast except where you meet the beach at **Garza**, about ten minutes before Nosara. This little hamlet is a good place to stop for a *refresco* at the *pulpería*, perhaps taking a dip in the sea.

Nosara itself is set some 3km inland, between a low ridge of mountains and the sea. Usually grouped together as **Playas Nosara**, the three beaches in the area – Nosara, Guiones and Pelada – are fine for **swimming**, although you can be buffeted by the crashing waves, and there are some rocky outcroppings. The whole area is great for beachside walks, and the vegetation, even in the dry season, is greener than further north. Some attempts have been made to limit development and to protect land: largely on the initiative of locals and foreign residents, a good deal of the land around Nosara has been designated a **Wildlife Refuge**.

Nosara is one of the most appealing villages in the whole of Costa Rica, prettily set with the low ridge of the Nicoya hills backing it to the east and tree-lined beaches to the west. The atmosphere is shady and slow, with the sweet smell of cow dung in the air and excitable voices drifting out from the local Evangelical church. People are friendly, and Nosara is still low-key, though it does get busy in the high season when foreigners flock here in search of seclusion. The area around the village can be very confusing, with little dirt and gravel roads radiating in all directions. If you look carefully, there are signs on the trees, most of them painted red, pointing the way to the villages and hotels, but there's a pretty good chance that you'll get lost anyway.

Refugio Nacional de Fauna Silvestre Ostional

Eight kilometres northeast of Nosara, **OSTIONAL** and its chocolate-coloured-sand beach make up the **REFUGIO NACIONAL DE FAUNA SILVESTRE OSTIONAL**, one of the most important nesting grounds in the country for **Olive Ridley** turtles who come ashore to lay their eggs between May and November. You can't swim here (it's too rough, and plagued by sharks).

If you're in town during the first few days of the *arribadas* you'll see local villagers with horses, carefully stuffing their big, thick bags full of eggs and slinging them over their shoulders, kids skipping alongside. This is quite legal; villagers of Ostional and Nosara are allowed to harvest eggs, for sale or consumption, during the first three days of the season only. Don't be surprised to see them barefoot, rocking back and forth on their heels as if they were crushing grapes in a winery; this is the surest way to pick up the telltale signs of eggs beneath the sand. It takes about fifteen minutes to drive the gravel-and-stone road from Nosara to the Refuge; alternately you can bike it or take a taxi (see below).

Nosara arrival, orientation and getting around

Travelair and *Sansa* **fly** to Nosara from San José, often via Sámara, landing at the small airstrip-cum-dance floor (see opposite). The San José **bus** comes in at the *Abastecedor* general store. There isn't much to the village itself but a soccer field, a couple of restaurants and a **gas station**. The latter is little more than a shack, with nothing, no pumps even, to show what it is. Gas is syphoned out of a barrel or canister, and they can also change tyres. *The Monkey Business* **tour shop** nearby sells souvenirs, clothes and *Travelair* tickets, as well as pizza and *refrescos*. There's a **correo** (Mon–Fri 7.30am–5pm) as you leave the town on the right.

Ask at the gas station about **taxis** to Ostional to see the turtles (about $15), or **rent a bike** from *Cyclo Nosara*, next door – also very useful for getting to the beaches. They also sell *Travelair* and *Sansa* tickets.

Nosara accommodation

If you want to stay on the **beach** you've got two options: posh **gringo-run accommodation** or **camping**. There's a group of economical cabinas and hotels in the village – but you'll need to rent a bike or count on doing a lot of walking to get to the ocean. For **long-term** stays, *Condominio las Flores* (☎680-0696), down the road from *Almost Paradise*, has air-conditioned apartments with private bath and kitchens from $550 per week.

Almost Paradise Cafe and Cabinas, signed from the left turn at *Hotel Playas Nosara* (☎223-3200 or 680-0763). Pink bungalow perched above town. Comfortable rooms with private bath, stupendous views, howler monkeys and birds in the garden, and a café. ④.

Cabinas Agnell, in the village (no phone). Basic, dark, thin-walled rooms with fans; a poor second to *Cabinas Chorotega*. ①.

Cabinas Chorotega, in the village (☎680-0836 – village public phone, leave message). Superb cabinas with large, spotless rooms, and a communal terrace with rocking chairs where you can sit with a beer and watch the stars plaster themselves across the sky. Friendly, homely atmosphere and very fairly priced. ②.

Estancia de Nosara, set back about 1km from Nosara beach; follow signs (☎680-0378). Upmarket foreign-owned hotel in landscaped grounds, with comfortable rooms with many small details. Quiet and well-run with a restaurant and tennis court. ⑤.

Hotel Playas Nosara, on hilltop, between Playas Guiones and Pelada; follow signs (☎680-0495). Quite simply one of the best views in Costa Rica: beaches, piney coastline, rocky headlands, and the sheer Pacific Ocean. Large, clean, cool rooms with fans, priced according to the quality of the view (not all rooms overlook the beach). ④–⑤.

Rancho Suiza Lodge, set back from Piáya Pelada, copiously signed (☎233-1888; fax 257-0404). One place you won't have trouble finding. Bungalows with hammocks, whirlpool, fan, heated water and fridge, and chattering birds in lovely landscaped grounds. Well-cared-for by friendly Swiss *dueños*. ④.

Nosara eating and drinking

Owing to Nosara's relative isolation, food can be pricey, and there's little choice. In the **village** there are a number of places around the soccer field. *Restaurant el Bambú* features the usual rice dishes; more popular for a night out, *Rancho*

THE RECORRIDO DE TOROS

If you're in Nosara on a weekend in January or February, or on a public holiday, be sure to get to the **recorrido de toros** (rodeo). *Recorridos*, held in many of the Nicoya Peninsula villages, are a rallying point for local communities, who travel long distances in bumpy communal trucks to join in the fun.

Typically, the village **redondel** (bullring) is no more than a rickety wooden circular stadium, held together with bundles of palm thatch, looking dangerously close to tumbling down. Here local radio announcers perform the kind of patter heard at local functions the world over – thanking local entrepreneurs, sending birthday wishes, introducing competitors and listing the weight and ferocity of the *toros*. Travelling **tuba bands**, many of them from Santa Cruz (see p.241), spend a couple of months a year doing the rodeo circuit. Usually comprising two saxophones, a clarinettist, a drummer and the biggest tuba known to man, they perform oddly Bavarian-sounding oom-pah-pah music at crucial moments in the shows of skill. For the most fun and the best-seasoned rodeo jokes, sit with the band – but avoid the seat right in front of the tuba.

The *recorrido* usually begins in the afternoon, with **"Best Bull" competitions**, and gets rowdier as evening falls – after dark, a single string of cloudy white light bulbs illuminates the derring-do – and more beer is consumed. *Sabanero* tricks on display are truly impressive: the mounted cowboy who gallops past the bull, twirls his rope, throws it behind his back and snags it as desultorily as you would loop a garden hose, has to be seen to be believed. The grand finale is the **bronco bull-riding**, during which a sinewy cowboy sticks like a burr to the huge spine of the Brahma bull who leaps and bucks with increasing fury. During the intervals, local men and boys engage in a strange ritual of wrestling in the arena, taking each other by the forearm and twirling each other round like windmills, faster and faster, until one loses his hold and flies straight out to land sprawling on the ground. These displays of macho bravado are followed by mock fights and tumbles, after which everyone slaps each other cordially on the back, sentimental through booze.

The *recorrido* is followed by a **dance**: in Nosara the *pista* (dance floor) takes up the largest flat space available – the airstrip. The white-line area where the planes are supposed to stop is turned into a giant outdoor bar, ringed by tables and chairs, while the *Discomovíl* (mobile disco) rolls out the flashing lightballs and blasts out salsa, reggae and countrified two-steps. Wear good shoes, as the asphalt is super-hard: you can almost see your soles smoking after a quick twirl with a hotshot cowboy.

The atmosphere at these events is friendly and beer-sodden: in villages where there's a big foreign community, you'll be sure to find someone to talk to if your Spanish isn't up to conversing with the *sabaneros*. **Food** is sold from stalls, where you can sample the usual *empanadas* or local Guanacastecan dishes such as *sopa de albondiagas* (meatball soup with egg) or *tanelas*.

Nosara has a sound system and serves food and drink at nice wooden tables. Further down the road, the simple restaurant at *Cabinas Chorotega* dishes up local dishes and very cold beer under a conical roof. Plushest of the **beach restaurants**, *Hotel Playas Nosara* is pricey, but worth it for the view alone; if you don't want a full meal, stop off at least for *refrescos* and coffee. To the left of *Hotel Playas Nosara*, there are more great views at the *Almost Paradise Café*, as well as fresh, healthy food. *Olga's*, on **Playa Pelada**, serves cold beer, good *casados* and fish, again with ocean views. The most ambitious restaurant in the area is the *churasscuría* at *Rancho Suiza*; head here for tasty fish, meat and Thai food (daily except Sat). They also do lunch in their very pretty seaside restaurant (daily 11am–5pm). For a **picnic** or budget meal, pick up something in the supermarket across from *Cabinas Chorotega*.

Parque Nacional Barra Honda and around

PARQUE NACIONAL BARRA HONDA (daily 8am–4pm; $15 on the day, $5 in advance), about 40km east of Nicoya and 13km west of the Río Tempisque, is popular with spelunkers for its forty-odd deep subterranean **caves**, unique in the country, and only discovered in the 1960s and 1970s. A visit to Barra Honda is not for claustrophobes, people afraid of heights (some of the caves are more than 200m deep) or anyone with an aversion to creepy crawlies. They are only open to visitors in the dry season (Dec–April).

The landscape around here is dominated by the **limestone plateau** of the Cerro Barra Honda, rising out of the otherwise flat lowlands of the eastern Nicoya Peninsula. About seventy million years ago this whole area – along with Palo Verde, across the Río Tempisque – was under water. Over the millennia, the porous limestone was eventually hollowed out, by rainfall and weathering, to gradually form caves.

The caves continue in an interconnecting network, catacomb-like, under the limestone ridge, but you can't necessarily pass from one to the other. Kitted out with a rope harness and a helmet with a lamp on it, you descend with a guide, who will normally take you down into just one; they can give verbal descriptions of each cave before you descend. The **main caves**, all within 2km of each other and of the ranger station, are the Terciopelo (so named not because the snakes actually live there, but because the remains of one were found at the bottom), the Trampa, Santa Ana, Pozo Hediondo and Nicoa, where remains of pre-Columbian peoples were recently found, along with burial ornaments and utensils, suspected of being over 2000 years old. Most people come wanting to see the huge needle-like **stalagmites** and **stalactites** at Terciopelo, or to see subterranean wildlife such as bats, blind salamanders, insects and even birds.

Down in the depths, you're faced with a sight reminiscent of old etchings of *Moby Dick*, with sleek, moist walls, jutting rib-like ridges, and strangely smooth protuberances. Some caves are big enough – almost cathedral-like, in fact, with their vaulting ceilings – to allow breathing room for those who don't like enclosed spaces, but it is still an eerie experience, like descending into a ruined subterranean Notre Dame inhabited by crawling things you can barely see. There's even an "organ" of fluted stalagmites in the Terciopelo cave; if knocked, each gives off a slightly different musical note.

CAVE ARCHITECTURE

Created by the interaction of H_2O, calcium bicarbonate and limestone, the distinctive cave formations of stalagmites and stalactites are often mistaken for each other. **Stalagmites** grow upwards from the floor of a cave, formed by drips of water saturated with calcium bicarbonate. **Stalactites**, made of a similar deposit of crystalline calcium bicarbonate, grow downwards, like icicles. They are formed by the percolating nature of H_2O and calcium bicarbonate filtering through limestone and partially dissolving it, elongating it downwards into ever-narrowing protrusions.

In limestone caves, stalagmites and stalactites are usually white (from the limestone) or brown; in caves where copper deposits are present colours might be more psychedelic, with iridescent greens and blues. They often become united, over time, in a single column – inspiration for the style of Moorish architecture seen in ancient mosques and buildings called **stalagmite halls** or processions, whereby rows of columns are sculpted one after the other in a kind of intricate latticework.

Above ground, three short **trails**, not well-marked, lead around the caves. It's easy to get lost, and you should walk them with your guide or with a ranger if there is one free, and take water with you. A few years ago two German hikers came with the idea of walking the trails independently, got lost and, because they were not carrying water, died of dehydration and heat exhaustion.

The endangered **scarlet macaw** sometimes nests here, and there's a variety of ground mammals about – including anteaters and deer – as usual, you'll be lucky to see any, though you'll certainly hear loud howler monkeys.

Practicalities

You need to be pretty serious about caves to go spelunking in Barra Honda. Quite apart from all the planning, what with the entrance fee, the payment to the guide and the price of renting equipment ($17–23), **costs** can add up. It's obligatory to go with a guide who provides equipment as well as advice; to do otherwise would be foolhardy, not to mention illegal. Contact the SPN in advance, either at the main office in San José or the regional headquarters in Bagaces (see p.211), for names of their approved guides. You should also tell them the date and approximate time of your arrival. Anyone who wants to follow the **trails** at Barra Honda has to tell the rangers where they are intending to walk and how long they intend to be. If you are going into the caves, your guide will let the rangers know in which cave you are descending and how long you will be.

If you speak Spanish, another good way to hook up with guides is to call Sr Olman Cubillo, president of the local community development association, at the *Complejo Ecoturistico Las Delicias* (☎685-5580) in **SANTA ANA**, the nearest hamlet to the caves. Recommended by both the SPN and the ACT, he can also give you **local information** about food, lodging, camping and horseback tours.

Driving to Barra Honda is possible even with a regular car. From the Nicoya–Tempisque road, the turnoff, 13km before the ferry, is well-signed. It's then a four-kilometre stretch along a good gravel road to the hamlet of Nacaome (also called Barra Honda), from where the Park is, again, signed. Continue about 6km further, passing the hamlet of Santa Ana – where, if you've arranged your trip with Sr Cubillo, you may have to meet your guide – until you reach the ranger station (most people arrange to meet their guide here).

There is a **campsite** inside the Park, with picnic tables and drinking water ($2 per person), and good basic **rooms** at *Proyecto Las Delicias* (①–②), nearby in Santa Ana. Most people who come to Barra Honda, however, stay in Nicoya (see p.244), or across the Río Tempisque on the mainland.

Leaving the Nicoya Peninsula

There are three alternatives when it comes to **leaving the peninsula** by bus or car from Nicoya. One is to drive north through **Santa Cruz** and around the cleft of the peninsula, picking up the Interamericana at Liberia. This drive takes two hours at most and, except for a few bad stretches along the paved road between Nicoya and Santa Cruz, is fairly easy. The most popular way to return to the mainland, however, is on the **Tempisque ferry**. Some bus services between Nicoya and San José take this ferry, while others take the longer land route via Liberia. Taking the Tempisque buses can cut the trip to Nicoya or San José by about an hour, even during busy holidays, as buses have priority over cars on the ferry (though see the caveat below).

The third, far less common way to leave the peninsula is to go from Nicoya by bus or car (4WD essential) and continue southeast about 72km to **Playa Naranjo**, from where a vehicle and passenger ferry sails to **Puntarenas**. However, the road to Playa Naranjo, especially after the Tempisque turnoff, is currently in such bad shape that even locals dissuade you from trying it, liberally applying the words "*fatal*" and "*pesadilla*" (nightmare). It can take as long as three hours, and it's a somewhat featureless journey, probably only of any interest to hardened explorers who will find satisfaction in the fact that barely any gringos come this way.

Travelling by bus to the **south of the peninsula** – Tambor/Bahía Ballena, say, or Montezuma – is very awkward. There is no public transport between Playa Naranjo, where the Nicoya buses stop and disgorge passengers on to the ferry, and Paquera, the town on the southeast tip of the peninsula from where you can get to Tambor and Montezuma. If you want to get there and don't have your own vehicle, you have to take the Naranjo ferry to Puntarenas (30min) then recross the gulf from Puntarenas on a passenger *lancha* to Paquera (1hr 30min). If you have your own car you can drive from Naranjo around to Paquera (45min) on bad dirt/gravel roads. For Naranjo ferry times, see p.276.

Río Tempisque ferry

The **Río Tempisque ferry** carries cars and passengers across the river between Puerto Moreno, 17km from the Nicoya–Carmona road, and a point 25km west of the Interamericana on the mainland. Crossing here will save you a 110-kilometre drive up and over the cleft of the peninsula, via Liberia, but leave yourself plenty of time on weekends (Fridays and Sundays especially) and holidays, when the line-up of traffic can mean waits of four to five hours. Whatever time you cross, and in whichever direction, be in line about an hour before departure. Unless curtailed by bad weather in the wet season, **eastbound** crossings take place on the half-hour between 6.30am and 8.30pm, **westbound** every hour on the hour from 6am to 8pm – it takes twenty minutes.

travel details

Buses

San José to: Cañas (5 daily; 3hr); Junquillal (1 daily; 5hr); Liberia (8 daily; 4hr); Nicoya (8 daily; 6hr); Nosara (1 daily; 6hr); Peñas Blancas, for Nicaragua (4 daily; 6hr); Playa Brasilito (2 daily; 6hr); Playa del Coco (1 daily; 5hr); Playa Flamingo (2 daily; 6hr); Playa Hermosa (1 daily; 5hr); Playa Panamá (1 daily; 5hr); Playa Potrero (2 daily; 6hr); Playa Sámara (1 daily; 6hr); Santa Cruz (5 daily; 5hr); Parque Nacional Santa Rosa (4 daily; 6hr); Tamarindo (1 daily; 6hr).

Cañas to: San José (5 daily; 6 Sun; 3hr).

Junquillal to: San José (1 daily; 5hr); Santa Cruz (1 daily; 1hr 30min).

Liberia to: Bagaces (3 daily; 40min); Cañas (3 daily; 50min); Cuajiniquil (1 daily; 1hr 30min); La Cruz (14 daily; 1hr); Nicoya (14 daily; 2hr); Peñas Blancas, for Nicaragua (5 daily; 2hr); Playa del Coco (3/4 daily; 1hr); Playa Hermosa (2 daily; 1hr); Playa Panamá (2 daily; 1hr); Puntarenas (5 daily; 3hr); San José (8 daily; 4hr); Santa Cruz (14 daily; 1hr); Parque Nacional Santa Rosa (5 daily; 1hr).

Nicoya to: Liberia (14 daily; 2hr); Nosara (1 daily; 2hr); Playa Sámara (3 daily; 2hr); San José (6 daily; 6hr); Santa Cruz (15 daily; 40min).

Nosara to: Nicoya (1 daily; 2hr); Sámara (1 daily; 40min); San José (1 daily; 6hr).

Peñas Blancas to: Liberia (9 daily; 2hr); San José (2 daily; 6hr).

Playa Brasilito to: San José (2 daily; 6hr); Santa Cruz (2 daily; 1hr 30min).

Playa del Coco to: Liberia (3/4 daily; 1hr); San José (1 daily; 5hr).

Playa Flamingo to: San José (2 daily; 6hr); Santa Cruz (2 daily; 1hr 30min).

Playa Hermosa to: Liberia (2 daily; 1hr); San José (1 daily; 5hr).

Playa Panamá to: Liberia (2 daily; 1hr); San José (1 daily; 5hr).

Playa Potrero to: San José (2 daily; 6hr); Santa Cruz (2 daily; 1hr 30min).

Playa Sámara to: Nicoya (2 daily; 2hr); San José (1 daily; 6hr).

Santa Cruz to: Junquillal (1 daily; 1hr 30min); Liberia (14 daily; 1hr); Nicoya (15 daily; 40min); Playa Brasilito (2 daily; 1hr 30min); Playa Flamingo (2 daily; 1hr 30min); Playa Potrero (2 daily; 1hr 30min); San José (5 daily; 5hr); Tamarindo (1 direct daily; 1hr).

Tamarindo to: Liberia (1 daily; 1–2hr); San José (1 daily; 6hr); Santa Cruz (1 direct daily; 1hr).

Flights

Travelair

San José to: Nosara (1 daily; 1hr 25min); Playa Sámara (1 daily; 1hr 45min); Tamarindo (1 daily; 40min).

Sansa

San José to: Nosara (3 weekly; 1hr 30min); Playa Sámara (10 weekly; 1hr 45min); Tamarindo (10 weekly; 40min).

Nosara to: San José (3 weekly; 1hr 30min).

Playa Sámara to: San José (10 weekly; 1hr 45min).

Tamarindo to: San José (6 weekly; 40min).

CHAPTER SIX

THE CENTRAL PACIFIC
AND SOUTHERN NICOYA

While Costa Rica's **Central Pacific** area is less of a geographical or cultural entity than the other regions of the country, it does contain several of its most popular tourist spots, among them the number one attraction, **Reserva Biológica Bosque Nuboso Monteverde** (Monteverde Cloudforest Reserve), draped over the ridge of the Cordillera de Tilarán. Along with the nearby **Reserva Santa Elena**, Monteverde protects some of the last remaining pristine **cloudforest** in the Americas. **Southern Nicoya**, effectively cut off by bad roads and a provincial boundary from the north of the peninsula (covered in our chapter on *Guanacaste*), is part of **Puntarenas** province. Its eponymous capital, a steamy tropical port across the Gulf of Nicoya on the mainland, is the only town of any size in the entire area.

The Central Pacific and Southern Nicoya also has a number of beautiful **beaches** which, along with those of Guanacaste are some of the best known in the country, with the advantage of being easily accessible from San José. Each one offers a distinctly different experience. A former tiny fishing village near the southwest tip of the Nicoya Peninsula, **Montezuma** is surrounded by a series of coves that, while picturesque in the extreme, are not great for swimming. But if you want to hang out and sunbathe, they can't be bettered. On the mainland coast, the rough water and huge waves at **Jacó** make it one of the best places to surf in the country. Further south, **Parque Nacional Manuel Antonio** has several extraordinarily lovely beaches, with the kind of white sand and azure water you equate with the Caribbean islands – though only one of them is calm enough to be safe for swimming. For years a well-kept secret among those who knew of its rugged natural beauty, in the past five years the Manuel Antonio area, which can be traced roughly from the Park itself to the sportsfishing town of **Quepos**, 7km north, has experienced an astounding tourism boom, with hotels springing up virtually overnight.

With the exception of the cool cloudforest of Monteverde, the **vegetation** is Pacific lowland: tropical, hot and rather dryer than in the south. It can be uncomfortably **hot** all over this region – about 30°C is a dry season average. It's not that much cooler in the wet months, when Quepos and Manuel Antonio, in particular, often receive torrential afternoon rains. Further north the so-called "green season" is less virulent, though high in the clouds of Monteverde it can bucket down, especially in the afternoons. However, as the Central Pacific is heavily touristed to the point of discomfort in the dry season, it is a good idea to **time your visit** to coincide with the wet, when the crowds have gone home, hotels in

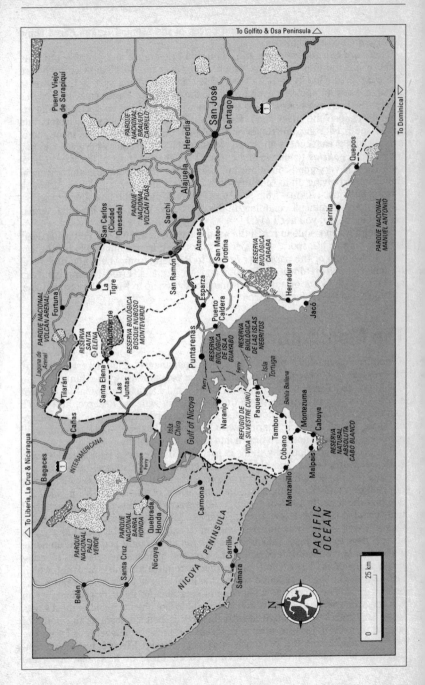

Monteverde actually have space, and prices in the Manuel Antonio area come down from the stratosphere.

There are two **routes from the capital** to Puntarenas and points south. The main road is the Interamericana, which climbs over the Cordillera Central before dropping precipitously into the Pacific lowlands, levelling out at the town of Esparza, a few kilometres beyond which is the turnoff for Puntarenas. In total this trip takes about two hours. Many travellers who are aiming for Jacó and Manuel Antonio choose the older road, Hwy-3, via Atenas, which passes Orotina and heads south, skirting the **Reserva Biológica Carara**. This is the nicer route, overall, with great scenery and good roadside stalls at Orotina where you can buy fudge, nuts, *galletas* (cookies) and crafts. From Orotina most of the way to Jacó, the road is in very good condition, and offers some of the least stressful driving in the country. Driving up to Monteverde is always a bit of an expedition. Although it is not far – just 170km – from San José, the roads along the final 35km or so are unpaved and in difficult condition. In the dry season you can do it with a regular car, but in the wet you need 4WD.

Though it is possible to reach the southern third of the Nicoya Peninsula overland by private transport, most people cross over from Puntarenas on the car ferry to Naranjo or the passenger *lancha* to Paquera, from where you can travel by public transport down to Tambor and Montezuma. From Naranjo you can continue south by car or north to Carmona and then up to Nicoya and Santa Cruz, but you'll need 4WD for either route.

The Monteverde area

Generally associated only with the eponymous Cloudforest Reserve, **Monteverde** is, properly, a much larger area, straddling the hump of the Cordillera de Tilarán between Volcán Arenal and Laguna de Arenal to the east and the low hills of Guanacaste to the west. Along with the Reserve, here you'll find the spread-out Quaker community of **Monteverde**, the neighbouring village of **Santa Elena** – which has its own Cloudforest Reserve – and several small hamlets which have not been drawn into any tourism activity.

The area's huge popularity stems in part from the **Reserva Biológica Bosque Nuboso Monteverde**, and also from the cultural and historical uniqueness of the Monteverde community, which was colonized in the early 1950s by a number of **Quaker** families, mostly from Alabama, some of whom had been jailed for dodging the draft. In 1950–51 the first settlers arrived in this remote area, at that time peopled only by a few farming familes. Monteverde's isolation suited the Quakers well – there was no road, only an ox-cart track, and it was a journey of several days to San José, 180km away. The families bought and settled on some 3000 acres of mountainside, dividing the land and building their houses, meeting house and school. The climate and terrain were ideal for **dairy farming**, which fast became the main economic earner; the local cheese factory (*la lechería*) was built in 1954. The area is now famous in Costa Rica for its dairy products – you will see Monteverde **cheese**, which tastes a little like cheddar, sold in most Costa Rican supermarkets – though abroad the area is better known as the home of several pioneering **private nature reserves**. Of these, Monteverde is by far the best known, although the less-touristed **Reserva Santa Elena** is just as interesting, with an equally pristine cloudforest cover. More or less adjacent is the

SANTA ELENA VS MONTEVERDE

Many people planning a trip to see the Monteverde cloudforest are confused by the relationship between the village of Santa Elena and the settlement of Monteverde. Hotels are often described as being "in" Monteverde when they are in fact in Santa Elena, outside the Monteverde community proper.

Santa Elena is the small hamlet where the buses stop and where you'll find most of the services and the cheaper places to sleep, eat and drink. Staying here, you can meet up with independent travellers and volunteers, and perhaps even a few locals. The Quaker community of **Monteverde**, on the other hand, spread out on the road from Santa Elena to the Monteverde Reserve, is altogether quieter. Most of the hotels around Monteverde and close to the Reserve are pricey, mainly used by tour groups and older, better-heeled tourists. While the majority of accommodation here is very comfortable, some travellers find the atmosphere a bit dour; perhaps because everything is so smoothly – rigidly, almost – organized. You get little sense of a community, partly because Monteverde is not an obvious settlement, and many of the houses are set back in pasture, hidden from the main road.

Bosque Eterno de los Niños, or Children's Eternal Rainforest, established with funds raised by schoolkids from all over the world.

If there's any downside at all to coming to the Monteverde area, it is the **expense**. Admission fees to the Reserves are high, and if you want to take a guided tour, you're looking at shelling out at least another $15. Accommodation near the Reserve tends to be expensive, though there you can find very good cheap lodging the further away from the entrance you get. Food, too, is fairly pricey, owing in part to the transport distance involved in trucking in things from San José, and perhaps, too, to the captive audience.

Though officially the low season, the **rainy season** (May–Nov) is the best time to visit Monteverde, to avoid not only the crowds of walkers and fully booked hotels, but also the usual afternoon fogs of the dry season. Ideally, try to come early or late in the wet season, when you can get the double benefit of lower crowds but reasonably good weather.

Getting to Monteverde

Getting to Monteverde independently from **San José**, especially in the dry season, entails some pre-planning. Make sure to buy your bus ticket as far in advance as possible, and once you've arrived buy your return ticket immediately. In the wet season you should be able to get away with buying your ticket just a day in advance. From **Puntarenas**, bus demand is somewhat less strained, so you can probably get away with not booking. Wherever you arrive from, in the dry months you should **book a room** in advance – most of the larger and plusher hotels, at least, are often full for weeks at a time with tour groups, and the rare cheaper ones are much in demand. In the wet season, especially midweek, you can probably get away with turning up on spec. Give yourself at least three days in the area; one to get up there, at least one to explore (two is better), and another to descend.

All the major operators offer **tours** to Monteverde from San José; usually two or three nights with accommodation, and sometimes meals, pre-paid. Transport

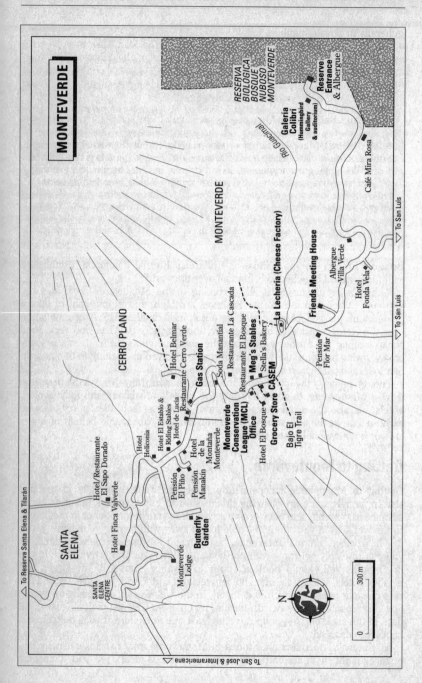

MONTEVERDE

(generally in private minibus) to and from the capital and, when in Monteverde, to and from the Reserve, is included in the price of the tour. They may even lay on wildlife-spotting treks with a private guide. The main difference between tours is the hotel they use, and whether the Reserve entrance fee is covered in the price.

By car

Driving from San José to Monteverde takes about four hours (3hr 30min if you drive fast) via the Interamericana – two hours to the turnoff (there's a choice of three; see below), then another two hours to make the final mountainous ascent. The question most drivers face is which **route** to take, and hardened two-day veterans of 4WD techniques argue endlessly – usually in hotel bars in the evening – about which way is more exciting and entails shifting into 4X4 mode more often.

One route, sometimes called the Sardinal route, is to take the Interamericana north from Puntarenas towards Liberia, branching off at the **Rancho Grande** turning to Monteverde. Buses go a shorter route, continuing past Rancho Grande to the **Río Lagarto** turnoff – just before Río Lagarto itself – which is signed to Santa Elena and Monteverde. The least well-known route, which local *taxistas* will swear on a book of lottery tickets is the best, is via **Las Juntas de Abangares**, a small town reached from a small road, labelled 145 on some maps, off the Interamericana. Once you've reached Las Juntas, drive past the main square, turn left and continue over a bridge; turn right, and follow the signs. The first 7km of this 37-kilometre road, via Candelaría, are paved, but have some spectacular hairpin bends – drive slowly. You can also reach Monteverde from **Tilarán**, near Laguna de Arenal. The road (40km) is often very rough, but provides spectacular views over the Laguna de Arenal and Volcán Arenal (both covered in our *Zona Norte* chapter).

Whichever route you take, you'll need **4WD** in the rainy season, unless you are very good at fishtailing up and down hills while dodging large stones. Indeed, some agencies will refuse to rent you a regular car to drive up to Monteverde in the rainy season, no doubt through long experience with cars breaking down or foundering in mud.

By bus

All **buses** pull in at Santa Elena. Some then continue along the road to Monteverde, making their last stop at the *Lodge Villa Verde*, one of the closest to the Reserve. Most people arrive on one of the two direct services from **San José**'s Tilarán terminal. Note that with the afternoon service you will arrive in the dark (it takes 3hr 30min minimum – more like 5hr, especially in the rainy season). From **Tilarán**, you can catch the 1pm bus (3hr). This service is only dependable in the dry season; in the rainy months you may have to walk for as long as an hour with your gear after the bus gives up. For more information, call *Autotransportes Soto Mena* at the *Iman* restaurant in Santa Elena (☎661-1255), or ask at the tourist office. From **Puntarenas**, a bus leaves for Santa Elena at 2.15pm and arrives three hours later. The Puntarenas bus does not continue beyond Santa Elena.

The **Santa Elena bus stop** is at the top of the "triangle", right across from the *Banco Nacional*, the local landmark from which all directions are given. From here, it's no more than 100m to anything you might need. If you are booked in to one of the hotels on the road to the Reserve, stay on the bus and ask the driver to drop you off, or, if you arrive on the bus from Puntarenas, arrange with your hotel to have a taxi meet you ($5–6).

TOURISM IN MONTEVERDE

Dazed travellers, stumbling off the bus from San José, often wonder why the **roads** to Monteverde are so bad. The obvious reasons are the terrain – mountainous, with a large run-off of soil in the wet season – and that these roads, like so many in Costa Rica, were built to serve small rural communities. The difference with Monteverde, though, is that tens of thousands of visitors make the journey up and down to see the Reserve, passing through villages that elsewhere in the country would not expect to see more than a handful of tourists each year.

Monteverde has become more popular than anyone ever really imagined. In 1980, it received 3100 visitors; in 1990, 26,000, and in 1992 about 64,000. It doesn't take a statistician to see that, by the end of the decade, at these rates of increase, the number of people visiting the area may reach 100,000 per annum. Although strict **rules** govern how many can enter the Reserve at any one time – indeed, studies have suggested that with proper management the Reserve can in fact accommodate this amount of visitors without large-scale environmental degradation – it is far more difficult to measure and to limit the **cultural impact** made by the number of people who currently pass through Monteverde and Santa Elena.

Tour operators regularly bemoan the state of the roads up to Monteverde. The considerable amount of time, not to mention discomfort, entailed in getting there renders the area off the day-trip agenda for people who are staying at the Guanacaste package beach resorts, and for the passengers on cruise ships that dock at Puntarenas. In response, however, the **Monteverde Conservation League** (MCL; see p.264) and the community in general, aware of the seemingly limitless demand for their cloudforest, have resisted suggestions that the road(s) up to Monteverde be paved. They argue that easier access would not only increase visitor intake to levels that would adversely affect the biological integrity of the Reserves, but also give rise to a short-stay day-tripper tourism culture that would threaten the integrity of the local communities. At the same time, Monteverdeans are fully aware that people having no choice but to spend at least a night in the area means that businesses, especially hotels, benefit. Whatever the future holds for Monteverde, it is unlikely that it will be "ruined": the community is too articulate and organized to permit itself be overrun by its own success.

Moving on from Monteverde, buses to San José leave Santa Elena at 6.30am and 2.30pm daily. For Tilarán, one bus leaves at 7am. Tickets are sold at the office next to the tourist office in Santa Elena (see p.264).

Accommodation

The cheapest place to stay in the Monteverde area is **Santa Elena**. All accommodation here is basic; but you'll get a bed and heated water at least, and, almost certainly a warm welcome. Many small *pensiones* are run by local families or couples and offer an array of services, from cooking for you – the prices we quote below are for room only – to laundry and horse rental. Some of the hotels right "downtown", in the village triangle, like *Pensión Santa Elena* and *Pensión el Tucán*, are convivial places to meet up and swap information with other travellers. You can also **camp for a** minimal charge on the grounds at the *Albergue Ecológico Arco Iris*.

Hotels in and around the **Monteverde** community aspire to European mountain-resort facilities and atmosphere, and with the exception of a couple of

ACCOMMODATION PRICE CODES

All the establishments in this book have been given price codes according to the following scale. The prices quoted are for the least expensive double room in high season, and do not include the national 18.46 percent tax automatically added on to hotel bills. Wherever an establishment offers dorm beds the prices of these are given in the text. For more details see p.26.

  ① less than $10   ③ $20–30   ⑤ $50–75   ⑦ $100–150

  ② $10–20   ④ $30–50   ⑥ $75–100   ⑧ $150 plus

cheap *pensiones*, tend to be expensive and "packaged", appealing to those who like their wilderness de luxe. You'll certainly be comfortable in the majority of these places – large rooms, running hot water, orthopedic mattresses, even saunas and jacuzzis, are the norm. Most hotels have a restaurant and, if you come on a package, meals may be included. Many of the larger places are set in extensive grounds and have their own private trails in the surrounding woods. While most have a small library and show slides of local flora and fauna, few have a television – the idea, it seems, is to escape from the modern world. Nightlife within the hotels is low-key to non-existent – some have a small bar, and that's about it.

Wherever you stay, if you haven't come on a tour or with private transport, you are going to have to do a lot of **walking** – 5km uphill from Santa Elena to either Reserve, or about 2km from the nearest hotels in Monteverde to the Monteverde Reserve entrance. Despite reports that people will give you a lift at least partway to either Reserve if you stick out your thumb, nobody seems to be that obliging.

Santa Elena

Albergue Ecológico Arco Iris (☎645-5067; fax 645-5022). Comfortable cabinas surrounded by nice gardens and owned by impressively multilingual *dueños*. Laundry service and good restaurant. ②–④.

Hospedaje el Banco, next to the *Banco Nacional* (no phone). Friendly and very basic – bed and heated water for the best prices in town. ①.

Pensión Colibrí (no phone). Family-run, simple accommodation; small rooms, with shared bath and heated water. They cook breakfast, and *casados* for lunch, and also rent horses. ②.

Don Taco, 500m north of the school (☎645-6023). Welcoming, clean cabinas a little more upscale than the others. Upstairs rooms are nicer, with private bath and heated water. ②–③.

Finca Valverde, just up the hill from Santa Elena towards Monteverde (☎645-5157). Mid-range hotel, with large rooms, some in two-storey cabinas with porches, and hot water. Good restaurant, open to the public (7am–9pm), and a small system of private trails. ⑤.

To Reserva Santa Elena (5 km)
Tilarán (Fortuna, Laguna de Arenal), Las Juntas (for the Interamericana; 40 km), Cabinas Don Taco & Marín (500 m), & Sunset Hotel (1 km)

SANTA ELENA

School

Albergue Ecológico Arco Iris

To the Interamericana (Vía Río Lagarto & Sardinal Routes)

Hospedaje el Banco

Pensión Colibrí

Bus Stop

Banco Nacional

Supermarket

Pensión Santa Elena

Chunchies

Police

Pensión El Sueño

Pensión el Tucán

Finca Valverde

To Cerro Plano & Monteverde

N

0   50 m

Cabinas Marín, 500m north of the school (☎645-6039). Rooms in an annexe near a family house. Small and basic, but clean, and with shared bath. ①.

Pensión Santa Elena, 50m south of the *Banco Nacional* (☎645-5051; fax 645-5147; Aptdo 11689-1000, San José). IYHF-affiliated (members get 10 percent discount) and a great deal under any circumstances. Comfortable and friendly, and a good place to meet other travellers, with kitchen, laundry, and a small restaurant (8am–5pm) serving good, plain food. ②.

Pensión el Sueño, 25m east of the *correo* (☎645-5021). Basic, clean accommodation with shared bath, or, for a few colones more, slightly nicer rooms with private bath. TV in a small lounge and friendly *dueños* who cook meals on request. ①–②.

Sunset Hotel, 1km north of town on the way to the Santa Elena Reserve (☎645-5048). Uninspired rooms with inspiring views west into, as the name says, the setting sun; fairly priced with private bath, hot water and breakfast. A good place to flee the crowds. ④.

Pensión el Tucán, 100m south of the *Banco Nacional* (☎645-5017). Most rooms are above the soda (which serves good food), with shared bath and heated water. Rooms with private bath cost a few dollars more. ①.

Monteverde and around

Albergue Reserva Biológica de Monteverde, at the entrance to the Monteverde Reserve (contact MCL; ☎645-5003). Comfortable, full-board accommodation. Often packed with researchers and students; tourists have second priority. Reservations essential. ③–④.

Belmar, 200m north of the gas station, Cerro Plano (☎645-5201; fax 645-5135). Lovely Chilean-owned, Swiss-chalet-type lodge. Rooms in the new building are best: spacious, with private bath and wonderful, uninterrupted views over the Gulf of Nicoya. Good restaurant and small bar. ⑤.

Hotel el Bosque, Monteverde, about 3km from the Reserve entrance (☎ and fax 645-5129). Good mid-priced option, next to the restaurant of the same name, with large rooms, private baths and views over the hills out towards the Gulf of Nicoya. ⑤.

El Establo, between Santa Elena and Cerro Plano (☎645-5033 or 5041). A family farm with some land in the cloudforest, offering trails, birdwatching and a large stable. Rooms are large, there's a comfortable restaurant, and the central fireplace gives it a homely feel. ⑤.

Pensión Flor Mar, about 2km before the Reserve entrance (☎645-5009; fax 645-5008; Aptdo 2498-1000, San José). One of the older *pensiones,* owned by an original founder of the Quaker community. Basic and good value, although rooms are small. Management is friendly and there's a nice restaurant. ③–④.

Fonda Vela, Monteverde (☎645-5125; fax 645-5119). Large rooms, though the ones at the back can be quite dark. Has its own trails, plus pleasant grounds with pre-Columbian statuary, and is convenient for the Reserve. Good restaurant, open to public. ⑤.

Heliconia, between Santa Elena and Cerro Plano (☎645-5109). Luxury hotel, with large, comfortable rooms in main lodge with porches or balconies, and cabinas set some distance away. The lodge has jacuzzi, sauna and a restaurant. ⑤.

Pensión Manakín, signed at Cerro Plano (☎645-5080). One of the best budget options, with homely atmosphere, friendly, basic dorm accommodation, or rooms with shared or private bath. Use of kitchen facilities. Ten percent discount for students with ID. ②.

Hotel de Montaña Monteverde, Cerro Plano (☎645-5046; fax 645-6079). Comfortable, rustic, lodge-like hotel, with jacuzzi and sauna, and a good restaurant serving "health food". Some birdwatching on its own private Reserve. ⑥.

Monteverde Lodge, Monteverde (contact *Costa Rica Expeditions*: ☎222-0333; in USA: ☎1-800/633-4734). One of the more luxurious hotels in Monteverde, popular with package tours. Large, well-furnished rooms, with bathrooms with tubs. Atrium, jacuzzi, restaurant, and nightly slide shows of the cloudforest and its animals. ⑥.

Pensión el Pino, Cerro Plano, next to *Pensión Manakín* (☎645-5130). Good budget rooms with shared bath and heated water in a small annexe next to a family house. ②.

El Sapo Dorado, east of Santa Elena (☎645-5010; fax 645-5180; Aptdo 09, CP 5655, Monteverde). Individual, roomy, rustic wooden chalets on a hill, with stupendous view of the

Gulf of Nicoya. Some with fireplaces and kitchenettes. Also guided walks on private paths by the Río Guácimal. The restaurant here is one of the best in Monteverde (see p.271). ⑤.

Lodge Villa Verde, about 2km from Reserve entrance (☎645-5025; fax 645-5115). Chalet-style accommodation with wraparound windows and huge verandah, some kitchen-equipped cabins, or rooms in small annexe – all with private bath. ⑤.

The communities

In recent years the tiny town of **SANTA ELENA** has benefited – economically, anyway – from the influx of visitors to the Monteverde Reserve and, increasingly, to the Santa Elena Reserve, 5km northeast. The centre of the village is actually a triangle, formed by three streets on which you'll find most of the businesses, services and a good number of the *pensiones*. The most sizable community in the area, it's a hub for all the farms spread out along the flanks of Monteverde. Here

---

CUÁQUERISMO

Many people who come to Monteverde don't quite know what to expect from a Quaker (*cuáquer*) community. **Quakerism** does not impose any obvious standards of dress or appearance upon its followers – you're not going to see the jolly old man on the oatmeal box walking by – nor does it manifest itself in any way that is immediately obvious to visitors, save, of course, for the lack of bars.

Also called the Society of Friends, Quakerism, an altruistic, optimistic belief system, was founded by **George Fox** (1624–91) an English man born near Manchester. He instilled in his followers the importance of comporting themselves in the best way to encourage the goodness in others – in other words, as he put it, to "answer that of God in every one". Quakers are encouraged to see God in everybody, even those who are doing evil. Another cornerstone of Quaker belief is **pacifism**. All war is seen as unlawful, as it impedes the call to bring out people's "inner light". From the beginning, Quakers placed themselves in opposition to many of the coercive instruments employed by the state and society, and they continue to embody a blend of the conservative, the non-conformist and absolute resistance to state control.

In 1656 Quakerism arrived in the New World, where initially followers were subject to severe discrimination. It was a deeply felt pacifism that led to the exodus of several **Alabama** Quaker families from the USA in the early 1950s to settle in the Monteverde area. Harassed to the point of imprisonment for refusing the draft, the Quakers were convinced by Costa Rica's abolition of its army a few years earlier in 1948 – an extraordinary move under any circumstances but particularly in the context of Central America – that they could live as they wanted, unmolested, in this remote corner of a remote country.

Quakers manage their **meeting houses** individually; there is no officiating minister and most meetings confine their agendas to the purely local. Gatherings are for the purpose of meditation, but anyone who is moved to say a few words or read simply speaks up, out of the silence. All verbal offerings in context are considered valid. Outsiders are welcome at the meeting houses, and there is no question of trying to "convert" them. In Monteverde visitors are invited to join the meetings at the **Friends Meeting House**, held on Sundays and Wednesdays (look for announcements on the various community noticeboards). San José's **Centro de los Amigos para la Paz** (Friends Peace Centre), C 15, Av 6 bis, is an excellent source of material on Quakers and other secular pacifist groups in Central America. They have leaflets, newsletters, newspapers and a small library, plus a café and weekly meetings and discussion groups (☎233-6168; fax 224-8910; Aptdo 1507-1000, San José).

you'll find the only bank, *correo* and large grocery store for miles. You'll also find things you wouldn't necessarily expect 37km up a mountain with dreadful roads in all directions, such as the *New York Times*, cappuccino, vegetarian *casados* and a sizable foreign community.

For **information**, head to the **tourist office** (daily 7am–7pm), across from the Catholic church, 75m west of *Banco Nacional*. Gringos hang out at *Chunchie's* (daily 9am–6pm), opposite the *Pensión Santa Elena*, which has a laundry, café serving espresso, US newspapers, and a useful noticeboard with details of tours, rooms and just about everything else. Its secondhand bookstore is especially good, with maps and guidebooks including the invaluable field guide *Birds of Costa Rica*. Though its better by far to bring plenty of colones, *Banco Nacional* (Mon–Fri 8am–3pm) can change **travellers' cheques**, a service also offered to guests by many of the upscale Monteverde hotels.

The **Monteverde Conservation League** (MCL) is about 25m before the gas station in the hamlet of **CERRO PLANO**, 1km from Santa Elena (for *Albergue Reserva Biológica de Monteverde* reservations: ☎645-5003; for information on local guides: ☎645-5220). They can answer general questions about the history of the area and the Reserve – don't bother them for restaurant recommendations and the like – and take donations, should you be moved to leave them.

Essentially a group of dairy farms and smallholdings strung out alongside the dirt road between Cerro Plano and the Monteverde Reserve, **MONTEVERDE** is a seemingly timeless place where milk cans are left out at the end of small dairy-farm driveways to be collected, modest houses sit perched above splendid forested views, and farmers trudge along the muddy roads in sturdy rubber boots. Many people speak English as easily as Spanish here, often in the same sentence, switching seamlessly between the two. The foreign presence is heavy, a giant contingent of biologists, conservationists, researchers and volunteers, many of them from the USA. The focal points of the community are the **lechería** (cheese factory), the **Friends Meeting House** and school, and the cluster of services around **CASEM**, the women's arts and crafts collective.

Reserva Biológica Bosque Nuboso Monteverde

By 1972, homesteading in the Monteverde area had spread to the the surrounding cloudforest. At the behest of two visiting American biologists and a number of local residents, plans to establish a Reserve were initiated. Funds provided by the World Wildlife Fund enabled the community to buy an additional 554 hectares, bringing the total protected area of **RESERVA BIOLÓGICA BOSQUE NUBOSO MONTEVERDE** (daily 7am–4.30pm; closed Oct 6 and 7; $8) to 10,500 hectares. Administered by the non-profit-making organization Centro Científico Tropical (Tropical Science Centre) based in San José, today the Reserve is hugely popular with both foreigners and Costa Ricans, who flock here in droves – especially during Easter week and school holidays – to walk trails through the last sizable pockets of primary cloudforest in Mesoamerica.

Few people fail to be impressed by its sheer diversity of **terrain**, from semi-dwarf stunted forest on the more wind-exposed areas, to thick bearded cloudforest vegetation, and some truly moving **views** from its various miradors. To describe them in detail is almost to spoil the effect, but suffice to say you find yourself looking out over a world of uninterrupted, dense green, the unimpeded wind whistling in your ears, with no sign of human habitation as far as the eye can see.

The Monteverde Reserve supports six different **life zones**, or eco-communities, hosting an estimated 2500 species of plants, more than 100 species of mammals, some 490 species of butterflies, including the blue morpho, and over 400 species of birds, including the **quetzal**, the unusual three-wattled bellbird, the bare-necked umbrella bird and some thirty types of hummingbird alone. Over 120 species of reptiles and amphibians have been identified here, including the **Monteverde golden toad** (*sapo dorado*), officially discovered in 1964, listed as endemic to the area and now feared to be extinct.

It's important to remember, however, that the cloudforest cover – dense, low-lit and heavy – makes it difficult to see, and many visitors leave the Reserve disappointed that they have not spotted more wildlife. Plant-spotting at Monteverde, however, is never unrewarding, especially if you take a **guided walk**, which will help you identify thick mosses, epiphytes, bromeliads, primitive ferns, leaf-cutter ants, poison dart frogs and other small fauna and flora – not to mention directing you towards the fantastic views. Serious rainforest walkers should plan on spending at least a day in the Reserve, and many people spend two or three days quite happily here.

Temperatures are cool, as you would expect at this altitude; 15° or 16°C is not uncommon, though in the sun it will feel more like 22° to 25°. The average **rainfall** is 3000mm, and mist and rain move in quickly, so dress in layers, and be sure to carry an umbrella and light rain gear, especially after 10 or 11am. You should also bring binoculars, fast-speed film and insect repellent. It's just about possible to get away without **rubber boots** in the dry season, but you will most definitely need them in the wet. The Reserve office and some hotels rent them out.

THE CLOUDFOREST

Many visitors are enchanted with the primeval, otherworldly feel of the **cloudforest**, often painted as a disturbingly impenetrable terrain of quetzals and jaguars and other near-mythical animals. The most obvious property of the cloudforest is its dense, dripping **wetness**. Even in the morning or in the dry season it looks as if everything has just been hosed down. Cloudforests are formed by a perennial near-100 percent humidity created by mists. In the Monteverde area, these mists are the product of northeasterly trade winds from the Caribbean that drift across to the high ridge of the continental divide, where they cool to become dense clouds and settle over this high-altitude forest.

The cloudforest can also be rather eerie, due to the sheer stacking and layering of vegetation, and the preponderance of **epiphytes**; everything seems to be growing on top of each other. You will notice, walking the Monteverde and Santa Elena trails, that many trees seem to be wholly carpeted by green mosses and other guests, while others seem to be choked by multiple layers of strangler vines, small plants, ferns and drooping lianas.

Leaves of cloudforest plants are often dotted with scores of **tiny holes**, as though gnawed by insects that have given up the ghost after only a few millimetres. This is, in effect, what happens. Many cloudforest plants have the ability to produce toxins to deter insects from eating the entire leaf or plant, producing the poisons from the excess energy conserved by not having to protect themselves against adverse weather conditions, such as a prolonged dry season and heavy winds and rain. Insects in turn guard themselves against being poisoned by eating only a very little of a leaf at any time, but also sampling a wide variety, thus juggling the different toxins consumed so that they are not overwhelmed by any one.

Practicalities

The Reserve **entrance** is 45 minutes' to an hour's walk from most of the hotels – despite reports that people will pick you up and give you a lift at least partway, this is often not the case. At the entrance, the **Galería Colibrí**, or Hummingbird Gallery (Mon–Sat 9.30am–4.30pm, Sun 10am–2pm), named after the birds that buzz in and out to feed at the sugared water fountains, sells nature slides, cards, jewellery and the like, as well as holding slide shows on cloudforest topics. The **Reserve office**, right at the entrance, is very well geared up to tourists, with a **visitor centre** where you can pick up maps of the Reserve, and buy useful inter- pretive booklets for the trails. It also has a good souvenir shop, and a small soda, which dishes out coffee, cold drinks and snacks plus vegetarian *casados* at lunch- time. For overnight and long-distance hikers, there are simple **shelter facilities** along the trails, which cost $4 per night plus a small deposit. They're not always open, however, so check with the MCL or the Resreve visitor centre. If you can't or don't want to go on the official **tours** organized by the Reserve – if you prefer to go in a small group, say, or if your schedule doesn't tally with the timing of the tours – a number of local people act as excellent and experienced **guides** for the Reserve and the entire Monteverde area. For more information and recommenda- tions, ask at the Santa Elena tourist office or at MCL (☎645-5220).

A number of **rules** govern entrance to Monteverde, in an attempt to limit human impact on the Reserve. Only **100 people** are allowed in at any time, or 125 in exceptional circumstances. The MCL strongly advises that serious birders, wildlife spotters and those who would prefer to walk the trails in quiet, avoid the **peak hours** of 8 till 10am, when the tour groups pour in. If you arrive at this time in the dry season it is almost sure to be full. An alternative is to book a ticket a **day in advance** – your hotel can reserve you a place for the following day – and get here by 5.30am (not earlier – it's still too dark), when, even though the visitor centre is closed, you are able to go on the trails. Bookings cannot be made any more than 24 hours in advance.

The trails

At 10,500 hectares, the Reserve is far, far bigger than the area covered by the nine **trails**, which are contained in a roughly triangular pocket known as **El Triángulo**. They are clearly marked and easily walkable (at least at the end of the dry season), many of them along wooden, wire-mesh-netted pathways. This some- what mars the feeling that you are hiking in a "real" wilderness, but at least you aren't slipping and sliding in seas of mud.

The visitor centre gives out a good map of El Triángulo, with accurate distances, and shows roughly where you pass the continental divide – there's no obvious indication when you're on the ground. If you're keen to plunge straight into the cloudforest, the self-guided **Sendero Bosque Nuboso** is the trail to make for, armed with the interpretive booklet sold at the visitor centre. Cover along this trail is literally dripping with moisture, each tree thickly encrusted with moss and epiphytes. You'll hear howler monkeys and a few flutters, but it is quite difficult to spot birds in this dense, dark cover. Your best bet is around the begin- ning of the trail, where the three-wattled bellbird and the bare-necked umbrella bird hang out. The spongy terrain efficiently preserves **animal tracks** – in the morning you may be able to see the marks of the agouti and coati.

El Camino, several metres higher in elevation, is a mini-version of the road up to Monteverde: stony, deeply rutted in spots, and muddy. There's a small **mira-**

dor, *La Ventana*, on the trail signed to **Peñas Blancas**, looking out to the thickly forested hills of the other side of the continental divide. It is reached via a virtual staircase of cement-laid steps leading to a high, wild, wind-sculpted garden, empty and pristine, dotted with stunted vegetation, and suspended over an amazingly green expanse of hills. It's a surreal place; the only sound the wind whizzing past your ears.

Clambering up and down both sides of the continental divide, the *Río*, *Pantanoso* and *Chomogo* trails are all fairly long, some steep, and more apt to be muddy than the others.

Tours and talks

If you're short of time, make a **guided natural history walk** your priority. They currently leave at 7am, 7.30am, 8am, 8.30am and 9am (maximum 10 people). Make sure to arrive on time, or they'll set off without you. The walks are slow-paced, focusing on plants and whatever insect and bird life comes along, and take about three hours.

Birdwatching tours currently run at 5.30am and 8.30am, with a guide provided by the Reserve. There are also occasional **orchid walks**, available only at certain times of the year. Ask at the visitor centre. **Night walks** begin at 7pm and, if there is demand, at 10pm, on Tuesdays and Thursdays. These are fascinating, eerie experiences – some guides are into catching bats – and recommended

---

WHAT TO SEE AT MONTEVERDE

Seeing a **quetzal** is almost a rite of passage for visitors to Monteverde, and many zealous, binocular-toting birders come here with this express purpose in mind. A member of the trogon family, this slim, aquiline bird, with sweet face and tiny beak, is extraordinarily colourful, with shimmering green feathers on the back and head, and a rich, carmine stomach. The male is the more spectacular, and it is he who has the long, picturesque tail and fuzzy crown. About a hundred pairs of quetzals mate at Monteverde, in monogamous pairs, between **March** and **June**. During this period they descend to slightly lower altitudes than their usual stratospheric heights, coming down to about 1000m to nest in dead or dying trees, hollowing out a niche in which to lay their blue eggs. However, even during nesting season you are not guaranteed a glimpse of them; the best chance is on a guided tour.

Other creatures to look out for at Monteverde are the **bare-necked umbrella bird** and the bizarre-looking **three-wattled bellbird** (March–Aug especially), with three black "wattles", or skin pockets, hanging down from its beak. Even if you don't see one, you'll almost certainly hear its distinctive metallic call, uncannily like a pinball machine. Several types of **cats**, all of them considered endangered, live in the Reserve, which gives them enough space for hunting; among them are the puma, jaguar, ocelot, jaguarundi and margay. As with all rainforest/cloudforest habitats, however, you certainly should not arrive expecting to come face to face with a jaguar – luckily the growls of big cats coming at you out of dense night-thick forest is usually unnerving enough to cure you of your desire to actually see one.

Another famous resident of the Monteverde area – who may in fact be extinct – is the **sapo dorado**, or golden toad, a vibrant red/orange/gold toad discovered in Monteverde in 1964. However, it has not been spotted since 1989. **Ithomiid butterflies**, better known as clearwings, have just that: transparent wings, fragile as the thinnest parchment. They are abundant in the Reserve, especially on the Sendero Bosque Nuboso, feeding on dead insects, flower water and bird droppings.

if you want to see a maximum of amphibian, reptile and insect life and don't spook easily. All walks end with a **slide show** in the auditorium near the *Galería Colibrí*, during which you'll see some of the creatures you encountered in the Reserve and many you did not, including the Monteverde golden toad.

Regular **discussions**, held at 7.30pm in the auditorium, cover such broad themes as "gender issues in sustainable development" and "sex lives of lesser-known insects", usually given by visiting academics and researchers. Look for notices posted at the hotels, at *Galería Colibrí* or in *Chunchie's* in Santa Elena. Often a bus will pick up carless people at the fork in the road at the *Pensión Flor Mar*. See notices for details.

Reserva Santa Elena

Less touristed than Monteverde, the **RESERVA SANTA ELENA** (daily 7am–4pm; $6), 5km northeast of the village of Santa Elena, offers just as illuminating an experience of the cloudforest. Higher than the Monteverde Reserve – poised at an elevation of 1650m – its 310-hectare area consists of mainly primary cover. Established in 1992, Santa Elena Reserve is a separate entity from the Monteverde Reserve and the MCL, largely community-owned and administered by the Centro Ecológico Bosque Nuboso de Monteverde (Monteverde Cloudforest Ecological Centre). It strives to be self-funding, assisted by donations and entrance fee revenue, and gives a percentage of its profit to local schools. For maintenance and building projects it depends greatly on **volunteers**, usually foreign students (see below).

There's a **visitor centre** at the entrance, with washrooms and an information booth where staff hand out maps and recommend guides. They also have an excellently succinct six-page leaflet discussing rainforests, cloudforests, epiphytes, seed dispersal patterns and describing some of the mammals you might see within the Reserve. A small interpretive display written and illustrated by local schoolchildren documents the life of the cloudforest ecosystem and the history of the Reserve itself.

Trails

Santa Elena's **trails** are confined to a roughly square area east of the entrance. At present 8km of trails are developed, with more to come. With the map from the visitor centre, which clearly states distances between points and the estimated time needed to walk them, you should be able to tackle even the more difficult trails such as **Sendero del Bajo**, which follows roughly the path of Quebrada la

---

VOLUNTEERING IN MONTEVERDE

Both the Santa Elena and Monteverde Reserves depend significantly on **volunteer labour**. Activities include trail maintenance, teaching English and general conservation work. In addition, the CIEE (Council on International Educational Exchange) offers a summer **education programme** in Monteverde, from about mid-June to mid-August, teaching (in English) on tropical community ecology and tropical diversity. For more details on volunteering and education programmes in Monteverde, contact MCL direct (☎645-5034), Instituto Monteverde (☎ and fax 645-5053), or Fundación Centro Ecológico Bosque Nuboso de Monteverde, Aptdo 57-5655, Santa Elena, Monteverde, Puntarenas (☎ and fax 645-5238).

Saca, the **Sendero Caño Negro** and **Sendero Encantado**. About an hour's walk from the visitor centre, two miradors afford incredible postcard-perfect views of Volcán Arenal in the distance. Get to the Reserve as early as possible, however, before cloud, mist and fog roll in to obliterate the volcano.

Some trails are virtual concrete walkways, while others are unmade. Bring rubber boots (you can rent them locally), rain gear or an umbrella, and some warm clothes. Though the average temperature is 18°C, it can feel cooler once the clouds move in. There is currently nowhere to eat or drink at the Santa Elena Reserve, so bring your own supplies from town.

Other Monteverde attractions

A number of attractions have sprung up in the Monteverde area. Though none is likely to detract you from the real business of getting to see the cloudforests, many of them are worth a look and make useful fallbacks should you need to fill an afternoon before heading off to the Reserves in the early morning. One of the most appealing is the **"Canopy Tour for Adventurers"**, based on three static suspended platforms at Finca Valverde, near Santa Elena. Having grappled up strangler figs to reach the top – which gives great views of life in the forest canopy – you can, if you're so inclined, go from platform to platform via pulleys strung on horizontal traverse cables. Dawn and dusk tours are provided on request. The Canopy Tour is moving to the *Cloud Forest Lodge* at some point; for details contact the "base camp" across from *Pensión el Tucan* in Santa Elena (☎645-5243), or in San José call ☎255-2463 (fax 255-3573). Unlike most such places in Costa Rica, the **Monteverde Butterfly Garden**, near Santa Elena (daily 9.30am–4pm; $5) is geared to research rather than export of pupae. You can take a guided tour, which illuminates the life cycle of butterflies, or use the leaflet they hand you to tour by yourself. The best times to visit are between 11am and 1pm, especially on a sunny day – butterflies tend to hide when it's raining.

Up the hill from Santa Elena on the way to Monteverde, the **Serpentario** (daily 9am–4pm) has a range of unnerving vipers in residence. Go here *after* you've walked the Reserves – you'll think twice about treading through pretty cloudforests if you are at all wary of snakes. About 2km from the Monteverde Reserve entrance, **la lechería**, or cheese factory (Mon–Sat 7.30am–noon & 1–3.30pm, Sun 7.30am–12.30pm) sells Monteverde cheese and *cajeta*, a butterscotch spread. **Guided tours** (☎645-5150 or 5029; $8) give you a behind-the-scenes glimpse into the production processes, with rivers of curd rushing into and out of various gleaming super-clean steel sloughs and troughs. Interesting enough for a few minutes, but probably only worth it for real cheese fanatics. Nearby, the women's arts and crafts cooperative **CASEM** (Mon–Sat 8am–5pm, Sun 10am–4pm; free) sells embroidered T-shirts, blouses and dresses, and some hand-painted T-shirts – lovely but expensive. Cards emblazoned with various representations of the quetzal are also popular.

The only part of the **Bosque Eterno de los Niños** (Children's Eternal Rainforest), that you are currently permitted to walk, the **Bajo el Tigre trail** (daily 7.30am–4.30pm; $4.50), offers a short, unchallenging trek at lower elevations than in the Cloudforest Reserves. Walks are always guided, geared up for groups, and include a sunset hike between 3pm and 5.30pm.

You can't **ride horses** on the trails in the Monteverde or Santa Elena Reserves, but a number of local outfitters rent them out for trips through the surrounding valleys and on private land. In Santa Elena ask at *pensiones Colibrí* and *el Tucán*, both of whom rent good, strong beasts for around $7 an hour. *Establos Santa Elena*, across from the *Banco Nacional* (☎645-5064) offers five-hour "jungle tours" to a mirador, from where you can see across to Volcán Arenal, provided it is not cloudy. *Meg's Stables*, next to *Stella's Bakery*, is similar. *El Establo* has thirty horses and offers various tours in the area.

Eating, drinking and nightlife

In **Santa Elena**, most people eat in their **pensiones**. The restaurants at the *Pensión Santa Elena* and *Pensión el Tucán* (closed Sun) serve good cheap food, especially *casados*. The *Arco Iris* has a nice restaurant with TV, an extensive menu, including grilled shrimp, and friendly service. Of the **restaurants**, *El Daiquirí*, in the centre of Santa Elena, has vegetarian dishes and a generally healthy menu, and good breakfasts that start at 6am (it closes at 10pm). For espresso, go to *Chunchie's*. If it's a **beer** you're after, you'll have more luck in Santa Elena than Monteverde.

Cuisine in many of the top-end **Monteverde** hotels is very good indeed, and most of them open their restaurants to the public. Menus are usually fixed, and meals are served at set times. Drop round in person to book for dinner and see what is on the menu. Most of the smaller eating places that have proliferated in the past couple of years are only open for breakfast and lunch. One way to avoid eating endless *casados*, although you won't necessarily save any money, is to buy your own **supplies**. You can pick up fruit and veg in the Santa Elena grocery store, across from the church and 25m west, or in the *Coop Santa Elena* store next to CASEM in Monteverde, which, added to cheese from the *lechería* and bread and cookies from *Stella's Bakery*, makes a good lunch.

Being a Quaker community, there is not much **drinking** to be done in Monteverde. Most restaurants do have alcohol on the menu, but you will notice a whiff of temperance in the air. Furthermore, everybody goes to bed and gets up early, and restaurants tend to **close** at about 9pm or 9.30pm. The one exception is *Restaurante la Cascada*, the only place in the area where you can **dance**.

Monteverde and around

Restaurante el Bosque, Monteverde, about 3km from the Reserve entrance. Good, filling *casados* – not especially cheap – and other *típico* food. Lunch specials are particularly recommended, but watch out if you arrive at the same time as a tour/hotel group; the kitchen puts you at the end of the queue.

Restaurante la Cascada, opposite *Soda Manantial*. Good food and a large vestibuled dining area; the main reason to come here, though, is for its disco (Thurs–Sun, after 8pm), the only place for miles where you can dance the salsa and merengue.

Restaurante Cerro Verde, at the foot of the road leading to the *bomba* and the *Hotel Belmar*. Small place for passable pizza, served on candlelit gingham tablecloths. Windows on all three sides make it a light place for lunch.

Restaurante Flor Mar, about 2km before the Reserve entrance. *Casados* – including a child-size serving – served in a light, plant-filled dining room. Also ice cream, drinks and cakes to take out. Relatively cheap, and very friendly – local *señoras* cook in an open kitchen.

Restaurante de Lucia, between Santa Elena and Cerro Plano, 150m south of the *Hotel Heliconia*. Extremely friendly, Chilean-owned restaurant, with excellent service and a fine, varied menu.

Café Mira Rosa, 500m before the Reserve entrance. The lunch menu of this pleasant American-run café, set in a cabin-like building just off the road in the woods, includes houmous and lentils, soup, salads, sandwiches and quiches, all served cafeteria-style at fair prices. Lunch and dinner Mon–Sat.

Soda Manantial, opposite *Restaurante la Cascada*. Tiny place overlooking a pretty stream. Basic food that is cheap (for Monteverde) and good, especially the lunchtime *casado*.

El Sapo Dorado, east of Santa Elena (☎645-5010). The poshest place in Monteverde, with an excellent changing menu of interesting, expensive, nouvelle-type dishes, such as ink pasta with squid and calamares. Classical music on the stereos, and jaw-dropping views out over the gulf from the open-air terrace in front. Open for dinner 6–9pm daily.

Stella's Bakery, opposite CASEM. Delicious chocolate chip cookies, strudel, brownies and coffee, in a pleasant café-like atmosphere. Daily 6.30am–4.30pm.

Around Monteverde

TILARÁN, 40km northeast of Monteverde and roughly the same distance west of Fortuna, is a useful stopoff between Guanacaste to the west and the Zona Norte to the east. It is also about the best place in the country for **windsurfing**. The *Tilawa Viento Surf & High Wind* centre (☎695-5050; fax 695-5766) can arrange all kind of rentals and advise on conditions on Laguna de Arenal. There are a few **cabinas** in Tilarán, and you can expect more in the future. Two good options are *Cabinas Mary,* with large rooms and private bath (☎695-5479; ②), and *Lago Lindo* (☎695-5977; ②), whose basic rooms have communal kitchen facilities. In addition to the service to Santa Elena (see p.259), Tilarán has good **bus** connections with Cañas and the Interamericana, from where you can head on to Liberia and the Guanacaste beaches, or south to Puntarenas.

Some 37km southwest of Santa Elena and 10km off the Interamericana, **LAS JUNTAS DE ABANGARES** was a small gold-mining centre in the late nineteenth and early twentieth centuries. Just off the road to Monteverde, 5km outside town, its **Ecomuseo Oro**, or Gold-mining "Ecological" Museum (daily 6am–5pm; donations) is one of the more bizarre uses of the eco-prefix in Costa Rica – gold mining is not exactly known for respecting ecological integrity. Commemorating the activities of the Abangares Gold Fields Company, this small-scale exhibit features dusty photographs of the mini-gold boom, along with a ragbag collection of mining artefacts. Surrounding the building, short trails pass through pockets of tropical dry forest.

To get to the museum from Monteverde, look for a fork on the left just before you hit the outskirts of Juntas. It is signed from here. You'll need 4WD, or could drop your car in Juntas and hop in one of the 4WD taxis waiting at the rank around the corner from the church.

Puntarenas

Poor **PUNTARENAS**, 110km west of San José, has the look of abandonment that haunts so many tropical port cities. What isn't rusting has long ago bleached out to a generic pastel, and its cracked, potholed streets, shaded by mop-headed mango trees, are lined with old wooden buildings painted in faded tutti-frutti colours. It's hard to believe now, but in the 1800s this was a prosperous port – the export point for much of Costa Rica's coffee to England – and a popular resort for holidaying Ticos. Today, vacationing Costa Ricans have long abandoned its dodgy beaches and somewhat tawdry charms in favour of the ocean playgrounds of Manuel Antonio and Guanacaste, and foreign tourists, who never spent much

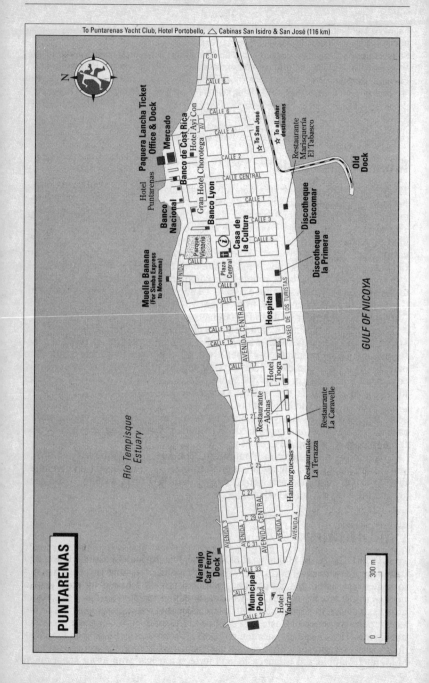

To Puntarenas Yacht Club, Hotel Portobello, △ Cabinas San Isidro & San José (116 km)

N

PUNTARENAS

C. 10
CALLE 8
CALLE 6
CALLE 4
CALLE 2
CALLE CENTRAL
CALLE 1
CALLE 3
CALLE 5
CALLE 7
CALLE 9
CALLE 11
CALLE 13
CALLE 15
CALLE 17
C. 19
C. 21
C. 23
C. 25
C. 27
C. 29
C. 31
CALLE 33
CALLE 35
CALLE 37

AVENIDA
AVENIDA CENTRAL
AVENIDA 2
AVENIDA 3
AVENIDA 4

Paquera Lancha Ticket Office & Dock
Mercado
Banco de Cost Rica
Hotel Ayi Con
Hotel Chorotega
AVT
To San José
★ To all other destinations
Restaurante Marisquería El Tabasco
Old Dock
Hotel Puntarenas
Gran Hotel Victoria
Banco Lyon
Banco Nacional
Discotheque Disconar
Casa de la Cultura
Discotheque la Primera
Parque Victoria
Plaza Central
Muelle Banana (For Simba Express to Montezuma)
Hospital
PASEO DE LOS TURISTAS
GULF OF NICOYA
Hotel Tioga
AV. 6 BIS
Restaurante Alohas
Restaurante La Caravelle
Río Tempisque Estuary
Restaurante La Terazza
Hamburguesas
Naranjo Car Ferry Dock
Municipal Pool
Hotel Yadran

0   300 m

time here anyway, come only to catch a *lancha* or ferry across to southern Nicoya or to go on a boat trip to pristine **Isla Tortuga**. Puntarenas carries on, however, as a working fishing town and a regional hub, with banks, businesses, hotels and transport facilities serving the populations of the southern Nicoya Peninsula and the Pacific coast.

In recent years Puntarenas has been the focus of a number of localized **health scares**, including minor outbreaks of cholera. It's one of the few places in Costa Rica where you might do better to drink **bottled water**, although supplies in the better hotels have usually been treated.

Arrival, orientation and getting around

Puntarenas means "sandy point", and that's what it is; a thin finger of sand pointing out into the Gulf of Nicoya, looking like a narrow-backed fish. You come into town from the east, on the narrow isthmus road that follows the old train tracks, becoming the **Avenida Central**. It seems to take for ever to get into the centre; if driving, look for the orange colonial-style building on your right. This is the **Casa de la Cultura**, and marks the centre of town.

Scores of **buses** arrive from San José every day. The bus stop is on the south side of C 2, near the old train tracks and the old dock that juts out into the gulf. **Local services** from Quepos and Manuel Antonio (3 daily; 3hr) arrive just across the street from the San José bus stop, as does the daily service from Liberia, which arrives at about 11am, and the daily run from Santa Elena, which currently arrives at about 9.30am.

Island-like, attached to the mainland by a narrow **isthmus**, Puntarenas is just five blocks wide at its most ample point, but more than sixty streets long. The **north shore** is the estuary side, where the Gulf of Nicoya eventually narrows into the Río Tempisque. The *lancha* to Paquera on the Nicoya Peninsula – from where you can head on to Playa Tambor and Montezuma – leaves from the busy docks here. The **south shore**, site of the old docks, gives you beautiful uninterrupted views out over the wide mouth of the Gulf of Nicoya and across to the Pacific. To the right is the southern tip of the Nicoya Peninsula; to the left, Costa Rica's long western coast.

Though it's easy enough to get around on foot, **taxis** scoot through the town, and can be flagged down. You can also wave down the **buses** that ply Avenida Central. The last stop is in front of the Playa Naranjo ferry dock, a couple of blocks' walk from the municipal swimming pool.

Information

Walking just one and a half blocks north and a few blocks west of the San José bus stop will get you into the town centre, where you'll find the the very helpful **tourist office** (Mon–Fri 9am–noon & 2–5pm, Sat 9am–2pm; ☎661-1985 or 1169). The office may not always be open, but, when it is, you can pick up town maps and make reservations for hotels and tours to Isla Tortuga. They also have the latest ferry and *lancha* schedules to the Nicoya Peninsula and offers a left-luggage facility. This is the place to come if you want to contact home: an AT&T **phone** connects you directly to the USA, you can call elsewhere at good rates, and there's a **fax**.

The *Banco de Costa Rica* and the *Banco Nacional*, virtually next to each other on the north shore near the docks area, offer **currency exchange** (both Mon–Fri 9am–3pm). Another good option, for those with *Citicorp* or *AmEx* travellers' cheques only, is the friendly *Banco Lyon* (Mon–Fri 9am–3pm, Sat 9am–1pm). If you get stuck, hotels like the *Gran Hotel Chorotega* can probably help you out. You could try the more upscale ones too, like the *Tioga*, although these normally only change dollars for their own guests.

Accommodation

The **cheap hotels** around the docks are useful if you want to catch an early *lancha* to Paquera. It's not a great area at night, however. More upmarket options – with the exception of the *Tioga* – congregate just east of the town centre, near the yacht club. Wherever you stay, make sure your room has a **fan** that works, otherwise you'll be as heat-baked as a ceramic pot by morning.

Ayi-Con, 50m south of the mercado on C 2 (☎661-0164 or 1477). Decent option near the Paquera *lancha* dock. Some rooms with a/c, but those with ceiling fans are fine and better value. Private or shared bath; cold water only. ②.

Gran Hotel Chorotega, C 1, Av 3 (☎661-0908). Very basic downtown hotel near the docks. Rooms have a table fan, just about adequate for this climate, and private or shared bath. Well-run and very popular, it's often full of dockers and refinery workers at weekends. ①–②.

Portobello, 3km east of downtown on the estuary (north) side (☎661-2122; fax 661-0036). The plushest place in Puntarenas, set in landscaped gardens, with swimming pools and restaurant: a nice, upscale, resort-style hotel without the outlandish prices. Good rooms with choice of a/c or sea breezes, and private bath with hot water. ⑤.

Hotel Puntarenas, 25m west of the mercado near the docks (☎661-2821). One of the cheapest – clean – places in town. Very basic, box-like rooms, hot, stuffy and dark, with paper-thin walls, but conveniently placed for the Paquera docks. ①.

Puntarenas Yacht Club, next to the *Portobello* (☎661-0784; fax 661-2518). Accommodates non-members if there's space. Rooms are nothing special but the ambience is very nice, and you get a/c, private bath with hot water; and a swimming pool. ⑤.

Cabinas San Isidro, in Puntarenas' San Isidro suburb, 8km east of downtown (☎221-1225; fax 221-6822). IYHF-affiliated (make reservations at *Toruma* in San José), and good value for members. Small beach nearby – not suitable for swimming – and a pool. ①–②.

Tioga, Paseo de los Turistas, C 17/19 (☎661-0271; fax 661-0127). The nicest downtown hotel, with elegant atmosphere, extra-friendly management and a/c rooms – those on the sea-facing side get the best views. Also a soothing interior courtyard and very pretty indoor pool. Rates include breakfast in cafeteria-style restaurant. ⑤.

Yadran, Paseo de los Turistas, C 35/37 (☎661-2662; fax 661-1944).While somewhat lacking in atmosphere, the rooms here are comfortable enough, carpeted, with TV, a/c and bath. Also a swimming pool and restaurant. ⑦.

The Town

By far the best thing in town is the clean, cheap and underused **municipal pool** (daily except Tues 9am–4pm; $1.25), at the western edge of town, on the very point of the sandspit. From the pool's landscaped terrace and gardens you have a marvellous view over the whole gulf and off to the brown humps of the Nicoya Peninsula in the distance.

Otherwise, there is little to see, though the place does have a certain sad charm. Even if Puntarenas does look like it is slowly expiring in the near-Equatorial sun, it is doing so with an affectingly anguished elegance. The forlorn air builds to moving proportions on its southerly, south-facing promenade, optimistically called **Paseo de los Turistas**, evoking happier days. A wide avenue, it is bordered on the town side with hotels and restaurants and a couple of discos, while the sea-facing side is home to a long painted promenade – the colours, of course, long since faded by the sun. The **beach** itself used to be polluted; these days the sand at least looks quite clean, backed by sparse landscaped greenery, but there's an unsettling, metallic whiff coming off the water, and the breezes do little to mitigate the intense heat. It's pleasant enough, however, to sit at one of the beachside restaurants or kiosks, where you can dig into good *pargo* (snapper) and other fresh fish while watching hulking Pacific-born clouds drift in across the Gulf of Nicoya.

From the eastern end of the Paseo, the long, skinny finger of the **old dock** crooks out into the gulf. This is where the bananas and coffee were loaded, before all the big shipping traffic shifted a few kilometres down the coast to the deeper harbour of Puerto Caldera. The docks on the **estuary** side, however, are a quite different matter, with a jungle of ketches and sturdy mini-trawlers testimony to a thriving fishing industry, and the *lancha* to Paquera chugging through daily. Despite the heat-driven lassitude you get the feeling that a lot of business is being done in the few blocks surrounding the docks, especially in the hectic **mercado**, a cacophany of noise, people and unfamiliar smells. Safe enough during the day, the docks area is best avoided at night.

West of the docks, the **Parque Victoria** is one of the least park-like *parques* in the country, little more than a long, thin strip of green, bordered by red benches and an unusual, pretty stone **church**, which looks like it might be more at home in England. A few metres south, the **Casa de la Cultura** (officially Mon–Fri 8am–noon & 1–4pm) exhibits evocative *fin-de-siècle* photographs documenting Puntarenas' lost prosperity – sepia images of tough fishermen clash with upright, white-clad Edwardian ladies, husbands made wealthy from coffee exports.

Eating, drinking and nightlife

For some reason, and everybody comments on this without being able to offer an adequate explanation, eating out in Puntarenas is **expensive**. Even fish is pricey: you'll be lucky to get *casados* or *platos del día* for less than $4 or $5. As usual the **mercado** is a good place to pick up a cheap meal and a *refresco*, although you should avoid drinking anything made with the local water. Puntarenas' mercado is particularly frantic, however. The beachside sodas and kiosks near the **old dock** are more appealing places to linger for a quiet drink or a seafood lunch.

For evening meals, if you've got money to spend, head for one of the several well-above-average restaurants that line the west side of the **Paseo de los Turistas**. As for **nightlife**, *El Primero* and *Discomar*, also on the Paseo, are the only two discos in town, offering mainly salsa and merengue. They're busy with young crowds at weekends and during holidays.

Alohas, Paseo de los Turistas, C 19/21. The most popular place in town for an evening drink. Extensive, expensive menu, and nice breezy tables where you can sit al fresco looking out to sea. Live music on Tues.

La Caravelle, 100m west of *Alohas* on the Paseo. Good honest French cuisine – not cheap, but a change from *casados* and burgers. Closed Mon.

Hamburguesas, 100m west of *La Terraza* on the Paseo. Good little hamburger stand offering tasty burgers and *típico* food – walk across the street and eat on the beach or on a bench.

MOVING ON FROM PUNTARENAS

BY FERRY

Puntarenas is a jumping-off point for foot, bicycle and motor vehicle traffic for the **southern Nicoya Peninsula**. The **Naranjo car ferry**, run by *Coonatramar* (☎661-1069; fax 661-2197) currently leaves five times daily (1hr 30min) from the docks at the western end of the estuary side of town. Check at the **tourist office** for the latest schedule. In the summer (Dec–April) especially, get there ninety minutes before sailing to ensure a space. Bear in mind that, though it is possible to drive around the Nicoya Peninsula from Naranjo, the roads are not in great shape, and you'll need 4WD.

The **passenger ferry** (*lancha*) to Paquera (for Tambor and Montezuma) currently leaves from behind the mercado (no longer from the *muelle banana* six blocks west), three times daily in the high season, twice daily in the low season (1hr 30min; $1.50). Schedules are posted outside the blue kiosk where you buy tickets. You can also store luggage at the kiosk for a minimal charge, should you not want to take all your gear over to the peninsula. Buses for Tambor and Montezuma are timed to meet the Paquera *lancha* and leave once everyone is on board. Rush to get off the ferry when it docks; this way you'll have a better chance of getting a seat. It takes about an hour to get to Montezuma, and about forty minutes to Tambor.

There's also a new **private passenger ferry service** between Puntarenas and Montezuma. The *Simba Express* ($15 one way) currently leaves the *muelle banana*, at 1pm every day (3hr) and returns from Montezuma at 7am the following morning. The schedule may well change; for information call the *Polar Bar* (☎661-0723) in Puntarenas. The boat has a capacity of thirty, so if you arrive early you might get away without a reservation.

BY BUS

Buses leave at least every hour on the hour (2hr) for **San José**. From the other side of the Paseo you can pick up services to **Liberia** (5 daily; 3hr) and **Santa Elena** (daily 2.15pm; 3hr 30min). For **Manuel Antonio**, take the Quepos service (3 daily; 3hr 30min). This bus will also drop you off just 2km from **Jacó**.

Marisquería el Tabasco, Paseo de los Turistas, C 1/3. Great surf'n'turf, including black mussels, fish *casados*, hamburgers, other hunks of meat and French fries. Not particularly cheap, and service is slow, but the beachside tables, under palms, are the nicest in town.

La Terraza, Paseo de los Turistas, C 21/23. Reasonably priced menu concentrating on seafood, pizza and pasta. The marinated mussels are a bargain at $4; the seafood salad is also good. It's a yellow, colonial-style building with a pretty outdoor terrace.

The southern Nicoya Peninsula

The ninety-minute ferry trip across the Gulf of Nicoya from Puntarenas is soothing: slow-paced, the boat purrs through usually calm waters, passing island bird sanctuaries along the way. In the distance are the low brown hills of the Nicoya Peninsula, ringed by a rugged coastline and pockets of intense jungly green.

Much of the southern peninsula has been cleared for farming or cattle grazing or, in the case of **Tambor**, given over to tourism development. **Cóbano**, 6km inland from Montezuma, is the main town in the southwest of the peninsula, with gas station, *correo*, *guardia rural* and a few bars. Most tourists pass right though on the way to **Montezuma**, one of the most popular beach hang-outs in the country, reached by a reasonable dirt road lined with cattle pasture on both sides. Like many parts of the Osa Peninsula (see p.322), this particular stretch of land gives you a startling vision of the future for the deforested tropics. Once covered with dense primary Pacific lowland forest, today the fields are stump-dotted, the red soil cutting rivulets down hills as it runs off, unimpeded by the natural drainage of the felled forest cover.

Refugio de Fauna Silvestre Curú

The small, privately owned **REFUGIO DE FAUNA SILVESTRE CURÚ**, 8km southwest of Paquera (☎661-2392; $6), protects a wide variety of flora, including many endangered **mangrove** species. Also within its grounds are some pretty white-sand **beaches**, dotted by rocky coves – a kind of mini-Montezuma. Deciduous forest areas are home to a great variety of **wildlife** which, due to the small number of people allowed in each day, have not become too shy. You are most likely to see or hear monkeys and agoutis. Live deer and wildcats also live here but are less forthcoming. At low tide the rocky tidal pools can yield crabs and assorted shellfish. All in all there is a network of seventeen **trails**; you can ask the owners for a map and directions, and some are signposted.

Practicalities

A number of **restrictions** govern visits to Curú. You cannot arrive here on your own, unannounced, but must call the owner, Sra Schutz, a week in advance, and let her know when to expect you, so she can make sure the gate is unlocked. Only thirty people are allowed in at any one time – students and field researchers

---

ISLA TORTUGA

One of the most popular day-trip destinations in Costa Rica, **Isla Tortuga** is actually two large (326 hectares in total) uninhabited islands, just off the coast of the Nicoya Peninsula in the Gulf of Nicoya, about 15km as the crow flies from Puntarenas. Characterized by its poster-perfect white sands, palm-lined beaches and lush, tropical deciduous vegetation, it's certainly a picturesque place, offering quiet – during the week, at least – sheltered swimming and snorkelling. At the weekend, however, a number of tour operators and boats disgorge their loads of passengers, roughly at the same time and the same place, marring somewhat its image as an isolated pristine tropical paradise.

   Cruises to Isla Tortuga usually leave **from Puntarenas** and take about one to three hours' sailing time each way. There's plenty of opportunity for spotting marine animals, including large whale sharks, depending upon the season. You also pass by Negritos and Guayabo island sanctuaries, where swarms of sea birds nest. On the island there's time for lunch (usually included in tour price) and snorkelling, followed by sunbathing or a little walking. Swimming in the warm water is perfectly safe.

   The majority of visitors to Tortuga actually come on day trips from **San José**. All in all, tours from the capital – including transport to and from Puntarenas – cost about $80, which is fairly steep, especially as you only get two to two-and-a-half hours on the island itself. One of the biggest operators is *Calypso Tours* (☎233-3617; fax 233-0401). An option for a more slow-paced, less-organized visit is to take a tour from **Tambor** or **Montezuma** on the Nicoya Peninsula.

have priority, and Curú's association with the University of Massachusetts means that it is often booked solid. Guides are available for about $15 per day or tour. Enquire when you telephone or talk to the Schutz family when you arrive.

No **camping** is allowed; but you could feasibly ask if there is space at the accommodation reserved for students and researchers. However, it's far easier to use Tambor as your base and travel here by taxi or bus.

Bahía Ballena and Tambor

Since 1992, when the Spanish hotel group Barceló completed its 400-room *Hotel de Playa Tambor*, the small village of **TAMBOR**, set in Bahía Ballena, has become synonymous with big-time tourist resort development. The hotel is currently the largest single hotel development in Costa Rica – though it will eventually be surpassed by the Papagayo Project in Guanacaste (see p.233).

The Playa Tambor project was dogged by controversy from the outset. At times the backers seemed wilfully bent on acting out every environmental and interpersonal gaffe possible. Not only was Barceló accused of illegally draining and filling ecologically valuable mangroves, similar to those protected by the nearby Curú Wildlife Refuge, but also of violating the Costa Rican law that states the first 50m of any beach is public property, with no development or habitation allowed. Continuous complaints about the group's working and management style were aired not only in private among residents of the traditionally fishing-oriented Tambor area, but also in the national press. Despite an order issued by the Costa Rican supreme court in 1992, ruling that the project be stopped, the government appeared unwilling to enforce the ruling. Barceló went ahead as planned and the hotel was opened in November the same year. Apparently, they have a number of such projects planned elsewhere in the country.

Despite the presence of the mega-hotel, set off by itself in the bay, with its own road, grounds and guards, the whole area remains rather remote in feel, and the village itself, surrounded on two sides by rising, thickly forested hills, is friendly and laid-back. There's not a lot to do other than go to the seal-grey, sandy beach, which stretches along a narrow horseshoe strip at the western end of the sheltered Bahía Ballena. Swimming is good, and whales are sometimes seen in the bay (hence the name – *ballena* means whale). The setting is pretty, but the sheltered position means you don't get a lot in the way of sea breeze, and there's a profusion of biting insects. If you fancy a trip out to Isla Tortuga (see p.277), enquire at the hotels or ask one of the local boatmen.

Tambor has an **airstrip**, mainly for flying in guests of the *Hotel de Playa Tambor*, although it also serves scheduled *Sansa* and *Travelair* flights. The **Montezuma–Paquera bus** passes right by on the road. You can be asked to be dropped off, and when leaving Tambor you can flag it down. For the most up-to-date information on schedules, ask locals. They know exactly what time the bus passes.

Accommodation

Cabinas el Bosque, in town (☎661-1122, ext 246). Nice, small place, owned by a local woman, just a few hundred metres from the beach. Comfortable, cool rooms with private bath (cold water only). The best deal in the area. ①–②.

Dos Lagartos, by the beach (☎661-1122, ext 236). Friendly, beautifully situated hotel with unremarkable rooms with fans. Choice of private and shared bathroom; the latter is particularly good value. Also a good restaurant. ③.

Tambor Tropical, by the beach (☎288-0491). Small, beachside, resort-type hotel, with comfortable hexagonal cabinas and a kitchen, set in very scenic grounds centring on a pool and jacuzzi. All very nice but very expensive, not to say overpriced. ⑧.

Hotel Tango Mar, by the beach (☎661-2798; fax 255-2697). Large resort-type hotel, which doesn't seem to have perpetrated any major ecological disasters, with swimming pool, tennis court and small golf course. Comfortable cabins with private bath are nice, if overpriced; weekly discounts and low-season bargains can make them affordable. ⑦–⑧.

Montezuma and around

The former fishing village of **MONTEZUMA**, about 25km west of Paquera at the southwestern tip of the Nicoya Peninsula, is in danger of becoming overwhelmed by its popularity. For a place that didn't even have electricity until six or seven years ago, it really has grown extremely quickly, shifting from a haunt for younger, budget tourists to include groups as diverse as honeymooners and "ecotourists".

What brings everyone here is the astounding beauty of the setting. Montezuma and the coast south to Cabo Blanco features some of the loveliest coastline in the country: white sand, dotted with jutting rocks and vertiginous, leaning palms, and backed by lush greenery, including rare Pacific lowland tropical forest. The village itself is surrounded by thickly forested hills sliced through by the needle-thin cascades of waterfalls. Views out into the Pacific are uninterrupted, and are especially wonderful at night, when the occasional lightning storm illuminates the horizon and silky waters.

Some fifteen or twenty years ago a handful of foreigners fell in love with Montezuma and settled here. In recent years, though, the **foreign influx** has been overwhelming. Arriving at night the place can look like the Quartier Latin-by-the-sea: lights twinkle, music pours out of the bar, and well-tanned, well-honed boys and girls sip cappuccino at cafés. Locals are understandably fed up with campers who, abusing the Costa Rican law that states that the first 50m of beach is public property, insist on setting up on the beach (often, in the past, with the express purpose of dealing drugs) and leave their mess behind – particularly arrogant as there are several campgrounds with complete water and sanitary services nearby. In response to the threats to their community that tourism poses, villagers have formed an articulate **residents' group**, CATUMO, and organize various collective projects, including brigades that regularly clean up the beach. Signs have been erected asking people nicely to use the litter bins, not to cut down trees, and not to park their 4WDs in the *parquecito*.

Arrival and information

Having plunged down a precipitous dip in the road from Cóbano, arriving at Montezuma you really do feel as if you have arrived at the outer edges of the country, if not the universe. From where you get off the bus, at the bottom of the hill, you can see pretty much all there is to see. *Chico's Bar* is straight ahead, as is the grocery store and the souvenir shop. The **information kiosk** is on your left. If you bring a car, respect the wishes of the local community and put it in the village *parqueo* behind the bus stop ($3 per day).

Monteaventuras (daily 8am–noon & 4–8pm; ☎ and fax 642-0025), adjacent to *Hotel el Jardín* acts as an all-purpose **information** service. As well as organizing tours (see p.282) they have a **fax**, an **international phone** line, and can reserve and confirm **flights** on *Sansa* and *Travelair*. There's also a very useful **leaflet**

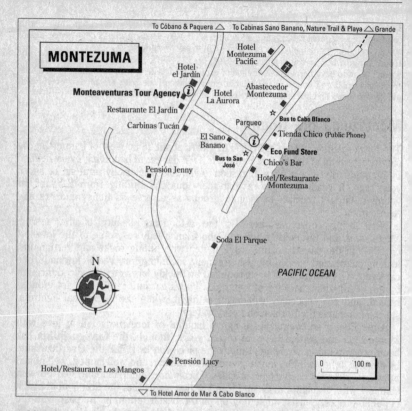

To Cóbano & Paquera △   To Cabinas Sano Banano, Nature Trail & Playa △ Grande

MONTEZUMA

Hotel Montezuma Pacific

Hotel el Jardín

Monteaventuras Tour Agency (i)

Hotel La Aurora

Abastecedor Montezuma

Restaurante El Jardín

Parqueo

☆ **Bus to Cabo Blanco**

Carbinas Tucán

El Sano Banano

(i)   • Tienda Chico (Public Phone)

☆ **Eco Fund Store**

Bus to San José   Chico's Bar

Pensión Jenny

Hotel/Restaurante Montezuma

Soda El Parque

N

PACIFIC OCEAN

0   100 m

● Pensión Lucy

Hotel/Restaurante Los Mangos

▽ To Hotel Amor de Mar & Cabo Blanco

published by the SPN, *Sugerencias al visitante del distrito de Cóbano* ("Suggestions for visiting the Cóbano area"), which, despite the Spanish title, is in both English and Spanish. As well as offering tips on excursions and activities, it outlines the general objectives of the local residents in terms of preserving their natural environment. A ferry and *lancha* schedule is printed on the back. Ask at the SPN office in San José.

Many businesses, including the information kiosk, **close down** for the afternoon, between noon, 1pm and 4pm. Bring lots of **colones**, as Montezuma is not really set up to change dollars or travellers' cheques, although the souvenir stores will accept the latter.

Montezuma has recently switched over from the old **telephone system**, whereby a central number (☎661-1122) served the whole of the southern peninsula, each business and resident being assigned an extension. Many places now have their own private numbers, but the system is still in flux. If you can't get through on any of the numbers that we've listed, call the local operator (☎113), ask for the Montezuma number, and request the establishment by name. The operator will give you the new number and connect you.

If you're heading on **to Puntarenas**, buy your ticket for the *Simba Express* (leaves 7am) from *Hotel el Jardín* or the information kiosk by the parking lot.

Accommodation

New places to stay are springing up every day in Montezuma, it seems. **Prices**, in the main, have remained moderate, as the village still caters to a young, studenty crowd who can't afford the outrageous rates of, say, Manuel Antonio. Though there's less of a high season/low season schism here than in most places, prices in some of the more upscale hotels do drop in the **low season**, by about $10 to $15. The cheaper accommodation tends to cost the same all year round.

Reservations are essential in the dry season. That said, this can be next to impossible to pull off. Although most of the places listed below now have their own private line, it can be difficult to reach hotels direct by phone, and the lines regularly go down. Mail, also, can take for ever. If you don't manage to book in advance, make sure you arrive as early as possible. Things are easier in the rainy season, when, although you'll do better to reserve, it's not quite so dire if you arrive at night without a room.

Staying in the **village** is convenient, saving you from having to walk in the dark back to your lodging, but it can be noisy, due to the shenanigans at *Chico's Bar*. Elsewhere it's wonderfully peaceful, with choices out on the **beach,** on the road that heads southwest to the Cabo Blanco Refuge, and on the sides of the steep hill about 1km above the village.

Hotel Amor de Mar, 600m southwest of village centre on beach (ext 262). Seafront hotel, in pretty landscaped gardens set on a rocky promontory, with hammocks swinging between giant mango trees. There's a small restaurant downstairs, and some rooms have kitchenette. Rooms upstairs and facing the sea are best, with nice views and cross-breezes. ⑤.

Hotel la Aurora, in the village (☎642-0051; fax 642-0025). Pleasant, environmentally conscious *pensión*, run by friendly Angela Jiménez, one of the driving forces in the local community. All rooms have mosquito nets or screens, fans, communal fridge, coffee- and tea-making facilities. Upstairs rooms, a little more expensive, have ceiling fans, cross-breezes, and hammocks. ②–③.

Hotel el Jardín, in the village (☎ and fax 642-2320). Attractive, spacious rooms with wooden ceilings, tiled bathrooms, verandahs or terraces with Sarchí leather rocking chairs. Some have fridges, and the upstairs rooms have a lovely view over the town and sea. ⑤.

Pensión Jenny, in the village (no phone). Good budget option, with basic rooms with shared bath, in a house on the side of the road, overlooking the beach. Upstairs rooms are quite large, and there's a verandah with a hammock. ①.

Cabinas/Pensión Lucy, in the village (no phone). A Montezuma stalwart that the government once attempted to have torn down, as it violates the *zona marítima*, which says you can't build on the first 50m of beach. Clean and basic, with cold water showers, and a nice seaside verandah upstairs. Pictures of autumnal New England adorn the walls. ①–②.

Los Mangos, 800m south of *Montezuma*, on road to Cabo Blanco (ext 258). Some bungalows, made out of what looks like very expensive wood, which makes them a bit dark, with large (hot water) showers, fan and palm roof. The cheaper rooms – the best are upstairs – in the main building down by the road are good value, particularly for groups of 4 or 6. The only hotel in town with a pool, and a good poolside restaurant (see below). ③–⑤.

Hotel Montezuma, in the centre of the village (ext 258). Popular with budget travellers, this is the cheapest place in town with shared bath (prices hike significantly for private bath) and ceiling fans. Management is not that friendly, however, and there's noise from *Chico's Bar* next door. Go for the upstairs rooms if you want to sleep. Accepts *Visa*. ②.

Hotel Montezuma Pacífico (☎222-7746, or ☎ and fax 642-0204). As usual, upstairs rooms are better, and more expensive; choose those with fans rather than a/c. Small lounge with TV, and breakfast area (in low season breakfast is included in room price). Also laundry and bike rental. Rooms with kitchen are planned. ④.

Sano Banano Cabinas, 15-min walk northeast of the centre, on the beach – ask for Patricia or Lenny in the restaurant of the same name for directions (☎642-0068; fax 642-0272). Truly wonderful circular cabinas with thatched roof, beachfront balcony, outside shower and kitch-enette. This is the place to stay if you want seclusion and don't mind the crabs who do the best to infiltrate your room. Bring a torch. ④–⑤.

Cabinas Tucán, in the village (☎642-0284). Good value, adequately clean, basic rooms in two-storey wooden house. Shared baths and ceiling or table fans, but no curtains. Upstairs rooms are marginally better. ②.

The village and around

There's nothing much to do in Montezuma itself, and even the swimming isn't that great, hampered by rocks and occasionally heavy surf. The **beach** features a lovely **nature trail** (1500m; 30min), founded by the late Karen Morgenson and her husband Olof Weissburg, conservationists and long-time residents of the area. Heading northeast, dipping in and out of several coves, up and down littoral vegetation, it ends at **Playa Grande**, a reasonable swimming beach, decent for surfing, with a small waterfall at its eastern edge. It's utterly deserted, usually – go early in the morning for the most solitude.

There are a number of interesting places to **shop** in Montezuma. *Ecofund*, run by a local cooperative, sells tiger balm – an all-purpose herbal remedy, especially good for sprains and muscle ache – and condoms, along with the usual T-shirts, sandals, hats and sunblock. The small shop next to *Monteaventuras* has some beautiful **Indonesian** sarongs and dresses, at better prices ($25 for a dress) than elsewhere – Manuel Antonio for example – as does the souvenir shop next to the *abastecedor* (general store), modelled to nice effect by the young women running the place. For **crafts** and **jewellery**, head for the streetside stalls between the bus stop and *Sano Banano* cabinas.

Montezuma and its environs is laced with a number of **waterfalls**, the closest of which is about a kilometre walk down the road towards Cabo Blanco and then another 800m on a path through the dense growth (signed). Bring your swimsuit, as you may be able to bathe – but always take care with waterfalls, especially in the wet season, on account of **flash floods**. If you insist on climbing the rocks by the waterfall, take care; people slip and have accidents every year, and one person was killed a few years ago. Local tour operators lead **horseback rides** to falls that are otherwise difficult or impossible to reach on foot.

Isla Tortuga (see p.277), off the coast of the peninsula, near Curú, is a popular place to snorkel, swim safely in calm and warm shallow waters, and sunbathe. Local boatmen can take you there and back for quite a bit less than you'd pay with one of the "cruise ship" companies doing the run from San José or

---

TOURS AND TREKS FROM MONTEZUMA

The **information kiosk**, when it is open (it is likely to be closed in low season, especially midweek) can advise regarding guides for the hike to nearby **waterfalls**, **horse rentals** for riding along the beach ($5–7/hr) and **boat trips** via the local boatmen's cooperative association to Isla Mercadoa, Isla Tortuga, Puntarenas, and around the west coast of the peninsula to Playa Sámara. They will also point you to places that rent **bikes** ($10/day).

Monteaventuras organize guided **walks** (30–90min) and **horseback** rides (4hr) to the **waterfalls**, snorkelling trips to **Isla Tortuga,** and a wildlife tour to Cabo Blanco (4hr natural history walks with qualified guide cost $15, transport included). They also rent **snorkelling** gear ($25/hr) and **scuba** equipment ($40/hr), **motorbikes** and **cars** (from $40 per day for motorbikes; $75 for a 4WD).

Puntarenas, although tours from Montezuma are less posh. Drinks, for instance, may be included, although lunch is usually not. Best to stock up in the village and ask the boatmen if they have a cooler you can use.

The single most popular excursion in town, however, is probably to the **Cabo Blanco** Reserve for a morning's walking. Although you can do this independently if you have your own (4WD) transport, most people take a tour or go on the clapped-out bus (see p.284). If you like **mountain biking** you could ride the 9km down to Cabo Blanco, walk the trails and bike back in a day. Mind the height of the two creeks en route, though, as you won't get through them at high tide.

Eating, drinking and nightlife

Just a few years ago all you could get to eat in Montezuma was fantastically fresh **fish**, practically right off the hook. This is still on offer, of course, along with vegetarian pizza, granola, mango shakes and paella, not to mention more exotic dishes. Eating three meals a day will set you back a few colones, though; Montezuma's accommodation may still be moderately priced, but food is a little on the **expensive** side. Many of the best places are linked to the hotels and cabinas; if you're staying at the *Sano Banano*, you can cut costs by grabbing pasta, sauce and a cold beer from the small grocery store in the centre of the village, and a papaya or two at the *pulpería* a few metres east.

For one of the **best restaurants** on the peninsula, head to **CABUYA**, the first hamlet beyond Montezuma on the way to Cabo Blanco. Here *El Ancla de Oro* dishes up the most delicious **lobster** in the •country, served in garlic butter (around $10). The red snapper is cheaper and just as good. They also have a few, simple **rooms** (①). The road to Cabuya is very bad, and you can only be guaranteed of getting there in the dry season (Dec–April) – even then, only with 4WD. Transport may be laid on from Montezuma village: ask at the information kiosk.

Nightlife in Montezuma centres around *Chico's Bar*, where the only thing to do is hang out and drink. More retiring types can take in the very popular nightly video shows at the *Sano Banano* (in English) at 7.30pm. You have to spend at least $2 in the restaurant to get in. The noticeboard outside *Monteaventuras* announces local dances and events.

Restaurante el Jardín, next to *Hotel el Jardín*. Espresso, good fruit drinks and semi-veggie dishes, including stuffed zucchini and burritos. The spaghetti and shrimp and fish fillet in ranchera sauce are good value.

Restaurante Pensión Jenny. Small restaurant in the back of the *pensión*, serving cheap *típico* food. Closed 2–4pm.

Restaurante Los Mangos, at the *Los Mangos* hotel. Nice poolside location with relentlessly cosmopolitan food, much of it Mediterranean: pastas, salads, seafood and the like. Friendly atmosphere and a good sound system in an open rancho-style building.

Restaurante Montezuma, in *Hotel Montezuma*. The Spanish chef cooks great paella and seafood, and they also serve delicious fresh bread. Lovely situation, upstairs, under palm trees and looking out to sea.

Soda el Parque, fronting the beach. Small soda, underneath the palms, serving great fresh fish – snapper, lobster, bass in garlic and oil – and traditional *gallo pinto* breakfasts. Avoid eating the *cambute* (conch), though, as it's on the verge of extinction and consumption is technically prohibited. Daily 7–10am & 6–9pm.

Soda la Playa, 700m west of *Hotel Montezuma*. Local foods – *gallo pinto*, *casados*, rice dishes for breakfast, lunch and dinner daily. Their small terrace overlooks the beach.

Sano Banano, middle of the village. Filling lunch specials of fish, baked potato, bread with garlic butter and salad, for around $6. Also crepes, vegetarian pizzas, vegetable *casados* with lentil fritters, yoghurt and beans. If you have nothing else, try a mango shake.

Reserva Natural Absoluta Cabo Blanco

RESERVA NATURAL ABSOLUTA CABO BLANCO (Wed–Sun 8am–4pm; $3), 9km southwest of Montezuma, is Costa Rica's oldest protected piece of land, established in 1963 by Karen Morgenson, a Danish immigrant to Costa Rica, and her Swedish husband Olof. Its name – the "absolute" bit – derives from the fact that, until 1989, no visitors were allowed here.

At 1172 hectares, Cabo Blanco occupies the entire southwest tip of the peninsula. The natural beauty of the area is complemented by its unique biodiversity, with pockets of **Pacific lowland tropical forest** of a type and mix that are found nowhere else in the country. It used to be said that animals in Cabo Blanco were more demonstrative than in any other Park or protected area in Costa Rica, a fact possibly explained by the lack of visitors until 1989. Even in the ensuing couple of years few people made the long trek out here. These days, however, as Montezuma's popularity has stepped up, so has demand for Cabo Blanco, to a degree that few, including founder Karen Morgenson (who died in 1994), expected. The more people that have flooded in, the shyer the animals have become, and there's now talk of imposing daily limits on visitors – about forty, probably – and/or closing the Reserve one or two days a week. Animals that live here include howler monkeys, plus sloths and squirrels. Agoutis and coati are common, as are snakes – so watch your step. Sea birds nest down by the shore, using the islands off the very tip of the peninsula as their prime site, and you'll often see clouds of frigate birds hovering above.

The **trail** (5km; 2hr) leads from the ranger station through tropical deciduous forest to **Playa Cabo Blanco** and **Playa Balsitas**; not great for swimming, but two very lovely, lonely spots. Be wary of the high tide – *marea* – ask the ranger at the entrance when and where you are likely to get cut off if walking on the beach. It's very **hot**: 30°C is not uncommon, so bring a hat, some water and sunblock.

Practicalities

There's an old road-hardened **bus** between Montezuma and Cabo Blanco, leaving from the side of Montezuma's *parqueo* (Wed–Sun 8am & 10am). This service may not run in the rainy season if it has been very wet. Though **roads** down to Cabo Blanco are bad, you can drive there with 4WD. Watch the two creeks, however, which are too deep – even for most 4WDs – at high tide.

You pay your entrance fee at the ranger hut, where they can also supply you with a map of the trail. There's no real need to take a **guide**, but if you would like one, the information kiosk in Montezuma can recommend local people. No camping is allowed, but there are a number of **places to stay** on the road from Montezuma. Fernando Morales' house about 5km southwest of Montezuma, and Sr Guevara's house, 500m before you reach the Cabo Blanco entrance, have **rooms** (①–②) and good **campgrounds**.

North of Cabo Blanco

Surfers with 4WD can try heading to **Manzanillo**, a great surfing beach on the western side of the peninsula. There are few facilities, and the beach is likely to be deserted, with long waves similar to Playa Junquillal in the north (see p.241). In the rainy season the drive really is not recommended, however: the creeks – at least a dozen of them – that cut the dirt road between Malpaís, Manzanillo and Sámara are likely to be high enough that you'll be pushing it in anything less than a Land Rover or large truck.

Roads all over this part of the peninsula are confusing, in bad shape, and liable to be nearly impassable in the rainy season. It's just about possible to get around in the dry season, with a good road map, some Spanish and camping gear – not to mention a 4WD. Some people, certainly locals, drive from Cóbano up to **Carmona** in the northeast, or from Manzanillo north to **Sámara**, but neither is an interesting enough drive to make it worth the trouble.

South of Puntarenas

On the mainland, south of Puntarenas, the coast road, sometimes marked as the **Costañera Sur**, leads down to Quepos and continues, in various states of paving, south to Dominical (covered in our *Zona Sur* chapter). At first the landscape is sparse and hilly, with the coast coming into view only intermittently. The road improves considerably once the huge trucks heading to the container docks and refineries at Puerto Caldera get out of the way. As soon as you cross the wide mouth of the Río Tárcoles, you come to the **Reserva Biológica Carara**, known for its rich birdlife. There are a number of lovely old ranches to stay in nearby, probably a better bet than the run-of-the-mill hotels at the resort town of **Jacó**. South of here, running down the coast from the hamlet of Parrita to Quepos, you enter a long corridor of **African palm oil plantations**, a surreal landscape of brooding, thick-girthed stout palms, imported for commercial growth.

Reserva Biológica Carara and Río Tárcoles

RESERVA BIOLÓGICA CARARA, 90km west of San José (daily 8am–4pm), is ecologically significant, a transition area between the hot tropical lowlands of Guanacaste and the humid, more verdant climate of the southern Pacific coast. Consequently, Carara teems with **wildlife**, much if it of the unnerving sort: huge crocodiles lounge in the bankside mud of the Río Tárcoles, and snakes (19 out of Costa Rica's 22 poisonous species) go about their business. Mammals include monkeys, agoutis and the big cats – the latter, of course, are very rarely seen. **Birding** is very good, however, and this is one of the best places in the country to witness the brightly coloured **scarlet macaw** in its natural habitat. Each night at twilight, around 5 or 5.30pm, they migrate from the lowland tropical forest areas to the swampy mangroves, setting flight from the tree branches and soaring off in a burst of red and blue against the darkening sky. Among other birds that frequent the treetops, you may see tóucans, trogons and guans, while riverside birds include herons, anhingas and storks. For migratory-bird-spotters, the **best time** to come is, as usual, the dry season, from December to April. Whatever time of the year you are here, it's a good idea to go with a nature **guide** in order to spot wildlife, and particularly birds. They can also take you into restricted areas where tourists are not allowed on their own.

Getting to Carara

Carara is reached **from San José** by taking the Orotina highway and turning left at the bridge on the Río Tárcoles. It's a drive of less than three hours. You will see many cars parked at the entrance; usually birders with binoculars trained on the river, or croc-spotters pointing at the lazing reptiles. From here it's 3km to the **ranger station**, where you pay your entrance fee. Staff have basic maps on hand

and will answer questions about the wildlife. There are also toilets and picnic tables. Recently Carara has been a magnet for **thieves** breaking into unattended cars, and vehicles should be left at the *parqueo* at the ranger station.

Carara is on the itineraries of a number of tour operators, and included in most of the serious **birding tours** from North America and the UK. In San José *Geotur* (☎234-1867; fax 253-6338) and *Costa Rica Expeditions* (☎257-0766) offer all-inclusive tours with trained guides (knowledgeable in the natural history of the area) transport and a small lunch for about $75. Another option, if you are staying there, is to take one of the boat tours from the *Dundee Ranch Hotel* (see below), on which you can spot crocodiles and river-borne bird life.

It's extremely **hot** at Carara, especially at midday, when 30°C temperatures are common, and it receives a good amount – 30mm – of rain per year, most of it in the rainy season. Take a hat, sunscreen and rain gear.

Accommodation

Although **camping** is not allowed, there are a number of very good accommodation options **near Carara**, a couple of them on working or former **ranches** with their own land. They all offer **birding tours** – *Tarcol Lodge* is one of the premier birding destinations in the country – and a couple of them are great destinations for horseriding and hiking. All are accessible to independent travellers.

Hacienda Doña Marta, Cascajal, near Orotina (☎253-6514; fax 269-9555; Aptdo 23-3009, Santa Barbara de Heredia). Family-run, working dairy farm with hectares of forest and river-side land. Offers horseriding and birding, and tours to Carara, 10min away. New cabinas, surrounding a pool, and home cooking served in the hacienda house. You'll need to reserve, and pay 30 days in advance. Good-value packages available, with meals, tours of the farm and horseriding included. ⑤.

Dundee Ranch Hotel, Cascajal, near Orotina (☎428-8776 or 8096; fax 267-7050; Aptdo 7812-1000, San José). Lovely former cattle ranch. Guests stay in the old ranch house. Recommended for enthusiastic riders and hikers, as the *peones* who work on the mango farm can take you on horse rides through rivers, rainforest, beautiful dry forest and mango planta-tions, with an abundance of wildlife all around. They also run trips to Carara, and have their own lake, fitted out with decks for great bird-spotting. The good restaurant serves food grilled to your liking, and there's a lovely pool. ⑤.

Tarcol Lodge, on the south bank of the Tárcoles (☎ and fax 267-7138; in US: Dept 1425, PO Box 025216, Miami, FL 33102-5216). Entirely dedicated to the needs of birdwatchers. At high tide the lodge is surrounded on three sides by water; the birds really come out, however, when the tide retreats and sand flats attract thousands of species. Local tours, all meals, lodg-ing and transport from San José included in their prices. ⑥.

Playa Jacó

The best thing you can say about **PLAYA JACÓ** is that, at just two or three hours away (102km), it's the closest beach to San José. Other than that, it's got little going for it. An old seaside resort, Jacó attracts a mix of surfers, weekenders and holidaying Ticos, from party-hearty students to working-class families. The other major presence – you'll notice the ingratiating flags flown everywhere – are Canadians, who descend during the winter on package tours.

If you have dreams of swimming in the Pacific off pristine white sands, don't come to Jacó. For one, the water is reported to be polluted near the estuaries, and elsewhere it can be dangerous. However, if you are stuck in San José and desper-ate to get to a beach, there are fast and frequent buses and good weekend specials at the larger hotels like *Jacófiesta* and *Jacó Beach*, both of which have swimming pools. Despite the caveats, Jacó remains popular, and you'll need reservations during the high season, especially at weekends.

Arrival and information

From San José **buses** leave for Jacó at 7.15am and 3.30pm daily. There are extra buses on holidays and holiday weekends but if you intend on travelling between Friday and Sunday, especially in the high season (Dec–April) or on holidays, buy your ticket three days in advance. Though the bus officially stops at the extreme north end of the village, by *Hotel el Jardín*, it does in fact continue 3km down the main street backing the town. If you know more or less where you want to get off and/or have gear, it's best to stay on until the bus finally terminates. If you are booked at the *Hotel Jacó Beach,* you can take their daily shuttle bus from the *Hotel Irazú,* just outside San José on the way to Alajuela; ask the hotel for details. Alternatively, a luxurious private bus, *American Limo Bus* leaves San José at 9am daily. This doesn't leave you enough time for a day trip, however, as it returns from Jacó at 2pm (☎222–8134; about $25).

The Jacó **tourist office**, on the main road, has information on accommodation, and local bus schedules. If you've come for the day, head to the *Nucleo de Turistas Bribrí*, where a locker, access to showers, toilets and parking will set you back $1. The *Banco Nacional* and the *Banco de Costa Rica* (both Mon–Fri 9am–3pm) can change **travellers' cheques**. Outside hours, head to any sizable hotel in this seasoned gringo town. The *ICE* office (Mon–Sat 8am–noon & 1–5pm) offers a **fax** and **phone** service to Europe and the US. Next door, the self-serve **laundry** has hot water, free soap and coin-operated machines.

Getting around

A **shuttle bus** runs through Jacó from the *Hotel Jacó Beach*, at the extreme north end of town. It leaves at 9am, 10.30am, 2pm, 3.30pm and 5pm; there's a flat fare of $1. Yell "¡parada!" when you want to get off. There's an abundance of places to **rent motorbikes**. More environmentally sound by far is to rent a **mountain bike** (though note that no bikes are allowed on the beach). Try *Fun Rentals*, next to the *Restaurante Flamboyant* on the main boulevard. You can also rent a **car**, to get, for example, to Manuel Antonio (although you can get there just fine by bus). *ADA* (☎643-3207), *Budget* (☎643-3112) and *Elegante* (☎643-3224) all have offices here, though prices are higher than in San José.

Accommodation

Jacó features a hodge-podge of places to stay, from **cabinas** catering to weekending hordes to a couple of older, all-inclusive **resort hotels**. In general, be prepared to pay far more than either the town or, in some cases, the accommodation, merits. At the really big hotels you can expect some sort of **discount** – up to 50 percent on the prices we've listed – for low-season (May–Nov) weekends. Keep an eye on the *Tico Times, Costa Rica Today* and *La Nación* for big splashy adverts. In addition, many places are geared up towards **surfers**, offering discounts in the low season, when the surf is at its best. You'll need to **reserve** at holiday times, like Easter and Christmas, and weekends, for any of the places listed below.

The large **campground** at *Tropical Camping* at the north end of Jacó, near the San José bus stop, has toilets, showers and picnic tables (about $4 per night). It gets crowded during Costa Rican holidays. *Camping Madrigal*, at the southern end of the beach has shade, toilet and showers ($3).

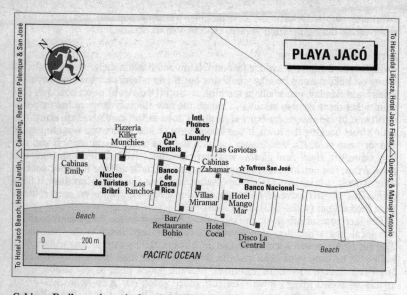

Cabinas Emily, on the main drag (☎643-3513 or 3328). Friendly hotel, filled with surfers on a budget, with rooms with rickety beds, shared bath and heated water. Also a restaurant. ③.

Cocal, off the main drag, towards the sea (☎643-3067; fax ☎643-3082). Rooms around a pool in nice tropical gardens. All have private bath and hot water, ceiling fans or a/c at a surcharge. Some have sea views. ⑤–⑥.

Las Gaviotas, off the main drag (☎ and fax 643-3092). Spick and span rooms with balconies, patios and small kitchens, all with private bath and hot water. There's a pool, too. ⑤.

Hotel Jacó Beach, north end of town (☎220-1441; fax 232-3159). King of the package holiday league. If you can get an off-season or weekend discount (breakfast included) it's worth it for the facilities alone: large clean pool, restaurant and disco, as well as kayaking, sportsfishing and sailiing lessons. Typically soulless rooms with private bath and a/c. ⑦.

Jacó Fiesta, south end of town (☎643-3147; fax 643-3148). Big package hotel, modern and efficient, with clean rooms with private bath, hot water, a/c, well-equipped kitchenettes and cable TV. Several swimming pools and a good restaurant. ⑦.

Hotel el Jardín, 100m from the official San José bus stop (☎643-3050). Good value, nice rooms with private bath and ceiling fans. Friendly owners and a French restaurant. ④.

Mango Mar, off the main drag, towards the sea (☎643-3670). Modern complex in beachside grounds, popular with package groups in the winter but offering good low-season rates. Spotless rooms with private bath, hot water and fans. Kitchenettes cost extra. The upstairs rooms have good views, and there's a small pool and jacuzzi. ④.

Villas Miramar, off the main drag, towards the sea (☎643-3003). One of the nicer upscale places, with landscaped gardens and a pool. Quiet, clean rooms, with kitchenettes and bathrooms with hot water. ⑤.

Los Ranchos, 50m west of *Banco de Costa Rica* (☎ and fax 643-3070). Friendly cabinas set around a pool, very popular with surfers and students. A variety of rooms and prices, from upstairs loft rooms, some with kitchenettes, to two-floor bungalows with kitchens. All are well-screened, with fans, and there's laundry service. Good value for groups. ③–⑤.

Cabinas Zabamar, just off the main drag, north of the San José bus stop (☎643-3174). Nicely equipped, well-screened rooms; choice of cold water and ceiling fans or hot water and a/c ($10 more). Also a good swimming pool. ④–⑤.

The Town and around

Jacó straggles along for about 3km, backed by one long avenida and with a few individual roads that head for the beach but never quite make it, petering out in groves of small palms or in dead ends. The beach itself has unattractive chocolate-brown sand, strewn with huge hunks of driftwood, and is notorious for its dangerous rip tides, with quite heavy surf – bad for swimming but wonderful for **surfing**, with some mean lefts and rights.

Jacó makes a good base for the many (most of them better) surfing beaches nearby. Little **Playa Herradura**, 7km north, deserves a mention particularly, not only for its good beach breaks; it also has the dubious distinction of having been a major location in *1492: Conquest of Paradise*, starring Gérard Depardieu. You can still see the remains of one of the docks built for the shoot – the film was obviously a big deal for the community, and locals still shake their heads in dismay at the antics of the cast and crew. Most visitors come to Herradura for the day or stay in Jacó, as there's nothing much in the way of accommodation.

South of Jacó, the wild and wave-crashed beaches – Playa Hermosa a couple of kilometres south, and continuing on to Esterillos Oeste, Esterillos Este and Bejuco – are of interest only to surfers: swimmers will get clobbered by waves and harassed by rip tides. You'll need 4WD to get to them, as the little roads leading off the Costañera Sur can be tricky in the rainy (best surfing) season. It's perfectly possible to beach-hop, but don't expect much in the way of accommodation between Jacó and Quepos.

A number of operators in town offer **tours** to Carara Biological Reserve, and perhaps some horseback riding and surfing. *Fantasy Tours* (☎643-3211) also run cruises on their own boat out from Jacó. *Horseback Riding Tours*, by the *Supermarket Rayo Azul* (☎643-3248), leads rides into the surrounding forest and on the beach. *Jacó Beach Central Tours* (☎643-3510) offers reasonably priced sportsfishing and snorkelling tours, inclusive of gear and beer.

Eating, drinking and nightlife

When it comes to **eating** in Jacó, there's a sharp divide between the places frequented by locals and the *turista* establishments. Though a number of the hotels have very good restaurants, as always in Costa Rica, if you're on a budget, make the lunchtime *casado* or *plato del día* your main meal. Some of the better **sodas** frequented by locals include *Restaurante Casita del Maíz*, which serves good *casados* made with fresh ingredients, and *Restaurante Doña Cecilia*, recommended for lunchtime specials.

For **breakfast**, head to *El Bosque* for *gallo pinto* and *huevos revueltos* and coffee – they may even have pancakes. Of the **restaurants**, *Bar y Restaurante Bohio*, right on the beach, is a great place for an evening drink, with a *típico* menu heavy on the rice. Check out the church-pew benches and tables, all under a ranch roof. They sometimes lay on a – very loud – disco. *Pizzería Killer Munchies* is, as the name suggests, a popular tourist place with fancy pizzas, including vegetarian and Hawaiian. *Restaurante/Grill Flamboyant,* on the main street, has a varied lunchtime menu of *típico* food. If you're craving upscale, **international** cuisine, *El Jardín* is the nicest (and most expensive) place to eat in Jacó, offering French food with sea views; you'll need to reserve for dinner on weekends. *Le Café de Paris* has espresso, cappuccino, croissants and omelettes, while *El Gran Palenque* serves good, pricey, Spanish food with flamenco guitar accompaniment (closed Tues).

MOVING ON FROM JACÓ

For San José, buses leave Jacó's north-end bus stop daily at 5am and 3pm (2hr 30min–3hr). It's also possible to continue to Quepos and the Manuel Antonio area by walking the 2km out to the Costañera Sur and flagging down the Puntarenas–Quepos or San José–Manuel Antonio buses that pass on the highway. Buses from Puntarenas to Quepos pass by about ninety minutes after departure (see p.276). Just to be sure, get out there on the highway twenty minutes early. Local people can help you out with directions and bus schedules.

Sedate during midweek in low season, Jacó transforms itself into beer-drinking-contest hell during the holidays. **Discos** are only really busy on weekends, especially during peak season and on holidays, when they get packed. Those at *Jacófiesta* and *Hotel Jacó Beach* are the swankiest, but usually open only on weekends. *Disco la Central*, on the beach right in the centre of town, is the most popular with gringos. *Upe's Disco* is more traditional, with music ranging from salsa, merengue, soca and calypso to a few House tunes.

Quepos and Parque Nacional Manuel Antonio

With one of the most stunning, picture-postcard backdrops in the country, the small corridor between the old banana-exporting town of **Quepos** and the little community of **Manuel Antonio** outside the **Parque Nacional Manuel Antonio**, has experienced one of the most dramatic tourist booms in the country. In addition to the huge variety of things to do – walking the Park's easy trails, whitewater rafting, ocean cruising and horseback riding, to name but a few – this is one of the lushest places in Costa Rica, with spectacular white-grey sand beaches fringed by thickly forested green hills. The beauty of the area is due in part to the unique **tómbolo** formation of **Punta Catedral**, which juts out into the Pacific from the Park. A rare geophysical phenomenon, a *tómbolo* results when an island becomes joined, slowly and over millennia, to the mainland, through accumulated sand deposits. Other smaller islands, some of them no more than rocky outcroppings, straggle off from Punta Catedral and, from high up in the hills, watching a fantastic sunset flower and die over the Pacific, it does seem as though Manuel Antonio is one of the more charmed places on earth.

That said, the huge tourist input has undeniably taken its toll on the whole area. The tiny village of Manuel Antonio has been practically drowned in a sea of hotels, cabinas, restaurants and bars and, in particular, there has been general concern over an inadequate to non-existent sewage system, which often causes fears that the area's waters are being **polluted**. Considering the number of tourists heading this way, the road from Jacó is in pretty bad condition, with entire sections of asphalt washed out and daunting potholes lying in wait for reckless drivers. It improves dramatically beyond the nondescript town of **Parrita**, where it runs through a surreal landscape of brooding **African oil palms** on plantations owned by United Brands. From here it's in better condition than your average airport runway, complete with meridian markings and Catseyes – almost unknown in Costa Rica. Bridges along this stretch are either in progress or periodically washed out, however, and driving is subject to delays as you wait to cross yet another makeshift bridge. Along with the forests of oil palms, you'll pass a series of "Company" villages, with identical two-storey bungalows on stilts, arranged around soccer fields. Bright blue once, but long since bleached to a uniform grey/green, the bungalows were originally built for the banana workers, before the onset of Panama disease in the 1950s ravaged the fruit plantations. Today they're bunkhouses for oil-palm workers and managers.

Quepos

Arriving at the town of **QUEPOS** it's immediately apparent that you've crossed into the lush, wetter southern Pacific region. The vegetation is thicker and greener than further north, and more often than not it has just started or just finished raining. Backed up against a thick hill, with a muddy beach in front (obscured by the seaside road out to the old dock), Quepos can look pretty ramshackle. Luckily it's a friendly place, a good place to meet fellow travellers, and with plenty of places to stay, eat and drink. The name "Quepos" derives from the indigenous language of the Quepoa people, part of the larger Borucas (or Bruncas, as they are sometimes called) group, who occupied this area for at least 1000 years before the arrival of Juan Vásques de Coronado in 1563. After the invasion the Quepoa went into predictably swift decline due to disease and enslavement.

Once a banana-exporting town, Quepos was severely hit by Panama disease, which caused United Fruit to pull out. It's had something of a resurgence in recent decades, with the importation of the African oil palms, and has also developed as one of the country's prime **sportsfishing** destinations. The waters around these parts are stuffed with big, hard-fighting fish, apt to set records for poundage caught. Of all the sportsfishing grounds in Costa Rica, the Quepos area has the most variety: Spanish mackerel, sailfish, wahoo, yellowfin tuna, dorado, blue marlin, white tip shark and cubera snapper among them. Posh sportfishing boats anchor in Blue Bay in front of town, and you will see drawings of marlin and other big-game fish all around the place, as well as many small tour agencies that cater more or less exclusively to sportsfishers.

Most important is its proximity to **Parque Nacional Manuel Antonio** and its beaches, 7km south. In comparison to the establishments along the road to the Park entrance, lodgings and restaurants in Quepos are quite affordable, and there are frequent buses to the Park, making it the most useful base in the area. English signs and menus in English proliferate; it looks like everyone's involved in the tourist trade. That said, other than sportsfishing, or simply hanging out, there's nothing to do in town – illustrated by the disaffected youth hanging out on the stone benches along the main drag or whizzing their mountain bikes back and forth to the old banana docks.

Arrival and orientation

Buses from San José's La Coca-Cola to Quepos (currently 7am, 10am, 2pm & 4pm daily; 4hr) are slower than the direct service, also leaving from La Coca-Cola, to Manuel Antonio (daily 6am, noon & 6pm; 3hr 30min). The latter continues beyond Quepos, dropping people off along the seven-kilometre stretch of road between the town and the Park entrance, and is convenient if you are staying at one of the hotels scattered between the two. For weekends, holidays and any time during the dry season, you need to buy your bus ticket for the Manuel

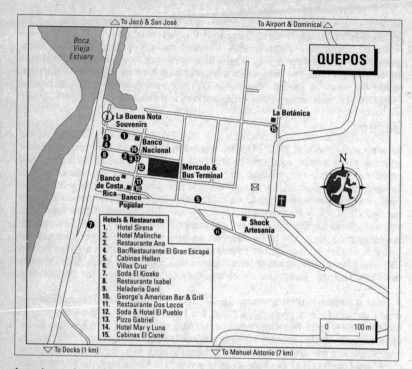

To Jacó & San José △   To Airport & Dominical △

Boca
Vieja
Estuary

QUEPOS

N

La Buena Nota
Souvenirs   La Botánica

Banco
Nacional

Mercado &
Bus Terminal

Banco
de Costa
Rica   Banco
Popular

Shock
Artesanía

Hotels & Restaurants
1. Hotel Sirena
2. Hotel Malinche
3. Restaurante Ana
4. Bar/Restaurante El Gran Escape
5. Cabinas Hellen
6. Villas Cruz
7. Soda El Kiosko
8. Restaurante Isabel
9. Heladería Daní
10. George's American Bar & Grill
11. Restaurante Dos Locos
12. Soda & Hotel El Pueblo
13. Pizza Gabriel
14. Hotel Mar y Luna
15. Cabinas El Cisne

0   100 m

▽ To Docks (1 km)   ▽ To Manuel Antonio (7 km)

Antonio service at least three days in advance, and your return ticket as soon as you arrive. All buses arrive in Quepos at the busy **terminal**, which doubles as the mercado, just one block east of the "centre". The **ticket office** is open daily (Mon–Sat 7–11am & 1–5pm, Sun 7–11am & 1–4pm).

Driving to Quepos, it's easy to miss the town and find yourself out on an old abandoned dock with nowhere to go but the Pacific. The entrance is actually on the left-hand side, down a narrow slip road, just after you cross the bridge.

You can **fly** in from San José with *Sansa* or *Travelair*, though flights are often booked weeks in advance, especially in the dry season. Quepos is also one of the most popular destinations in the country to charter an aircraft (see *Basics*, p.23). The airstrip is about 5km north of town.

Quepos does have street names – numbered avenidas and calles – but nobody uses them. The town itself is tiny, three blocks or so by four. "Downtown" consists of the main road along the front (sea side) and the three blocks that run around it. You can stumble off the bus right into a hotel, be in a good restaurant or bar in another two minutes, and then pick up the local bus service to Manuel Antonio in about another thirty seconds.

Information

Quepos has no official **tourist office**, although *La Buena Nota* souvenir shop, on the main street, 50m before the exit to San José (☎777-0345), functions as an information centre for the area, as well as selling foreign papers and magazines. Here you'll find the best selection of swimsuits, locally made and hand-crafted clothing, including some with *molas* (designs from the Panamanian Kuna peoples). They also sell film and the *New York Times*. There is a larger branch on the road to Manuel Antonio between the *Hotel Karahé* and the *Hotel Pisces* (☎777-1002). *Shock Artesanía*, on the south side of the soccer field, sells good **maps** of Costa Rica not found elsewhere, including wildlife guides, maps showing indigenous reservations and protected areas, along with crafts from Costa Rica and the rest of Central America. *La Botánica*, northeast of the centre (Mon–Fri 8am–4pm) is dedicated to all things **herbal**, including vanilla and sachets of herbal tea grown on the owner's nearby farm.

For **currency exchange**, head for the *Banco de Costa Rica*, 75m west of the mercado and bus terminal, or the *Banco Popular*, 25m south (both Mon–Fri 9am–3pm). Many businesses in town will change dollars. Note that there is a trend towards not accepting **credit cards** in the Manuel Antonio area – banking must be awkward – and where you can use a credit card, it will usually incur a 6 percent service charge. The **correo** (Mon–Fri 8am–5pm) is on the north side of the soccer field at the far western end of town. *Estrella Tours* (daily 8.30–10.30am & 4–6pm; ☎777-1286 or 1068) **rent bikes** at $5 per hour.

You have to take a few more precautions against **theft** in the Manuel Antonio area than in the rest of Costa Rica. Never leave anything on the beach when you are swimming and, if you take the bus, do not let anyone handle your luggage: best to keep it with you in the bus, too, if it is small enough to be put in the overhead rack, as things have been taken from the baggage compartments. Wherever you stay, ensure your hotel room is locked at all times.

Accommodation

Budget travellers will have a hard time in Quepos – and in the entire Manuel Antonio area – especially in the dry season, when hotels are full and charging their highest prices. Plan well ahead, and if you want to come here anywhere near **Christmas**, make sure you have **reserved** and **paid** at least three or four months in advance. As ever, things are cheaper and easier in the wet season. Despite the fact that so many hotels are very expensive, few take credit cards, so make sure you have plenty of **cash** – colones or dollars – and/or travellers' cheques.

Cabinas el Cisne (☎777-0590). Plain, good-value budget cabinas, away from the centre of town. Cement block rooms are slightly enlivened by the colourful painted floors; private bath, cold water and fans. ③.

Villas Cruz (☎777-0271). Friendly place with spacious, clean rooms with great mattresses and private bath; cold water only. ③.

Cabinas Hellen (☎777-0504). Owned by the same people as *Villas Cruz*, with clean cabinas in the back of a family home. Large rooms, with private bath, hot water and fridge, fans, small table and chairs, and a small patio; *dueños* will do laundry. Secure, and recommended for those travelling with children. Good single rates also. ②–③.

Hotel Malinche (☎777-0093). Modern, "American"-style, a/c rooms, with carpet, TV and balcony, and cheaper, older rooms with none of the above. All good value, especially for singles. If you don't like the first room they show you, ask to see another. ②–③.

Mar y Luna (☎777-0394). Central, friendly, budget hotel. Rooms have private bath, heated water and fans, and there's a small communal balcony, shared fridge and free coffee. ③.

Hotel el Pueblo (☎777-1003). Spanking clean new rooms, bright and basic, with private bath and fans. Above the spotless soda of the same name. ③.

Hotel Sirena (☎ and fax 777-0528). The only Quepos hotel with a pool; plus poolside bar and restaurant. Simple rooms – the nicest are upstairs – with private bath, hot water and a/c. They can fix up horseback-riding tours. Reserve by fax, and pay 8 days in advance. They'll pick you up at the airstrip. ⑤–⑥.

Eating and drinking

Even more than in the rest of Costa Rica, Quepos' eating scene is distinctly split into places owned by and geared towards gringos, and those owned by locals and frequented by Ticos. For cheap lunchtime *casados*, head for the sodas scattered around the **mercado**, or *Restaurante Ana*. **Fish** is predictably good – order grilled *pargo* (snapper), and you can't go wrong. You can also eat **"international"**, with macrobiotic, American and continental breakfasts at *Restaurante Isabel*, and burgers at *George's*.

Restaurante Ana, on the main street, south of *La Buena Nota*. Solid Tico soda for cheap, cheerful lunches – *arroz con camarones* in he-man portions. They also keep the music down.

Boquitos, above *Adobe Bike Rentals*. Popular second-storey bar, one of the best places to drink at night in Quepos.

TOURS FROM THE QUEPOS AREA

There is a huge variety of **tours** from the Quepos area. If you're staying at one of the upmarket hotels in town or on the road to Manuel Antonio, you can book any of the following from reception. Most of the day tours include equipment rental and guides where necessary, along with lunch and/or snacks.

Sportsfishing outfitters include *Bluefin Sportsfishing Charters*, across from the soccer field (☎777-1676), and *Costa Rican Dreams* (☎777-0593), next to *Restaurante Ana*.

You can theoretically visit **Bahía Drake and the Osa Peninsula** – including Isla del Caño just off the coast of Osa – from Quepos, although it's far cheaper to get there from Palmar (see p.314) or Golfito (see p.317) in the Zona Sur. *Lynch Tours* across from *Soda el Pueblo* (Mon–Fri 8am–6pm, Sun 9am–12.30pm) can take you to Corcovado, Drake Bay, Isla del Caño and Savegre, and organize horseriding tours, sportsfishing, and day cruises in the Quepos area. *Taximar* sea shuttle, across from *Hotel Malinche* (☎777-1647) runs to Corcovado, Drake Bay and Isla del Caño. They also go to Dominical, departing daily at 7am and returning at 4pm.

A variety of guided **horse rides** are offered by *Equus Stables* (contact them via the *Hotel Mariposa*, ☎777-0355; fax 777-0050), including a two-hour trek to the beach. *Rancho Savegre*, 17km south of Quepos (☎ and fax 777-0528; in USA: ☎1-800/355-BETY) also do a great day horseback tour through their farm, passing rivers, palm-oil plantations, rice fields, lowland tropical forests and mangroves around the Río Savegre. Good bilingual guides point out monkeys, crocodiles and birds; you end up on the beach, which is great for riding.

Rafting outfitters *Ríos Tropicales* have an office between Quepos and Manuel Antonio at *Centro "Si como No"* (☎ and fax 777-1262). They organize **sea kayaking** tours to the Isla Damas estuary just north of Quepos, along with a more challenging coastal paddle, and whitewater rafting on the Río Savegre (Class II and III, good for wildlife viewing) or on the Río Naranjo (Class III–IV, more difficult, with zigzag rapids). They also rent mountain bikes and sell **discounted tickets** to **Parque Nacional Manuel Antonio**. *High Tide Tours* (☎777-0403) do a three-hour **snorkelling** tour of Manuel Antonio, taking you to off-the-track coves, and sea kayaking along the beaches and coves of the surrounding coast. In Quepos, *Tarzan's Mother* (☎777-1257 or 0191) offer day cruises to see porpoises, marlin and other fish that jump about in the waters, and sunset **catamaran cruises**.

Many visitors to Quepos take the popular day trip to **Hacienda Barú**, a private hacienda-cum-nature-reserve much closer – 2km – to Dominical than Quepos (☎771-1903). They have a canopy observation platform, from where you get a birds' eye view of the upper rainforest canopy, and also offer horseback riding.

MOVING ON FROM QUEPOS

Buses to Manuel Antonio leave from the terminal at the mercado (15 daily; 20min) between 5.30am and 9.30pm; there are slightly fewer in the rainy season. For bus information, call ☎777-0263. **Taxis** line up at the rank at the south end of the terminal/mercado, or you can ring *Quepos Taxi* (☎777-0277) who will take you to the Park for $5.

San José, Puntarenas and San Isidro in the Zona Sur are reached over the new road via **Dominical**, 44km south of Quepos. You used to need a sturdy 4WD to negiotiate this terrible road, but it is currently being paved and should be passable to regular cars. From Quepos the service to **San José** (3hr 30min) currently departs at 5am, 8am, 2pm and 4pm. To **Puntarenas** buses leave at 4.30am, 10.30am and 3pm (3hr); and to **San Isidro**, at 5am and 1.30pm (3hr 30min).

A number of agencies sell **air** tickets. *Lynch Tours*, across from *Soda el Pueblo*, is the agent for *Sansa*, while *Costa Rican Dreams*, next to *Restaurante Ana*, sells *Travelair* tickets.

Heladería Dani, next to *Hotel Malinche*. Fresh fruit ice cream from a street-side window.

Dos Locos, southwest of the mercado. Cosmopolitan menu, including large healthy sandwiches, open-to-the-street with nice roadside tables and gringo clientele.

Pizza Gabriel, west of the mercado. Small, quiet restaurant with gingham tablecloths, serving nice, simple, fairly cheap pizzas.

George's American Bar and Grill, south of the mercado. Good, if fairly expensive, thick steaks and burgers. US-college-type atmosphere, augmented by cable TV from the US.

El Gran Escape, on the main street, south of *La Buena Nota*. Sportsfisherman's bar, with hundreds of photos of record marlin/wahoo catches on the walls. Closed Tues.

Restaurante Isabel, on the main street. Pleasant washed-out orange wooden house with soft wicker chairs. Serves macrobiotic breakfasts, salads, pasta and rice dishes. Friendly and fast service, and individual polystyrene coolers for your beer.

Soda el Kiosko, just across from the sea wall. Pleasant, floral-decorated open soda serving cheap and filling *gallo pinto* breakfasts and great *refrescos*.

Pirates Bar, round the corner from *Dos Locos*. Gringo hang-out, with big bar stock. Very popular and usually packed.

Soda el Pueblo, west of the mercado. Great, spotless soda, with huge menu and long hours (7am–midnight). The place to come if you're suffering a peanut butter craving.

Quepos to Parque Nacional Manuel Antonio

Southeast of Quepos, a seven-kilometre stretch of road winds over the surrounding hills, pitching up at the loop at the entrance to Parque Nacional Manuel Antonio. In recent years there has been a tremendous influx of new **hotels** in this corridor, mostly European-owned, and driving the road from Quepos to the Park you come upon some sort of accommodation every few metres. The most exclusive – and expensive – places are hidden away in the surrounding hills, reached by side roads, and can promise you luxury and pampering, not to mention wonderful ocean and sunset views. The very best overlook Punta Catedral, or Cathedral Point, which juts out so picturesquely into the Pacific.

Though there are some reasonably **affordable** places near the Park entrance, and the occasional low-season discount, prices are likely to rise as the seemingly inexhaustible popularity of the area continues to draw travellers. Few places accept **credit cards** (and if they do, it's often with a 6 percent surcharge slapped on), so bring enough cash and travellers' cheques to cover the considerable costs. You should also make sure to **reserve** well in advance.

The hotels below are listed in the order you encounter them from Quepos. More than anywhere else in the *Guide* the choice is partial, representing the best value in their price range.

Hotels

Cabinas Pedro Miguel, 500m beyond Quepos, on right-hand side (☎777-0035). The friendliest place in the area, locally owned and managed. Rooms in the main complex are nothing special, but comfortable, with balcony/patio and sunset views; go instead for the two little *casitas* backed up against the rainforest, with mosquito nets, kitchenette and basic furnishings. They're well-screened, open to the sounds of birds and monkeys. Small pool and great cook-your-own restaurant (see below). Very popular, so book ahead. Low-season midweek (Mon–Wed) and weekend (Thurs–Sun) discounts of 25 and 15 percent respectively. ③–⑤.

Hotel Plinios, Aptdo 71, Quepos (☎777-0055; fax 777-0558). Rooms vary, some are dark, but all are well-screened, and nicely decorated with Guatemalan prints. The highest rooms give spectacular sunset views from a raised platform bed. Landscaped tropical gardens, pool and very good restaurant, plus 4-km-long nature trail, with stupendous views from top. Good off-season discounts. ④–⑤.

Makanda-by-the-sea (☎777-0442). One of the pricier accommodations in the area, with rooms running to $200. Quiet and secluded individual villas with kitchen, private bath and hot water. Spectacular ocean views, both from the villas and the new pool. No children under 15; reservations must be pre-paid (credit cards accepted). ⑧.

Tulemar, Aptdo 225-6350, Manuel Antonio (☎777-0580; fax 777-1579). Beautiful octagonal bungalows, on stilts and set into the hillside, with panoramic views over Punta Catedral. Skylit, roomy and airy, with a/c, VCR and TV, phones and well-equipped kitchenettes. ⑥.

Villas Nicolas (☎ and fax 777-0451). Very classy, but not overpriced, accommodation, suspended high above the surrounding landscape, with lovely views. All villas have private bath, hot water and ceiling fans; some have kitchens. Also a small pool. ⑤–⑥.

Hotel Nina, 2500m from Park entrance. Romantic hideaway with lovely balconied rooms. Rates include breakfast, and there's a pool, rooftop bar and sloths and monkeys in the trees. The best value in this price range. ⑤.

Hotel y Villa Mogotes, Aptdo 120, Quepos (☎777-1043; fax 777-0582). All rooms have a/c, private bath with hot water, and phone; most have balconies with panoramic ocean views. Restaurant, bar and pool, plus a short nature trail, good for monkey-spotting. This was the summer residence of American folk-rock singer Jim Croce. ⑦.

El Colibrí, Aptdo 94, Manuel Antonio (☎ and fax 777-0432). Clean, spacious hotel, with nice atmosphere. Rooms are attractively ranged around a pool, with kitchens, verandahs and hammocks. Well-priced, friendly and efficient. ③–⑤.

Casitas Eclipse (☎777-0408). Individual white villas set around a pool, with private bath, hot water, and ceiling fans. Some have kitchens. Good value. ⑦.

La Quinta, Aptdo 76-6350, Manuel Antonio (☎777-0434). Good, well-established hotel, one of the first in the area, with very friendly, professional management. Beautiful pool, and poolside French restaurant with the best view in Manuel Antonio. Variety of spacious, attractive rooms in individual houses, with kitchen, private bath with hot water and balcony. Fairly priced, and good for families. ④–⑤.

Costa Verde, Aptdo 89, Escazú (☎777-0584; fax ☎777-0560; in the USA: ☎1-800/231-RICA). Spacious, luxurious studio apartments, with modern furnishings and balconies for terrific ocean views. Very quiet area. ⑥–⑦.

Karahé, 500m from the Park entrance (☎ and fax 777-0152; Aptdo 100-6350, Quepos). One of the best established hotels in the area. Cabinas with incredible views, perched high on the hill. Newer ones have a/c, older ones have ceiling fan and fridges – all are good value. There's a pool and small restaurant on the grounds. Rates include breakfast. ⑥.

Cabinas Piscis, just north of Playa Espadilla (☎777-0046; Aptdo 207, Quepos). One of the best budget places in Manuel Antonio, with student and group discounts available. Big, clean, basic cabina rooms, with cement floors and private bath with cold water. The pleasant garden area leads to the beach, where a little restaurant serves juices and sandwiches (high season only). Friendly *dueños*. Very popular, so reserve in advance. ③.

Cabinas Ramirez, Playa Espadillas Sur, Manuel Antonio village. Pretty basic, with stuffy rooms and cold water only, but at least it gets you on the beach. Noise from the disco can be a problem at weekends. ②.

Costa Linda, Manuel Antonio village (☎777-0304). The cheapest accommodation around, with small, plain, stuffy rooms, with shared bath and cold water. Good restaurant. ①.

Villabosque, Manuel Antonio village, 125m from the Park entrance (☎777-0463; fax 777-0401). One of the most expensive places in Manuel Antonio village. Nicely furnished, clean and bright rooms, with wicker chairs, private bath with hot water, and a choice of a/c and ceiling fans. Restaurant, bar and small swimming pool. ⑥.

Los Almendros, Aptdo 68-6350 (☎777-0225). Good value – if not exactly budget – option close to the beach. Rooms with cold water and fans are cheaper than those with a/c and hot water. Good restaurant attached. ④.

Eating and drinking

Most of the **hotel-restaurants** along this stretch are very good, if expensive. Cheaper places can be found in the village right next to the Park entrance, where a cluster of beachside and roadside **sodas** serve Tico food.

Some restaurants, especially the best ones, close or have restricted hours in the rainy season. Drop by either branch of *La Buena Nota* to ask which ones are open, or ring ahead where numbers are given. For the more popular places – *Plinios*, *Karola's* and *Vela Bar* among them – you should call or stop by to make a reservation, especially on weekends, and especially in the high season.

Barba Roja, next to the *Divisimar Hotel*, on road to Manuel Antonio, about 2500m from the Park entrance. Friendly, popular place for high-quality American cuisine, including burgers and desserts.

Karola's, near *Barba Roja*. Mexican cuisine, with burritos, seafood, vegetarian dishes and a macadamia nut pie that has entered local food legend. Closed Wed and in the low season.

Restaurante Manuel Antonio, Manuel Antonio village, close to the Park entrance. Friendly and popular, with *típico* food, rice dishes and good *refrescos*.

Mar y Sombra, Manuel Antonio village, 500m from the Park entrance, on the beach. In a grove of shady palm trees, this sprawling, cheap place is the most popular in the village. You can have a drink on the beach, and eat *típico* food including good *casados*, and there's a disco at weekends.

Las Olas, Manuel Antonio village, near the Park entrance. Cheap, cheerful soda for rice dishes, *casados* and *refrescos*.

Restaurante Pedro Miguel, signed immediately as you leave Quepos, in *Cabinas Pedro Miguel*. Wonderful, open-air barbecue-your-own steak restaurant with rough-hewn wooden tables and chairs, set right next to the forest. Choose your cut of meat or fish, then cook it to your liking on the big outdoor grill. Extremely popular, and lots of fun. Dec–April only.

Plinios, directly opposite *Pedro Miguel* (☎777-0055; fax 777-0558). Quite simply one of the best restaurants in the country, locally famous for its eggplant parmesan. Also pot roast in red wine, tiramisu, and reasonable Chilean wine. Nice bar, too; relaxed, with good music. Seven percent surcharge on credit cards. Breakfast 6–10am, lunch 11am–1pm, dinner 5–9.30pm.

Vela Bar, Manuel Antonio village. Traditionally the swankiest food in the area, with good grilled fish, some vegetarian choices and paella. Not cheap, though, starting at around $7.

298/THE CENTRAL PACIFIC AND SOUTHERN NICOYA

Playa Espadilla

Playa Espadilla, also sometimes called Playa Manuel Antonio, or Playa Numero Uno, is outside the Park, immediately north of the entrance and of Punta Catedral. One of the most popular beaches in the country – wide, with smooth light-grey sand – it is also very dangerous, plagued by **rip tides** that travel between six and ten kilometres per hour. However, lots of people do swim here – or rather, paddle and wade – and live to tell the tale. Now the professional lifeguards are around, it is considerably safer; in the dry season, at least.

GUARDAVIVAS AT PLAYA ESPADILLA

Until recently very few of Costa Rica's beaches had lifeguards (in Spanish, **guardavivas**). Like most South and Central American countries graced with good beaches, the nation lacks the resources to make them safe for swimmers. This goes some way to explaining why 200 lives are lost from drownings in Costa Rica every year – one of the highest rates in the world, and the country's second leading cause of accidental death (after car crashes).

In 1993, members of Quepos' and Manuel Antonio's business community – spearheaded by Donald Melton and Anita Myketuk, co-owners of the *La Buena Nota* shops – contributed funds to form Costa Rica's first professional **surf rescue lifeguards**. This eleven-strong team, of professionally trained locals who know the currents well, has made eighty surf rescues at Playa Espadilla since December 1993 and has reduced the number of drownings to zero. Before the lifeguards, the beach usually claimed between five to ten lives a year. Funds, donated by local businesses dependent on tourism, the US Lifesaving Association and the University of California's Ocean Initiative Group, are currently sufficient only to guard the beaches in the **high season**, between December and April.

Parque Nacional Manuel Antonio

By far the smallest Park in Costa Rica's system, **PARQUE NACIONAL MANUEL ANTONIO** (Tues–Sun 8am–4pm; $15 on the day, $10 in advance), some 150km southwest of San José, fights it out with Parque Nacional Volcán Poás in the Valle Central for the title of the most popular Park in the country. It is hard not to appreciate the foresight that went into the establishment of Manuel Antonio as a National Park in 1972; considering the number of hotels and restaurants sidling up to its borders, you can just imagine how developed the near-limestone white sands Playa Espadilla Sur would be today. Still, the Park is suffering from the numbers of visitors it receives, and sometimes reaches its quota of 600 visitors a day. The current system of closing the Park on Mondays is a half-measure to try to give the animals a rest and rangers and trail maintenance people a chance to work.

Covering an area of just 683 hectares, Manuel Antonio preserves not only the lovely **beaches** and the unique *tómbolo* formation (see p.290) of Punta Catedral, but also **mangroves** and humid tropical **forest**. Visitors can walk only on the sea-side section of the Park. The eastern *montaña*, or mountain section, off limits to the public, is regularly patrolled by rangers to deter poaching, which is rife in the area, and incursions into the Park from surrounding farmers and *campesinos*.

Rangers at Manuel Antonio know their terrain well and are happy to talk to you about the Park if they are not too busy – telling fond stories about boa constrictors, and the antics of the *monos titi*, or **squirrel monkeys**. Manuel Antonio is one of the few remaining natural habitats for the squirrel monkeys, whose cuteness is their own nemesis – highly sought after as pets and for zoos, they used to be prime targets for poachers. Smaller than their primate cousins – the howler, white-faced, spider and capuchin monkeys – they have close-set bright eyes and a delicate, white-haired face. You're unlikely to see them nowadays, as they've become tired of being gawped at and have largely retreated from the trails. Besides being quiet, the other thing you can do to help preserve the habitat of the squirrel monkeys – and the other animals who live in Manuel Antonio – is not to feed them and not to leave any litter.

Other **mammals** in the Park – you're likely to see many of the smaller ones – are the racoon, the coati, the agouti, the two-toed sloth and white-faced capuchin monkey. **Birdlife** is also abundant, including the shimmering green **kingfisher**, the brown pelican, who can often be seen fishing off the rocks, and the laughing falcon. Beware the snakes that do a mean imitation of a vine, draping themselves over the trails; you may not see them, but they're here.

The **climate** is hot, humid and wet, all year round. Though the rains ease off in the dry season (Dec–April), they never disappear entirely. The average temperature all year is 27°C, and it can easily go to 30°C and above.

Trails

Manuel Antonio has a tiny system of short **trails**, all of them easy, except when it's rainy and they can get slippery. The most popular (**no 1** on the maps) is the small loop around Punta Catedral. There's a wonderful view of the Pacific, dotted with jagged-edged little islands, from the mirador at the very tip of the point. If you loop round this trail you come back to the main beachside trail, **El Perezoso** ("sloth"; no 2), which takes you to Playa Blanca, the best beach for swimming (see below). The **Puerto Escondido** trail (no 3) and the **Mirador** trail (4) head through relatively dense humid tropical forest cover, crossing a small creek and eventually reaching rocky Playa Puerto Escondido. You can clamber across Puerto Escondido at low tide (although you must check with the rangers regarding the hours of high and low tide to avoid getting cut off – see below). All in all it's pretty untaxing walking, although the views are fabulous, and after you're good and sweaty you can go for a swim.

BEACHES WITHIN MANUEL ANTONIO

Beaches in Parque Nacional Manuel Antonio can be confusing, called by a number of different names. Because some are not safe for swimming, it is important to grasp which one is which. Follow the rangers' advice and swim only at **Playa Blanca**, which is where everyone else will be, anyway. From the north to the south they are, and conditions are, as follows:

Playa Espadilla Sur is the first beach within the Park, on the south side of Punta Catedral. It is also sometimes referred to as playa numero dos, or, confusingly, playa numero uno (as it's the first one in the Park). The brochures the SNP hands out on Manuel Antonio suggest you can swim here with no problems, but in reality rangers take a dim view of swimming at this beach; the surf can be rough.

Playa Blanca (also called playa numero dos, or tres) is by far the best swimming

beach. Immediately south of Punta Catedral, it is in a protected, deeper bay than the others. Numero dos is very calm – like a swimming pool, say the rangers – but you can still get clobbered by the deceptively gentle-looking waves as they hit the shore. Be careful getting in and out. Unfortunately it's quite narrow and can get crowded. Early morning before 10am is the best time to come.

Playa Puerto Escondido (sometimes called playa numero tres, or quatro) is a pretty, white horseshoe-shaped beach which can be reached along the Puerto Escondido trail (see above). Do not set out here without checking with the rangers about the *marea* first. At high tide you cannot get across Puerto Escondido, nor can you cross it from the dense forest behind. At best it will be a waste of time; at worst you'll get cut off on the other side for a few hours. You can't swim here anyway, as the currents are dangerous.

Practicalities

You may be able to buy **discounted tickets** for Parque Nacional Manuel Antonio ($7 as opposed to $10) at a number of operators in Quepos, including *Lynch Tours* and *Ríos Tropicales*. **Buses** from Quepos and San José can let you off right in front of the *Restaurante Sol y Mar*, about 500m before the Park, if you want to grab lunch or go to Playa Espadilla for a swim. Otherwise it continues round the loop before returning to Quepos. The driver stops on request, so ask him to let you off at your hotel.

If you're driving, note that there isn't much **parking** at the loop at the end of Manuel Antonio village; arrive early in the morning for the best (shady) spot, and pay the kids who guard cars about 150 to 200 colones. To get to the Park entrance from here you have to wade across a creek. At low tide it's ankle-deep, and at high tide it can come up to your shoulders. Use common sense and wait for it to go down. The entrance hut is across the creek and about 50m up a track. Here you can pick up a basic photocopied **map** (50¢), which marks the beaches and trails. **Facilities** within the Park are minimal. Beyond the entrance hut and the toilets and showers staked out at close intervals along the trails, the only other buildings are administrative. There are no **guides** for the Park, but you hardly need them. Rangers are often on patrol. There have been problems with **theft** in Manuel Antonio, usually as a result of people leaving valuables (like cameras) on the beach: the rangers, who often sit at the picnic tables, might be able to look after your stuff, but ask nicely, as it's not actually part of their job.

travel details

Buses

San José to: Jacó (2 daily; 2hr 30min–3hr); Manuel Antonio (express service, 3 daily; 3hr 30min–4hr); Monteverde/Santa Elena (2 daily; 4–5hr); Puntarenas (14 daily; 2hr); Quepos (stopping service, 5 daily; 5hr).

Jacó to: Quepos (via Puntarenas service, 3 daily; 1hr); San José (2 daily; 2hr 30min–3hr).

Monteverde/Santa Elena to: Puntarenas (from Santa Elena only, 1 daily; 3hr 30 min); San José (2 daily; 4–5hr); Tilarán (1 daily; 3hr).

Montezuma to: Paquera (for ferry to Puntarenas, 3 daily; 1hr); Tambor (3 daily; 30min).

Paquera to: Montezuma (3 daily; 1hr); Tambor (3 daily; 40min).

Puntarenas to: Liberia (1 daily; 3 hr); Quepos (3 daily; 3hr 30min); San José (14 daily; 2hr); Santa Elena, for Monteverde (1 daily; 3hr 30min).

Quepos to: Dominical and San Isidro (2 daily; 3hr 30min); Puntarenas (3 daily; 3hr 30min); San José (express service, 3 daily; 3hr 30min–4hr; stopping service, 4 daily; 5hr).

Tilarán to: Santa Elena (1 daily; 3hr).

Ferries

Naranjo to: Puntarenas (car/passenger ferry, 5 daily; 1hr 30min).

Paquera to: Puntarenas (passenger ferry, 3–4 daily; 1hr 30min).

Puntarenas to: Montezuma (passenger ferry, via Paquera, 3–4 daily; 1hr 30min; car/passenger ferry, via Naranjo, 5 daily; 1hr 30min).

Flights

Sansa

San José to: Quepos (Mon–Sat 2 daily, Sun 1 daily; 20 min); Tambor (1 daily; 20min).

Quepos to: San José (Mon–Sat 2 daily, Sun 1 daily; 20min).

Tambor to: San José (1 daily; 20min).

Travelair

San José to: Quepos (3 daily high season, 1 daily low season; 20min).

Quepos to: San José (3 daily high season, 1 daily low season; 20min).

CHAPTER SEVEN

ZONA SUR

osta Rica's **Zona Sur** (southern zone) is the country's least-known region, both for Ticos and for travellers. Geographically, it's a diverse area, varying from the agricultural heartland of the Valle de el General to high mountain peaks, most notably the mountain pass at Cerro de la Muerte ("Death Mountain"), and Cerro el Chirripó – at 3819m the highest peak in Central America. Both of these crown the top of the Cordillera de Talamanca, which falls away quickly into the river-cut lowlands of the Valle de Diquis and the coffee-growing Valle de Coto Brus.

The region is particularly popular with hikers, many of whom come to climb Chirripó, set in the chilly, rugged terrain of **Parque Nacional Chirripó**. In the extreme southwest, the Osa Peninsula is the site of **Parque Nacional Corcovado**, one of the prime rainforest hiking destinations in the country. Its soaring canopy trees constitute the last chunk of tropical wet forest on the entire Pacific side of the Central American isthmus. Bordering Parque Nacional Chirripó, the giant Costa Rica–Panamá-administered **Parque Internacional la Amistad**, a UNESCO-declared Biosphere Reserve and a World Heritage Site, protects an enormous swathe of land along Costa Rica's southern border, and is for the most part inaccessible to all but the most experienced hikers.

For those bent on getting to remote places, there are plenty, including the picturesque **Bahía Drake** on the hump of the Osa Peninsula, and nearby **Reserva Biológica Isla del Caño**, scattered with lithic spheres formed by the Diquis. **Parque Nacional Isla del Coco**, some 500km off the southwest coast is unsurprisingly almost entirely unvisited. Less off the beaten track, and one of the most recent areas in the country to open up to tourism, there's the **Playa Dominical** area of the Pacific coast, a surfing destination whose tremendous tropical beauty is beginning to draw snorkellers and swimmers, especially since road improvements made it accessible without a 4WD. Further asphalting has made it possible to continue south from Dominical to the small hamlet of **Uvita**, and on to **Palmar**, from where you can take a bus or drive south to **Golfito**, the only town of any size in the region. For years after the pull-out of the United Fruit Company's banana operations in 1985, Golfito received a bad press, painted as a town of ill repute. However, it has been attacting more visitors of late, since being made a tax-free zone (called the *depósito libre*) for manufactured goods from Panamá. Costa Ricans who previously never dreamed of journeying out to this part of the country now hop in their cars and cart back refrigerators. For foreign visitors, it is more useful as a base for moving on to the Osa Peninsula and Corcovado.

Despite the profusion of cheap basic accommodation – in many areas you can get a good clean room for half the price of the more heavily touristed parts of the country – you'll find yourself spending more than you bargained for simply because of the time, distance and planning involved in getting to many of the region's more beautiful spots. This is the case particularly if you stay in one of the very comfortable private **"rainforest lodges"** in the Osa, Golfito and Bahía

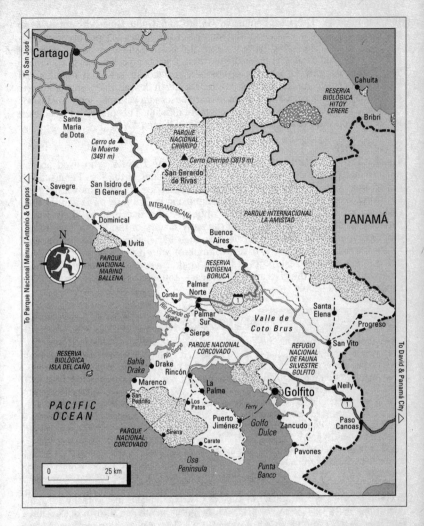

Drake areas. Many people prefer to take a package rather than travel independently; and travellers who stay at the rainforest lodges often choose to fly in. Even doing Corcovado on the cheap, taking buses and camping, can set you back a bit, as the bus journeys are more expensive than elsewhere, and food is in short and relatively expensive supply. Bear in mind, too, that many of the communities down here are not used to seeing strangers – certainly women travelling alone are in for some curiosity.

Climatically the Zona Sur has two distinct regions. The Pacific lowlands, from south of Quepos roughly to the Río Sierpe delta at the top of the Osa Peninsula, experience a dry season (Dec–April), as do the upland Valle de el General and the Talamancas. The Osa Peninsula, Golfito and Golfo Dulce do not have so marked a dry season – although the months of December to April are less wet – and, due to localized wind patterns from the Pacific, these areas get very wet indeed, receiving as much rain as the northern Caribbean coast – up to 5000mm a year. From roughly October to December, spectacular seasonal thunder and lightning storms canter in from across the Pacific. In the rainy season, some parts of Parque Nacional Corcovado become more or less unwalkable, local mud roads become undrivable, and everything gets more difficult. This makes it a good time to come if you want to avoid the crowds, but you'll need 4WD.

Some history

The earliest inhabitants of the Zona Sur were the **Diquis**, who lived around modern-day Palmar and Bahía Drake, on the shoulder of the Osa Peninsula – a region that is still known as the Valle de Diquis. They are best known for **gold-smithing** (see the Museo de Oro Precolumbiano in *San José*, p.74) and for their crafting and transportation of **lithic spheres**, characterized by their almost perfect roundness. Less is known of the early history of the Diquis than of any other group in Costa Rica, chiefly because their burial sites have been plundered by *huaqueros* (grave-robbers/treasure hunters) who have in some cases dynamited tombs in their zeal to get at buried gold. These days the only indigenous group of any size in the area are the Borucas – sometimes called the Bruncas – a subgroup of the Diquis.

THE DIQUIS

Very little is known about the history of the **Diquis region** before 1000 BC, but, because of cultural affiliations, it is considered to be part of the larger Greater Chiriquí region, which takes its name from the province in southwestern Panamá. Archeologists date the famous **lithic spheres** from some time between 1000 BC and 500 AD; between 700/800 and 1600 AD the Diquis began fashioning **gold** pendants, breastplates, headbands and chains, becoming master goldsmiths within a hundred years or so. Between 500 and 800 AD drastic changes occurred in the culture of the Diquis. Archeologists posit the impact of the arrival of sea-going peoples from Colombia or possibly the Andes – a theory borne out by their metates and pottery, which show llama or guanaco figures, animals that would have been unknown on the isthmus. In the Diquis' own artisanry, both the ingenious – often cheeky – goldwork and the voluptuous pottery display a unique humour as well as superlative attention to detail.

The Diquis were in a state of constant **warfare** among themselves and with foreign groups. Like the Chorotegas to the north in Greater Nicoya (see p.210), they seem to have engaged in sacrifice, ritually beheading war captives. Huge metates unearthed at Barilles in Panamá show images of these rituals, while smaller crucible-like dishes suggest ritual inebriation; it seems coca leaves, yucca or maize may have been crushed and fermented inside.

The indigenous peoples of the Zona Sur first met the Spaniards in 1522 when the *cacique* of the Térraba group graciously hosted Captain **Gil González** for a fortnight. González was on his way from near the present-day Panamá border, where his ship had run aground, to Nicaragua. Despite infirmity (he was in his fifties), he was walking all the way. The Diquis seem to have declined abruptly after this initial contact, most likely felled by influenza, smallpox, the plague, and other diseases brought by Spanish settlers.

The modern history of the Zona Sur has been defined by its isolation. Before the building of the **Interamericana** in the 1950s, which today scythes its irregular course from San José to Panamá, transport across the Cerro de la Muerte was by mule only. **Charcoal-burning** was until very recently the main economic activity up in these heights, using the majestic local oaks. *Campesinos* in the area are now being discouraged from charcoal-burning, due to its deforesting effects, but for a glimpse of how the *carboneros* lived before the building of the Interamericana, read the short story "The Carbonero" by Costa Rican writer Carlos Salazar Herera, translated into English and anthologized in *Costa Rica: A Traveller's Literary Companion* (see *Contexts*).

San José to San Isidro

The quality of the trip from the capital, via Cartago, southwest to the market town of **San Isidro de el General**, 136km southwest of San José, is governed by the current condition of the San José–Panamá stretch of the Interamericana, which winds its way about 2000m up from the bowl of Cartago's surrounding valley to the chilly heights of the 3491-metre **Cerro de la Muerte** pass. Rockslides and mudslides are frequent along this road, and there have been isolated reports of drivers being flagged down and robbed by *banditos*, although this normally happens to intercontinental truckers and not tourists. Still, it is not a good idea to drive at lonely times of night – not just because of the chance of robbery, but more crucially because you may not be able to see. Fog, mist, rain and general lack of visibility are a constant threat, and the road lacks shoulder or meridian markings. Also, if you have just arrived in Costa Rica, remember that you may be prone to a bit of altitude or **mountain sickness** caused by too quick an ascent to the pass. The drop into San Isidro is perhaps even more spectacular than the views from the top. An enormous valley falls in front of you, green and tame, centring on the white modernist church, glinting like Mecca in the sun. This whole area is defined by the **Interamericana** (also known here as Hwy-2), heaving with international transport trucks and other large vehicles. Yellow-topped kilometre markings line the highway, and villages and hamlets are often referred to by these numbers (for example, Km-37 is Briseño, which everybody calls "kilómetro treintesiete").

About 60km south of San José, the *Albergue de Montaña Tapantí* (☎232-0436; ⑤), enjoys a fantastic setting high on a ridge. Accommodation is warm and cosy, in comfortable bungalow-like chalets, with private bath and hot water. The lodge also hosts unique small-scale **cultural tours** of the area, where for $10 you can spend the morning with a local *campesino* family (who receive the entire fee). If your Spanish is good, this can be a worthwhile encounter for both parties; you can find out about local farming methods, tour smallholdings, perhaps do a bit of trout fishing and watch milk being churned into cheese.

A little less than 20km further on, a turnoff leads to the hamlet of **SAN GERARDO DE DOTA**, where the *Albergue de Montaña Río Savegre* – more commonly known as *Cabinas Chacon* (☎771-1732; ⑤) – is well known among birders for the number of quetzal that nest on or near its property. If you're really keen on seeing a quetzal and can't make it to Monteverde (see p.256, this is probably the next best place to come, especially in nesting season (March–June). The very friendly *dueños* have trail maps, can arrange guides (which cost extra), and will give bird-spotting tips. They also offer trout fishing in the Río Savegre.

San Isidro and the Valle de el General

Arriving at **SAN ISIDRO DE EL GENERAL**, just 702m above sea level, brings you halfway back into tropical climes after the chilly ride over Cerro de la Muerte. In Costa Rica, San Isidro is seen as an increasingly attractive place to live, with its clean, country-town atmosphere. While the Talamancas are a non-volcanic range, and the Valle de el General lacks the fertile volcanic fallout that enriches the soils of the Valle Central, there is still considerable local agricultural activity, with pineapples growing particularly well. The town hosts an **agricultural fair** in the first week in February, when farmers don their finery, put their produce up for competition and sell great fresh food in the streets. In May, the **month of San Isidro** – patron saint of farmers and animals – is celebrated by fiestas, ox-cart parades, dog shows, and the erection of gaudy ferris wheels. The one museum, the **Museo Regional de Pérez Zeledón**, 75m north of the church, is devoted to the *campesino* history of the area (Mon–Fri 8am–noon & 1–4.30pm, though it's often closed).

Practicalities

Buses to San Isidro from San José are run by *MUSA* and *TRACOPA*, whose services continue to Golfito, Palmar or Paso Canoas. San Isidro's new **bus terminal** is at Av 6, C 0/2, although *TRACOPA* buses stop right on the Interamericana at the corner of C 3 and *MUSA* picks up passengers across the road.

The best **accommodation** in town is the *Chirripó*, C 1, Av 2/4 (☎771-0529; ②), with a good restaurant. The *Hotel del Sur*, about 6km southwest of San Isidro on the Interamericana (☎771-3033; ⑤), has rooms with private bath, tennis courts, a swimming pool and a good restaurant. Despite being just off the main road, it is set in nice grounds and is quiet.

As regards **moving on**, if travelling **south** to Palmar, Golfito or Paso Canoas (schedules are posted on the bus stop), it's far better to get a bus that originates in San Isidro rather than one that's coming through from San José, as they're often full and you could find yourself standing all the way to Panamá. Buses for **Quepos** (3 daily; 3hr 30min) and **Dominical** (2 daily; 40min–1hr) currently leave from C 1, Av 4/6, but may shift to the new terminal. Buses for **San Gerardo de Rivas** currently leave at 5am and 2pm (40min; call ☎233-4160 for information). At present they leave from the Parque Central but, again, may move to the new terminal. For all local services, buy your ticket on the bus.

Parque Nacional Chirripó

PARQUE NACIONAL CHIRRIPÓ, some 20km northeast of San Isidro ($10) is named after the **Cerro el Chirripó**, which lies at its centre – at 3819m the highest peak in Central America south of Guatemala. Ever since the conquest of the peak in 1904 by a missionary priest, Father Agustín Blessing (local indigenous peoples may of course have climbed it before), visitors have been flocking to Chirripó to do the same.

The **terrain** varies widely, and is governed mainly by altitude, from cloudforest to rocky mountaintops. Between the two lies the interesting alpine **páramo** – high moorland, punctuated by rocks, shrubs and hardy clump grasses, more usually associated with the Andean heights. Colours are muted yellows and browns, with the occasional deep purple. Below the *páramo* lie areas of **oak forest**, now much depleted through continued charcoal burning. Chirripó is also the only place in Costa Rica where you can observe vestiges of the **glaciers** that scraped across here about 30,000 years ago: narrow, U-shaped valleys, moraines (heaps of rock and soil left behind by retreating glaciers) and glacial lakes, as well as the distinctive **crestones**, or heavily weathered fingers of rock, which look as though they might be more at home in Montana than Costa Rica. The land is generally waterlogged, with a few bogs – take care where you step, as sometimes it's so chilly you won't want to get your feet wet.

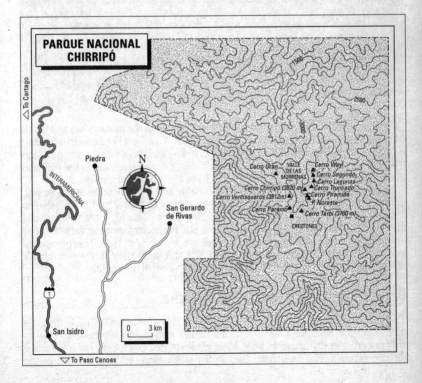

PLANNING A TRIP TO CHIRRIPÓ

Climbing Chirripó requires advance **planning**. First, you have to contact the SPN – preferably before you come to Costa Rica – and reserve a place. This is especially important during the dry season. A maxiumum of forty hikers are allowed in the Park on any one day, and, at the most popular times (around March and April – especially Easter – and Christmas), demand far outstrips capacity. There are sometimes **cancellations**, however, and you should ask the SPN about this. Under no circumstances can you **camp** in the Park, nor can you make a fire (forest fires frequently devastate the area, some caused by an improperly put-out campfire). You must stay in the basic **accommodation huts**, which have twenty bunks and cold water showers, a cooking area and a big sink where you can wash clothes.

To make **advance reservations** call or fax the SPN in San José (see p.65), stating your preferred dates. Most hikers find two or three nights sufficient. You may have to **pay in advance and** in full – $10 per day, plus $4 per night for accommodation – although it's sometimes possible to leave a deposit. Ask that they fax you a receipt. Without proof of payment, it will be impossible to get your **permit**, which you must collect from the San José office. Things are easier in the **wet season** (May–Nov), when you may be able to sort it all out in San José. Even then, you will still need to be flexible, and the procedure can take time. Best to try it at the beginning of your trip.

While Chirripó is hot at midday, it frequently drops to freezing at the higher altitudes at night. You should **bring** warm clothing and a proper sleeping bag (though these can be rented on site), a blanket, water, food (including snacks) and a propane gas stove. A short list of clothing and other essentials might include a good pair of boots, socks, long trousers, T-shirt, shirt, sweater, woolly hat and jacket, lots of insect repellent, sunglasses, first aid (for cuts and scratches), gloves (for rocks and the cold), binoculars and a torch – the accommodation huts have no lights.

Though walking off the trails isn't recommended – there's a good chance of getting lost and suffering hypothermia – if you do want to set out on your own, check at the SPN office whether they can offer you any advice on detailed **contour maps**. The *Instituto Geográfico* (see p.16) may sell an ordnance-survey-type map.

Many **mammals** live in the Park, and you may see spider monkeys as you climb from the lower montane to the montane rainforest. Your best bet for **bird-spotting** is in the lower elevations. Through the oak, mixed and cloudforest sections of the trail you may spot hawks, trogons, woodpeckers and even quetzals. In the cold and inhospitable terrain up high, the most you'll see are robins and hawks.

The **weather** in Chirripó is extremely variable and unpredictable. It can be hot, humid and rainy between May and December, but is clearer and drier between January and April ("peak season" for climbing the mountain). Even then, clouds may roll in at the top and obscure your view, and rainstorms move in very fast. The only months you can be sure of a dry spell are March and April. **Temperatures** may drop to below 0°C at night and rise to 20°C during the day. At the summit, it's so cold that it's hard to believe that you're just 9° north of the equator.

Practicalities: San Gerardo de Rivas

The tiny town of **SAN GERARDO DE RIVAS**, 17km from San Isidro, is the gateway to Parque Nacional Chirripó, with a ranger station and several very reasonably priced, friendly places to stay. Most climbers bed down here before starting for the summit. The **bus** from San Isidro stops more or less in front of the entrance to the Park, where you must show your permit. Here you can pick up an adequate map, which shows some altitude markings, but will not suffice if you are determined to walk off the beaten path (which is not recommended, in any case; see above).You can **rent a guide** and a horse to carry your gear up the trail to the accommodation huts. Ask the SPN for recommendations.

Accommodation

Most of San Gerardo's hotels don't have have their own phones. To **reserve** (essential at peak times), you must call the local number (☎771-0433, ext 106), ask the person who answers to convey a message to the accommodation of your choice, and request that they call you back at a specified number and time. Try and get somewhere with **hot water**, as it can get very cold at night. Many of the places listed below offer rental of key equipment like sleeping bags and cooking stoves – ask when you arrive.

Albergue Turístico Chirripó (no phone). Very friendly lodge offering nice, basic rooms with heated water, and overlooking the river. ①.

Posada del Descanso (no phone). Private house, owned by the long-time local Elizondo family, who can advise on Chirripó activities, quetzal-spotting, local culture and the like. If your Spanish is good enough, try to talk to Don Rafael or his brother Don Francisco, who can arrange a local guide for climbing Chirripó or exploring the area. ①.

Cabinas Marín (no phone). Comfortable, if spartan, accommodation with heated water, some inside the house, some in an annexe behind. ①.

Pensión Quetzal Dorado (no phone). As its name suggests, this rustic place is great for quetzal-spotting. It's set some 10km above the village of Herradura, which is itself several hundred metres above San Gerardo de Rivas – from where it is a 3-hr hike. To arrange horse and guide to get there ($25), either arrive in San Gerardo or Herradura and ask to speak to Sr Vargas, or call the public phone in Herradura (☎771-0433, ext 109) and leave a message for him asking him to call you back at a given time. Shared baths with cold water, but all meals are included. Dec–April only. ①.

Visiting the Park

Almost everyone who climbs Chirripó goes up to the accommodation huts first, rests there overnight, and then takes another day or two to explore the summit, surrounding peaks and *páramo*. During high season, you will have company on the path up the mountain, and the trail is well-marked with signs stating the altitude and the distance to the summit. Watch out for **altitude sickness**, though; if you have made a quick descent from the lowland beach areas, you could find yourself becoming short of breath, experiencing pins and needles, nausea and exhaustion. If this happens, stop and rest. The main thing to keep in mind is **not to go off the trail** or exploring on your own without telling anyone, especially in the higher patches. Off the trail, definite landscape markers are few, and it is easy to get confused.

The hike

The **hike** begins at 1219m and ends at 3819m – the peak. It's almost entirely uphill, and exhausting to an extent that you may have trouble appreciating the scenery. On the first day, most hikers make the fourteen-kilometre trek to the accommodation huts in twelve to sixteen hours, although really fit and experienced walkers can do it in half this. You can make the huts your base while you hike to the summit and back, which is easily done in a day, perhaps taking in some of the nearby lagoons.

The walk **begins** in pastureland, with cows munching contentedly, and passes through thick cloudforest, which is very dark, especially if it has been raining. It's here hikers usually stop and try to spot **quetzals** (March–May are the best months). After the cloudforest, there's a relatively flat stretch of several kilometres, where you're likely to be plagued by various biting insects. About midway between the start and the accommodation huts is the **rest station**; some people stay here, splitting the hike into a less taxing two days, but conditions are extremely rustic, with three sides open to the wind. The **Cuesta de los Arrepentidos** ("Hill of the Repentants", meaning you're sorry at this point that you came) is the real push, all uphill, for at least 3km. At **Monte Sin Fé** ("Faithless•Mountain"), about 10km into the trail, is another patch of tropical montane forest, more open than the cloudforest. Keep your eye out for the *refugio natural*, a big cave where you can sleep in an emergency – not desirable, really – from where it's just 3km to the **accommodation huts**. At the huts, the land looks like a greener version of Scotland: bare moss cover, grasslands, and a waterlogged area where the lagoons congregate. There are no trees, and little obvious wildlife in evidence.

The **rangers** based up here are friendly, and in the high season (Jan–April) you can ask to accompany them on walks near the summit, thus sidestepping the possibility of getting lost. Do not *expect* this, however, as it is not their job to lead guided walks. It is really not a good idea to go off the trails on your own, but if you do, let others at the accommodation huts or rangers know which part you intend to explore and how long you intend to be. Whatever you do, you'll need to set off by dawn because clear weather at the peak is really only guaranteed until 9am or 10am.

Though the **summit** is just ninety minutes' walk from the accommodation huts, you should allow a day. There's a bit of grappling involved, but no hard climbing or mountaineering. The trail is well-marked, both on the free map and on the ground. At the summit there's a little book in a metal box that you can sign with your "I did it" message; but you'll need to bring a pen. From the top, if it is clear, you can see right across to the Pacific. However, you're above the cloud line up here, and the surrounding mountains may often be obscured by drifting milky clouds.

The Dominical area

As you drive along the coastal road south from Quepos (covered in our chapter *Central Pacific and Southern Nicoya*) to the booming beach town of **Dominical**, the first settlement of any size you'll come upon is **MATAPALO**, about halfway along. **Playa Matapalo** itself is a wide, white-sand beach, mostly deserted, and good for bathing; but ask about currents. *Cabinas el Coquito* (☎233-1731; fax 222-8849; ④) have comfortable **rooms** with private bath and fan, a bar-restaurant on the premises, and direct access to the beach.

The **Bahía Ballena** area, 17km south of Dominical, is one of the most pristine in Costa Rica. It features **Parque Nacional Marino las Ballenas** – 5575 hectares of water around Punta Uvita and Isla Ballena – which was created to safeguard the ecological integrity of the local marine life. Further south, **Playa Tortuga** is an undiscovered shallow bay, draped with palms.

Dominical

DOMINICAL, 44km south of Quepos and 29km southwest of San Isidro, was until recently relatively undiscovered, due mainly to the lack of a good road. However, since the road has been paved, the once quiet fishing village has been discovered by foreigners, lured by the beauty of the surroundings, the romantic sunsets and the get-away-from-it-all atmosphere. Though it seems poised to become the country's next Manuel Antonio, development remains – for the time being at least – relatively low-key.

There's nothing to do, really, except explore the beach and surrounding forest. Lodges and hotels can arrange visits with a guide to two nearby **waterfalls**, both of which are warm and safe for swimming. The **Dominicalito** falls are most accessible, 6km south of the village, while the 45-metre **San Cristo** falls lie 10km from the village of Tinamaste.

Wide and long, Dominical **beach** is postcard-pretty, although its sand is dark, backed by a wall of palms. It is often deserted, and never crowded, except perhaps with **surfers** at certain times. **Sportsfishing** and **snorkelling** are big here, too; though, as usual with surfing beaches, the swimming varies from not great to downright dangerous, plagued by rip tides and crashing surf. About twenty minutes' walk south along the beach brings you to a small cove, where the water is calmer and you can paddle and snorkel.

Nowadays any vehicle *should* be able to make the trip to Dominical, from either approach, although it makes sense to rent a 4WD if you want to explore the surrounding area. **From San José** it is more convenient and faster to come via San Isidro; **from Guanacaste** and the Central Pacific, you'll do best to take the road south from Quepos. **Buses** from Quepos arrive at around 6.30am and 3pm daily, and continue to San Isidro (2hr). Buses from San Isidro go on to Uvita.

Accommodation in the Dominical area

Though most **accommodation** in the Dominical, Uvita and Bahía Ballena area is still considered basic – in the past, the area catered mainly for surfers – a number of more upmarket places, usually owned by foreigners, are springing up fast. For the moment it is still possible to find very reasonably priced rooms, on the whole owned by locals, in the $20–30 range. The most expensive hotels are wonderful hideaways, good for honeymoons, romantics and escapists.

There are currently no private phones installed in this area; locals communicate via CB radio. However, Jack Ewing, long-time resident and owner of *Hacienda Barú*, has set up a local **reservation service**, *Selva Mar*, through which you can book any of the accommodation listed below, either in advance or by dropping into their office in the centre of Dominical (☎ and fax 771-1903).

Hacienda Barú, 1km north of Dominical on the road to Quepos (☎ and fax 771-1903). Good-value, comfortable cabinas. With 330 hectares of rainforest, a fixed canopy platform, mangroves and horseriding tours, this is the largest, most upscale accommodation in the area. Good for birders and orchid lovers (there are 250 varieties scattered around). ③.

Finca Bella Vista, above Dominical in the hills (☎ and fax 771-1903). Comfortable guest lodge and working ranch, set 300m above the coast. You need quite a vehicle to get up here, especially if it's wet: ask at *Selva Mar* to see if they can pick you up. The sunset views are worth the trouble, and there are horse rides to the beach and nearby waterfalls. ④.

Finca Brian y Milena, 300m above Dominical, on the road to Escaleras (☎ and fax 771-1903). One of the nicest small-scale family farm operations, doubling as a wildlife sanctuary, experimental fruit farm, botanical garden and guest lodge. You can't drive here, so call *Selva Mar* and have the owners come and meet you with horses. Most people arrive on packages, which include hikes in the surrounding rainforest and meals. ⑤.

El Chaman, Playa Bahía Ballena/Uvita, 1km past the turnoff to Uvita (☎ and fax 771-1903). Very near the beach and very rustic, backed by mountains. A romantic hideaway atmosphere, quiet and secluded, with dinner served by candlelight. Convenient for Parque Nacional Marino Las Ballenas. No electricity, so bring a torch. ④.

Cabinas el Coco Tico, Playa Uvita (☎ and fax 771-1903). Basic cabinas with private bath. They will cook on request. ③.

Diu Wak Hotel, 400m from *San Clemente Bar and Grill* on the main road in Dominical (☎233-8195). Just 50m from the beach. Comfortable cabinas with private bath, hot water, ceiling fans and verandahs; there's an on-site jacuzzi, too. ④.

Cabinas los Laureles, Playa Uvita (☎ and fax 771-1903). Rustic, clean cabinas with private baths, surrounded by laurel trees. Good local food, and meals can be included. ③.

Cabinas Nayarit, Dominical (☎ and fax 771-1878). Comfortable, basic rooms, with private bath, fan, and hammocks strung between palm trees. A/c (not necessary) costs extra. ④.

Pacific Edge, 3km south of Dominical (☎771-1903). Secluded, simple and comfortable, on a ridge above the sea, with beautiful mountain and beach views. Four roomy chalets each have private shower, porches and hammocks. Meals cost extra. The owners offer tours to nearby waterfalls and to Bahía Drake, and good-value packages. You need 4WD to get here. ④.

Hotel Río Lindo, Dominical (☎771-2009; fax 771-1725). New hotel with nicely furnished, a/c rooms. Pool and whirlpool on the grounds. ⑤.

Villas Río Mar, Dominical (☎771-2264; in San José: ☎225-5712). Upscale accommodation with swimming pool, bar, tennis court and jacuzzi. Comfortable rooms in individual chalets, set in extensive tropical gardens, with terraces. Rates include three good meals per day. ⑥.

Albergue Willdale, Dominical (☎ and fax 771-1903). Also known as *Cabinas Willi*. Very basic but clean cabinas with fan and hammocks; the owner is planning renovations so they may become more fancy (and expensive). ③.

Eating and drinking

There's a *pulpería* in Dominical, but if you're **self-catering**, stock up in the mercado in Quepos or in San Isidro. Many local **hotels** include meals or will cook for you for a small charge. Of the **restaurants**, in Dominical *Marisquería Maui* serves fish and seafood, while the *San Clemente Bar and Grill* has a Tex-Mex menu with a little Italian and Cajun thrown in. The pizzas are highly recommended. The *Restaurante y Cabinas Roca Verde*, 2km south, has the only barbecue in the area, plus a beautiful sea view; its disco is a meeting place for surfers, travellers and young locals.

Parque Nacional las Ballenas, Uvita and Bahía Ballena

In the last decade or so, access to the lovely **Bahía Ballena** has become relatively easy (albeit by sturdy 4WD), but the tiny hamlets of Bahía and Uvita are still little-visited, and hardly geared up for tourism. Efforts to get here are amply rewarded, however, with wide beaches washed by lazy breakers, palms swaying on the shore, and a hot, serene, very quiet atmosphere. This will no doubt change, as more people "discover" Bahía Ballena, but for the time being it's likely to remain extremely unspoilt.

There's not a lot to do. If you like hanging out on the beach, surfing and walking through rock shoals and along the sand, you'll be happy. At certain times of year (usually May–Oct), Olive Ridley and hawksbill **turtles** may come ashore to nest, but nowhere near to the same extent as elsewhere in the country. The beach is currently unregulated, so if you do want to see them, remember the ground rules of turtle-watching: come at night with a torch, watch where you walk (partly for snakes), keep well back from the beach, and don't shine the light right on the turtles. You may also see **dolphins** frolicking in the water. Ask around for a boat tour. Make sure the boat has a good outboard motor and life-jackets on board, as out here you're on the open Pacific. Though nowhere yet rents scuba-diving or snorkelling equipment or offers tours, with your own equipment you should be able to **snorkel** to your heart's content.

The tiny village of **BAHÍA**, 2km south of Uvita across a creek, is right next to the Marine National Park. It is strung out along just one road, and at the moment tourist infastructure is limited. There are, however, a couple of **places to stay**: *Cabinas Hegalua* has basic rooms, and will throw in breakfast and dinner (③), while *Cabinas Punta Uvita* has clean, if not especially cheap, doubles and singles (②). As for **eating**, there's a *pulpería*, and you can arrange for meals to be cooked at your cabina. From San Isidro, **buses** leave C 1, Av 4/6 at 3pm daily, heading for Uvita via Dominical (1hr 30min). They return at about 6.30am.

Parque Nacional Marino las Ballenas

Created in 1990, the **PARQUE NACIONAL MARINO LAS BALLENAS** protects one of the biggest chunks of **coral reef** left on the Pacific coast. It is also the habitat of **humpback whales** – although they are spotted very infrequently (Dec–April is best) – and **dolphins**. The main threats to the ecological survival of these waters is the disturbance caused by shrimp trawling, sedimentation caused by deforestation – rivers bring silt and pollutants into the sea and kill the coral – and dragnet fishing, which often entraps whales and dolphins. On land, 110 hectares of sandy and rocky beaches and coastal areas are protected, as is the *tómbolo* of **Punta Uvita** – a former island connected to the mainland by a narrow sea-created land bridge. There are minimal **services** to speak of; while rangers are on duty, there are no trails and nothing to stop you from **snorkelling** or paddling in the calm bay when the tide is out. This may all change, however, as the SPN accord more infrastructure to the area.

Playa Tortuga

Heading south on the Costanera Sur, you'll come to **Playa Tortuga**, about half-way between Dominical and Palmar Norte. A few years ago this beach got an award as the cleanest in Costa Rica: no wonder, as practically nobody did the bone-shaking trip here then (unless they had a Land Rover). Not too many people venture here now, either, though the road has improved and is passable with 4WD. A couple of **hotels** have opened (both owned by Québecois, who constitute a mini foreign colony) in the last few years, and more will probably follow. The very secluded, friendly and modern *Paraíso del Pacífico* (☎786-6534; fax 786-6365; ⑤) is perched on the hill, with great views out to the ocean and the Talamancas, and has comfortable cabinas with private bath and fan. There's also a pool, bar and restaurant. The similarly friendly *Posada de la Playa Tortuga* (no phone, try through *Selva Mar*, see p.311; ⑤) also has excellent views, big comfortable rooms with private bath and fan, a pool and barbecue terrace.

Palmar to Bahía Drake

About 100km north of the Panamá border, the small and prefab town of **PALMAR** is the hub for the banana plantations of the area. This is a good place to see **lithic spheres**, scattered on the lands of several nearby plantations and on the way to **SIERPE**, 15km south, on the Río Sierpe. Ask politely for the "*esferas de piedra*"; if the banana workers are not too busy – don't pressure them – they may be able to show you where to look. Palmar is also a useful jumping-off point for the beautiful **Bahía Drake** – via Sierpe – and for the Marenco/San Pedrillo entrance to **Parque Nacional Corcovado** on the Osa Peninsula.

The town is divided in two by the Río Grande de Térraba. Palmar Sur is where the plane lands; most of the services, including hotels and buses to points beyond, are in **Palmar Norte**. *Osa Tours*, in the Centro Comercial del Norte, Palmar Norte (☎786-6534; fax 786-6335), offers **tourist information**, help with reservations and transport, as well as selling stamps; you can also make international telephone calls and receive money cabled by *Western Union*. **Accommodation** is very basic. Both *Cabinas Tico Aleman* (☎786-6232; ②) and *Casa Amarilla*, 300m east of the *TRACOPA* bus stop (☎786-6251; ①), have clean rooms with private bath and fan. Upstairs rooms at the *Amarilla* have balconies and better ventilation.

From San José, *TRACOPA* **buses** run to Palmar Norte six times daily, returning to the capital only three times. Buses for **Sierpe** leave Palmar Norte from the *Supermercado Térraba* (5 daily; first bus at 6am; 30min).

Bahía Drake and around

Bahía Drake (pronounced "Dra-kay") is named after Sir Francis Drake, who anchored here, and indeed set foot on land, in 1579. Today a favourite of **yachters**, the calm waters of the bay are dotted with flotillas of swish-looking boats. This has to be one of the most stunning areas in Costa Rica: the scenery, with fire-orange Pacific sunsets plunging like meteors into the water and Isla del Caño's blue wedge floating just off the coast, is pure tropics. The bay is rich in marine life, and a number of **boat trips** offer opportunities for spotting manta rays, marine turtles, porpoises and even whales. You can also go hiking or horse-riding, or take a tour to **Isla del Caño**, about 20km off the coast of the Osa Peninsula (and easily visible from Drake).

Bahía Drake and the tiny hamlet of **DRAKE** make a good base for Parque Nacional Corcovado on the northwest of the Osa Peninsula – the San Pedrillo entrance is walkable from here, and hikers can combine serious walking with serious comfort at either end of their trip to the Park by staying at one of the upscale rainforest "eco-lodge"-type hotels that have sprung up in recent years.

Getting to Bahía Drake: the Río Sierpe route

Like many other places in the Zona Sur, **getting to Bahía Drake** requires some planning. There are three choices: the really tough way, hiking in from Corcovado; the cheap way, by bus from San José and then by boat along the Río Sierpe; and the *lujo* or luxury way, by flying from San José to Palmar or Sierpe, and taking one of the many **packages** offered by hotels in the area. If you do this, transport to your lodge is taken care of.

LITHIC SPHERES

Aside from goldworking, the Diquis are known for their precise fashioning of large stone **spheres** – most of them nearly, within a centimetre or two, exactly circular, which is an astounding feat for a culture without technology. Thousands have been found in southwestern Costa Rica and a few in northern Panamá. Some are located in sites of obvious significance, like burial mounds, others in the middle of nowhere, and range in size from that of a tennis ball up to about two metres in diameter.

Neither recorded history nor the spheres themselves divulge their meaning, but when unearthed or found in groups, they seem to have been positioned in a way as to reflect the constellations. In many cases the Diquis transported them a considerable distance, rafting them across rivers or the open sea (the only explanation for their presence on Isla del Caño). This indicates that their placement and meaning must be deliberate and significant.

As well as around Río Sierpe, you can see lithic spheres most easily by visiting **Isla del Caño**. Tours are available from the Quepos/Manuel Antonio area (see p.290) and Dominical hotels (see p.311). Some of the posher Valle Central residences even have stone spheres – purchased by the inhabitants at great price – sitting in their front gardens as lawn sculpture.

Travelling **independently** you will need to get a bus from San José to Palmar (6 daily; 5hr 30min); depending on what time you get in, you can then either bed down in Palmar Norte or get a local bus (see opposite) or taxi to **Sierpe** (about $12), where there are a few cabinas. In Sierpe, you must find a **boatman** to take you the 30km downriver to Bahía Drake (2hr). You need someone with experience, a motorized *lancha*, and lifejackets. Emiliano González is recommended; he can take you practically anywhere on the peninsula (☎771-2336). You can also hook up with a boatman in *Bar Las Vegas*, a rendezvous for tourists and boat captains – try out the ancient jukebox while you wait. The going rate for a one-way trip to Drake is currently about $20 per person or around $70–80 per boatload (maximum usually 8); ask around for the best rates.

The trip down the Río Sierpe (2hr) is calm enough, with mangroves lining either side of the bank (you can spot monkeys, sloths and sometimes kingfishers), until you see the Pacific rolling in at the river mouth. The Sierpe is very wide where it meets the sea, and huge breakers crash in from the ocean, making it a turbulent and treacherous crossing. Sharks reportedly await here for their dinner. If the tide is right and the boatman knows his water, you'll be fine. All the *lanchas* used by the lodges have powerful outboard motors, and there's minimal chance of accident; all the same, some find this part of the trip a bit disconcerting. Once you are out in Bahía Drake the water is calm.

Accommodation in and around Bahía Drake

Virtually all the **eco-lodges** listed below do a range of **tours**, from accompanied excursions to Corcovado to boating in Bahía Drake and trips to Isla del Caño. The larger lodges are accustomed to bringing guests on packages from San José and can include transport from the capital, from Palmar, or from Sierpe. The packages (and the prices we give below) usually include three meals a day – there are few eating options in Drake otherwise. Although hoteliers will tell you you can't **camp** in the Drake area, people do – but you should do your best to be courteous as to where you pitch your tent, and make sure to leave no litter.

Aguila de Osa (☎ and fax 232-7722). Upmarket, nicely furnished, huge rooms with private bath and running hot water. Snorkelling and scuba trips offered, and meals available. ⑥.

Cabinas Cecilia, Agujitas (☎771-2336: this is the number of the *pulpería*; leave message for Doña Cecilia). Small, unpretentious cabinas with friendly *dueña* who can arrange horseriding and boating tours, and will cook for you. The lowest prives in the area; rooms have six bunks so are extra-cheap for groups. ③.

Cocalito Lodge (☎ and fax 786-6150). Small and family-run, with cabinas scattered around the main lodge, and delicious meals served. They rent mountain bikes and you can swim safely from the small beach in front. ⑤.

Bahía Drake Wilderness Camp (☎ and fax 771-2436). The most-established lodge in the area, providing a buffer zone between tourist and wilderness with rustic, comfortable cabinas – or, if you want to rough it a bit, nice tents. Both options are well-screened. Good local food, and snorkelling and canoeing available. It's popular, so best book and pay in advance. ⑥–⑨.

Albergue Jinetes de Osa (☎253-6909). Simple bunk accommodation with shared bath. Meals served. Can connect you with boat, horseriding tours and treks. ③.

Marenco Lodge, 7km south of Drake (☎221-1594 or 233-9101; fax 255-1340). Secluded accommodation in an ex-biological station, with thatched-roof cabinas and beautiful views of Isla del Caño. Snorkelling and swimming spots and good birdwatching, too. It's 5km north of Corcovado's San Pedrillo entrance, and a good starting point for hiking the San Pedrillo–Sirena trail (see p.330). Because of limited access (it can take 2hr to walk here from Drake) most guests come on all-inclusive packages. ⑥.

La Paloma, in Drake (☎ and fax 239-0954). Beautiful, rustic thatched-roof rooms in hilltop bungalows, with private bath (cold water), balconies and hammocks. Spectacular views, and great sunsets. They rent *pangas* – traditional canoes – so you can paddle on the Río Agujitas behind the lodge. Rates include three hearty meals; good value in this price range. ⑥.

Río Sierpe Lodge, on the Río Sierpe, near the mouth of Bahía Drake (☎223-9945; fax 233-2886). Family atmosphere with restaurant, library, rustic rooms with private bath, screens and fans. They can take you on boat trips to Playa Violin at the mouth of the Sierpe, Playa Blanca, and other remote coves. Also sportsfishing, diving, horseriding and snorkelling. ⑤.

Tent Camp, between Drake and Marenco (☎777-0368; fax 777-1248). Luxury camping with tents on raised wooden platforms, beds, shared bath and hammocks. Meals are served; packages are a bit on the pricey side. ⑥.

GETTING TO CORCOVADO FROM DRAKE

From Drake you can follow the **beachside trail** via Marenco to the San Pedrillo entrance of **Parque Nacional Corcovado** (see p.325). At a leisurely pace, it will take twelve hours, though fit hikers can do it in eight or less. You can camp at San Pedrillo, although the SPN much prefer that you advise them in advance of your intention to do this. If you are staying at any of the Bahía Drake lodges, they should be able to contact the Puerto Jiménez office of Corcovado, and you can make a reservation to stay and eat in San Pedrillo with the rangers.

Isla del Caño

The tiny, tabletop **RESERVA BIOLÓGICA ISLA DEL CAÑO** sits placidly in the ocean some 20km due west of Bahía Drake. Just 3km long by 2km wide, the island is probably the exposed part of an underwater mountain, thrown up by an ancient collision of the two tectonic plates on either side of Costa Rica. It's a pretty sight in the distance, and going there is even better – if you can afford it. You can't get there on your own, but sometimes a **tour** is included in the package price of the Drake lodges. Otherwise tours are run by many operators in the Manuel Antonio area (see p.290) and, increasingly, from Dominical (p.310).

The island is thought to have been a burial ground of the Diquis, who would have brought their famed **lithic spheres** here from the mainland in large, ocean-going canoes. Your guide can take you hiking into the thick rainforest interior to look for examples near the top of the 110-metre high crest, and you'll certainly come across some as you wander around – they're lying about all over the place. Caño is also a prime **snorkelling** and diving destination. Under water you'll see coral beds and various **marine life**, including spiny lobsters and sea cucumber, snapper, sea urchins, manta rays, octopus and the occasional barracuda. On the surface, porpoises and Olive Ridley marine turtles are regularly spotted; it's less common to catch a glimpse of humpback and sometimes sperm whales.

Golfito and around

The former banana port of **GOLFITO**, 33km north of the Panamanian border, straggles for 2500m along the water of the same name (*golfito* means "little gulf"). The town's **setting** is spectacular, backed up against thickly forested, steep hills on the east, and with the glorious Golfo Dulce – one of the deepest gulfs of its size in the world, formed by volcanic activity – to the west. The low shadow of the Osa Peninsula shimmers in the distance, and everywhere the vegetation has the soft muted look of the undisturbed tropics. It is also very **wet** – even if you speak no Spanish, you'll certainly pick up the local expression "*va a caer baldazos*": "it's gonna pour".

Golfito's **history** is inextricably intertwined with the giant transnational **United Brands** company – locally known as *La Yunai* – which first set up in this area in 1938, twenty years before the Interamericana hit town. The company built schools, and brought doctors and police to the area, as well as prosperity. "Problems" with labour union organizers began just ten years later, and came to characterize the relationship between company and town. What with fluctuating banana prices, a three-month strike by workers and local social unrest, the company eventually decided Golfito was too much trouble and pulled out in a hurry in 1985. The town died, and in the public eye became synonymous with rampant unemployment, alcoholism, abandoned children, prostitution and general unruliness.

Today, at the big old *muelle bananero*, container ships are still loaded up with bananas processed further up toward Palmar. This residual traffic, along with tourism – Golfito is a good base for getting to **Parque Nacional Corcovado** by *lancha* or plane, as well as a major **sportsfishing** centre – have combined to help revive the local economy. The real rescue, though, came from the Costa Rican government, who in the early 1990s established in the town a **depósito libre**, or tax-free zone, where Costa Ricans can buy manufactured goods imported from Panamá without the 100 percent tax normally levied. Ticos who come to shop here have to buy their tickets for the *depósito* 24 hours in advance, obliging them to spend a night, and therefore colones, in the town.

Golfito straggles for ages without any clear centre, and in some stretches where the main road is hemmed in by hills on one side and the lapping waters of the *golfito* on the other. The town is effectively divided – by the poverty line as well as architecturally – into two parts. In the north is the **zona americana**, where the banana company execs used to live and where better-off residents still

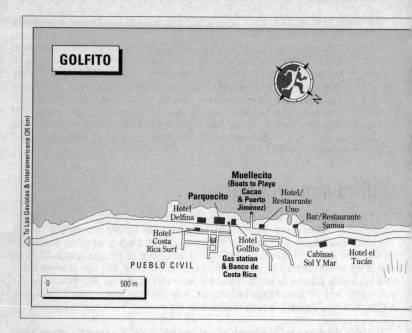

live, in beautiful wooden houses shaded by dignified palms. It is the site of the *depósito libre*, an unaesthetic outdoor mall ringed by a circular wall of concrete, with a cattle-auction atmosphere. South of the *parquecito*, the **pueblo civil** (civilian town), is a very small, tight nest of streets; hotter, noiser and more crowded than the *zona*. It's here you'll find the good-value hotels and sodas, as well as the *lancha* across the Golfo Dulce to Puerto Jiménez and the Osa Peninsula. Although the *pueblo civil* is perfectly civil in the daytime, tourists are warned not to wander around at night – although exactly why not is unclear. That there is prostitution and heavy drinking is no secret.

Arrival and information

Buses from San José currently leave *TRACOPA*'s terminal at 7am, 11am and 3pm (8hr). Buy your return ticket (see below) as soon as you disembark. You can also **fly** here with *Sansa*; the airstrip is in the *zona americana*.

    Banco de Costa Rica, in the *pueblo civil* next to the gas station, and *Banco Nacional*, in the *zona americana* next to the *TRACOPA* terminal (both Mon–Fri 8am–3.45pm) will theoretically change **travellers' cheques** but it's best to bring lots of cash just in case. The **correo** (Mon–Fri 7.30am–5pm) is a few blocks south of the *Banco de Costa Rica*. **VHF radio**, rather than telephone, is often used to communicate in this area, but there is an ICE office in the *pueblo civil*, across from the *muellecito*.

    Incidentally, it is especially important in Golfito to **carry ID** at all times, as the local police have been known to approach tourists in the streets, demanding to see passports (show a photocopy first, even if you have the real thing on you, and don't let anyone take your passport away).

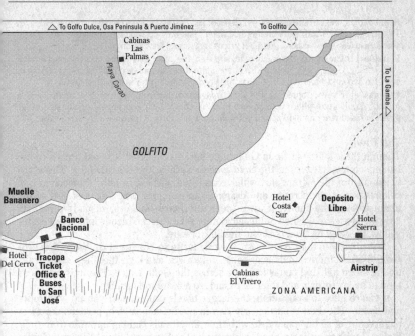

To Golfo Dulce, Osa Peninsula & Puerto Jiménez △   To Golfito △

Cabinas Las Palmas

Playa Cacao

To La Gamba △

GOLFITO

Muelle Bananero

Banco Nacional

Hotel Costa Sur

Depósito Libre

Hotel Sierra

Hotel Del Cerro   Tracopa Ticket Office & Buses to San José

Cabinas El Vivero

Airstrip

ZONA AMERICANA

Accommodation

Accommodation in Golfito comes in two varieties: swish places in the *zona americana*, catering to businesspeople and shoppers at the *depósito*, and decent, basic rooms in the *pueblo civil*.

Hotel del Cerro, between the *pueblo civil* and the *zona americana* (☎775-0006; fax 775-0551). Good-value, friendly budget option: they can help with tourist information and reservations. Rooms with choice of shared or private bath, heated water and ceiling fans. ②.

Hotel Costa Sur, in the *pueblo civil* (☎ and fax 775-0871). The nicest place to stay in the middle of the *pueblo civil*, although a bit noisy. Comfortable rooms with private bath (cold water only); a/c costs more than ceiling fans. Restaurant and bar on the premises. ③.

Hotel Delfina, in the *pueblo civil* (☎775-0043). An older house, converted into a warren of widely varying rooms. Some are good value, others are dark; those at the back are quieter, and overlook the water. Cheap rooms (shared bath, ceiling fan) are better value than those with private bath and ancient, groaning a/c. ②.

Esquinas Rainforest Lodge, La Gamba, 4km from Km-37 on the Interamericana (☎775-0849 or 0131; fax 775-0849 or 0631). Friendly, family-owned lodge, about 15min from Golfito. It's set in primary rainforest cover, with animals on the grounds. You can hike the on-site trails yourself or with a guide, and they offer a variety of tours, including to Corcovado and Wilson Botanical Gardens. Member of a local co-op, the lodge shares profits with the small community of La Gamba. Fantastic cooking; rates include meals. Packages available. ⑤.

Las Gaviotas, south end of the *pueblo civil* (☎775-0062; fax 775-0544). Without doubt the plushest hotel in town, right beside the water. Rooms in modern individual chalets have porches, private bath with heated water, ceiling fans or a/c ($10 more). There's a pool, outdoor restaurant with BBQ, and a private dock for yachts. ⑥.

Hotel Golfito, in the *pueblo civil* beside the gas station (☎775-0047). The cheapest deal around; stuffy, dark rooms, with private bath (cold water only) and ceiling fans. Most rooms sleep three, and single rates aren't bad. The back balcony has a nice view. ①.

Hotel Sierra, next to the airstrip (☎775-0666; fax 775-0087). Large modern rooms with a/c, TV, phone, private bath and running hot water. The only drawback is the occasional musty smell. Also a swimming pool, good but pricey restaurant, bar and disco. ⑤.

Pensión el Tucán, on the main road between the *zona americana* and the *pueblo civil* (☎775-0553). Good, cheap rooms. Most are quite dark, so look around, but all have private bath, fan and cold water only. The very friendly *dueña* will throw in breakfast for $2.50. ①.

Cabinas el Vivero, signed, in the *zona americana*. Big, simply furnished rooms, and a friendly family atmosphere with shared kitchen. *Dueño* Don Bob grows orchids and other plants in his nursery next door, and is a walking oral history of the area. Very good value. ①.

The Town

Though there's little to do in Golfito, be sure to check out the old homes of the banana company execs in the *zona americana* near the *depósito libre*. These are obvious from their grandeur: wide-verandahed, painted in jolly, if bleached out, colours, with huge screens and draping sun canopies. One line, just east of the main street in the centre of town (near the *Banco Nacional*) displays a particularly fine series of washed-out tropical hues – lime green blends into faded oyster yellow, followed by tired pink and metallic orange.

Immediately to the east of town, the tiny **Refugio Nacional de Vida Silvestre Golfito** is not immediately accessible to tourists, although there are some trails up the steep hill, and fantastic views across the Golfo Dulce. The trail entrances tend to be overgrown and difficult to find, so ask around locally.

If you're here to **sportsfish**, the larger hotels can connect you up with tours and tackle. The area is particularly rich in marlin and sailfish, perhaps the most picturesque of all big-game fish, with their fluted sails fanning upwards from their bodies. **Swimming** is no good, however, as the bay is polluted. All along Golfito you'll see oil in the water and various bits of floating refuse. Your best bet for a swim is to head across to Playa Cacao, or to move south down the Burica Peninsula.

Eating and drinking

There's no shortage of **places to eat** in Golfito. For *casados* and *platos del día* there are two conglomerations of simple **sodas**: one is near the *depósito libre*, and caters to Ticos who have come to Golfito on shopping trips. Slightly better value are the sodas in the *pueblo civil*, most of which are on the main drag or in the surrounding few streets. *Soda Magnolio* is a nice corner-side place, good for beer or a *refresco*, on the sea-facing side of the main road. At t-he tiny, cheap and cheerful *Soda Patricia*, you can sit in booths or at the formica counter: ask for their daily specials. With a nice breezy view of the water, *Restaurante la Eurekita* serves solidly *típico* food at prices slightly higher than you'd expect – the filet mignon, however, is good value.

Of the **hotel-restaurants**, *Hotel las Gaviotas*, south of the *pueblo civil*, has an all-you-can-eat barbecue on Friday and Saturday evenings from 6pm, open to non-guests. The meat is good, and they even have a reasonable wine list. The best thing about this place, though, is the waterside location, floating out over the *golfito*. The restaurant at the *Hotel Sierra* is also recommended, although expensive, dishing up tasty grilled shrimp and fish. Their continental breakfast is a good deal. Outside the hotel-restaurants, the beachside *Bar/Restaurante Samoa Sur*, 200m north of *Hotel Uno,* has a huge *palenque* roof and a garden. The menu includes seafood and pizza, and it's a nice place for an evening beer.

MOVING ON FROM GOLFITO

Buses to San José leave daily at 5am and 1pm. If you're getting the 5am bus you will need to have bought your return ticket in advance. There are also flights to San José on *Sansa*. For **Corcovado**, you can take the *lancha Arco Iris* across the Golfo Dulce to Puerto Jiménez (daily 11am; 1hr 30min; ☎735-5036; $3), or a small plane to Jiménez. The ten-minute flight can cost anywhere from $20 to a fortune, depending on the number of passengers (5 max). Contact *Aeronaves de Costa Rica* (☎775-0278) or *Aero Taxi* (☎735-5178).

Daily buses to Niely and San Vito leave from in front of the *muelle bananero*, where in the dry season only, you can also pick up buses south to **Playas Zancudo** and **Pavones** (2hr 30min–3hr). Getting to the beaches by road in the wet season is tricky, however, as buses do not run. It's just about manageable with a 4WD, but you need to check the levels of the creeks and fords that you have to pass. You can, however, get to them by water.

There are two competing **boatmen's associations** in Golfito. The official group, the Golfito Boatmen's Association, come and go from the old *muello bananero*. The smaller Independent Boatmen's Association, who seem just as well-equipped, are based at the municipal dock, called the *muellecito*, near the *pueblo civil*. All boats are motorized *lanchas*, and prices seem to be about the same for either group. Whichever you go with, make sure there are lifejackets on board; the Golfo Dulce is usually calm but winds can come up suddenly and waves are unexpectedly high. Boats can take you almost anywhere in the Golfo Dulce area – including Playa Cacao, Playa Cativo, Playa Zancudo and Puerto Jiménez – you'll get a better price by far if you gather a group together.

Around Golfito

Golfito is the jumping-off point for a couple of very isolated **beaches**, set on the **Burica Peninsula**, a thin-fingered, pristine stretch that is shared with Panamá. Ask anyone in town where you can swim without braving the sharks of the Osa Peninsula or the big clobbering waves that come ashore elsewhere, and they'll direct you to black-sand **Playa Zancudo**, 15km southwest of Golfito, facing the Golfo Dulce and bordered on one side by the Río Coto Colorado. During summer weekends (Dec–April) you may be joined by Zona Sur Ticos taking a beach break, otherwise it's very low-key, except for a small colony of US ex-pats. About 12km further south is **Playa Pavones** (marked on most maps as Bahía de Pavón, but locally called Pavones), famed among surfers for having the longest continuous wave in the world – exactly how long, they do not divulge. The waves are biggest and best from May to November. Needless to say the water's too rough for anything else. There's absolutely nothing to do either at Zancudo or Pavones other than swim (Zancudo) or wade (Pavones) and admire either the surfers' snazzy 4WDs or the view across to the Osa Peninsula, hovering on the distant horizon. Both beaches are a little over two hours' drive from Golfito, and entail crossing the Río Coto Colorado on a tiny ferry. You need 4WD, whatever the season.

After another 10km or so you come to **Punta Banco**, site of the beautiful *Tiskita Lodge* (☎255-2011 or 233-6890; fax 255-3529 or 4410; ⑤) a friendly, extremely comfortable rainforest lodge – which doubles as a biological research station – with cabinas overlooking the beach. Trails weave through the surrounding forest, birdwatching is good, and you can tour their fruit farm (the owner is an agronomist). They also offer good-value packages, including flight from San José and three high-quality meals a day.

North of Golfito are a couple of beaches accessible by boat. Although the beach is a little grimy, swimming is good at **Playa Cacao**, diagonally across the *golfito*. You can **stay** at *Cabinas Palmas* (☎775-0357; fax 775-0373; Aptdo 98, Golfito; ④), in well-equipped chalets right on the water. The friendly owners offer jungle walks and no-frills fishing tours, and there are a number of decent bars and restaurants nearby. You can get to Cacao by *lancha* from Golfito, or in the dry season drive a rough unfinished track from the turnoff right in front of the *guardia*, bearing left.

At **Playa Cativo**, thirty minutes by boat from Golfito, *Rainbow Adventures* (☎775-0220; in the US: ☎503/690-7750; fax 503/690-7735; ⑥) is one of the premier places of its kind in Costa Rica, with luxurious, tastefully decorated individual chalets next to a beautiful, pristine beach. They offer tours in the surrounding rainforest, as well snorkelling and birdwatching, and serve excellent food in the dining-room.

The Osa Peninsula

In the extreme southwest of the country, the **Osa Peninsula** is an area of immense biological diversity, semi-separate from the mainland. In the early years of the twentieth century, Osa was something of a **penal colony**; a place to which men were either sent forcibly or went, machete in hand, to forget. Consequently, a violent, frontierlands folklore permeates the whole peninsula, and old-time residents of **Puerto Jiménez** – the only town of any size – are only too happy to regale you with hosts of gory tales. Some may be apocryphal, but they certainly add colour to the place.

It was on the Osa Peninsula that the Diquis found **gold** in such abundant supply that they hardly had to pan or dig. Gold is still around, as is the odd *orero* (goldminer/panner). When **Parque Nacional Corcovado** was established, in the mid-1970s, substantial numbers of miners were panning within its boundaries, but the heaviest influx of *oreros* stemmed directly from the pull-out of the United Brands Company in 1985. Many were laid-off banana plantation workers with no alternate means of making an living: a case of the pull-out of a large-scale employer leading to immediate and serious environmental threat. In 1986 the *oreros* were forcibly deported from the Park by the Costa Rican police. Today, several well-known international conservationist groups are involved in protecting and maintaining Osa's ecological integrity, and recently successfully fought off an attempt to establish a wood-chip mill here.

Few will fail to be moved by Osa's beauty. Whether you approach the peninsula by *lancha* from Golfito or Bahía Drake, on the Jiménez bus, or driving in from the mainland, you will see what looks to be a floating island, an intricate mesh of blue and green, with tall canopy trees sailing high and flat like elaborate floral hats. You'll also see a revealing picture of *precarista* (squatter) life on the country's extreme geographical margins. Since the mid- to late 1980s the improvement of the road between Jiménez and Rincón has brought many families seeking land. Most have built simple shacks and cultivated a little roadside plot, burning away the forest to do so. They plant a few vegetables and a banana patch and may keep a few cattle. Soil here is classically tropical, with few nutrients, poor absorption and minimal regenerative capacity. In a few years it will have exhausted itself and the smallholders will have to cultivate new areas or move on.

You could feasibly "do" the whole peninsula in four days, but this would be rushing it, especially if you want to spend time walking the trails and wildlife-spotting at Corcovado. Most people allot five to seven days for the area, taking it at a relaxed pace, and more if they want to stay in and explore Bahía Drake (see p.314). Hikers and walkers who come to Osa without their own car tend to use Puerto Jiménez as a base: a place where it's easy to strike up a conversation, people are relaxed, environmentally conscientious, and not yet overwhelmed by tourism.

Puerto Jiménez

The friendly town of **PUERTO JIMÉNEZ** – known locally as just Jiménez – has plenty of places to stay and eat and good public transport connections. There's also the possibility of grabbing a lift with a truck to **Carate**, 43km southwest, from where you can enter Corcovado (see p.325). Drivers shouldn't try going further south – including to Carate – in anything less than a 4WD, at any time of year. What looks like a good, patted-down dirt road can turn into a quagmire after a sudden downpour.

Arrival and information

Two **buses** daily arrive from San José via San Isidro (6am & noon; 8–9hr) returning at 5am and 11am. The ticket office in Jiménez is open daily (7–11am & 1–5pm). There's a **lancha** from Golfito (1 daily; 1hr 30min), and you can **fly** in from San José with *Sansa*, or from Golfito on the *avioneta*. The *lancha* back to Golfito leaves at 6am (☎735-5036).

The **Corcovado administration and information office** (Mon–Fri 8am–4pm; ☎735-5036) is staffed by friendly rangers who can answer questions, arrange accommodation at the *puestos* (if you haven't already done so – in most cases you should have before coming) and radio ahead if you want to share your meals with the rangers (there's a small charge). For other **tourist information**, try Cecilia Solano's office at *Península de Osa S.A.* on the main drag (daily 7.30–11.30am & 1–5pm). You can make reservations here for area accommodation, and may be able to pay to use her phone and fax to call elsewhere or abroad (☎735-5138; fax 735-5073). Next door to the Park information office, the tiny *Banco Nacional* (Mon–Fri 8am–3pm; may close over lunch) may be able to change **travellers' cheques**, but the accepted wisdom is to come with all the colones you'll need. You can **telephone** from a few hotels.

The **town truck to Carate** goes most mornings in the dry season at about 6am, but you'd do best to confirm this locally. Ask Cecilia Solano, the Park information office, or staff at *Restaurante Carolina*. In the wet season it goes less often, about three days a week. If you don't get a place on the truck, a number of places **rent 4WD taxis**: Oscar Blanco at *Cabinas Puerto Jiménez* will take you to Carate and return at a fixed day or time to pick you up (about $50 per carload).

Accommodation

Jiménez's **hotels** are reasonably priced, clean and basic. Though in the dry season it's best to reserve, this may not always be possible, as phone and fax lines sometimes go down. In the rainy season there are far fewer people about and you

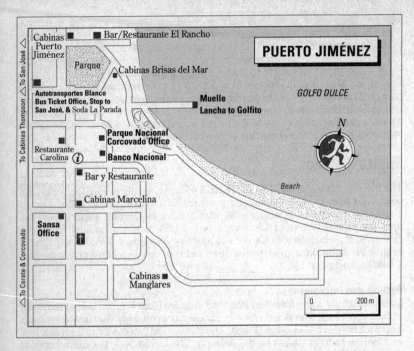

shouldn't need to worry about booking in advance. **Between Jiménez and Carate**, around the lower hump of the peninsula, are a few comfort-in-the-wilderness places, a couple of which make great **retreats** or honeymoon spots.

IN JIMÉNEZ

Iguana Iguana (☎735-5158). Good rooms, with private or shared bath, cold water only. There's a *sodita* – small restaurant – on the grounds, and a larger bar-restaurant is planned, along with six more cabinas. The friendly *dueña* will advise on transport to Corcovado or will drive guests there and back (pre-arrange pick-up time) for about $30. ②.

Cabinas Manglares, towards the airstrip (☎735-5002). The most upscale cabinas in town, in quiet surroundings, next to a mangrove swamp. Private bath (cold water) and ceiling fans, and a restaurant-bar on site. ④.

Cabinas Marcelina, right in town, east of the main drag. Big, basic rooms with shelf space, table fan, and private bath (cold water only); owned by friendly family. ①.

Cabinas Puerto Jiménez, next to *El Rancho*. Quiet (unless the adjacent disco is on – ask around) cabinas next to the water. Simple, clean, nicely furnished rooms, well-screened, with bath and fan. Some can be dark, so ask to see a few. ②.

Cabinas Thompson, 25m west of the San José bus stop (☎735-5140). Rock-bottom budget rooms with cement floors; can be airless, despite fans. Pity about the noisy local dogs. ①.

BETWEEN PUERTO JIMÉNEZ AND CARATE

The following are ordered in order of their distance from Puerto Jiménez. The first, *Tierra de Milagros*, is 20km south from Jiménez. The last, *Corcovado Tent Camp*, sidles right up to the Park entrance. All are signed.

Tierra de Milagros (☎735-5073). Rustic lodge in a nature preserve. You sleep in an open (no walls, but a roof) *rancho* in hammocks or sleeping bag. All meals are vegetarian or fish, and no smoking is allowed. Proceeds help fund a local reforestation project. ②.

Lapa Ríos (☎735-5130; fax 735-5179; in USA: PO Box 025216-SJO 706, Miami, FL 33102-5216). One of the most comfortable and impressive "jungle lodges" in the country, set in a private nature reserve of more than 1000 acres. Rooms have big beds and mosquito nets, and blend into surrounding forest. There's a huge thatch-roofed restaurant, complete with spiral staircase, and a swimming pool on site (you can't swim in the ocean due to sharks and currents). Excellent birdwatching on the grounds. ⑦.

Bosque del Cabo, above Playa Matapalo, down private road to the left (☎735-5206; fax 735-5073). Very secluded, comfortable bungalows, with stupendous views out to the Pacific. The owners are helping to repopulate scarlet macaws, and there are lots around. Waterfall and swimming hole nearby, and a good restaurant. ⑤.

Corcovado Tent Camp, about 45-min walk along the beach from Carate (book via *Costa Rica Expeditions*; see p.25). Eight self-contained "tent-camps" fully screened, elevated on short stilts, with bedroom and screened verandah, in an amazing beachside location in front of breakers, sheltered behind a little clutch of palm trees. Communal baths, and good local cooking served on site (rates include meals). Very good value; packages available, some that will fly you right to Carate. ④.

Eating and drinking

There's not much choice when it comes to **eating** in Jiménez, but you certainly won't starve. Everybody goes to *Restaurante Carolina*, on the main drag, which has a *comida típica* menu. The soda beside the *Transportes Blanco* bus stop is as good a place as any to have a *casado* or *plato del día*. For **evening meals** the friendly, gringo-run restaurant on the corner 100m north of *Cabinas Marcelina* is the nicest, with good fish, cold beers, a CD collection and a few outside tables.

Parque Nacional Corcovado

Created in 1975, **PARQUE NACIONAL CORCOVADO** ("hunchback"), 368km southwest of San José (daily 8am–4pm; $15 on the day, $7 in advance), protects a fascinating, biologically complex area of land, most of it on the peninsula itself. It also covers one mainland area just north of Golfito, which may soon be made into a National Park in its own right.

It's an undeniably beautiful Park, with deserted beaches, some laced with waterfalls, high canopy trees and better than average wildlife-spotting opportunities. Many people come with the express purpose of spotting a **margay, ocelot, tapir** and other rarely seen animals. Of course, it's all down to luck, but if you walk quietly and there aren't too many other humans around, you should have a better chance of seeing some of these creatures here than elsewhere.

Serious walking in Corcovado is not for the faint-hearted. Quite apart from the distances and the terrain, **hazards** include insects (*lots* of them, especially in the rainy season: take a mosquito net, tons of repellent, and all the precautions you can think of), herds of peccaries – who have been known to menace hikers – rivers full of crocodiles (and in one case, sharks), and nasty snakes, including the *terciopelo* and bushmaster who can attack without provocation. That said, most of these are present elsewhere in the country anyway, and everybody seems to make it through Corcovado just fine. But you must at least be prepared to get wet, dirty, incredibly hot, and also be ready to resist the temptation to jump in the sea to cool off (there are many sharks).

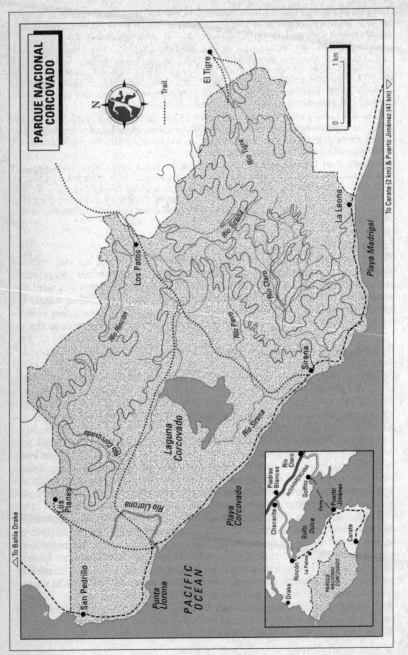

PARQUE NACIONAL
CORCOVADO

N

········· Trail

0 ___ 1 km

To Bahía Drake ◁

PACIFIC
OCEAN

San Pedrillo

Punta
Llorona

Los
Planes

Río Llorona

Río Corcovado

Río Rincón

Laguna
Corcovado

Playa
Corcovado

Río Sirena

Los Patos

Sirena

Río Sirena

Río Pavo

Río Claro

La Leona

Playa Madrigal

Río Tigre

El Tigre

To Carate (2 km) & Puerto Jiménez (41 km) ▷

Chacarita
Piedras
Blancas
Río
Claro
INTERAMERICANA
Golfito
Golfo
Dulce
Puerto
Jiménez
Ferry
Rincón
La Palma
Drake
Carate
PARQUE
NACIONAL
CORCOVADO

The **terrain** in Corcovado varies from beaches of packed or soft sand, riverways, mangroves, *holillo* (palm) swamps to dense forest, although most of it is at lowland elevations. Hikers can expect to spend most of their time on the beach trails that ring the outer perimeters of the peninsular section of the Park. Inland, the broad alluvial Corcovado plain contains the **Corcovado lagoon**, and for the most part the cover constitutes the only sizable chunk of tropical **premontane wet forest** (also called tropical humid forest) on the Pacific side of Central America. The Osa forest is as visually and biologically magnificent as any on the subcontinent: biologists often compare the tree heights and density here with that of the Amazon basin cover – practically the only place in the entire isthmus of which this can still be said.

The coastal areas of the peninsular section of the Park receive at least 3800mm of **rain** a year, with precipitation rising to about 5000mm in the higher elevations of the interior. This intense wetness, combined with a sunny respite, is ideal for the growth and development of the intricate, densely matted cover associated with tropical wet forests. There's a dry season (Dec–March). The inland lowland areas, especially those around the lagoon, can be amazingly **hot**, even for those accustomed to tropical temperatures.

Practicalities

Unless you are coming to Corcovado with *Costa Rica Expeditions* and staying in their tent camp (see p.325), you have to **reserve** in advance, by visiting, faxing or phoning the SPN in San José (see p.65). They will make you a reservation for meals, camping space or lodging at the *puesto* of your choice (see below). You have to specify your dates and stick to them. In the rainy season or off-peak times (generally after Easter and before Christmas), it's possible to do all this at the Corcovado administration and information office in Jiménez, but the SPN prefer that you go through their San José office. Current prices for **staying** at the *puestos* are $2 per night for camping, or $4 for sleeping under the attic roof at Sirena. You can either take **meals** with the rangers ($4 for breakfast, $6 for lunch and dinner – you pay in colones at the *puesto*) or bring your own food and utensils and use their stove. Food is basic – rice and beans or fish – but filling.

The SPN suggest that you come in a group of at least two people, that you **bring** your own tent, mosquito net, sleeping bag, food and water – though you can fill up at the beachside waterfalls at at the *puestos* – and advise that you be more or less experienced in hiking in this kind of terrain. You should plan to **hike** early in the day – not before dawn, due to snakes – and take shelter at midday. Corcovado is set up so that the rangers at each *puesto* always know how many people are on a given trail, and how long they are expected to be. If you are late getting back, they will go looking for you. This gives a measure of security, but, all the same, take **precautions**. There have been no mishaps (like people getting lost) in the Park of late, but always check with the rangers or ask around in Jiménez regarding current conditions. A few years ago things were tense between the *oreros* who still mine, some of them illegally, in and around Corcovado, and the rangers, whose job it is to stop them. Though no tourist has been hurt, the *oreros* may well be suspicious of strangers, and it's best not to walk alone just in case.

Incidentally, it's especially important when coming to Corcovado to brush up on your **Spanish**. You'll be asking the rangers for a lot of crucial information, and few, if any, of them speak English. Bring a phrase book if you're not fluent.

Puestos and routes through the Park

In the village of **Carate**, about 43km from Jiménez, Sr Morale's *pulpería* sells basic foodstuffs. You can also pitch your **tent** right outside; he charges a minimal amount for use of his toilets and showers. From here it is a 45-minute walk along the beach to enter Corcovado at the **La Leona** *puesto*. It's then a sixteen-kilometre hike to **Sirena**, where you can stay for a day or two in the simple lodge, exploring the local trails around the Río Sirena. Sirena, the biggest *puesto* in the Park, is also a research station, often full of biologists. Hikers coming from the Bahía Drake area enter at **San Pedrillo** and walk to Sirena from here.

The small hamlet of La Palma, 24km north of Puerto Jiménez, is the starting point for getting to the **Los Patos** *puesto*. It's a twelve-kilometre walk to the Park, much of it through hot lowland terrain. You need to arrive at Los Patos soon after dawn; if you want to stay in La Palma and get up early, *Cabinas Corcovado* (①–②) are a good bet. The relatively new **El Tigre** *puesto*, at the eastern inland entrance to the Park, is the largest and most comfortable of all the Corcovado *puestos*, a good place to take breakfast or lunch with the ranger(s) before setting off on the local trails. To get there from Jiménez, drive 10km north and take the second left, a dirt track, signed to El Tigre and Dos Brazos.

All puestos have camping areas, drinking water, information, toilets and telephone or radio telephone contact. Wherever you enter, jot down the **marea** (tide tables) which are posted in prominent positions. You'll need to cross most of the rivers at low tide. To do otherwise is dangerous. Rangers can advise on conditions.

LOCAL GUIDES

In recent years a programme to train local men and women between the ages of 18 and 35 as **naturalist guides** has been initiated at Rincón de Osa, a village about 35km north of Jiménez, snug in the curve of the Golfo Dulce. The programme is typical in Costa Rica – Rara Avis and Selva Verde in Sarapiquí, among others, have similar schemes – enabling people to not only make a living from their naturally acquired local knowledge, but also to appreciate the many ways in which a rainforest can be sustainable. Guides are taught to identify some of the 367 or more species of birds recorded in the area, the 177 amphibians and reptiles, nearly 6000 insects, 140 mammals and 1000 trees – Corcovado's biodiversity makes for a lot of homework. They are also given lectures in tourism and tutored by working professional guides. If you wish to hire a local guide, ask in Rincón or at the Fundación Neotrópica office in San José for details. This arrangement works best if you are planning to hike around the El Tigre *puesto* or on the Los Patos–Sirena trail, as these are the nearest entrances to Rincón.

Walking the trails

The fifteen-kilometre trail from **La Leona to Sirena** runs nearly entirely upon the beach. You can only walk its full length at low tide, as at high tide you may be cut off from getting across a couple of headlands. If you do get caught out, the only thing to do is wait for the water to recede. With few tide problems you should be able to make the walk in five hours, although most hikers take six, taking time to look out for birds. The walk can get a bit monotonous, but the beaches are uniformly lovely and deserted, and if you are lucky you may spot a flock of **scarlet**

WHAT TO SEE AT CORCOVADO

Walking through Corcovado you will see many lianas, vines, mosses and **spectacularly tall trees** – some of them 50m or 60m tall, and a few more than 80m high. All in all, Corcovado's area is home to about a quarter, or five hundred, of all the tree species in the country, including the **silkwood** (or *ceiba pentandra*), characterized by its height (it is thought to be the largest tree in Central America) and its smooth grey bark. One silkwood, near the Llorona–San Pedrillo section of the trail, is over 80m high and 3m in diameter. You'll also notice huge **buttresses**: above-ground roots shot out by the silkwoods and other tall canopy species. These are used to help anchor the massive tree in thin tropics soil where drainage is particularly poor.

Corcovado supports a higher volume of **large mammals** than most other areas of the country, except perhaps the wild and rugged Talamancas. **Jaguars** need more than 100 square kilometres each for their hunting and territorial grounds; if you are a good tracker you may be able to spot their tracks within the Park, especially in the fresh mud along trails and riverbeds. Initially they look identical to those made by a large dog, but the four toes are of unequal size – the outermost one is the smallest – and the fore footprint should be wider than its length. You might, too, see the **margay**, a spotted wildcat about the size of a large domesticated house cat, which comes down from the forest to sun itself on rocks at midday. The **ocelot**, a larger spotted cat, is even shyer; rarely seen for more than a second, poking its head out of the dense cover and then melting away into the forest again immediately.

With a body shape somewhere between a large pig and a cow, the **Baird's tapir** is an odd-looking animal, most immediately recognizable for its funny-looking snout, a truncated elephant-type trunk. Tapirs are *very* shy – and have been made even more so through large-scale hunting – and not aggressive. You would have to be exceptionally lucky to see one here or anywhere. More threatening are the packs of white-collared **peccaries**, a type of wild pig, who in Corcovado typically group themselves in packs of about thirty. They are often seen along the trails and should be treated with caution. The accepted wisdom is to climb a tree if they come at you threateningly, clacking their jaws and growling – this, of course, means you have to be good at climbing trees, some of which have painful spines.

More common mammals that you will almost certainly catch a glimpse of are the ubiquitous **agoutis** (also called pacas), foraging in the underbrush. Essentially a large rodent with smooth, glossy hair, the agouti looks similar to a large squirrel. The **coati**, a member of the racoon family, with a long ringed tail, is sure to cross your path. Another mammal found in significant numbers in the Park – and all over the peninsula – is the **tayra** (*tolumuco*), a mink-like creature, small and swift. They will in most cases run from you, but should not be approached; they have teeth and can be aggressive.

Among the birds that call Corcovado home is the **scarlet macaw**. Around 300 or so live in the Park; more, in terms of birds per square kilometre, than anywhere else in the country. Macaws are highly prized as caged birds, and despite the efforts of the SPN, poaching is still a problem in Corcovado, as their (relative) abundance makes them easy prey. Around the Río Sirena estuary especially, keep an eye out for the **boat-billed heron**, whose wide bill gives it a lopsided quality. The big black **king vulture** is present at Corcovado; a forager rather than a hunter, it still looks pretty ominous. There are many other smaller birds in Corcovado including, perhaps, the fluffy-headed **harpy eagle**. Though the harpy is thought to be extinct in Costa Rica, ornithologists reckon there is a chance that a few pairs still live in Corcovado, and in the Parque Internacional la Amistad on the Talamanca coast (see p.333).

macaws in the coastal trees – a rare sight. You will probably see (or hear) monkeys, too. You need to take lots of sunscreen, a big hat and at least five litres of water per person; it is very hot on this trail, despite sea breezes.

The really heroic walk in Corcovado, all 25km of it, is from **Sirena to San Pedrillo** – the stretch along which you'll see the most impressive trees. It's a two-day trek, so you need a tent, sleeping bag and mosquito net, and must not be worried by pitching in the jungle. Fording the **Río Sirena**, just 1km beyond the Sirena *puesto*, is the biggest obstacle: this is the deepest, with the strongest out-tow current, of all the rivers on the peninsula. It has to be crossed with care, at low tide only. At high tide, sharks come in and out in search of food. Get the latest information from the Sirena rangers before you set out.

About half of the walk is spent slogging it out on the beach, where the sand is more tightly packed than along the La Leona–Sirena stretch. Some hikers do the beach section of the walk well before dawn or after dark; there are fewer dangers (like snakes) at night on the beach and as long as you have a good torch with lots of batteries and/or the moon is out, this is a reasonable option. You can pitch a tent well up on the beach, but it is best to ask the rangers to recommend a good spot. The other half – a seven-hour stint – is in the jungle, most of the time following the coast. Beyond the jungle you come once more to the beach; here you are only about 40 minutes to an hour away from the Río San Pedrillo and just 10km from Bahía Drake, easily walkable along the coast.

All in all, the trail across the peninsula from **Los Patos to Sirena** is twenty-kilometres long. You may want to take a rest at the entrance, as this is an immediately demanding walk, continuing uphill for about 6 to 8km and taking you into high, wet and dense rainforest. After that you've still got 14km or so of incredibly hot lowland walking to go. This is the trail for experienced rainforest hikers and hopeful **mammal**-spotters: taking you through the interior, it gives you a reasonable chance of coming across, for example, a margay, or the tracks of tapirs and jaguars. That said, some hikers come away very disappointed, having not seen a thing. It's a gruelling trek, especially with the hot inland temperatures (at least 26°C and 100 percent humidity), and the lack of sea breezes. It's not the route to take if you have not done much rainforest hiking before.

The **El Tigre** area, at the eastern inland entrance to the Park, is gradually becoming more developed, with short walking trails cut around the *puesto*. These provide an introduction to Corcovado without having to slog it out on the marathon trails, and can easily be covered in a morning or afternoon.

Parque Nacional Isla del Coco

Integrated into the National Park system in 1978, these days the remote **PARQUE NACIONAL ISLA DEL COCO**, 500km southwest off Costa Rica's southern Pacific coast ($15) is most famous for being the location of Dinosaur Island in Steven Spielberg's blockbuster *Jurassic Park*. In the opening frames of the film, a helicopter swoops over azure seas to a remote, emerald-green isle: that's Coco. At 12km long and 5km wide, Coco is the only island in this part of the Pacific that receives enough rain to support the growth of a **rainforest**. It also has an extraordinary wealth of **endemic species**: seventy plant species, sixty-four insect species, three local spiders and four types of bird, all of which are found nowhere else in the world. Besides researchers and rangers, Coco has no human inhabitants.

Though evidence suggests that the island was known by pre-Columbian sea-going peoples from Ecuador and Columbia, in the modern age it was "discovered" by the navigator and sea captain Joan Cabezas in 1526. In the early twentieth century, attempts were made to establish a colony, would-be settlers bringing their pigs and coffee plants with them. Today wild versions of the pigs and flourishing coffee plants have upset the island's Galapagos-like ecosystem. Other threats include illegal fishing in its waters; the SPN has extremely limited resources for policing the island, as simply getting there by sea is so expensive. Besides biologists and divers Coco attracts treasure hunters. It is said that over the centuries nefarious pirates buried bullion here, but in more than five hundred expeditions by tenacious treasure hunters, no one has yet found it.

Getting to Coco entails major expense. It is, as you'd expect, a pristine and undisturbed destination for qualified divers only. In the North American winter months the ship *Okeanos* leaves from Puntarenas (see p.271) for specialist ten-day **diving tours**. The price is about $2600 per person, excluding transport to Costa Rica and equipment rental, which is available once you arrive (in the US, call ☎1-800/348-2628).

The Interamericana to Panamá

On the Interamericana, 25km south of the turnoff for the mountain town of **Buenos Aires** (just off the Interamericana 64km south of San Isidro), you come to the **Paso Real ferry**. From here you can continue on the Interamericana, or take the tiny car ferry and drive a little-touristed route along the new paved road, which takes you through some spectacularly scenic country. The latter is little used by tourists except those few heading to the pretty mountain town of **San Vito**, jumping-off point for the **Wilson Botanical Gardens** and **Parque Internacional la Amistad**. Most people stick to the Interamericana, which switch-backs its way to the Panamá border following the fast-running and wide **Río Grande de Térraba**. The river cuts a giant path through the almost unbearably hot lowland landscape, its banks red-lipped with tropical soils and low forested hills rising on the other side. Very simple dwellings and almost no towns line the roadside, where locals wait patiently for the few buses that ply this area. Rainstorms seem to steamroller in with the express purpose of washing everything away, and you can almost see the river rise with each fresh torrent. The area is prone to landslides in the rainy season, when you can find yourself stranded by a sea of mud. The last section of the trip down to **Panamá** is through something of a no-man's-land, with the highway being the major feature of the landscape. There are few towns or hamlets in this universal limboland of border regions.

Boruca and Reserva Indígena Boruca

About 12km past the turnoff for Buenos Aires on the Interamericana, and then 18km up a bad road, is the village of **BORUCA**. This is officially within an **indigenous reserve** and, technically, foreign tourists need a better reason to come than simply to look around. However, because of its proximity to the highway, tourists do occasionally turn up, usually looking to buy local **crafts**. The women of Boruca make small tablecloths and purses on home-made looms; the men make balsa-wood masks, some of which are expressly intended for the *diablitos* (little devils)

THE BORUCAS AND THE FIESTA DE LOS DIABLITOS

Many indigenous peoples throughout the isthmus, and all the way north to Mexico, enact the **fiesta de los diablitos** – a resonant spectacle that is both disturbing and humorous. In Costa Rica the Borucas use it to celebrate New Year and to re-enact the Spanish invasion, with Columbus, Cortez and his men reborn every year. The fiesta takes place over three days and is a village affair: foreigners and tourists are not encouraged to come as spectators. On the first day a village man is appointed to play the bull; others disguise themselves as little devils (*diablitos*), with masks carved from balsawood, and burlap sacks. The *diablitos* taunt the bull, teasing him with sticks, while the bull responds in kind. At midnight on December 30 the *diablitos* congregate on the top of a hill, joined by musicians playing simple flutes and horns fashioned from conch shells. During the whole night and over the next three days, the group proceeds from house to house, visiting everyone in the village, enjoying a drink of home brew (*chicha*) and indulging in general conviviality. On the third day, the "bull" is ritually killed. The symbolism is indirect, but the bull, of course, represents the Spaniard(s), and the *diablitos* the indigenous people. The bull is always vanquished and the *diablitos* always win – which of course is not quite how it turned out, in the end.

ceremony and procession that takes place on New Year's Eve. You can buy only from the artisans themselves – there's no store or co-op – which entails a good knowledge of Spanish. Local people have little other outlet for their crafts (you won't find them in the San José shops) so a visit can be a good way of contributing to the local economy – though once again you'll need a 4WD to get here.

San Vito

The road from **Paso Real**, 28km south of Buenos Aires, to San Vito is newly paved: steep and winding, it offers beautiful views. Just beyond Paso Real a tiny (two cars only) ferry crosses the Río Térraba on demand. Stop at *Soda la Balsa* for a *refresco* or a piece of pineapple. Even though the roads around here have improved, you'll have more peace of mind if you have a 4WD, to deal with occasional washouts and landslides (May–Nov especially).

Settled largely by post WWII immigrants from Italy, **SAN VITO** is a clean, prosperous agricultural town with a lovely setting in the Talamancas. At nearly 1000m above sea level, it has a wonderfully refreshing climate, as well as great views over the Valle de Coto Brus, below. The town is growing as Costa Ricans discover its attributes and will soon be an important regional hub; for now, though, there's nothing to do around here but visit the nearby **Wilson Botanical Gardens**, 6km south (Tues–Sun 7.30am–4pm; $5). Owned by the OTS (see p.199), the gardens are the best in the country, and on the itineraries of many specialist birdwatching and natural history tours. They make an excellent day trip if you already happen to be in the area, but unless you have a keen interest it is probably not worth making a special trip from San José. The huge tract of land is home to orchids, interesting tropical trees, and exotic flowers such as heliconias. There's good **birding**, too, on the paths and in the surrounding lands: more than 300 species in total. You can **stay** at the Gardens, in OTS bunkhouses or cabinas with private bath (②–⑥). Students and reserachers with ID get reduced rates. Contact the OTS (☎240-6696; fax 240-6738) for details; you must reserve in advance.

Parque Internacional la Amistad

Created in 1982 as a Biosphere Reserve, **PARQUE INTERNACIONAL LA AMISTAD** (daily 8am–4pm; $5 in advance, $15 on the day), is a joint venture by the governments of Panamá and Costa Rica to protect the Talamancan mountainous areas on both sides of their shared border. Amistad also encompasses several **indigenous reserves**, the most geographically isolated in the country, where Bribrí and Cabecar peoples are able to live with minimal interference from the Valle Central. It is the largest Park in the country, covering 207,000 hectares of Costa Rican territory.

In 1983 Amistad was designated a World Heritage site, thanks to its immense scientific wealth. The Central American isthmus is often described as being a crossroads or filter for the meeting of the North and South American ecocommunities; the Amistad area is itself a "biological bridge" within the isthmus, where an extraordinary number of habitats, life zones, topographical features, soils, terrains, animal and plant life can be found. Its **terrain**, while mainly mountainous, is extremely varied on account of shifting altitudes, and ranges from wet tropical forest to high peaks where the temperature can go down to below freezing at night. According to the classification system devised by LR Holdridge (see *Contexts*), Amistad has at least seven (some say eight or nine) **life zones**, along with six transition zones. Even more important is Amistad's function as the last bastion of some of the species in most danger of **extinction** in both Costa Rica and the isthmus. Within its boundaries roam the jaguar and the puma, the ocelot, and the tapir. Along with Corcovado on the Osa Peninsula, Amistad may also be the last holdout of the harpy eagle, feared extinct in Costa Rica.

Too bad for keen natural historians and animal spotters, then, that the terrain is so rugged, for there is only limited access to Amistad. Indeed, only serious and experienced walkers and hikers should consider it a destination. There are few rangers in relation to the area they need to cover, and getting lost and/or running out of water and food is potentially fatal. Drinking from the many streams and rivers is not recommended, due to the presence of the giardia bacterium.

Practicalities

If you are really serious about exploring La Amistad's limited (and often unmarked and uncleared) trails, contact the SPN office in San José in advance. They may be able to hook you up with a local guide who knows the area well. The small hamlet of **Progreso**, 40km northwest of San Vito, functions as the Park headquarters, with a *puesto* maintained by a full-time ranger who can provide information. You'll need 4WD to get here, whatever the season. From Progreso you can walk a demanding ten-kilometre-long trail, most of it uphill, to a flat ridge called **Las Tablas**, where it is possible to **camp**. Take water, tent and a three-season sleeping bag.

Near Las Tablas, bordering the Park, *La Amistad Lodge*, 3km from the hamlet of Las Mellizas on the way to Sabalito (☎773-3193; in San José: ☎233-8228; ⑤) is a new hotel, with comfortable rustic rooms. It's on the Montero family farm, which also grows organic coffee. The Monteros have hewn a few kilometres of trails in the surrounding woods, and can provide transport if you ask in advance.

Virtually the only **organized tour** to Amistad is a specialist birdwatching excursion run by San-José-based *Costa Rica Expeditions* (see p.25; tours run on demand, minimum 4 people).

Paso Canoas and the Panamanian border

Dutyfree shops and stalls lining the Interamericana announce the approach to **PASO CANOAS**. As you come into town, either driving or on the *TRACOPA* or international *Ticabus* service, you'll pass the Costa Rican customs checkpoint, where everybody gets a going-over. Foreigners don't attract much interest, however; customs officials are far more concerned with nabbing Costa Ricans coming back over the border with an unauthorized amount of cheap consumer goods.

To cross from Costa Rica into Panamá most nationalities need a **tourist card**: exceptions include nationals of the UK, Austria, Germany, Finland, Spain and Switzerland, who need only bring their passport. Tourist cards should be collected in advance from the **Panamanian consulate**, or from the office of *Copa*, Panama's national airline, in San José. The Paso Canoas *migración* is notorious for running out of them, and you won't be allowed to enter without one. Many people should also have a **visa** – Canadians, Australians and New Zealanders among them. Requirements change, often at short notice, so always check with the Panamanian consulate before setting off.

The **migración** is on the Costa Rican side, next to the *TRACOPA* bus terminal. You'll have to wait in line, maybe for several hours, especially if a San José–David–Panamá City *Ticabus* comes through, as all international bus passengers are processed together. Arrive early (8am) to get through fastest. There's no problem **changing currency**; on the Costa Rican side of the border there is a *Banco Nacional* (Mon–Fri 8am–4pm) and, beyond that, plenty of moneychangers. Note that Panamá has no paper currency of its own, and US dollars, here called *balboas*, are used. It does have its own coin currency, which is interchangeable with US coins and notes.

If you absolutely have to bed down in Paso Canoas, there are about a dozen rock-bottom cheap **cabinas** and *hospedajes*. These are all extremely basic, with cell rooms, private bath and cold water. They can be full on weekends. One place a cut above the pack is *Cabinas Interamericano*, on a sideroad to the right after the *TRACOPA* bus terminal, heading towards the border (①). Rooms are not bad, and there's a restaurant.

Note that you cannot take any fruit or vegetables across the border – even if they're your lunch. They will be confiscated.

On to David

DAVID, the first city of any size in Panamá, is about ninety minutes beyond the border. Buses run from the Panamanian bus terminal every hour or so until 5pm. From David it's easy to pick up local services, including the *Ticabus* to Panamá City, which you can't pick up at the border.

travel details

Buses

San José to: Golfito (3 daily; 8hr); Palmar Norte (6 daily; 5hr 30min); Paso Canoas (4 daily; 9hr); Puerto Jiménez (2 daily; 8–9hr); San Isidro (12 daily; 3hr).

Dominical to: Quepos (2 daily; 2hr); San Isidro (2 daily; 40min–1hr).

Golfito to: Playas Pavones and Zancudo (dry season only, 1 daily; 2hr 30min); San José (2 daily; 8hr).

Palmar Norte to: San José (3 daily; 5hr 30min); Sierpe (5 daily; 30min).

Paso Canoas to: San Isidro (2 daily; 6hr); San José (4 daily; 9hr).

Playas Pavones/Zancudo to: Golfito (dry season only, 1 daily; 2hr 30min).

Puerto Jiménez to: San Isidro (2 daily; 5hr); San José (2 daily; 8–9hr).

San Gerardo de Rivas to: San Isidro (2 daily; 40min).

San Isidro to: Dominical (2 daily; 40min–1hr); Puerto Jiménez (2 daily; 5hr); Quepos (2 daily; 3hr 30min); San Gerardo de Rivas, for Chirripó (2 daily; 40min); San José (12 daily; 3hr); Uvita (1 daily; 1hr 30min).

Sierpe to: Palmar Norte (5 daily; 30min).

Uvita to: San Isidro (1 daily; 1hr 30min).

Flights

Sansa

San José to: Golfito (1 daily Mon–Sat, 2 daily Wed–Fri); Palmar Sur (1 daily Tues, 2 daily Mon, Wed, Thurs, Fri & Sat); Puerto Jiménez (1 daily Mon–Sat).

Golfito to: San José (1 daily Mon–Sat, 2 daily Wed–Fri).

Palmar to: San José (3 daily Mon & Sat, 2 daily Wed, Thurs, Fri – always indirect, via Quepos, Puerto Jiménez or Coto 47).

Puerto Jiménez to: San José (1 daily Mon–Sat).

Ferries

The *lancha Arco Iris* leaves Golfito daily at 11am (1hr 30min), returning from Jiménez at 6am.

PART THREE

THE
CONTEXTS

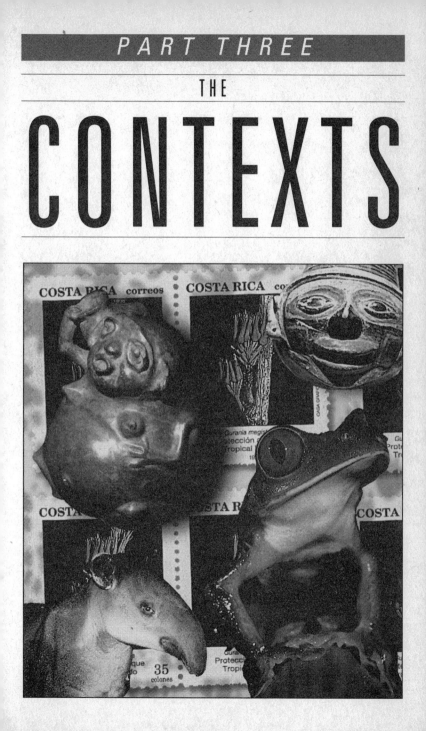

A BRIEF HISTORY OF COSTA RICA

The peopling of Costa Rica probably took place sometime around 10,000 BC, about 25,000 years after the first *homo sapiens* had crossed the Bering Strait into what is now the Americas. The only thing to attest to this tentative date is a single flint arrowhead excavated in the 1890s in Guanacaste. Archeologists know almost nothing of the various people who inhabited modern-day Costa Rica until about 1000 BC. Certainly no written records were left.

What is known is that Costa Rica was a contact zone – a corridor for merchants and trading expeditions – between the Mesoamerican empires to the north and the Andean empire to the south. Excavations of pottery, jade and trade goods, and accounts of cultural traditions have shown that the pre-Columbian peoples of Costa Rica adopted liberally from both areas.

When the Spaniards arrived in Costa Rica in the early sixteenth century, it was inhabited by as many as 27 different groups or clans. Most clans were assigned names by the invaders, which they took from the *cacique* (chief) with whom they dealt. The modern-day Zona Norte was home to the **Catapas**, the **Votos** and the **Suerres**; the extreme south of the Talamancas held the **Cabécars** and the **Guayamís**, whose influence spread to the modern-day Zona Sur and the Osa Peninsula. In the nearby Valle de Diquis and Valle de el General were the **Térrabas** and their sub-group the **Borucas**. The Valle Central contained the **Huetars**. Modern-day Guanacaste was the most heavily populated and farmed area in pre-Columbian Costa Rica, home to the **Chorotegas** and the older Nicoyan peoples.

Many of these groups had affinities with their neighbours in Nicaragua to the north and Panamá to the south. The Chorotegas in particular showed signs of cultural inheritance from the Olmec peoples of southern Mexico, while those of the extreme south and Osa Peninsula had affinities with peoples in Panamá and Colombia.

About 1000 BC, most of these groups would have been involved in **subsistence farming**. They also existed in a state of almost constant warfare. However, unlike in the Mesoamerican states and in the Inca empire, where war and domination had led to the establishment of complex, far-reaching empires, in Costa Rica no one group gained ascendancy, and the political position of the clans seemed to remain more or less constant throughout the ages, with no group imposing its language or customs on the rest. One reason could be that although these groups were only too willing to go to **war**, they did not do so in order to increase their territory. Perennially low population density in ancient Costa Rica meant that there was plenty of land, and plenty of space into which persecuted or vanquished groups could escape. Like the forest-dwelling tribes in Amazonia to the south, these pre-Columbian peoples waged war to capture slaves, victims for potential sacrifice, marriage partners, or simply for revenge.

As for **religion**, the clans were highly complex and specialized. Shamans were respected members of society, officiating at funerals, which were the most important rites-of-passage, especially in the Talamancan groups. Some clans had animal taboos that prevented them from hunting and killing certain beasts. The taboos neatly complemented each other: one group might not be able to hunt the tapir, for example, while the neighbouring clan in turn would be prohibited from hunting the main prey of another group. This delicate balance played itself out on various levels, promoting harmony between man and nature.

Like everywhere from southern Mexico to Brazil, the jaguar was much revered among all the groups, and only hunted to provide shamans with pelts, teeth and other ritualistic articles.

Gender divisions were, to an extent, along familiar lines: men made war and performed religious duties, while women were confined to domestic roles. However, women of the Boruca group in the southwest went to war alongside men, and the Votos of the Zona Norte regularly had women chiefs. In many clans the inheritance of names and objects was matrilineal.

People lived **communally** in stockaded villages – especially in the Talamancan groups – called *palenques* by the Spaniards. Whole groups, not necessarily related by kin, would live kibbutz-like in a village big house. They organized work "gangs" who would tackle labour projects, usually agricultural. In most cases land was held communally and harvests shared to ensure the survival of all. **Social hierarchy** was complex, with an ascending scale of *caciques* and shamans occupying the elite positions.

The Chorotegas in Guanacaste in particular developed a "high" level of **cultural expression**, possessing a written symbol-based language, and harvesting and trading such diverse products as honey, natural dyes, and cotton.

COSTA RICA "DISCOVERED"

On September 18, 1502, on his fourth and last voyage to the Americas, **Columbus** sighted Costa Rica. Battered by a storm, he ordered his ships to drop anchor just off Isla Uvita, 1km offshore from present-day Puerto Limón. The group stayed seventeen days, making minor forays into the heavily forested coast and its few villages. The indigenous peoples that Columbus met, he could not fail to notice, were liberally attired in gold headbands, mirrored breastplates, bracelets and the like, convincing him of potential riches. In fact, the **gold** worn by those first welcoming envoys would have been traded or come to the peoples of the Caribbean coast through inter-tribal warfare. There was very little gold in the area known as the Atlantic watershed – the eastern slopes of the Cordilleras Central and Talamanca. Rather it came from the southwest of the country near the Valle de Diquís, over the near-impenetrable

GOLD, LAND AND SOULS

The first **Spanish accounts** of Costa Rican indigenous peoples were made in the sixteenth century by "chroniclers", the official scribes who accompanied mapping and evangelical expeditions. In general these were either soldiers or missionaries who showed almost no talent for ethnography. Rather, they approached the pre-Columbian world as inventory-takers or suspicious accountants, writing terse and unimaginative reports liberally spiced with numbers and accounts of gold (although they found almost none). It was they who started the trend of portraying the cultures of the indigenous peoples of Costa Rica as "low" and underdeveloped; what they in fact meant was that there was little that could be expropriated for the Crown. Of the narratives which stand out is one by **Columbus** himself, who described the small welcoming party he received in 1502 in vivid and rather romanticized prose in his *lettera rarissima*, meant for the eyes of his sovereign.

Another, more important, account is by **Gonzalo Fernández de Oviedo**, whose comprehensive, nineteen-volume *Historía General de las Indias, Islas y Tierra Firme del Mar Oceano* was first published in 1535. Oviedo spent only ten or twelve days with the Chorotega peoples, but he had a fine eye for detail, and recorded many of the known details of the Chorotega diet, dress, and social customs. He also noticed that they spoke a form of Nahua, the language of the Aztecs and the *lingua franca* of Mesoamerica, an observation which has since convinced most historians of a direct cultural link between the empires to the north and the peoples of pre-Columbian Costa Rica and Nicaragua.

One of the first things the Spanish chroniclers noticed was that the indigenous peoples in the Talamancas in the southeast and also the peoples of Greater Chiriquí in the southwest practised ritual sacrifice. Every full moon, prisoners captured in the most recent raid would be ritually beheaded. The Spanish, of course, were repelled, and so began the systematic baptism campaigns, and the destruction of indigenous "idolatry".

For details of the best available ethnographic title on the early chroniclers – Elías Zamora Acosta's *Ethnografía histórica de Costa Rica, 1561 y 1615* – see *Books* on p.374.

hump of the Cordillera de Talamanca. With dreams of wealth, Columbus sailed on, charting the entire coastal area from Honduras to Panamá, including Costa Rica, and naming it **Veragua**.

In 1506 King Ferdinand of Spain dispatched Diego de Nicuesa to govern what would become Costa Rica. From the start his mission was beset by hardship, beginning when their ship ran aground on the coast of Panamá, forcing the party to walk up the Caribbean shore. There they met native people who, unlike those who had welcomed Columbus tentatively but politely with their shows of gold, burned their crops rather than submit to the authority of the Spanish. This, together with the impenetrable jungles – and the creatures who lived there – and tropical diseases, meant that the expedition had to be abandoned.

Next came **Gil González** in 1521–22, who concentrated on Costa Rica's Pacific coast, which offered safer anchorages. Gonzalez and his men covered practically the entire length of Pacific Costa Rica on foot, baptizing as they went: the expedition priest later claimed that some 32,000 souls had been saved in the name of the king of Spain.

The indigenous peoples, meanwhile, began a campaign of **resistance** that was to last nearly thirty years, employing guerrilla tactics, full-scale flight, infanticide, attacks on colonist settlements and burning their own villages. There were massacres, defeats and submissions on both sides, but by 1540 Costa Rica was officially a Royal Province of Spain, and a decade later, the Conquest was more or less complete. Most of the key areas of the country had been charted or settled, with the exception of the Talamanca region, which remained largely unexplored for centuries.

INDIGENOUS PEOPLES IN THE COLONIAL PERIOD

During the first years of the Spanish invasion, the main factors that governed the lives of indigenous Costa Ricans were **social organization** and **disease**. Those who grouped themselves in large settlements, like the Chorotegas, proved more easily subjected to the will of the Spaniards, and were carted off to work in the mines, forced to build the first Costa Rican towns, or co-opted to general slavery in the guise of farmwork. The more scattered groups fared better, in the main exiling themselves to the rugged Talamancas.

By then, however, the real conquerors of the New World had arrived: smallpox, influenza, and measles. In the seventeenth and eighteenth centuries huge pandemics swept the country, among them the so-called **Great Pandemic** of 1611–60, in which whole towns and villages disappeared virtually overnight. *Caciques* as well as commoners died, leaving groups with no leadership structure. Although colonial censuses are notoriously inaccurate, in 1563, it is reckoned that an estimated 80,000 indigenous peoples lived in Costa Rica; by 1714 the official count was 999. Today there are only about 5000 indigenous people in the country, out of a population of nearly 3.5 million. For more on the current status of indigenous people in Costa Rica, see p.349.

In 1560 **Juan de Cavallon** and **Juan Vásquez de Coronado** – the first true conquistadors of Costa Rica – succeeded in penetrating the Valle Central, the area that would become most significant in the development of the nation. As Cortés had done in Mexico, the Spaniards of Costa Rica took advantage of existing rivalries among the aboriginal groups and played them off against each other. In this way they managed to dominate the groups of the Pacific coast with the help of tribes from the Valle Central.

In the early years of the colony, the Spaniards quickly established the **encomienda**, a system widespread in the Spanish crown's Central American possessions, that gave the conquistadors and their descendants the right to demand tribute or labour from the indigenous population. The *encomienda* applied to all aboriginal males in Costa Rica between the ages of 18 and 50, and to a lesser extent to women. Quotas were set for the donation of foods such as cacao fruit, corn, chicken, honey and chilli peppers. Although these are all foodstuffs the settlers could have grown and harvested themselves, the capacity for the *encomienda* to enrich the colonies was immense. From the Spanish point of view, this was compensation for the risks and hazards involved in coming to the New World. As many people have said, no man came to America to be poorer than he as in Europe.

Costa Rica's indigenous peoples **resisted** servitude to the colonials quite fiercely, although, in the words of one *cacique* they did get tired of "running around in the jungle and hiding all the time." Nor was there total acceptance of the way the aboriginal peoples were treated during this period. High-ranking clergymen expressed distress to their Spanish overlords, and as early as 1542 the **New Laws**, influenced by the passionate appeals on the part of the aboriginal peoples of Mesoamerica by Fray Bartolomé de las Casas, decreed that colonizers had a duty to "protect" the indigenous peoples. In 1711 the Bishop of Nicaragua, Fray Benito Garret y Arlovi, informed on the governor of Costa Rica for his brutal policies against the *índios*. These decrees assuaged the conscience of the Spanish crown but what happened on the ground in the colonies, of course, was quite a different matter.

THE EARLY SETTLERS

It seems more appropriate to discuss Costa Rica's *lack of* colonial experience, rather than a bona fide colonization. In 1562, **Juan Vásquez de Coronado** became the second governor of Costa Rica. Coronado has always been portrayed as the good guy, reputed for his favourable, if not benevolent, treatment of the indigenous peoples he encountered in his migration from the Pacific coast to the Valle Central. It was under his administration that the first settlement of any size or importance was established, and **Cartago**, in the heart of the Valle Central, was made capital of the colony. During the next century settlers confined themselves more or less to the centre of the country. The Caribbean coast was the haunt of buccaneers – mainly English – who put ashore and wintered here after plundering the lucrative Spanish Main; the Pacific coast saw its share of pirate activity too, most famously when Sir Francis Drake put ashore briefly in the modern-day Bahía Drake in 1579.

This first epoch of the colony is remembered as one of unremitting **poverty**. Within a decade of its invasion Costa Rica was notorious and widely disparaged throughout the Spanish empire for its lack of gold. The settlers and their descendants, unlike those to the north and the south, who became wealthy on the gold of the Aztecs and Inca, never achieved their dreams of instant aristocracy. Instead, they were confronted with almost insuperable obstacles, including tropical fever, hunger, and belligerence from the indigenous peoples. The Valle Central land was fertile, but there was uncertainty as to what crops to grow. Coffee had not yet been imported to Costa Rica, nor had tobacco, so it was to subsistence agriculture that most settlers turned, growing just enough to live on. There were no export crops and no national markets for foodstuffs. Spanish fabrics, manufactured goods and currency became so scarce that by 1709 Valle Central settlers were forced to adopt cacao beans as currency. Goat's hair and bark were used as clothing fabrics, making your average eighteenth-century Costa Rican farmer look as wild and uncivilized as Romulus and Remus before the founding of Rome. In 1719, the governor of Costa Rica famously complained that he had to till his own land. To make matters worse, Volcán Irazú blew its top in 1723, nearly destroying the capital. In escaping the hot dry plains of Andalucía or of northern Spain the first settlers must have thought they had come to a fresh hell.

With the emphasis on agriculture, and with little industry or trade, Costa Rica was unsurprisingly slow in founding urban settlements. 1706 saw the establishment of the second city (after Cartago) of Cubujuquí (modern-day Heredia); in 1737 Villa Nueva de la Boca del Monte (later shortened, thankfully, to San José) was founded; in 1782 it was Villa Hermosa's turn (today Alajuela).

The tough yeoman **settler farmer**, who survived these conditions, is the most distinct figure in the early colonial history, his independent state of poverty widely believed to be the root of the country's modern-day egalitarianism. Recent historical works, however, concede that while everybody in the early days of the colony may have been equally poor, social distinctions still counted, and where they did not exist, were manufactured, albeit in a much less virulent form than in other Central American possessions of the Spanish crown.

Two other crucial factors prevailed in the making of the modern-day nation. One was **coffee**, eventually to become Costa Rica's main export, a crop that requires many smallholders rather than large hacienda systems. Another factor in the unique development of the colony is **ethnic**: quite simply, the vast majority of peasants in Costa Rica are descendants of the Spanish colonists, rather than *indigenos* or *mestizos*, and as such, treated as equals by the ruling elite, who saw them as *hermaniticos*, or little brothers.

INDEPENDENCE

The **nineteenth century** was the most significant era in the development of the modern nation state of Costa Rica. Initially, after 1821, when Central America declared **independence** from Spain, freedom made little difference to Costa Ricans. Although granted on September 15, 1823, the news did not reach Costa Rica until a month later, when a mule messenger arrived from Nicaragua to tell the astonished citizens of Cartago the good news. Rather than rejoicing in being freed from the Spanish – Spain had not paid much attention to the poor isolated province anyway – a **civil war** promptly broke out among the inhabitants of the Valle Central, dividing the citizens of Alajuela and San José from those of Heredia and Cartago. This struggle for power was won by the Alajuela-San José faction, and **San José** became the capital city in 1823.

BANANA REPUBLIC: THE UNITED FRUIT COMPANY AND RACE RELATIONS

The history of **banana-growing** in Costa Rica is inextricably linked to the establishment of the **railroads**. Initially the brainchild of Costa Rican president Tomas Guardia, the San José–Puerto Limón railway – the Jungle Train – was built by American capitalist Minor Keith. From the outset in 1871, the idea behind the proposed railway was to establish an easy route for Valle Central coffee to reach the Caribbean coast, thus circumventing both the fluvial method of transporting the beans via the Río Sarapiquí, and the Puntarenas route, by which the crop had to travel around Cape Horn.

Almost immediately after construction began on the Jungle Train, the contractors faced a labour shortage. The lowlands of Limón province have a particularly brutal climate: continously hot, muggy, and lashed by heavy rain. Yellow fever, venomous serpents, raids by bands of indigenous peoples and general exhaustion conspired to fell much of the workforce, initially made up of Highlanders, imported Chinese "coolie" labour, and Italians.

Due to economic conditions in Jamaica at the time, there was a ready pool of black labour. Between 1874 and 1891 some 11,000 Jamaicans arrived in Costa Rica. The Highland majority did not respond well to this immigration, largely on grounds of race. Costa Ricans thought of themselves as white and often compared themselves favourably with the darker-skinned inhabitants of neighbouring countries. It is generally held that for the first half of this century a law existed prohibiting the migration of Afro-Caribbeans to the Valle Central.

In 1890 the train finally sparked and puffed its way out of the capital. Minor Keith's involvement in the history of Costa Rica did not stop here, as he had ingeniously planted bananas along the tracks in order to help pay for the train's construction. The fruit flourished and, as new markets opened up in Europe and the US, it became an exportable commodity: Costa Rica was the first Central American republic to grow bananas in bulk. In 1899 Keith and a colleague founded the **United Fruit Company**. The company, or *Yunai*, as it was called locally, came to transform the social, political and cultural face of Central America, and of all the countries in which it operated, it had the biggest dealings in Costa Rica.

Opinions of the *Yunai* oscillate between the belief that it was a capitalist scourge that gave Costa Rica its Banana Republic burden, and that it was the saving grace of the nation. Almost from the beginning, United Brands – as it came to call itself – gained a reputation for anti-union practice, deserting entire areas once labour showed any signs of being organized. They also fled, more understandably, when banana-attacking diseases forced them out.

However, the *bananeros* have always offered high **salaries** in comparison with other forms of economic activity – like small-scale farming – available to lowland dwellers, and particularly to Afro-Caribbeans. Many Highlanders would spend a year or two working on the banana plantations with the express purpose of getting together enough money to start a small farm, although workers would more often spend their salaries – for many years given in redeemable scrip instead of cash – on drink and dissipation. To a degree

Continued overleaf

BANANA REPUBLIC: THE UNITED FRUIT COMPANY AND RACE RELATIONS (continued)

this was a deliberate plan by the company to have their labour force continuously in hock and therefore pliable.

As long as the *bananeros* of the United Fruit Company provided a steady flow of jobs, there was no real temptation for the Jamaicans and their descendants to leave the Caribbean where they had effectively transported their own culture intact. In isolated Limón they could retain their traditional food, Protestantism, and play West Indian games like cricket, preserving their culture in the face of a much larger Highland majority. They could also use their ability to speak English to advantage – often Afro-Caribbeans attained high-ranking positions in the *bananeros* because they could communicate with the American foremen in their own language.

When the plantations began to close down in Limón in 1925 as a result of the dreaded banana maladies *Sigatoka* and Panama disease, the fortunes of the Jamaicans changed. In the face of a pestilence so virulent that plantations could only run for about two or three years, the United Fruit company had to look elsewhere in the country for possible locations for their operations. While keeping their Limón plantations open, in 1934 they began acquiring land and planting bananas in the area around modern-day Quepos in the Central Pacific, and Golfito in the Zona Sur. This spelled bad news for the Afro-Caribbean workers as, unbeknown to them, United Fruit had signed a contract with the Costa Rican government stipulating that employment preference be given to native Costa Ricans. When the contract became public in September 1930, racial tensions rose to boiling point in Limón. Afro-Caribbeans were caught, unable to afford the passage home to Jamaica on the one hand and prohibited from taking work elsewhere in the country on the other. It seems that United Fruit itself did not have any qualms about employing Afro-Caribbeans; quite the opposite. Rather it was the government, along with the white plantation workers and the Highland elite who felt most threatened, and who in 1933 petitioned Congress to prohibit the entry of blacks into the country " because they are of a race inferior to ours."

In 1934 the most virulent strike yet seen in the Costa Rican *bananeros* began. It was organized by **Carlos Luis Fallas**, labour activist and novelist, who had been exiled by the judges to Limón as a result of his militancy on behalf of labour organizations in the Valle Central. As historian Michael Seligson puts it, sending Fallas to the *bananeros*

"was like throwing Brer Rabbit into the briar patch. For the judges Limón was the Siberia of Costa Rica; for Fallas, it was the Nirvana of union organizers."

Fallas proved a brilliant organizer. Initially the proposals he put forward to the Company were quite mild, requesting things like malaria drugs, snakebite serum, and payment in cash rather than scrip, which could easily be squandered. Nonetheless, the Company refused to recognize these proposals, and in August 1934 the strike began in earnest, tenaciously holding on in the face of physical harassment by the Company and police forces. For the next four years strikes and worker opposition raged on. In 1938 the Company finally pulled out of Limón province for good, deserting it for the Pacific coast.

Left behind in the economic devastation and unable to migrate within the country in search of work, the Afro-Caribbean population either took up cacao cultivation, hacked out their own smallholdings, or took to fishing or other subsistence activities. Overnight the schools, bunkhouses, American dollars, scrip economy, liquor and cigarettes disappeared, as did the US foremen and the ample plantation-style homes they had occupied. From about 1934 to 1970 the region was virtually destitute, without much of a cash economy or any large-scale employers. It is only now beginning to recover in terms of banana production – under the aegis of the national banana-franchise operators Standard Fruit Company – and only at considerable cost to the environment as more tropical forests are felled and more rivers polluted with the pesticides used on the fruit.

It is hard to appreciate the overwhelming presence that the *Yunai* wielded in communities until you have seen the schools and hospitals that it established, the dolorous plantation-house style accommodation it built for its managers, and the rows upon rows of army compound-like houses it provided for its workers. You can get a flavour of this in the banana towns of Limón's Estrella Valley and on the road from Jacó to Quepos, where you pass through a long corridor of African palm oil farms, United Brands' only major investment remaining in Costa Rica. The Company also left its mark on the collective consciousness of the region. Carlos Luis Fallas' novels *Mamita Yunai* and *Gentes y gentecillas*, Garcia Marquez's *One Hundred Years of Solitude*, and Guatemalan Asturias's masterly *El Papa Verde* all document the power of the Company in the everyday life of the *pueblitos* of Central America.

GRANO D'ORO–THE GOLDEN BEAN

Costa Rica made remarkable progress in the latter half of the nineteenth century, building roads, bridges, and railways and filling San José with neo-Baroque, Europeanate edifices. Virtually all this activity was fuelled by the **coffee** trade, bringing wealth that the settlers just a century earlier could hardly have dreamed of. Today high-grade export coffee is still popularly known as *grano d'oro*. The coffee story begins as early as 1808, when beans from Cuba or Jamaica – depending on which sources you believe – were first planted in the Valle Central. The plants thrived in the highland climate and by 1820 citizens of Cartago were being encouraged – ordered, even – to plant coffee in their backyards. But most significant in the early history of the coffee trade was the arrival in 1844 of English merchant **William Le Lacheur**. His ship, the *Monarch*, had emptied her hold of its cargo, and Le Lacheur arrived in the Pacific port of Puntarenas looking for ballast to take his ship back to Liverpool. He travelled to the Valle Central, where he secured a cargo of coffee beans, which he bought on credit, promising to return and pay in two years' time.

Until that point, most of Costa Rica's coffee had made its way to Chile, where it was mixed with a lower-grade South American bean, packaged for export under the brand of *Café de Valparíso*, and sent to England, taking the long way around Cape Horn. With Le Lacheur's shipment, however, British tastebuds were won round to the wonderfully smooth and mellow, high-quality hard bean. A trading partnership began that saw the Costa Rican upper classes using Sheffield steel cutlery and Manchester linens for most of the 1800s.

The **coffee bourgeoisie** played a vital role in the cultural and political development of the country, and in 1848 the newly influential *cafetaleros* elected to the presidency their chosen candidate, Juan Rafael Mora. Extremely conservative and pro-trade, Mora came to distinguish himself in the battle against the American-backed filibusterer William Walker in 1856, only to fall from grace and be executed in 1860 (see p.229).

THE EARLY TWENTIETH CENTURY

The first years of the **twentieth century** represent an unstable route toward democracy in Costa Rica. Universal male suffrage had been in effect since the last years of the nineteenth century, but class and power conflicts still dogged the country, with several *caudillo* (authoritarian) leaders, familiar figures in other Latin American countries, hijacking power. But in general these figures ended up in exile (in contrast to facing the firing squads of the previous century) and neither the army nor the church gained much of a foothold in politics.

In 1917 Federico Tinoco, the Minister of War and the Navy, overthrew the unpopular González Flores and instated himself as president, establishing a particularly repressive dicatorship, abrogating the liberal constitution of 1871. In 1919 he was forced to resign and democratic elections resumed. Meanwhile, inspired by the Russian revolution, a number of radical labour initiatives were created. However, for most of the twentieth century Costa Rica's successive administrations, whatever their political colour, have proved no friend of labour relations, beginning in 1924 when most **strikes** were outlawed. In 1931 the Communist party was formed, followed quickly by the National Republican party in 1932. The latter dominated the political scene for most of the 1940s, with the election in 1940 of the Republican (PRN) candidate **Rafael Calderón Guardia**, a doctor educated in part in Belgium and a devout Catholic.

It was Calderón who instigated the social reforms and state support for which Costa Rica is still almost unique in the region. In 1941 he established a new **Labour Code**, which reinstated the right of workers to organize and strike, and a social security system providing free schooling for all. Calderón also paved the way for the establishment of the University of Costa Rica, health insurance, income security and assistance schemes, and thus won the support of the impoverished and the lower classes and the suspicion of the governing élites. One of those less than convinced by Calderón's policies was the man who would come to be known as **"Don Pepe"**, the coffee farmer José Figueres Ferrer, who denounced Calderón and his expensive reforms in a radio broadcast in 1941 and was then abuptly forced into exile in Mexico, from where he plotted his return.

THE "REVOLUTION" OF 1948 AND AFTER

The **elections of 1948** heralded the most eventful year of this century for Costa Rica. Constitutionally, Costa Rican presidents could not serve consecutive terms, so the election battle that year was between **Teodorico Picado**, widely considered to be a Calderón puppet, and **Ulate**, an ally of Figueres, who during two years in exile had become an heroic figure in some circles, returning to Costa Rica to play a key part in the *Acción Democratica*, a loose group of anti-Calderónistas. Ulate won the presidency, but the PRN won the majority in Congress – a fact that effectively annulled the election results.

For his part, **Figueres** was back on the scene and intent upon overthrowing Picado, who had stepped in and declared himself president in the face of the annulment. Figueres soon formed an opposition party, ideologically opposed to the PRN, calling them, somewhat ironically in view of the "republican" in their name, "communists". In March, **fighting** around Cartago began, culminating in an attack by the Figueres rebels on San José. To a degree, the battles were fought to safeguard the system of democratic election in the face of influence-peddling and corruption, and in order to stem the clannishness and cults of personality that dogged all Costa Rican political parties and presidential campaigns.

While Figueres' rebel forces were well equipped with arms, some supplied through CIA contacts, the militia defending president Picado was not: the national army consisted of only about 300 men at the time, and had to be supplemented by machete-wielding banana workers. Two thousand were dead by mid-April, when hostilities ceased. May saw the formation of the **Junta of the Second Republic**, with Figueres as acting president, despite an after-the-fact attack from Nicaraguan Picado supporters in December.

Figueres wanted above all to engineer a complete break with the country's past and especially the policies and legacies of the Calderónistas. Seeing himself as fighting both communism and corruption, he not only outlawed the PVP, the Popular Vanguard Party – formerly known as the Communist Party – but also nationalized the banks and devised a tax to hit the rich particularly hard, thus alienating the establishment.

The new **constitution** drawn up in 1949 gave full citizenship to Afro-Caribbeans, full suffrage to women and abolished Costa Rica's army. In a way, the **abolition of the army** fitted with political precedents in Costa Rica. Nearly thirty years before, in 1922, former president Ricardo Jiménez Oreamuno had given a famous speech in which he said "the school shall kill militarism, or militarism shall kill the Republic…we are a country with more teachers than soldiers…and a country that turns military headquarters into schools." Although the warming sentiment behind Jiménez's words is oft-repeated in Costa Rica, the truth is somewhat darker. Figueres' motives were not utopian but rather a pragmatic bid to limit the political instability that had been the scourge of so many Latin American countries, and an attempt to save valuable resources. Today, while the country still has no army, the police forces are powerful, highly specialized and, in some cases, heavily armed. **Paramilitary** organizations do exist. Chief among them is the Free Costa Rica Movement (MCRL), formed in 1961 and still active, which has allegedly been involved in a number of deeds more in the vein of the Guatemalan army's death squads than a harmonious and army-free Costa Rica.

In 1951 Figueres formed the **National Liberation Party**, or PLN, in order to be legitimately elected. He was a virtual genius in drawing together disparate strands of society: when the elections came around the following year he got the agricultural smallholder vote, while winning the support of the urban working classes with his retention of the welfare state. At the same time he appeased the right-of-centrists with his essentially free-marketeering and staunch anti-communist stance.

The **1960s** and **70s** were a period of prosperity and stability in Costa Rica, when the welfare state was developed to reach nearly all sectors of society. In 1977 the **indigenous bill** established the right of aboriginal peoples to their own land reserves – a progressive measure at the time, although indigenous peoples today are not convinced the system has served them well (see p.349). At the end of the 1970s, regional conflicts took the attention away from the domestic agenda, with the Carazo (1978–82) administration announcing its support for the FSLN revolutionary movement in Nicaragua, who had finally managed to despatch the Somoza family into exile.

STORM IN THE ISTHMUS: THE 1980s

Against all odds, Costa Rica in the 1980s and 1990s not only saw its way through the serious political conflicts of its neighbours, but also successfully managed predatory US interventionism, economic crisis and staggering debt.

Like many Latin American countries, Costa Rica had taken out bank and government **loans** in the 1960s and 70s to finance vital development. But in the early 1980s, the slump of prices for coffee and bananas on international commodity markets put the country's current account in the red to the tune of millions. In September 1981, Costa Rica defaulted on its interest payment on these loans, becoming the first third-world country to do so, and sparking off a chain of similar defaults in Latin America that resonated throughout the 1980s and threw the international banking community into crisis. Despite its defaults, Costa Rica's debt continued to accumulate, and by 1989 had reached a staggering $5 billion, one of the highest per capita debt loads in the world.

To compound the economic crisis came the simultaneous political escalation of the **Nicaraguan civil war**. During the entire decade Costa Rica's foreign policy and to an extent its domestic agenda would be overshadowed by tensions with Nicaragua on the one hand and with the US on the other. Initially, the Monge PLN administration (1982–86) more or less capitulated to US demands that Costa Rica be used as a supply line for the Contras and Costa Rica also accepted military training for its police force from the US. Simultaneously, the country's first agreement for a structural adjustment loan with the IMF was signed. It seemed increasingly clear that Costa Rica was on the path to both violating its declared neutrality in the conflicts of its neighbours and condemning its population to wage freezes, price increases and other side-effects associated with the IMF dose. In May 1984 the situation escalated with the events at the **La Penca** press conference, where attending journalists were expecting no more than another harangue against the Sandinistas on the part of US-backed Contra leader Edén Pastora. Held in a simple hut on the banks of the Río San Juan, roughly where it joins the Río San Carlos in the Zona Norte, the conference had minimal security. The bomb was apparently carried in to the hut by a "Danish" cameraman and concealed within an equipment case, and was intended to kill all. Miraculously, an aide of Pastora's accidentally kicked the case over while handing the leader coffee, knocking it on its side, so that when it was detonated by the perpetrator, who had gone outside, the force of the blast went up and down instead of sideways, thus saving the lives of most of those within. While Pastora himself survived the attack, and was sped off upriver with leg injuries, three foreign journalists – including a *Tico Times* reporter – were killed.

Although nobody is quite sure who was behind the bombing, it seems that the point of the carnage was to implicate Managua, thus cutting off international support and destabilizing the Sandinista government further. Both the CIA and freelance Argentine terrorists have been implicated. The immediate effect was to shock the Costa Rican government and the international community into paying more attention to the deadly conflicts of Nicaragua and, by association, El Salvador and Guatemala. As for its immediate target, Pastora ended up spending a long stint in exile in Costa Rica, some of it as an unsuccessful fisherman on the Nicoya Peninsula.

THE ARIAS PEACE PLAN

In 1986 PLN candidate **Oscar Arias Sánchez** was elected to the presidency, and Costa Rica's relations with the United States and, by association, with Nicaragua, took a different tack. The former political scientist began to play the role of peace broker in the conflicts of Nicaragua, El Salvador, and, to a lesser extent, Honduras and Guatemala, mediating between these countries and also between domestic factions within them. In October 1987, just eighteen months after taking office, Arias was awarded the **Nobel Prize for Peace**, bringing worldwide attention to this tiny country.

His **peace plan** focused on regional objectives, tying individual and domestic conflicts into the larger picture: the stability of the isthmus. It officially called for a ceasefire, the discontinuation of military aid to the Contra insurrectionists, amnesties for political prisoners and for guerrillas who voluntarily relinquished the fight, and, lastly and perhaps most importantly, intergovernmental negotiations leading to free and fair elections. The peace plan began, rather than ended, with the awarding of the Nobel Prize, dragging on throughout 1987 and 1988 and running into obstacles as, almost immediately, all nations involved charged one another with non-compliance or other violations. The situation deteriorated when the US stationed troops in southern Honduras, ready for attack into northern Nicaragua.

Meanwhile, Washington continued to undermine Costa Rica's declared neutrality. White House representative Morris Busby made an official request to Arias in April 1988 that he approve Costa Rican territory as a corridor for "humanitarian aid" to the Contras. The same month, Arias met with US president Bush in Washington. Arias' agenda included a request for more aid to meet its debt payments, external balance of payments, and continued funds for health care, education and the other social services which Costa Ricans had come to expect. For its part, the last thing the US wanted was internal unrest in Costa Rica, its natural (if not entirely compliant) ally in the conflicts of the region, as a stable democracy with no military forces, a staunch anti-communist and anti-labour union stance, and no interest in becoming involved in the conflicts of its neighbours. Oscar Arias's diplomatic credibility, solid public relations profile, and the international standing accorded him by winning not only the Peace Prize but also the Inter-American Leadership prize, awarded in 1988 by the Pan-American Development Fund ensured his success. He played the US masterfully, securing millions of dollars worth of US aid for Costa Rica, without compromising the country politically.

However, while Arias had obviously stalled on the US using Costa Rica's northern border, he seemed to have fewer quibbles about what was happening in the south, in Panamá. In July 1989, CIA-supported anti-Noriega guerrilla forces (many of them ex-Contras) amassed along the Costa Rica–Panamá border in preparation for the US invasion of Panamá that would take place in December.

Though Arias had gained the admiration of statesmen around the world, he proved to be less than popular at home. Many Costa Ricans saw him as diverting valuable resources and time to foreign affairs when he should have been paying attention to the domestic agenda. Increasing prices in response to the IMF's economic demands meant that conditions had not improved much in Costa Rica.

THE 1990s

In 1990 the mantle of power shifted to **Rafael Calderón Fournier** (son of Calderón Guardia) who in the 1980s had been instrumental in consolidating the opposition that became the free-marketeering Partido Unidad Social Cristiana, or PUSC.

A year later, Costa Rica was rocked by its most powerful **earthquake** since the one that laid waste to most of Cartago in 1910. Centred in Limón province, the quake killed 62 people and caused expensive structural damage. At the same time, nationals of El Salvador, Honduras, Guatemala and especially Nicaragua were looking to Costa Rica – the only stable country in the region – for asylum, and tension rose as the **refugees** poured in. In 1992 Costa Rica faced more trouble as it was brought to law in US courts for its failure to abide by international labour laws, maintaining **labour relations** as a black mark on the country's copybook for most of the twentieth century.

Until 1994, elections in Costa Rica had been relatively genteel affairs, involving lots of flag-waving and displays of national pride in democratic traditions. The elections of that year, however, were probably the dirtiest yet. Costa Rica is a republic, with a political power structure resembling that of the United States. The government is divided into legislative, executive and judicial branches, all guaranteed by a formal constitution, which long decreed that no president could rule for more than one four-year term consecutively. In 1969 an amendment added that no president may be re-elected to office once he has served his term. Since 1948 most of the country's elections have been a bipolar fight between the PLN candidate and the opposition party-of-the-moment, with the PLN winning office about once every other four years.

The campaign for the 1994 **elections** opened and closed with an unprecedented bout of mudslinging and attempts to smear the reputations of both candidates, tactics which shocked many Costa Ricans. The PLN candidate – the choice of the left, for his promises to maintain the role of the state in the economy – was none other than **José María Figueres**, the son of Don Pepe, who had died four years previously. During the campaign Figueres was accused of shady investment rackets and influence-peddling. His free-market PUSC opposition candidate, Miguel Angel Rodriguez, fared no better, having admitted to being involved in a tainted-beef scandal in the 1980s.

Figueres won, narrowly. A populist, at least in rhetoric, he was also considered a charismatic campaigner and continues to appeal to a broad base: visiting outlying areas, recognizing the concerns of *campesinos*, and winching himself up giant rainforest trees in a show of support for conservation issues. On the other hand, his term in office has already been plagued by a series of serious scandals. In August 1994, four OIJ (judicial investigation authorities) officers were accused of murdering known drug-trafficker Ciro Monge, prompting the resignation in November of the OIJ director. Hot on the heels in September came the *Banco Anglo Costarricense* scandal, in which a number of directors of Costa Rica's third national bank were alleged to have squandered the bank's credit resources on worthless Venezuelan bonds. In October, the US Drug Enforcement Administration (DEA) announced that it had discovered Costa Rican connections to international drugs and money-laundering operations.

On a more positive note, recent events have moved away from these scandals, centring on trade and economic relations. In January 1995, a Free Trade agreement was signed with Mexico in order to try to redress the lack of preference given to Costa Rican goods in the US market by the signing of NAFTA.

THE FUTURE

Fittingly, for a country in which traditional values still dominate, Costa Rica's economic **future** rides on a wave created in the past, a

INDIGENOUS PEOPLES IN MODERN COSTA RICA

Today you won't see much evidence of native traditions, crafts, dances, rituals, song, clothing, speech or any legacies of the once-populous civilizations in Costa Rica. Only about 1 percent of the country's population is of aboriginal extraction, and the dispersion of the various groups ensures that they frequently do not share the same concerns and agendas. Contact between them, apart from areas such as CONAI – the national indigenous affairs body – is minimal.

Although a system of **indigenous reserves** was set up by the Costa Rican administration in 1977, giving aboriginal peoples the right to remain in self-governing communities, titles to the reserve lands were withheld, so that while the communities may live on the land, they do not actually *own* it. This has led to government contracts being handed out to, for example, mining operations in the Talamanca area, leading to infringements on the communities themselves, which are further hampered by the presence of missionaries in settlements like Amubrí and San José Cabécar. The twelve "Indian reserves" scattered around the country are viewed by their inhabitants with some ambivalence. As in North America, establishing a reservation system has led in many cases to a banishing of indigenous peoples to poor quality land where poverty enclaves soon develop.

Although nothing like the scale of persecution of native peoples that goes on in Guatemala occurs in Costa Rica, in recent years there have been a number of disturbing **indigenous rights violations** in Costa Rica, many of them documented by CODEHUCA (comisión para la defensa de los derechos humanos en centroamérica).

At the same time there is growing recognition of the importance of preserving indigenous culture and for providing reserves with increased services and self-sufficiency. In 1994 the first **indigenous bank** was set up in Suretka, Talamanca, by the Bribrí and Cabecar groups. Formed to counter the fact that major banks have often refused indigenous business and initiatives credit, the bank received $500,000 in start-up funds from the Inter-American Development Bank. In addition, indigenous groups from around the country, realizing they need a cohesive voice and common agenda, have banded together to fund the rental of a building in San José. **Sejëktö** (also called *La voz del indio*) is to be used as a headquarters or capital seat.

constant see-sawing between the price of the country's bananas and coffee on world markets and the amount it pays for imports. Still, the economy continues to grow, in large part fuelled by **tourism**, and Figueres' government is beginning to claw back the massive public sector deficit through increased **taxation**, on basic services like electricity and water, along with restaurant meals and hotel bills, all of which has made it highly un-popular with the lower and middle classes.

As the Costa Rican economy grows, however, so do other indicators: **inflation** runs around 17 percent, and the annual **population** growth is as high as 3.2 percent per annum. Costa Rica has the highest rural population density in Latin America, so there is tremendous pressure on **land**. The prognosis for the *campesino*, that now nearly-forgotten former backbone of the country, is not good, as peasant agriculture becomes increasingly anachronistic in the face of the big banana, coffee, palmito and pineapple plantations.

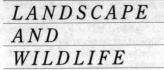

LANDSCAPE AND WILDLIFE

New World animals are believed to have crossed from Asia via the Bering Strait land bridge and migrated steadily southward through North America, evolving and populating regions on the way. Because of Costa Rica's own celebrated position as a land bridge between the temperate (Nearctic) zone to the north and the Neotropics to the south, its varied animal life features tropical forms like the jaguar, temperate zone animals like the deer, and some unusual, seemingly hybrid combinations such as the coati.

HABITATS

Although roughly the size of West Virginia, Nova Scotia, or Wales, Costa Rica has nearly as many **habitats** as the whole of the United States, including forests, riverside mangroves, seasonal wetlands and offshore marine forms such as coral reefs. Costa Rica has a remarkably varied **terrain** for its size, ranging from the plains of Guanacaste, where there is often no rain for five months of the year, to the Caribbean lowlands, thick-forested and deluged with a liberal 6000mm of annual precipitation. Meanwhile, from the very hot and humid lowlands of Corcovado, the terrain rises within 150km to the chilly heights of Cerro Chirripó, at 3819m. For a detailed account of the lay of the land, and the effect that altitude has on temperature and rainfall, see *Basics*.

LIFE ZONES

Because Costa Rica's territory is almost bewilderingly varied, with similar geographical features found in many different places, it makes sense to speak of **life zones**, a detailed system of categorization, referring primarily to forest habitats, developed in 1947 by biologist LR Holdridge to describe particular characteristics of terrain, climate and the life they support. Although he conceived the system in Haiti, with temperature and rainfall being the main determinants, this system has been used to create ecological maps of various countries, including Costa Rica. Among the most common or unusual life zones in Costa Rica are the following; there are also a number of gradations in between. To read more about the cloudforest see p.265; for the dry forest, turn to p.214.

The most endangered of all the life zones in Costa Rica is the **tropical dry forest**, which needs about six dry months a year to deserve the name. Most trees in a tropical dry forest are deciduous or semi-deciduous; some lose their leaves near the end of the dry season, primarily to conserve water. They have less of a multi-strata character than rainforests, with two layers rather than three or four, and appear far less dense. Orchids flower in the silver and brown branches, and bees, wasps and moths proliferate. Animal inhabitants include iguanas, white-tailed deer and some of the larger mammals, including the jaguar. The best examples are in the northwest, especially Guanacaste and **Santa Rosa National Park**.

The **tropical wet forest** is home, metre per metre, to the greatest number of species of flora and fauna, including the bushmaster snake and tapir, along with jaguar and other wild cats. Here the canopy trees can be very tall (55m and more, up to 70 or even 80m), and true to its name, it receives an enormous amount of rain – typically 5000–6000mm per year. Found in lowland areas, tropical wet forest is now confined to large protected blocks, chiefly the **Sarapiquí–Tortuguero** area and the large chunk protected by **Corcovado National Park** on the Osa Peninsula.

Premontane wet forests are found upon many of Costa Rica's mountains. Some trees are evergreen and most are covered with a thick carpet of moss. These forests typically exist at a high altitude and receive a lot of rain: the cover in **Tapantí National Park** in the southwest Valle Central is a good example, as is **Braulio Carrillo** – which has all five of the montane life zones within its boundaries. Many of the same animals that exist in the tropical wet forest exist here, along with brocket deer and peccaries.

Perhaps the most famous of Costa Rica's life zones are the **tropical lower montane wet forests**, or **cloudforests**, which occur in very isolated patches, mainly south of Cartago and on the Pacific slopes of the Cordillera de Tilarán. The cloudforest hosts many bromeliads, including orchids, and has a vine-thick understorey; its animal-life includes tapirs, pumas and quetzals. Costa Rica's best known cloudforest is at **Monteverde**.

Tropical montane rainforest occurs at the highest altitudes; the tops of **Poás and Irazú** volcanos are good examples. Although large mosses and ferns can be seen, much of the vegetation has a shrunken, or dwarfed aspect, due to the biting wind and lofty altitude. Animals that live here include the Poás squirrel (endemic to the volcano) and some of the larger birds, including raptors and vultures.

At the very top of the country near **Cerro el Chirripó** is the only place you'll find **tropical subalpine rain páramo**, inhospitably cold, with almost no trees. Costa Rica is the northern frontier of this particular Andean type of *páramo*. Except for hardy hawks and vultures, birds tend to shun this cold milieu, although at lower elevations you may spot a quetzal.

MANGROVES, WETLANDS AND RIVERS

The **mangrove** is an increasingly fragile and endangered ecosystem that occurs along tropical coastlines and is particularly vulnerable to dredging: both the Papagayo Project in Guanacaste and the Tambor Beach Hotel in the Central Pacific have been accused of irresponsibly draining mangroves. With their extensive root system, mangrove trees are unique for their ability to adapt to the salinity of seaside or tidal waters, or to areas where freshwater rivers empty into the ocean. Because they absorb the thrust of waves and tides, they act as a buffer zone behind which species of aquatic and landbased life can flourish unmolested. Meanwhile, the beer-coloured mangrove swamp water is like a nutritious primordial soup where a range of species can grow, including crustaceans and shrimp as well as turtles, caimans and crocodiles, and their banks are home to a range of bird life. The thick palmy swamps you see in the **Tortuguero** lagoons and in the waterways of **Corcovado National Park** are called **hollilos**, or, in the case of the rare examples in the Gandoca–Manzanillo Wildlife Refuge in the southeast of the country, **orey**, which is endemic to this corner of Costa Rica and to Panamá, across the border.

Birds and reptiles are especially abundant in the country's remaining **wetlands**, which are typically seasonal, caused by the flooding of rivers with the rains, only to shrink back to pleated mud flats in the dry season. The Caño Negro seasonal wetlands in the Zona Norte, and the Río Tempisque within the bounds of Palo Verde National Park in Guanacaste, are the prime wetlands in Costa Rica.

Despite increasing silting and pollution caused largely by the banana plantations, Costa Rica's rivers support a variety of life, from fish, including the tarpon, to migratory birds, crocodiles, caimans and freshwater turtles. The waterways that yield the best wildlife-watching are the Tortuguero canals, Ríos San Juan and Sarapiquí, Río Sierpe, and the Río Tárcoles in the Carara Biological Reserve on the central Pacific coast.

MARINE HABITATS

Costa Rica's **coral reefs**, never as extensive as those in Belize, are under threat. On the **Caribbean coast**, much of the coast was seriously damaged by the 1991 earthquake, which heaved the reefs up above the water. The last remaining on this side of the country are **Cahuita** and a smaller one further south at **Manzanillo** in the Gandoca–Manzanillo Wildlife Refuge. Though the Cahuita reef has been for some time under siege by silting caused by clearing of land for banana plantations, and pesiticides used in banana cultivation, you can still see some fine – extremely localized – specimens of **moose horn** and **deer horn** coral. On the **Pacific coast** the most pristine reef is at Bahía Ballena, protected within Costa Rica's first Marine National Park of the same name, and also the reef that fringes Isla del Caño, about 20km offshore from the north coast of the Osa Peninsula.

WILDLIFE

It is a source of constant woe for guides in Costa Rica to have to deal with tourists who have paid their National Park entrance fees and then expect to be reimbursed in kind by seeing a **tapir**, **jaguar** or **ocelot**. Many of the more exotic **mammals** that inhabit the country are either nocturnal, endangered, or made shy through years of hunting and human encroachment. Although encounters do occur, they are usually brief, with the animal in question fleeing in a haze of colour and fur or dipping quietly back into the shadows from which it first emerged. That said, however, it's very possible you will come in (usually fleeting) contact with some of the smaller and more abundant mammals.

Despite its reputation, Costa Rica does not have Central America's most diverse vertebrate fauna – that title goes to Guatemala. However, Costa Rican **insects** and **birds** are particularly numerous, with 850 species of birds (including migratory ones) – more than the US and Canada combined. Costa Rica is also home to a quarter of the world's known **butterflies** – more than in all Africa – thousands of moths, and scores of bees and wasps.

BIRDS (PÁJAROS, AVES)

Bird life, both migratory and indigenous, is abundant in Costa Rica and includes some of the most colourful birds in the Americas: the **quetzal**, the **toucan** and the **scarlet macaw**. Many are best observed while feeding. Guides often point out quetzals, for instance, when they are feeding from their favoured *aguacatillo* tree, and you might catch a glimpse of the hummingbird hovering over a bright flower as it feeds on its nectar.

It's only fair that any discussion of birds in Costa Rica start with the one that so many people come see: the brilliant green and red **quetzal**. With a range historically extending from southern Mexico to northern Panamá – more or less the deliniations of Mesoamerica – the dazzling quetzal was highly prized by the

Aztecs and the Maya. In the language of the Aztecs, *quetzali* means, roughly, "beautiful", and along with jade, the shimmering, jewel-coloured feathers were used as currency in Maya cities. The feathers were also worn by Maya nobles to signify religious qualities and social superiority, and formed the headdress of the plumed serpent Quetzalcoatl, the Aztec over-god.

Hunting quetzals is particularly cruel, as it is well known that the bird cannot (or will not) live in captivity, a poignant stance which has made it a symbol of freedom throughout Mesoamerica. The male in particular, who possesses the distinctive feather train, up to 1.5m long, is still pursued by poachers. The quetzal is further endangered because of the destruction of its favoured cloudforest habitat. These days the remaining cloudforests (particularly **Monteverde**) are among the best places to try to see the birds (March–May is best), although they are always difficult to spot, in part due to shyness and in part because the vibrant green of their feathers, seemingly so eye-catchingly bright, actually means that they blend in well with the wet and shimmering cloudforest. Quetzals are officially protected in Costa Rica in Braulio Carrillo and Volcán Poás National Parks in the Valle Central, in Chirripó in the Zona Sur, and in Monteverde.

The increasingly rare technicolour **scarlet macaw** (*lapa*) with its liberal splashes of red, yellow and blue, was once common on the Pacific coast of southern Mexico and Central America. The birds, which are monogamous, live in lowland forested areas, but these days your only chance of spotting them is in Corcovado National Park on the Osa Peninsula, and perhaps the Carara Biological Refuge in the Central Pacific, Palo Verde National Park or Lomas Barbudal Biological Refuge in Guanacaste. They are usually spotted in or near their nesting holes (they nest in tree trunks), in the upper branches, or while flying high and calling to one another with their distinctive raucous sqawk.

Parakeets are still fairly numerous and are most often seen in the lowland forested areas of the Pacific coast. You're also likely to see the **chestnut-mandibled** and **keel-billed toucans** (*tucánes*), with their ridiculous-but-beautiful banana-shaped beaks. The chestnut-mandibled is the largest; their bills are two-tone brown and yellow. Keel-billed toucans have the more rainbow-coloured beaks and are smaller, which is sometimes taken advantage of by their larger cousins, who may drive them away from a cache of food or hound them out of a particular tree. At other times, though, both types seem to commune quite happily. Other than humans, the toucan is thought to have few predators. They can be found in both higher and lower elevations, but in Costa Rica you are most likely to see them in the Caribbean lowlands, particularly the Sarapiquí area. They are most often spotted at dawn and in the afternoon as early as 4pm or 4.30pm – although dusk is best – sitting in the open upper branches of secondary forest. They also often fly low over the road from Guápiles to Las Horquetas.

In the **waterways** and **wetlands** of the country, most birds you see are **migratory** species from the north, including herons, gulls, sandpipers and plovers. Larger marine birds – pelicans and frigatebirds for example – come from much further afield, often making the journey from New Zealand or Cape Horn. Most migratory species are in residence between January and April, though a few arrive as early as November. The seasonal lagoons of the **Río Tempisque** basin in Guanacaste are home to the largest diversity and number of freshwater birds – both migratory and resident, in Central America. **Caño Negro** in the Zona Norte is another rewarding area for birdwatching.

Permanent residents of Costa Rican river areas include **cormorants**, and **anhingas** (sometimes called "snakebirds" in English, due to their sinuous necks). *Anhingas* are fishermen, impaling their prey on the knife-point of their beaks before swallowing. The elegant, long-limbed white **ibis** often stands motionless on river-level branches and banks; harder to spot and more endangered is the giant **jabirú stork**, most often seen in Caño Negro and on the Río Tempisque in Palo Verde National Park.

Travelling the Tortuguero canals or on the Río Sierpe down to Bahía Drake on the Osa Peninsula, you are likely to see a **kingfisher** (*martín pescador*). The green kingfisher, with its deep forest-green back and distinctive crown is particularly lovely. The largest colony of the Nicaraguan **grackle** (*zanate*) makes regular appearances in Caño Negro; the only place in Costa Rica where these dark, crow-like

birds nest. Other water birds are **brown pelicans** (*buchón*) and the pretty pink **roseate spoonbills**, found mainly in the Río Tempisque basin, where you can also see huge clumps of nesting **night-herons** (*cuacu*). The most common bird, and the one you're likely to come across hiking or riding in cattle country, is the unprepossessing grey-white **egret** (*garça*).

Of the raptors (hawks and eagles) the **laughing falcon** (*guaco*), which is found all over the country, probably has the most distinct call, which sounds exactly like it's Spanish name. The "laughing" bit comes from a much lower-pitched variation, which resembles muted human laughter. The laughing falcon preys on reptiles, including venomous snakes, biting off the head before bringing the body back to its eyrie, where it drapes it over a branch, sings a duet with its mate, and proceeds to dine. The sharp-eyed, mottled brown **osprey** eagle still has a reasonably good species count, despite the blows that deforestation have dealt to its rainforest habitat. You're most likely to see ospreys patrolling the skies of the canals between Barra del Colorado and Limón or in the Gandoca–Manzanillo Wildlife Refuge. The **harpy** eagles have not fared so well, and are thought to be locally extinct, due to widespread destruction of its favoured upper-canopy habitat. There is a chance that some may still live and hunt in the interior of Corcovado National Park on the Osa Peninsula, or within the rugged La Amistad International Park in the south of the country. Their bushy crowns give them a tousled look, rather than the usual fierce appearance of raptors, and they have a delicate, hooked beak.

You're unlikely to see much of owls, as they are nocturnal, but the **tropical screech owl** (*sorococa*) is commonly heard, even in the suburbs of San José, with its distinctive whirring call that builds to a screech or laugh as it takes flight.

The unremarkable brown **oropéndola**, relative of the oriole, is best-known for its distinctive basketweave nest, which looks like a lacrosse net and droops conspicuously from tree limbs all over the country, especially in the Valle Central and Chirripó.

Hardly anyone gets through a day or two in Monteverde or Santa Elena without at least hearing the distinctive, metallic call of the **three-wattled bellbird**. If you catch a glimpse of them you'll find that they look even stranger than their *clunk*-sounding clarion call, with three worm-like black sacks hanging off their beak. Monteverde is also a good place to watch the antics of the tiny thumb-sized **hummingbirds**,(*colibrís*) who buzz about like particularly swift, engorged bees. Thanks to their wings' unusual round hinges, hummingbirds can feed on flower nectar while actually hovering. They are numerous in Costa Rica, and some local types, like the purple-throated hummingbird, are particularly pretty.

The shrunk-shouldered **vulture** (*zópilote*) is not usually considered of interest to birders. That said, it is the one bird that almost everyone will see at some point, hanging out opportunistically on the side of major highways waiting for rabbits and iguanas to be thumped beneath the wheels of a passing vehicle.

MAMMALS (FAUNA, ANIMALES)

Costa Rica's mammals range from the fairly unexotic (at least for North Americans and Europeans) **white-tailed deer** (*venado cola blanca*) and **brocket deer** (*cabra de monte*) to the seemingly antidiluvean – **Baird's tapir** (or "mountain cow"; *danta* in Spanish) for instance – to the preternatural or semi-sacred **jaguar** (*tigre*).

Now an engandered species, the jaguar is endemic to the New World tropics and has a range from southern Mexico to northern Argentina. Although it was once common throughout Central America, especially in the lowland forests and mangroves of coastal areas, the jaguar's main foe has long been man, who has hunted it for its valuable pelt and because of its reputation among farmers as a predator of calves and pigs. It is easily tracked, due to its distinctive footprint. Incredibly, sport hunting of jaguars was allowed into the 1980s, although the trade was hampered by the fact that it is illegal to import the pelts into most countries, including the United States. Though you won't see a jaguar in the wild, one of the sorriest sights you may come across in Costa Rica is the caged jaguar, in a hotel's private zoo for example, and is typically kept in small cramped cages where it can do little but pace back and forth. Considered sacred by the Maya, jaguars are a very beautiful mid-sized cat; nearly always golden with black spots, and much more rarely a sleek,

beautiful black. They feed on smaller mammals such as agoutis, monkeys and peccaries, and may also eat fish and birds.

Not to be confused with the jaguar, the **jaguarundi** is a small cat, very rarely seen, that ranges in colour from reddish to black. Little-studied, the jaguarundi has short legs and a low-slung body, and is sometimes confused for the tayra, or tropical mink. They are swift and shy, and although they live in many lowland areas and forests, are very rarely encountered by walkers.

Along with the jaguar, the **tapir** is perhaps the most fantastical form inhabiting the Neotropical rainforest, where it is called Baird's tapir. A distant relative of the rhinoceros, the tapir also occurs in the tropics of southeast Asia. Rather homely, with eyes set back on either side of its head, the tapir looks something between a horse and an overgrown pig, with a stout grey-skinned body and a head that suggests an elephant with a truncated trunk. Their antidiluvean look comes from their prehensile snout, small ears, and delicate cloven feet. Weighting as much as 300 kilograms and vegetarian, they are extremely shy in the wild, largely nocturnal, and stick to densely forested or rugged land: consequently they are very rarely spotted by casual rainforest walkers. The tapir has proved to be very amiable in captivity, and is certain to be unaggressive should you be lucky enough to come upon it. Like the jaguar, its main foe is man, who hunts it for its succulent meat. Nowadays the tapir is protected to a degree in the National Parks and preserves.

Along with the tapir, all the cats have been made extremely shy through centuries of hunting. The one exception, which does not yield a big enough pelt, is the small, sinuous-necked **margay** (*tigrillo*), with its complex black-spotted markings and large, inquisitive eyes. It has been known to peek out of the shadows and even sun itself on the rocks. The **ocelot** (*manigordo*) is similar, somewhere between the margay and jaguar in size, but is another animal you are very unlikely to see. Of all the cats, the sandstone-coloured **mountain lion** (*puma*) is said to be the most forthcoming. It's a big animal, and although not usually aggressive toward humans, should be treated with respect.

Some of the animals you are more likely to see – because of their abundance and diurnal activity – look like outsize versions or variations on temperate zone mammals: the **agouti** or **paca** (*tepezcuintle*), a large water-rodent, for example, or the mink-like **tayra** (*tolumuco*), who may flash by you on its way up a tree. Notable for its lustrous coat and snake-like sinuosity, the tayra can be fierce if cornered. The Neotropical **river otter** (*nutria*) is an altogether friendlier creature, although extremely shy. The **coati** (often mistakenly called coatimundi; *pizote* in Spanish) looks like a confused combination of a racoon, domestic cat and an anteater. There is also a tropical **racoon** (*mapache*) that looks like its northern neighbour, complete with eye mask. Nearly all of these are foragers and forest-floor dwellers.

The **peccary** (*saíno*), usually described as a wild pig or boar, comes in two little-differentiated species in Costa Rica: collared or white-lipped. They can be menacing when encountered in packs, when, if they get a whiff of you – their sight is poor so they'll smell you before they see you – they may clack their teeth and growl a bit. The usual advice, especially in Corcovado National Park where they travel in groups as large as thirty, is to climb a tree. However, peccaries are not on the whole dangerous and in captivity have proved to be very affectionate, rubbing themselves against you delightedly at the least opportunity.

You may well see an **anteater** (*hormiguero*) vacuuming an anthill at some point. Of the two species that inhabit Costa Rica, you're much more likely to see the **northern tamandua**, although it is largely nocturnal. It hunts ants, occasionally bees, and termites, digging into nests using its sharp claws and inserting its proboscis-like snout into the mound to lick up its prey. Far rarer, the **silky anteater** is arboreal, a lovely golden in colour, and hardly ever seen.

Costa Rica is home to four species of monkey. Most people can expect to at least hear, if not see, the **howler monkey** (*mono congo*), especially in the lowland forests: the male has a mechanism in its thick throat by which it can make sounds which sound like those from a gorilla. Their whoops are most often heard at dawn or dusk. The **white-faced or capuchin** (*carablanca*) monkey is slighter than the howler, with a distinctly humanoid expression on its delicate face. This, combined with its intelligence, often consigns it to being a pet in a hotel or private zoo. The **spider monkey** (*araña*) takes its name from its spider-like ability to move through the trees employing its three limbs – the third one is its prehensile tail, which it uses to grip branches. The **squirrel monkey** (*mono tití*) is presently only found in and south of Manuel Antonio National Park.

GUISES AND DISGUISES

Rainforest fauna and flora have an elaborate repertoire of ruses, flamboyancies, poisons and camouflage, which they put to a variety of uses, from self-protection to pollination.

Many tropical animals are well-known for their gaudy **colour**, which can mean one of two things: warning potential predators to keep away, or flaunting an invulnerable position at the top of the food chain. Particularly notable are the birds that inhabit the rainforest canopy: toucans, parakeets and scarlet macaws, not to mention the resplendent quetzal. Unfortunately, while flaunting the fact that they have hardly any predators, these beautiful birds make themselves vulnerable to perhaps the most threatening adversary of them all – humans. Advertising **toxicity** is another ingenious evolutionary development. The amazingly colourful **poison dart frogs** are a case in point, as is the venomous **coral snake**. These reptiles give the "Keep Away" signal loud and clear to potential predators, some of whom, after successive bad experiences, build up a species memory and cease preying upon them.

Some animals are **camouflage** experts. Again, camouflage serves one of two purposes: to be able to hide in order to ensnare prey, or to hide in order to avoid predators. The predatorial jaguar looks exactly like the mottled light of the ground floor of the rainforest, making it easier to both hide and hunt, while the clear-winged butterfly literally disappears into the air. Sloths, too, hide from their attackers, with a greasy green algae growing on their fur, making them look even more like the clump of leaves that they already resemble.

Then there are the **mimics**, usually insects, who have an evolutionary ability to look like something which they are not. The *asilidae* family in particular features many mimics: flies impersonate wasps and wasps disguise themselves as bees, all in the pursuit of safety or predation.

Their delicate grey and white faces have long made them attractive to pet owners and zoos, and consequently they have been hunted to near extinction in Costa Rica. However, they are extremely gregarious – though they can be easily put off by too many people tramping through Manuel Antonio – and you may well catch sight of one.

Two types of **sloths** (*perezsosos*) live in Costa Rica: the **three-toed** sloth, active by day, and the nocturnal **two-toed** sloth. True to their name, sloths move very little during the day and have an extremely slow metabolism. They are excellently camouflaged from their main predators, eagles, by the algae that often covers their brown hair. In the first instance at least they are very difficult to spot on your own; a guide will usually point one out. Scan the V-intersections in trees, particularly the middle and upper elevations: from a distance they resemble a ball of fur or a hornet's nest. Sloths present something of a mystery in their defecating habits, risking life and limb to descend to the forest floor, once a week, to defecate. Their sharp taloned claws are best suited to the arboreal universe, and outside the tree limbs they are a bit lost, exposing themselves to predation by jaguars and other animals. No one has yet come up with a solid hypothesis as to this irrational behaviour.

Costa Rica has many species of **bats** (*murciélagos*) which literally hang out sleeping on the underside of branches, where they look like rows of small grey triangles. In Tortuguero, you may see a **fishing bat** skimming the water, casting its aural net in front in search of food: being blind, it fishes by sonar. For the best bat-viewing opportunities, head to Barra Honda caves on the Nicoya Peninsula, where they roost in huge numbers.

AMPHIBIANS AND REPTILES (ANFÍBIOS, REPTILES)

There are many, many **frogs** (*ranas*) and **toads** (*sapos*) in Costa Rica. Though they seem vulnerable – small, and with few defenses – many tropical frogs look after themselves by secreting poison through their skin. Using some of the most powerful natural toxins known, the frog can directly target the heart muscle of the predator, paralysing it and causing immediate death. As these poisons are transmittable through skin contact, you should never touch a Costa Rican frog. Probably the best-known, and most toxic, of the frogs, is the colourful **poison dart frog**, usually quite small, and found in various combinations of bright red and blue or green and black. Even the innocuous-looking **shore** or **beach frog** can shoot out a jet of toxins; while it may not be fatal to humans, it can kill heedless cats and dogs who try to pick it up in their mouths.

The more common ways in which tropical frogs defend themselves are through camouflage (usually mottled brown, green or variations thereon, they blend perfectly into the tropical cover) or by jumping, a good method of escape in thick ground cover. Jumping also throws snakes – who hunt by scent, and are probably their most prevalent predator – off track. You will most likely see frogs around dusk or at night; some of them make a regular and dignified procession down paths and trails, sitting motionless for long periods before hopping off again. The chief thing you'll notice about the more common frogs is their size: they're much stouter than temperate zone frogs. Look out for the gaudy **leaf frog** (*rana calzonudo*), star of many a frog calendar. Relatively large, it is an alarming bright green, with orange hands and feet and dark blue thighs. Its sides are purple, and its eyes are pure red, to scare off potential predators.

Travelling along or past Costa Rica's waterways, you may well see **caimans** and **crocodiles**. Crocs hang out on the muddy banks, basking in the sun, while the smaller, shyer caimans will sometimes perch on submerged tree-branches, scuttling away at your approach. Both are under constant threat from hunters, who sell their skin to make shoes and handbags.

Pot-bellied **iguanas** are the most ubiquitous of Costa Rica's lizards, as common here as chickens are in Europe or the US. Masters of camouflage, they can occasionally be spotted on the middle and lower branches of trees and on the ground. Despite their dragon-like appearance, they are very shy, and if you do spot them, it's likely that they'll be scurrying away in an ungainly fashion. In wetlands and on rivers, watch out for a tiny form skittering across the water: this is the **"Jesus Christ" lizard** (*basilisk*), so-called for its web-like foot and speed, which allows it to "walk" on water.

Costa Rica is home to a vast array of **snakes** (*serpientes, culebras*). Many of them both venomous and non-venomous, are amazingly beautiful: this can be appreciated more if you see them in captivity than if you come across one in the wild. That said, chances of the latter happening – let alone getting bitten – are very slim. Snakes are largely nocturnal, and for the most part far more wary of you than you are of them.

Out of 162 species found in the country, only 22 are venomous. These are usually well camouflaged, but some advertise their danger with a flamboyance of colour. One such is the highly venomous **coral** (same in Spanish) snake, which although retiring, is easily spotted – and avoided – with its bright rings of carmine red, yellow and black. The **false coral** snake, which is not venomous, looks very similar; a guide or a ranger will be able to point out the subtle differences. Of all the Costa Rican snakes the **bushmaster** (*cascabela, matabuey*) is the one of which even *guardaparques* are afraid. The bushmaster, whose range extends from southern Mexico to Brazil, is the largest venomous snake in the Americas – in Costa Rica it can reach a size of nearly 2m. The most aggressive of snakes, it will actually chase people, if it is so inclined. The good news is that you are extremely unlikely to encounter one, as it prefers dense and mountainous territory – Braulio Carrillo, the Sarapiquí region and Corcovado, for example – and rarely emerges during the day.

Once the inhabitant of the rainforests, the **fer-de-lance** (*terciopelo*) has adapted quite well to cleared areas, grassy uplands, and even some inhabited stretches, although you are far more likely to see them in places which have heavy rainfall (like the Limón coast) and near streams or rivers at night. Though it can reach more than 2m in length, the *terciopelo* (as it is most often called, in English or Spanish) is well-camouflaged and very difficult to spot, resembling a big pile of leaves with its greyblack skin with a light crisscross pattern. Along with the bushmaster, the *terciopelo* is one of the few snakes who may attack without provocation. They are usually killed when encountered, due to their venom and fairly healthy species count. These are the ones you'll see coiled in jars of formaldehyde at rainforest lodges, often on display beside the supper table.

The very pretty **eyelash viper** (*bocaracá*) is usually tan or green, but sometimes brilliant yellow when inhabiting golden palm fruit groves. Largely arboreal and generally well-camouflaged, it takes its name from the raised scales around its eyes. They are quite venomous to humans and should be given a wide berth if seen hanging from a branch or negotiating a path through the groves.

Considering the competition, it's not hard to see why the **boa constrictor** (*boa*) wins the title of most congenial snake. Often with beautiful semi-triangular markings, largely retiring and shy of people, the boa is one of the few snakes you may see in the daytime. Although they are largely torpid, it is not a good idea to bother them. They have big teeth and can bite though they are not venomous, and are unlikely to stir unless startled. If you encounter one, either on the move or lying still, the best thing is to walk around it slowly, giving it a good 5m berth.

For more details on precautions when dealing with snakes, see p.14 in *Basics*.

INSECTS (*INSECTOS, BICHOS*)

Costa Rica supports an enormous diversity of insects, of which the **butterflies** (*mariposas*) are the most flamboyant and sought after. Active during the day, they can be seen, especially from about 8am to noon, almost anywhere in the country. Most adult butterflies take their typical food of nectar – usually from red flowers – through a proboscis. Others feed on fungi, dung and rotting fruit. Best-known, and quite often spotted, especially along the forest trails, is the fast-flying **blue morpho**, whose titanium-bright wings seem to shimmer electrically. Like other garish butterflies, the morpho uses its colourfulness to startle or shock potential predators. Far more difficult to spot, for obvious reasons, is the **clear-winged butterfly**.

Of the annoying insects, you'll surely get acqainted with **mosquitos**, a few of which carry malaria and Dengue Fever (see p.14). In hot, slightly swampy lowland areas such as the coastal Osa or the southern Nicoya peninsulas, you may also come across **purrujas**, similar to blackflies or midges. They can inflict itchy bites, as can the **chiggers** (*colorados*) that inhabit scrub and secondary growth areas, attaching themselves to the skin, leech-like, in order to feed. Though not really bothersome, the **lantern fly** (*machaca*) emits an amazingly strong mint-blue light, like a mini lightning streak – if you have one in your hotel room you'll know it as soon as you turn out the light.

The ant kingdom is well-represented in Costa Rica. Chief among the rainforest salarymen are the **leaf-cutter ants**, who work in businesslike cadres, carrying bits of leaf to and fro to build their distinctive nests. The ones to watch out for are the big **bullet ants**, that resemble moving blackberries (their colloquial name is *veintequatro* – "24" – meaning that if you get bitten by one it will hurt for 24 hours). Endemic to the Neotropics, carniverous **army ants** are often encountered in the forest, typically living in large colonies, some of more than a million individuals. They are most famous for their "dawn raids", when they pour out of a hideaway, typically a log, and divide into several columns to create a swarm. In this columnar formation they go off in search of prey – other ants and insects – which they carry back to the nest to consume.

Among the many **bees and wasps** (*abejas, avispas*) are aggressive **Africanized bees**, which migrated from Africa to Brazil and then north to Costa Rica, where they have colonized certain localities in earnest. Although you have to disturb their nests before they'll bother you, people sensitive or allergic to bee-stings should avoid Palo Verde National Park.

MARINE LIFE

Among Costa Rica's **marine mammals** is the sea-cow or **manatee** (*manati*), elephantine in size, lumbering, good-natured and well-intentioned, not to mention endangered. Manatees all over the Caribbean and Florida are declining in number, due to the disappearance and pollution of the fresh or saltwater riverways in which they live. In Costa Rica your only reasonable chance of seeing one is in the Tortuguero canals in Limón province, where they sometimes break the surface. At first you might mistake it for a tarpon, but the manatee's overlapping snout and long whiskers are quite distinctive.

Five species of **marine turtle** nest on Costa Rica's shores. Nesting takes place mostly at night and mostly in the context of *arribadas*; giant invasions of turtles who come ashore in their thousands on the same beach (or spot of

beach) at a certain time of year, laying hundreds of thousands of eggs. Greens, hawksbills and leatherbacks come ashore on both coasts, while the Olive Ridley comes ashore only on the Pacific. The strange blunt-nosed **loggerhead**, which seems not to nest in Costa Rica, can sometimes be seen in Caribbean coastal waters.

The **green turtle**, long-prized for the delicacy of its flesh, has become nearly synonymous with its favoured nesting grounds in Tortuguero. In the 1950s it was classified as endangered, and, thanks in part to the protection offered by areas like Tortuguero, is making a comeback. Some greens make herculean journeys of as much as 2000km to their breeding beaches at Tortuguero, returning to the same stretch year after year. *Arribadas* are most concentrated in June and October. Green turtles are careful nesters: if a female is disturbed by human presence she will go back to the ocean and return only when all is clear.

The **hawksbill** (*carey*), so-named for its distinctive down-curving "beak", is found all over the tropics, often preferring rocky shores and coral reefs. it used to be hunted extensively on the Caribbean coast for its meat and shell, but this is now banned. Poaching does still occur, however, and you should avoid buying any tortoiseshell that you see for sale. Hawksbills do not come ashore in *arribadas* to the extent that green turtles do, preferring to nest alone.

Capable of growing to a length of 5m, the **leatherback** (*baula*) is the largest reptile in the world. Its "shell" is actually a network of bones overlaid with a very tough leathery skin. Though it nests most concentratedly at Parque Nacional las Baulas on the western Nicoya Peninsula, it also comes ashore elsewhere, including Tortuguero on the Caribbean coast.

The **Olive Ridley** (*lora, carpintera* – also called Pacific Ridley) turtle nests on just a few beaches, among them Playa Nancite in Santa Rosa National Park and Ostional near Nosara on the Nicoya Peninsula. They come ashore in massive *arribadas*, and, unusually, often nest during the day. Olive Ridley eggs are as prized as any, but its species count seems to be fairly healthy.

Among the freshwater **turtles** (*tortugas*) in Costa Rica is the **yellow turtle** (*tortuga amarilla*), most often seen in Caño Negro. The

black river turtle and the **snapping turtle**, about whom little is known (except that it snaps), also inhabit rivers and mangrove swamps, and may occasionally be spotted on the riverbanks.

Though **dolphins** (*delfínes*) and **whales** thread themselves through the waters of the Pacific coast, it is rare to see them. Dolphins are sighted in the Manuel Antonio and Dominical areas: for the best chance of a glimpse, take a boat trip at the Ballena Marine National Park. Getting to see a **whale** (*ballena*) is even harder. Though around Dominical, Bahía Drake and Isla del Caño, both sperm and humpback whales may be around in April and May, they are not dependable in their arrivals.

FISH (PESCAS)

Costa Rica is one of the richest sportsfishing grounds in the Neotropics. The best-known big-game fish in Costa Rica is the startlingly huge white **tarpon**. Other big fish prized for their fighting spirit are **snook, marlin**, and **wahoo** – all of which ply the waters of Barra del Colorado, Quepos and Golfito on the Pacific coast, and Playa Flamingo in Guanacaste. More laid-back are the **trout** (*trucha*) and **rainbow bass** (*guapote*) that live in the fresh-water rivers and in Laguna de Arenal. Costa Rica also features a few oddities and evolutionary throwbacks, including the undeniably homely **garfish**, which inhabits the Caño Negro wetlands and the canals of Limón province. Snorkellers will see a number of exotic fish, including enormous, plate-flat **manta rays** and the **parrotfish**, so-called less for its rich colouring than for its distinctive "beak" (actually a number or tiny teeth, welded together) which is used to munch on coral. There's another set of teeth at the back of the mouth that then grinds the coral down in order to digest it. Many of the white-sand beaches throughout the Caribbean, including the one just south of Cahuita, are the result of eons of coral excreted by these fish. Other sea creatures include stingrays, oysters, sponges, ugly moray eels, sea urchins, starfish, spiny lobsters, and fat, slug-like **sea cucumbers** that lie half submerged in the sea bed, digesting and excreting sand and mud.

Sharks are generally found on beaches where turtles nest, especially along the northern Caribbean coast, on Playa Ostional in the Nicoya Peninsula – although not further south in Playas Nosara – and in the waters surrounding Corcovado.

TIME RUNNING OUT: THE TROPICAL FOREST

Many myths are perpetuated about the rainforest: that it is a representation of disorder (a natural chaos); that it is full of loud and startling sounds; that it is thick and impenetrable as well as mysterious. Along with these ideas, conveyed through fiction, poetry and the more colourful representations of the first European explorers of the tropics, go the colonial notions that it is a world unfinished, awaiting the seed of civilization, and it is in itself valueless and unprofitable.

Meanwhile, it's likely that in just forty years time the world's rainforests may not exist at all outside officially protected areas. Throughout the 1980s Costa Rica had one of the highest rates of **deforestation** in the world. So much of Costa Rica's forest is being logged, cleared or otherwise destroyed that it is estimated that by the year 2000 Costa Rica will not only have no forests left outside the protected areas, but will actually be importing timber: until twenty years ago, bringing wood to Costa Rica would have been the equivalent of taking coals to Newcastle.

TALES FROM THE RAINFOREST

Tropical forests exist only in a thin band roughly ten degrees on either side of the equator. Chief among their characteristics is the diversity of life they support. They are home to around 40 to 50 percent of all living things on earth (barring marine ecosystems). But in biological terms, the tropical rainforest is still the Great Unknown. Scientists have catalogued fewer than one in six of their two million species, and it is often said that, scientifically speaking, we know less about the workings of the rainforest than we know about the surface of the moon.

Though "rainforest" describes the typically diverse, typically wet tropical forests you encounter in most areas of Costa Rica, there are minute differences in altitude and climate. The unifying factor is, of course, rain. To qualify, a true rainforest must receive more than 2000mm annually, dispersed relatively equitably throughout the year — many receive as much as 5000mm or 6000mm. Most of what is discussed below pertains to **primary rainforest** (*bosque primario*) which has not been disturbed for several hundreds, even thousands, of years. **Secondary growth** is the vegetation that springs up in the wake of some disturbance, like cutting, cultivation or habitation.

THE HORIZONTAL UNIVERSE

A tropical rainforest is characterized by the presence of several layers. At its most complex it will have four layers: the **canopy**, about 40–70m high, at the very top of which are **emergent** trees, often flat-topped; the **subcanopy** beneath the emergent trees; followed by the **understorey** trees, typically 10–20m in height; and finally the **shrub**, or ground, layer. Each strata is interconnected by a mesh of horizontal lianas and climbers.

The canopy often looks like a moth-eaten umbrella opened over the lower layers. The chief function of these very tall trees is to **protect** the layers below and to filter light. In very harsh downpours or tropical storms, it is the canopy that takes the brunt of the driving wind and rain, sometimes lightning, often being lashed about like a cat-o-nine-tails in the process. Sometimes they may be felled in particularly virulent storms, falling with a great crash and creating a hole in the upper layer through which light filters to feed the under-storey below.

Up to 50 percent of the rainforests' mammalian population may at some point live in the trees, compared to about 15 percent of mammals in temperate-zone forests. The majority of the animals, especially insects, remain most of the time in a specific layer of the forest; some never leave their particular "floor". Species loss — in some cases leading to local extinction, as with the canopy-dwelling harpy eagle — takes place when the rainforest is felled, in part because many animals are not able to adapt to the new topography: they need their floor in order to survive.

INTERDEPENDENCY

Rainforest vegetation has a muffled quality. Mosses beard trees, vines and lianas seemingly strangle their host trees, and huge clumps of plants sprout from the armpits formed by tree branches. This results from **co-** or **interdependency** (sometimes called mutuality), another distinct feature of the tropical rainforest. Over millennia, birds and plants have had the entire year in which to engage in ecological interactions, unlike in the temperate zones where winter shuts both plants and animals down for part of the year.

Rainforest **epiphytes**, plants which grow on other plants, present an example of **commensualism**, a form of symbiosis in which one species profits from its association with another without harming or benefiting the host. Sometimes the relationship is more parasitic, with the epiphyte taking nutrients from its hosts, as is the case with **bromeliads**, which resemble the leafy top of a pineapple turned upside down and stuck on a tree. **Orchids** are the flowering parts of these pineapple-like "weeds", as are pineapples. Bromeliads' leaves trap moisture; otherwise they take their nutrients from their host.

Co-evolution is where two species evolve more or less together due to mutual influence. Flowering plants and their insect pollinators are the best example you'll see in the rainforest. Birds, too, are important in this game of mutual survival. Hummingbirds, for example, pollinate flowers by picking up small quantities of pollen when they insert their long beaks into the flower to drink nectar, then transporting it to another flower. Some plants and birds build tight-knit relationships; deep flowers are pollinated only by long-beaked hummingbirds, more shallow ones by shorter-billed birds.

EXPERIENCING THE RAINFOREST

Among the celebrated but false characteristics attributed to rainforests are **giganticism** and **density**. In reality, most rainforest tree trunks are thin, with the taller trees seeming to rise emaciated into the sun, sprouting like mushrooms atop the other layers in their search for light. Neither is primary rainforest as impenetrable as many visitors expect. It's actually roomy on the ground. Most growth goes on above your head – what the German explorer Alexander von Humbolt called "a forest above a forest". It is the **secondary forest** which grows up after the destruction of a primary growth that is bushy and hard to penetrate.

During the day the primary forest cover can be quite **light**, except in perennially misty cloudforests or when it is raining. It's true that aside from secondary growth or where a tree has crashed, leaving a hole in the canopy, about 90 percent of the sunlight is captured by the upper layers before it reaches the ground. But when the sun is out, the rainforest light is almost bright in its translucence, a "light darkness", that is neither day nor night; rather as if a mesh of cheesecloth has been thrown over your head.

The true tropical rainforest is also not that **colourful**, unless you take into account incrementally differing shades of green and bark. Most orchids, for instance, grow in the upper canopy, as much as 40m above the ground, although you may see flashes of red in the form of heliconias, smiling-lip-shaped red flowers that grow in symmetrical bunches at eye level or lower.

Rather than hearing frightening screeches and feeling yourself being watched from all corners by the unseen eyes of tapirs and jaguars, you are likely to feel unexpectedly lonely in the largely **silent** tropical rainforest. Most walkers, unless they are trained or with a guide, do not see very much at all of other living creatures. Almost every living thing inside a tropical rainforest is shy of humans and/or well camouflaged, and many spend its days in semi-torpor or completely hidden. During the day it can be very quiet, except for birds and howler monkeys, two of the more voluble rainforest-dwellers. Once twilight begins to fall, though, the buzz and hum of the tropical forest crescendoes noticeably, with the intertwined croaks of frogs, the mating calls of toads, the whirr of crickets and the night cries of birds.

STRANGER THAN FICTION

Among the most fantastic of the rainforest trees is the **walking palm**, whose finger-like roots are prehensile; in fact, they can actually move. If it is so inclined, the palm can "walk" more than 1m in its lifetime in search of water, stepping over inconvenient obstacles like logs. **Strangler vines** initially look disturbing; a sort of arboreal version of the boa constrictor that doesn't strangle, but rather out-competes host trees for light, eventually dehydrating them to death. Everywhere in the rainforest you will see dried-up, hollowed-out dead trees surrounded by the healthy stranglers they once supported. The loops of **lianas and vines** – stranglers and otherwise – are amazingly intricate, spiralling endlessly into complex *pas-de-deux*.

One of the most startling characteristics of some rainforest trees are their **buttresses**, which help anchor the tree in thin soil where runoff is considerable. These sometimes massive above-ground roots have bark that ranges from cement-hard to long peeling strips, called **exfoliating bark**. Some trunks also have huge **spines** that look as though they could have defended a medieval garrison. These are a protective mechanism, making it difficult for animals or humans to climb the tree.

RAINFOREST DESTRUCTION

What the large-scale **destruction** of the rainforest will mean in terms of climatic change and the chemical composition of the air is not known. We do know that the tropical rainforest performs vital photosynthisizing processes, affects **weather** patterns, and mitigates the greenhouse effect and a range of other changes occuring as a result of humankind's misuse of its environment. Tropical forests, particularly those in higher altitude areas, do the usually richer lowland soils a big favour by acting as **watersheds** and absorbing most of the tremendous rainfall of the tropical climate. Without them, lowland agricultural soils would be washed away by torrents of water. Each year in Costa Rica about 725 million tons of **topsoil** are lost to wind erosion and water runoff – 83 percent of this happens in areas cleared and put under pasture. When it's bucketing down in the Valle Central in October, visitors will have a hard time believing that Costa Rica has a problem with water supply, or even desertification, as is the case in Guanacaste, but the watershed deterioration caused by deforestation has put the country at risk from both.

Many of the lower order of living things that inhabit rainforests, like fungi and bacteria, have provided **medicine** with some of its most effective treatments against serious illnesses – good arguments, in human terms, for preserving the rainforest and the medical secrets it may divulge. Also lost when rainforests are felled are forest-dwelling indigenous **peoples** and their cultures. **Animals** and birds, including jaguars, tapirs, macaws, toucans and quetzals, lose their habitats or are hounded out into the open where they are easily killed by hunters.

THE PERPETRATORS

The reason that such destruction takes place is, quite simply, that there is serious **money** to be made from the felling of tropical forests. **Loggers** fell the forest for the hardwoods it yields, using them to make expensive furniture prized for its durability and beauty. The most famous endangered hardwoods are **mahogany** and **purpleheart**, whose names evoke their lovely deep-blooded colour. Meanwhile, the big old oak trees of the cloudforests are depleted for timber and charcoal. Although the major deforesters often have the implicit support of the national government because they are earners of much needed foreign currency or foreign investment, they do not have total *carte blanche*. Loggers need a government permit, and the export of many rare tropical hardwood species is prohibited. But between a certain level of corruption and illegality, logging still takes place: the Costa Rican Forestry Office reckons that illegal cutting of rainforest trees accounted for 80 percent of forest losses between 1989 and 1991. Travellers who spend any amount of time on the nation's highways can expect at some point to find themselves stuck behind a slow-moving truck loaded with incredibly massive tree trunks swathed in chains – these are tropical hardwoods, trees hundreds or even thousands of years old, that are being lost for good.

Other perpetrators fell the trees for the land the forest stands on. **Bananas**, another large foreign-currency earner, only grow well in the hot, wet tropical lowlands. Other major **agro-exports** include coffee, tea and macadamia nut plantations, all grown for the foreign market.

Cattle-ranchers have been clearing areas of rainforest for years. The first horses and cows were brought to Costa Rica by the Spanish as early as 1561. By 1950, approximately an eighth of the country was under pasture. The cattle industry in Costa Rica grew rapidly from the 1960s to the 80s, largely funded by loans from the US to encourage lower-grade beef production and by rising beef prices on the international market. During much of the 1980s Costa Rica was the world's biggest exporter of beef to the US.

Cattle ranching takes up more land and yields less than any other type of farming and ranches create little local employment in comparison to banana or coffee plantations. The tropical soils of the pasture the cattle feed on are exhausted quickly, usually within three to ten years. By 1983 about 30 percent of the country was pastureland, much of it abandoned. Of all the forests cut during the 1960s and 70s to make way for the growth of the cattle industry, about 90 percent are not regenerable. Meanwhile, since the late 1980s, tastes, both domestic and foreign, have changed, and the consumption and price of beef has dropped to such an extent that the future of large-scale cattle ranching seems in doubt.

Despite this, the cattle continues to feature heavily in Costa Rica – especially in Guanacaste where the cowboy and hacienda culture reigns. Many haciendas have turned to non-traditional activities like tourism and have scaled down their herds in order to concentrate on the new trade, although in aspect and essence they remain working cattle farms. At the other end of the scale, the smallholder keeps cattle as a way of safeguarding against the risks of subsistence-level agriculture. Cows can be milked, slaughtered or sold, and in hard times – or in an inflationary economy such as Costa Rica's – they are a good investment for the *campesino*.

Another principal threat to the survival of the tropical forest is **agriculture**. The very act of felling the rainforest renders the soil useless after a couple of years. Rainforest soils are, in fact, very poor in nutrients. The complex, dense appearance of the trees represents an attempt to compensate for this, as they have to build a store of crucial chemicals above ground, in their leaves and bark. When a rainforest tree is felled by a storm or by wind and comes crashing down, the nutrients are recycled by the ground vegetation within a matter of weeks (rather than months, as in the temperate zone). In this way essential chemicals are kept in constant exchange. These chemicals are located in the thin uppermost layer of soil – the **humus** – which is easily washed away, turned over for cultivation, or tramped into nonexistence by cows' hooves.

The main exponent of **slash-and-burn** techniques in Costa Rica is usually the *precarista*, or squatter *campesino*, victim of unequal land distribution, poverty and a lack of viable alternatives.

Costa Rica has the highest rural population density in Latin America, so there is tremendous pressure on **land**. Until the second half of this century, deforestation came under the legal definition of "improvement of the land", and the state still encourages deforestation by allowing the *campesino* to establish title to isolated patches of "unwanted" land, usually in remote areas, if he clears or otherwise "improves" it. (This is not just a Costa Rican phenomenon: in the eighteenth century, pioneer settlers to Canada and the United States were granted title to land according to the same criteria.) The effects of this colonization are most conspicuous along the roadsides and in the smaller communities of the Zona Norte, where you see smallholders' shacks built on poor, stump-studded land, dotted with the odd banana tree, vegetable patches, and a few cattle and pigs.

Archeologists and biologists speculate that the pre-columbian isthmus peoples used the slash-and-burn method to plant crops of maize and *pejibaye*, and that this did not do long-term damage to the regenerative capacities of complex forest systems (for more on this, see p.200). Rather it is large-scale colonization, followed by burning, that ensure that the rainforest will never recover. Burning renders long-term cultivation of anything from grasses to carrots impossible, as it definitively destroys the humus at the topmost layer of the former rainforest soil.

FORESTS OF THE FUTURE

Any **real solutions** to the problem of deforestation – rather than the preservation of existing forests – appear complex or unattainable. Historically, fault for the near total deforestation of the Central American isthmus lies with – who else – the conquistadors, who, in the search for domestic wealth, disrupted indigenous forms of sustainable cultivation to grow export crops, effectively turning the country into a coffee-and-banana Republic. The concerns of the domestic elites and the consumer demands of the countries that import Costa Rican goods make it difficult to break the pattern. In an essentially third world country with little economic room for manoeuvre, under pressure from all sides, it seems Costa Rica's rainforest can no longer just exist: it must pay its own way in order to achieve eternal preservation – it must be **sustainable**.

A recent development in the sustainable use of rainforests is the entry of large **pharmaceutical** companies into the conservation effort. INbio (National Institute of Biodiversity), was founded in San José in 1989 as the first institute of its kind in the world, and is devoted to taking an entire inventory of Costa Rica's species, and training locals in species collection procedures.

Many lower-order rainforest flora like fungi and bacteria are suspected to possess potential anti-cancer, rheumatoid, and hypertension agents. INbio has recently signed a lucrative contract with Merck, one of the world's largest pharmeceutical companies, who have guaranteed that INbio (and the state) will receive "royalties" on any drugs successfully developed from samples INbio sends for investigation.

Debt payments and ecological concerns can even be successfully intertwined in **"debt-for-nature"** swaps. A complex arrangement still in the pioneering stage, this scheme allows organizations like the World Wildlife Fund to purchase a piece of Costa Rica's foreign debt, usually at a discount. Costa Rica's government in return issues short-term government bonds. The funds raised by selling these bonds to investors are funnelled into conservation. For the first world foreign banks and organizations who participate, debt-for-nature is seen in purely economic terms: an investment in the environment. Philosophically speaking, though, some justify it as the Third World being "paid back" for the First World's ravages, including carbon monoxide emissions and the deforestation that has long been encouraged by the markets and tastes of the developed world.

CONSERVATION AND TOURISM

Costa Rica is widely regarded to be at the cutting edge of worldwide conservation strategy, an impressive feat for a tiny Central American nation. At the centre of Costa Rica's internationally applauded conservation effort is a complex system of National Parks and Wildlife Refuges, which protect a full 25 percent of its territory, making it the nation with the largest percentage of protected land in the western hemisphere. These statistics are used with great effect to attract tourists, and along with Belize, Costa Rica has become virtually synonymous with eco-tourism in Central America.

On the other hand, the National Parks service does not possess the funds to protect adequately more than half the boundaries and ecological integrity of these areas, which are under constant pressure from logging and squatters (*precaristas*) and to a lesser extent from mining interests. To illustrate this you could take a river trip from Puerto Viejo de Sarapiquí to Barra del Colorado Wildlife Refuge or fly over the western perimeter of Tortuguero National Park. In addition, the question uppermost in the minds of conservationists and biologists who undertook field studies in Costa Rica long before it was "discovered", is: what, if any, damage is caused by so many feet walking through the rainforests?

CONSERVATION IN THE NEW WORLD TROPICS

The **traditional view** of conservation is an old-world European one, of preserving, museum-like, pretty animals and flowers; an idea that was conceived and upheld by relatively wealthy countries in which the majority of the forests have long-since disappeared. In the contemporary world, this definition of conservation no longer works, and certainly not in the New World tropics, besieged as they are by lack of resources, huge income inequalities, legislation that lacks bite, and the continual appetite of the world market for tropical hardwoods, not to mention First-World zeal for coffee and picture-perfect supermarket fruits.

There's a **leftist perspective** on conservation that sees an imperialistic, bourgeois and anti-*campesino* agenda among the large conservation organizations of the North. By this reckoning, saving the environment is all very well but does little for the day-to-day realities of the 38 percent or so of Costa Rica's population who live below the poverty line. These people have, in many cases, been made landless and resource-poor by, for instance, absentee landowners speculating on land (in the Zona Norte and in Guanacaste) or the pulling-out of a major employer like the United Fruit Company (in the Zona Sur near Golfito and on the Osa Peninsula). Many are left with simply no choice but to engage in the kind of activity – be it gold-panning or slash-and-burn agriculture – universally condemned by conservationists in the North.

Into this situation step **eco-tourists** with dollars to spend, which is also a problematic issue. There is an argument on the far fringe of eco-militancy which says, in sum, if you love the rainforest, then stay at home and donate money to conservation organizations rather than travelling abroad to tramp through it and change local economies with influxes of *dólares*.

CONSERVATION IN COSTA RICA

Costa Rica has a long **history** of conservation-consciousness, although it has taken several different forms and guises. As early as 1775 a number of laws were passed to limit the destructive impact of *quemas*, or brush-burning. Meanwhile, a vogue developed in Europe for **botanical gardens**. The period from 1635 to 1812 saw the birth of some of Europe's most splendid gardens – including the *doyenne* of them all, London's Kew Gardens, founded in 1730. Scientists-cum-adventurers in search of knowledge and botanists in search of flora descended upon the Neotropics, bringing attention to the potential foreign interest in Costa Rica's plant and animal life.

The bulk of **preservation laws** were passed after 1845, concurrent with Costa Rica's period of greatest economic and cultural growth. That said, most of this legislation was directed at protecting resource extraction rather than the areas themselves – to guard fishing and hunting grounds and to conserve what were already seen as valuable timber supplies. In 1895 laws were passed protecting water supplies and the establishment of *guardabosques* (forest rangers) to fight the *quemas* caused by the regular burning of deforested land and pasture by cattle-ranchers. The forerunners of several institutions later to be important to the development of conservation in Costa Rica were founded by the end of the nineteenth century, including the Museo Nacional and the Instituto Físico Geográfico.

THE NATIONAL PARKS

Much of the credit for the initial phases of the present system of National Parks in Costa Rica has to go to **Olof Wessberg** and **Karen Morgenson**, longtime foreign residents who in 1963 founded the **Reserva Natura Absoluta Cabo Blanco** near their home on the southwest tip of the Nicoya Peninsula, largely through their own efforts. Wessberg and Morgenson helped raise national consciousness through an extensive letter-writing and fundraising campaign in the mid-Sixties so that by the end of the decade there was broad support for the founding of a National Parks service. In 1969 Santa Rosa National Monument and Park was declared, and in 1970 the SPN (Servicio de Parques Nacionales) was officially inaugurated. Spearheaded by a recently graduated forester, Mario Boza, the system developed slowly at first, as the law which established Santa Rosa really existed only on paper: neighbouring farmers and ranchers continued their encroachment on the land for pasture and brush-burning as before.

Although it remains a mystery, the murder of Olof Wessberg in 1975 on the Osa Peninsula

THE CASE OF TORTUGUERO

National Parks are now such an entrenched part of Costa Rica's landcape that they might be taken to have always been there. In fact most have been established in the last twenty-five years and the process of creating them is not always smooth. **Tortuguero National Park** on the Caribbean coast is a case in point.

Turtle Bogue (the old Miskito name for Tortuguero) had always been isolated. Even today access is by fluvial transport or air only, and before the dredging of the main canal in the 1960s it was even more cut off from the rest of the country. Most of the local people were of Miskito or Afro-Caribbean extraction, hunting and fishing and living almost completely without consumer goods. There was virtually no cash economy in the village, with local trade and barter being sufficient for most people's needs.

In the 1940s, **lumbering** began in earnest in the area. A sawmill was built in the village, and during the next two decades the area experienced a boom. The local lumber exhausted itself by the 1960s, but in the twenty-year interim it brought outsiders and a dependence on cash-obtainable consumer goods.

Simultaneously, the number of **green sea turtles** was declining rapidly, due to overfishing and egg harvesting, and by the 1950s the once-numerous turtle was officially endangered. The alarm raised by biologists over the green turtle's preciptous decline paved the way for the establishment, in 1970, of Tortuguero National Park, protecting 30 of the 35 kilometres of turtle-nesting beach and extending to more than 20,000 hectares of surrounding forests, canals and waterways. The establishment of this protective area made former sources of income off-limits to local populations, and villagers who had benefited from the wood-and-turtle economy either reverted to the subsistence and agricultural life they had known before or left the area in search of a better one. Nowadays, twenty years after the Park was officially established, many locals make a good living off the increasing amount of tourism it brings, especially those with their own independent businesses, although others are relegated to low-paid positions in hotels and other services.

The establishment of the National Park effectively broke the boom-and-bust cycle so prevalent in the tropics, whereby local resources are used to extinction, often by foreign interests, and no viable alternatives are left after the storm has passed. In Tortuguero the hardwoods have made a bit of a comeback, and the green turtle's numbers are up dramatically from their low point in the 1950s and 1960s. Considering the popularity of the National Park and its lagoons and turtle tours, there's no doubt that conservation and protection of Tortuguero's wildlands will have lasting benefits to locals, although there is some question as to how a tiny community like Tortuguero can absorb such high levels of tourism and retain its cultural integrity.

is an illustration of the powerful interests that are thwarted by conservation. Wessberg was conducting a preliminary survey in Osa to assess the possibility of a National Park there (the site of modern-day Corcovado). Although his assailant – the man who had offered to guide him – was caught, a motive was never discovered and the crime has not been satisfactorily solved.

Under the Arias government a national conservation strategy was drafted in 1988, and soon after his election victory in 1994, current president José Maria Figueres proclaimed, "We will build a constructive alliance with nature". The money to back these plans has come chiefly from increased taxation, something the country's middle and lower classes resent. His government has recently introduced a comprehensive range of tax hikes, including an electricity tax to encourage energy conservation and a carbon tax whose revenue will be directed to replanting tropical forests on exhausted cattle pastures. Figueres has also pleged to double the area of the country covered by National Parks and Wildlife Refuges.

In autumn 1994 the government and the SPN raised entrance fees to most of the country's parks overnight by 1000 percent to $15. Uproar ensued, and even Costa Ricans (who continue to pay $1.50) could be heard to comment that the prices foreigners were being asked to pay were simply too high. Now the dust has settled, it is hoped that the fees will result in improved management, higher salaries and better training for rangers, and the purchase of more lands for preservation.

ECO-PARADISE LOST: PESTICIDES AND POLLUTION

There are, however, flaws in this Garden of Eden. Chief among them is the importance of the **agro-export** economy. The growth of the large scale agro-industries depends upon a continual supply of cheap labour, and of land, and the **pollution** wreaked by the pesticides used in banana plantations – the country's major agro-export – is becoming an increasing threat. Foreign consumers attach an amazing level of importance to the appearance of supermarket bananas and pineapples. About 20 percent of potentially dangerous **pesticides** used in the cultivation of bananas serve only to improve the look of the fruit and not, as it is often thought, to control pestilence. Travellers who pass through banana plantations in Costa Rica or who take river trips, especially along the Río Sarapiquí, can't fail to notice the ubiquitous blue plastic bags. The pristine appearance of Costa Rican bananas are due largely to the fact that they grow inside these pesticide-lined bags, which make their way into waterways where they are fatally consumed by fish, mammals (such as the manatee) or iguanas. In the Río Tempisque basin armadillos and crocodiles are thought to have been virtually exterminated by agricultural pesticides.

Animals are not alone in being at risk from pesticides. In 1987 a hundred Costa Rican plantation workers sued Standard Fruit, Dow Chemical, and Shell Oil for producing a pesticide that is a known cause of sterility in banana-plantation workers. Although the workers' claims were upheld in US courts, the companies have appealed. Since then several harmful pesticides have been banned, although every year 6 percent of all Costa Rican banana-workers have reason to present claims for incidents of dangerous intoxications involving pesticides – the highest such incidence in the world.

CONSERVATION INITIATIVES

In recent years Mario Boza, a founder of the National Parks System and prominent conservationist, has been advocating a strategy of **macro-conservation**. By uniting concerns and "joining up" chunks of protected land, he argued, the macro-areas will allow larger protected areas for animals who need room to hunt, like jaguars and pumas. Most of all, they will allow countries to make more effective joint conservation policies and decisions. Macro-conservation projects include the Proyeto Paseo Pantera (all of Mesoamerica), El Mundo Maya (Belize, El Salvador, Guatemala, Honduras and Mexico), Si-a-Paz (Nicaragua and Costa Rica) and La Amistad International Park and Biosphere Reserve (Costa Rica and Panamá).

Arguably, however, the most revolutionary change in conservation management, and the one likeliest to have the biggest pay-off in the long term, is the shift toward **local initiatives**. Some projects are truly local, such as the tiny grassroots organization TUVA and its

CONSERVATION ORGANIZATIONS IN COSTA RICA

The following list represents just a sample of the large number of conservationist organizations working in Costa Rica. There are many more local operations. For details of voluntary conservation opportunities in Costa Rica, see p.54.

Fundación Neotropica, Aptdo 236-1002, Paseo de los Estudiantes, San José (☎253-2130; fax 253-4210).

Well-established organization that works with several small-scale and typically local conservation initiatives in Costa Rica. Their Curridabat office sells posters, books and T-shirts in aid of funds. Accepts donations.

Rainforest Action Costa Rica, PO Box 99 Saxmundham, Suffolk, IP17 2LB, UK (☎01728/668501; fax 01728/668680).

A new programme run by the UK-based World Wide Land Conservation Trust. All donations of £25 go toward purchase of an acre (£50 per acre is the going price) of Costa Rican rainforest. Working closely with the Massachusetts Audobon society, they are particularly active on the Osa Peninsula, where they have been instrumental in blocking a planned woodchip mill and dock.

World Wide Fund for Nature, 1250 24th St NW, Washington DC, 20037 USA (☎202/293-4800); 90 Eglington Ave E, Suite 504, Toronto, Ontario M4P 2Z7 (☎416/489-8800); Panda House, Weyside Park, Godalming, Surrey GU7 1XR (☎01483/26444).

Long a donor to projects in the Monteverde area WWF has recently expanded their funding to CATIE, a tropical agriculture research centre, which acts as their Costa Rica office. They also supported negotiations for debt-for-nature swaps.

---

selective logging of naturally felled rainforest trees on the Osa Peninsula, or the eco-tourism co-operative of Las Delicias in Barra Honda on the Nicoya Peninsula.

Another initiative, even more promising in terms of how it affects the lives of many rural-based Costa Ricans, is the creation of **"buffer zones"** around some National Parks. In these zones *campesinos* and other smallholders can do part-time farming, are allowed restricted hunting rights and receive education as to the ecological and economic value of the forest. Locals may be trained as nature guides, and *campesinos* may be given incentives to enter into non-traditional forms of agriculture and ways of making a living which are not so distressing to the environment.

In recent years Costa Rica's **waste disposal problems** have given the country a garbage nightmare, culminating in a scandal in 1995 over the overflowing of the Río Azul site, San José's main dump. The government fully recognizes the irony of this – rubbish lining the streets of a country with such a high conservation profile – and in an admirable, typically Tico grass-roots initiative, legions of schoolkids are now sent on rubbish-collecting after-school projects and weekend brigades. Even more ingenious is the national movement which sends Costa Rican schoolchildren to National Parks and other preserves as **volunteers** to work on conservation projects during school holidays, thus planting the seeds for a future generation of dedicated, or at least aware, conservationists.

TOURISM

In 1993 more than 700,000 tourists came to Costa Rica – mostly from the US, Canada and Europe – an incredible number, considering that the population of the country itself is only 3.34 million. In 1994, revenue to Costa Rica from tourism was $700 million or more, surpassing earnings by banana exports for the first time in the country's history. In the North American winter months of December to March, it is estimated that the country's hotel rooms are at near 100 percent occupancy.

Ten or even five years ago it seemed unlikely that this small Central American country, peaceful but off the beaten track, would attract so many visitors. Along with the considerable charms of the country itself, its popularity today is linked with the growing trend toward eco-tourism.

ECO-TOURISM

If managed properly, low-impact **eco-tourism** is one of the best ways in which forests, beaches, rivers, mangroves, volcanos and other natural formations can pay their way – in *dólares* – while remaining pristine and intact. However, eco-tourism is a difficult term to **define**. It was often seen in relation to what it was not: package tourism, wherein visitors have limited contact with nature and with the day-to-day lives of local people. But as more and more organizations and businesses hijack the "eco" prefix for dubious uses, the authentic eco-tourism experience has become increasingly difficult to pin down. One of the best attempts has been put forward by **ATEC**, the Talamancan Eco-tourism and Conservation Association, which seeks to promote, as it says, "socially responsible tourism" by integrating local Bribrí and Afro-Caribbean culture into tourists' experience of the area, as well as giving residents pride in their unique cultural heritage and natural environment. Their definition is:

"Eco-tourism means more than bird books and binoculars. Eco-tourism means more than native art hanging on hotel walls or ethnic dishes on the restaurant menu. Eco-tourism is not mass tourism behind a green mask.

Eco-tourism means a constant struggle to defend the earth and to protect and sustain traditional communities. Eco-tourism is a cooperative relationship between the non-wealthy local community and those sincere, open-minded tourists who want to enjoy themselves in a Third World setting and, at the same time, enrich their consciousness by means of significant educational and cultural experience."

There are more cynical views. For some, eco-tourism is a PR concept with a nice ring,

but all in all no less destructive or voyeuristic than regular (package holiday) tourism. Most, though, argue that if people are going to travel, they may as well do so in a low-impact manner that reduces destruction of the visited environment, and promotes cultural exchange.

Several pioneering projects in Costa Rica have set out to combine tourism with sustainable methods of farming, rainforest preservation, and scientific research. Some of these, like the **Rainforest Aerial Tram** and the **Monteverde Cloudforest Reserve**, are the most advanced of their kind in the Americas, if not the world. Not only does the Aerial Tram provide a fascinating glimpse of the tropical canopy – normally completely inaccessible to human eyes – but also a rare safe and stable method for biologists to investigate this little-known habitat. Income from visitors is funnelled into maintaining and augmenting the surrounding reserve. Monteverde, meanwhile, merely in preserving a large piece of complex tropical forest, gives scientists a valuable and fast-disappearing stomping ground for taxonomic study. Tourism is just one of the main activities in the reserve, which has been a research ground for tropical biologists from all over the world, and provides revenue for maintenance and, hopefully, future expansion.

Rara Avis, a private rainforest preserve in the Sarapiquí area northeast of San José, is one of the larger and better established of such projects. The result of years of work by Amos Bien, a former administrator at nearby La Selva Biological Station, Rara Avis seeks not only to

ECO-TOURISM CODES OF CONDUCT

Though well-meaning, eco-tourism **codes of conduct** can seem preachy and presumptuous. Still, in any attempt to define the term, or to go any way towards understanding its aims, it's useful to know what the locally accepted guidelines are.

The Ascociación Tsuli, the Costa Rican branch of the Audubon Society, has developed its own short code of conduct for "Environmental Ethics for Nature Travel":

1 Wildlife and natural habitats must not be needlessly disturbed

2 Waste should be disposed of properly.

3 Tourism should be a positive influence on local communities.

4 Tourism should be managed and sustainable.

5 Tourism should be culturally sensitive.

6 There must be no commerce in wildlife, wildlife products, or native plants.

7 Tourists should leave with a greater understanding and appreciation of nature, conservation and the environment.

8 Tourism should strengthen the conservation effort and enhance the natural integrity of places visited.

provide a memorable experience for those interested in tropical rainforests, but also to find ways of profitably harvesting rainforest products and at the same time give something back to the local community, offering small farmers living on the edges of deforested land a chance to make a profit from the forest without clearcutting for cattle.

TOURISM AND THE FUTURE

The huge growth of tourism in the country worries many Costa Ricans, even those who make their living from it. Is it just a fad that will fade away, only to be replaced by another unprepared country-of-the-moment? What – if any – are the advantages of having an economy led by tourism instead of the traditional exports of bananas and coffee?

More alarming is what many Costa Ricans see as the virtual purchase of their country by foreigners. Though many hotels and businesses are still Costa Rican-owned and managed, entire areas on the Pacific coast may as well be plastered with "Se Vende" signs as the government gears itself up to sell off yet more national resources and industries in its quest for foreign investment. It remains to be seen what the effect this might have on small communities and local cultures.

At times the government seems bent on turning the country into a high-income tourist enclave. North Americans and Europeans will still consider many things quite cheap, but Costa Rica is already the most expensive country to visit in the region, and recently the tourism minister was quoted in the national press as saying that he had no qualms about discouraging "backpackers" (ie budget tourists) from coming to Costa Rica. Better-heeled tourists, the thinking goes, not only make a more significant investment in the country dollar for dollar, but are more easily controlled, choosing in the main to travel in tour groups or to stay in big holiday resorts such as the Papagayo Project in Guanacaste and the Hotel Playa Tambor on the Nicoya Peninsula.

However, tourists with a genuine concern and interest in the country's flora, fauna and cultural life can choose from a variety of places to spend their money constructively, including top-notch "rainforest lodges" that have worked hard to integrate themselves with their surroundings. And those who want to rough it can still do so heroically in places like Corcovado and Chirripó. For now, at least, Costa Rica is one of the few countries in the world where eco-tourism can viably outlast and out-compete other, potentially more damaging, types of tourism.

BOOKS

The most comprehensive volumes written on Costa Rica tend to be about natural history. Many of these are accessible to the lay reader and make better introductions to what you may see in the country than the limp and glossy literature pumped out by the government tourist board and most guidebooks. Those interested in Costa Rican fiction (which is alive and well although not extensively translated or known abroad) will have much richer and varied reading with some knowledge of Spanish. Frustratingly many of the most informative works on both natural and cultural history are, unfortunately, out of date or out of print. You'll find a number of the titles listed below in San José bookshops, but you should not expect to see them elsewhere in the country.

TRAVEL NARRATIVES AND GUIDES

There are relatively few **travel narratives** dealing with Costa Rica. There has been, however, a virtual explosion of travel guides in the past few years, mostly enthusiastic and commercial in tone.

Beatrice Blake and Anne Becher *Key to Costa Rica* (US, Ulysses). Dependable guide, especially useful for those intending to stay in Costa Rica for some time, be they *pensionados* or long-term travellers. Good chapters on negotiating the horrible *trámites* involved should you want to become a resident. The upbeat tone appears to gloss over problem areas and insalubrious aspects of the country, but is mitigated by subtle asides and observations.

Peter Ford *Tekkin a Waalk* (UK, Flamingo, o/p). Journalist Ford was based in Managua for most of the terrible 1980s. After that his idea of a holiday seems to have been to *tek a waalk* along the eastern coast of the isthmus. In the very short part of the book that deals with Costa Rica, Ford's boatmen overshoot the river entrance to Greytown, Nicaragua, and end up in the northeastern Costa Rican village of Barra del Colorado, much to the chagrin of the *migración* – Ford must be one of the few people ever to be deported from Costa Rica.

Paul Theroux *The Old Patagonian Express: By Train through the Americas* (US, Pocket Books, o/p/UK, Penguin). Somewhat out of date, (Theroux went through about fifteen years ago) but a great read nonetheless. Laced with the author's usual tetchy black humour and general misanthropy, the descriptions of his two Costa Rican train journeys (neither of which still run) to Limón and to Puntarenas remain apt – as is the account of passing through San José, where he meets American men on sex-and-booze vacations.

CULTURE AND FOLK TRADITIONS

Most books dealing with Costa Rica's **culture** and **music** come from and are about Guanacaste, the "home of Costa Rican folklore". There are also a couple of very good titles on the Talamanca region's unique ethnicity. The following, specialist-interest only (and, with one exception, Spanish-only) titles are all that is currently available in print.

Jorge Luis Acevedo *La Musica en Guanacaste* (San José, Editorial de la universidad de Costa Rica). Written music and lyrics express the tango/flamenco-like intensity and military precision of local dances. Also features intriguing accounts of ingenious handmade instruments only found in Guanacaste. In the same vein and by the same author is the *Anthología de la musica guanacasteca*.

Roberto Cabrera *Santa Cruz Guanacaste: una approximación a la historia y la cultura popular* (San José, Ediciones Guayacán). The best cultural history of Guanacaste, written by a respected Guanacastecan sociologist. Verbal snapshots of nineteenth- and twentieth-century hacienda life, accounts of bull riding, and details of micro-regional dances such as the *punto guanacasteco* (adopted as the national dance), *El torito* and the veiled dance.

Paula Palmer *What Happen: A Folk History of the Talamanca Coast* (San José, Ecodesarrolos). The definitive – although now dated – folk history of the Afro-Caribbean community on Limón province's Talamancan coast. Palmer first went to Cahuita in the early 1970s as a Peace Corps volunteer, later to return as a sociologist, collecting oral histories from older members of the local communities. Great stories and atmospheric testimonies of pirate treasure, ghosts and the like; complemented by photos and accounts of local agriculture, foods and traditional remedies. Available in English and Spanish (in Costa Rica only).

Paula Palmer, Juanita Sánchez and Gloria Mayorga *Taking Care of Sibö's Gifts* (San José, Editorarama). Manifesto for the future of Bribrí culture, ecological survival of the *Talamanqueña* ecosystems and a concise explication of differing views of the land and people's relationship to it held by the *ladinos* and Bribrí on the KéköLdi indigenous reserve.

CONSERVATION

Many of the tomes devoted to **conservation** and **rainforests** refer to Costa Rica only briefly, concentrating on other Neotropical countries, mainly Brazil. Several give a good introduction to the issues surrounding the economic interests involved in worldwide deforestation, however, and it's not much of a stretch to apply their points to Costa Rica.

Catherine Caulfield *In the Rainforest* (US, Knopf, o/p). One of the best introductory volumes to rainforests, dealing in an accessible, discursive fashion with many of the issues covered in the more academic or specialized titles. Her chapter on Costa Rica is a wary elucidation of the destruction that cattle ranching in particular wreaks, as well as an interesting profile of the farming methods used by the Monteverde community.

Marcus Colcheser and Larry Lohmann (eds) *The Struggle for Land and the Fate of the Forests* (US, Humanities Press/UK, Zed Books). A volume of essays that divides rainforest issues into general theoretical discussions, followed by case studies. Although Costa Rica is covered

only in passing, the chapter on Guatemala introduces relevant points, while the brief and accessible history of agrarian reform in Latin America puts the *campesino* and landlessness issues of Costa Rica in context.

Luis Fournier *Desarrollo y perspectivas del movimiento conservacionista costarricense* (San José, EDUCA). Seminal, if dry, survey of conservation policy from the dawn of the nation until present, by one of Costa Rica's most eminent scientists and conservationists.

Susanna Hecht and Alexander Cockburn *The Fate of the Forest: Developers, Destroyers and Defenders of the Amazon* (US, Schocken, o/ p/UK, Penguin). The best single book readily available on rainforest destruction, this exhaustive volume is written with a sound knowledge of Amazonian history. The beautiful prose dissects some of the more pervasive myths about rainforest destruction, and it's comprehensive enough to be applicable to any forested areas under threat in the New World tropics.

William Weinberg *War on the Land: Ecology and Politics in Central America* (US, Humanities Press/UK, Zed Books). Just one chapter, but a good one, devoted to Costa Rica. While not failing to congratulate the country for its conservation achievements, the author also reveals the internal wranglings of conservationist policy.

HISTORY AND CURRENT AFFAIRS

Although there are some very critical contemporary books on Costa Rican **current affairs** in print, it's more of a struggle to find a good **historical survey**. Those available in English tend to have a promotional and self-congratulatory tone; the best are in Spanish only. Not listed here are also some fantastically detailed multi-volumed titles, available only in Spanish and in San José, which rake over the country's history with a fine-tooth comb.

Between Continents, Between Seas: Precolumbian Art of Costa Rica (US, Harry Abrams, o/p). Produced as a catalogue to accompany the exhibit that toured the US in 1982, this is the best single volume on pre-Conquest history and craftsmanship, with illuminating accounts of the lives, beliefs and customs of Costa Rica's pre-Columbian peoples as interpreted through artefacts and excavations. The photographs, whether of jade pendants, Chorotega pottery or the more diabolical of the Diquís' gold pieces, are uniformly wonderful.

Elías Zamora Acosta *Etnografía histórica de Costa Rica, 1561 y 1615* (Spain, Universidad de Sevilla). Hugely impressive archival research that reconstructs the economic, political and social life in the province in the years immediately following the Spanish invasion. A masterwork, distressingly difficult to get hold of.

Tony Avirgan and Martha Honey *La Penca: On Trial in Costa Rica: The CIA vs. the Press* (San José, Editorial Porvenir). Avirgan, a journalist and longtime resident in San José, was wounded at the La Penca news conference bombing in 1984. After this, he and Honey sunk their teeth into the "dark underbelly" of US/CIA politics and operations in the area during the years of the Nicaraguan Civil War. In contrast to her more recent and more definitive book (see below), Honey concludes here that the attack was carried out by the CIA.

Richard Biesanz, Karen Zubris Biesanz and Mavis Hiltunen Biesanz *The Costa Ricans* (US, Prentice Hall, o/p). Rather outdated generalizations and idealizations about the Costa Rican "character". However, though descriptive rather than analytical, many of the authors' observations and conclusions, especially about sexual conduct, inequality and marriage, ring true.

Marc Edelman and Joanne Kenen (eds) *The Costa Rica Reader* (US, Grove Atlantic, o/p). The best single title for the general reader. The chronologically arranged essays are mainly by respected Costa Rican historians, academic in tone but not inaccessible. See especially Chilean sociologist Diego Palma's essay on current Costa Rican politics and class conflict, which penetrates the picture of Costa Rica as a haven of middle-class democracy.

Omar Hernandez, Eugenia Ibarra and Juan Rafael Quesada (eds) *Discriminación y racismo en la historia costarricense* (San José, Editorial de la Universidad de Costa Rica). Most of these essays are written in the language and form of legal case studies, but nonetheless provide a history of the racial bias of legal discrimination in Costa Rica, and that of ethnicity in human rights abuses. Interesting counterpoint to Costa Rica's reputation for harmonious social relations, although probably only of use to specialists and those with a particular interest in race issues.

Martha Honey *Hostile Acts – US Policy in Costa Rica in the 1980s* (US & UK, University of Florida Press). Those sceptical of elaborate conspiracy theories may have their minds changed by this exhaustively researched, weighty volume detailing the United States' "dual diplomacy" against Costa Rica in the 1980s. In this heroic volume Honey concludes that the La Penca bomber was a leftist Argentine terrorist with connections to Nicaragua's Sandinista government.

Silvia Lara and Tom Barry *Inside Costa Rica* (US, Inter-hemispheric Resource Center). One title that will bring you up to date with most aspects of the country, although it has little to say about tourism, conservation, and culture. Left-leaning, argumentative, and analytical, the authors refuse to toe the party line on Costa Rica, and though the style is factual and somewhat dry, it is enlivened by flashes of humour and apt, well-supported conclusions.

Michael A Seligson *Peasants of Costa Rica and the Development of Agrarian Capitalism* (US & UK, University of Wisconsin). The best single history available in English, although only a university or specialist library will have it. Much wider in scope than the title suggests, this is an excellent intermeshing of ethnic and racial issues, economics and sociology along with hard-core analysis of the rise and fall of the Costa Rican peasant.

WILDLIFE/NATURAL HISTORY/FIELD GUIDES

Field guides to Costa Rican flora and fauna are typically excellent, weighty and expensive. Some, like *Costa Rican Natural History*, however valuable, are too big to be easily portable. You will find some locally produced and locally oriented field guides in Costa Rica (in English), usually focusing on a specific reserve, like La Selva or Monteverde. Also included in the list below are a couple of highly readable **natural history/narrative hybrids**.

Paul H Allen *The Rainforests of the Golfo Dulce* (US, Stanford University Press). Obviously a labour of love, this is the best descriptive account of the lush rainforest cover found in the southwest of the country. It's a scientific book, with complete taxonomic accounts, although still very readable and with interesting photographs.

Mario A Boza Costa Rica's National Parks (Spain, Incafo; available in San José from Editoral Heliconia). Essentially a coffee-table book, this informed volume is a great taster for what you will find in the National Parks. The text is in Spanish and English, and there are uniformly stunning photographs.

A S and P P Calvert A Year of Costa Rican Natural History (US, Macmillan). Although now very old – the year in question is 1910 – this is a brilliant, insightful and charmingly enthusiastic travelogue/natural history/autobiography by American biologist and zoologist husband and wife team. It features much, much more than natural history, with sections such as Blood Sucking Flies, Fiestas in Santa Cruz and Earthquakes. The best single title ever written on Costa Rica – the only problem is finding it. Try good libraries and specialist bookstores.

Stephen E Cornelius The Sea Turtles of Santa Rosa National Park (San José, Fundación de Parques Nacionales, o/p). Field guide to the four species of marine turtles who nest in Santa Rosa, and elsewhere. Full of detail about marine turtles' habits. Difficult to find.

Philip J De Vries The Butterflies of Costa Rica and their Natural History (US & UK Princeton University Press). Much-admired volume, really for serious butterfly enthusiasts or scientists only, but illustrated with beautiful colour plates so you can marvel at the incremental differences between various butterflies.

Louise H Emmons and François Feer Neotropical Rainforest Mammals – a Field Guide (US & UK, University of Chicago Press, o/p in UK). Not written specifically for Costa Rica, but most mammals found in the country are covered here. Huge but portable, with more than 300 illustrations, and useful for identifying the flash of colour and fur that speeds past you as you make yet another fleeting contact with a rainforest mammal.

Daniel H Janzen Costa Rican Natural History (US & UK, University of Chicago Press, o/p in UK). The definitive reference source, with accessible, continuously fascinating species-by-species accounts, written by a highly influential

figure, involved on a policy level in the governing of the National Parks system. If nothing else the introduction is worth reading, as it deals in a cursory, lively fashion with tectonics, meteorology, history and archeology. Illustrated throughout with gripping photographs. Available in paperback, but still doorstep-thick.

Michael W Mayfield and Raphael E Gallow The Rivers of Costa Rica: A Canoeing, Kayaking and Rafting Guide (US, Menasha Ridge Press). An essential book for serious whitewater rafters and river or sea kayakers. Stretch-by-stretch and rapid-by-rapid accounts of the best rafting rivers south of the Colorado, including the Reventazon and Pacuaré.

Sam Mitchell Pura Vida: The Waterfalls and Hot Springs of Costa Rica (US, Menasha Ridge). Jolly, personably written guide to the many little-known waterholes, cascades, and waterfalls of Costa Rica. Complete with detailed directions and accounts of surrounding trails. Available in English in San José.

Donald Perry Life Above the Jungle Floor (US, Simon & Schuster, o/p/). Nicely poised, lyrical account of biologist Perry's trials and tribulations in conceiving and mounting his Rainforest Aerial Tram (see p.121). Most of the book deals with his time at Rara Avis, where he conceived and tested his Tram prototype, the Automated Web for Canopy Exploration.

F Gary Stiles and Alexander F Skutch A Guide to the Birds of Costa Rica (US, Cornell University Press/UK, Black Press). All over Costa Rica you'll see guides clutching well-thumbed copies of this seminal tome, illustrated with colour plates to aid identification. Hefty, even in paperback, and too pricey for the amateur, but you may be able to pick up good secondhand copies in Costa Rica.

Allen M Young Sarapiquí Chronicle: A Naturalist in Costa Rica (US & UK, Smithsonian Institute Press). Lavishly produced book on entomologist Young's twenty years off-and-on work in the Sarapiquí area. A fluid and well-written combination of autobiography, travelogue and natural science, centring on the insect life he encounters.

FICTION

Costa Rica has no single internationally recognized towering figure in its national literature, and in sharp contrast to other countries in the region the most sophisticated and best-known writers in the country are **women**. Carmen Naranjo is the most widely translated, with six novels and two short-story collections (plus some of the country's most prestigious literary awards) to her name, but there are a number of lesser-read writers, including the brilliant Yolanda Oreomuno, and an upsurge of younger women, tackling contemporary social issues like domestic violence and alcoholism in their fiction and poetry. The publication in the 1930s of Carlos Luis Fallas' seminal novel *Mamita Yunai*, about labour conditions in the United Fruit Company banana fields of Limón province sparked a wave of **"proletarian"** novels, which became the dominant form in Costa Rican fiction until well into the 1970s.

Until recently Costa Rican fiction also leant heavily on picturesque stories of **rural life** with some writers – usually men – drawing on the country's wealth of fauna. There are a number of *cuentos* (stories), fable-like in their simplicity and not a little ponderous in their symbolism, featuring turtles, fish and rabbits as characters.

Miguel Benavides (trans Joan Henry) *The Children of Mariplata* (UK, Forest Books). A short collection of even shorter stories, most of which are good examples of vaguely tiresome fable-like or allegorical Costa Rican *cuentos*. Many are written in an anthropomorphized voice of an animal; others, like *The Twilight which lost its Colour* are searing slices of poverty-stricken life.

Fabián Dobles *Ese Que Llaman Pueblo* (San José, Editorial Costa Rica). Born in 1918, Dobles is Costa Rica's elder statesman of letters. Set in the countryside among *campesinos*, this title is a typical "proletarian" novel.

Carlos Luis Fallas *Mamita Yunai: El Infierdo de las Bananeras* (San José). Exuberant, full of local colour, culture and diction: this entertaining, leftist novel depicting life in the hell of the banana plantations is a great read. It's set in the La Estrella valley in Limón province, where Fallas was a pioneer labour organizer, instrumental in forcing the United Brands conglomerate to take workers' welfare into account in the 1930s and 1940s.

Amanda Hopkinson (ed, trans) *Lovers and Comrades: Women's Resistance Poetry in Central America* (US, Interlink/UK, Women's Press). Heartfelt contributions by Costa Rican poets Janina Fernandez, Eulalia Bernard and Lily Guardia. Poems such as Bernard's "We are the nation of threes" shows that Costa Rican poetry is no less political and no less felt than the more numerous contributions from the countries torn by war in the 1980s.

Enrique Jaramillo Levi (ed) *When New Flowers Bloomed: Short Stories by Women Writers from Costa Rica and Panamá* (US, Latin American Literary Review Press). Collection of the best-known Costa Rican women writers, including Rima de Vallbona, Carmen Naranjo, Carmen Lyra and Yolanda Oreamuno. Most of the stories are from the late 1980s, with shared themes of domestic violence – a persistent problem in Costa Rica – sexual and economic inequality, and the tyrannies of female anatomy and desire. Look out especially for Emilia Macaya, a younger writer.

Carmen Naranjo *Los perros no ladraron* (1966), *Responso por el niño Juan Manuel* (1968), *Ondina* (1982) and *Sobrepunto* (1985). In keeping with a tradition in Latin American letters but unusual for a woman, Naranjo has occupied several posts of public office, including Secretary of Culture, director of the publishing house EDUCA and Ambassador to Israel. She is widely considered an experimentalist. Her novels are accessible in Costa Rica, and her collection of stories *There Never Was Once Upon a Time* (US, Latin American Literary Review Press) is available in English.

Yolanda Oreamuno *La ruta de su evasión* (San José, EDUCA). Oreamuno had a short life, dying at the age of 40 in 1956. By the time she was 24, however, she had distinguished herself as the most promising writer of her generation with her novel *Por Tierra Firme*. Technically brilliant, she is a great scénariste, with a continually surprising lyrical style. *La ruta* concerns a child sent to look for his father, who has disappeared, possibly on a drinking binge. The search is both actual and spiritual; the novel a complex weave of themes.

Barbara Ras *Costa Rica: A Traveller's Literary Companion* (US, Whereabouts Press). Flowing, well-translated, with stories arranged by geographical zone, this is probably the most accessible starting point for readers interested in Costa Rican literature. The best stories are also the most heartrending – read "The Girl Who Came from the Moon" and "The Carbonero" for a glimpse of real life beyond the tourist-brochure images.

Anachristina Rossi *La loca de Gandoca* (San José, EDUCA). One of the most popular novels to be published in Costa Rica in recent years, Rossi's book is really "faction", documenting in businesslike prose and with tongue firmly in cheek the bizarre and byzantine wranglings over the Gandoca-Manzanillo refuge, including the surveying and defining of the indigenous Bribrí KéköLdi reserve.

Rosario Santos (ed) *And We Sold the Rain: Contemporary Fiction from Central America* (UK, Ryan Publishing). Put together in the late 1980s, this collection attempts to show the faces of real people behind the newspaper headlines about guerrillas and militaries during the poltical conflicts of that decade. The introduction, by Jo Anne Englebert, gives an overview, and there are Costa Rican stories by Samuel Rovinski, Carmen Naranjo and Fabian Dobles.

Rogelio Sotela (ed) *Escritores de Costa Rica* (San José, Lehmann, o/p). Outdated, out-of-print and inaccessible in all but the best libraries, this is still the definitive volume of Costa Rican literaure up until the 1940s. Several fascinating sections, including one devoted to folklore. Much dreadful poetry, though.

Rima de Vallbona (trans Lillian Lorca de Tabgle) *Flowering Inferno: Tales of Sinking Hearts* (US, Latin American Literary Review Press). Slim volume of affecting short stories by one of Costa Rica's most respected (and widely translated) writers on social life, customs, and the position of women.

LANGUAGE

Although it is commonly said that everyone speaks English in Costa Rica, it is not really the case. Certainly many who work in the tourist trade speak some English, and there are a number of expats who speak anything from English to German to Dutch, but the people you'll meet day to day speak only Spanish. The one area where you will hear English widely spoken is on the Caribbean coast, where many of the Afro-Caribbean inhabitants are of Jamaican descent, and speak a distinctive regional creole (for more on Limón patois, see p.142).

If you want to get to know Costa Ricans, then, it makes sense to acquire some Spanish before you arrive. Ticos are polite, patient and forgiving interlocutors, and will not only tolerate but appreciate any attempts you make to speak their language. The rules of **pronunciation** are pretty straightforward, and strictly observed. Unless there's an accent, all words ending in l, r and z are stressed on the last syllable, all others on the second last. Unlike in the rest of Latin America, in Costa Rica the final "d" in many words sometimes gets dropped; thus you'll hear "usté" for "usted" or "¿verdá?" for "¿verdad?" Other Costa Rican peculiarities are the ll and r sounds. All vowels are pure and short.

A somewhere between the A sound in "back" and that in "father".

E as in "get".

I as in "police".

O as in "hot".

U as in "rule".

C is soft before E and I, hard otherwise: cerca is pronounced "serka".

G works the same way: a guttural H sound (like the ch in "loch") before E or I, a hard G elsewhere: *gigante* becomes "higante".

H is always silent.

J the same sound as a guttural G: *jamon* is pronounced "hamon".

LL may be pronouned as a soft J (as in parts of Chile and Argentina) instead of Y: *ballena* (whale) becomes "bajzhena" instead of "bayena".

N is as in English, unless it has a tilde (accent) over it, when it becomes NY: *mañana* sounds like manyana.

QU is pronounced like the English K.

R is not rolled Scottish burr-like as much as in other Spanish-speaking countries: *carro* is said "cahro", with a soft rather than a rolled R.

V sounds more like B: *vino* becomes "beano".

Z is the same as a soft C: *cerveza* is thus "servesa".

A COSTA RICAN DICTIONARY

Mario Quesada Pacheco *Nuevo Diccionario de Costarriequeñismos* (San José, Editorial de la Universidad Technologica de Costa Rica). An entertaining, illustrated dictionary of slang and *dichos* (sayings) for Spanish-speakers interested in understanding heavily argot-spiced Costa Rican spoken Spanish. It's a fascinating compendium, giving the regional location of word usage and sayings, what age group uses them, and some etymology. It also reveals a fascinating wealth of localisms developed to describe local phenomena – witness, for example the number of different words for "wasp".

A SPANISH LANGUAGE GUIDE

BASICS

Yes, No	*Sí, No*	Open, Closed	*Abierto/a, Cerrado/a*
Please, Thank you	*Por favor, Gracias*	With, Without	*Con, Sin*
Where, When	*Dónde, Cuando*	Good, Bad	*Buen(o)/a, Mal(o)/a*
What, How much	*Qué, Cuanto*	Big, Small	*Gran(de), Pequeño/a*
Here, There	*Aquí, Allí*	More, Less	*Mas, Menos*
This, That	*Este, Eso*	Today, Tomorrow	*Hoy, Mañana*
Now, Later	*Ahora, Mas tarde*	Yesterday	*Ayer*

GREETINGS AND RESPONSES

Hello, Goodbye	*Hola, Adiós*	Not at all/You're welcome	*De nada*
Good morning	*Buenos días*		
Good afternoon/night	*Buenas tardes/noches*	Do you speak English?	*¿Habla (usted) Inglés?*
See you later	*Hasta luego*	I don't speak Spanish	*(No) Hablo Español*
Sorry	*Lo siento/disculpeme*	My name is . . .	*Me llamo . . .*
Excuse me	*Con permiso/perdón*	What's your name?	*¿Como se llama usted?*
How are you?	*¿Cómo está (usted)?*	I am English/	*Soy/Ingles(a)/*
I (don't) understand	*(No) Entiendo*	Australian	*Australiano(a).*
What did you say?	*¿Cómo?*		

NEEDS – HOTELS AND TRANSPORT

I want	*Quiero*	How do I get to . . . ?	*¿Por donde se va a . . . ?*
I'd like	*Quisiera*		
Do you know . . . ?	*¿Sabe . . . ?*	Left, right, straight on	*Izquierda, derecha, derecho*
I don't know	*No sé*		
There is (is there)?	*(¿)Hay(?)*	Where is . . . ?	*¿Dónde está . . . ?*
Give me . . .	*Deme . . .*	. . . the bus station	*. . . el estación autobuses*
(one like that)	*(uno así)*		
Do you have . . . ?	*¿Tiene . . . ?*	. . . the nearest bank	*. . . el banco mas cercano*
. . . the time	*. . . la hora*		
. . . a room	*. . . un cuarto*	. . . the post office	*. . . el correo*
. . . with two beds/ double bed	*. . . con dos camas/ cama matrimonial*	. . . the toilet	*. . . el baño/servicio*
It's for one person (two people)	*Es para una persona (dos personas)*	Where does the bus to . . . leave from?	*¿De donde sale el autobus para . . . ?*
. . . for one night (one week)	*. . . para una noche (una semana)*	I'd like a (return) ticket to . . .	*Quisiera un tiquete (de ida y vuelta) para . . .*
It's fine, how much is it?	*¿Está bien, cuanto es?*		
It's too expensive	*Es demasiado caro*	What time does it leave (arrive in . . .)?	*¿A qué hora sale (llega en . . .)?*
Don't you have anything cheaper?	*¿No tiene algo más barato?*		
Can one . . . ?	*¿Se puede . . . ?*	What is there to eat?	*¿Qué hay para comer?*
. . . camp (near) here?	*¿ . . . acampar aqui (cerca)?*	What's that?	*¿Qué es eso?*
Is there a hotel nearby?	*¿Hay un hotel aquí cerca?*	What's this called in Spanish?	*¿Como se llama este en Español?*

NUMBERS AND DAYS

1	un/uno/una	20	veinte	1990	mil novocientos
2	dos	21	veintiuno		noventa
3	tres	30	treinta	1991	. . . y uno
4	cuatro	40	cuarenta	first	primero/a
5	cinco	50	cincuenta	second	segundo/a
6	seis	60	sesenta	third	tercero/a
7	siete	70	setenta		
8	ocho	80	ochenta	Monday	lunes
9	nueve	90	noventa	Tuesday	martes
10	diez	100	cien(to)	Wednesday	miércoles
11	once	101	ciento uno	Thursday	jueves
12	doce	200	doscientos	Friday	viernes
13	trece	201	doscientos uno	Saturday	sabado
14	catorce	500	quinientos	Sunday	domingo
15	quince	1000	mil		
16	diez y seis	2000	dos mil		

INTIMATE ADDRESS

It is difficult to get your head round forms of **second-person address** in Costa Rica. Children are often spoken to in the "usted" form, which is technically formal and reserved for showing respect (in other Spanish-speaking countries you *never* hear this; children are always addressed as "tu"). Even friends who have known each other for years in Costa Rica will address each other as "usted". But the single most confounding irregularity of Costa Rican speech for those who already speak Spanish is the use of **"vos"** as personal intimate address – generally between friends and *compañeros* of the same age. Many people on a short trip to the country never quite get to grips with it.

Now archaic, "vos" is only used widely in the New World in Argentina and Costa Rica. It has an interesting rhythm and sound, with verbs ending on a kind of dipthong-ized stress: *vos sabeís, vos queréis* (you know, you want), as opposed to *tu sabes/usted sabe* or *tu quieres/usted quiere*. In reflexive verbs the reflexive pronoun of the "tu" form is used: *vos te laváis* (you wash). It is most often used among young people, especially by those around university age. If you are addressed in the "vos" form it is a sign of friendship, and you should try to use it back if you can. It is an affront to use "vos" improperly, with someone you don't know well, when it can be seen as being patronizing.

Again, Costa Ricans are good-hearted in this respect, however, and put errors down to the fact that you are a foreigner.

EL IDIOMA AND TIQUISMOS

Costa Rican Spanish is a living language full of flux and argot. Local slang and usage are often referred to as **Tiquismos** (from *Costarriqueñismos*, or Costa Ricanisms) or, as Costa Ricans will say when enlightening the foreigner as to their meaning, "*palabras muy ticas*". Some of the expressions and terms discussed below may be heard in other countries in the region, especially in Nicaragua and El Salvador, but still they are highly regional. Others are purely endemic, including *barbarismos* (bastardizations) and *provincialismos* (words particular to specific regions of Costa Rica).

EVERYDAY EXPRESSIONS

Here are some everyday **peculiarities** that most visitors to Costa Rica will become familiar with pretty quickly:

¡acharál! expression of regret: "what a pity", like "*¡qué lástima!*"

adios "hi", used primarily in the *campo* (country) when greeting someone on the road or street. Confusingly, as in the rest of Latin America, *adiós* is also "goodbye", but only if you are going away for a long time.

¿diay? slightly melancholic interjection in the vein of "ah, but what can you expect?".

fatal reserved for the absolutely worst possible eventuality: "*esta carretera para Golfito es fatal*" means "the road to Golfito is the very worst".

feo literally "ugly", but can also mean rotten or lousy, as in "*Todos los caminos en Costa Rica estan muy feos*" ("All the roads in Costa Rica are in really bad shape").

maje literally "dummy", used between young men as an affirmation of their friendship/ maleness: it's used like "buddy, pal" (US) or "mate" (UK). There is no equivalent for women, unfortunately.

pura vida perhaps the best-known *tiquismo*, meaning "great, OK," or "cool".

que mala/buena nota expression of disapproval/ approval – "how uncool/great".

LUCK AND GOD

Both **luck** and **God** come into conversation often in Costa Rica. Thus you get the pattern:

"*¿Cómo amaneció?*"
"*Muy bien, por dicha, ¿y usted?*"
"*Muy bien, gracias a Dios.*"

"How did you sleep?" (Literally, "how did you wake up?")
"Very well, fortunately, and you?"
"Very well, thank God."

Also, you will hear *dicha* and *Dios* used in situations that seem to have not much to do with luck or divine intervention: "*¡Qué dicha que usted llegó!*" ("What luck that you arrived!"), along with such phrases as "*Vamanos a la playa esta fin de semana, sí Dios quiere*" ("We'll go to the beach this weekend, God willing"). Even a shrug of the shoulders elicits a "*¡Dios sabe!*" "God only knows." And the usual forms "*hasta luego*" or "*hasta la vista*" become in Costa Rica the much more God-fearing "*Que Dios le acompañe*" ("may God go with you").

NICKNAMES

Nicknames and a delight in the informal mix with a quite proper formal tone in spoken Costa Rican Spanish. Nicknames centre on your most obvious physical characteristic: popular ones include *flaco/a* (thin); *gordo/a* (fat), and *macho/*

a (light-skinned). Terms of endearment are also very current in popular speech; along with the ubiquitous *mí amor*, you may also get called *jóven*: young one.

DIMINUTION

The noun "Tico" used as a short form for (a) Costa Rican comes less from a desire to shorten "Costarricense" than from the traditional trend toward **diminution** which is supposed to signal classlessness, eagerness to band together and desire not to cause offence. In Costa Rica the common Spanish diminution of "ito" – applied as a suffix at the end of the word, as in "herman*ito*"; "little brother" – often becomes "itico" ("herman*itico*"). That said, you hear the -ito or -itico endings less and less nowadays.

POLITESSE

Costa Rican Spanish often displays an astounding **formality** that borders on servility. Instead of "*de nada*" ("you're welcome") many Costa Ricans will say, "*para servirle*", which means, literally, "I'm here to serve you." When they meet you, Costa Ricans will say "*con mucho gusto*"; "it's a pleasure", and you should do the same. Even when you leave people you do not know well, you will be told "*que le vaya bien*" ("may all go well with you"), a formal, heartfelt, sentiment that at times seems to border on benediction.

"¿WHERE IS YOUR BOYFRIEND?"

"*¿Dónde está su novio?/padres?*" ("Where is your boyfriend/family?") is a query women, especially those travelling alone, will hear often. **Family** is very important in explaining to many Costa Ricans who you are and where you come from, and people will place you by asking how many brothers and sisters you have, where your family (*padres*) live, whether your *abuela* (grandmother) is still alive... It's a good idea to get to grips with the following:

madre/padre mother/father
abuela/abuelo father/grandmother
hijo/hija daughter/son
hermano/hermana brother/sister
tía/tío aunt/uncle
prima/primo cousin

GLOSSARY

abastecedor a general store, usually in a rural area or *barrio* (neighbourhood) that keeps a stock of groceries and basic toiletries.

agringarse (verb) to adopt the ways of the gringos.

aguacero downpour.

ahorita right now (any time within the coming hour).

barrio neighbourhood (usually urban).

bomba gas station.

burro can refer to the animal, but is usually an adjective denoting "really big", as in "*vea este bicho sí burro*": "come see this *really* big insect".

campesino peasant farmer, smallholder.

campo literally countryside, but more often in Costa Rica "space", as in "seat" when travelling. Thus "*¿Hay un campo en este autobus?*": "is there a (free) seat on this bus?"

cantina bar, usually patronized by the working class or rural labouring class.

carro car (not *coche*, as in the rest of Central America).

cazadora literally, huntress; a beaten up old schoolbus that serves as public transport in rural areas.

chance widely used anglicism to denote chance, or opportunity; like *opportunidad.*

chiquillos kids; also *chiquititos, chiquiticos.*

chorreador sack-and-metal coffee-filter contraption, still widely used.

choteo quick-witted sarcasm, something Costa Ricans admire, provided it's not too sharp-tongued.

conchos yokels, hicks from the sticks.

cordillera mountain range.

dando cuerda colloquial expression meaning, roughly, to "make eyes at", in an approximation of sexual interest (men to women, hardly ever the other way around).

evangélico usually refers to anyone who is of a religion other than Catholic, but particularly Protestant even if they are not evangelical. Such religions are also called *cultos,* belying a general wariness and disapproval for anything other than Catholicism.

finca farm or plantation.

finquero coffee grower.

foco flashlight/torch.

gambas buttresses, the giant above-ground roots that some rainforest trees put out.

gaseosa fizzy drink.

gasolinera gas station.

gringo not at all pejorative term for a North American. A European is usually "*el Europeo*".

guaca pre-Columbian burial ground or tomb.

güisqui whisky (usually bad, unless imported, and astronomically expensive).

hacienda big farm, usually a ranch.

hospedaje very basic *pensión.*

humilde humble, simple; an appearance and quality that is widely respected.

ICT Instituto Costarricense de Turismo, the national tourist board.

indígena an indigenous person; preferred term among indigenous groups in Costa Rica, rather than the less polite *índio:* indian.

invierno winter (May–Nov).

jornaleros day labourers, usually landless peasants who are paid by the day, for instance to pick coffee in season.

mal educado literally, badly educated; a gentle if effective insult, especially useful for women harassed by hissing, leering men.

malecón seaside promenade.

marimba type of xylophone played mainly in Guanacaste. Also refers to the style of music.

mestizo person of mixed race indigenous/Spanish; not usually pejorative.

metate pre-Columbian stone table used for grinding corn, especially by the Chorotega people of Guanacaste. Many of the archeological finds in Costa Rica are metates.

mirador lookout.

morenos offensive term for Afro-Caribbeans. The best term to use is *negros* or *Limónenses.*

muelle dock.

Neotrópicos Neotropics: tropics of the New World.

Nica Nicaraguan, from *Nicaragüense.*

palenque a thatched-roofed longhouse inhabited by indigenous people; more or less equivalent to the Native North American longhouse.

pasear to be on vacation/holiday; literally, to be passing through.

PLA National Liberation Party, the dominant political party.

peón farm labourer, usually landless.

personaje someone of importance, a VIP, although usually used pejoratively to indicate someone who is putting on airs.

PUSC Social Christian Unity Party, the opposition party-of-the-moment.

pulpería general store or corner store. Also sometimes serves cooked food and drinks.

purrujas spectacularly annoying, tiny biting insect, encountered in lowland areas.

rancho palm-thatched roof, also smallholding.

redondel de toros bull-ring, not used for bull fighting but for local rodeos.

refresco drink, usually made with fresh fruit or water, sometimes fizzy drink, although this is most often called *gaseosa*.

regalar (verb) usually to give, as in to give a present, but in Costa Rica the usual command or request of "*deme uno de estos*" ("give me one of those"), becomes "*regaleme*". Thus "*regaleme un cafecito, por favor*": "could you give me a coffee?".

rejas security grille, popularly known in English as The Cage: the iron grille you see around all but the most humble dwellings in an effort to discourage burglary.

sabanero Costa Rican cowboy.

soda cafeteria or diner; in the rest of Central America it's usually called a *comedor*.

temporada season: *la temporada de lluvia* is the rainy season.

temporales early morning rains in the wet season (mainly in the Valle Central).

terreno land, small farm.

UCR Universidad de Costa Rica (in San Pedro, San José).

UNA Universidad Nacional (in Heredia).

verano summer (Dec–April).

INDEX

A

Accommodation 26
ALAJUELA 105–108
  Accommodation 106
  Arrival 106
  Bars 108
  Juan Santamaría Cultural-
    Historical Museum 107
  Moving on 108
  Nightlife 108
  Restaurants 108
  Santo Cristo de la Agonía 107
Amistad *see* Parque
  Internacional la Amistad
Amubrí 172
Animals 351–360
Arenal *see* Parque Nacional
  Volcán Arenal
ATEC 169, 370

B

Bagaces 211
Bahía 312
Bahía Ballena 278
Bahía Culebra 233
Bahía Drake 314–316
Balneario Tabacón 187
Banks 19
Barra del Colorado 148–150
Barra Honda *see* Parque
  Nacional Barra Honda
Bars 32
Barva 122
Birdwatching 49
Books 372–377
Boruca 331
Braulio Carrillo *see* Parque
  Nacional Braulio Carrillo
Bribrí 175
Buses in Costa Rica 21, 95, 96,
  98

C

Cabo Blanco *see* Reserva
  Natural Absoluta Cabo
  Blanco
Café Britt *finca* 122
Cahuita *see* Parque Nacional
  Cahuita
Cahuita village 157–163

Camping 28
Caño Negro *see* Refugio
  Nacional de Vida Silvestre
  Caño Negro
Car rental 22
Carara *see* Reserva Biológica
  Carara 285
CARTAGO 124–127
  Accommodation 125
  Arrival 125
  Basílica de Nuestra Señora de
    Los Angeles 126
  Iglesia de la Parroquía 126
  Las Ruinas 126
  Moving on 127
  Restaurants 126
Catarata de La Fortuna 186
CATIE 132
Cerro de la Muerte 305
Children, travelling with 53
Chirripó *see* Parque Nacional
  Chirripó
Chorotegas, The 210, 243
Ciudad Quesada *see* San
  Carlos
Climate 39
Cloudforest 265
Cóbano 276
Coffee 33, 345
Conservation 366–371
Corcovado *see* Parque
  Nacional Corcovado
Costs 18
Creole cuisine 136
Crime 37
Currency 18
Curú *see* Refugio de Fauna
  Silvestre Curú
Cycling 24, 50

D

Diquis, The 304
Diving 48
Dominical 310–312
Drinking 29
Driving in Costa Rica 22
Dry Forests 214
Dulce Nombre de Coronado
  124

E

Eating 29
Eco-tourism 369–371
**Estación Biológica La
  Selva** 199–201

F

Fishing 49
Flights, domestic 23
Flights from Australasia 10
Flights from Britain 6
Flights from North America 3
Flights in Costa Rica 23, 98
Food 29
Fortuna *see* La Fortuna de San
  Carlos

G

Gandoca-Manzanillo *see*
  Refugio Nacional de Vida
  Silvestre Gandoca-
  Manzanillo
Gay and lesbian Costa Rica 52
Glossary 382
Gold 75, 340
Golfito 317–321
Ground operators 25
Guaitíl 243
Guápiles 139
Guápiles Highway 139

H

Health 13
HEREDIA 115–118
  Accommodation 116
  Arrival 115
  Bars 117
  Basílica de la Inmaculada
    Concepción 116
  El Fortín 116
  Mercado Central 116
  Moving on 118
  Nightlife 117
  Restaurants 117
Hiking 46
History 339–350
Hitoy-Cerere *see* Reserva
  Biológica Hitoy-Cerere
Holidays 51
Horseriding 50

I

ICT (Instituto Costarricense de
  Turismo) 16
Instituto Clodomiro Picado 124
Insurance 11
Irazú *see* Parque Nacional
  Volcán Irazú
Isla del Caño *see* Reserva
  Biológica Isla del Caño

Isla del Coco *see* Parque Nacional Isla del Coco
Isla Tortuga 277

K

Kayaking 50
KéköLdi indigenous reserve 169, 174

L

La Cruz 231
LA FORTUNA DE SAN CARLOS 182–185
Accommodation 182
Arrival 182
Bars 185
Moving on 185
Restaurants 185
Tours 184
La Fortuna *see* La Fortuna de San Carlos
La Garita 114
La Guácima Butterfly Farm 114
La Selva *see* Estación Biológica La Selva
Laguna de Arenal 188
Language 378–381
Language courses 55
Lankaster Gardens 128
Las Ballenas *see* Parque Nacional Marino las Ballenas
Las Baulas *see* Parque Nacional Marino las Baulas
Las Juntas de Abangares 271
LIBERIA 215–220
Accommodation 217
Arrival 216
Bars 219
Moving on 220
Museo de Sabanero 218
Nightlife 219
Restaurants 219
Tours 217
Lomas Barbudal *see* Reserva Biológica Lomas Barbudal
Los Angeles Cloudforest Reserve 113
Los Chiles 189–192

M

Mail 34
Manuel Antonio *see* Parque Nacional Manuel Antonio
Manuel Antonio area accommodation 295–298

Manzanillo (Limón province) 173
Manzanillo (southern Nicoya) 284
Maps of Costa Rica 16
Matapalo 310
Media, the 35
Micro-climates 39
Money 18
Monteverde 256–271
Monteverde cloudforest *see* Reserva Biológica Bosque Nuboso Monteverde
Montezuma 279–283
Monumento Nacional Guayabo 131
Mountain biking 50

N

National Parks 40–46
Newspapers 35
Nicoya 244
Nosara 247–250

O

Orosí 129
Osa Peninsula 322–330
Overland to Costa Rica 5

P

Palmar 314
Palo Verde *see* Parque Nacional Palo Verde 212
Papagayo Project 233
Parque Internacional la Amistad 333
Parque Nacional Barra Honda 250–252
Parque Nacional Braulio Carrillo 118–121
Parque Nacional Cahuita 163–165
Parque Nacional Chirripó 307–310
Parque Nacional Corcovado 325–330
Parque Nacional Guanacaste 229
Parque Nacional Isla del Coco 330
Parque Nacional Manuel Antonio 298–301
Parque Nacional Marino las Ballenas 312

Parque Nacional Marino las Baulas 237
Parque Nacional Palo Verde 212
Parque Nacional Rincón de la Vieja 221–224
Parque Nacional Santa Rosa 224–229
Parque Nacional Tapantí 130
Parque Nacional Tortuguero 150–156, 367
Parque Nacional Volcán Arenal 179, 183–185
Parque Nacional Volcán Irazú 127–128
Parque Nacional Volcán Poás 109–111
Paso Canoas 334
Peñas Blancas 231
Phones 35
Playa Cacao 322
Playa Cativo 322
Playa del Coco 233–236
Playa Conchal 236
Playa Espadilla 298
Playa Grande 237
Playa Hermosa 234
Playa Herradura 289
Playa Jacó 286–290
Playa Junquillal 241
Playa Manzanillo 170
Playa Ocotal 236
Playa Panamá 234
Playa Pavones 321
Playa Sámara 245–247
Playa Tortuga 313
Playa Zancudo 321
Poás *see* Parque Nacional Volcán Poás
Pottery *see* Chorotegas, The
Public holidays 51
Puerto Jiménez 323–325
PUERTO LIMÓN 140–146
Accommodation 142
Arrival 140
Bars 145
Carnaval 144
Mercado Central 144
Moving on 146
Nightlife 145
Parque Vargas 144
Patois 142
Playa Bonita 142
Portete 142

Restaurants 145
Tourist information 141
Puerto Viejo de Sarapiquí
201–203
Puerto Viejo de Talamanca
165–170
Punta Banco 321
Punta Uva 172
PUNTARENAS 271–276
Accommodation 274
Arrival 273
Bars 275
Moving on 276
Nightlife 275
Restaurants 275
Tourist information 274

Q
Quepos 290–295

R
Radio 36
Rainforest Aerial Tram 121
Rainforests 361–365
Rara Avis 196–199
Refugio de Fauna Silvestre
Curú 277
Refugio Nacional de Fauna
Silvestre Barra del Colorado
148
**Refugio Nacional de Vida
Silvestre Caño Negro** 192–
195
**Refugio Nacional de Vida
Silvestre Gandoca-
Manzanillo** 171–174
Research projects 54
**Reserva Biológica Bosque
Nuboso Monteverde** 264–
268
Reserva Biológica Carara 285
**Reserva Biológica Hitoy-
Cerere** 147
Reserva Biológica Isla del
Caño 316
Reserva Biológica Lomas
Barbudal 213
Reserva Natural Absoluta
Cabo Blanco 284
Reserva Santa Elena 268
Rincón de la Vieja see Parque
Nacional Rincón de la Vieja
Río San Juan 149
Río Tárcoles 285

Río Tempisque ferry 252
Rip tides 48
Rodeos 249

S
San Carlos 180
San Gerardo de Dota 306
San Gerardo de Rivas 308
San Isidro 306
SAN JOSÉ 61–99
Accommodation 68
Alianza Francesa 77
Arrival 63
Arts, The 90
Avenida Central 74
Barrio Amón 77
Barrio Otoya 77
Bars 88
Biblioteca Nacional 78
Bishop's Castle 77
Boca bars 88
Bus companies 95
Buses from San José: domestic
96
Buses from San José:
international 98
Buses in San José 66
Buses to San José 64
Cafés 86
Casa Matute 90
Centro Comercial El Pueblo 78
Centro Cultural Costarricense-
Norteamericano 80
Cinemas 91
City transport 65
Cycling in San José 67
Discos 90
Drinking 86
Driving in San José 67
Eating out 83
Edificio Metálica 76
Escuela Metálica 76
Flights, domestic 98
Flights to San José 63
Galería Nacional de Arte
Contemporáneo 79
Gay and lesbian nightlife 89
Goethe Institut 80
ICT 64
Jade Museum see Marco Fidel
Tristan Museo de Jade
La California 80
Listings 92
Live music 86
Los Yoses 80
Marco Fidel Tristan Museo de
Jade 76

Markets 92
Mercado Central 81
Museo Criminalógico 80
Museo de Arte Costarricense 82
Museo de Arte y Diseño
Contemporáneo 77
Museo de Ciencias Natural La
Salle 82
Museo de Moneda 75
Museo de Oro Precolumbiano 74
Museo Dr Rafael Angel Calderón
Guardia 80
Museo Ferrocarril 78
Museo Nacional 79
Museo Postal, Telegráfico y
Filatelico 81
Museum of Contemporary Art and
Design see Museo de Arte y
Diseño Contemporáneo
National Parks Office 65
Nightlife 86
Palacio Nacional 78
Parque Central 74
Parque España 76
Parque Morazón 76
Parque Nacional 78
Parque la Sabana 82
Parque Zoológico Simón Bolívar
77
Paseo Colón 82
Plaza de la Cultura 74
Pre-Columbian Gold Museum see
Museo de Oro Precolumbiano
Railway Museum see Museo
Ferrocarril
Restaurants 84
Salsa schools 87
San Pedro 80
Serpentario 79
Shopping 92
Sodas 85
Spirogyra Jardín de Mariposas 78
SPN 65
Taxis in San José 66
Teatro Nacional 75
Theatres 91
Tourist information 64
UCR 81
University of Costa Rica 81
San Rafael de Guatuso 188
San Vicente de Moravia 123
San Vito 332
Santa Cruz 241–243
Santa Elena 257, 260, 261, 263
Santa Rosa see Parque
Nacional Santa Rosa
Sarapiquí region 195–205

Sarchí 111–113
Seasons 39
Selva Verde Lodge 204
Shopping 52
Siquerres 139
Sixaola 175
Snorkelling 48
Sportsfishing 49
Study programmes 55
Surfing 48
Swimming 47

T

Tabacón Hot Springs *see*
  Balneario Tabacón
Tamarindo 237–240
Tambor 278
Tapantí *see* Parque Nacional
  Tapantí
Telecommunications 34
Television 36
Tilarán 271

Tipping 57
Tortuguero *see* Parque
  Nacional Tortuguero
Tortuguero village 152–154
Tour operators in Costa Rica
  25
Tourist information 16
Tropical Dry Forest 214
Tropical Forests 361–365
Turrialba 130
Turtles 154–156, 225–227,
  237

U

Ujarras 129
United Fruit Company 343
Uvita 312

V

Valle de el General 306
Venado Caves 188
Visas 11

Volcán Arenal *see* Parque
  Nacional Volcán Arenal
Volcán Barva 122
Volcán Irazú *see* Parque
  Nacional Volcán Irazú
Volcán Poás *see* Parque
  Nacional Volcán Poás
Volunteer work 54, 268

W

Walker, William 228
Walking 46
Whitewater rafting 47
Wildlife 351–360
Women travellers 38

Y

Youth hostels 28

Z

Zarcero 114
Zoo-Ave 114

HELP US UPDATE

We've gone to a lot of effort to ensure that the first edition of the *Rough Guide to Costa Rica* is up-to-date and accurate. However, things do change, and any suggestions, comments or corrections would be much appreciated. We'll send a copy of the next edition (or any other *Rough Guide* if you prefer) for the best contributions. Please mark letters "Rough Guide Costa Rica update" and send to:
Rough Guides, 1 Mercer St, London WC2H 9QJ
or Rough Guides, 375 Hudson St, 9thfloor, New York NY 10014

DIRECT ORDERS IN THE UK

Title	ISBN	Price
Amsterdam	1858280869	£7.99
Andalucia	185828094X	£8.99
Australia	1858281415	£12.99
Barcelona & Catalunya	1858281067	£8.99
Berlin	1858281296	£8.99
Big Island of Hawaii	185828158X	£8.99
Brazil	1858281024	£9.99
Brittany & Normandy	1858281261	£8.99
Bulgaria	1858280478	£8.99
California	1858280907	£9.99
Canada	185828130X	£10.99
Classical Music on CD	185828113X	£12.99
Corsica	1858280893	£8.99
Crete	1858281326	£8.99
Cyprus	185828032X	£8.99
Czech & Slovak Republics	185828029X	£8.99
Egypt	1858280753	£10.99
England	1858280788	£9.99
Europe	185828077X	£14.99
Florida	1858280109	£8.99
France	1858281245	£10.99
Germany	1858281288	£11.99
Goa	1858281563	£8.99
Greece	1858281318	£9.99
Greek Islands	1858281636	£8.99
Guatemala & Belize	1858280451	£9.99
Holland, Belgium & Luxembourg	1858280877	£9.99
Hong Kong & Macau	1858280664	£8.99
Hungary	1858281237	£8.99
India	1858281040	£13.99
Ireland	1858280958	£9.99
Italy	1858280311	£12.99
Jazz	1858281377	£16.99
Kenya	1858280435	£9.99
London	1858291172	£8.99
Mediterranean Wildlife	0747100993	£7.95
Malaysia, Singapore & Brunei	1858281032	£9.99
Mexico	1858280443	£10.99
Morocco	1858280400	£9.99
Moscow	185828118 0	£8.99
Nepal	185828046X	£8.99
New York	1858280583	£8.99
Nothing Ventured	0747102082	£7.99
Pacific Northwest	1858280923	£9.99
Paris	1858281253	£7.99
Poland	1858280346	£9.99
Portugal	1858280842	£9.99
Prague	185828015X	£7.99
Provence & the Côte d'Azur	1858280230	£8.99
Pyrenees	1858280931	£8.99
Romania	1858280974	£9.99
St Petersburg	1858281334	£8.99
San Francisco	1858280826	£8.99
Scandinavia	1858280397	£10.99
Scotland	1858280834	£8.99
Sicily	1858280370	£8.99
Singapore	1858281350	£8.99
Spain	1858280818	£9.99
Thailand	1858281407	£10.99
Tunisia	1858280656	£8.99
Turkey	1858280885	£9.99
Tuscany & Umbria	1858280915	£8.99
USA	185828080X	£12.99
Venice	1858281709	£8.99
Wales	1858280966	£8.99
West Africa	1858280141	£12.99
More Women Travel	1858280982	£9.99
World Music	1858280176	£14.99
Zimbabwe & Botswana	1858280419	£10.99

Rough Guide Phrasebooks

Czech	1858281482	£3.50
French	185828144X	£3.50
German	1858281466	£3.50
Greek	1858281458	£3.50
Italian	1858281431	£3.50
Spanish	1858281474	£3.50

Rough Guides can be obtained directly in the UK* from Penguin by contacting:
Penguin Direct, Penguin Books Ltd, Bath Road, Harmondsworth, West Drayton,
Middlesex UB7 0DA; or telephone our credit line on 0181-899 4036 (9am–5pm)
and ask for Penguin Direct. Visa, Access and Amex accepted. Delivery will
normally be within 14 working days. Penguin Direct ordering facilities are
only available in the UK.

The availability and published prices quoted are correct at the time
of going to press but are subject to alteration without prior notice.

DIRECT ORDERS IN THE USA

Title	ISBN	Price
Amsterdam	1858280869	$13.59
Andalucia	185828094X	$14.95
Australia	1858281415	$19.95
Barcelona & Catalunya	1858281067	$17.99
Berlin	1858281296	$14.95
Big Island of Hawaii	185828158X	$12.95
Brazil	1858281024	$15.95
Brittany & Normandy	1858281261	$14.95
Bulgaria	1858280478	$14.99
California	1858280907	$14.95
Canada	185828130X	$14.95
Classical Music on CD	185828113X	$19.95
Corsica	1858280893	$14.95
Crete	1858281326	$14.95
Cyprus	185828032X	$13.99
Czech & Slovak Republics	185828029X	$14.95
Egypt	1858280753	$17.95
England	1858280788	$16.95
Europe	185828077X	$18.95
Florida	1858280109	$14.95
France	1858281245	$16.95
Germany	1858281288	$17.95
Goa	1858281563	$14.95
Greece	1858281318	$16.95
Greek Islands	1858281636	$14.95
Guatemala & Belize	1858280451	$14.95
Holland, Belgium & Luxembourg	1858280877	$15.95
Hong Kong & Macau	1858280664	$13.95
Hungary	1858281237	$14.95
India	1858281040	$22.95
Ireland	1858280958	$16.95
Italy	1858280311	$17.95
Jazz	1858281377	$24.95
Kenya	1858280435	$15.95
London	1858291172	$12.95
Mediterranean Wildlife	0747100993	$15.95
Malaysia, Singapore & Brunei	1858281032	$16.95
Mexico	1858280443	$16.95
Morocco	1858280400	$16.95
Moscow	1858281180	$14.95
Nepal	185828046X	$13.95
New York	1858280583	$13.95
Nothing Ventured	0747102082	$19.95
Pacific Northwest	1858280923	$14.95
Paris	1858281253	$12.95
Poland	1858280346	$16.95
Portugal	1858280842	$15.95
Prague	1858281229	$14.95
Provence & the Côte d'Azur	1858280230	$14.95
Pyrenees	1858280931	$15.95
Romania	1858280974	$15.95
St Petersburg	1858281334	$14.95
San Francisco	1858280826	$13.95
Scandinavia	1858280397	$16.99
Scotland	1858280834	$14.95
Sicily	1858280370	$14.99
Singapore	1858281350	$14.95
Spain	1858280818	$16.95
Thailand	1858281407	$17.95
Tunisia	1858280656	$15.95
Turkey	1858280885	$16.95
Tuscany & Umbria	1858280915	$15.95
USA	185828080X	$18.95
Venice	1858281709	$14.95
Wales	1858280966	$14.95
West Africa	1858280141	$24.95
More Women Travel	1858280982	$14.95
World Music	1858280176	$19.95
Zimbabwe & Botswana	1858280419	$16.95

Rough Guide Phrasebooks

Title	ISBN	Price
Czech	1858281482	$5.00
French	185828144X	$5.00
German	1858281466	$5.00
Greek	1858281458	$5.00
Italian	1858281431	$5.00
Spanish	1858281474	$5.00

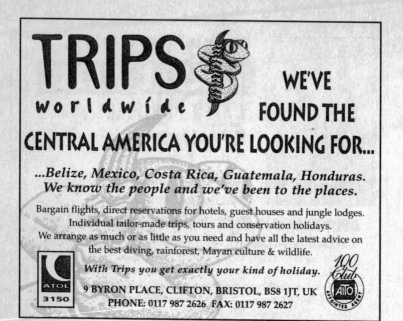

CAMINO
T R A V E L

Our One Stop Travel Shop offers you everything you need to have a great time in Costa Rica!

Prepare your vacation as you like! We can design your vacation according to your budget, time and interests.

We offer:

• Travel itineraries whether by bus, car hire, private driver or guided minibus.

• Hotel & Lodge bookings throughout the country

• Local flights

• Advanced ticket purchase for public buses

• Document delivery in the San José area

• Free T-shirt with sales above $500 (cash) or $700 (credit card)

And with your Rough Guide you will receive our updated public transportation list free!

You can contact us previous to your arrival (by fax or mail) or upon arrival in our downtown office!

Camino Travel Calle 1, between 1st & Central Avenues. San José, Costa Rica
Tel: (506) 234 2530 or (506) 225 0263
FAX: (506) 225 6143

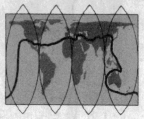

You are
A STUDENT

You travel
THE WORLD

You want
TO SAVE MONEY

Here's how

The International Student Identity Card

International Student Identity Card

Family name/Nom de famille
Sian
First name/Vorname/Prénom
Sharoush
Born/Geburtsdatum/Né
20/8/1973
Nationality/Nationalität/Nationalité
French
Student at/Hochschule, Schule/Etablissement
University of Paris

STUDENT

Available at Student Travel Offices Worldwide.

Entitles you to discounts and special services worldwide.

TECHNICAL COLLEGE